FLOWER

Exploring the
World in Bloom

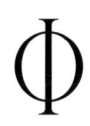

Phaidon Press Limited
2 Cooperage Yard
London E15 2QR

Phaidon Press Inc.
111 Broadway
New York, NY 10006

Phaidon SARL
55, rue Traversière
75012 Paris

phaidon.com

First published 2020
Reprinted 2021, 2022, 2023, 2024
Reprinted in this compact format 2026
© 2020 Phaidon Press Limited

ISBN 978 1 83729 145 8

A CIP catalogue record for this book is available from the
British Library and the Library of Congress.

Commissioning Editor: Victoria Clarke
Project Editors: Lynne Ciccaglione and Rosie Pickles
Production Controller: Jane Harman
Design: Hans Stofregen
Artwork: Cantina

Printed in China

It is almost impossible to imagine a time when the grace, beauty, charm and delicacy of flowers did not seduce us. We turn to them for all the great milestones of our lives. We celebrate birthdays with them. We surround brides with them. We name children after them, fill our homes with their images on curtains, coffee cups and wallpaper. And when we die, we are sent on our way mounded over with sweet-smelling roses and bouquets of lilies.

Flowers have always had this power. Long before the first book was ever printed, monks painted delicate little columbines, fat double daisies and heartsease in the borders of their manuscripts. Before flowers even had official names, people cultivated them in gardens, first because they were useful – most medicines were based on extracts of plants – but also because they were beautiful. Transplanted into new habitats, cosseted, protected from grazing animals, the plants prospered and increased. We thought we were using them – or was it, perhaps, the other way around?

Unspoken associations developed around certain flowers such as lilies, irises, roses or lotuses. Depictions of the Virgin Mary often show her with a white lily, a symbol of purity; the flower is still called the Madonna Lily. In the fifteenth century, the rose, another religious symbol, was reinvented as a political one. In England's War of the Roses, the House of Lancaster, which took the red *Rosa gallica* as its emblem, warred with the House of York, which fought under the white *R. centifolia*. The marriage of Henry VII to Elizabeth of York brought the two together beneath the emblem of the Tudor rose.

The power of flowers shines out from every page of the rich collection of images brought together in *Flower: Exploring the World in Bloom*. The images range much further than the iconic flower still lifes painted by Dutch Golden Age artists such as Jan Brueghel the Elder and Jan van Huysum (see pp.268, 142). Here are extraordinarily complex examples of the maker's skill: ceramics, metalwork, jewellery, tapestries, furniture, manuscripts, books, as well as enchanting ephemera such as seed packets, postage stamps and cigarette cards. From the world of fashion come the bold black-and-white daisy logo adopted in the 1960s by Mary Quant, which quickly became synonymous with her name (see p.286), a stylized cover for French *Vogue* by American designer Helen Dryden in 1921 (see p.62) and Karl Lagerfeld's couture wedding dress for Chanel in 2005, which incorporated 2,500 hand-made miniature camellias (see p.255).

In the decorative arts, particularly from the seventeenth century onwards, flowers bloomed with abandon. They were painted on money chests and inlaid in mother-of-pearl on cases used to display natural curiosities. Flowers were flamed in stained glass; curled round the bowls of wassail cups; engraved on silver plates and spoons; stitched into bed hangings, curtains and quilts; and woven into the borders of Flemish tapestries. Most of all, they blossomed on china and pottery, such as a blue-and-white moon flask made early in the early fifteenth century in the imperial kilns in China and an exquisite set of porcelain plates made at the Sèvres factory in France decorated with roses and asters (see pp.218, 299). At the Paul Revere pottery near Boston, Sara Galner was one of the amateur 'Saturday Evening Girls' at evening classes for poor immigrants but became a professional whose elegant vase of 1915 shows white Queen Anne's lace against bands of blue and green glaze (see p.259).

The images in this book range over many countries and thousands of years. One of the oldest is a fresco of Flora, goddess of flowers and the season of spring, gathering flowers, which was painted on the wall of a Roman villa near Pompeii sometime between 1–45 AD (see p.70). One of the most recent is a hyperreal image of roses taken on a smartphone by British photographer Nick Knight and processed through Instagram – the 'gallery' of the twenty-first century (see p.127). The instant smartphone image is the latest in a long series of techniques developed and exploited by artists and craftspeople to capture nature's beauties, from early printed woodcuts to later etchings and lithographs, cyanotypes and photographs. All are represented in this wide-ranging volume.

The images in this superb collection could have been arranged by chronology or theme, but instead pictures have been cleverly paired on facing pages to highlight revealing or stimulating similarities or contrasts. René Magritte's twentieth-century painting of a rose marooned on a rocky island is teamed with photographer Martin Parr's image of brilliant pink roses on a Dorset campsite taken in 1999 (see pp.196, 197). An image of lavender formally portrayed in Pietro Andrea Mattioli's sixteenth-century *Kreüterbuch* is partnered by a radical display by the Australian floral artist Ruby Barber from the 2019 Flora International Flower Festival in Córdoba, Spain (see pp.238, 239).

The florist, now as glamorous a creature as a fashion model, is a relatively new arrival in the world of flowers.

We take for granted the fact that we can buy a bunch of flowers so easily, but growing flowers for sale is quite a recent phenomenon: in Britain, it only began towards the end of the nineteenth century. When *Gardeners' Magazine* first started to publish prices from the Covent Garden flower market in London, Parma violets cost eight shillings a bunch — at a time when 'a thoroughly experienced head gardener' earned about 28 shillings a week. Arranging flowers in the 'big house' would have been one of the gardener's duties and most of them would have been home-grown, not bought. Arranging flowers has moved a long way from the pioneering work of British florist Constance Spry in the 1930s (see p.270). Floral designers now make whole installations, such as the Brussels-based florist Thierry Boutemy's *Lost Garden*, created in 2006 in a Belgian glasshouse (see p.302). The American studio Lewis Miller Design subverts the discipline with Flower Flashes – guerrilla arrangements displaying leftover flowers at traffic lights, in bus shelters and rubbish bins on the streets of New York (see p.271).

Certain flowers continually reappear in different guises throughout this book: the sunflower, the orchid, the tulip, the rose, the iris, the lily, the poppy all became particular favourites, both with artists and craftspeople. 'The sunflower is mine,' said Vincent van Gogh, who perhaps did make the flower uniquely his own with his famous depictions in the 1880s (see p.47). But much earlier, the sunflower had signified devotion to the Catholic Church, standing also for love and loyalty. The oddly unreal, mesmerizing aspect of the orchid attracted artists over a wide range of disciplines. In the 1890s, American designer Paulding Farnham was inspired by the South American species *Oncidium jonesianum* to make a beautiful orchid brooch for Tiffany & Co. (see p.164). More than a hundred years later, after visiting Singapore's National Orchid Gardens, milliner Philip Treacy was motivated by an extraordinary paphiopedilum to create fantastic orchid hats (see p.316). The flower itself does not change, only the way in which different artists and craftspeople see it and employ it for their own ends – and our delight.

Early Depictions
From early times, flowers decorated houses and the things used in them. In western Europe we think of myrtle and roses on the walls of villas at Pompeii and Herculaneum; saffron crocus, iris and Madonna lilies on frescoes at Knossos; the moulded flowers decorating a Minoan vessel of 1700 BC(see p.148); the fabulous wall paintings of sea daffodils (see p.43) from the House of Ladies on the Greek island of Santorini (*c*.1600 BC). Myrtle was sacred in Greek mythology, worn as a crown by the goddess Aphrodite. It symbolized love and is still, by tradition, included in a bride's wedding bouquet.

But it took a while before someone had the idea of making plant portraits for their own sake, not just as elements in a decorative scheme. One of the earliest references to plant illustration is made by the Roman author, Pliny, around 77 AD, who noted the difficulties involved: plants had many colours, the painters of the time had few. The palette was limited to one kind of green per plant, a blue, a thick coffee-coloured brown for the roots and various ochre-based yellows and oranges for the flowers. The earliest pictures in herbals and medical treatises were single snapshots: the plant in its prime with roots, stem, leaves and flower all present. But Pliny pointed out that, 'It is not enough for each plant to be painted at one period only of its life, since it alters its appearance with the fourfold changes of the year.' In copying nature, which of nature's seasons do you choose to portray?

Early illustrators were particularly keen on showing roots, as many medicines were prepared from them, rather than leaves, seeds or flowers. Long before the iris acquired its religious symbolism, it had an important place in early herbals. The roots, ground up, were good for coughs and helped insomniacs sleep. Iris was an antidote to snakebites, eased sciatica, cleansed ulcers, eased headaches and calmed sunburn – a paragon among flowers.

Despite the technical constraints, early painters created some beautiful plant illustrations. Around 512 AD for instance, the residents of Honorata in Constantinople presented a grand volume to their imperial patron, Juliana Anicia, in gratitude for giving them a church. This exquisite ragbag of knowledge, the *Juliana Anicia Codex*, includes illustrations of 383 plants: spurges and a gorgeous asphodel (see p.24), a rose and an autumn-flowering cyclamen. It is the earliest surviving plant book – and one of the most magnificent ever produced.

In terms of picturing flowers that looked like the real thing, no progress was made in the Middle Ages in Europe. The magic of plants remained as important as any medical attribute they might possess. No traveller, for instance, could set out without mugwort (*Artemisia vulgaris*) in his or her pocket to take away tiredness and ward off robbers. There was nothing, it seems, that mugwort could not do. The superstitions persist. In a British survey in the 1980s, hawthorn was chosen as the most unlucky of flowers, closely followed by lilac. If either were brought into a house, disaster, even death, would follow.

Advances in Visualizing Flowers
During the Renaissance, the boundaries between art and science were blurred. It was certainly not a distinction

recognized by Leonardo da Vinci, who by the time he was thirty was working as an engineer for the Duke of Milan, but was also making superb pen-and-ink studies of flowers (see p.108). He also made leaf prints – physiotypes – by coating their undersurfaces with the soot of a candle flame and pressing the leaves face-down on paper.

The German printmaker Albrecht Dürer instinctively caught the habit of a plant – the way the head of a cowslip is placed on its stem (see p.295), the way lily of the valley emerges from its enclosing sheath – without seeming so overtly interested in their structure. But he did share with da Vinci an absolute reliance on the evidence of his own eyes. Artists were the great naturalists of the period from the late fourteenth to the middle of the sixteenth century, but they could only be articulate in one particular way. They could open eyes, but they could not, on their own, promote debate until writers caught up with them. Even the simple word 'petal' was not brought into the language until 1592, when the Italian scholar Fabio Colonna suggested it in his book *Phytobasanos*.

The invention of printing in Europe had a cataclysmic effect on the spread of floral images. The first printed herbal to be a bestseller throughout the continent was produced in 1530. It owed its success to the woodcuts contributed by Hans Weiditz (see p.144), draughtsman, engraver and pupil of Dürer, who had taught him to 'be guided by nature'. Drawing directly from life, Weiditz created the first printed images of flowers – the pasqueflower, the white-flowered water lily – that were unequivocally recognized throughout Europe.

The arrival of printing was a great landmark, but the best paintings were still to come during the Golden Age of Dutch still lifes in the seventeenth century: Jan Brueghel the Elder's *Flowers in a Vase* of 1606 (see p.268), Crispijn van de Passe II's *Hortus Floridus* of 1614 (see p.294), Balthasar van der Ast's *Flowers in a Snail Shell* (see p.267). In the latter half of the century, Jan Davidsz. de Heem produced thundering still lifes of flowers spilling out of their containers, filling every inch of the canvas (see p.125). With extraordinary verisimilitude, cabinetmakers such as Jan van Mekeren emulated the artists' works with huge arrangements of tulips, daffodils and lilies, executed not in paint but in exotic wood veneers (see p.298).

A Floral Obsession
This Golden Age of Dutch flower painting was fuelled by the arrival in Europe of a host of flamboyant superstars from Central Asia – fritillaries, narcotically scented hyacinths, anemones – spearheading the first great wave of strangers to enter European gardens. The most spectacular of them all was the tulip, which arrived in Europe in the baggage of a Flemish diplomat called Ogier de Busbecq.

The Netherlands became the setting for one of the tulip's strangest escapades: tulipomania. At the height of the fever, in the mid-1630s, a single tulip bulb, such as the beautiful 'Schoon Solffer', could sell for the equivalent of fifteen years' wages for an Amsterdam bricklayer. This was partly a matter of timing – the activities of the Dutch East India Company were the basis of an era of great prosperity – and partly a trick of nature, for the flower itself had a unique characteristic. A plain red tulip might emerge the following spring with its petals 'broken': feathered and flamed in intricate patterns of contrasting colours. 'Broken' flowers commanded the most outrageous prices, but they lacked vigour and were slow to produce 'offsets', or immature bulbs. (We now know that the 'breaks' were caused by a virus, spread by aphids.) Supply was always short and that, too, increased the bulbs' value.

The flamboyance of the tulip, its brilliant colours, its elegant shape, soon caught the imagination of painters in Europe. Those who could not afford the tulips themselves commissioned artists to paint them instead. The grand masters of Dutch flower painting could rarely command more than 5,000 guilders for their work, but at auction in February 1637, a single bulb of the tulip 'Admiral Liefkens' changed hands for 4,400 guilders.

A tenuous line marked the advance of the tulip to the New World, where it was unknown in the wild. In his letters home, Adriaen van der Donck, who had settled in New Amsterdam (now Manhattan) in 1642, described the European flowers that bravely colonized the settlers' gardens. Today, in the deep basements of Fifth Avenue's skyscrapers lie the ghosts of the very first tulips ever to grow on American soil.

When the tulip finally lost its place in the stylish gardens of Europe, it was rescued by a different class of grower, who developed a different kind of tulip: the English Florists' tulip. The florists were working men – cutlers, shoemakers, barbers, weavers and potters, such as the Derby florist, William Pegg, born in 1775. As a boy, Pegg was apprenticed to a china painter, working fifteen hours a day at the Derby China Works. The beautiful tulips he grew in his tenement garden found their way into his sketchbooks and, from there, onto the expensive porcelain produced at the Derby works. The tulip, together with other florists' flowers, such as the auricula and the carnation, were what the decorators knew best and they became favourite motifs on the plates, bowls and teacups of the period.

In Turkey, tulips became such an obsession that an entire historical period in the early 1700s has been labelled the Tulip Era. Whereas English florists favoured round, wide-petalled tulips, the Turks wanted dagger-shaped tulips with petals as pointed as needles (see p.308). The best of these

Ottoman tulips live on in the pages of a leather-bound manuscript, the only illustrated book of Turkish tulips known to exist. Forty-nine different varieties are painted on thick Indian paper. All have the etiolated shape and narrow petals so familiar from Iznik tiles and pottery of the period.

Further east, Chinese and Japanese artists turned to nature for inspiration. In making representations of their favourite flowers – cherry blossom was particularly associated with both cultures – painters showed them as if they were growing, not arranged in a vase. In Japan the bold, graphic prints produced by artists such as Katsushika Hokusai and Utagawa Hiroshige (see pp.258, 231) became an important influence on the group of painters in France we know as the Impressionists. When Japan was forced to open its ports to shipping, Western plant hunters sent back plants such as the big-rayed lily, *Lilium auratum*, which became an immediate sensation. It is the star of John Singer Sargent's painting *Carnation, Lily, Lily, Rose* (see p.192). From Japan, too, came cherries, such as the famous 'Hokusai', and big Japanese chrysanthemums. Claude Monet so loved the painting of chrysanthemums by his friend Gustave Caillebotte that he bought it for himself (see p.282).

When Monet started to make his famous water garden, his farming neighbours turned hostile. Nevertheless, Monet got his lily pond with its famous wooden bridge based on a Japanese print, together with bamboos, Japanese cherries and water lilies. But the new garden lay alongside an unsurfaced road and constant traffic created clouds of dust, which settled thickly on the water lily pads. Even *plein-air* painters have their breaking points and eventually Monet paid for the whole of the road alongside the water garden to be tarred. Gazing at the artist's translucent images of his water lilies (see p.169), it is easy to forget that the tranquil pond was born out of conflict and hard labour.

Flowers continued to bloom in the paintings of twentieth-century artists, but they were a more eclectic bunch, not so easy to categorize as the Impressionists or the painters of the Dutch Golden Age. In the decade that American artist Georgia O'Keeffe was producing her huge hard-edged images of *Datura innoxia* (see p.59) and iris, the Englishman Sir Cedric Morris was painting the same beautiful flowers in a lush, romantic style that owed far more to the nineteenth century than the twentieth (see p.37). Morris knew his flowers, for he bred them as well as painted them. 'Only a modest man can paint a flower,' he wrote in *The Studio* magazine. The Surrealist Max Ernst showed flowers in bold, collaged forms (see p.81), while American sculptor Harry Bertoia created dandelion heads from the finest strands of stainless steel (see p.284). The techniques among artists of the modern age could not be more varied, but the subject matter remains universal.

A New Golden Age

Universal, but also more diverse. The earliest painters of flowers, in the main, knew only their native blooms, that is, until in Renaissance Italy patrons such as Francesco I de' Medici collected foreign plants and commissioned portraits of them from artists such as Jacopo Ligozzi and Girolamo Pini (see p.280). After the first influx into Europe of flowers from Central Asia, a second wave arrived in the seventeenth century: strange and wonderful flowers from the New World, woodsy creatures such as trilliums and erythroniums. This owed much to the enterprise of John Bartram, the American botanist and plant collector, who from his nursery at Kingsessing, Philadelphia, first sent plants such as the white-flowered franklinia to Europe. Then on 12 July 1771, a little Whitby collier called *Endeavour* sailed into port at Dover, bringing with her the wonders of the great, then-unknown, landmass, Terra Australis: Australia.

On board the *Endeavour* was the naturalist Joseph Banks, with a retinue of artists, including Sydney Parkinson (see p.29). From that voyage to the Pacific and Australasia, Parkinson produced more than 900 drawings, many made under hideous conditions. In Tahiti, for instance, swarms of flies blacked out his drawing paper and ate his paint as well.

Expedition artists were hired for practical reasons: drawings were likely to survive in better condition than the plants themselves. Parkinson's plant portraits, expertly engraved, constituted a new, but different kind of golden age of flower painting. Now artists specialized not in elaborate still lifes of flowers, but in precise and accurate portraits of them: Georg Ehret (see p.20) was one of the first of these botanical artists, followed by Pierre Joseph Redouté, who, for the Empress Josephine, produced *Les Liliacées* (see p.109). These portraits of bulbous plants such as amaryllis and delicate alliums remain among the greatest works of botanical art ever made. Redouté had studied under the fine flower painter Gerard van Spaendonck (see p.201), himself a pupil of Jan van Huysum (see p.142). Three consummate masters of flower painting are connected by a single thread.

Alongside this was a strong amateur tradition of botanical painting. The well-connected Mary Delany produced flower pictures built up from layer upon layer of tissue paper (see p.145). Her models were plants from her patroness and friend, the Duchess of Portland, and from the botanic gardens at Kew in London. Kew holds more than a million portraits of plants, with a particularly golden period from 1759 to 1820. The pictures reflect the horticultural fads of different generations of plant collectors and gardeners: the rhododendrons flooding in from China and the Himalayas, recorded in stunning lithographs by Joseph Dalton Hooker and

Walter Hood Fitch (see p.146); the mania for rare orchids in the middle of the nineteenth century, when they were grown by a small band of obsessive collectors such as the industrialist James Bateman, who grew them in hothouses at Biddulph Grange, Staffordshire. When he was only twenty-five, Bateman began to produce his *Orchidaceae of Mexico and Guatemala*. The volume, which is made up of huge, hand-coloured lithographs of rarities by Mrs Augusta Withers (see p.165), is the largest botanical book ever published. The cartoonist George Cruikshank depicted the vast volume being hauled up with pulleys by an army of struggling workers. Only 125 copies were ever published – and no wonder.

Wild orchids were imported from Central and South America, the Philippines and India, where more than a thousand wild species grew naturally. Here, Indian artists trained in the traditional Mughal style adapted their skills to suit the more naturalistic tastes of rich British patrons. They produced gorgeous and intensely poetic images of plants, animals and flowers in rich colours, often heightened by gum arabic, that were thrilling – if not shocking – to Western eyes used to wan watercolours. Flowers had a long history in the decorative arts of India. They appear on the famous friezes of the Taj Mahal, in metal filigree work, woven into textiles, or decorating ceramics and glass, such as the gorgeous opium poppies curving round a glass water pipe (*huqqa*) made around 1700 (see p.293).

The use of the flower as a motif was universal, but each culture used different forms to create images of the plants with which they were most familiar. The lotus (*Nelumbo nucifera*) frequently appeared in ancient Egypt, for instance, where it was a symbol of regeneration linked with the sun god Ra. Among Hindus in India, the lotus was associated with divinities such as Vishnu and Lakshmi, who were often shown seated on stylized lotus thrones. The flower became a symbol of perfection, of purity overcoming squalor, as the lotus itself rises from muddy waters.

One of the most significant aspects of Chinese culture is reverence for custom and tradition. China has an immensely rich and varied native flora, but in Chinese gardens, the same half dozen plants are constantly used. Gardeners grow the plants cultivated by their ancestors: the tree peony, symbolizing wealth, honour, love and elegance; plum blossom, *Prunus mume*, symbolizing perseverance and hope; the cherry, symbolizing strength of will, long life, good fortune, fecundity. The implicit message of the 'hundred flowers' scheme used on vases and bowls by artists of the Qianlong Imperial Workshop (see p.110) was that the Qing dynasty would last forever.

Of course, it didn't. The Qing dynasty was overthrown in 1911 – but flowers continued to rule. In Western Europe and America at that time, they were constant motifs of the movement known as Art Nouveau. Soft, sinuous and romantic, the artefacts produced by geniuses such as French glassmaker and jewellery designer René Lalique (see p.249) and American designer Louis Comfort Tiffany (see p.232) still resonate today. Preceded by the Arts and Crafts movement, embodied in the textile designs of William Morris (see p.160), succeeded by the Art Deco designs of the 1920s and 1930s, which used flower motifs in a harder, more sophisticated and graphic style, the Tiffany lamps, the furniture, textiles and pewter photo frames of the Art Nouveau period mark a high point in flower-inspired decorative arts.

Flowers Frozen in Time

'From today painting is dead!' cried the artist Paul Delaroche when, in 1839, he first saw a daguerreotype. Painting survived, of course, but it was the beginning of a new kind of magic – a way to arrest a moment in all its riveting detail. The disadvantage of the daguerreotype was that it produced only a single image; the photograph (the word was coined by the astronomer Sir John Herschel) fixed a negative from which any number of prints could be made.

Herschel was a friend of pioneering inventor William Henry Fox Talbot, who was also a keen plantsman, so it was not surprising that some of his first photographs were of flowers. But the first person to publish a plant book illustrated with photographic images was Anna Atkins (see p.34), who brought out *Cyanotypes of British Algae* in 1843. Cyanotypes, called blueprints after their distinctive Prussian-blue colour, were made by placing specimens directly onto paper coated with ferric ammonium citrate and potassium ferricyanide, then exposing them to sunlight to produce ghostly silhouettes. It's a process still used by experimental photographers today.

At the beginning, photography was as much about science as art, with its silver nitrate, bitumen and iodine crystals. Its pioneers were a closely connected group of intellectuals, with plenty of spare time for experiments. Charles Jones, who between 1895 and 1910 produced an extraordinary series of prints of fruit, vegetables and flowers, was very different (see p.36). Jones, the son of a Wolverhampton butcher, was a professional gardener who at some stage acquired a camera and started making portraits of flowers and vegetables, captured in a timeless series of gold-toned prints. Jones died in 1959 without any recognition, but more than twenty years later his prints came to light in London's Bermondsey Market, each named and initialled, but not dated. None of the original glass negatives were with the prints, but a photograph taken by Jones's daughter rather tragically shows them being used as glass cloches to shelter young onions.

Karl Blossfeldt, another plant portraitist, who made stunning silver prints of flowers between 1900 and 1925, said he valued his images as 'totally artistic and architectural structures' (see p.273). He was driven by his professional interest in design. Jones's photographs acknowledge and celebrate a gardener's achievement. The long exposures he used give his images the depth and serenity of a Dutch still life.

Many early masters of photography, such as the Frenchmen Charles Aubry and Adolphe Braun or the Americans Henry Troth and Edward Steichen, specialized in the still life, the frozen flower (see pp.194, 182, 16, 181). Their images celebrated a curious contradiction: the flower was by nature fleeting, evanescent, yet a photograph could preserve it forever. When, at the end of the nineteenth century, the Lumière brothers (see p.152) introduced the first autochrome plate, they added a vital element to the new art form: colour. It was a sensational breakthrough.

The flower still life had existed for centuries, but photography offered a new opportunity to record the way people lived – as with Eugène Atget's great project documenting Paris in the 1920s (see p.240) – and, crucially, to capture and preserve images that became metaphors for particular events: Marc Riboud's photograph of a girl with a flower facing the rifles of the American National Guard in protest against the Vietnam War (see p.326), or Henri Cartier-Bresson's image of flowers heaped in front of the gates of Kensington Palace after the death of Diana, Princess of Wales (see p.198). The introduction of the Kodak camera in 1888 first demystified the process of photography. The introduction of the smartphone in 2000 turned it into everyone's art form.

A Tradition of Flowers

Through all these the new processes of recording and interpreting, the flower reigned supreme. In the magnificent rebirth of the Renaissance, artists began to paint flowers simply because they were intriguing and beautiful, not just because a doctor or apothecary needed to be able to identify them. Flowers escaped from herbals into tapestries such as the famous unicorn tapestries at the Metropolitan Museum of Art in New York. They illuminated manuscripts and decorated books of hours, such as the sumptuous beauties painted by Jean Bourdichon for the Queen of France (see p.18). They bloomed on the great bronze doors that Lorenzo Ghiberti made for the baptistery of Florence Cathedral. Flowers took on their own symbolism. The way they close at night but open again each morning became in itself an important symbol of longevity, as did their 'death' in winter and 'rebirth' in spring.

Over many centuries, flowers have become an integral part of our lives, attracting particular customs and iconography.

In the east, lotus flowers have long been associated with representations of Buddha; the real blooms, beautifully presented, are still offered for sale to pilgrims at both Hindu and Buddhist temples in India. In Europe, there was an early belief that violets had come into bloom at the very moment the Virgin Mary learned from the angel Gabriel of the baby she was to bear; violets were often used by painters as symbols of the modesty, innocence and everlasting love imbued in the mother figure. A small bunch of violets remains the traditional gift to bring home on Mothering Sunday. The beauty of the real thing is the catalyst, which, for more than two thousand years, has inspired artists and craftspeople in cultures all over the world to create the glorious images laid out on the following pages.

Anna Pavord
Gardener and author of *The Tulip*

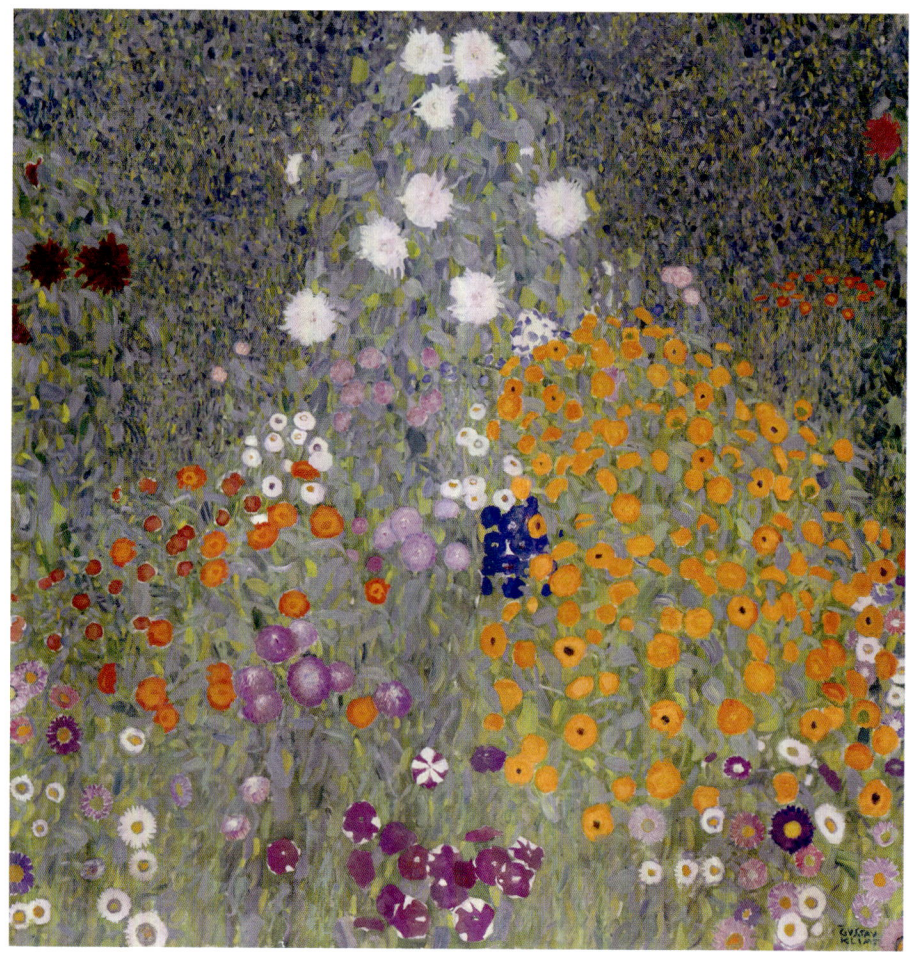

Gustav Klimt

Flower Garden, 1905–07
Oil on canvas, 1.1 × 1.1 m / 3 ft 7 in × 3 ft 7 in
Private collection

A kaleidoscopic explosion of flowers fills the entire canvas: red poppies, white daisies and orange zinnias; all structured around a verdant blue-green foliage causing the flower heads to dance in excitement. Austrian artist Gustav Klimt (1862–1918) flips the usual recessional spatial perspective of the scene so the garden is presented as flat and wall-like; upright in front of us, rather than receding into the background. To heighten this effect, he deliberately leaves out any negative space, so that every inch is decorated in the natural world. The painting has a tapestry-like quality, crescendoing up towards the shower of white blossoms. Klimt painted *Flower Garden* in the summer of 1907 in the rustic garden of the Mayr-Hof near Lake Attersee, Austria, while spending time with friends and family. He was a founding member of the Vienna Secession, an art movement whose main aim was the creation of a 'total art', unifying painting, architecture and the decorative arts. *Flower Garden* is a perfect demonstration of that objective, with its exploration of pattern and texture and its seeming shifts between different formats. Transcending any one visual medium, it could almost be hand-painted wallpaper, a textile print or even the decorative surface of a piece of avant-garde jewellery.

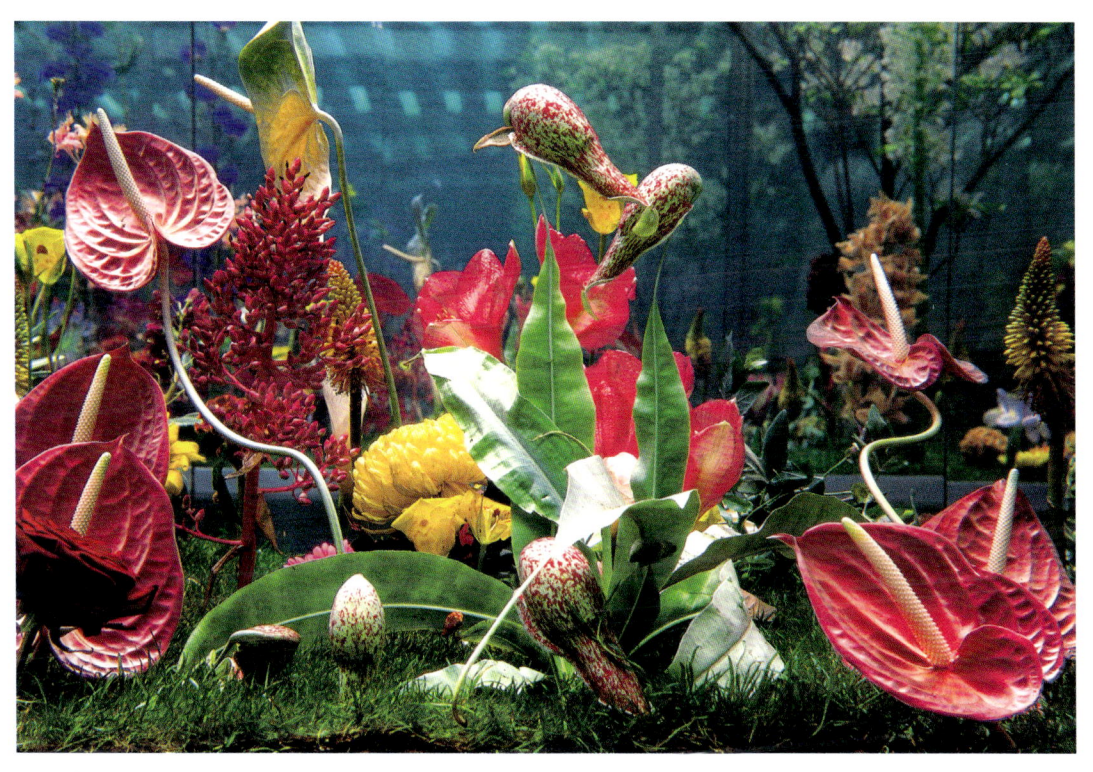

Marc Quinn

Garden, 2000
Cold room, stainless steel, heated glass,
refrigerating equipment, mirrors, turf, real plants,
acrylic tank, low viscosity silicon oil held at -20°C,
3.2 × 12.7 × 5.4 m / 10 ft 6 in × 41 ft 8 in × 17 ft 10 in
Private collection

Anthuriums, pink speckled pitcher plants,
a dahlia, a yellow-flowered red hot poker and
a bromeliad inflorescence harmoniously spring
from the manicured evenness of a tidy English
lawn. The colours and shapes are breathtaking,
but something is awry. Nothing is out of place;
everything is silent. No leaf quivers in a gentle
breeze and no petal shows the signs of time's
passing. Housed in a massive glass tank, this
tableau by the contemporary British artist Marc
Quinn (born 1964) is submerged in 22.5 tonnes
(25 tons) of low-viscosity silicon kept at −20°C
(−4° F). The plants look vibrantly alive but are
in fact frozen solid, preserved in an impossible
dream – a fragment of the Garden of Eden mate-
rialized by the artifice of art and the complicity
of high-end technology. The silicon is kept at the
correct temperature by a refrigerating system,
power generators and a set of custom-made
cold lights. What seems at first glance natural
could not be more artificial. Closer inspection
reveals that all the varieties in Quinn's enchanted
garden are cultivars, plants selected and cross-
bred by humans over hundreds of years. The
colours, shapes and sizes of their flowers are
the tangible result of society's desires. Quinn's
garden reminds us that all gardens are special
places, not quite nature yet not mere artifice:
places in which our relationship with plants
becomes gorgeously complicated by our desire
to test the natural boundaries of beauty.

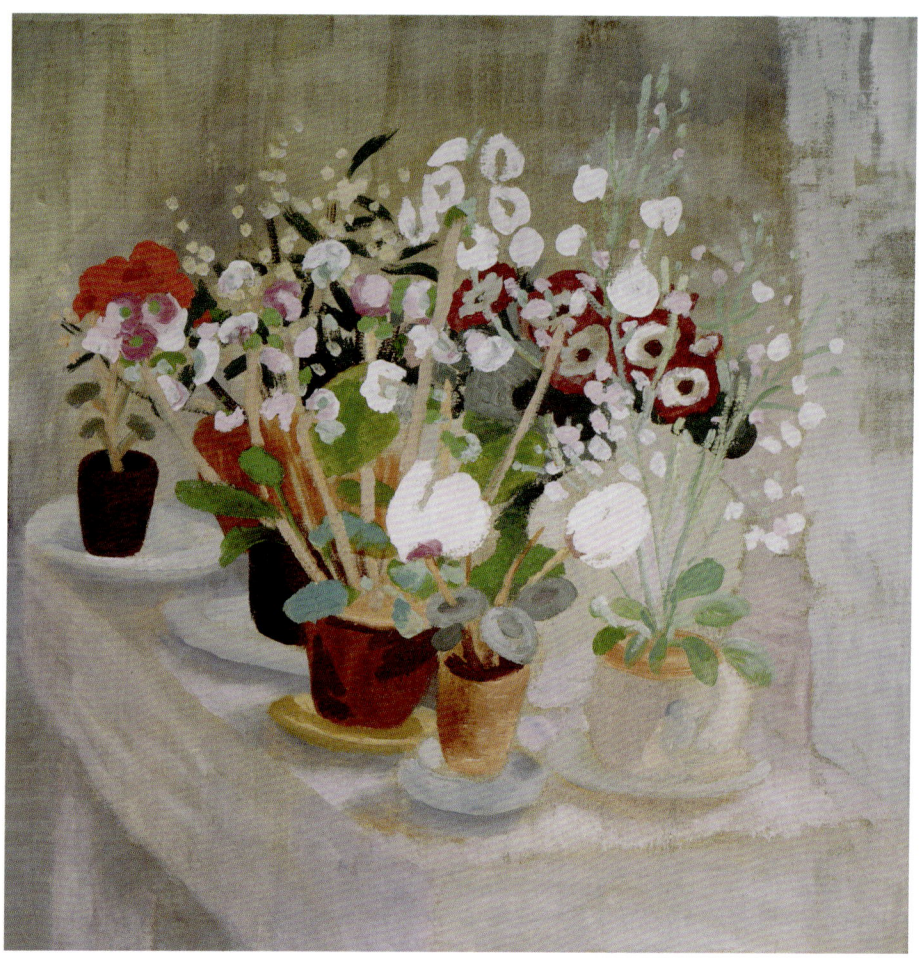

Winifred Nicholson

Cineraria and Cyclamen, 1927
Oil on canvas, 60.5 × 60.5 cm / 24 × 24 in
Private collection

With splashes of vibrant colour and bold brush-strokes, British artist Winifred Nicholson (1893–1981) playfully renders creamy cyclamen petals and cineraria's distinctive crimson and white flowers. Celebrating the vitality of these early spring blooms, the canvas is typical of Nicholson's impressionistic style and her renowned use of dynamic colours. Flowers were one of the painter's favourite subjects;

Nicholson loved their intricate and unruly forms, as well as their thrilling and endlessly varied hues. Throughout her career she painted a vast range of species and regularly collected bunches of wildflowers while walking at her countryside home in Cumbria in England's Lake District. Her compositions frequently feature arrangements of pots and vases of flowers on windowsills, often setting up relationships between the domestic and landscape settings. For *Cineraria and Cyclamen*, however, Nicholson focuses solely on the effusive display of the flowers' dancing colours, which stand out against a muted

background. It was likely painted at Bankshead, a farmhouse built on Hadrian's Wall that Nicholson purchased in 1923, where many of her flower and landscape pictures were executed. The painting was included in the works Nicholson exhibited at London's Beaux Arts Gallery in 1927, in a joint show with Christopher Wood, the potter William Staite Murray and her husband, Ben Nicholson.

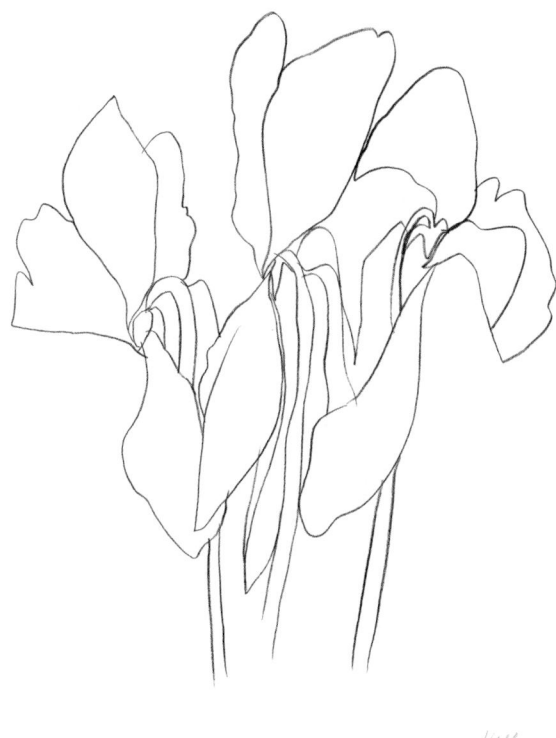

Ellsworth Kelly

Cyclamen V, from *Suite of Plant Lithographs*, 1964–65
Lithograph, 90.5 × 61.6 cm / 35½ × 24¼ in
Museum of Modern Art, New York

Beginning as early as 1949 and continuing throughout his career, Ellsworth Kelly (1923–2015) created more than a thousand images of plant forms, tirelessly drawing leaves, fruit and flowers. Always with a refined composition and elegant line, these drawings form a substantial portion of Kelly's artistic output, though they are less known than his familiar abstract work. Although seemingly disparate, the abstract work and the plant drawings both draw on Kelly's interest in observing the natural world: all of his work comes from physical observation rather than imagination or algorithm. As a keen observer of nature, his plant drawings are a logical counterpoint to his distilled abstraction and he pursued both means of expression simultaneously throughout his career. Many of these plant and flower forms were created as lithographs, as Kelly was partial to the quality of line produced by a lithographic crayon, something he could not achieve with a pencil or ink drawing. Kelly journeyed to Paris in 1964 and soon after embarked on two monumental series of lithographs. One project consisted of twenty-seven images of strongly coloured abstract forms and the second was twenty-eight images of plants and flowers, including *Cyclamen V* – indicating that both subject matters were equally important to him. Also present is the influence of line drawings by Henri Matisse and Pablo Picasso (see pp.19, 297), whose presence was still deeply felt in Paris at that time and were both greatly admired by Kelly.

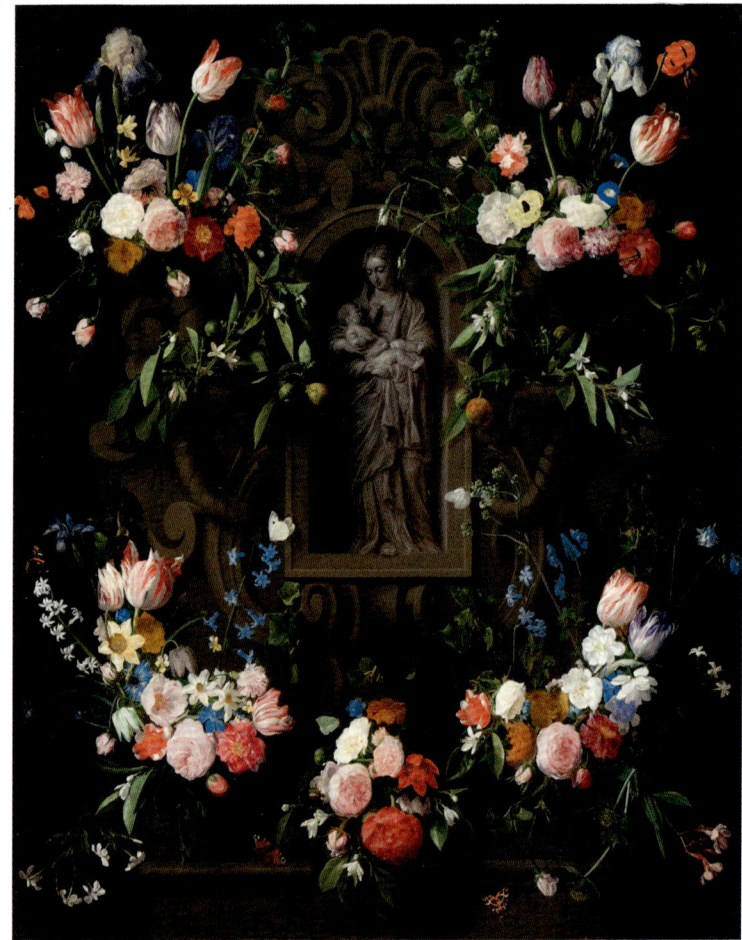

Daniël Seghers and Thomas Willeboirts Bosschaert

Abundant floral offerings surround a devotional image of the Virgin Mary in a collaboration of two Dutch masters: Daniël Seghers (1590–1661) and Thomas Willeboirts Bosschaert (c.1613/14–1654). Bosschaert was responsible for the monochromatic depiction of Mary, while Seghers painted the stone cartouche and garland; this type of ring of flowers around a devotional image or portrait had been introduced earlier in the seventeenth century by his teacher, Jan Brueghel the Elder (see pp.130, 268). Flowers were – and, indeed, still are – an integral aspect of all religions: showcased at religious festivals, worn in garlands, used to decorate shrines and scattered before statues of the saints. Many had individual symbolic meanings. Of those depicted here, roses, lilies and columbines were especially associated with the Virgin, while white flowers such as jasmine and narcissus signified purity and their sweet scent – like spirituality – was invisible, but potent. Seghers perfected a pure, clear blue that recalls the sky, and therefore heaven, as seen in his hyacinths, irises, and morning glories. The sprays of orange blossom and oranges had special significance, as the work was painted for Frederik Hendrik, Prince of Orange and Stadtholder of the Dutch Republic, as a gift from the Jesuit order to which Seghers belonged. This gifting turned Seghers's paintings into collectors' items among princes and prelates – even Protestants, like the ruling family of the Netherlands, who hung the painting in their palace in the Hague.

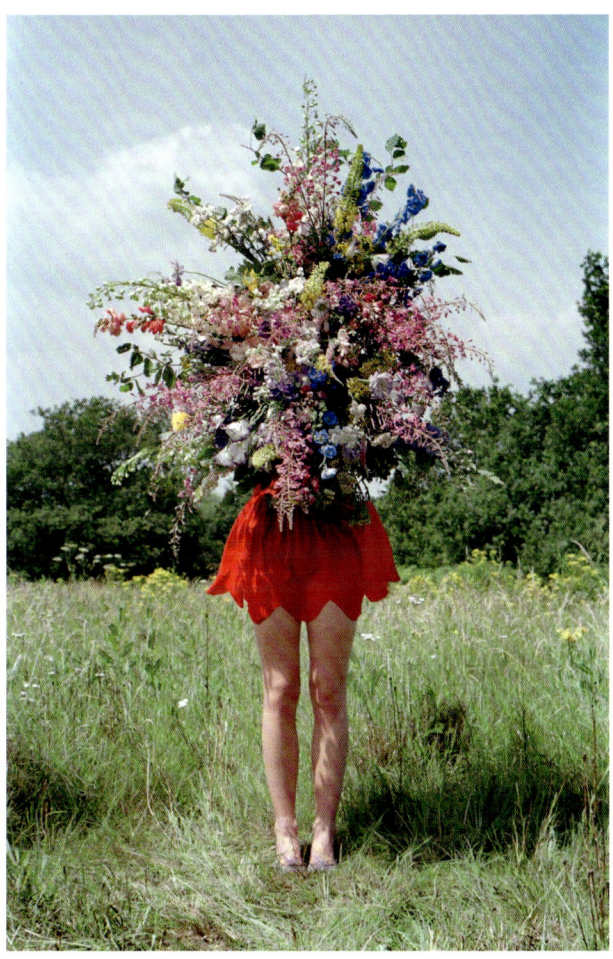

Tim Walker

Siobhan Finnigan, 1998

A young woman stands in a summer field holding an enormous bunch of foxtail lilies, delphiniums, fireweed and mixed foliage that entirely conceals the top half of her body. Only a red miniskirt, with an undulating hem like a fairy costume, is visible beneath the floral display. This image taken in 1998 is one of the earliest pictures taken by British photographer Tim Walker (born 1970), yet it speaks volumes about the obsessions that would later define his work: a celebration of quirky Englishness,

a deep love of the countryside and the pastoral and a sense of surrealism – where a bunch of almost psychedelic flowers can form the top half of a woman's body. Walker later recalled that he had scraped together the money to buy a large bunch of flowers at a florist's in Fulham, London but still did not have enough, so he added foraged wildflowers, foliage, grasses and weeds from a park in nearby Putney. Flowers have featured regularly in Walker's fantastical images, which have appeared in the pages of British, Italian and American *Vogue*, and they are a key part of his storytelling – spilling across tables

and up the walls of grand country houses, filling chintzy bedrooms or setting the scene in fairy-tale fields and magical woodlands.

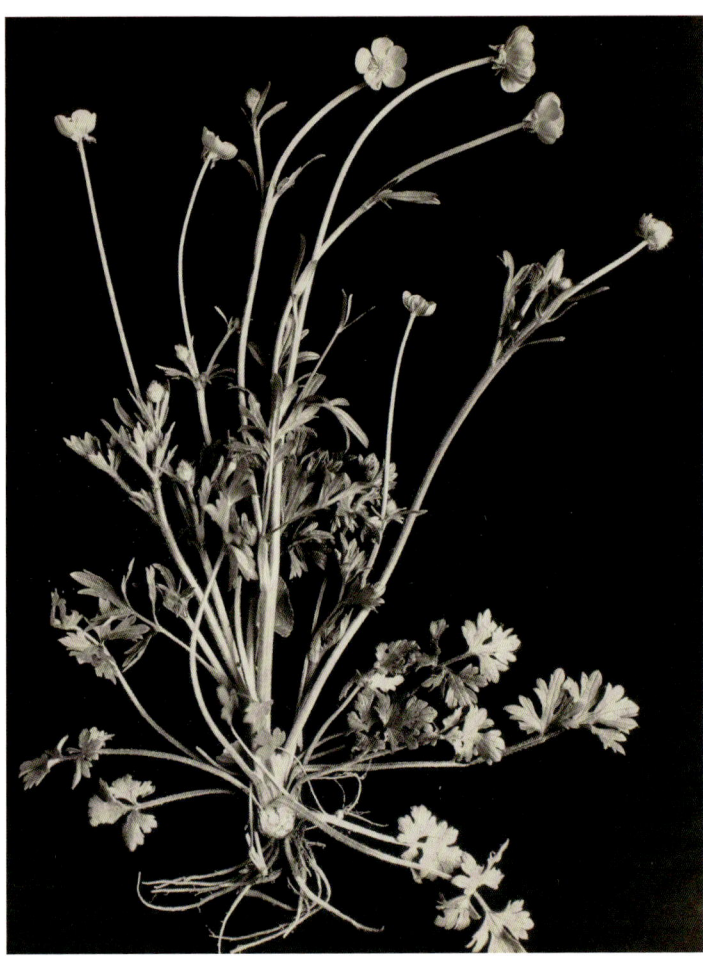

Henry Troth

Buttercup, c.1900
Gelatin silver print, 22.3 × 17.5 cm / 8¾ × 7 in
George Eastman Museum, Rochester, New York

An unadorned buttercup, shot in black and white, lies on a plain background. The effect is magical: the plant is almost porcelain and sculptural in its beauty. Although it must have been shot from above, lying on its side, the image is arranged to suggest that nature has been removed to leave nothing but the plant. In this way we are invited to examine how its roots would burrow into the soil and its flower heads turn towards the sun, seeking out its warming rays. This is one of hundreds of photographs of flowers and landscapes taken by the renowned American photographer Henry Troth (1863–1948), who worked throughout North America at the turn of the nineteenth century. Troth's work is often referred to as belonging to 'pictorialism', an international aesthetic movement that challenged preconceived ideas about photography. At the time, the medium was criticized as being purely functional, and for only being capable of showing the viewer exactly what was in front of the photographer at the time – in other words, just showing us what we already knew, and so not worthy of being seen as a form of art. Troth soundly refutes such an idea. He takes what could have been a very standard photo – a floral still life – and by shooting it as plainly as possible, in a setting removed from the normal world, he depicts far more than what is simply before our eyes.

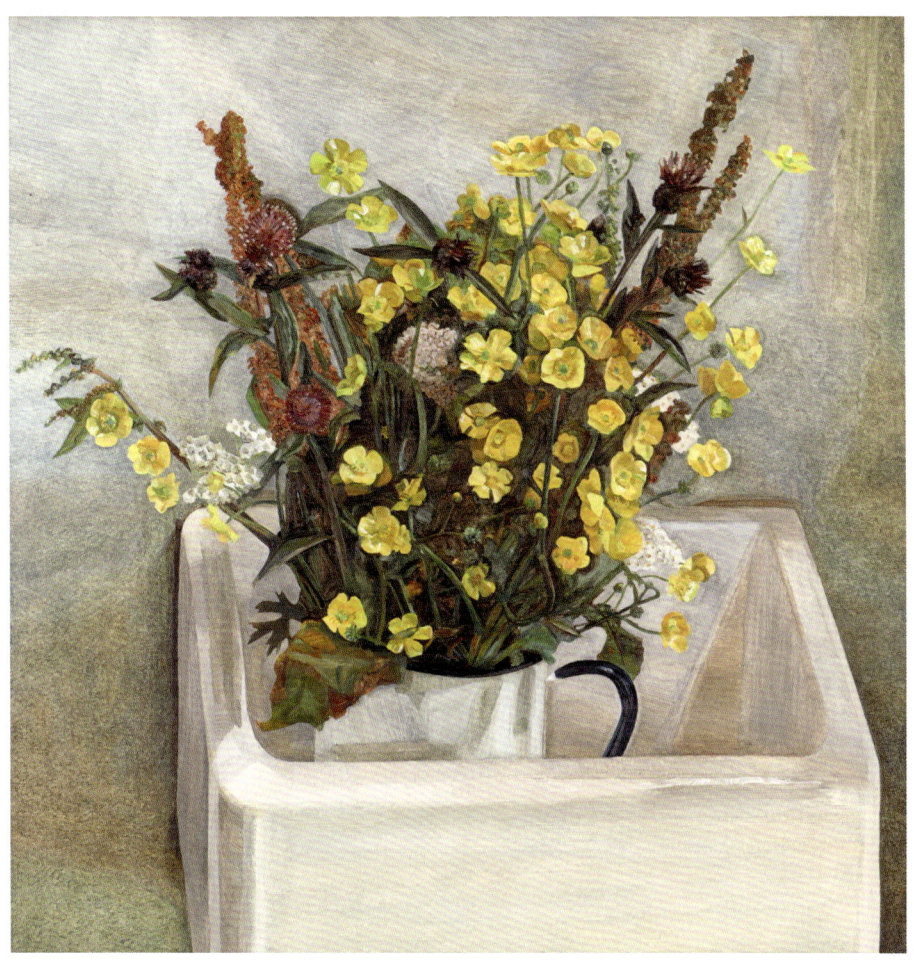

Lucian Freud

Buttercups, 1968
Oil on canvas, 61 × 61 cm / 24 × 24 in
Private collection

The freshness of an early summer morning is masterfully summoned by the vibrant colours and humble setting of *Buttercups*, by British artist Lucian Freud (1922–2011). Bunched together in a simple tin jug are meadow buttercups (*Ranunculus acris*), sorrel (*Rumex acetosa*), red clover (*Trifolium pratense*), white clover (*T. repens*), knapweed (*Centaurea nigra*) and yarrow (*Achillea millefolium*). A far cry from the opulence of eighteenth-century still-life flower compositions, where variegated exotic varieties reigned supreme, *Buttercups* retains a sense of genuine wonder for spontaneous flowering plants – those usually dismissed as weeds. To heighten the lack of sophistication, Freud placed the flowers in a modest white ceramic sink and discards the dark and moody backdrops of the Baroque tradition, favouring the brightness of a bare white wall. Such aesthetic simplicity allowed Freud to capture flowers precisely for what they are, including their imperfections. Similarly, in contrast to the symbolic tradition of flower painting, the artist's intent was not to remind us of the relentless passing of time. Throughout his career, Freud strove to strip off the layers of symbolic meaning humans impose on animals, plants or objects. The history of classical art is filled with beautiful cultivars that symbolically speak of loss, love and purity. In a stark departure from this tradition, Freud's reinvention of the still-life genre portrays truly silent flowers unconcerned with human desires.

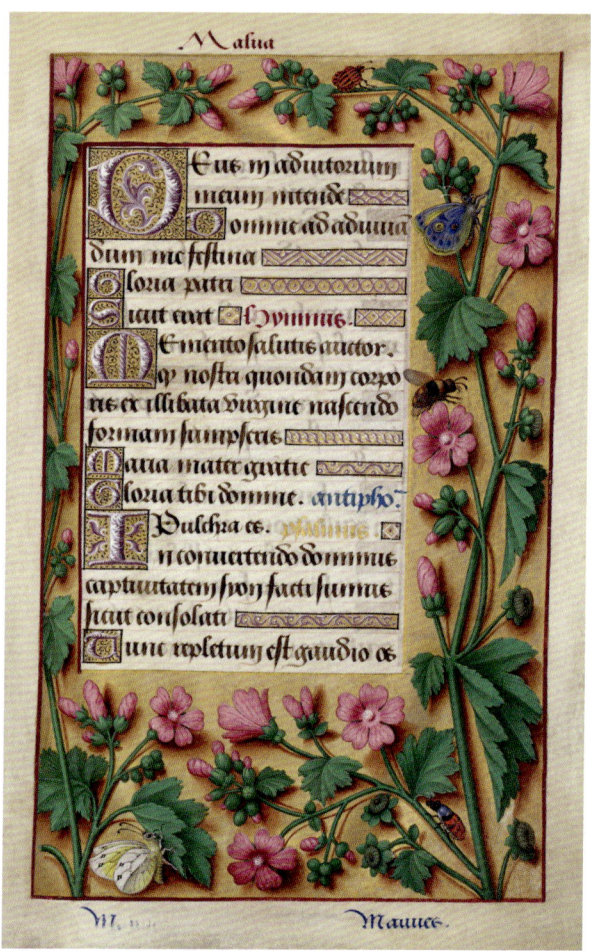

Jean Bourdichon

Folio 71r: Malva, from *Grandes Heures of Anne de Bretagne*, 1505–10
Parchment manuscript, 30 × 19 cm / 11¾ × 7½ in
Bibliothèque nationale de France, Paris

Lying against golden backgrounds, the lush pink flowers and vivid green leaves and stems of mallow frame an evening prayer. Illuminated by French court artist Jean Bourdichon (1457?–1521), this book of hours, or prayer book, was commissioned in 1508 by Anne of Brittany, Queen of France. Bourdichon painted more than 300 different plants, flowers and fruits from

Anne's royal gardens and the countryside to surround the text, casting *trompe l'oeil* shadows as insects clamber among them, increasing the illusion of reality. Bourdichon typically showed only one variety on each page, with the plant's name recorded in both Latin and French on most pages, including mostly traditional favourites but also some plants depicted for the first time, including snowdrops and black currants. The book is considered an important early florilegium, as it recorded a particular historic collection. Much of Bourdichon's career can be traced in and around the French town

of Tours, and as he was paid by the Queen at Blois, it is thought that many of the illustrations were inspired by the plants that grew in the châteaux gardens of the Loire. Many would have been grown as medicinal plants, including mallows, which produce a mucilage or gum with natural anti-inflammatory properties, making it useful for healing ointments or to soothe a sore throat. The plant family name, *Malva*, is from the Greek *malakos*, meaning 'soft', and can be traced back to the ancient Greek herbals that originally described these medicinal values.

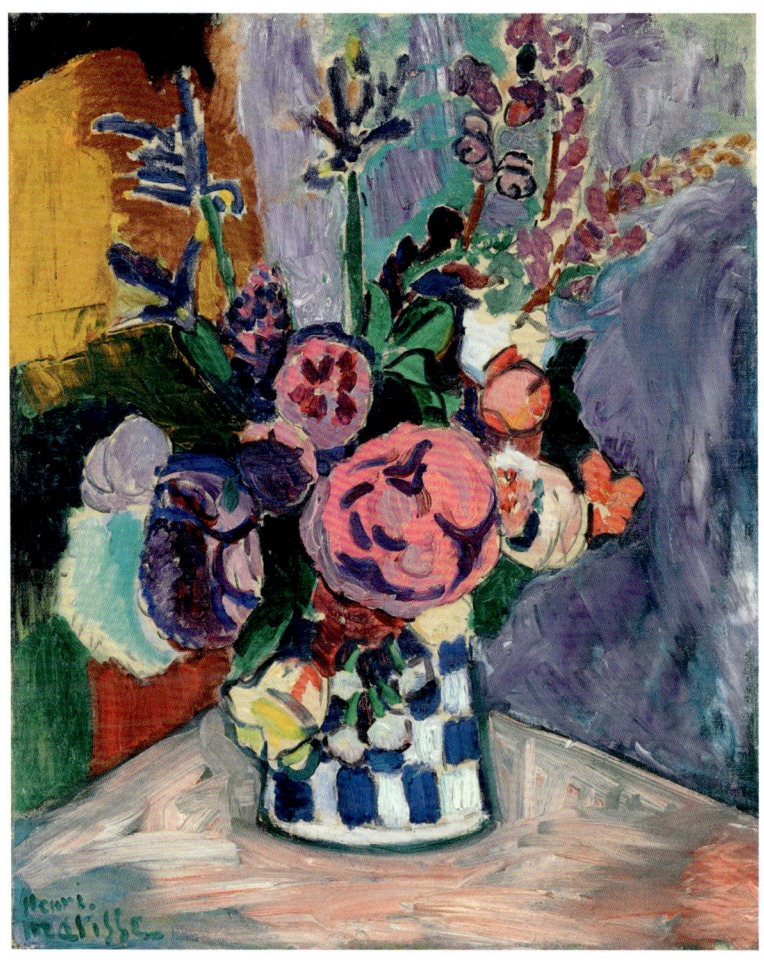

Henri Matisse

Les Pivoines, 1907
Oil on canvas, 65 × 54.6 cm / 25½ × 21½ in
Private collection

Magenta peonies, purple irises and pink fox-gloves sit quietly arranged in a low vase decorated with blue and white squares in a composition that plays the organic against the geometric. Renowned French artist Henri Matisse (1869–1954) sets the rounded exuberance of the peony heads against the spindly and flattened forms of the irises, which recede into pure pattern. The gestural nature of the marks and the brilliance of the colours – created with dynamic strokes of pigment applied separately on a white primed canvas – produces a painting that vibrates with energy. Matisse painted *Les Pivoines* (*The Peonies*) in Collioure, on the Mediterranean coast in the south of France, in the late spring of 1907 at the age of thirty-seven. He had first visited the remote fishing village in 1905, and the time he spent there coincided with his movement away from the representational values of the Impressionists towards the radical, more experimental approach to colour and form adopted by the Fauvists – the 'Wild Beasts' – characterized as the first real revolution in twentieth-century art. Within weeks of its creation, *Les Pivoines* was acquired by art critic Félix Fénéon for the Galerie Bernheim-Jeune in Paris, where it featured in an exhibition of still lifes a few months later, in November 1907. When Matisse put together a solo retrospective at the same he considered the painting sufficiently important in the narrative of his artistic development to select it for the show.

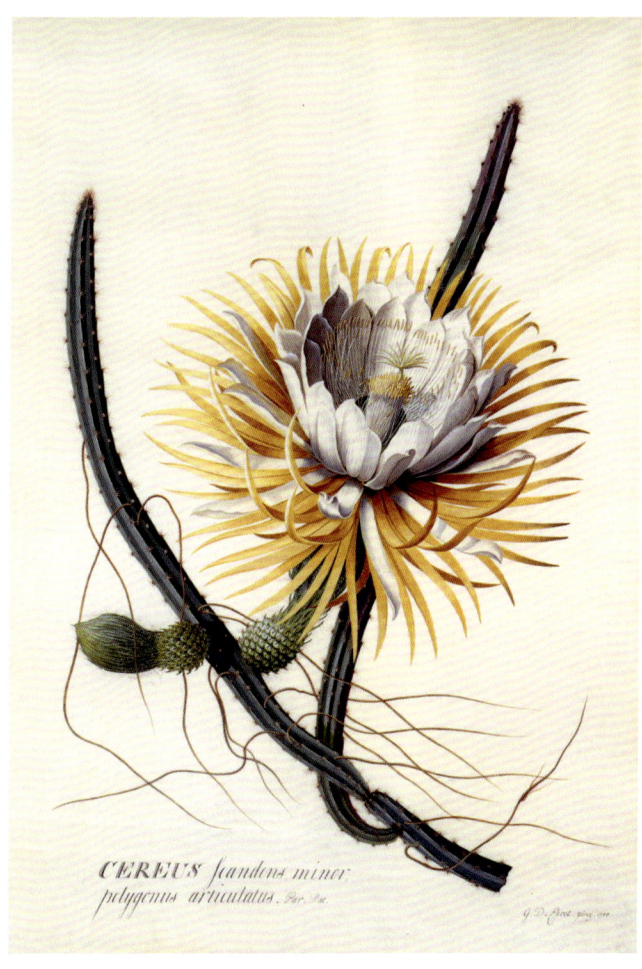

CEREUS *scandens minor*
polygonus articulatus. Par. 9a.

G. D. Ehret pinx. 1750

Georg Dionysius Ehret

Cereus scandens, minor, polygonus, articulatus,
from *Plantae Selectae*, 1750–73
Hand-coloured engraving, 51.4 × 35.6 cm /
20¼ × 14 in
Private collection

Aptly called the queen of the night, this ungainly vining cactus produces spectacular flowers that individually bloom for only one evening each year. The flower petals unfurl and release an intoxicating, vanilla-like scent that attracts nocturnal pollinators; having completed its brief mission, the flower slowly closes and drops to the ground. This dynamic image by German painter Georg Ehret (1708–70) perfectly captures the allure of this flower, which became a popular hothouse plant during the nineteenth century. While it is now known as *Selenicereus grandiflorus*, the painting's title includes Latin descriptors used before the adoption of the Linnaen binomial system. In his youth Ehret was apprenticed as a gardener and learned to paint from his father before securing employment as an illustrator of plants. Eventually, the life-long patronage of the Nuremberg physician Christoph Jacob Trew enabled Ehret to travel through Germany, Holland, France and England and paint many of the plants that had been introduced into Europe, many of which were published in Trew's *Plantae Selectae* (1750–73). Ehret gained the esteem of the scientific community in Germany and England, and was elected the first foreign member of the Royal Society. He created hundreds of paintings for the Duchess of Portland and the Royal Physician Richard Mead and taught flower painting to the daughters of the British aristocracy. Ehret's painting style influenced not only his peers but future generations of botanical artists.

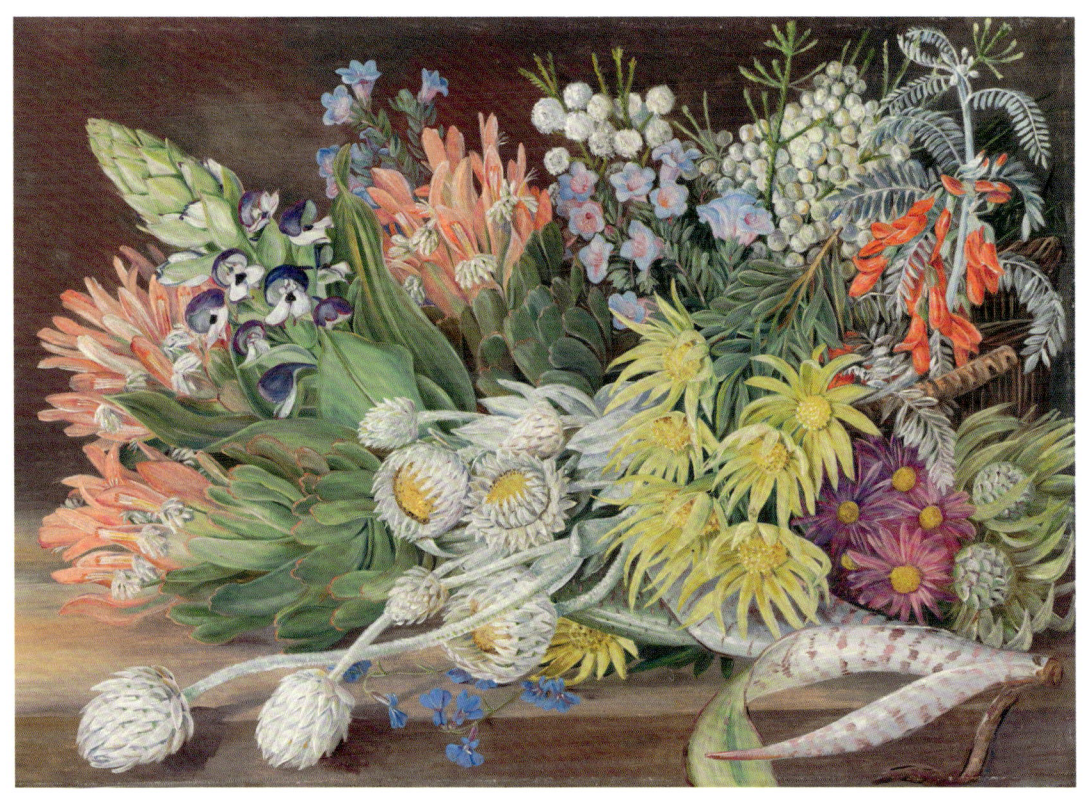

Marianne North

*A Medley of Flowers from Table Mountain,
Cape of Good Hope, c.1882*
Oil on board, 35.2 × 50.5 cm / 14 × 20 in
Marianne North Gallery, Royal Botanic Gardens,
Kew, London

This luscious medley of native South African plants – including *Sutherlandia frutescens*, a legume noted for its medicinal properties, *Brunia*, a member of the borage family, *Lobostemon* and *Leucadendron platyspermum*, noted for its large cones – is just one of a remarkable 800-plus works painted by British biologist and botanical artist

Marianne North (1830–90) during a thirteen-year odyssey spanning six continents. Born in 1830 in Hastings, North became fascinated by exotic plants during visits to the Royal Botanic Gardens at Kew. When her father died in 1869, leaving her a comfortable legacy, she was free to indulge her passion for plants, painting and travel. In 1871, North set out on a journey from Canada to Brazil and then from Ceylon to Australia and New Zealand, the last two at the behest of her friend Charles Darwin. She travelled alone and – unusually for a botanical artist – painted in oils, a sensible choice in a tropical climate. By using

tints of green, blue or orange – rather than black – to modify tones, she achieved a vivid, almost hyperreal palette. On her return from India in 1879, she wrote to Sir Joseph Hooker, director at Kew, offering both her paintings and funding for a gallery. With its mosaic of some 832 paintings, organized geographically, the Marianne North Gallery is a virtual journey around the world, a treasure trove of botanical art and a testament to an intrepid, extraordinary woman.

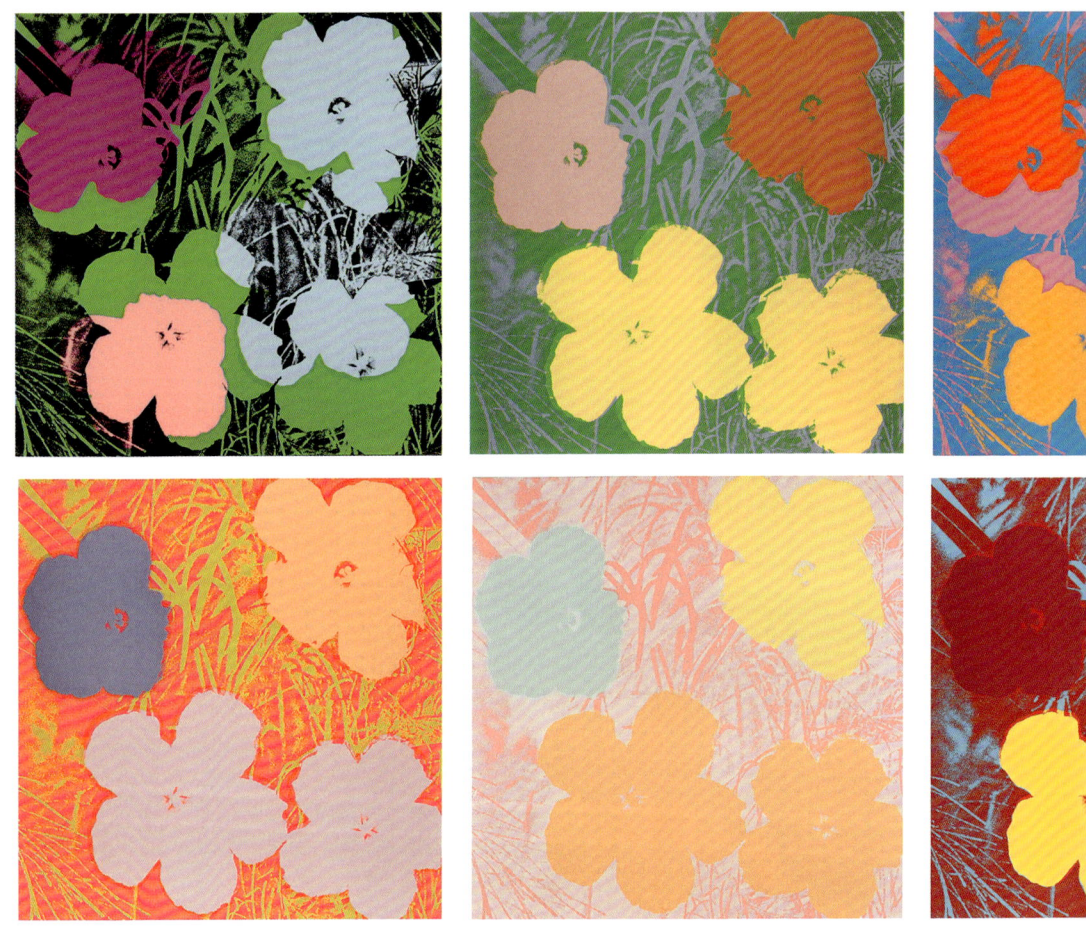

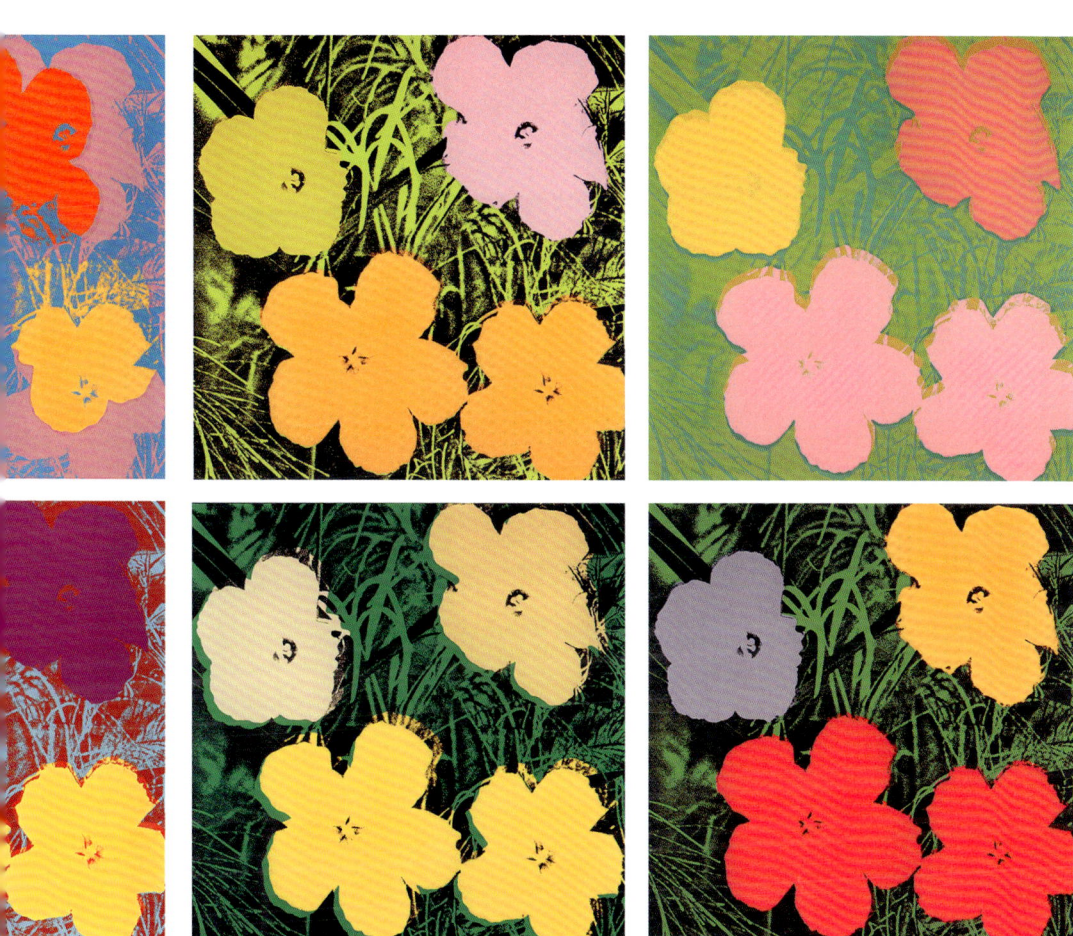

Andy Warhol

Flowers, 1970
Colour screen prints on wove paper, each sheet:
91.4 × 91.4 cm / 36 × 36 in
Private collection

Flowers represented a new subject for the renowned American artist Andy Warhol (1928–87) and marked a pivotal moment in his career. Warhol was apparently encouraged by his friend Henry Geldzahler, the legendary curator at the Museum of Modern Art in New York, in 1964 to consider happier subjects than the disaster images that typically preoccupied him. Flowers were an ideal choice. On the one hand they were positive and life-affirming, but on the other they carried associations with death and decay that appealed to Warhol's darker sensibilities. Warhol produced images of flowers for several years based on an image of hibiscus flowers originally used to illustrate an article about variations in colour photography in *Modern Photography Magazine*. Warhol produced screen prints of *Flowers* in varying sizes and colours, both on paper and on canvas, and the image remains one of the icons of Pop Art. In this set of ten, he introduces substantial variation into the repeated image by using vibrant and sometimes harsh combinations of unlikely colours. Warhol's interest in the serial nature of images and in screen printing as a medium would carry throughout his entire career. Warhol's use of this photograph, meanwhile, resulted in a long lawsuit that defined the boundaries of artistic appropriation for decades – and that forced Warhol to agree to give a portion of all proceeds from the work to the photographer.

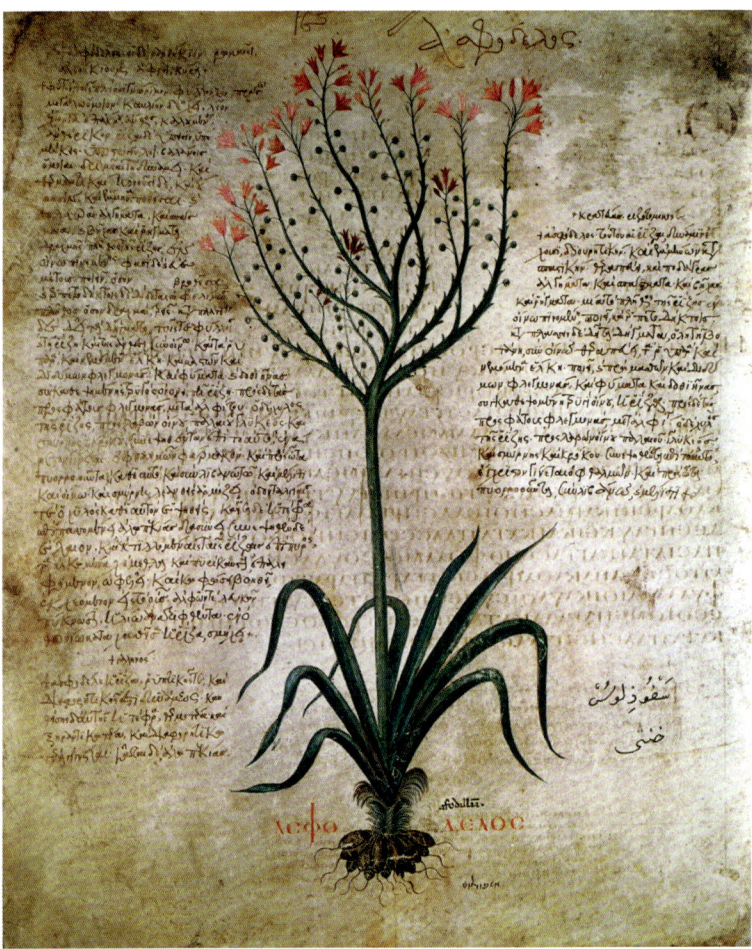

Pedanius Dioscorides

Asphodelos, from *Vienna Dioscorides*, *c*.512 AD
Tempera and ink on vellum, approx. 30 × 37 cm /
11¾ × 14½ in
Österreichische Nationalbibliothek, Vienna

Created more than 1,500 years ago, this Byzantine illustration by an unknown artist of an asphodel beautifully captures the plant's elongated stalk topped with pale pink flowers. The image comes from the oldest known manuscript of the *Codex Vindobonensis*, prepared around 512 AD, also known as the *Juliana Anicia Codex*, after the princess of the Roman Empire to whom the book was

presented. The original codex was created by the Greek physician Pedanius Dioscorides (*c*. 40–90 AD), who was an army doctor with the Roman legions in Greece, Italy, Asia Minor and Provence. As well as recording the existence and therapeutic value of hundreds of plants during his travels, Dioscorides also had access to the library at Alexandria. In about 70 AD he compiled an extensive list of herbs and their medicinal value – around a thousand remedies using around 600 plants. Dioscorides not only described the practical applications of each specimen, but also frequently detailed the structure of their

roots, foliage and flowers. The asphodel here (*Asphodelus aestivus*) – a plant Homer describes as the flower of death, carpeting a particularly gloomy part of the underworld – was noted to have uses ranging from a poultice for sores to a snake-bite antidote. The treatise created by Dioscorides is the oldest work in the history of botany and pharmacology and remained the authority on its subject for over 1,500 years. Since no original copy of Dioscorides' herbal has been found, it is uncertain whether his work incorporated illustrations.

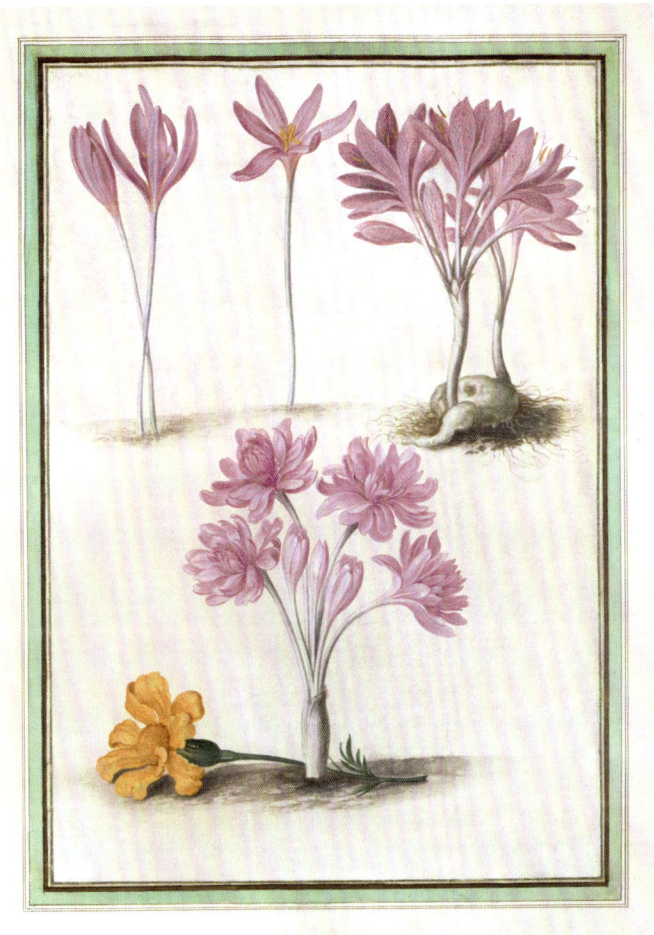

Johann Jakob Walther

Page from *Simulacrum Scenographicum
Celeberrimi Horti Itzsteinensis*, 1654
Watercolour on paper, 60 × 46.2 cm / 23¾ × 18 in
Victoria and Albert Museum, London

A bright yellow French marigold adds a decorative counterpoint to the tender pink of two autumn crocuses, *Colchicum autumnale*, also known as meadow saffron, and *Colchicum tenorii*. This delicate watercolour is one of 133 painted by the Strasbourg artist Johann Jakob Walther (1604–77) to catalogue the flowers and fruits growing in the celebrated garden created by Count Johann of

Nassau-Idstein at his castle near Frankfurt, Germany. The vivid plant portraits that comprise the *Nassau Florilegium* were painted over a period of twenty years, between about 1651 and 1672, during which Walther visited Idstein at least eight times, staying for around six months on each occasion – from April to September – in order to sketch the plants in situ. He then finished the paintings at home in Strasbourg. The florilegium celebrated the count's garden as essentially a collection of ephemeral exhibits, a living extension of the fashionable 'cabinets of curiosities' that brought together examples of the rare

and wonderful in art and nature. It is likely that Walther's florilegium was inspired by, if not directly modelled on, Basilius Besler's magnificent two-volume *Hortus Eystettensis* published in 1613, with its fine engraved illustrations (see p.243). Like Besler before him, Walther ordered the plants by their season of flowering, and often grouped several varieties of each species on one page to create a decorative composition.

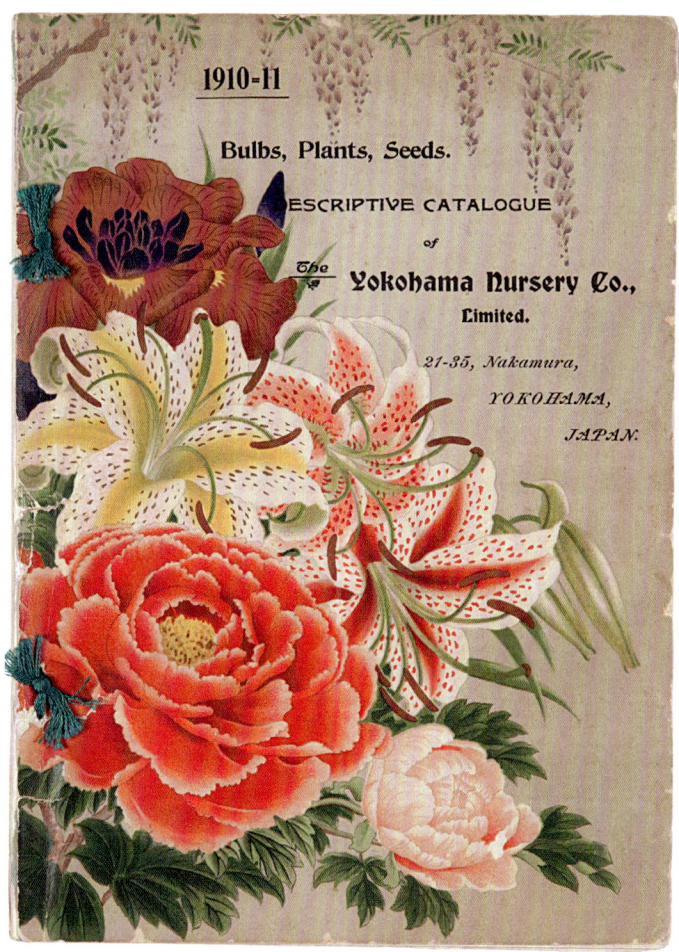

Yokohama Nursery Co. Ltd.

Bulbs, Plants, Seeds. Descriptive Catalogue of the Yokohama Nursery Co., 1910
Chromolithograph print, 26 × 18 cm / 10¼ × 7 in
Caroline Simpson Library & Research Collection, Sydney Living Museums

Vibrant peonies, lilies and irises framed by lush green leaves and hanging wisteria decorate the cover of this Japanese flower catalogue from the early twentieth century, luring buyers with the appeal of the 'exotic East'. Capitalizing on the increasingly fashionable *japonisme* aesthetic that became popular in the West during the second half of the nineteenth century, the Yokohama Nursery Company attained worldwide success as a globally respected horticulture company. Founded in 1890 by Ueki Suzuki in the Japanese city of Yokohama, the nursery later opened branches in cities such as London, Tokyo and New York. People from the West increasingly travelled to Japan in the late nineteenth century, leading to the widespread dissemination of the country's arts and crafts traditions. The company specialized in Japanese plants and flowers, such as bamboo, Japanese laurel, cherry trees and magnolias, and in 1893 it presented the themes of 'bonsai' and 'Japanese garden' at the World's Columbian Exposition held in Chicago. This catalogue exemplifies how such plants impacted the gardening scene worldwide. Its chromolithographic plates use a late Art Nouveau style, rendered with undulating lines and tendril loops, as well as stylized typography. The plants for sale range from peonies and camellias to cherries, lilies and irises, as well as bonsai trees, porcelain flowerpots and stone lanterns that were all typical of this period in Japan's aesthetic history.

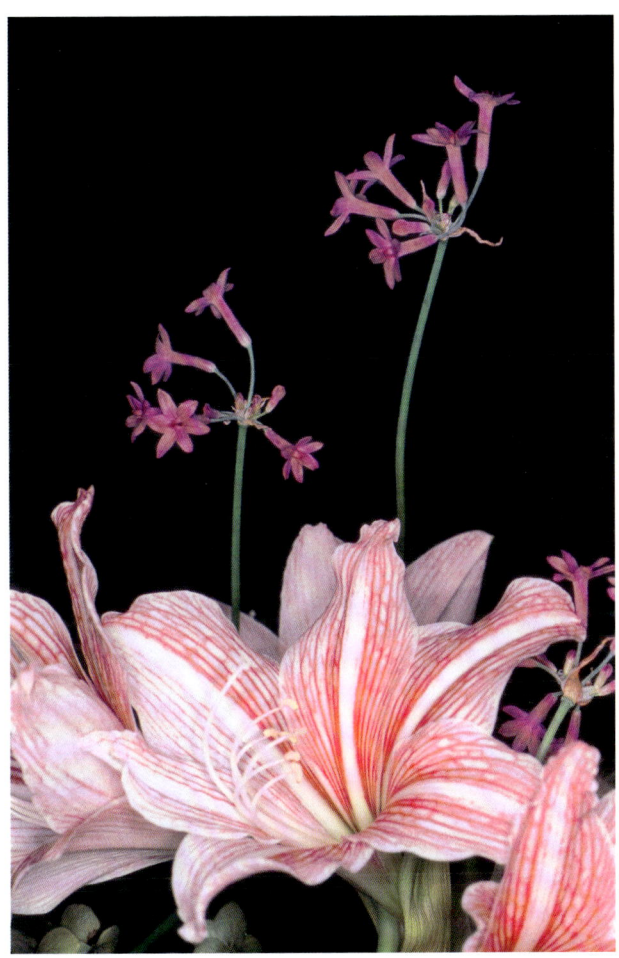

Nobuyoshi Araki

Untitled, from *Flower Rondo*, 1997
Colour photograph, dimensions variable

A strikingly exotic flower arrangement is captured in all its seductive glory by Japanese photographer Nobuyoshi Araki (born 1940). The dominant flowers' large petals are striped in lurid pink, sucking inwards, while delicate tendrils of anthers and filaments appear like upturned fingers, almost hidden yet beckoning gently. Here, the small purple flowers stand in for the intended target: insects, who are needed to ensure pollination, and thus ensure the survival of the species. They hover in front, selecting an orifice into which to crawl. Intriguingly, Araki does not name the flowers in the title of the work – they are in fact from the *Amaryllidaceae* family; the larger is a cultivar (*Hippeastrum* 'Fairy Tale'), with South African *Tulbaghia violacea* behind – and, despite the Japanese artist's reference to his home country's style of flower arranging, *ikebana*, he does not seem concerned solely with the aesthetic quality of these flowers. Rather they are a conduit for other ideas. In his wider practice Araki photographs flowers that are analogous to internal body parts that seemingly ooze, flop or even pulsate. Herein we find one of the artist's driving concerns: to draw parallels between flowers and the human body – and that most primal of shared concerns, reproduction. In this work Araki demonstrates a very real parallel between humans and flowers. In a very raw way, both are engaged in a struggle to attract and seduce, offering their body parts to willing suitors for the continuation of their species.

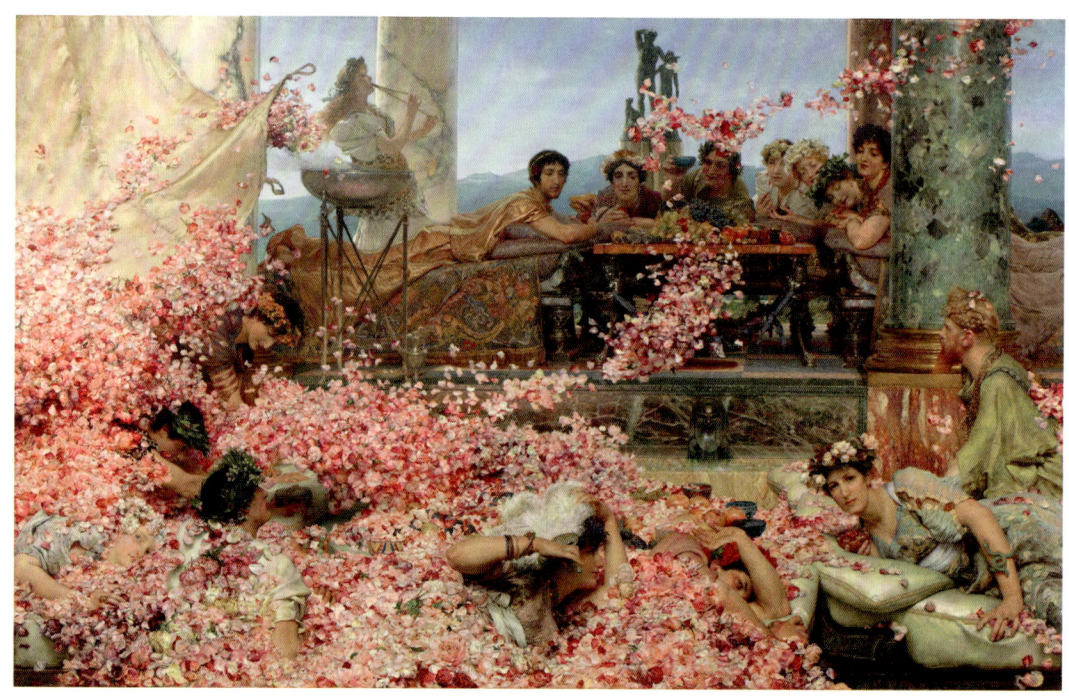

Lawrence Alma-Tadema

The Roses of Heliogabalus, 1888
Oil on canvas, 1.3 × 2.1 m / 4 ft 4 in × 7 ft
Private collection

What at first glance appears to be a celebratory and decadent Roman feast featuring a luxurious blanket of velvet rose petals warming their wearers turns out to be anything but. At the top of the painting, Dutch-English artist Lawrence Alma-Tadema (1836–1912) depicts the Roman emperor Heliogabalus, wearing a gold cape as he hosts a meal, raising a drink to his lips as his friends smile and laugh. Surrounding them are the trappings of the classical world: marble columns, bronze sculptures, burning braziers. Among the flora below, however, are the anguished faces of other guests – the emperor's subjects – drowning and suffocating in a wave of petals. Pink and white rose petals block out most of their bodies, leaving just their heads or a pair of desperately flailing arms, heightening the agony of the scene. According to what was likely a fictional account from the *Historia Augusta*, Heliogabalus – for his pleasure – deliberately smothered his guests with petals of 'violets and other flowers' released from a false ceiling. The flowers being thrown over the guests like a cape or tunic become a metaphor for the power and tyranny wielded by the heartless rulers of Imperial Rome. Painting the canvas in the winter months of 1887, Alma-Tadema arranged for a fresh supply of roses to be sent weekly from the French Riviera to London until the painting was completed, so that he could accurately depict the petals.

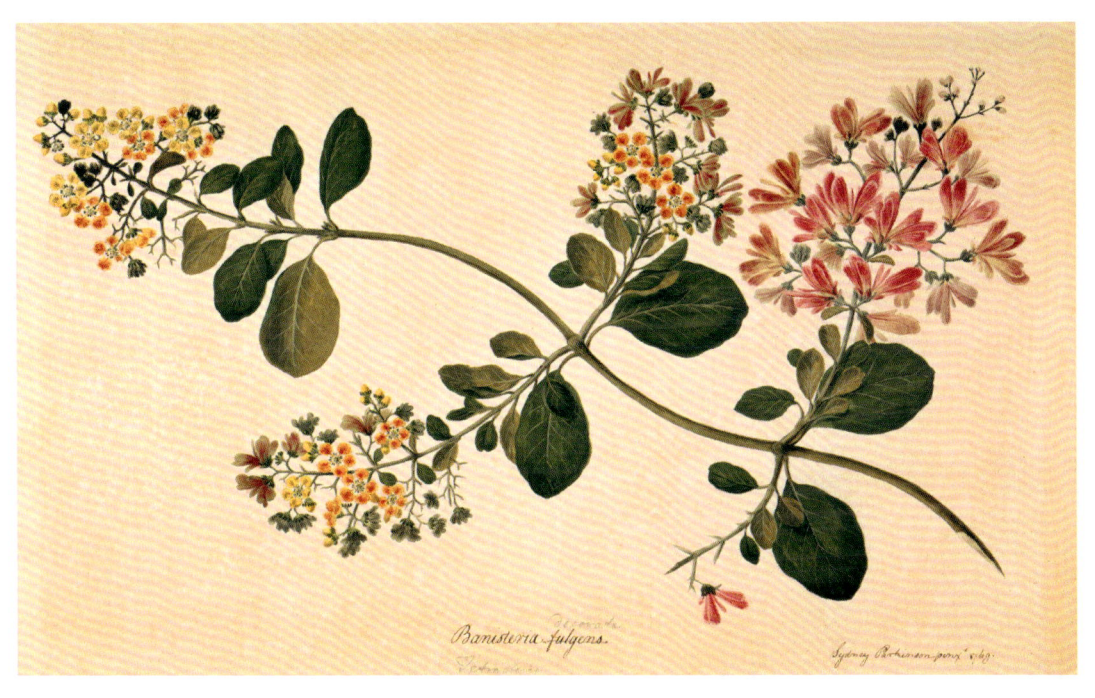

Banisteria fulgens.

Sydney Parkinson pinx.t 1769

Sydney Parkinson

Banisteria fulgens (Tetrapterys phlomoides), 1769
Watercolour, 28 × 46.5 cm / 11 × 18¼ in
Natural History Museum, London

This stem sprawling across the page with clustered flowers in varied hues of pink, yellow and
orange is noted as *Banisteria fulgens* but is in fact
a sprig of *Tetrapterys phlomoides*, a flowering tree
or shrub found exclusively in the states of Espírito
Santo and Rio de Janeiro on the east coast
of Brazil. It was first discovered by Europeans
in 1769, when it was collected by English naturalist Sir Joseph Banks, who was sailing

on Captain James Cook's HMS *Endeavour*,
en route to Tahiti. Accompanying this voyage
was Sydney Parkinson (1745–71), a Scottish
Quaker and botanical illustrator who had worked
for Banks briefly at Kew Gardens in London.
Only twenty-three when he set sail, Parkinson
would become the first European artist to set
foot on Australia, New Zealand and Tahiti, and
to draw their native flora and fauna from direct
observation. Parkinson made some 900 sketches
of plants and animals, and almost 300 fully
coloured paintings, of which this is one; he also
recorded people and landscapes after the

expedition's topographical artist, Alexander
Buchan, died in Tahiti. Parkinson himself con-
tracted fatal dysentery on the homeward voyage;
he was buried at sea in January 1771 on the way
to the African Cape. *Journal of a Voyage to the
South Seas, in His Majesty's Ship, the Endeavour*,
based on Parkinson's diaries, was published
in 1773. Later, engravings of his drawings
appeared in 1900 in James Britten's *Illustrations
of the Botany of Captain Cook's Voyage Round
the World in H.M.S. Endeavour in 1768–71*.

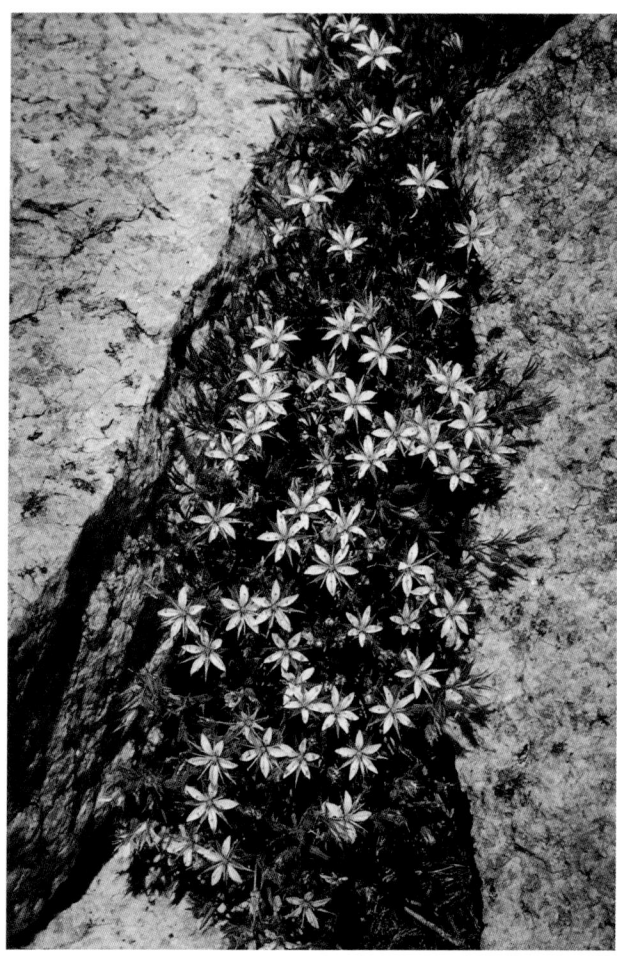

Ansel Adams

Flowers and Rock, San Joaquin Sierra, 1936
Gelatin silver print, 21.7 × 14.6 cm / 8½ × 5¾ in
Collection Center for Creative Photography,
University of Arizona, Tuscon

Delicately beautiful wildflowers shelter inside
the crevice of a rock in California's Sierra Nevada
mountains. This black-and-white image of
Franklin's sandwort (*Eremogone franklinii*) is representative of the iconic style of the prolific
American photographer Ansel Adams (1902–84):
documenting the small nuances and beautiful
moments seen in nature that are almost impossible
to actualize. Adams's photographs are magical yet
stunningly real, showcasing landscapes that
are both invigorating and humbling, reminding
us of how small humans are when seen against
the grandness of nature. *Flowers and Rock, San
Joaquin Sierra* is a photograph included in Adams's
epic 1938 work *Sierra Nevada: The John Muir Trail*.
Adams worked for nearly a year on the project,
which was used as a sophisticated lobbying tool
during the time the United States Congress was
voting on the proposed establishment of Kings
Canyon Grand National Park. Here, Adams's
photograph at once shows the vulnerability of the
flowers and the role of the rock as their protector,
relating the importance of the balance of nature
– a subtle yet powerful example of the need to
preserve our natural treasures. President Franklin
D. Roosevelt kept a copy of the book for the
White House, and in 1940 the areas documented
were officially declared national parks. A lifelong
environmentalist and advocate for conservation
efforts, Adams was awarded the Presidential
Medal of Freedom in 1980.

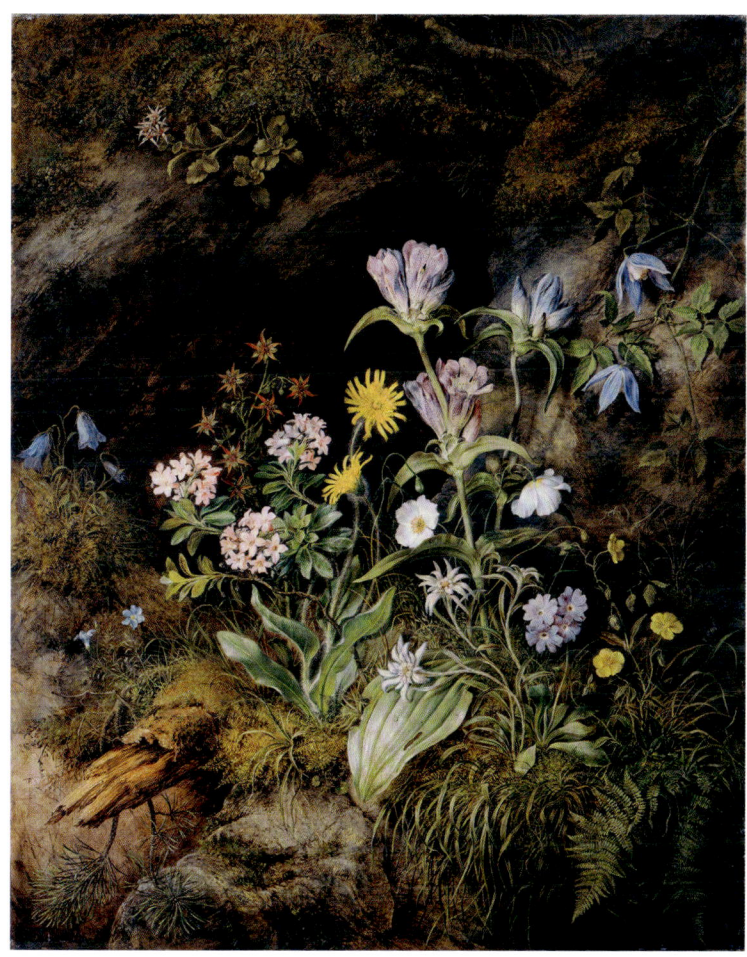

Theodor Josef Petter

Alpine Flora, 1853
Oil on canvas, 89 × 72 cm / 35 × 28⅛ in
Belvedere, Vienna

Grouped in almost bouquet-like proximity, this assemblage of wild alpine flowers was depicted by Austrian painter Theodor Josef Petter (1822–72) with such accuracy that it is possible to identify each individual species – although it is unlikely that they would have been encountered growing so close together at the same time. Blooming in stages throughout the spring and summer, Alpine flowers have evolved to withstand habitats with rocky soil and often below-freezing temperatures. The plants are mostly low to the ground avoiding strong and constant winds. The central stem, thrusting upwards at an angle, is notably a gentian, possibly a purple gentian (*Gentiana purpurea*), while trailing down from the rocks behind are the large blue flowers of alpine clematis (*Clematis alpina*). At left, the drooping blue flowers of a bellflower (*Campanula* sp.) and pink-flowered *Daphne cneorum* grow from a mossy mound, while centre-stage we see the yellow flower heads of alpine hawkweed (*Hieracium alpinum*). In the foreground, pride of place is given to edelweiss (*Leontopodium alpinum*), with its white, woolly flower heads. Petter was the son of Franz Xavier Petter, a famous floral still-life painter, and Theodor benefitted from his father's teachings. Although Theodor was best known for his botanical paintings, he was also an accomplished portrait painter. He studied under Friedrich von Amerling, a famous portrait painter in Emperor Franz Josef's court, and attended the Viennese Academy of Fine Arts and later the Munich Academy of Fine Arts.

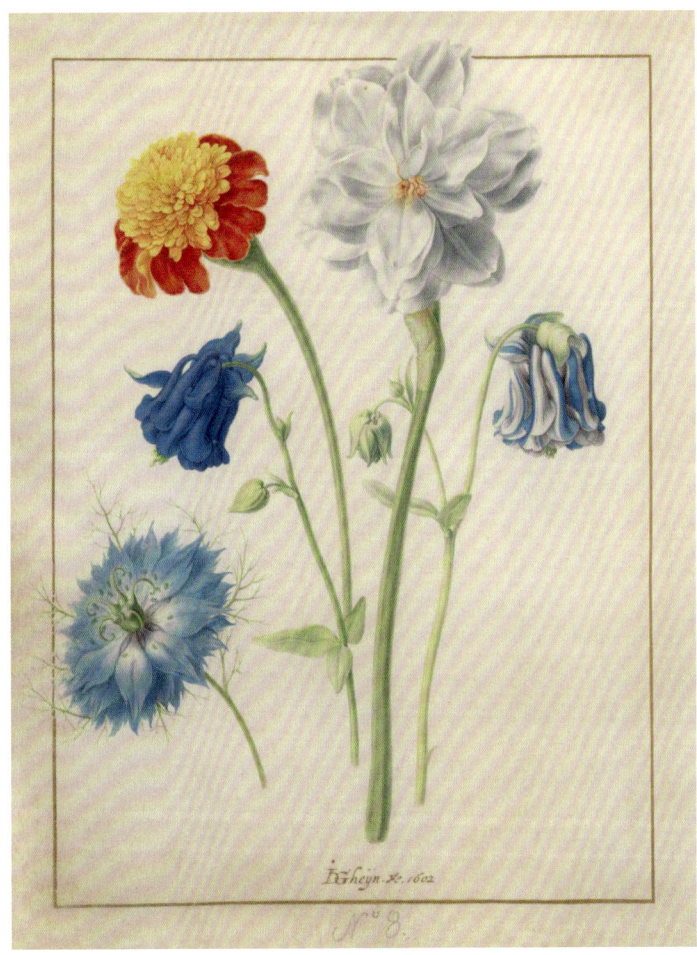

Jacques de Gheyn II

Five Flowers, from an album of 22 drawings of flowers, insects and animals, 1602
Watercolour and tempera on vellum, 21.9 × 16 cm / 8½ × 6¼ in
Fondation Custodia, Collection Frits Lugt, Paris

Framed with a thin line of gold, this watercolour painting by Dutch artist Jacques de Gheyn II (1565–1629) delicately depicts five flowers, including a marigold, poet's narcissus, columbine and *Nigella damascena*, which is seductively nicknamed love-in-a mist. Although native to different parts of the world – the marigold to South and Central

America and especially Mexico, and the columbine to meadows and woodlands throughout the Northern Hemisphere, for example – the flowers are brought together in a single composition, their bright colours offsetting one another. The vibrant orange of the marigold makes the centre of the poet's narcissus stand out, while the blue petals of the other flowers complement one another with shades from royal blue to turquoise. Born in Antwerp in the mid-sixteenth century, de Gheyn worked both as a painter and an engraver. During the course of his career, he moved from the Northern Mannerist style to Dutch realism.

He began as a glass painter and draftsman – and is credited with creating nearly 1,500 drawings in his lifetime, which included numerous landscapes – until shifting his focus to painting and etching from around 1600. Part of the entourage of Dutch royalty, he depicted some of the earliest examples of floral still lifes, female nudes and the *vanitas* genre in Dutch painting. A man of many talents, he even designed a garden that included two grottoes for Prince Maurice of Orange.

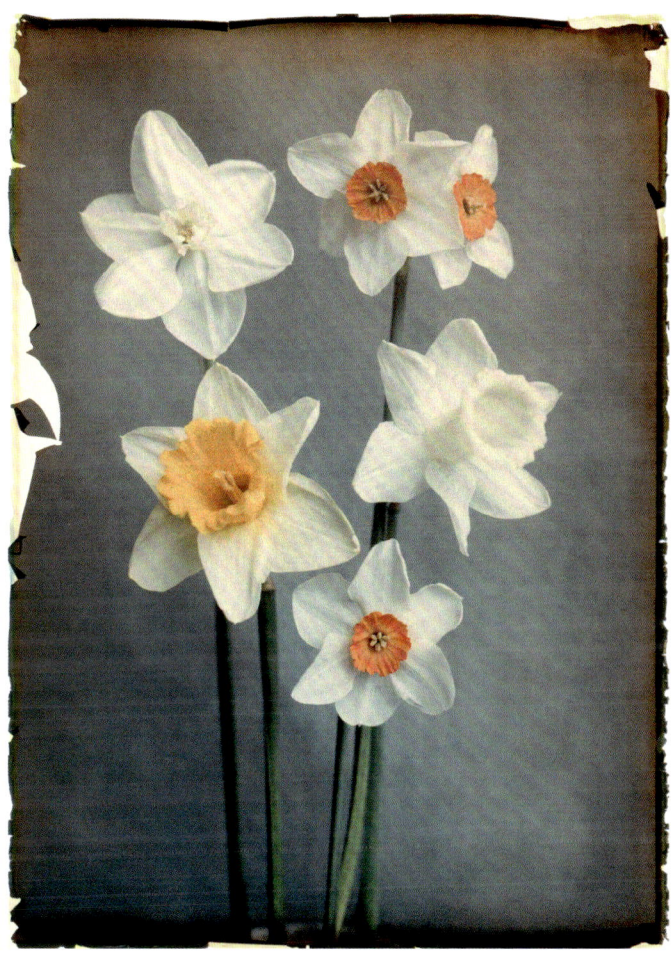

Leendert Blok

*Daffodils, c.*1927
Autochrome photograph, 18 × 13 cm / 7 × 5 in
Nationaal Archief/Collectie Spaarnestad,
The Hague

Four varieties of narcissus are arranged at different heights so as to display their petals with clarity and minimal overlap. Despite being highly staged for commercial purposes, the image retains a pronounced atmospheric freshness that enhances the essential traits of each individual flower – the trademark style of Dutch photographer Leendert Blok (1895–1986). Blok's images of flowers have had a major impact on the history of botanical photography. The clarity of composition and the plain background reference the tradition of botanical illustration. However, the artist not only focused his lens on the minute details of petals and leaves but also bathed his subjects in a uniform soft lighting to accentuate the nuanced textures and forms. Colour photography was invented in 1861, but it was not until the early 1920s that the quality of prints could satisfy botanists and naturalists. For the images included in his *Silent Beauties* series, Blok relied on the richness of colour, and three-dimensional breadth, offered by the Lumière autochrome process (see p.152). While some of Blok's photographs reflect artistic flair, the artist worked closely with botanists and growers interested in producing reliable, realistic images for sales catalogues of Dutch flowers. With their modern sensibility, aesthetic subtlety and balance, Blok's images are a timeless representation of the beauty of flowers.

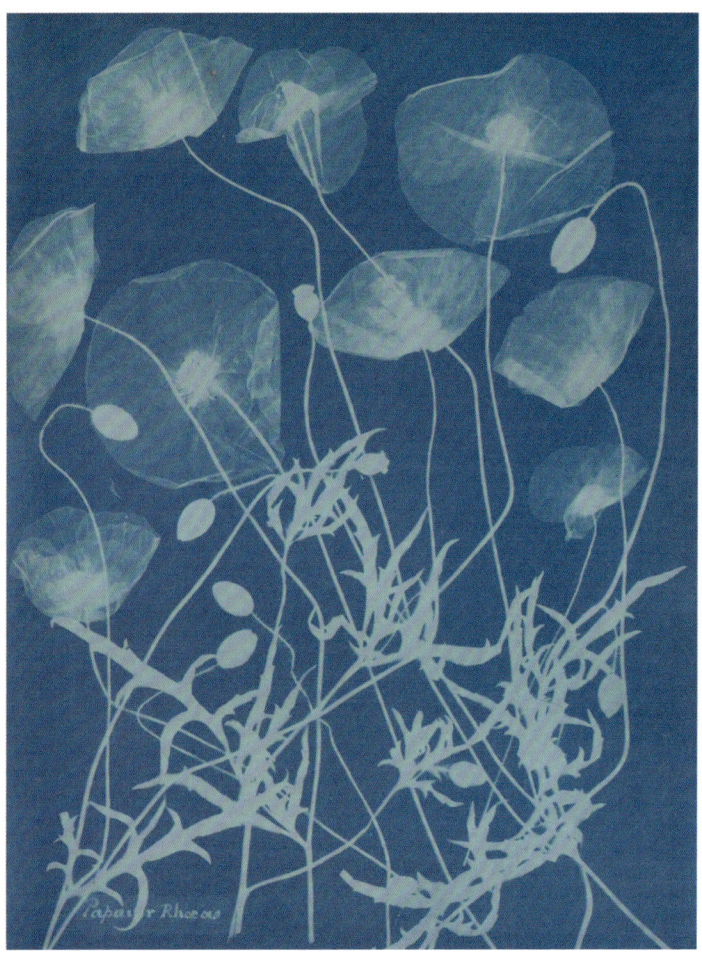

Papaver rhoeas

Anna Atkins and Anne Dixon

*Papaver rhoeas, c.*1851–54
Cyanotype photogram, 25.4 × 19 cm / 10 × 7½ in
Private collection, courtesy of Hans P. Kraus Jr.,
New York

A handful of common poppies (*Papaver rhoeas*)
is artfully cast across the page, revealing
a diaphanous cluster of petals that contrast with
opaque stems and leaves. What might appear
a straightforward image, however, is the result
of remarkable photographic innovation and a rare
example of scientific endeavour by a woman
of the Victorian age. Anna Atkins (1799–1871),

widely acknowledged to be the first female
photographer, had a keen interest in science,
a passion that was fostered by her father, scientist John George Children, and which led her
to experiment with cyanotype only a year after
the form was invented. The technique involves
positioning specimens on paper coated with iron
compounds that creates an image when exposed
to sunlight. Although she was a gifted illustrator,
Atkins seized upon the technique to make precise botanical images of plants, each rendered
negative on a deep cyan background. This plate
is part of a collection of garden specimens

originally included in an album presented
to Henry Dixon, nephew of Atkins's sometime
collaborator and childhood friend, Anne Dixon.
Atkins was the first person to create an illustrated photographic book – her self-published
three-part volume, *Photographs of British Algae:
Cyanotype Impressions*. Begun in 1843, it was
prescient in its appreciation of the value of photography to the scientific study of nature.

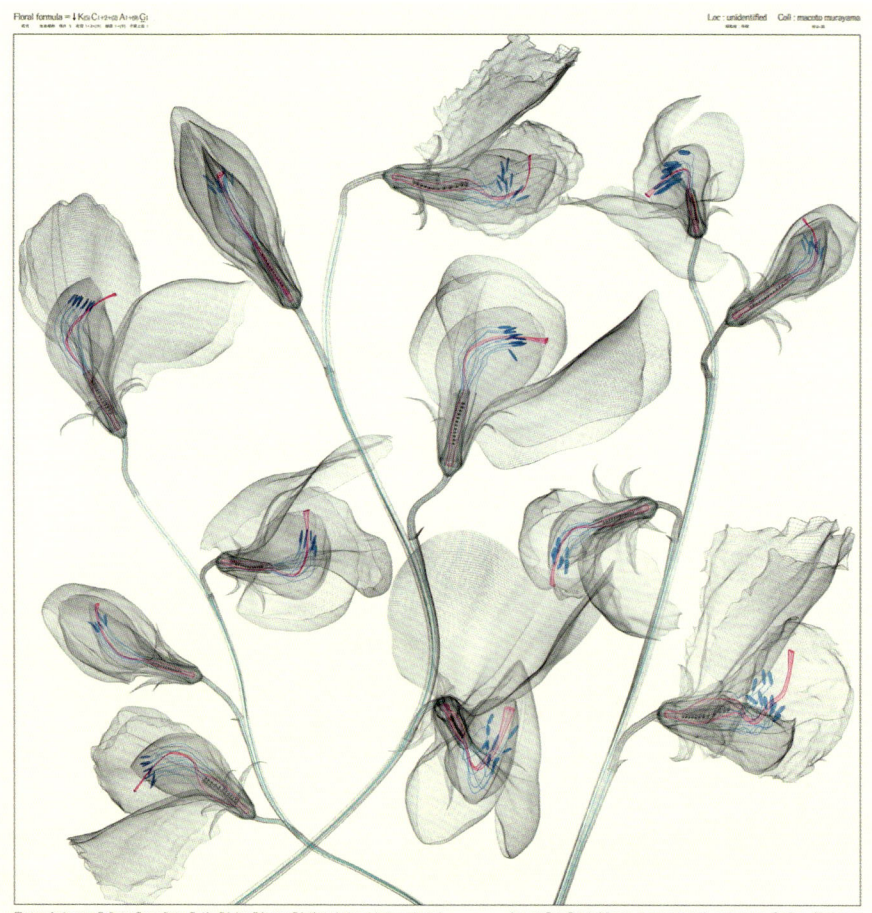

Plantae › Angiosperm › Eudicots › Core eudicots › Rosids › Fabales › Fabaceae › Faboideae › Lathyrus › Lathyrus odoratus L.   Inorganic flora - Botanical diagram - Lathyrus odoratus L. - ecology view   S = 7 : 1   SI units = μm

Macoto Murayama

Lathyrus odoratus L. – Ecology View, 2012
Digital, dimensions variable

Carefully arranged to fill the page in the same manner as traditional botanical plates, these delicate sweet pea flowers are evidence of how the complicity of art and science can reveal plants in new and exciting ways. Since the Middle Ages, botanical illustrators have attempted to capture the realistic structures and colours of plants, yet from the stylized renditions of early herbals to the detailed plates of eighteenth-century colonial explorers, botanical illustration has always entailed a compromise between the material essence of the plant and its reproduction on a two-dimensional surface. Like other art forms, botanical illustration has therefore always entailed a certain level of idealization, commonly adjusting lighting and perspective to visualize all the important parts of the plant at once. Japanese artist Macoto Murayama (born 1984) creates exceptional three-dimensionally rendered botanical illustrations with the help of Autodesk 3ds Max, a computer graphics software frequently used in video-game design and animation. While outstandingly beautiful, the futuristic allure of Murayama's images also alludes to a desire to discover the secrets of the botanical world, underlined by the way the artist collects, dissects, draws and photographs specimens to gather as much information as possible from different viewpoints. Like industrial blueprints, the resulting images simultaneously show the inside and outside of specific flowers in ways that neither botanical illustration nor photography ever could.

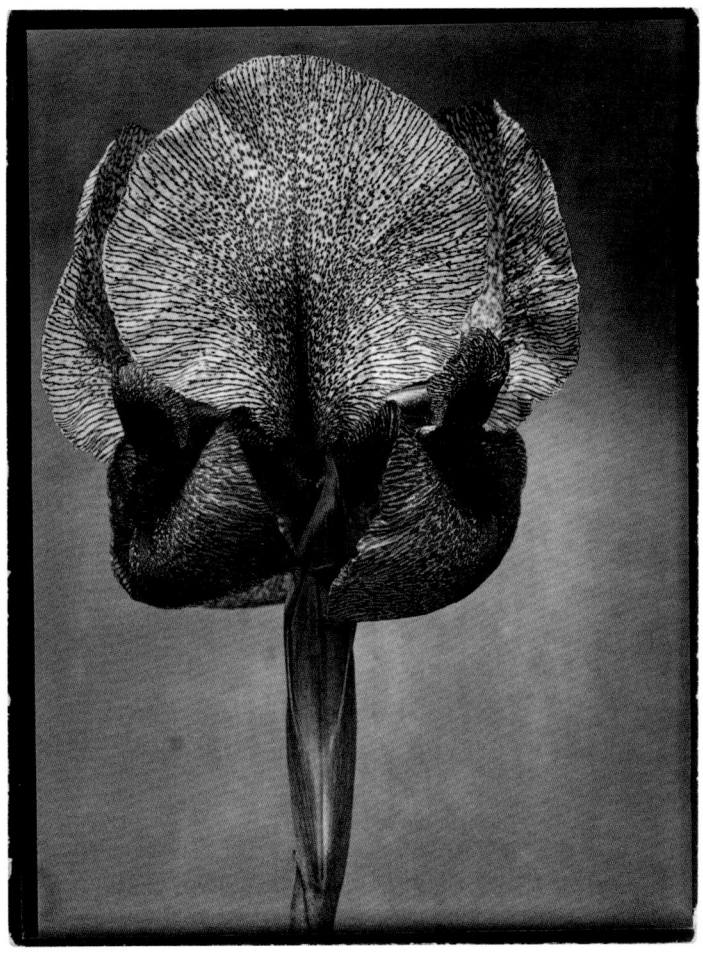

Charles Jones

Iris susiana, c.1895–1910
Gelatin silver print, 21.6 × 16.5 cm / 8½ × 6½ in
Private collection

An isolated specimen, *Iris susiana*, is photographed in tight close-up against a neutral, dark background, with all unnecessary detail stripped away. Captured by British horticulturalist and photographer Charles Jones (1866–1959), the flower, a native of Lebanon and Syria, also known as the 'mourning iris' for its striking purple-black and grey petals, has extraordinary presence. Born in the industrial town of Wolverhampton, Jones

trained as a gardener and worked at a number of private estates across England. From around 1895 onwards, he produced a series of remarkable gelatin silver prints of fruit, vegetables and flowers. Although his distinctive style prefigures the work of such modernist photographers as Edward Weston and Karl Blossfeldt (see p.273), Jones's work was not exhibited in his lifetime, and he left behind no negatives, journals or papers. His work might never have come to light but for the chance discovery in 1981 by Irish-born photographic collector Sean Sexton of a suitcase crammed with hundreds of carefully annotated photographs at a London

antiques market. Since then Jones, who resorted to using his glass plate negatives as cloche covers in his impoverished later years, has gained recognition for the timeless beauty of his images. How he was able to produce such a large body of work and develop such a refined aesthetic while apparently working in complete isolation, however, will remain a mystery forever.

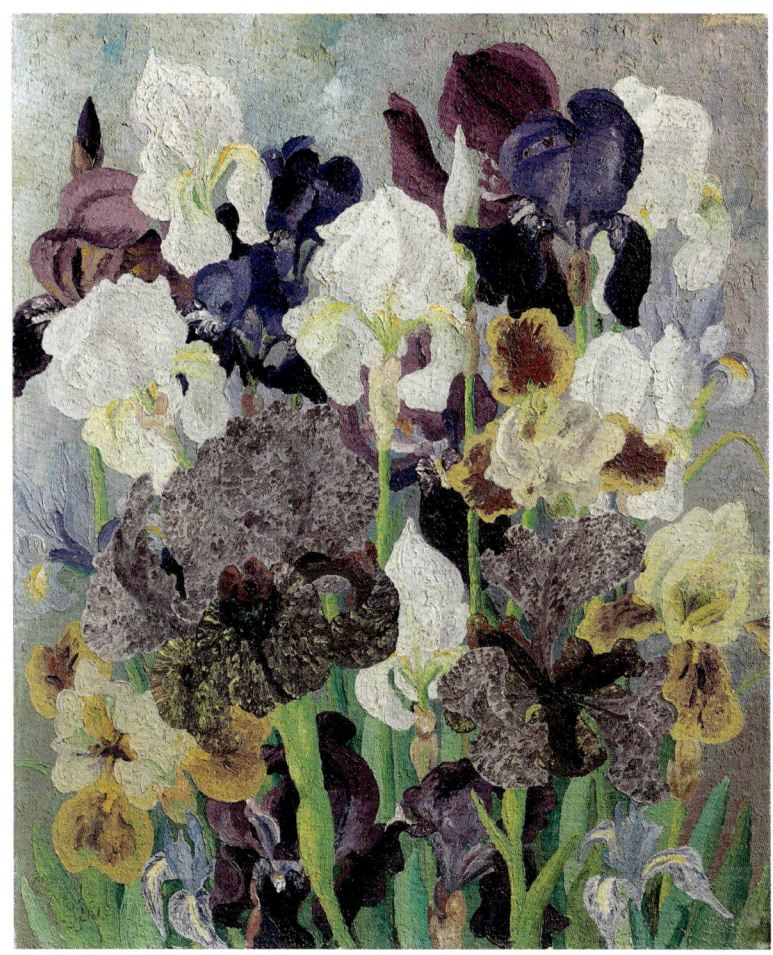

Cedric Morris

May Flowering Irises No. 2, 1935
Oil on canvas, 65 × 54 cm / 25½ × 21¼ in
Private collection

Bold purple, blue and white flowers mingle with golden yellow and chocolate brown in a sensuous array of luscious iris blooms, showcasing the wide variations – there are up to 300 species – that attracted British painter Cedric Morris (1889–1982) to his favourite subject. Morris strived to capture the subtlety and character of individual flowers almost as if painting portraits of individual people. Here, no single flower dominates the composition; each is rendered with small daubs of oil paint, creating a surface of slightly raised impasto brushstrokes. This canvas was painted in Morris's garden studio at Pound Farm in Suffolk where, with his partner Arthur Lett-Haines, he established the East Anglian School of Painting and Drawing, whose students included Lucian Freud (see p.17) and Maggi Hambling. It was also at Pound Farm that Morris first experimented with growing flowers from seeds he had collected on his international travels, going on to gain a reputation as a breeder of irises. He formally registered more than forty different cultivars, including 'Benton Menace', named after his pet cat, and 'Benton Rubeo', which commemorates the macaw given to him by Stella Gwynne, mother of the renowned cookery writer Elizabeth David. Morris, who loved horticulture as much as painting, referred to himself as an 'artist-plantsman', a description that appears on his epitaph in Friars Road Cemetery in Hadleigh, Suffolk.

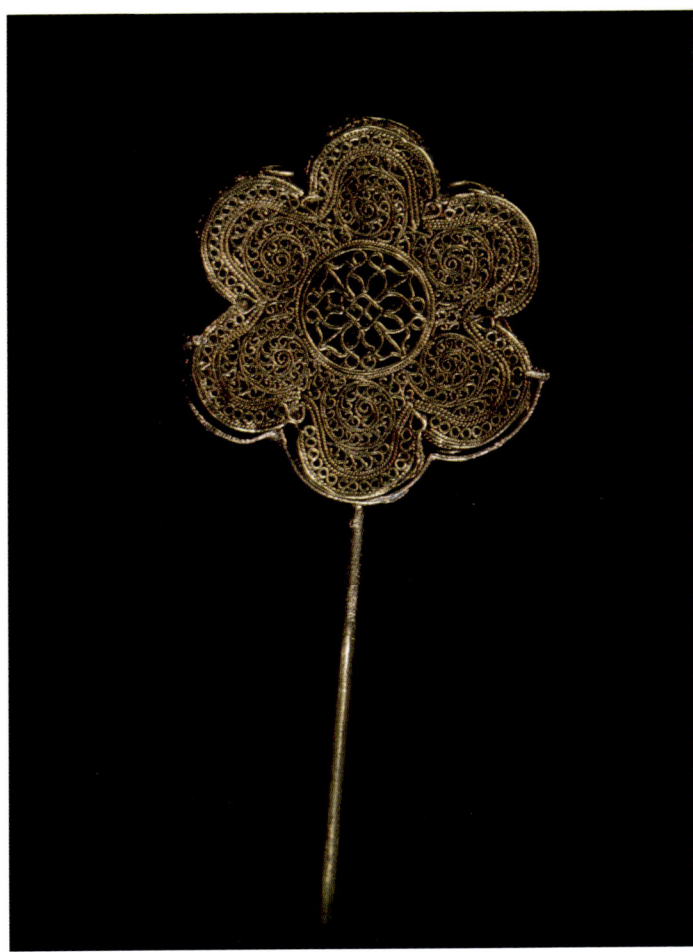

Anonymous

Flower hairpin, 909–1171 AD
Gold filigree

The overall form of this stunning golden flower, rendered in lace-like tracery, is basic and stylized to the point that it is hard to identify from which specific flower it might be derived. Six petals of equal shape and size surround a circle where disk florets might be found, as with the centre of a daisy. The fine gold filigree of this hairpin displays its dramatic opulence: in the petals we see tight swirls like fiddleheads packed close together and, in the very centre, a complex and delicate Islamic pattern. The hair pin would have been worn by a lady in the upper echelons of society under the Fatimids, a Shia caliphate that included a large area of North Africa and was governed from Cairo from the tenth to late twelfth centuries. The dynasty was remarkably wealthy, deriving its riches from its control of the trade in spices, silks and slaves. Constructed from such gossamer golden threads, this pin would have made the wearer's hair shimmer and glint in the light, but it is unlikely this object would have been worn for merely aesthetic purposes. Beyond acting as an important item of wealth – retained by the woman, even if she were to divorce – the symbol of a flower would have had a potent specific meaning, now lost to us.

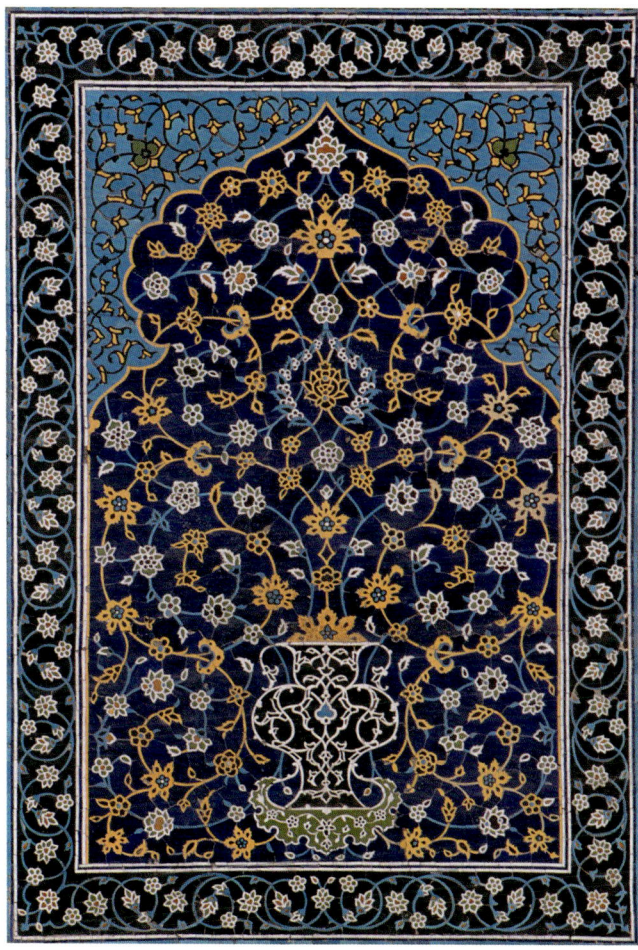

Anonymous

Entrance portal (detail), 1706–14
Ceramic tiles
Madar-i-Shah Madrasa, Isfahan, Iran

Vine-like spirals studded with blossom emerge from an ornate white vase, like seeds growing towards the light, signifying the progression of creation from a single Creator to eternity. This Islamic tilework decorates the entrance to the Madar-i-Shah *madrasa*, or theological college, in Isfahan, in what is now Iran; the madrasa was part of a vast urban complex begun under the last Safavid emperor that also included a mosque, caravanserai and bazaar. The quality of the work belies the notion of inevitable aesthetic decline at the end of a dynasty; indeed, early Safavid traditions are reflected in both the colours and the design. Calligraphy, geometric shapes and plant-based schemes are the main elements of Islamic decoration, and the last, in particular, became increasingly complex and stylized over time, influenced most notably by Byzantine and Chinese design. The scrolling flowers and leaves in this design, probably representing local flora, spring from two intertwined spiral motifs – one in blue with white-outlined flowers and leaves, the other yellow. A separate blue-and-white spiral fills the border, and a lighter blue-and-yellow variant occupies the upper corners. The form of the central vase contrasts with the spirals in being composed of a set of self-contained shapes, called *kapali*. The pattern is strictly symmetrical and repetitive, the floral motifs carefully positioned so that only the image of the vase from which everything springs stands out; the design otherwise oscillates rhythmically and evenly.

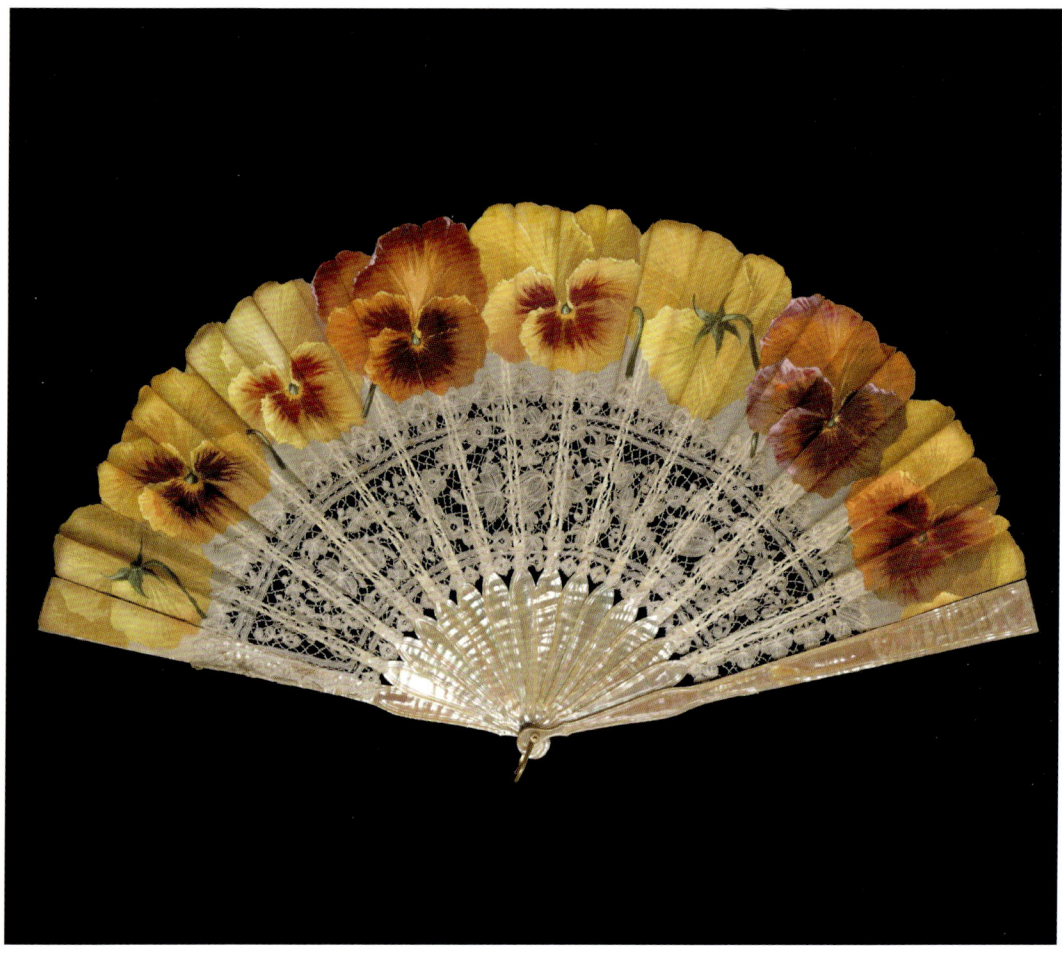

Ronot-Tutin

Fan, 1890–1900
Painted silk gauze and bobbin lace leaf, with mother-of-pearl sticks and guards, 37.5 × 66.5 × 3.3 cm /
14¾ × 26 × 1¼ in
Victoria and Albert Museum, London

The heads of eight pansies in full bloom form an arc of blossoms at the edge of a delicate ladies' fan. French artist Ronot-Tutin hand-painted the flowers onto the fan, which was intricately crafted out of iridescent mother-of-pearl sticks and guards, bobbin lace and gossamer-thin silk gauze to create an impression of refinement, elegance and class.

Although fans are still used today to keep cool, this ornamental example had an additional function, which the image of flowers served to heighten. At a time of comparatively strict cultural and sartorial rules in which revealing the skin was seen as brash and crude, the fan could become an aid to the art of seduction, hiding and revealing the user. The pansies' petals – luscious and smooth – act as a metaphor for skin itself, while the lace would have partially hidden the skin of the hands and hinted at what lay beneath the clothes. An active adornment, the fan could be held to shield the face as its owner glanced at potential suitors,

so that the bright flowers drew attention to her eyes before they were hidden again behind the fan. Intriguingly, two of the pansies turn their heads coquettishly from the viewer, once more alluding to the game of hiding and revealing that is taking place both within and outside the fan.

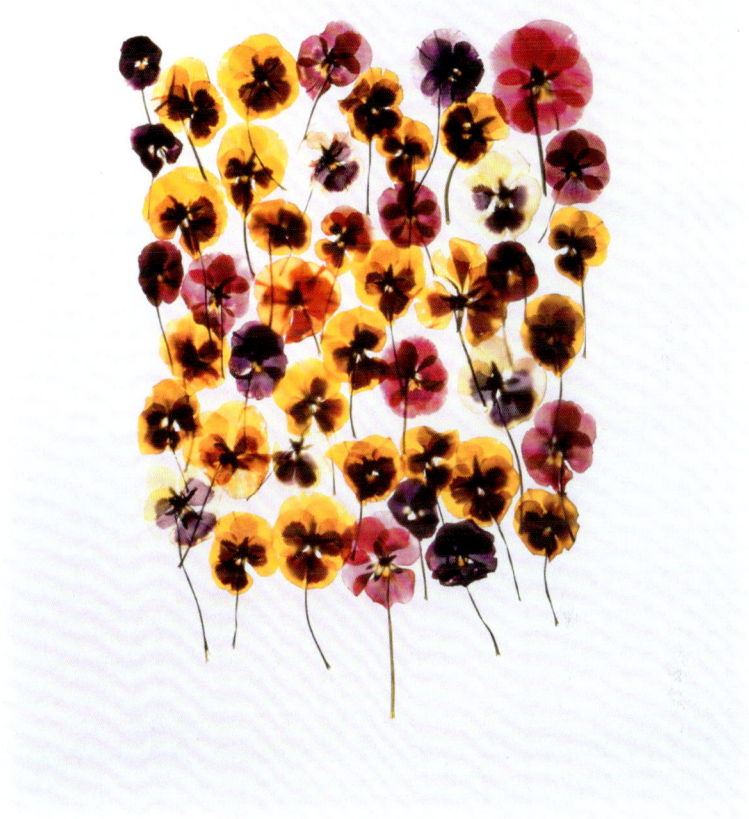

Adam Fuss

Untitled, 1994
Cibachrome photogram, 24 × 20 in / 61 × 50.8 cm
Private collection

At first glance these scattered pansies, with overlapping petals arranged in a flattened composition, may look like pressed flowers. But British-born American photographer Adam Fuss (born 1961) has instead placed pansies directly onto Cibachrome paper and exposed them to light. Growing up in rural England, Fuss documented the natural world through photography from an early age. This led him to experiment with early photographic techniques and eventually to ditch his analogue camera to produce images using camera-less processes, including pinhole images, daguerreotypes and photograms. In a revival of the photogram technique, pioneered by William Henry Fox Talbot and Anna Atkins (see p.34), and later developed by Man Ray with his 'rayographs', botanical specimens – flowers, petals, leaves, stems – are placed directly on a photographic medium. Here, Fuss's use of the Cibachrome technique is based on the chromolytic process, which uses a direct positive rather than relying on a traditional photographic negative. Using a silver-dye bleach with high concentrations of cyan, magenta and yellow, the dyes are incorporated in the emulsion of the paper, instead of being formed chemically in washes. Each layer contains a complementary colour to the sensitivity of that particular layer. The dyes are bleached away to reveal colour and to form a positive photograph. The resulting image has a distinctive and exceptional colour brilliance and the print appears to have a sharp, high-gloss, almost metallic finish.

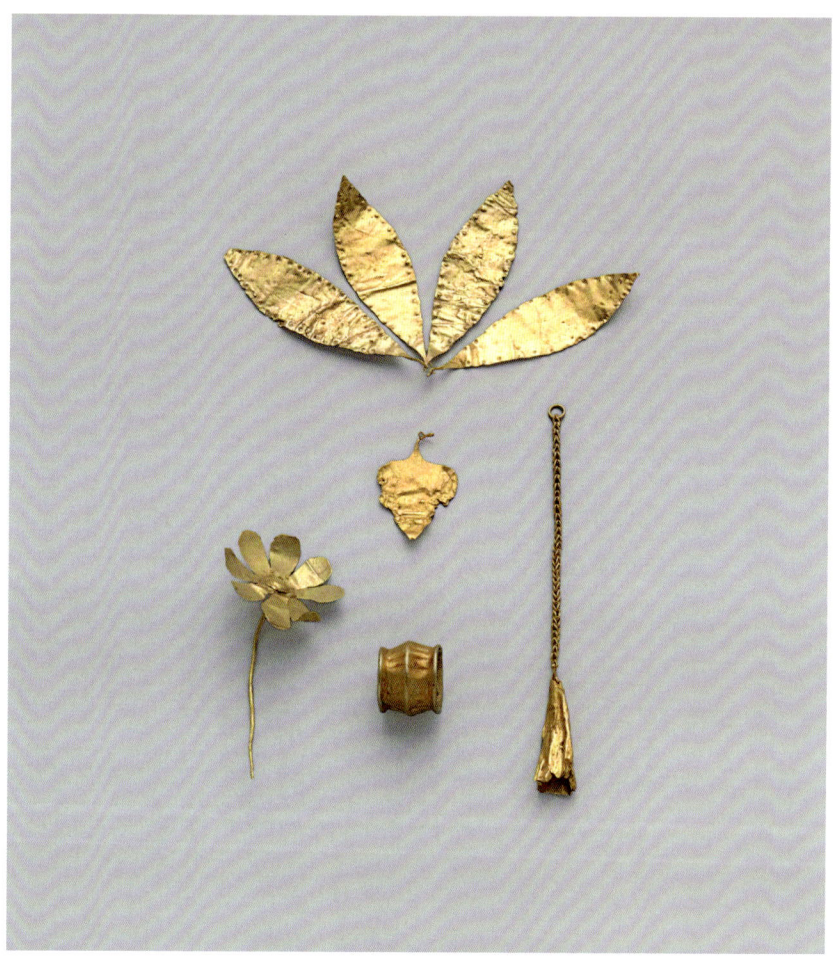

Anonymous

Gold ornaments, *c*.2300–2100 BC
Gold, dimensions variable
Metropolitan Museum of Art, New York

Individual leaves, a flower pendant suspended on a chain, a three-dimensional bead and a hairpin wrought into the shape of a flower are among the collection of small gold objects discovered by American archaeologist Richard Seager on the island of Mochlos, off the coast of Crete. Flowers and leaves were an enduring symbol of new life and celebration in Minoan and later Greek culture, and these graceful ornaments are part of a series of objects discovered in the tombs of wealthy residents of the settlement. As such, the delicately formed, hand-beaten gold objects reflect details of Minoan life in the Early Bronze Age. Just as importantly, however, they also demonstrate the existence of a community with an established hierarchical structure from as early as the third millennium BC. Seager donated much of his archaeological collection to the Metropolitan Museum on his death in 1926, including these gold ornaments, which form part of the museum's collection of Early Minoan works, along with stone and bronze tools, bowls, terracotta vases and other gold jewellery. Together, this valuable contribution has shaped a wider understanding of Greek life during the Bronze Age.

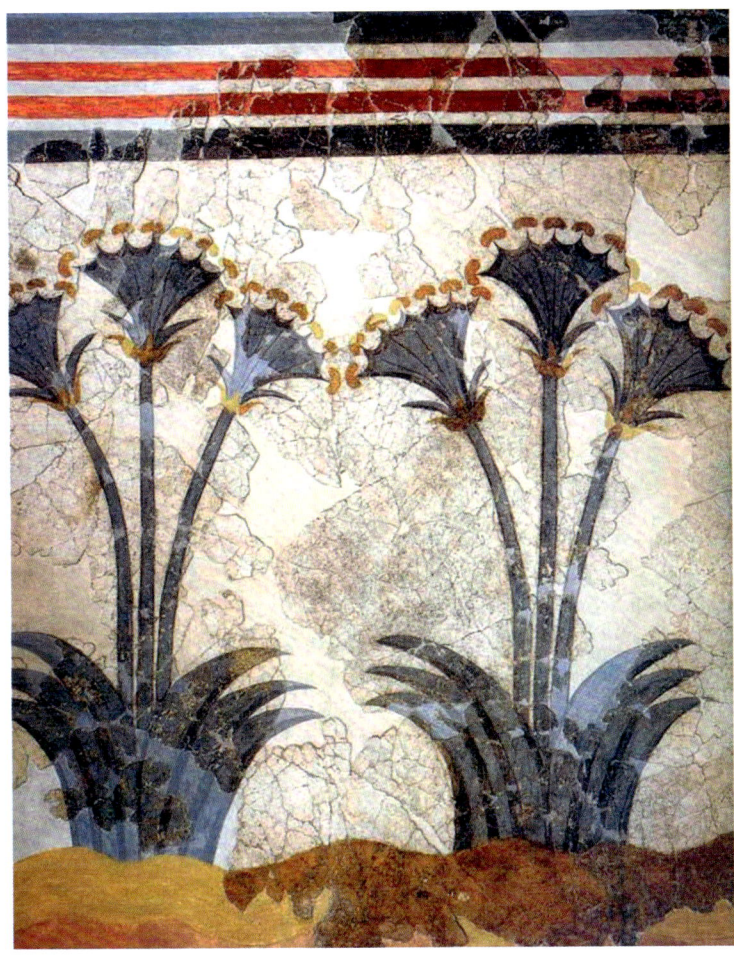

Anonymous

Sea daffodil fresco (detail), *c.*1600 BC
Mineral paints and organic material
Room 1, House of the Ladies, Akrotiri,
Santorini, Greece

After nearly 3,600 years, this fresco at a site on the Aegean island of Santorini, re-emerged from the rubble caused by a catastrophic volcanic eruption that triggered earthquakes, tsunamis and a subsequent fall of ash and pumice in around 1600 BC. Excavated by a team of Greek archaeologists, the wall painting is located in Room 1 of the so-called 'House of the Ladies' built near the present-day village of Akrotiri on the southwestern tip of Santorini. Conventionally the plants depicted are interpreted as sea daffodils (*Pancratium maritimum*), a common and widespread bulbous plant that grows along the coasts of the Mediterranean. However, in this depiction the six petals have been removed to show only the six white stamens with their yellow anthers. While the stamens are fused into a tube in nature, they are shown here spread out as if in a carefully pressed specimen in a herbarium, with even the short bracts on the base of the flowers being represented. Why the painter of the fresco decided to depict flowers with their petals removed is unclear. Only a small number of rooms in this Bronze Age settlement were decorated with frescoes, and only a fraction of those are strictly botanical in theme – but another fresco at Akrotiri depicts two ladies who are thought to be picking the flowers of saffron (*Crocus sativus*), its thread-like stigmas having possibly been used for seasonings, fragrance and dye.

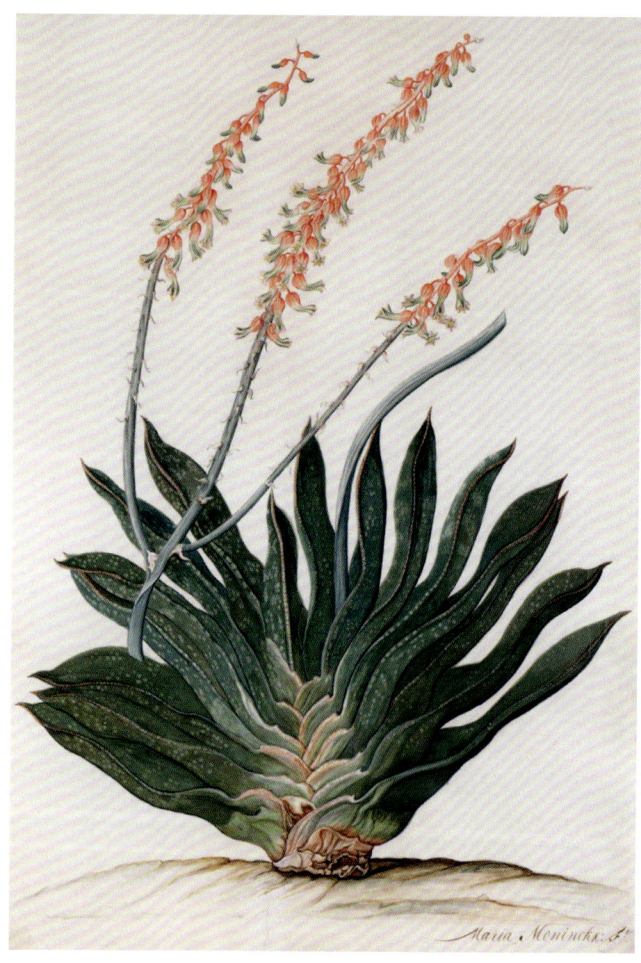

Maria Moninckx

Gasteria nigricans (Haw.) Duval, from the
Moninckx Atlas, *c.*1686–1706
Watercolour on parchment, 60 × 44.5 cm /
23½ × 17½ in
Library of the University of Amsterdam

This elegant and detailed illustration of *Gasteria nigricans*, now known as *G. disticha*, is part of a colossal nine-volume herbal known as the *Moninckx Atlas* after Jan and Maria Moninckx (1673–1757), Dutch father and daughter botanical artists who created it between 1686 and 1706. The herbal includes 420 large watercolours of plants from the renowned Hortus Medicus garden in Amsterdam, which included many varieties of medicinal plants as well as ornamentals, making it one of the most comprehensive collections in Europe. Because of its variety and breadth, the book became a reference for painters as well as an invaluable resource for botanists such as Carl Linnaeus (see p.208). This plate, one of more than a hundred executed by Maria Moninckx, shows *G. disticha* in bloom. Gasteria is an aloe-like, medium-sized, succulent plant with smooth leaves arranged in a sculptural, fan-like arrangement. Originally from the Western Cape region of South Africa, it has more recently become a houseplant favourite because of its versatility and resilience. The inflorescence is a raceme that can reach up to 90 centimetres (3 feet) in height, while the small tubular flowers are shaded in pink and orange. The specimen portrayed here was likely among the very first brought to Amsterdam by German-born South African botanist Henrik Oldenland from the Willowmore district of the Cape, who participated in an expedition in 1689 headed by German explorer Isaq Schrijver, in service of the Dutch East India Company.

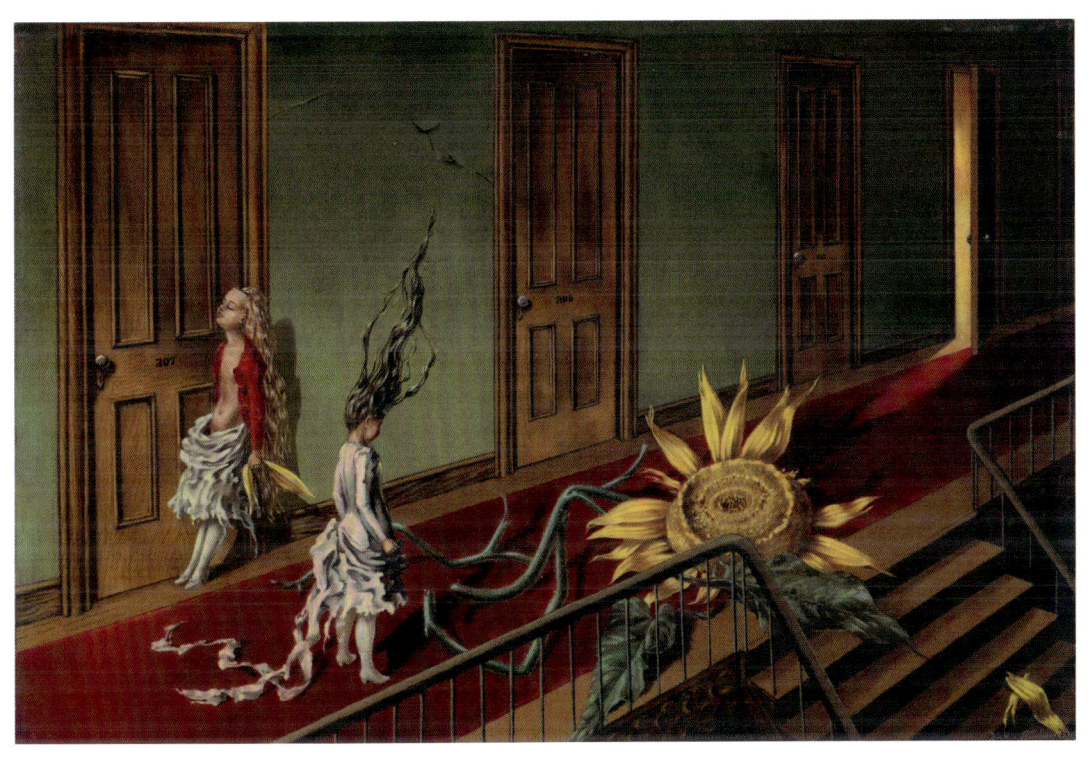

Dorothea Tanning

Eine Kleine Nachtmusik (A Little Night Music), 1943
Oil paint on canvas, 40.7 × 61 cm / 16 × 24 in
Tate, London

An enormous sunflower with plucked petals lies on a hotel landing; its broken stem creeps like a thick, green tentacle towards a girl in a tattered dress whose long hair stands on end. Nearby, a strange, doll-like figure leans against a door, holding one of the sunflower's yellow petals in its hand. More petals lie strewn on the staircase while an eerie light emanates from an open door. American artist Dorothea Tanning (1910–2012)

painted this surreal canvas while she was visiting the artist Max Ernst in Sedona, Arizona, where the couple would later live together. It was here that Tanning became fascinated with sunflowers, which she described as 'aggressive'. For her, the invasive plants came to symbolize the enduring battle humanity wages against the dark forces of evil, as reflected by the paranormal atmosphere of the painting, in which the dishevelled clothing and torn petals suggest a struggle with a supernatural power. One of Tanning's strongest works, *Eine Kleine Nachtmusik* also shows the influence of the Gothic horror novels that she loved, and

the otherworldly characteristics admired by the Surrealists with whom she associated in the 1940s. Sunflowers appear in several of Tanning's paintings, including a portrait of Ernst, *Sunflower Landscape* (1943), and are often depicted as towering, anthropomorphic plants that are at once menacing and seductive.

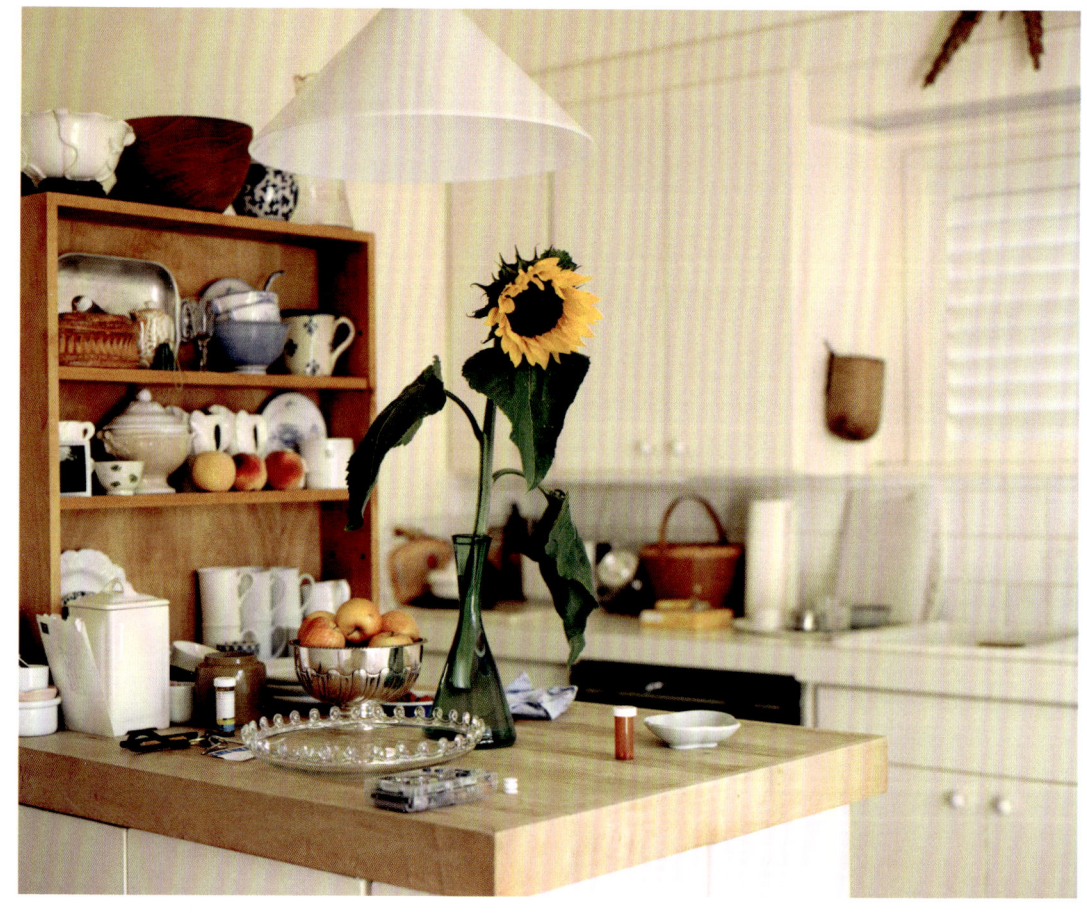

Jeff Wall

A Sunflower, 1995
Transparency in light box, 74 × 90 cm /
29¼ × 35½ in

Amid the mundane objects that populate a bright kitchen interior, a lone sunflower with its head tilted down looks oddly out of place. The style of Canadian photographer Jeff Wall (born 1946) can elevate the everyday and focus our attention on otherwise irrelevant details. Despite the casual appearance, everything in Wall's image is carefully positioned and staged like the elements of a classical painting or a film set. The effortlessness of what seems natural is the result of thoroughly calculated artifice. The silence of the scene is palpable. Beside the flower vase is a plastic prescription vial, while a nearby Nintendo video game suggests the presence of a child or teenager. The various objects sketch the first lines of an open-ended narrative. And what is the meaning of the sunflower? In Native American cultures, sunflowers symbolize abundance; in China, they are a good luck charm; in classical mythology, they tell the story of unrequited love between the nymph Clytie and the sun-god Apollo. But what meaning can be ascribed to the flower in the context of this interior? Is this sunflower a romantic gift? Or was it purchased at the supermarket simply to adorn the room? Despite its domestic simplicity, Wall's photograph reminds us of the broad range of meanings flowers can take on through our lives. From symbols of love to commemorative markers of loss, their presence in a home is never quite the same as that of the objects that surround them.

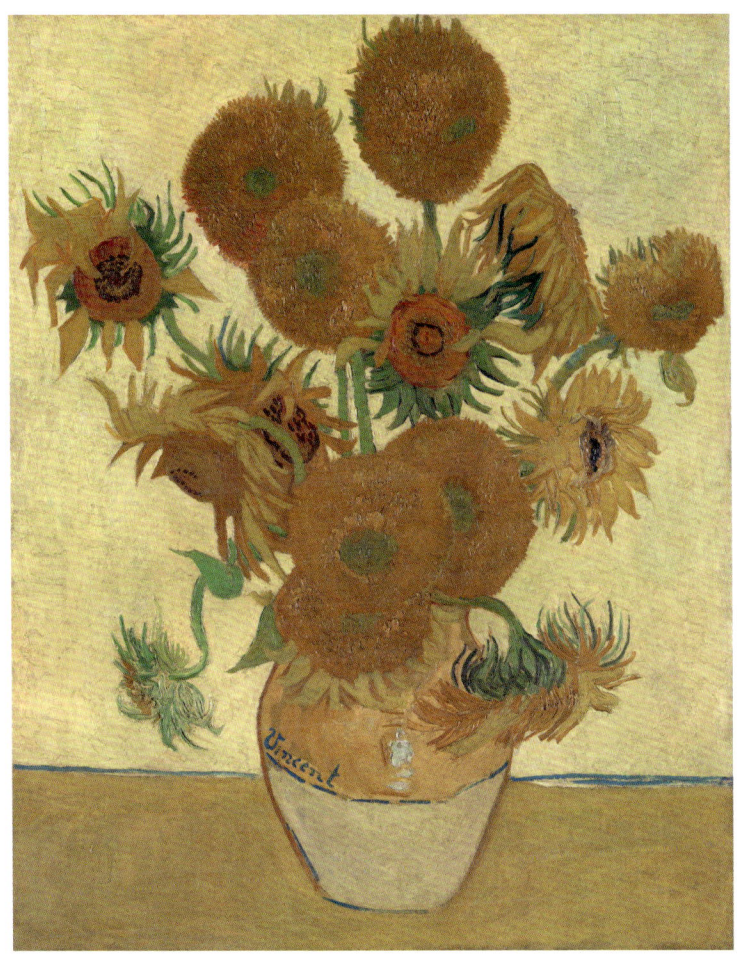

Vincent van Gogh

Sunflowers, 1888
Oil on canvas, 92.1 × 73 cm / 36¼ × 28¾ in
National Gallery, London

The Dutch artist Vincent van Gogh (1853–90) once declared, 'The sunflower is mine', and his sunflower paintings remain iconic symbols of the painter. Following in the vanitas tradition of seventeenth-century Dutch flower painting, the fifteen blossoms on this canvas traverse the whole life cycle of the sunflower: some flowers are in full bloom, while others droop, beginning to turn to seed. One stem, at lower left, is still in bud. The curving lines of the leaves and stems reflect Art Nouveau design, and the thick impasto effects wrought by new nineteenth-century oil paints lift the petals and seed heads off the canvas. As a failed missionary, van Gogh would have been aware of the sunflower's association with the idea of Christian love, as it tracks the sun the way a believer follows Christ. Closer to hand, van Gogh loved the sunflower for its beauty and vitality, and it became a symbol of friendship between him and French painter Paul Gauguin. Gauguin had admired van Gogh's sunflower still lifes painted in Paris, and van Gogh decided to welcome his friend to their shared house in Arles with a series of twelve paintings of the subject. Ultimately, he made only seven – four in August 1888, and three replicas in January 1889 – two of which, including this canvas, were hung in the guest room used by Gauguin. Sadly, Gauguin was to stay for only two months, leaving just before Christmas following a fight with van Gogh, after which the younger painter cut off part of his ear.

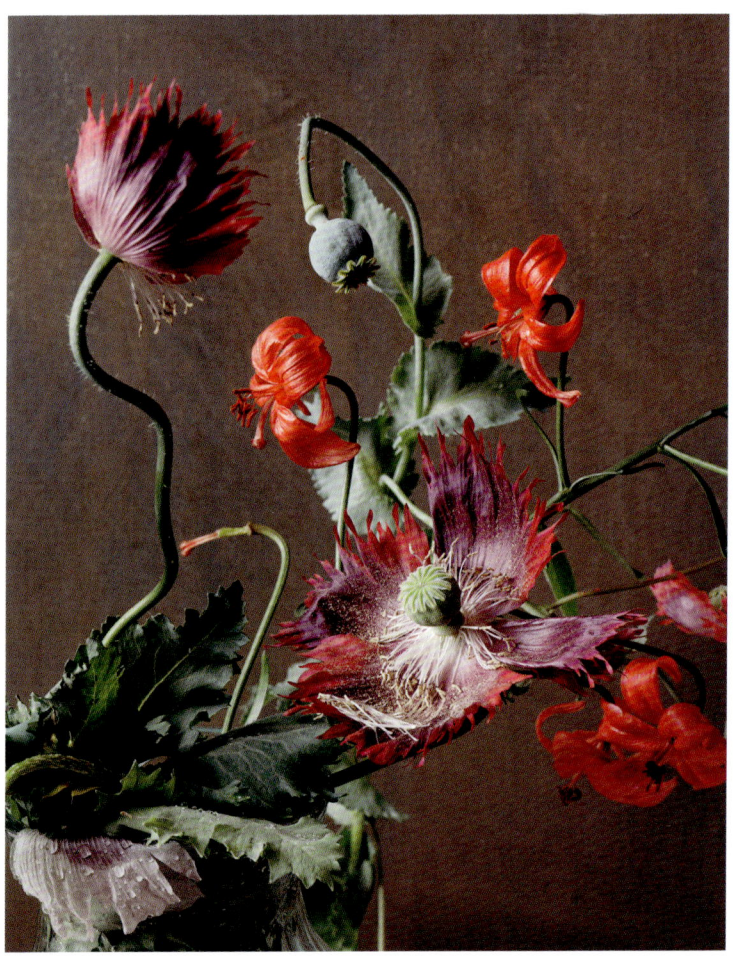

Sharon Core

Untitled (Drama Queen), 2014
Archival pigment print, 93.3 × 73.7 cm /
36¾ × 29 in

As the head of one poppy (*Papaver somniferum* 'Drama Queen') arcs away from the viewer, another has opened, showing off its beauty in the foreground but with its stamens already in the first stages of decay, about to fade and drop its delicate petals. In the background, coral lilies (*Lilium pumilum*) curl into the frame, fecund and ripe, as fleeting symbols of beauty. Along with beauty, there is an inherent tension in this photograph – in the arrangement and disorderly movement of the flowers, and in the timing of the blooms teetering on the edge of death. Challenging our ideas of reproduction and originality, the floral still-life series *1606–1907* by American photographer Sharon Core (born 1965) reimagines masterpieces of the past as modern photographs. Finding her inspiration in Dutch baroque, early Flemish painters and French nineteenth-century masters such as Jan van Huysum (see p.142), Rachel Ruysch (see p.86), Ambrosius Bosschaert the Elder (see p.177) and Jan Brueghel the Elder (see p.268) to the modernists Odilon Redon (see p.185) and Henri Fantin-Latour (see p.129), Core sources seeds and bulbs to grow the subjects of her photographs, selecting specific and period-accurate flowers. By using a 5 × 4 analogue film camera instead of digital she works from large negatives, creating the illusion of a flat, two-dimensional painted surface. Using chiaroscuro, Core's backgrounds are submerged in shadows – she positions directional lighting to highlight and pick out exquisite detail.

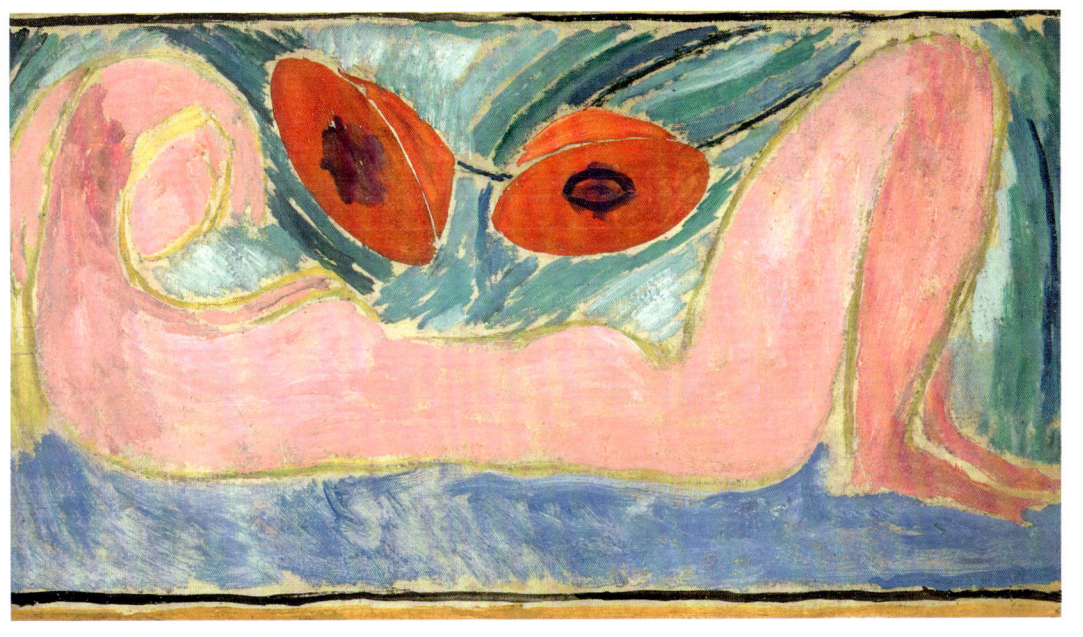

Vanessa Bell

Nude with Poppies, 1916
Oil on canvas, 39.1 × 58.1 cm / 15¼ × 23 in
Swindon Collection of Modern British Art, UK

A background of bright blues and greens, applied in broad brushstrokes, heightens the contrast between the floating scarlet poppies and the delicate pink shades of a woman's bare skin in this painting by British artist Vanessa Bell (1879–1961). In addition to being a leading member of the Bloomsbury Group of artists, writers and intellectuals, Bell was also an interior designer and the sister of the writer Virginia Woolf. Her

considerable output spans a wide range of styles, from her many floral still lifes to naturalistic landscapes, representational portraits, and more abstract paintings such as *Nude with Poppies* – created as either an open-minded or a mocking gift for her husband's lover. When she painted it during World War I (1914–18), Bell was experimenting with simplified forms and the bold use of a limited range of colours, inspired by the Second Post-Impressionist exhibition of 1912 in London, where her work featured alongside established artists including Henri Matisse and Pablo Picasso (see pp.19, 297). Bell's innovative

use of abstract colour and form set her apart from her contemporaries and made her one of the most influential British modernists. Born in London, she studied at the Royal Academy Schools, where her tutors included artist John Singer Sargent (see p.192). In 1916, Bell moved to a farmhouse in Charleston, a village in East Sussex, where her husband, Clive Bell, and their friends came and went, establishing a haven of artistic and literary endeavour in which freedom of expression was fundamental.

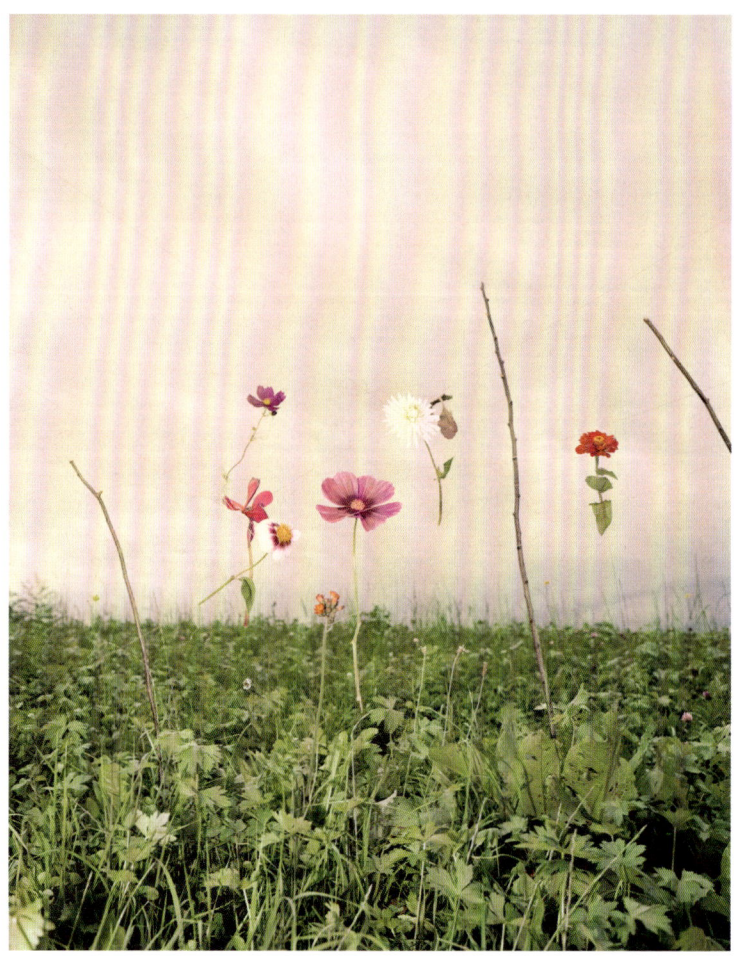

Collier Schorr

Arrangement #14 (Blumen), 2008

Cosmos, dahlias, zinnias and nasturtiums are caught in a near-invisible web above a meadow of grasses and wildflowers that contrasts starkly with the cloudy sky. This surreal image from the series *Blumen* (*Flowers*) captures what American artist Collier Schorr (born 1963) calls floral 'trespassers' – flowers picked, uprooted and sometimes stolen from their natural homes and brought to a new location where she stages an arrangement tied with fishing line between sticks. Unlike traditional still lifes, these compositions take minutes to set up and minutes to destroy, as the fragile stems have only fleeting moments of perfection before they begin to wilt and die. Schorr has spent the past eighteen years returning regularly to Schwäbisch Gmünd in Germany, where she photographed the series, to document life, both real and imagined, exploring themes of identity, gender, human nature and the environment. With *Blumen*, Schorr wanted to make portraits of something beyond nationality and identity. By reconstructing the landscape, first with the removal of flowers and then by repositioning them on public land, she asks questions about belonging. Inspired by Robert Mapplethorpe's bondage portraits, Schorr creates images that explore the polarities of transience and permanence, the idea of uprooting and restraint. The resulting 'public' sculpture captured in her photographs asks questions about time, constructed realities and our relationship with nature.

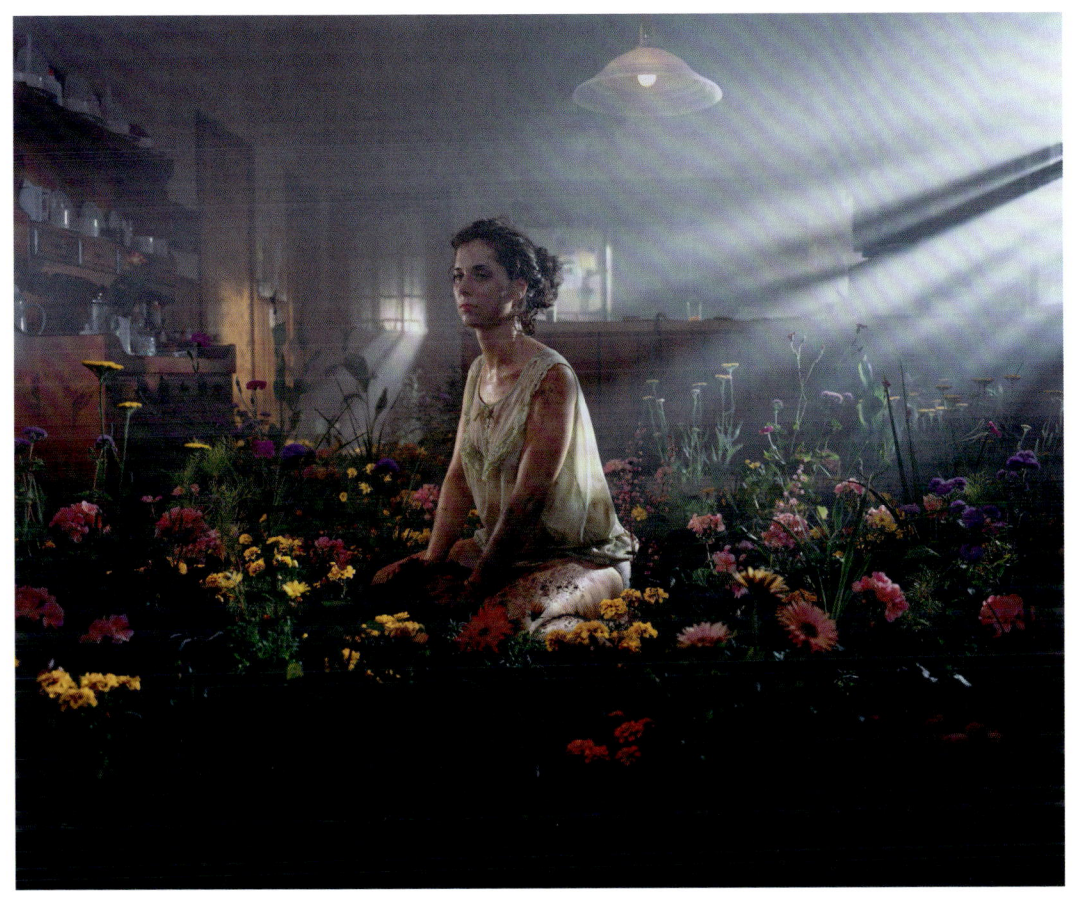

Gregory Crewdson

Untitled, 1998–2002
Digital C-print, 1.2 × 1.5 m / 4 ft × 5 ft

A woman sits in a garden surrounded by colourful flowers, her skin glistening and speckled with mud. The garden grows within a kitchen; plates and teapots sit on a nearby shelf and the fridge behind is peppered with scraps of paper. Marigolds, geraniums, cornflowers, daisies, yarrow and other blooms shine in the dimness, illuminated by shafts of twilight sun streaming in through the windows, casting a hazy, dream-like aura on the domestic interior. American photographer Gregory Crewdson (born 1962) is known for capturing subjects that appear at the cusp of some significant transition amid staged cinematic panoramas of American suburbia, turning the mundane into the bizarre and magical. As such, he shifts the real into the fictional or imagined. The scenes he creates are laden with mystery and a hint of an eerie supernatural atmosphere, often with elements that are dislocated from their normal surroundings: where did this garden originate? Who is this woman and what lies buried in the dirt beneath her hands? Crewdson does not answer, instead wanting 'the story to remain unsolved'. He employs vast crews to realize his large-scale photographs, a process that employs not only complicated lighting schemes, but teams for make-up, wardrobe and digital post-production work. The fantastical quality of this interior garden takes inspiration from the surreal worlds of filmmakers including Alfred Hitchcock and David Lynch, as well as the painter Edward Hopper and the photographer Diane Arbus.

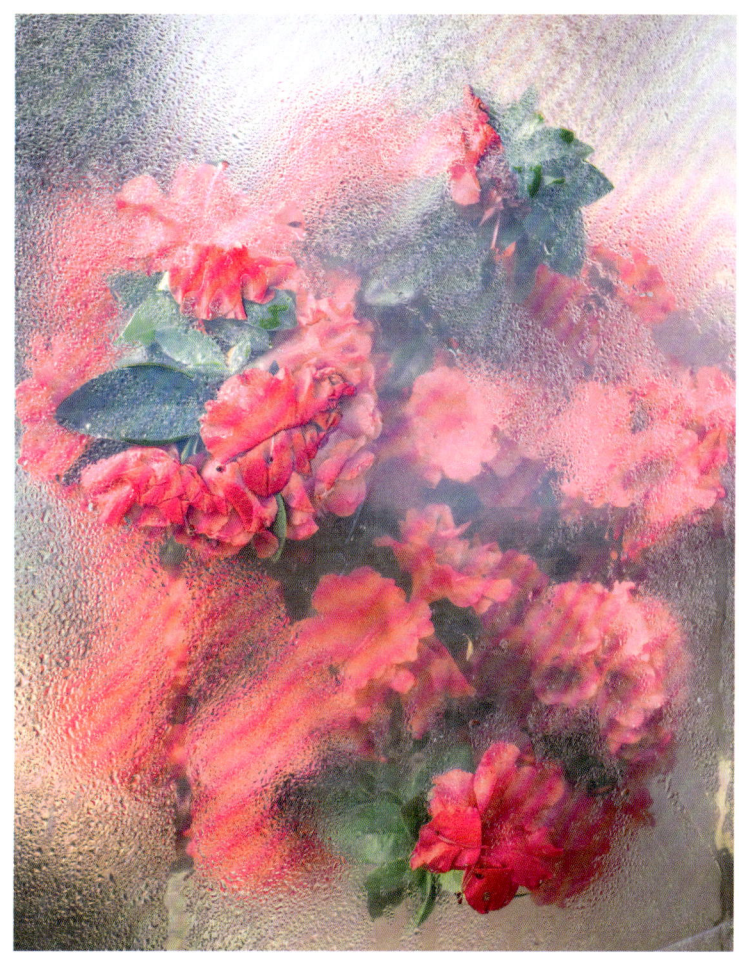

Cig Harvey

Azalea (Pressing), 2018
C-print, 1 × 0.8 m / 3 ft 4 in × 2 ft 6 in

With all its vegetal might, this deep pink azalea captured by British photographer Cig Harvey (born 1973) pushes against a windowpane. The flower's sublime beauty is simultaneously accentuated and compromised by the mist that diffuses its glory into an abstract burst of colour. Under the pressure, some of the ruffled petals momentarily transfigure into human lips awaiting a kiss, or perhaps about to part and speak. Whether incidental or intentional, the detail in Harvey's

photograph charges the azalea with an uncanny vividness, as if its captivity behind glass can no longer be endured. Harvey's work focuses intensely on the beauty and magic of nature and how humans interact with the natural world in everyday life. Native to the hilly regions of Asia and North America, azaleas can grow up to 3 metres (10 feet) tall. In mid-spring, they smother themselves with shrouds of blooms that, in some cases, last up to a couple of weeks. The hybrid seen in Harvey's photograph is a cultivar selected because of its compact demeanour and contained height. Hybridization of azaleas began during

the Edo period in Japan (1603–1867), and it is believed that Buddhist monks were among the first to crossbreed Japanese varieties with those that originated in China. So-called 'compact varieties' have been specifically engineered for indoor settings and can rebloom year after year if cared for appropriately.

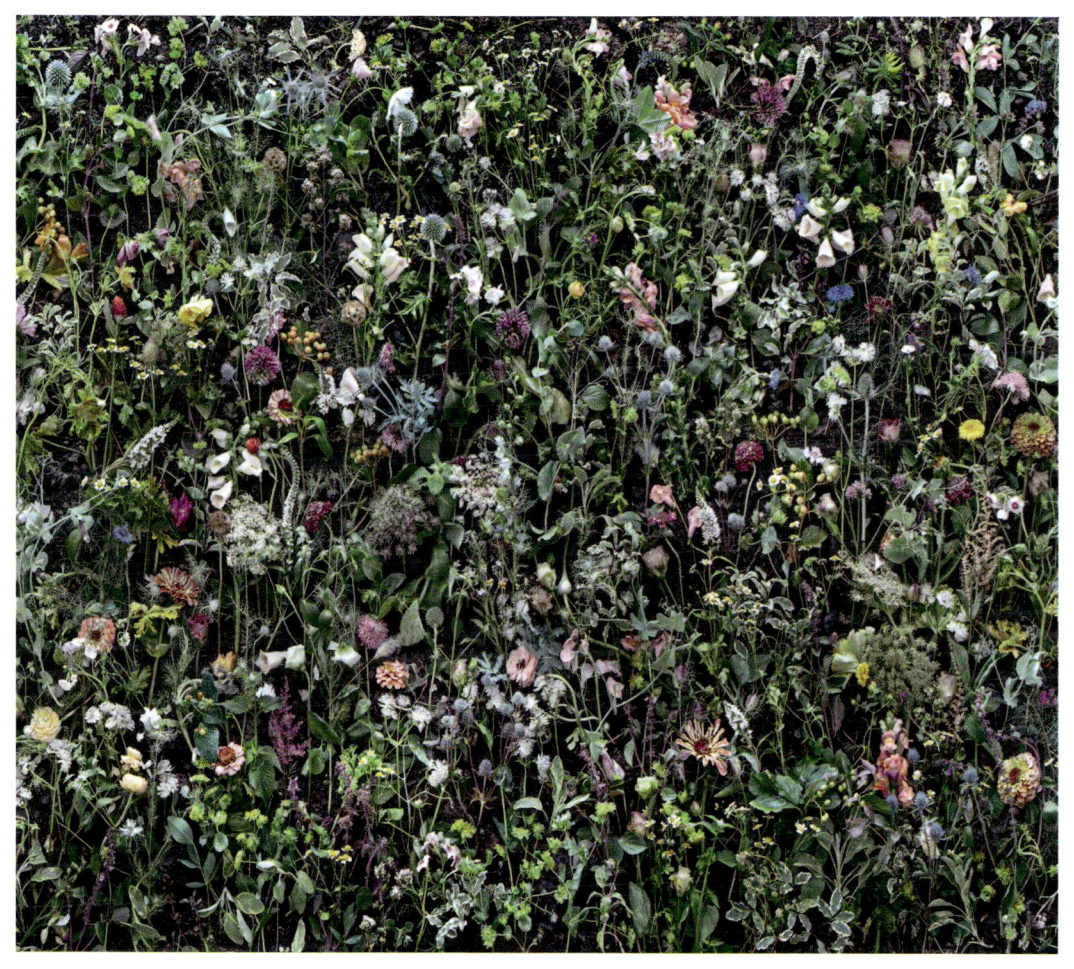

Tanya Marcuse

Woven Nº 28 (detail), 2018
Pigment print, 1.6 × 3.2 m / 5 ft 2 in × 10 ft 4 in
Private collection

Reminiscent of a Jackson Pollock painting or medieval tapestry, this enormous photograph shows a dense sea of flowers that cuts across its entire panorama. Amid the visually rich, all-over composition are roses, thistles, gooseneck loose-strife, foxgloves and chrysanthemums, among other garden and wildflowers. Yet the colours of each plant are muted; leaves appear dull and petals are beginning to wilt and shrivel. Created as part of her *Woven* series, American photographer Tanya Marcuse (born 1964) invites viewers to ponder the fragility of life and the natural cycles of growth and decay. As with all the works in the series, *Woven Nº 28* was composed around a purpose-built structure, with each flower painstakingly fixed into place. By capturing these flowers on the cusp of death, Marcuse references the Dutch vanitas tradition, a style of still-life painting popular in the seventeenth century that referenced the vanity of worldly pleasures in the face of death. Artists working in this genre often made their point using flowers, reminding viewers that earthly life is as fragile as a petal. Another major influence on Marcuse is the biblical story of the Fall, which offers an account of how death came into the world after Adam and Eve ate the forbidden fruit. But Marcuse's vision of a decaying paradise also contains hope, with the rotting flowers providing nutrients for new life.

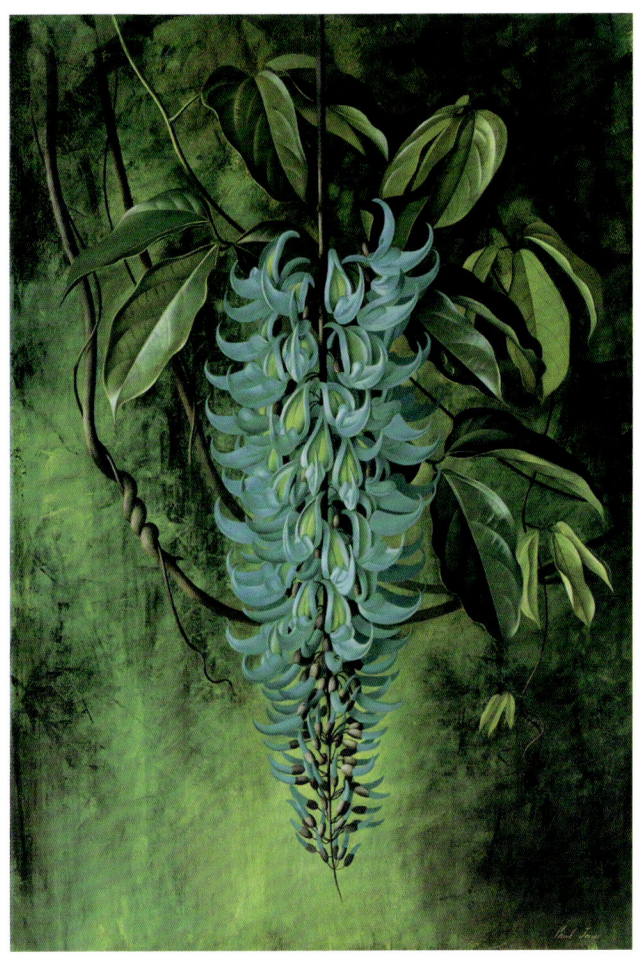

Paul Jones

Strongylodon macrobotrys (Jade Vine),
from *Flora Superba*, 1971
Lithograph, 36.8 × 52.7 cm / 14½ × 20¾ in
Private collection

Jade vine (*Strongylodon macrobotrys*) is one of the world's strangest and most beautiful flowers. Native to rainforests on a handful of islands in the Philippines, it is endangered through loss of its favoured habitat; however, the vine is not hard to cultivate under glass and is a star attraction in several botanic gardens. A member of the pea family, jade vine produces large clusters of green flowers that dangle from thin, wiry clambering stems. These pendent trusses, also called pseudo-racemes, can be up to 3 metres (nearly 10 feet) long, with each claw-shaped flower measuring up to 6 centimetres (2½ inches). The flowers have a waxy consistency and a distinctly luminous quality that increases their allure to their main pollinator: bats. At twilight, the bats seek out the flowers and sip the nectar as they hang upside down. As a bat feeds, the flower brushes its head with pollen, some of which may then be transferred to the flower of another vine on a later visit, fertilizing it. Painted in fine naturalistic detail, this depiction of jade vine was created by Australian artist Paul Osborne Jones (1921–97) for the publication *Flora Superba* in 1971. The book was printed in a limited edition of 406 copies with 16 colour lithographs of Jones's work – a modern interpretation of Robert Thornton's *Temple of Flora* (see p.161). His showcase of this exquisite creeper captures the contrast between the ghostly pale blue-green flowers and the deep green backdrop of the plant's natural habitat.

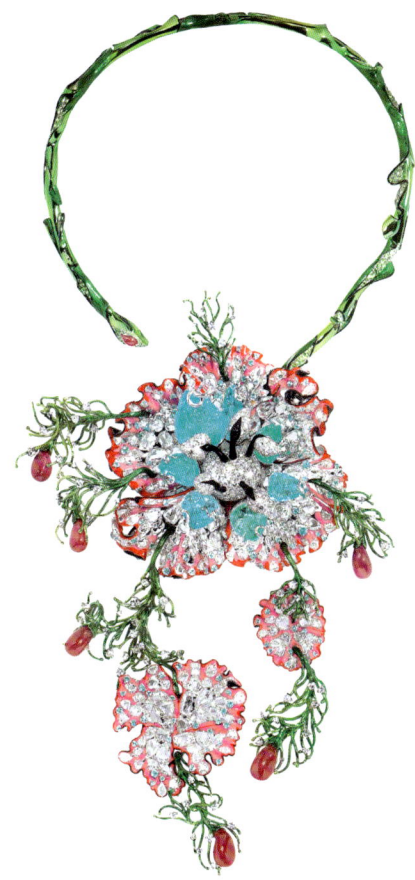

Victoire de Castellane for Dior Fine Jewelry

Reina Magnifica Sangria necklace, from the
Belladone Island collection, 2007
White gold, diamonds, Paraiba tourmalines,
rubies, demantoid garnets and lacquer,
dimensions variable
Private collection

A mysterious bejewelled flower in turquoise
stones and free-cut diamonds on hot pink lacquered gold hangs from a vivid green serpent
necklace; from the main flower, spinels hang
like drops of blood from green leaves speckled
with diamond 'dew drops'. This idiosyncratic

flower necklace by French jewellery designer
Victoire de Castellane (born 1962) for Dior
Joaillerie is typical of her fantastical, hyper-
colourful and extreme designs. The *Belladone*
collection took two years to create and featured
one-of-a-kind pieces snapped up by collectors
around the world. Based on a fictional island
where the poisonous belladonna flower thrives,
the collection was an imaginary herbarium
of plants from which magical potions were
derived, as reflected in the names of each piece,
including *Reina Magnifica Sangria* (shown),
Fleuro Poisonus Spinella and *Carnivo Papidevorus*.

De Castellane became creative director of Dior
Joaillerie in 1998, after fourteen years at Chanel,
where she oversaw the brand's costume jewellery.
After a meeting with Dior chairman Bernard
Arnault in 1997, she was tasked with setting up
the house's fine jewellery division and quickly
became known for her subversive approach, using
unusual colours, out-of-favour gems and enormous 80-carat stones in her debut *Incroyables
et Merveilleuses* collection in 1999. Castellane
is inspired by nature, pop culture, B-movies, cartoons and fairy tales – and frequently by the
flowers that are so integral to the history of Dior.

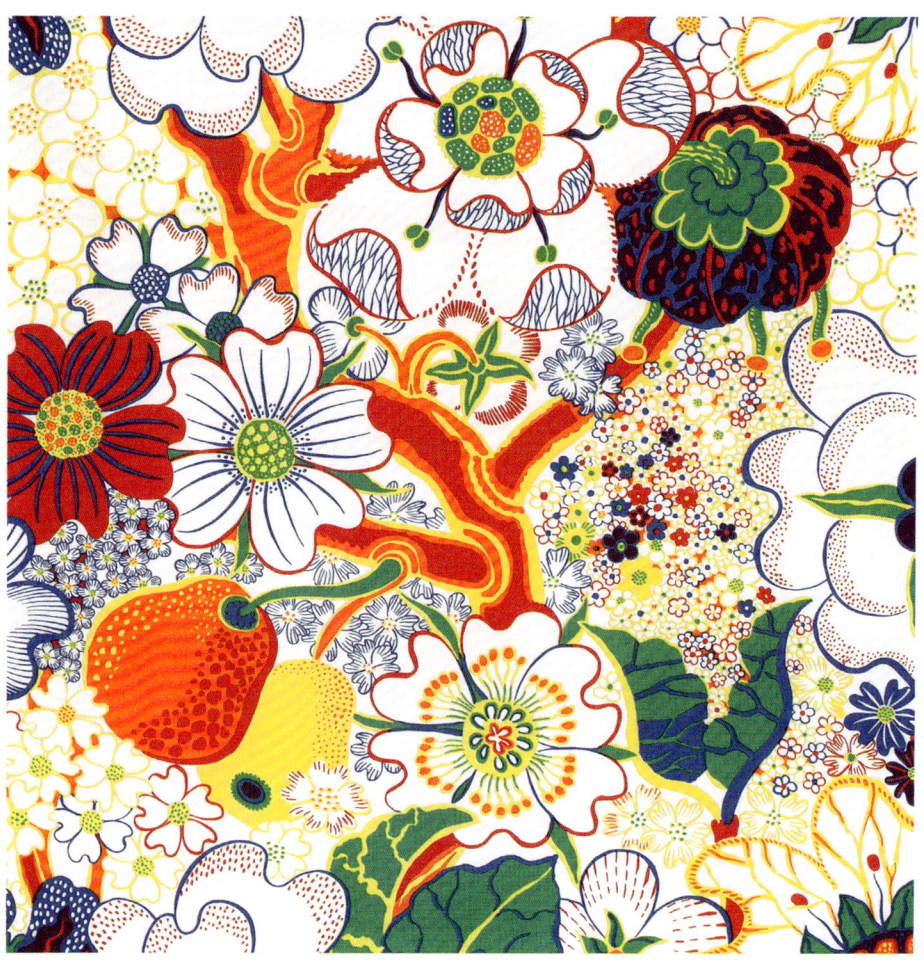

Josef Frank

Nippon, 1943–45
Screen-printed linen, dimensions variable
Svenskt Tenn, Stockholm

The vibrant, hugely influential prints and patterns designed by Austrian-born Swedish artist and architect Josef Frank (1885–1967) during the middle decades of the twentieth century have endured for decades. *Nippon* is emblematic of Frank's intense colour and dreamlike forms, here rooted in typically Japanese fruits and flowers such as daisies and chrysanthemums. Reimagined with clashing pop colours and an idiosyncratic play on scale and repetition, Frank's floral prints are never literal or simplistic. Often whimsical and slightly psychedelic, his dazzling designs have become representative of the modernist movement, particularly of Swedish modern style. His life-enhancing, joyful prints combine imaginary blooms with real flowers, commonly featuring varieties such as daisies, violets, crocuses, hyacinths, tulips and roses, among dozens of others. A socialist, Frank taught at the Vienna School of Arts and Crafts from 1919 to 1925, where he also designed public housing complexes, but left the city with his wife, Anna, and resettled in Stockholm in 1933. A year later, he began to produce fabric designs as well as furniture, lighting, accessories and interiors for Estrid Ericson's shop, Svenskt Tenn. Many of Frank's fabric designs, featuring abstracted florals as well as birds, insects and plants, are still in production today; his archive includes 2,000 furniture designs and 160 textile designs.

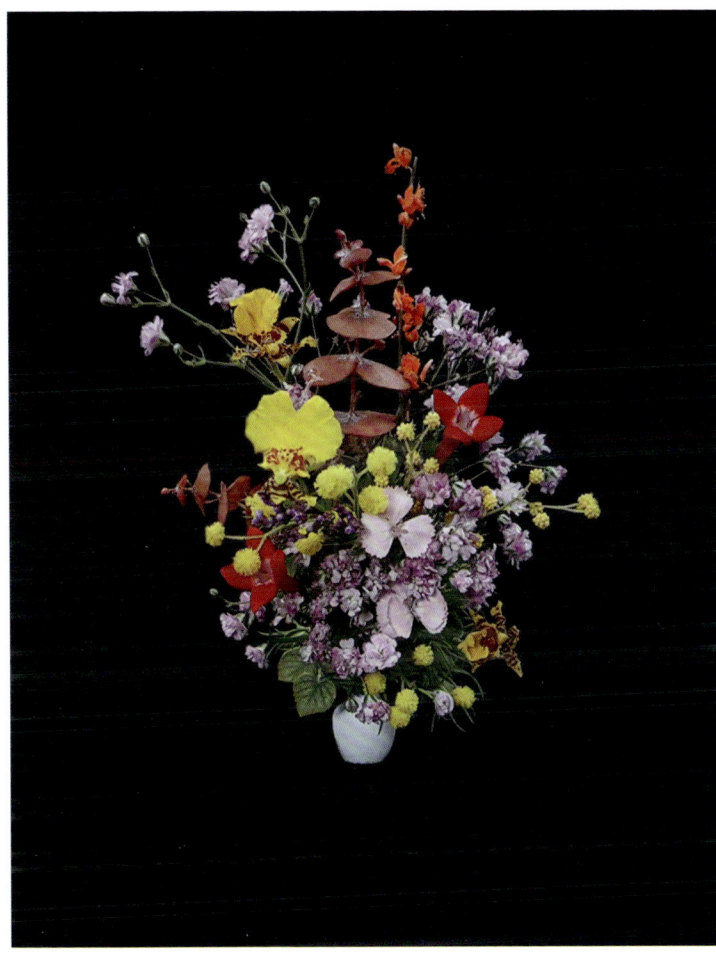

Harriet Parry

Ode to Vogue – Miniature Flower Arrangement, 2018
Floral arrangement, 10 × 5 × 5 cm / 4 × 2 × 2 in

A miniature ceramic vase more suited to a doll's house holds a tiny arrangement of flowers: pink gypsophila fizz next to a small stem of bouvardia, while eucalyptus, ginestra, mimosa and pink sweet William bump up next to delicate golden shower orchids. British floral artist Harriet Parry (born 1985) plays with a scale that is both disorienting and voyeuristic. In *Ode to Vogue*, the arrangement of individual flowers takes on a new life as a living miniature that is a celebration of form, like tiny beautiful jewels. Parry's microscopic attention to detail creates an imaginary world – but one that uses very real flowers. Working on such a small scale invites viewers into a personal, intimate relationship with the piece. In our fast-paced world you can easily grab attention by going big, but by using such a minute scale, Parry brings the shape of the flowers and their physiology into sharp focus. Breaking down the blooms into smaller parts reimagines familiar flowers and invites the viewer to look again at these everyday forms and see our world from a different perspective. You can almost feel the artist's intensity from the precision demanded to create these arrangements. With her use of real flowers, Parry puts a time limit on her pieces. Her flowers are a fleeting treat that remain elusive in their short-lived existence.

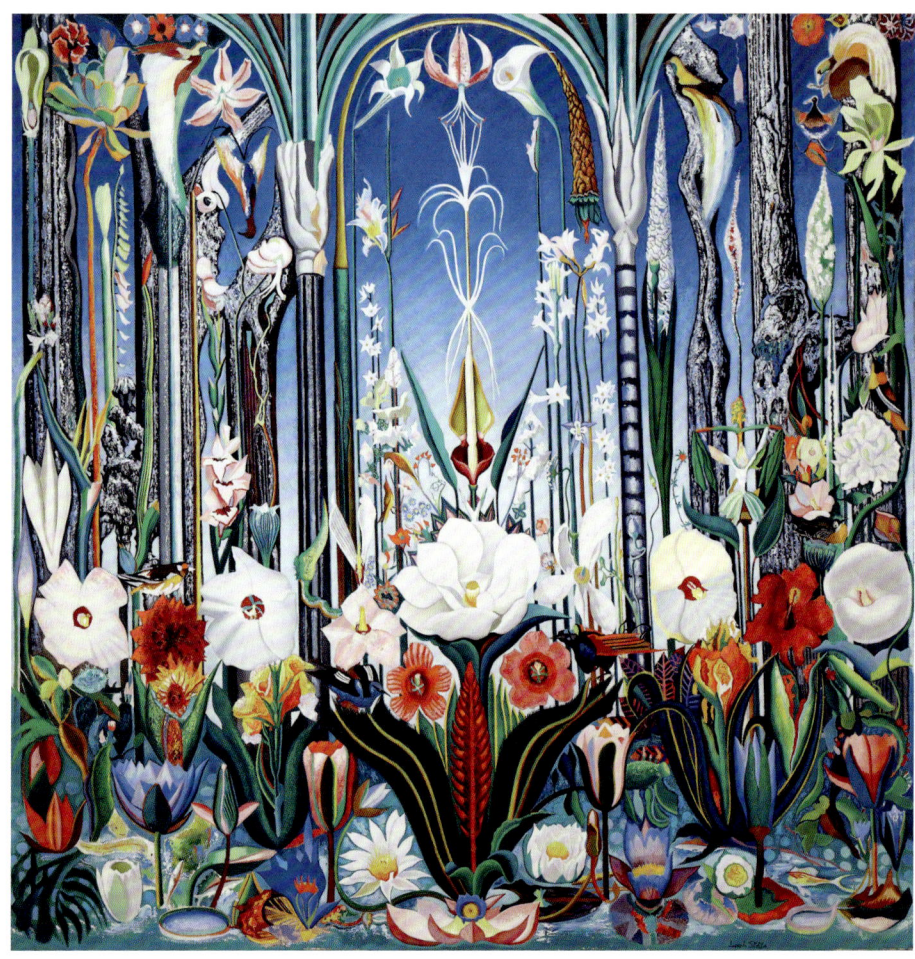

Joseph Stella

Flowers, Italy, 1931
Oil on canvas, 1.9 × 1.9 m / 6 ft 3 in × 6 ft 3 in
Phoenix Art Museum, Arizona

Hibiscus, calla lilies, birds of paradise, water lilies and scores of other flowers combine in a kaleidoscopic array, painted by Italian-born American Futurist Joseph Stella (1877–1946). *Flowers, Italy* epitomizes the different cultures that inform Stella's work, which stands at the intersection of American Precisionism and Italian Futurism. This large work depicts a blooming flower garden with such extreme attention to detail that it becomes

almost unnatural, arranged carefully before the backdrop of an idyllic blue sky. The vertical geometry of Manhattan, Stella's adopted city, is reflected in the rigid upright patterns: even when exaggerated, the flowers' stamens and petals serve a practical purpose in imposing structure on the work. On closer inspection, architectural elements emerge in the garden, set within three arches reminiscent of the vaults of a cathedral. This combination of nature and architecture may be an expression of Stella's scepticism towards the mechanical age and an attempt to reconcile the bucolic Italian countryside of his childhood with New

York's urban landscape. Stella's flowers are baroque, surreal, theatrical and strangely realistic, visibly at odds not just with any single art trend of the time – Fauvism, Cubism, Art Deco, Futurism, Dada, Precisionism, Surrealism – but also with Stella's own earlier work. *Flowers, Italy* may simply be a demonstration of the artist's determination to assert his own voice amid the contending movements within the international art world.

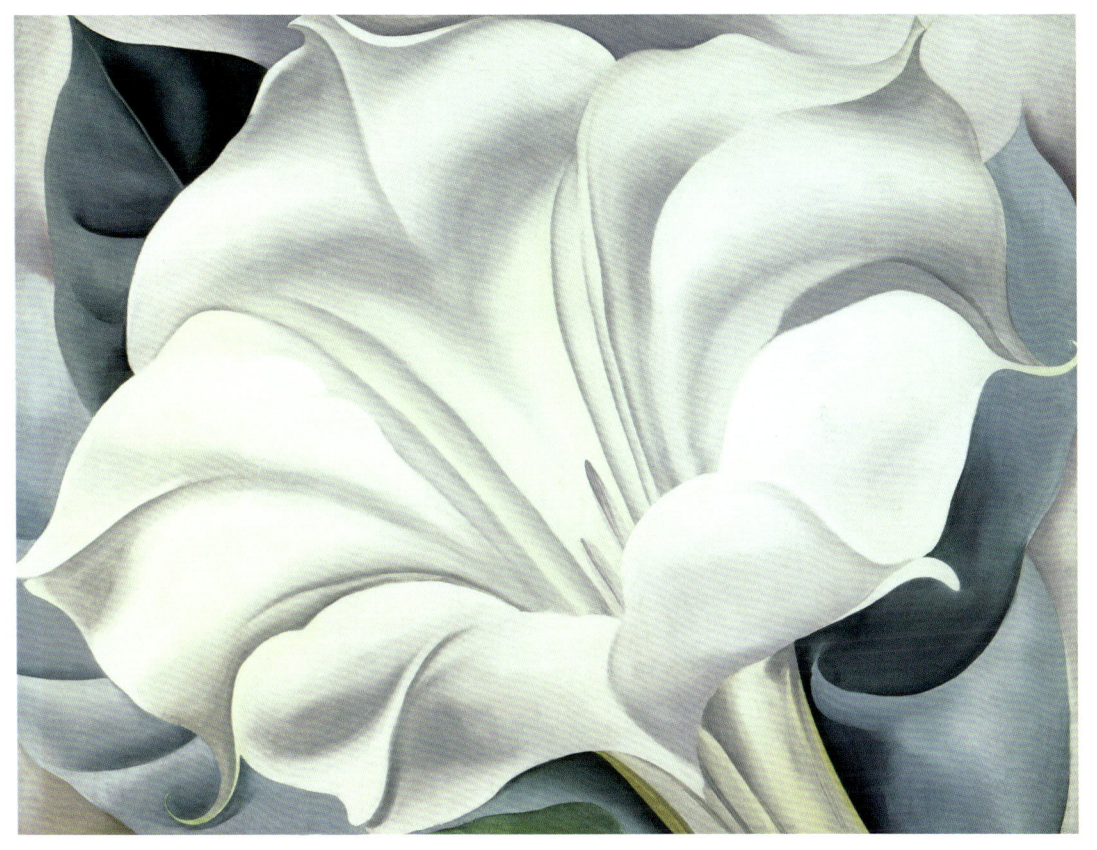

Georgia O'Keeffe

The White Flower (White Trumpet Flower), 1932
Oil on canvas, 0.8 × 1 m / 2 ft 6 in × 3 ft 4 in
San Diego Museum of Art, California

A white trumpet flower (the poisonous angel's trumpet or *Datura innoxia*) fills the canvas as if under a microscope. The American artist Georgia O'Keeffe (1887–1986) explained that her habit of enlarging the image in this way was an attempt to surprise viewers into taking the time to look as closely as she did. Trained in Chicago and New York, O'Keeffe began painting her large-scale flower canvases in 1924, the year she married the photographer and gallerist Alfred Stieglitz. One of Stieglitz's artists, the modernist photographer Paul Strand, influenced her techniques of close cropping and unconventional viewpoints. This is one of several large images of white trumpet flowers that O'Keeffe painted in 1932, a stressful year that ended with a nervous breakdown and her abandonment of all painting for more than a year. One of those works would eventually sell for $44.4 million, the most expensive painting by a female artist ever sold at auction. Some of O'Keeffe's celebrated flower paintings – mostly painted from the 1920s to the 1950s – were seen as metaphors for female genitalia by authorities ranging from Stieglitz to the feminist art historian Linda Nochlin, but the artist always resisted such interpretations of her works. 'When you took time to really notice my flower', she wrote in 1944, 'you hung all your own associations [on it] ... as if I think and see what you think and see ... and I don't.'

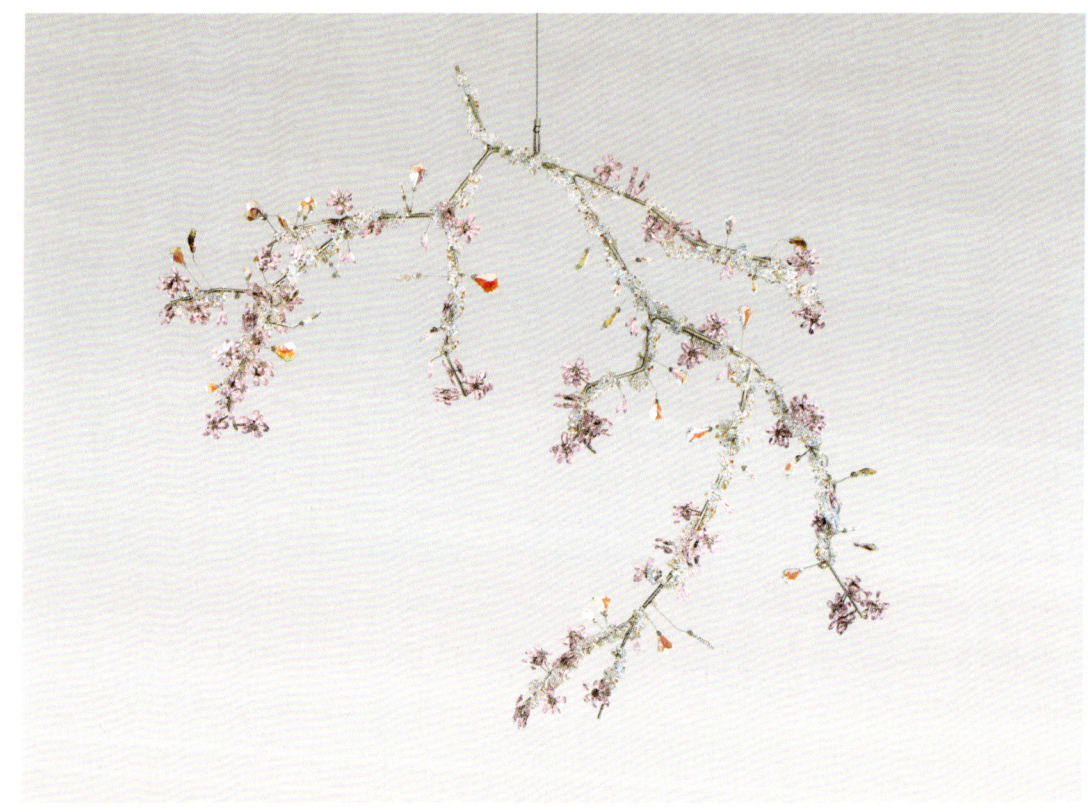

Tord Boontje for Swarovski Crystal Palace

Blossom Chandelier, 2002
Swarovski crystal, enamelled steel and LED
bulbs, 1.4 × 1.5 × 0.3 m / 4 ft 7 in × 4 ft 11 in × 1 ft
Private collection

For the Dutch designer Tord Boontje (born 1968), an invitation to use cut crystal as a medium sparked an unlikely botanical memory. Looking at the crystals, Boontje saw the shapes of flower petals and leaves, recalling a glittering branch of frozen blossom he had once seen as a child after an ice storm. The result was this blossom chandelier, with its organic shape and romantic concept

featuring silvery blossom sprigs with crystal leaves and petals. Not only did the work become a design icon of its time, it also introduced asymmetry into chandelier design. Boontje's design was the most emblematic result of the Crystal Palace project launched in 2002 by the Austrian jeweller Swarovski, which invited interior designers and architects to use cut crystal to push the boundaries of modern lighting. Boontje would go on to create other versions of the light for Swarovski, including a night version using inky blue and black crystals, a monochromatic white and black winter rendition, and a vivid green crystal spring blossom

branch. Boontje originally studied at the Design Academy Eindhoven and the Royal College of Art (RCA) in London, where he set up his own studio in 1996. In 2009 he shifted his focus to education, becoming professor and head of design products at the RCA, a post he held for four years. Boontje continues to produce nature-inspired lighting, furniture, textiles, glassworks, tableware and even jewellery, all with his signature contemporary yet whimsical aesthetic.

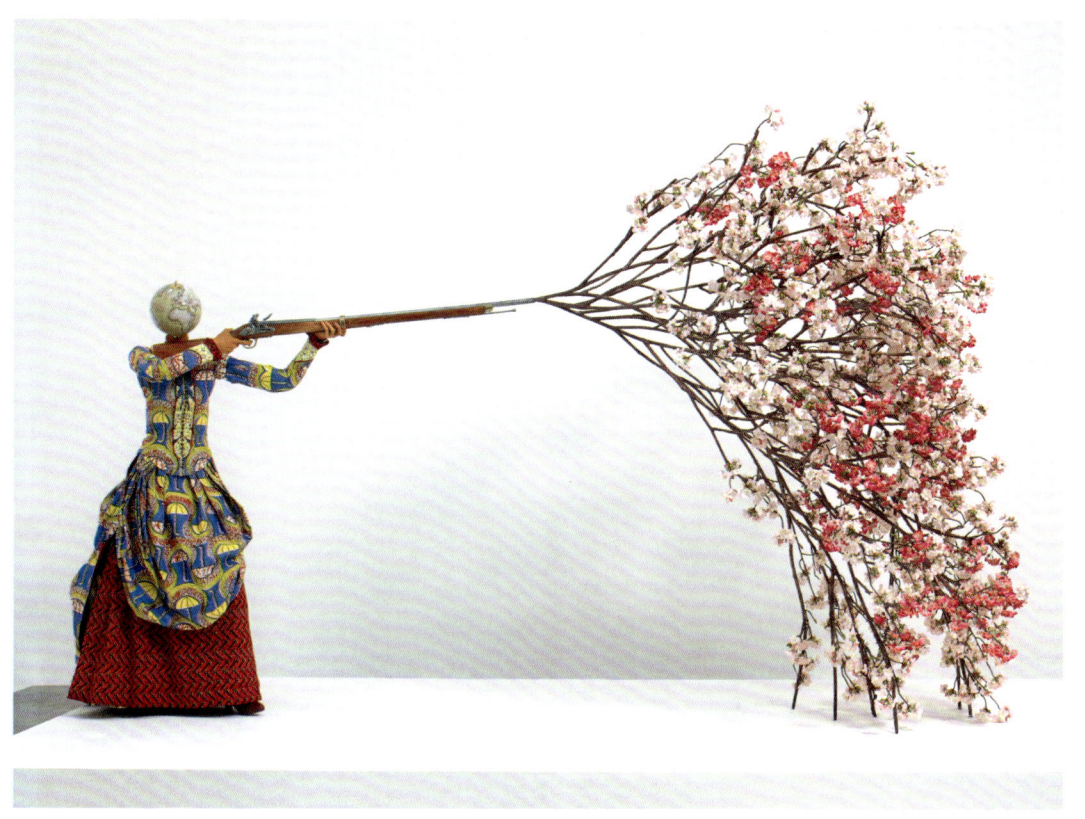

Yinka Shonibare

Woman Shooting Cherry Blossoms, 2019
Fibreglass, Dutch wax-printed cotton textile,
bespoke hand-coloured globe, steel, brass,
zamak, wood, resin and silk, 2.4 × 1.9 × 4.4 m /
8 ft × 6 ft 4 in × 14 ft 5 in
Fukuoka Art Museum, Japan

An arresting mix of global influences is united
in this multilayered sculpture by British-Nigerian
artist Yinka Shonibare (born 1962). Commissioned by the Fukuoka Art Museum in Japan for
the 2019 exhibition *Flower Power*, *Woman Shooting
Cherry Blossoms* was Shonibare's first work on

a Japanese theme. The cherry blossoms, or *sakura*,
are a national symbol in Japan, where they signify the arrival of spring and renewal of life. The
woman's dress, meanwhile, is fashioned in the
Western Edwardian style popular during Japan's
Meiji period from 1868 to 1912, but makes use of
'African'-style Dutch wax prints: bold, colourful
block designs based on Indonesian batik that were
mass-produced by Dutch colonists and exported
to African nations (see p.162). The woman is
depicted in a position of power, holding her rifle
high, which is reinforced by the names of female
activists from around the world inscribed on

the globe that creates her head. Every detail
of Shonibare's sculpture is laden with meaning,
combining to form an exploration of colonial-
ism, cross-cultural identity and the impacts
of globalization. These themes are in part drawn
from Shonibare's own experience. He was born
in London, but his family relocated to Lagos,
Nigeria, where he lived until the age of seventeen.
He returned to England for schooling, going
on to study fine art first at Central Saint Martins
and then Goldsmiths in London, where he graduated with other members of the group known
as the 'Young British Artists'.

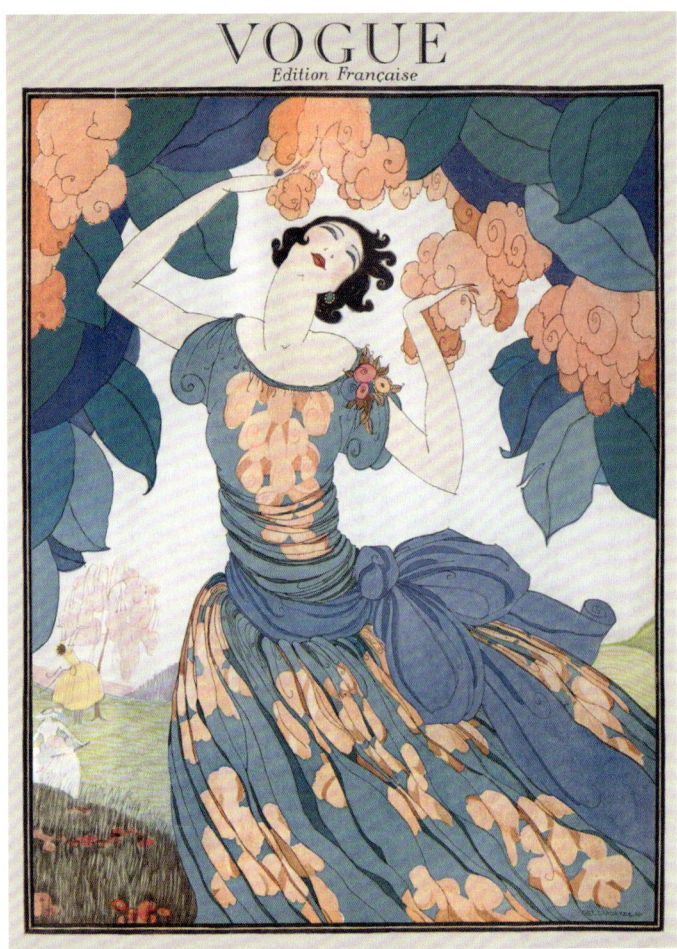

Helen Dryden

Vogue Edition Française, February 1921
Cover illustration, 32 × 24.5 cm / 12⅝ × 9⅝ in

A young raven-haired woman frolics among trees drenched in coral flowers as spring blooms in Paris. She wears a feminine, drop-waisted floral silk dress that mirrors the colours of nature around her. This illustration by American artist Helen Dryden (1882–1972) is typical of her work for *Vogue* between 1910 and 1922. Her covers featured imagined settings that drew on the highly stylized look of early Art Deco, with its feminine curves, rich colour and distinctive decorative

elements. Dryden's illustrations were often completed with swirling flowers, clouds or water. Like much of her work, this cover was influenced by the style and rich colours of the Ballets Russes and Leon Bakst. The dress design is typical of the flowing and soft, romantic look of contemporary Parisian designers such as Jeanne Lanvin and in direct contrast to the boyish, flapper look so often associated with the 1920s. Dryden was born in Baltimore and moved to New York in 1909, determined to become an artist; after a year of rejections, she signed a contract with Condé Nast and went on to create more than a hundred

designs for *Vogue* during her tenure. She also worked on costume design for Broadway as well as interiors, textiles, murals and product design, and would later also carve out a new career as a designer in the car industry. Dryden was a household name during her working life and was often cited as the highest paid female artist in America.

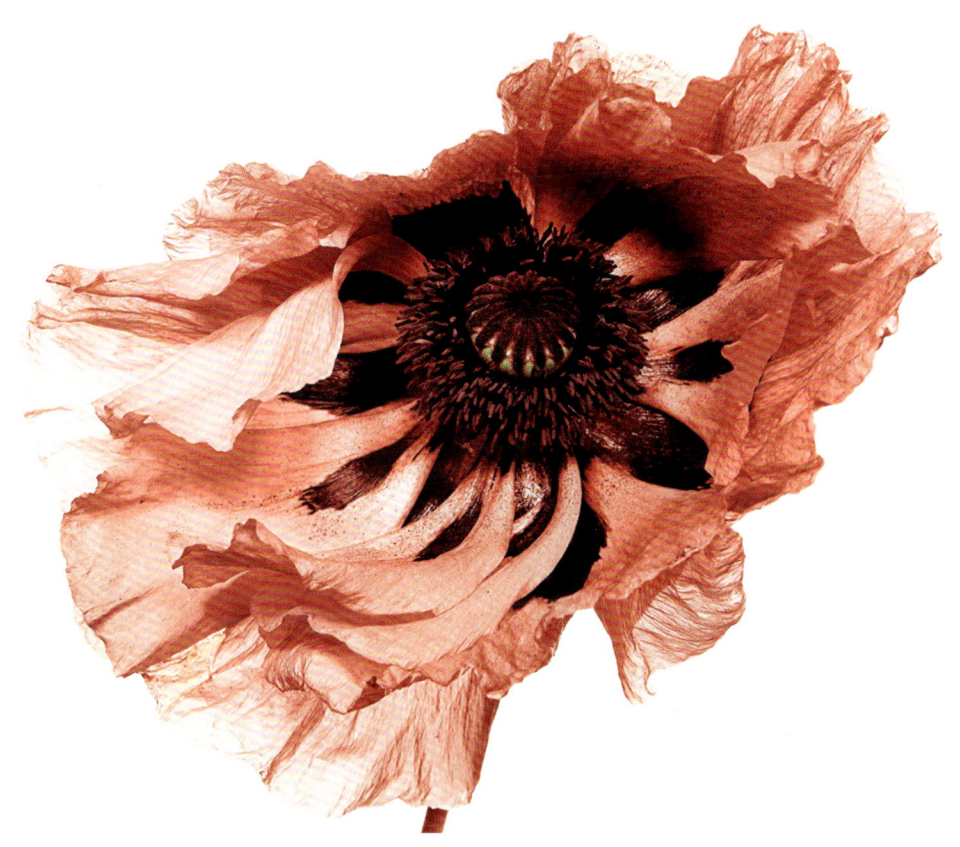

Irving Penn

Poppy: Showgirl, New York, 1968
Dye transfer print, printed 1989, 43.2 × 55.6 cm /
17 × 21¾ in

With its translucent petals curling inwards as if under the burden of time, Irving Penn's portrait of a poppy is as elegant as it is honest. A photographer renowned for crafting iconic images by distilling the essence of larger-than-life personalities from Marlene Dietrich to Pablo Picasso (see p.297) and Miles Davis, Penn (1917–2009) gave his flowers the same kind of star treatment. He began taking photographs of flowers for *Vogue* magazine in the summer of 1967. For seven consecutive years, he focused on a different flower, starkly positioned and brightly lit against a white background. Like others in the series, *Poppy* reveals a beautiful fragility, a sense of vulnerability that often eludes both classical still-life paintings and botanical illustration. This is the paradox underlying Penn's images: every detail of the flower's body is mercilessly exposed to heighten rather than dissolve its iconic essence. As a result, *Poppy* exudes individualistic character: it is the portrait of a moment in the life of a specific bloom, rather than an objective view of a scientific representative of its species. Neither is this poppy related to the metaphor of sleep, as the flower symbolically anchored the narratives of many Victorian paintings. Penn allows this bloom to remain proudly wrapped up in its mystery, forever frozen in ephemeral glory.

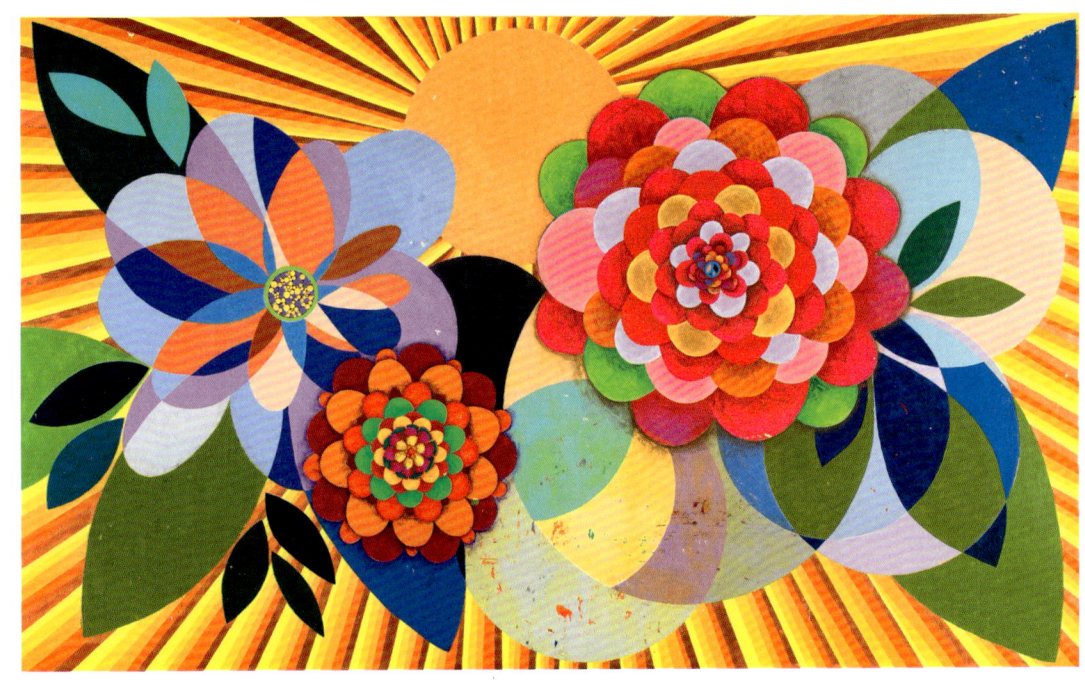

Beatriz Milhazes

Summer Love, from the polyptych
Gamboa Seasons, 2010
Acrylic on canvas, 3 × 5 m / 9 ft 10 in × 16 ft 5 in
Private collection

A riot of carnivalesque colour sweeps across this enormous canvas, evoking the tropical climate and flora of Brazil. Dominating the composition are three vividly coloured flower forms comprising pink, blue, green and red geometric shapes superimposed over a radiant sun emitting yellow and orange rays. The painting, which represents summer, is the first in a series embodying the four seasons by Brazilian artist Beatriz Milhazes (born 1960) – although, as the artist has noted, Brazil's seasons are not clearly defined and so each painting instead expresses a 'variation of heat'. Milhazes does not paint her floral motifs and geometric designs directly onto the canvas, preferring to compose them on plastic sheets. Once dry, she carefully peels the forms off and sticks them to the support like a collage. By slowly building up her images layer upon layer, she achieves a super-flat surface with little trace of her hand and no brushstrokes. This way of working recalls Henri Matisse's paper cut-outs, which have had a significant influence on Milhazes's celebrated practice. Other sources of inspiration include Brazilian modernist painters such as Tarsila do Amaral, British abstract painter Bridget Riley, American Pop artists such as Roy Lichtenstein, and the view from her own Rio de Janeiro studio, which overlooks the city's botanical gardens.

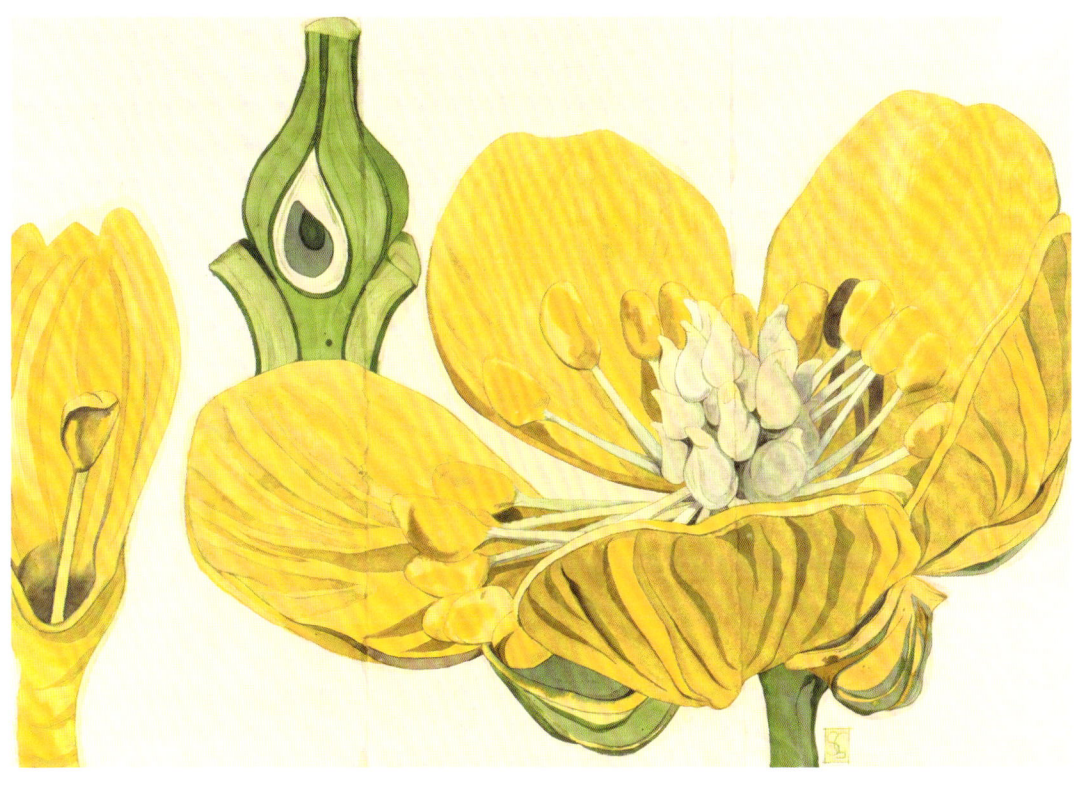

Sarah Graham

Nuphar and Ranunculus, 2016
Ink on paper, 1.2 × 1.8 m / 3 ft 11 in × 5 ft 11 in
Private collection

With their overwhelming scale, organic materials and surreal compositions, the works of artist Sarah Graham (born 1973) take traditional botanical drawing bravely into the twenty-first century. Graham is uncompromising about the monumental size of her drawings – most measure nearly 2 metres (6 feet 6 inches) long. Reinforcing her subject matter, Graham also uses organic materials: the papers are all hand-made from natural fibre and her intense colours are achieved by using pure inks distilled from natural dyes. Graham often seeks out unusual specimens from the natural world for inspiration. Based in London, she has a lending arrangement with Kew Gardens and the Natural History Museum, allowing her to borrow specimens and objects from each museum's collections. Working closely with the museum curators, she has an endless supply of subjects. *Nuphar and Ranunculus* is not in fact drawn from an actual flower but a Brendel papier-mâché model. These enlarged, didactic replicas of plants were used as teaching tools in nineteenth-century France. Although aware of the long history of botanical drawing, Graham's contemporary approach is concerned with self expression above empirical observation. She shifts the focus to drawings that are ambiguous, surreal and sensual rather than purely descriptive. Here, the characteristic golden colour and rounded shape of *Nuphar lutea*, also called a yellow pond lily, is blended with the stamen and other botanical structures of a ranunculus.

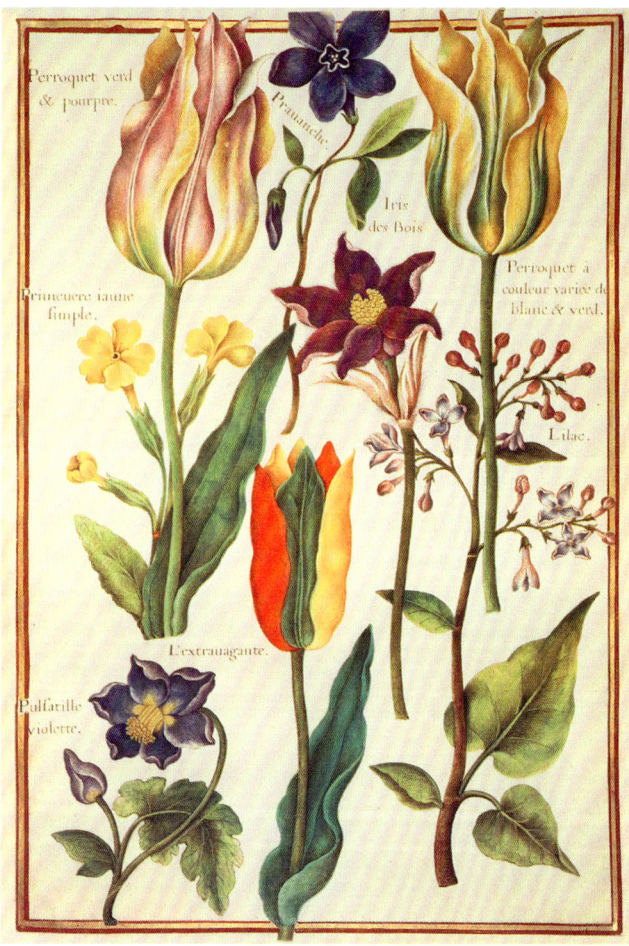

Nicolas Robert

Flower Studies, 17th century
Watercolour on vellum, 31.1 × 22.2 cm /
12¼ × 8¾ in
Fitzwilliam Museum, Cambridge, UK

A lyrical gathering of popular seventeenth-century garden flowers overlaps the gold border fencing them in, as if growing beyond the boundaries of the page. Delicate strokes of watercolour and gouache on vellum from the masterful hand of French miniaturist Nicolas Robert (1614–85) bring to life pasqueflower, lilac, primrose, parrot tulips and an iris. *Flower Studies* may have been painted during Robert's early years in the service of Gaston, Duke of Orléans, during which he documented the extensive collection of plants, animals and birds on the duke's garden estate in Blois, France. From around the age of thirty, Robert advanced his facility there as a botanical illustrator and completed paintings of singular subjects that filled five folios. After Gaston's death in 1660, the paintings were bequeathed to his nephew, King Louis XIV, and subsequently transferred to the Jardin du Roi (now Jardin des Plantes) in Paris – planted in 1635 by Louis XIII's physician originally as a garden for medicinal plants and later expanding to become the most important botanical garden in France. Appointed painter of miniatures by Louis in 1664, Robert continued to produce more than 700 paintings of plants from the Jardin and birds from the Versailles aviary. He was the first in a long line of artists appointed to add to *Les Vélins*, as these vellum illustrations are known. The collection of more than 7,000 paintings illustrates the progression of scientific collecting practices across three centuries.

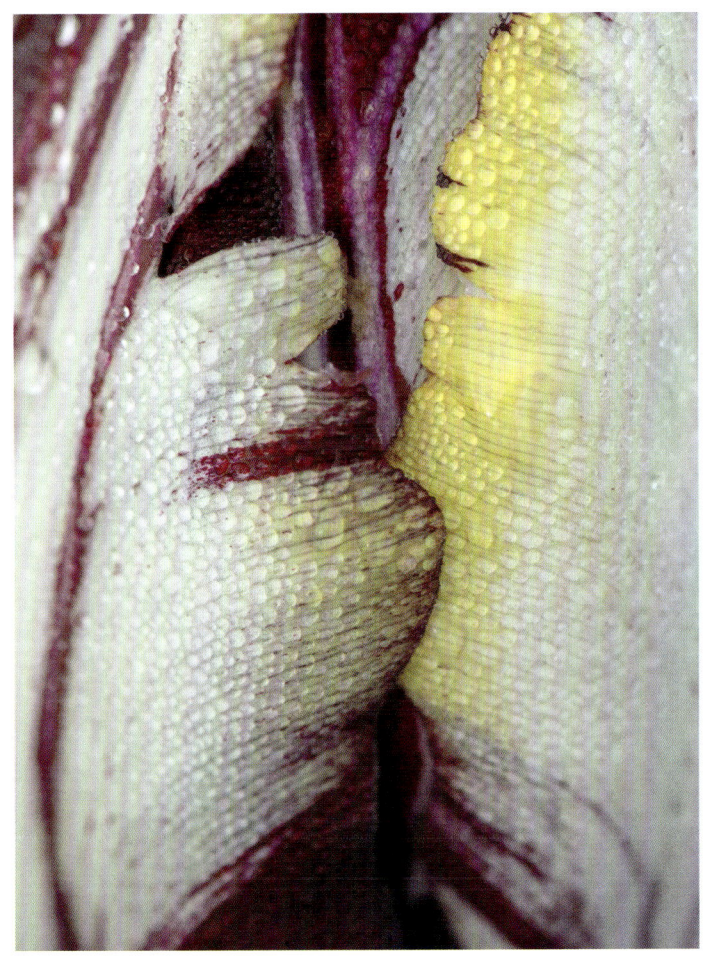

Clive Nichols

Bayntun Flowers: Close Up Plant Portrait of Heritage Broken Tulip – Tulipa Rembrandt, 2019
Photograph, dimensions variable
Private collection

In this close-up image, a Rembrandt tulip is abstracted into a compositional pattern – droplets of dew enhance the texture and colour of its flamed petals, emphasizing the edges which cross as if to conceal a secret. This striking image is a notable example of the unique ability developed by British photographer Clive Nichols (born 1962) – over three decades spent photographing gardens, plants and flowers – to capture the fleeting beauty of botanical subjects. During the mid-1630s, new varieties of tulip bulbs became extremely fashionable and much sought-after status symbols, and intricate feathering streaks on petals became the obsession of Dutch Golden Age collectors. Broken tulips, so named because of the 'shattered' colour of the petals, rose uncontrollably in value over a short period, creating the first market bubble in modern history. It was only three hundred years later that researchers discovered the secret of the unusually dramatic colouration: it was neither natural nor the result of careful hybridization, but the symptom of a mosaic virus spread by aphids. Regardless of their beauty, with each new generation, bulbs grow weaker and lack vigour, making them more difficult to grow. The original broken tulip varieties are now extinct and broken tulips have been outlawed in Holland, as they are generally feared by breeders around the world. *Tulipa* 'Rembrandt' is a benevolent impostor, however: it has been selectively bred to resemble its broken ancestors, but carries no virus.

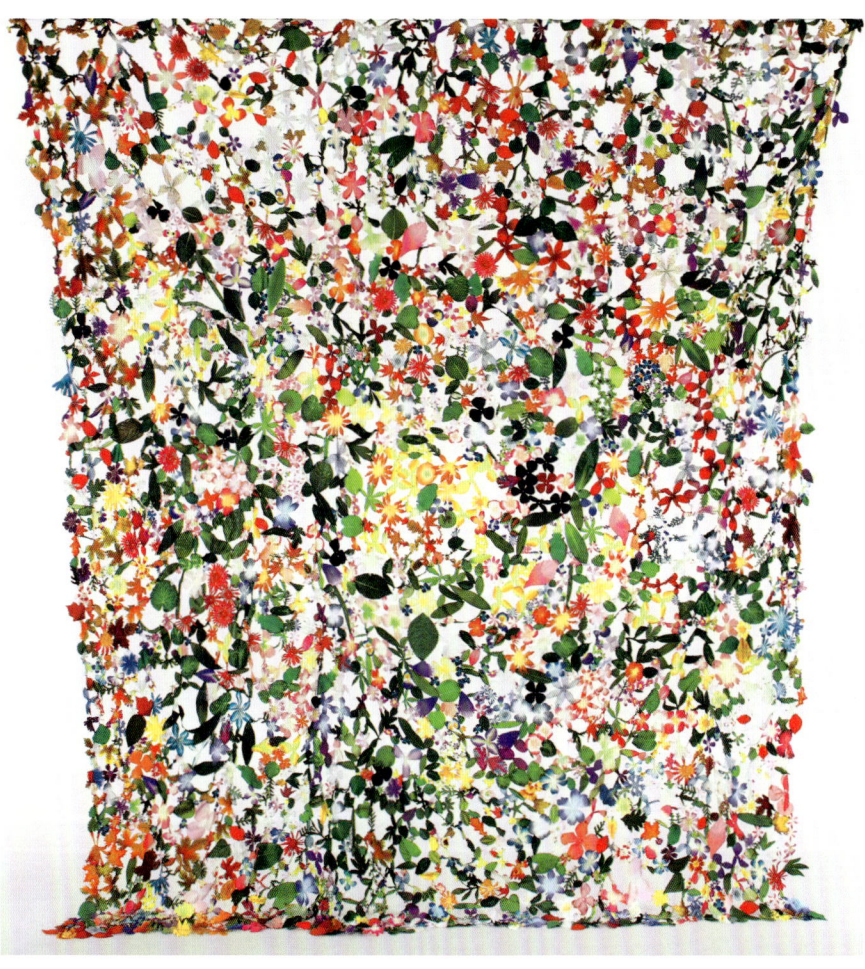

Jim Hodges

From Our Side, 1995
Silk, cotton, polyester and thread, 3.7 × 3.7 m /
12 × 12 ft
Private collection

Silk flowers, petals and leaves of every shape
and size are stitched densely together to form
a kaleidoscopic curtain cascading from a height
of nearly 4 metres (12 feet) down to the floor.
From Our Side is one of many pieces by American
artist Jim Hodges (born 1957) that incorporates
flowers, touching on fundamental subjects such
as fragility, temporality, beauty and power.

Hodges first presented the theme in 1994, with
A Diary of Flowers at CRC Art in New York – an
exhibition that featured 565 doodles of petals
on restaurant napkins. The series had been initiated three years earlier and was prompted,
among other things, by Hodges' examination
and deconstruction of silk flowers in his studio,
creating a desire to return the flowers to fabric.
'I was interested in the history of each petal. How
the material had been transformed: cut, painted,
sculptured, and given a flower identity. I wanted
to re-establish that material's fabric nature.'
In the following years, Hodges' flower works

would become an integral part of his practice,
underlining his interest in the relationship
between the spiritual and physical dimensions.
Such dichotomies are well represented in *From
Our Side*; as the title suggests, the curtain creates
a dividing presence between two unidentified
entities. On the surface, Hodges perhaps refers
to the creator and the viewer; or it could be that
his piece literally and metaphorically celebrates
the wallflower – the odd person out who finally
gets an opportunity to re-establish his or herself.

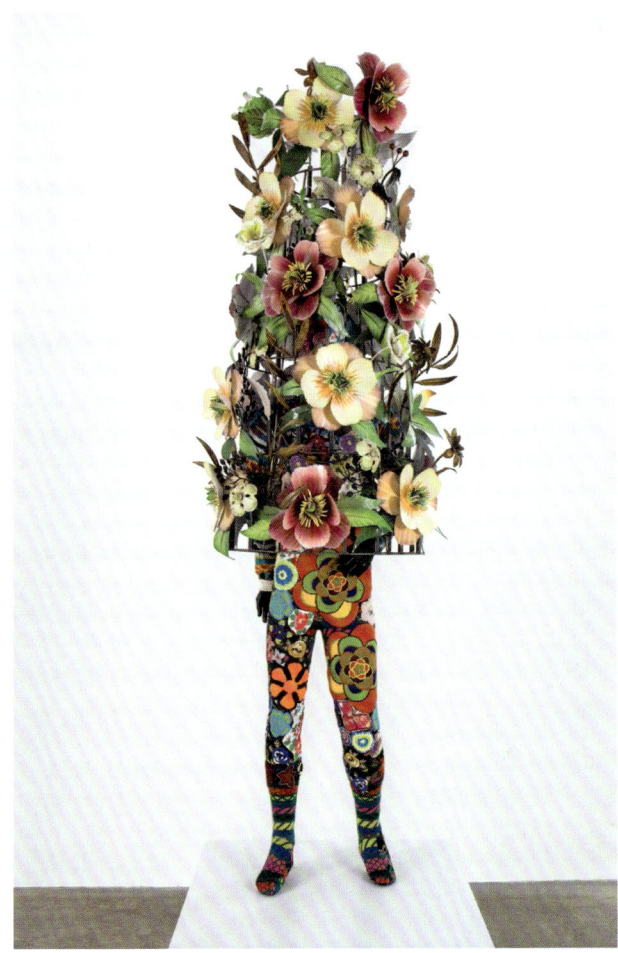

Nick Cave

Soundsuit, 2008
Fabric, fibreglass and metal, 2.6 × 0.9 × 0.7 m /
8 ft 6 in × 3 ft × 2 ft 4 in
Rubell Museum, Miami

Designed as an armour of plastic and metal hellebore flowers, this 'soundsuit' fully disguises
the body of the wearer, generating a second skin
to prevent onlookers from determining any identifying traits such as gender, race and class.
The soundsuit was first conceived in 1991 by Afro-
American artist Nick Cave (born 1959) in response
to the well-documented beating of Rodney King
by four police officers in Los Angeles. Over the
years Cave's outfits – featuring both flowers and,
frequently, musical instruments – have served
different purposes, acting both as sculptures and
as costumes for the artist's dance performances,
and earning iconic status as a vehicle of change.
On top of the limitations of weight and movement, the soundsuits' erasure of the identity
of their users, while simultaneously providing
protection, formulates an invitation to step into
the unknown. While there are historical prece-
dents in art for the anthropomorphic value
of flowers – chief among them the work
of sixteenth-century Italian painter Giuseppe
Arcimboldo (see p.149) – Cave's coverings also
refer to the traditional use of vegetation as cam-
ouflage, and function as an output for 'queerness'.
With time the soundsuits have expanded the
range of materials they are made of to encompass fabrics, buttons and African masks, but
without renouncing their power of liberating
performers and viewers from the social barriers
that could potentially inhibit or define their
personal relationship.

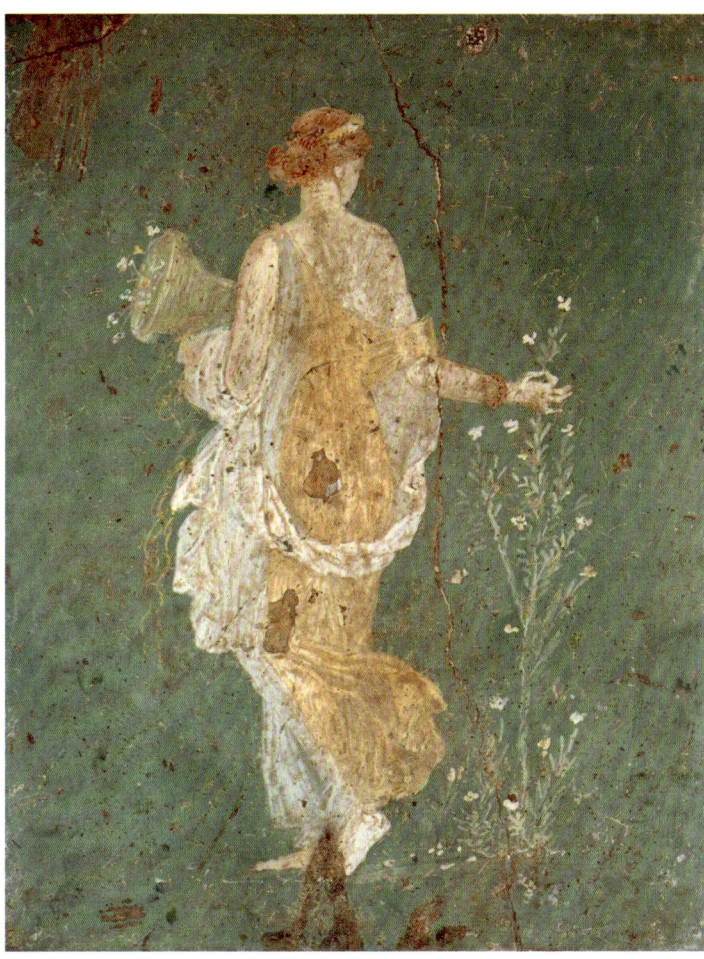

Anonymous

Flora, from the Villa of Ariadne, Stabiae, 1–45 AD
Fresco, 38 × 32 cm / 15 × 12½ in
Museo Archeologico Nazionale di Napoli, Italy

Flora, the Roman goddess of flowers and spring-time, faces away from the viewer with flowing pale robes and golden hair, carrying a basket of delicate white blooms against a fertile green ground as she picks flowers. The goddess is an apt allegory for the setting in which she was discovered: on the existing remnant of a fresco from the Villa Ariadne, one of the sumptuous seaside palaces in the town of Stabiae on the Gulf of Naples

where wealthy Romans took their summer pleasures. Abandoned following the eruption of Vesuvius in 79 AD, the mansions at Stabiae were unusually well preserved, unlike many in the neighbouring towns of Pompeii and Herculaneum. This fragment is one of four Graces – the others were Diana, Medea and Leda – each set within a wall of the villa's *cubiculum* (bedroom). The raw green was a costly material, along with the red and the blue pigments seen in the portraits of the other Graces. A preserve of wealthy clients, such colours gave the artists – who were probably expert Roman or Greek painters – a rich choice

of tonal expression. Flora is derived from the Greek goddess Chloris, and the use of Greek mythological figures also symbolizes the villa owner's cultural prestige, reflecting prized knowledge of the Hellenistic tradition that is expressed here pictorially.

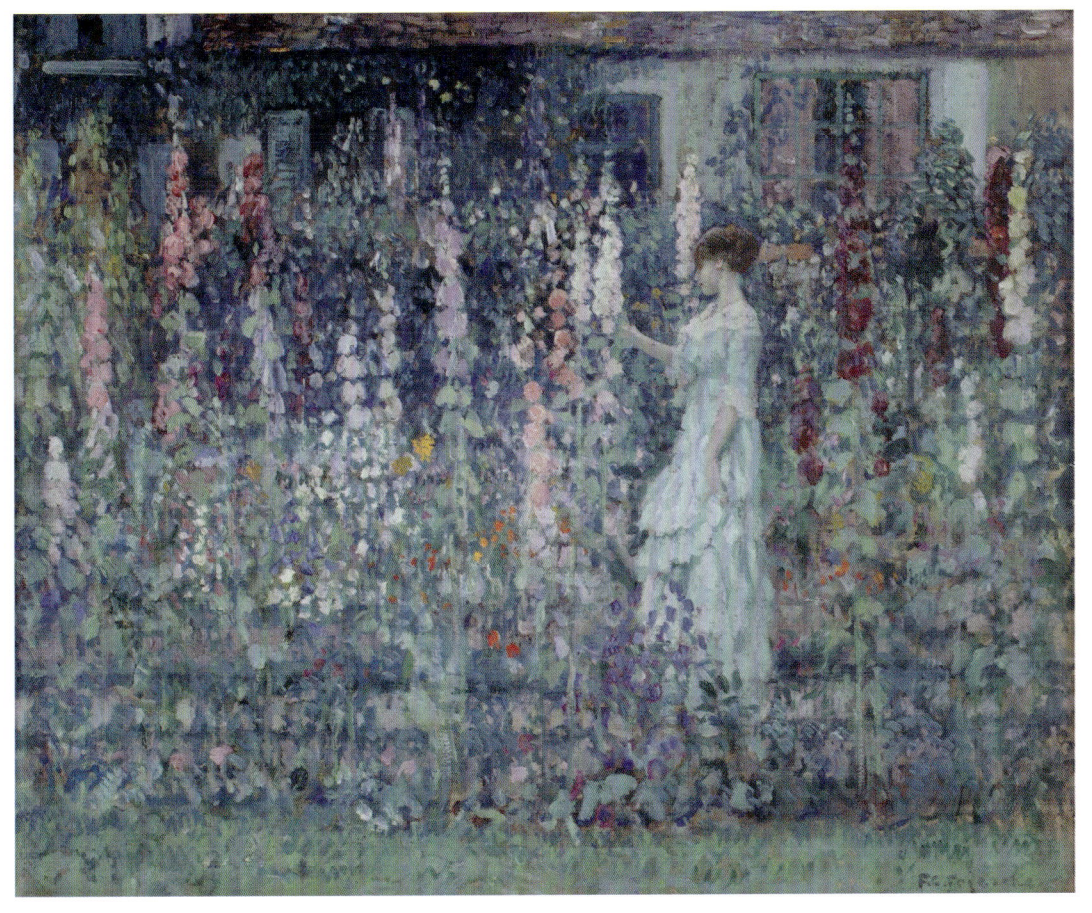

Frederick Frieseke

Hollyhocks, by 1911
Oil on canvas, 64.7 × 81.3 cm / 25½ × 32 in
National Academy of Design, New York

In its subject, composition and treatment –
a figure in a garden, among brilliantly coloured
hollyhocks, with contrasting hues used to convey an impression of heat and light – this picture
is entirely characteristic of a style which, for
a time, made Frederick Frieseke (1874–1939) one
of the most popular of all living American artists. Born in Owosso, Michigan, in 1874, Frieseke
left the United States for France in 1898, after

a brief period of artistic training in Chicago and
New York. Just a few years later he was exhibiting
at the Salon of the Société Nationale des Beaux-
Arts in Paris. A leading member of the second generation of Americans in the Giverny art colony,
Frieseke spent many summers in a house neighbouring Claude Monet (see p.169), but the two
did not become close acquaintances, nor did the
American regard the older French artist as a significant influence, citing instead the impact
of Pierre-Auguste Renoir's work (see p. 244) on his
development. While contemporaries such as
Henri Matisse (see p.19) and his fellow Fauvists

were pursuing more radical and experimental
approaches, Frieseke chose to continue to practice in the late Impressionist style. He painted
Hollyhocks in the garden of Le Hameau in Giverny,
adhering precisely to his own pronouncement:
'If you are looking at a mass of flowers in the
sunlight out of doors, you see a sparkle of spots
of different colours – then paint them that way.'

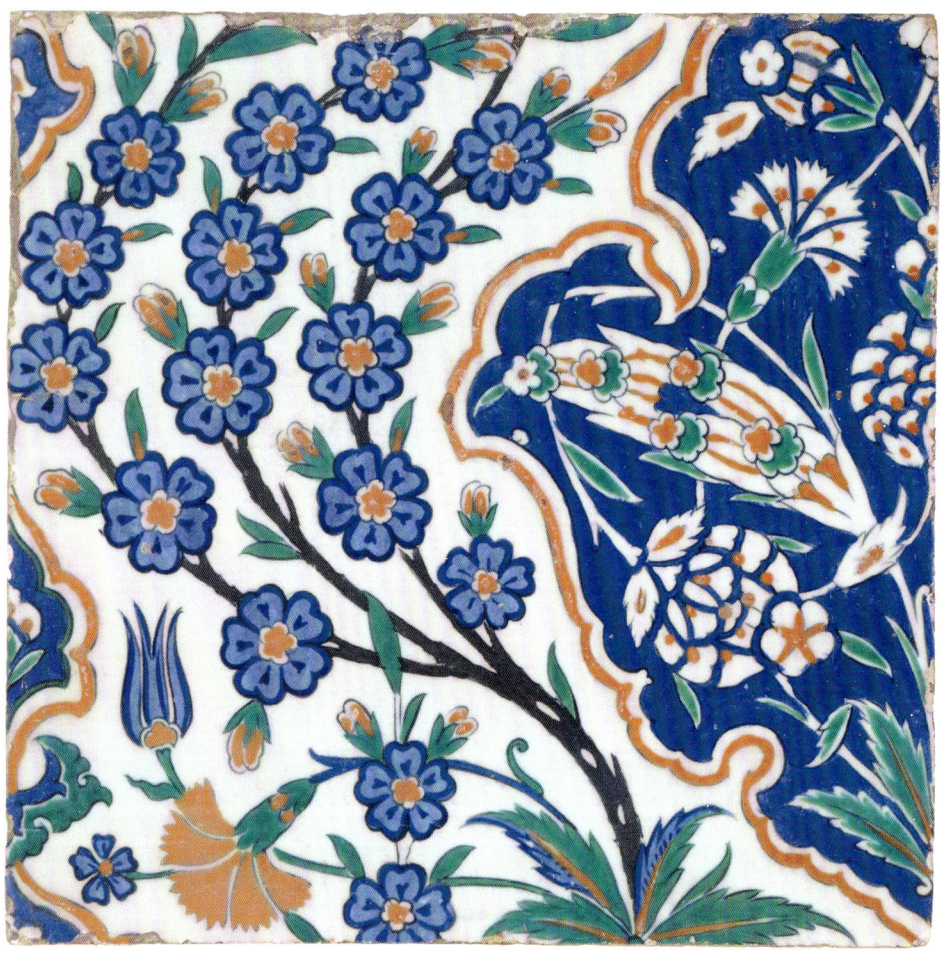

Anonymous

Iznik tile, c.1601–21
Clay, majolica, 23.5 × 34 cm / 9¼ × 13¼ in
Museum für Angewandte Kunst,
Cologne, Germany

Although the floral motifs on this seventeenth-century Iznik tile are highly stylized,
there are in fact four recognizable varieties
of flowers to be found. Within the cobalt blue
medallion at right, white segmented roses and
carnations surround an embellished feathery
saz leaf. To the left, separated by a thin outline
of bole red, are sprays of sinuous blue prunus

blossom, a solitary blue tulip with pointed
petals and a red carnation. Tufts of green anchor
the swirling black stems of the flowers, and the
colour is repeated through the pattern as small
leaves and sepals. The lack of symmetry within
the design – typical of this period – suggests
that the tile was part of a larger panel. The presence of four distinct flowers gave rise to the
term *quatre fleurs*, a style that became popular
from the middle of the sixteenth century. The
tulip, as the most exalted and revered flower
within Ottoman culture, was generally the
focal point. Carnations, seen as symbols of life,

were usually present, while the other blooms
included roses and hyacinths. Peonies and prunus
were also commonly depicted. The Ottoman city
of Iznik in northwest Anatolia, modern-day
Turkey, was the centre of tile production for the
whole of the Ottoman Empire, and industrial-
sized quantities of tiles were created to feed the
construction of monumental mosques and palaces. The combination of repeated glazing and
firing processes gave the pottery immense durability and preserved the brilliant colours and pure
white grounds that make this style so distinctive.

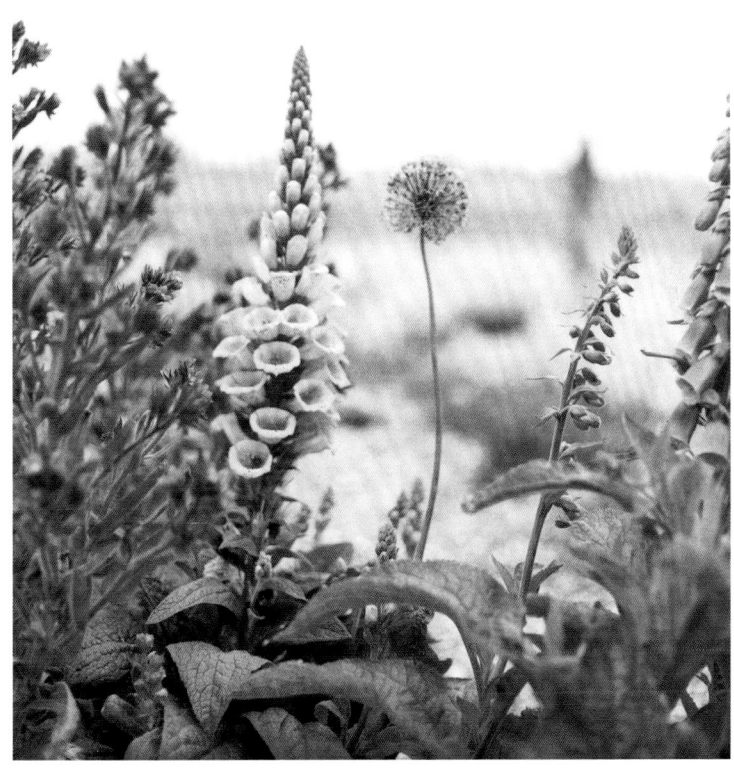

Howard Sooley

Foxglove, Dungeness, 1993
Photograph, 30.5 × 24.1 cm / 9½ × 12 in
Private collection

In 1991 Howard Sooley (born 1963) was commissioned to photograph the artist and filmmaker Derek Jarman (see p.116), marking the start of a deep friendship and a long and fruitful artistic collaboration centred on the unique garden Jarman created around his cottage on the bleak shingle bank at Dungeness on England's south coast. As they gardened together, Sooley would break off to photograph the flowers and sculptures around them, working with a spontaneity that is beautifully reflected in this image. Using a medium-format camera and no tripod, Sooley forgoes depth of field in order to capture a mood and a moment. In doing so, he also foregrounds the flowers – here, foxgloves and viper's bugloss or echium, both of which grow in the wild on the Ness, punctuated by the bold exclamation mark of the drumstick allium head, deliberately planted there by Jarman. The use of black and white puts the emphasis on structure, the vertical spires of the foxgloves echoing the blurry sculpture that can just be made out in the background, and on the spaces between the flowers as well as the flowers themselves. Like Jarman's renowned garden itself – with its absence of boundaries, its treasure trove of found objects and its embrace of self-sown and wildflowers, the whole nevertheless carefully curated by an artist's eye – the image is the perfect mix of randomness and art.

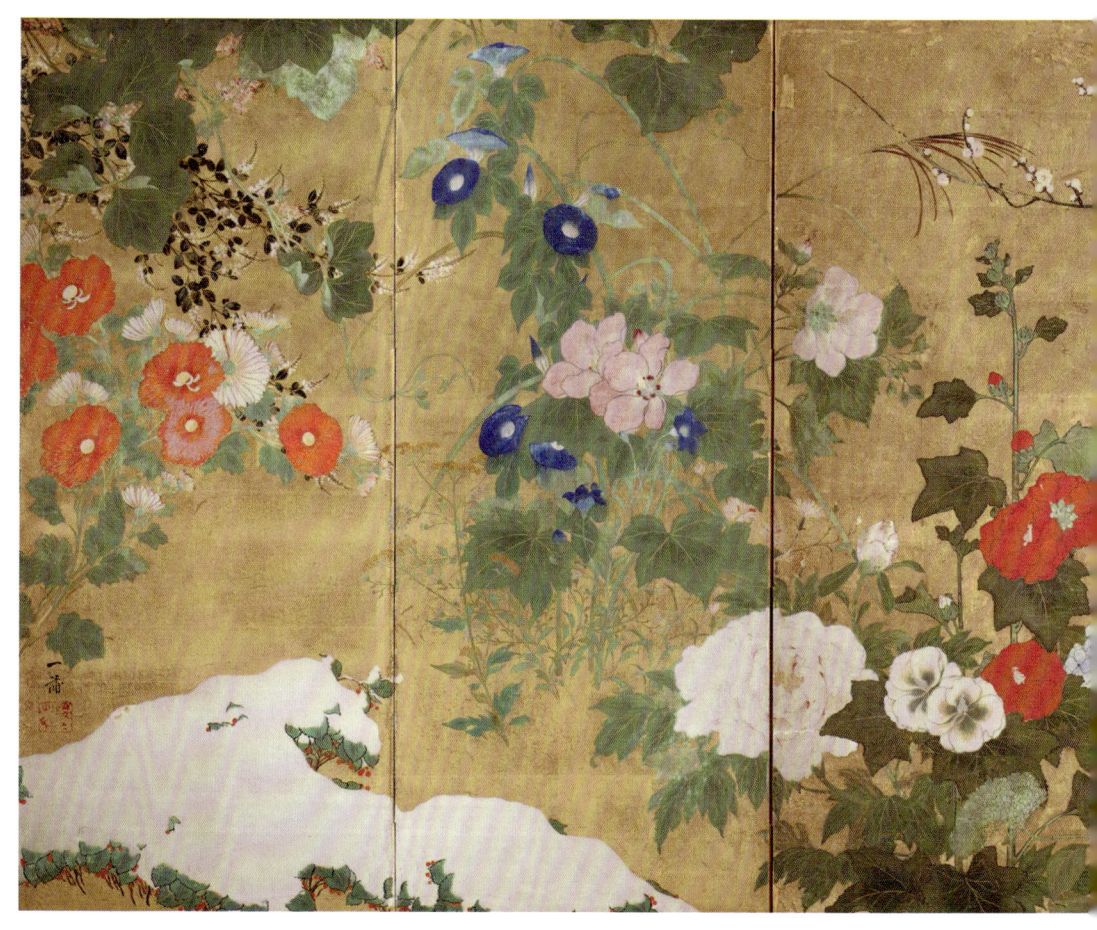

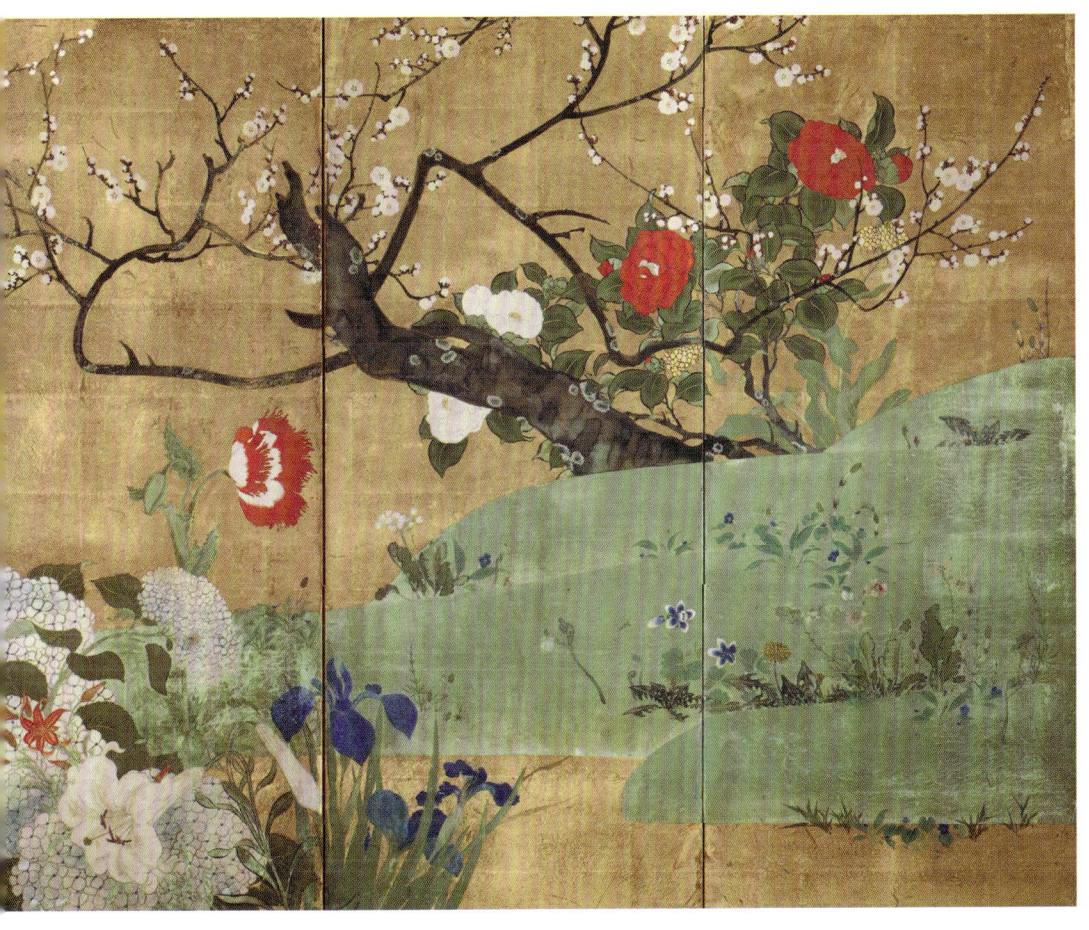

Saitō Ippo

Flowers of the Four Seasons, early 19th century
Ink and colour on gold leaf, 1 × 2.4 m /
3 ft 2 in × 8 ft
Minneapolis Institute of Arts, Minnesota

Against a glowing backdrop of gold leaf, this panoramic six-panel screen from Japan takes us on a floral journey through the four seasons. At the far right we see the flowers of spring, with dandelions, violets and both red and white camellias. Leaning across towards the centre of the screen is a cherry or plum tree, leafless, but already bearing a galaxy of small white blossoms. In the foreground of the central panels is a collection of summer-flowering peonies, hydrangeas and hollyhocks, with a small cluster of blue *Iris ensata* beside them. To the left of the irises, rises a single stem of *siro-yuri* or white lily (*Lilium longiflorum*) known in the west as the Easter lily. A covering of snow over the vegetation at the far left indicates the transition from autumn into winter, above which some species are still in flower, including deep blue blooms on the clambering vine of morning glory and sprays of chrysanthemums. The chrysanthemum (*kiku*), which starts to bloom in the autumn, is a deeply symbolic flower in Japanese culture, representing longevity and rejuvenation. Flowering cherry (*sakura*) is also central to Japanese life, and the arrival of cherry blossom is widely celebrated as marking the beginning of spring. Little is known about the artist, Saitō Ippo, beyond the fact that he was an official at the Asakusa Temple in Edo (modern Tokyo) in the early part of the nineteenth century. This is one of very few of his works to survive.

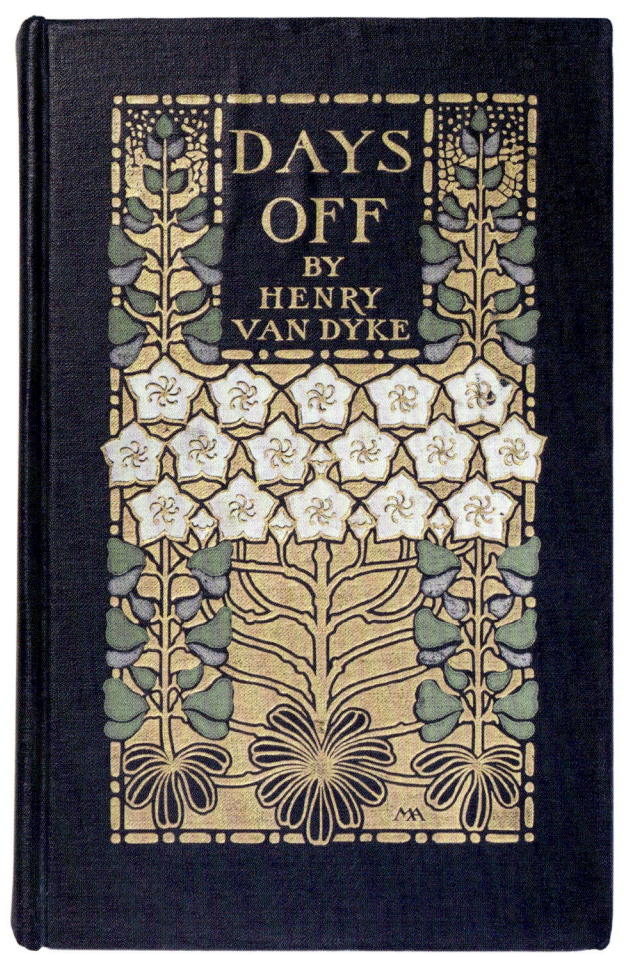

Margaret Neilson Armstrong

Cover of *Days Off* by Henry Van Dyke, 1907
Foil on cloth case, 19 × 12 cm / 7½ × 4¾ in
Private collection

A band of sixteen white, star-like flower heads forms the centrepiece of a bejewelled and gilded book cover that reflects not a realistic depiction but an unmistakable, stylized Art Nouveau style: the flowers' stems radiate both above and below the blossoms and the roots spray outwards, appearing almost like petals themselves. This book cover was designed by American illustrator Margaret Neilson Armstrong (1867–1944) for the

first edition of *Days Off*, a book of essays by the author Henry Van Dyke, published in 1907. Showcasing the Art Nouveau aesthetic mode at its most intense and beautiful, the cover applies symmetrical rigour to its various elements: the main stem of the flowers forms the backbone of the work, almost as if it were leadwork in stained glass – the medium in which Armstrong's father worked. At the centre of the white flowers, a swirling shape makes the flower head seem to spin like a child's windmill toy, giving the cover a sense of movement. Armstrong was a prolific book designer,

producing more than 270 book covers in a career spanning from the 1880s to the early 1910s, when dust jackets became the new fashion. She was also an enthusiastic naturalist with a particular interest in botany. From 1911 to 1914, she travelled the western United States and Canada, discovering several unidentified plant species that she documented and illustrated – nearly 550 of them – in her *Field Book of Western Wild Flowers* (1915).

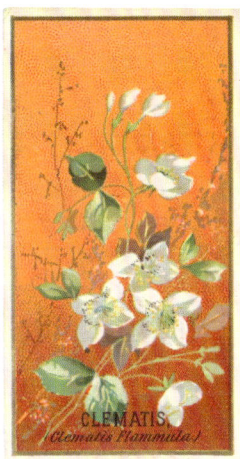

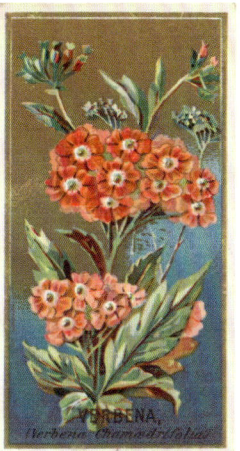

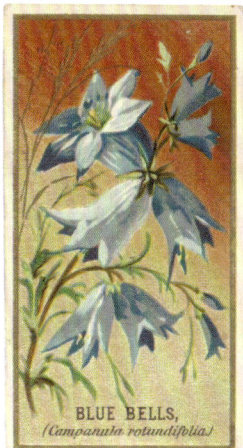

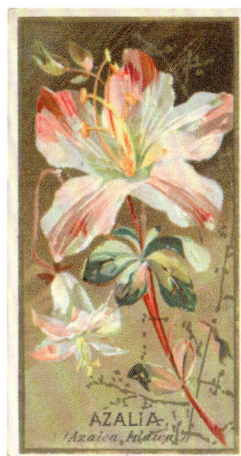

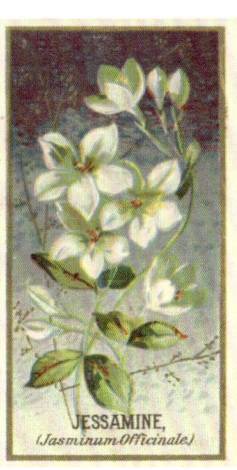

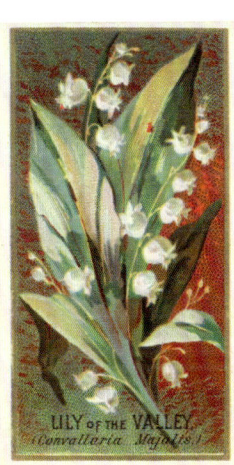

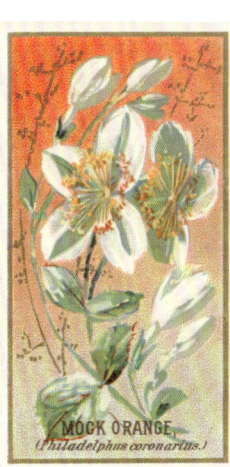

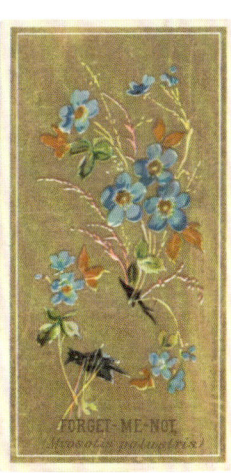

Goodwin & Company

Flowers trading cards, from a series promoting Old Judge Cigarettes, 1890
Colour lithographs, each 7 × 3.8 cm / 2¾ × 1½ in
Metropolitan Museum of Art, New York

These trading cards come from a set of fifty painted in a semi-pointillist style by an unknown artist for Goodwin & Company in 1890 to promote its Old Judge cigarette brand. In the top row, *Clematis flammula*, the deciduous climber with pure white petals, is set against a rich orange background. The bright red petals of verbena (*Verbena peruviana*) are followed by distinctive blue bells (*Campanula rotundifolia*) and the abundant blooms of azalea (*Rhododendron indicum*). In the bottom row we see the starry jasmine (*Jasminum officinale*), the delicate flowers of lily of the valley (*Convallaria majalis*), the ornamental mock orange (*Philadelphus coronarius*) and the blue and yellow blossoms of forget-me-not (*Myosotis palustris*). The *Flowers* series of cards, given away in packs of cigarettes, included obvious choices such as roses, hollyhocks and daffodils but also less familiar examples such as the small perennial wildflower Quaker lady (*Houstonia caerulea*); one curious image entitled 'sea flower' in fact shows a sea anemone. Many of the flowers are set against coloured backgrounds, although some are shown in their natural habitats, such as a water lily pictured on water accompanied by bulrushes. Goodwin & Company was one of the first companies to issue trading cards, first using sepia-toned photographic prints and later lithographic reproductions. Such printed ephemera encouraged brand loyalty and, although tobacco was bought by adults, it was predominantly children who collected and traded the cards.

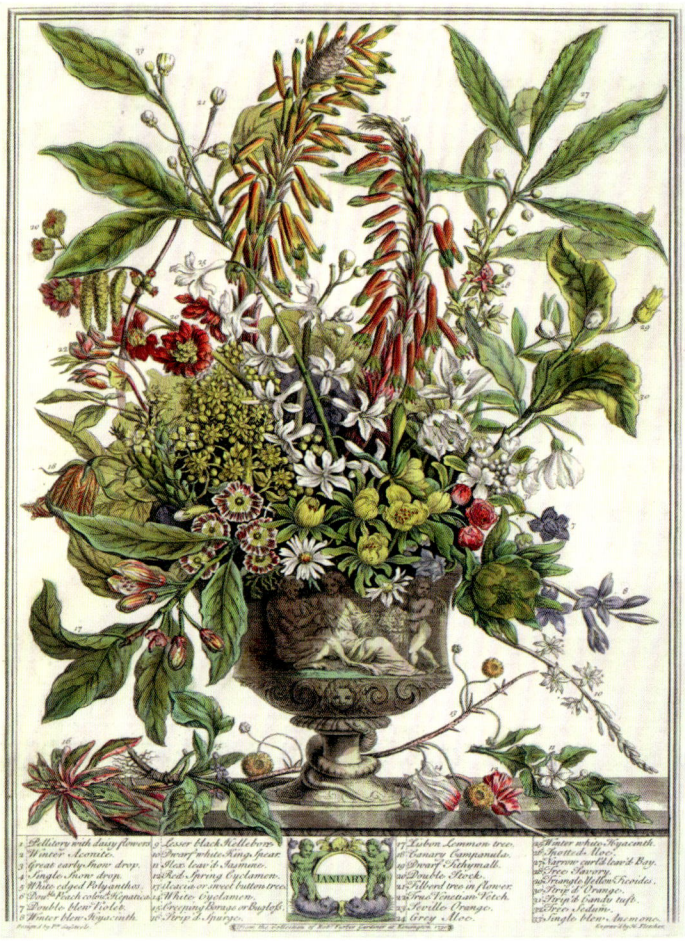

Pieter Casteels III and Robert Furber

January, from *Twelve Months of Flowers*, *c.*1730–50
Hand-coloured engraving, 40.8 × 30.4 cm /
16 × 12 in
Victoria and Albert Museum, London

A bountiful yet rather wild and somewhat unkempt flower arrangement in a classically decorated baroque urn dominates the frame. In total some thirty-three varieties of flower are shown, each numbered in the illustration and listed in the key below. In the centre of the key appears the label 'January', placing this image at the beginning of a cycle of twelve prints designed by

Pieter Casteels III (1684–1749) and published by British horticulturist and author Robert Furber (1674–1756), each designed to illustrate the flowers in bloom during that particular month. Here, we see among other flowers white cyclamen (14), red spring cyclamen (12) and single snowdrops (4). Although winter is typically a dormant time for flowers, Casteels presents a scene of exuberance and a profusion of blooms – as, indeed, he does with each month. Despite Furber's desire for the illustration to educate viewers it also had a commercial function. Furber owned a nursery in Kensington, London, where he sold native

and imported plants. This print would have served not just as an instructive or attractive engraving, but also as a means for customers to browse by month and point to the seed or plant they wanted to order, making it a revolutionary form of early gardening catalogue.

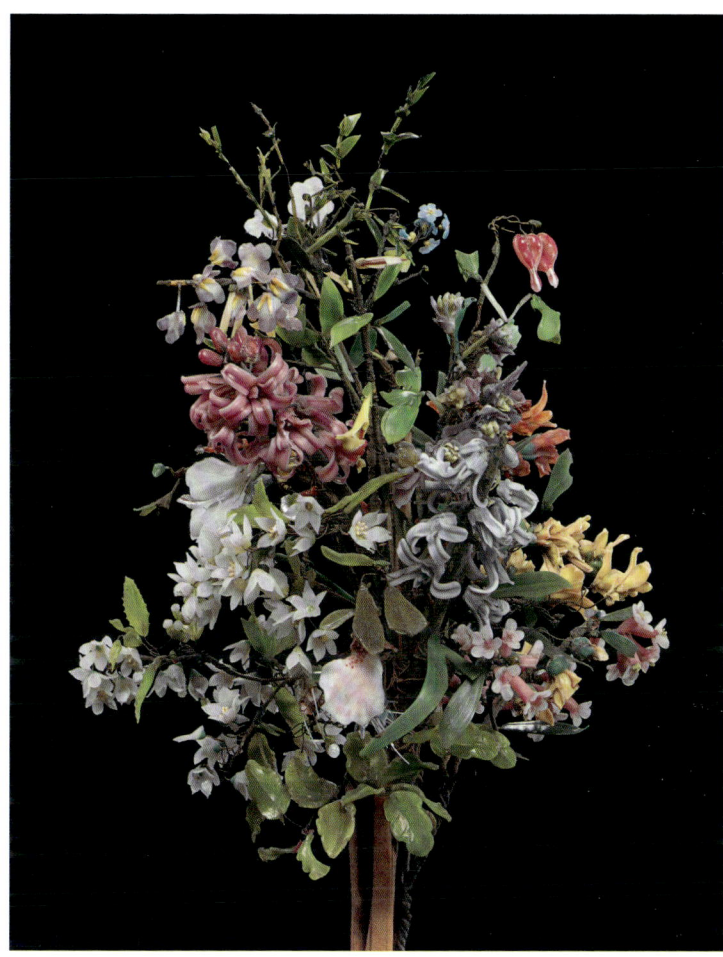

Leopold Blaschka

Bouquet of Flowers, 1857–1890
Glass, wood, wire, metal, paint, H. 36 cm / 14 in
Corning Museum of Glass, New York

On close inspection, a bouquet of spring ephemerals – bleeding heart, forget-me-not, hyacinth and others – is revealed as glass flowers with wire armatures and wooden stems. Each petal curve and leaf vein are produced by the lampwork (or flamework) process – melting glass rods or tubes, manipulating the forms with tools and fusing them with heat. This bouquet was created by the third-generation Bohemian glass artist

Leopold Blaschka (1822–95) who, with his son Rudolf, later pushed the limits of the process using coloured and painted clear glass. Leopold joined the family business, making costume jewellery and glass eyes for humans and museum taxidermy, but later focused on painting and making glass flower models. Commissions for glass orchids and sea anemones by Prince Camille de Rohan and the natural history museum in Dresden, respectively, furthered Blaschka's reputation and requests streamed in from universities and museums throughout Europe. With accessible public education and a widespread

interest in the sciences in the mid-to-late nineteenth century, models became an important teaching aide in university classrooms. The transparency and detail of Blaschka's glass models superseded other mediums. The Blaschkas are best known for the Ware Collection of Glass Models of Plants at the Botanical Museum of Harvard University, created between 1887 and 1936. Like any scientific illustrator, they sketched these plants from life in order to achieve the utmost accuracy and detail in glass.

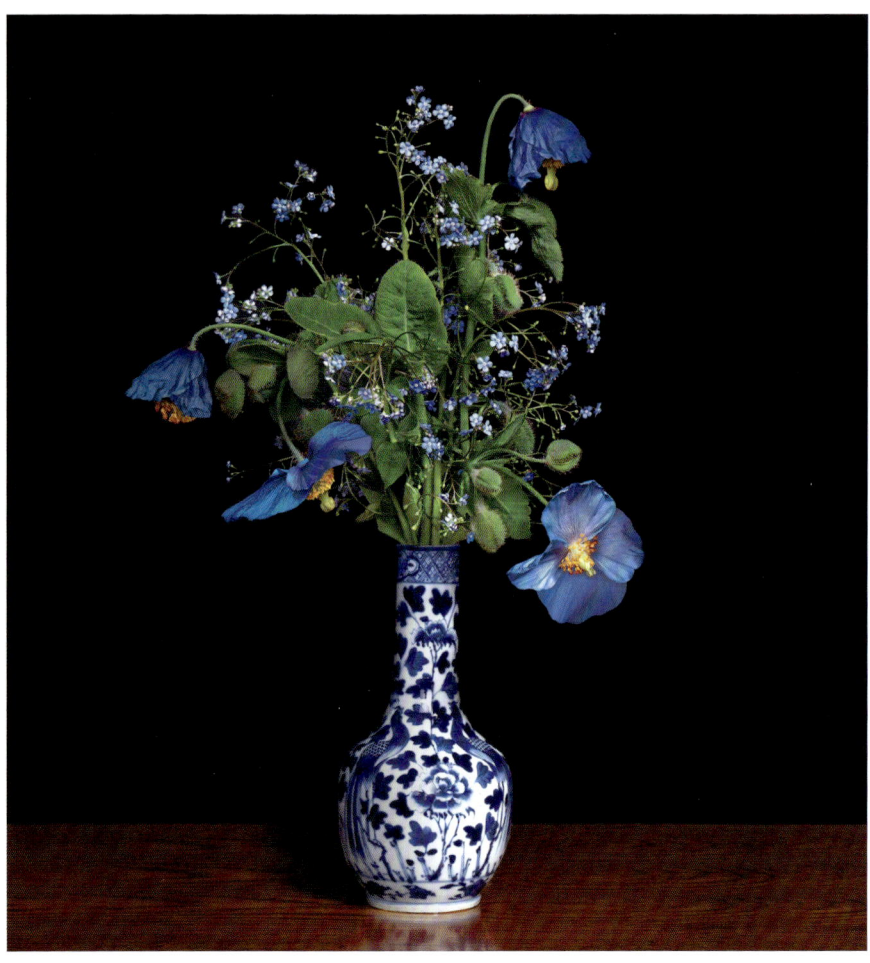

T.M. Glass

Blue Poppy in a Blue and White Chinese Vase, 2018
Archival pigment print, dimensions variable

Set against a uniform black background, the textures of every petal, bud, leaf and stem in this floral arrangement have been captured with stunning clarity. In such exquisite detail, the drooping flowers of the two uppermost Himalayan blue poppies reveal the beautifully wrinkled surfaces of the petals, which take on the quality of silken skirts. The poppies and the intermingled clustered flowering stems of forget-me-nots have been placed in a blue and white Chinese vase to create a harmonious combination. The tableau is the creation of Canadian artist T.M. Glass, who combines state-of-the-art digital photography and digital painting to create portraits of flowers that are then printed in archival limited-edition pigment prints at very high resolution. Although the result may echo historical still-life painting, Glass has fully embraced technology and the latest digital tools to mix colours, collage pieces of the imagery together and refine the picture with digital rather than physical brushstrokes. The still-life flower series, which began with cut blooms from Glass's own garden and collection of vessels, has grown to include flowers from renowned gardens around the world and fine vessels from museums and distinguished collections. Glass has worked in collaboration with a range of institutions, including the Royal Lodge and Royal Collection in Windsor, the Jaipur City Palace in India, the Royal Ontario Museum and, as here, the Jardin de Métis (Reford Gardens) in Québec.

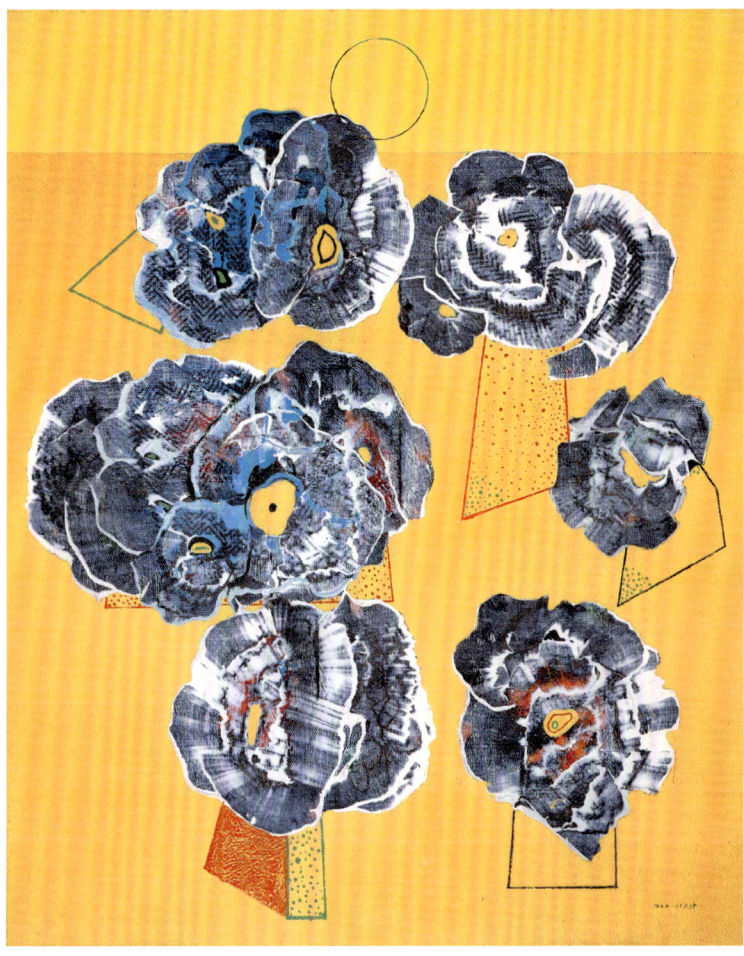

Max Ernst

Flowers on a Yellow Ground, 1929
Oil on canvas, 1 × 0.8 m / 3 ft 3 in × 2 ft 8 in
Albertina, Vienna

Slate blue flowers bloom in a peculiar yellow desert while the blazing sun – rendered as a simple line-drawn circle – is at its zenith against a yellow sky, the two yellow tones indicating, in the most basic way, some kind of planet-like surface. Flower heads emerge as clean-edged cut-outs rather than with softer, conventionally shaped petals. The 'stem' of each flower is shown as a polygon apart from the lowest, which has

a three-dimensional form. The overall impression is unsettling. This is a world without formal logic where humans are strangers, a world dreamt up or even painted from the inspiration of a nightmare. It will come as little surprise that the artist, the German Max Ernst (1891–1976), was a key member of first the Dada art group and then the Surrealist movement in Europe in the 1910s and 1920s, painting a series of hellish and otherworldly landscapes full of varying types of terror. Here, pictorial quirks add to the sense of disjointedness: the sun overlaps the uppermost flower, suggesting that it is somehow actually

in front of the bloom. Even the flowers themselves are bizarre: the pistil of each appears to be transparent, revealing the desert behind. The image depicts a world turned inside out, where the unbelievable is made possible and the subconscious is brought to the surface, illustrating the deeper recesses of the artist's mind.

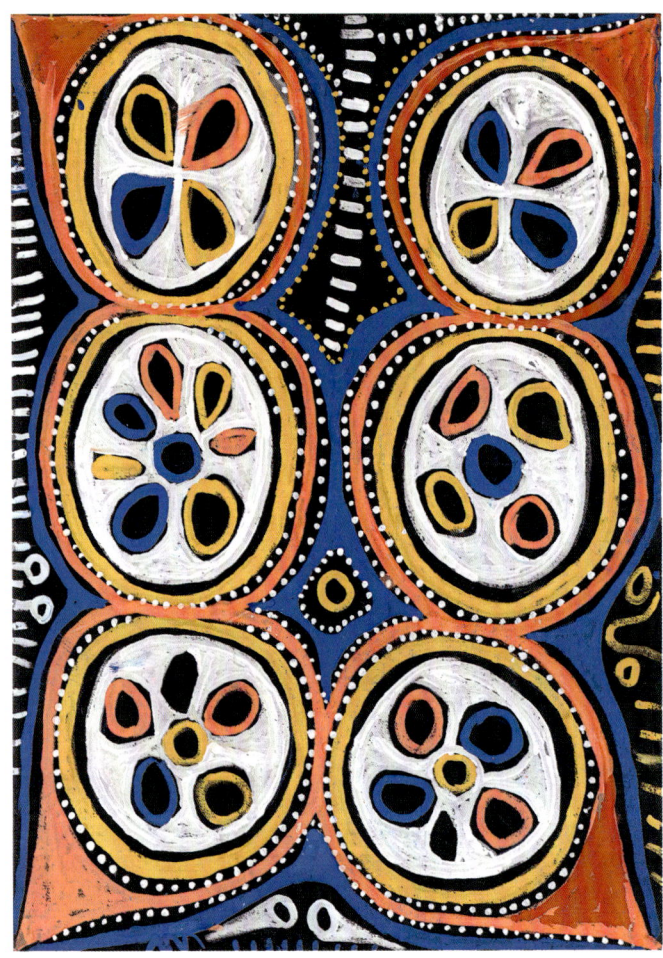

Apakwinya

Ukumba: Flower of the Water Lily Plant, 1973
Gouache on paper, 1 × 0.7 m / 3 ft 4 in × 2 ft 4 in
National Gallery of Victoria, Melbourne

Bright stylized flowers, approximately symmetrical in composition, stand out in striking contrast to a black background. Recognizable by the intense use of colour, this contemporary painting by an artist named Apakwinya is typical of the traditional bark paintings of the Kwoma people of the East Sepik province in Papua New Guinea. The flowers – a type of water lily that grows in the lagoons surrounding the Washkuk Hills –

have a totemic significance for the Kwoma, and their edible seeds are a source of food. Bark paintings were originally created with natural mineral pigments using black, white, yellow and red, but more recently they use acrylic or gouache. This painting, collected by anthropologist Ross Bowden in 1973, is based on one of many motifs of flowers, animals and plants that Kwoma artists use to decorate the ceilings of their ceremonial houses. Throughout Papua New Guinea, ceremonial houses – the *korumbo* or *koromb* (spirit house) – are the traditional artistic 'hub' of villages, where a rich tradition of art was focused,

both for decoration and for ceremonial purposes. The koromb was generally the largest and the most important sacred building in the village, and entry was usually restricted to initiated men, although women and children could enter for specific events. Nearly all important male rituals – including initiation rites for young boys – took place in these ceremonial houses. More recently the koromb is used as an informal gathering place for community events.

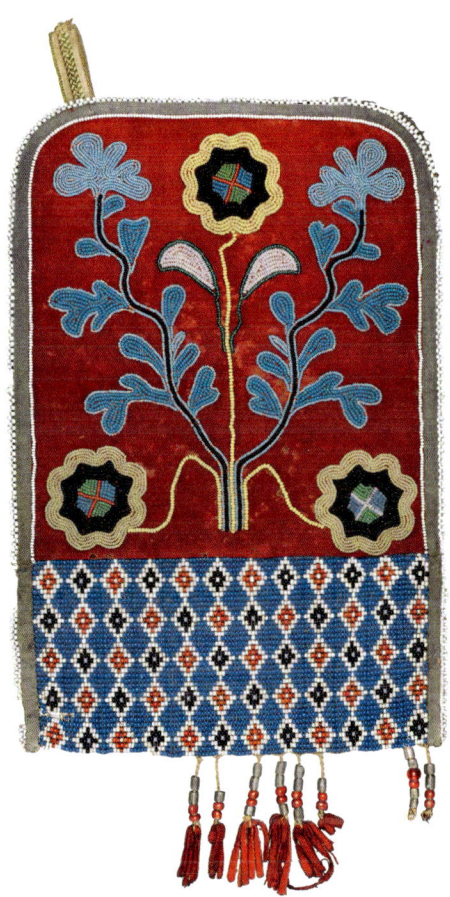

Anonymous

Bag, c.1850–1900
Beadwork on cloth, 30.5 × 20.4 cm / 12 × 8 in
Cleveland Museum of Art, Ohio

Arranged on a red background above a panel of geometric beadwork, three graphically stylized flower heads edged in serpentine rows of yellow beads are supported on slender yellow stems. Emerging from the same central stalk sprouts voluptuous turquoise foliage. Made in the second half of the nineteenth century by the Nêhiyawak or Métis peoples of Canada and the United States, the golden detailing of the flowers purposefully evokes the form of the sun regarded by the native peoples of the Northeast Woodlands as the supreme spirit. This colourful bag is beaded on both sides, the reverse depicting a different plant variety that symmetrically spreads its multicoloured leaves and flowers across a dark background. According to the animist belief system, every element of the universe – animals, birds, fish, plants, trees, rivers, mountains and rocks – has a soul or spirit. From the eighteenth century onwards, contact with European traders meant that imagery capturing this world view, which had traditionally been painted, etched, tattooed, woven and quilled, was also rendered in glass beads. By the second half of the nineteenth century, beadwork had become the dominant form of artwork and had absorbed, too, the European preference for curvilinear floral patterns, in combination with older tribal traditions of geometric abstraction.

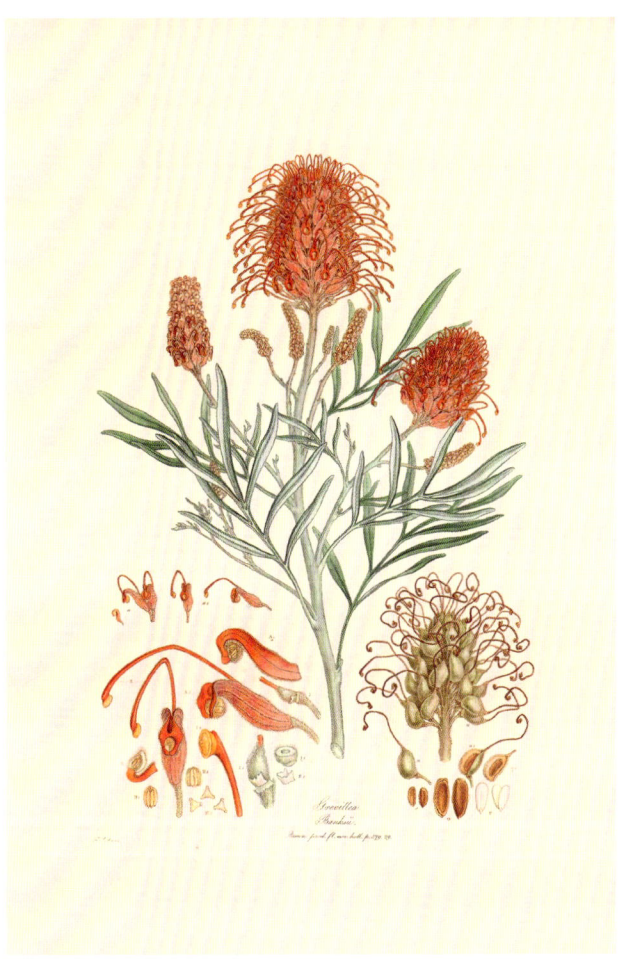

Ferdinand Bauer

Grevillea banksii, from *Illustrationes Florae Novae Hollandiae*, 1813
Hand-coloured line and stipple engraving,
51 × 34 cm / 20 × 13¼ in
Allport Library and Museum of Fine Arts,
Tasmanian Archive and Heritage Office,
Hobart, Australia

Austrian artist Ferdinand Bauer (1760–1826)
depicts not only the fiery red flowers of *Grevillea
banksii* but also dissected views to show every
element of the plant in minute detail, to enable
its classification according to the binomial system

introduced by Carl Linnaeus (see p.208). Having
worked alongside his brother Franz (see p.317)
as a botanical artist in Vienna, Ferdinand was
coaxed away in 1786 by English botanist John
Sibthorp, who invited Ferdinand to travel with
him as the recording artist on an expedition to
Greece. The duo returned a year later with nearly
1,500 sketches, of which 966 would be included
as illustrations in Sibthorp's ten volume *Flora
Graeca*. By the time the first volume was published
in 1806, Bauer had circumnavigated Australia as
botanical artist aboard the HMS *Investigator* at
the request of English scientist Sir Joseph Banks,

completing some 2,000 field sketches and collecting hundreds of plant specimens with botanist Robert Brown. Bauer's works were published
in *Illustrationes Florae Novae Hollandiae* from
1813, and included varieties such as this *G. banksii*.
Grevilleas are native to central eastern Queensland
and are now known as garden cultivars, but to
Australian Aborigines they were important for
their nectar. Banks named the plant genus after
Charles Greville – co-founder of the Horticultural
Society of London, now the Royal Horticultural
Society – and the species after himself.

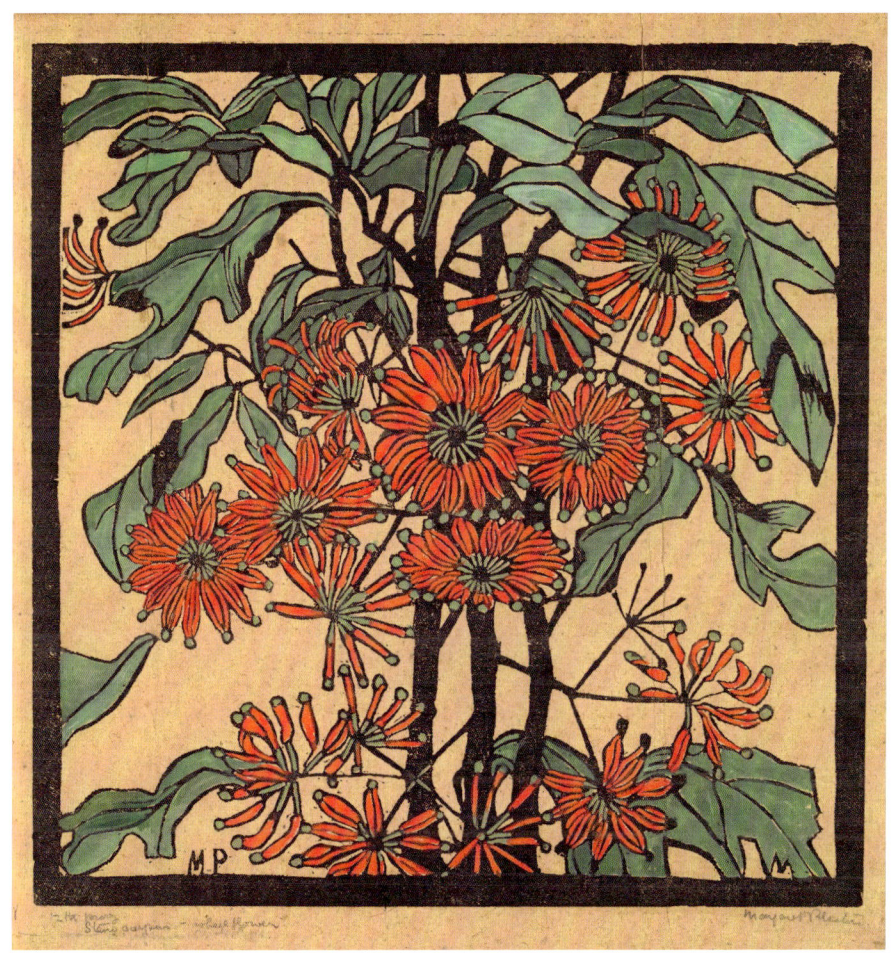

Margaret Preston

Wheelflower, c.1929
Hand-coloured woodcut on brown hand-made paper, 48.4 × 47.1 cm / 19 × 18½ in
National Gallery of Victoria, Melbourne

The firewheel tree (*Stenocarpus sinuatus*) that bursts across the page in contrasting reds and greens is native to Australia, but the strong graphic language of this hand-coloured woodcut – bold black outlines and layers of flat colour – echoes the manner of Japanese prints and the techniques of Paul Gauguin and Henri Matisse (see p.19). One of Australia's best-known female artists, Margaret Preston (1875–1963) studied Japanese prints and pioneering European painting at the cusp of the late nineteenth and early twentieth centuries, when she travelled from Adelaide to Europe. On returning to Sydney, Preston began experimenting with these ideas in still-life compositions of floral specimens, becoming noted for her bold use of indigenous flora and the uncompromising, modern methods with which she represented them. Her unconventional eye was drawn to native Australian species such as banksias and eucalypti, which became a signature of her prints. *Wheelflower* eschews conventional still-life arrangements staged in vases, instead drawn *en plein air*, with pinwheels of yellow-tipped flowers and the glossy foliage of long, leathery leaves. The firewheel tree can reach heights of 30 metres (100 feet) in native tropical and subtropical rainforests of Australia, but smaller trees are widely cultivated as ornamentals.

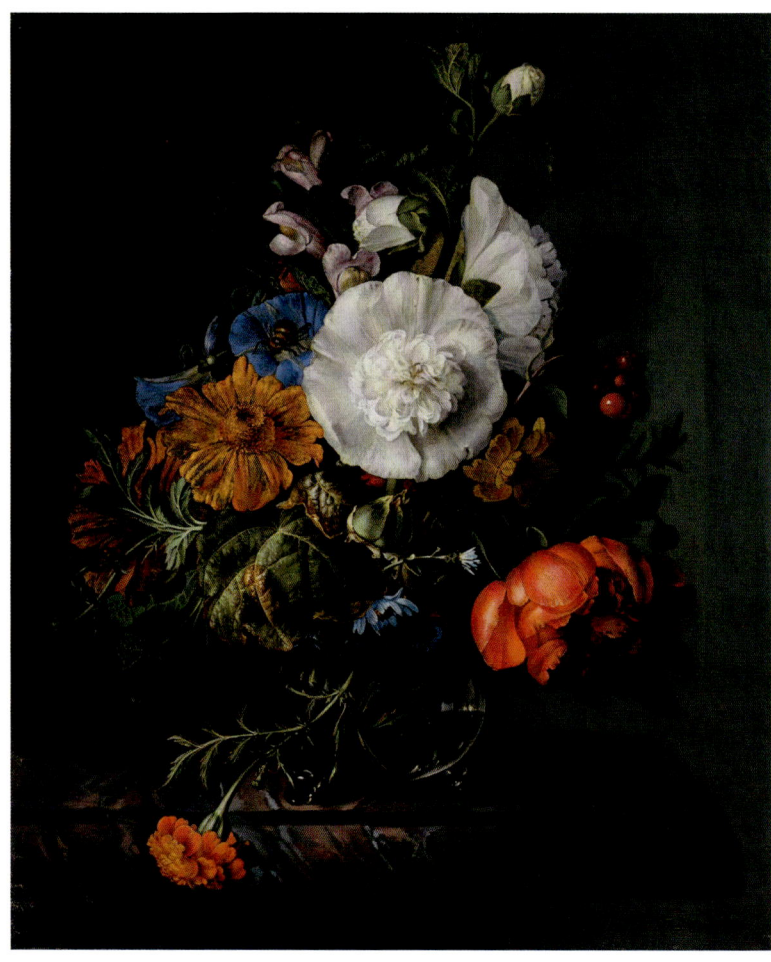

Rachel Ruysch

*Still Life of Flowers in a Glass Vase
on a Marble Ledge*, 1745
Oil on canvas, 38.2 × 32.2 cm / 15 × 12¾ in
Private collection

In this charming bouquet, a radiant sprig of white hollyhock takes pride of place, surrounded by African marigolds, morning glories, a snapdragon, a peony and several smaller flowers and berries. All of the blooms in this arrangement are relatively common species, but Dutch painter Rachel Ruysch (1664–1750) had a keen interest in botany and featured botanical rarities in many of her bouquets. Here, all the flowers are at the height of their bloom – indeed, a bumblebee has settled on a fresh morning glory – and there is no indication in the blossoms of the sense of transience and vanitas often apparent in Ruysch's earlier flower paintings. Adding to the celebration of the beauty of these flowers, they are presented in a costly vase of clear glass – perhaps Venetian – allowing a view of the stems within, and placed on a marble ledge. Ruysch's father, a prominent anatomist, apprenticed her at a young age to the still-life painter Willem van Aelst, and by the age of seventeen she was already producing remarkable flower pieces, which she continued until her last known work painted at age eighty-four. At the height of her career, Ruysch was the leading Dutch female painter, creating still lifes for prestigious patrons. She was appointed court painter to Johann Wilhelm, Elector Palatine, in Düsseldorf in 1708. The floral still life shown here testifies to the fact that she was still highly skilled in 1745, when she proudly inscribed it with her age: eighty-one.

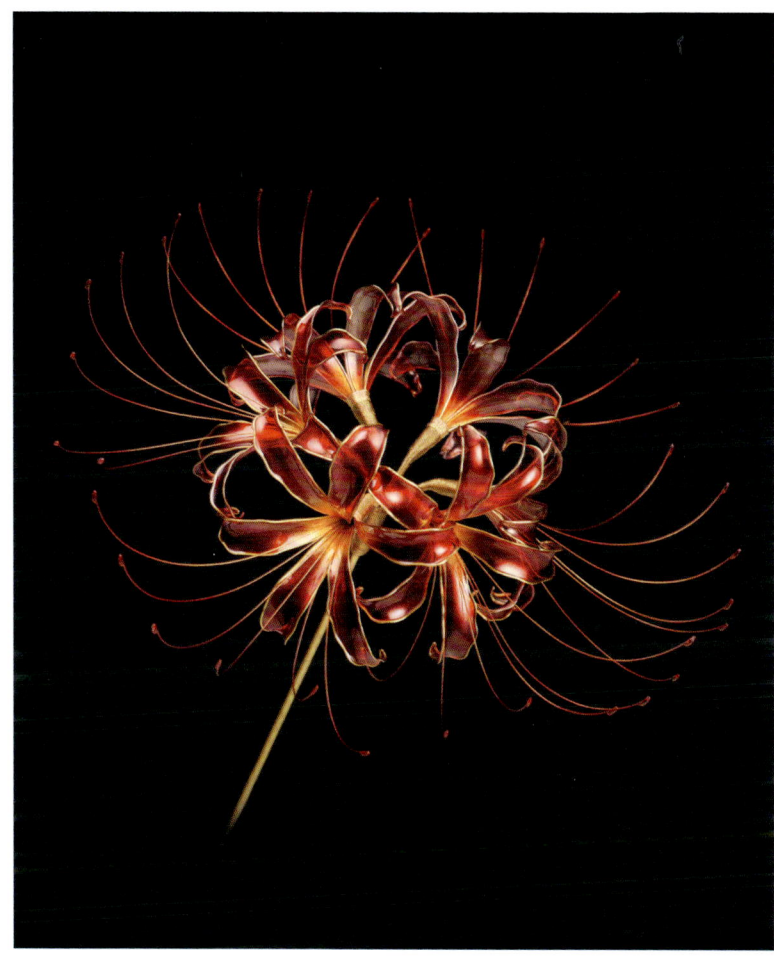

Sakae

Lycoris, Red Spider Lily Hairpin, 2017
Wire and liquid resin, Diam. 18.5 cm / 7¼ in
Private collection

Gloriously realistic, the curved petals of the individual blooms of this lily's inflorescence seem to glow in reflected light as the narrow, spidery stamens arch outwards from the centre of each flower. The contemporary Japanese artist Sakae (born 1974) specializes in making delicate hairpins like this, known as *kanzashi*, taking her inspiration from nature and crafting mainly flowers and butterflies. Sakae works with coloured resin and wire in a process that involves sculpting the basic floral shape with metallic wire and then dipping it into liquid plastic to produce a glass-like yet faithful representation of a living flower. Kanzashi are traditional hair ornaments worn with kimonos by Japanese women for special occasions such as weddings or tea ceremonies; they were typically made from folded pieces of cloth before new materials were introduced. The fashion of wearing hair ornaments has a long history in Japan, where they were traditionally considered to have the power to ward off evil spirits.

Sakae has taken this tradition to a new level by turning such adornments into true works of art. Her subject here is the red spider lily (*Lycoris radiata*), a plant native to China, Korea, Nepal and Japan, where it is commonly grown in gardens as well as around rice paddies and in cemeteries. Known also as the resurrection lily, it blooms in late summer and autumn, often following a rainfall, the tall flowering stems growing and opening ahead of the foliage.

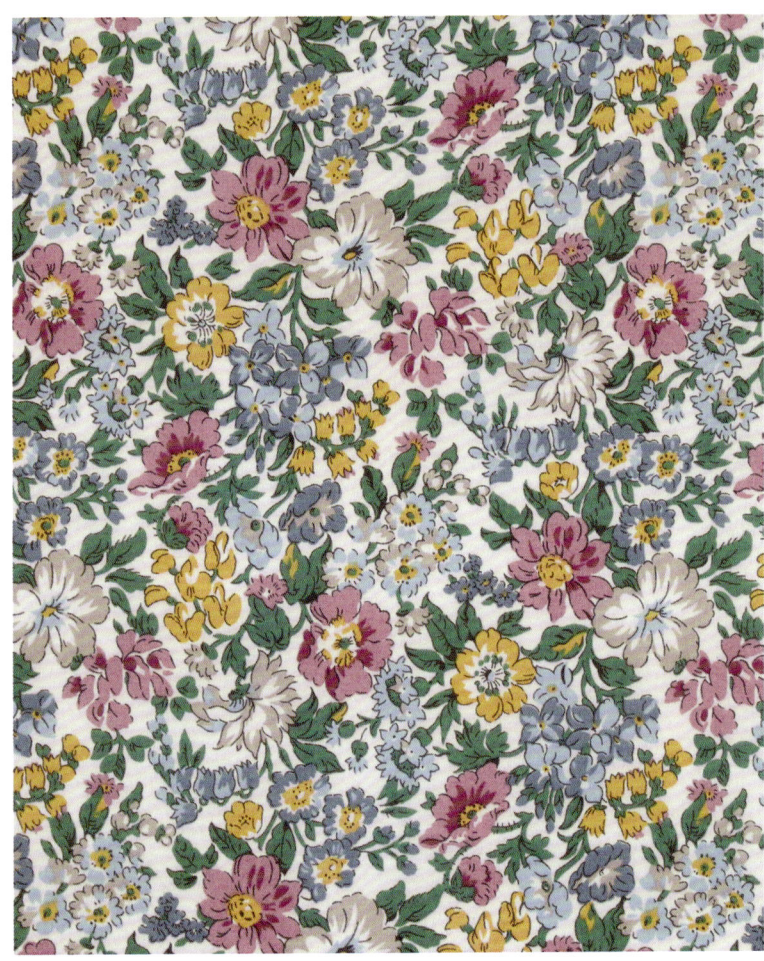

Liberty & Co. Ltd.

*Honeydew, c.*1930
Tana Lawn cotton, dimensions variable

Dahlias, poppies, anemones, daisies and bell-flowers mingle in a beautiful print bursting with a palette of bright summer colours. This classic floral print, *Honeydew*, was designed in the 1930s and represents the storied history of the London design and department store, Liberty & Co. Founded in the late nineteenth century by Arthur Lasenby Liberty (1843–1917), the company's ascendant motif is its floral-patterned fabrics, particularly those printed on Tana Lawn cotton.

Liberty's vision originated in a shop bountiful with goods from the East, as well as undyed, imported fabrics hand-printed in England. Bringing together an exotic aesthetic with British craftsmanship, his forward-looking approach paid off. Liberty commissioned leading artists of the day, such as William Morris (see p.160) and Charles Voysey, to produce imaginative textile designs, with a range of floral interpretations. Similarly inventive were later projects with starry fashion brands, such as Yves Saint Laurent, Jean Muir and Cacharel. Artistic circles quickly adopted the brand's signature prints, bedecked with blooms

of all varieties and colours. Queen Elizabeth II and Princess Margaret often sported floral Liberty frocks, while David Bowie's Liberty-print jumpsuit embellishes *The Rise and Fall of Ziggy Stardust* record sleeve of 1972. Liberty London, as it is now known, continues the innovative work of its founder, collaborating with fashion figures that range from avant-garde Vivienne Westwood to Japanese high-street giant Uniqlo.

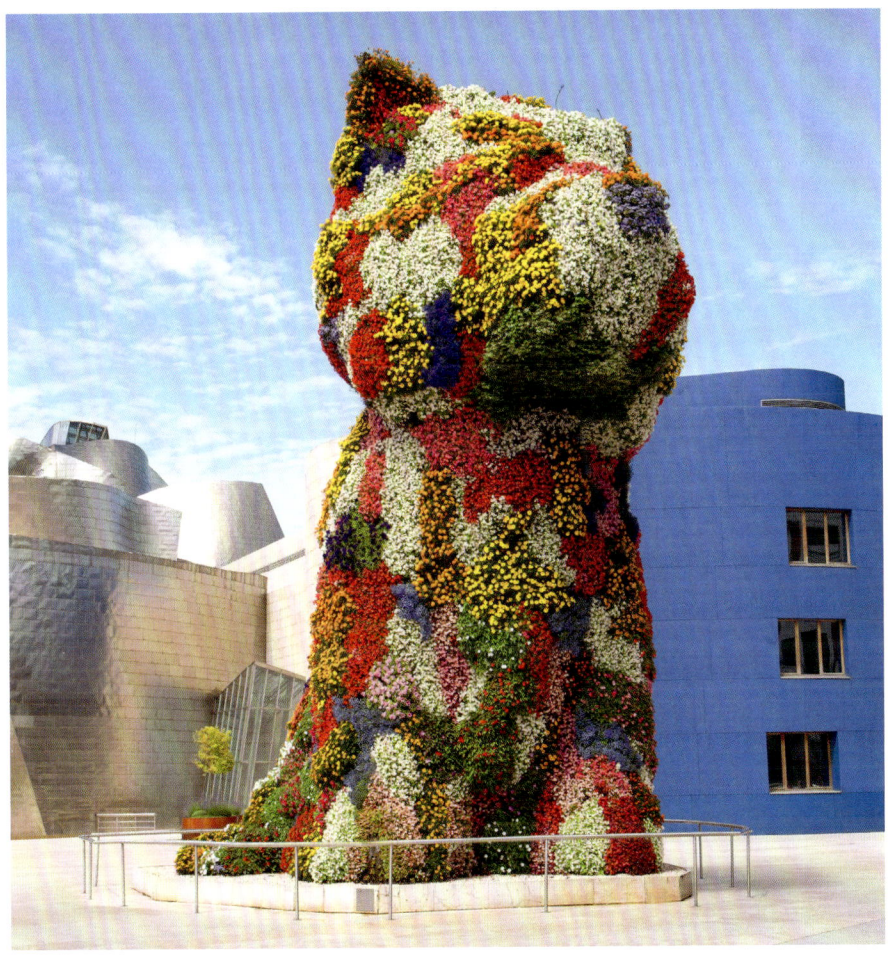

Jeff Koons

Puppy, 1992
Stainless steel, soil, geotextile fabric, internal irrigation system and live flowering plants,
12.4 × 8.3 × 9.1 m / 40 ft 8 in × 27 ft × 30 ft
Guggenheim Bilbao Museoa, Spain

This towering sculpture of a West Highland terrier by American artist Jeff Koons (born 1955) was purchased by the Guggenheim Bilbao Museoa in Spain, and installed for the highly anticipated inauguration of the museum. While Koons intended the sculpture as a positive piece to instil 'confidence and security', its position at the museum's gates, seemingly guarding them, caused controversy throughout the Basque counties of Spain and beyond. *Puppy* has since become a welcome fixture at the museum, where the nearly 38,000 plants are changed twice a year to mark the transition of seasons from autumn to winter and spring to summer. While the exterior looks dense with foliage of green leaves and brightly coloured flowers, the hidden structure within contains a system of pumps that deliver fertilizer and, depending on weather conditions, water daily. *Puppy* was inspired by the eighteenth-century formal European garden, which used the aesthetic ideal of the Baroque and Rococo styles in Europe, while in England classical literature from the likes of Virgil, as well as pastoral poetry, influenced landscapes of sweeping, undulating lines, lakes and even Palladian temples. Koons' works often combine references to high and low culture as part of his interest in contemporary modes of consumerism and the language of advertising. Continuing the history of Marcel Duchamp's readymade, Koons uses pre-existing objects as part of his art, such as basketballs, vacuum cleaners and even the Pink Panther.

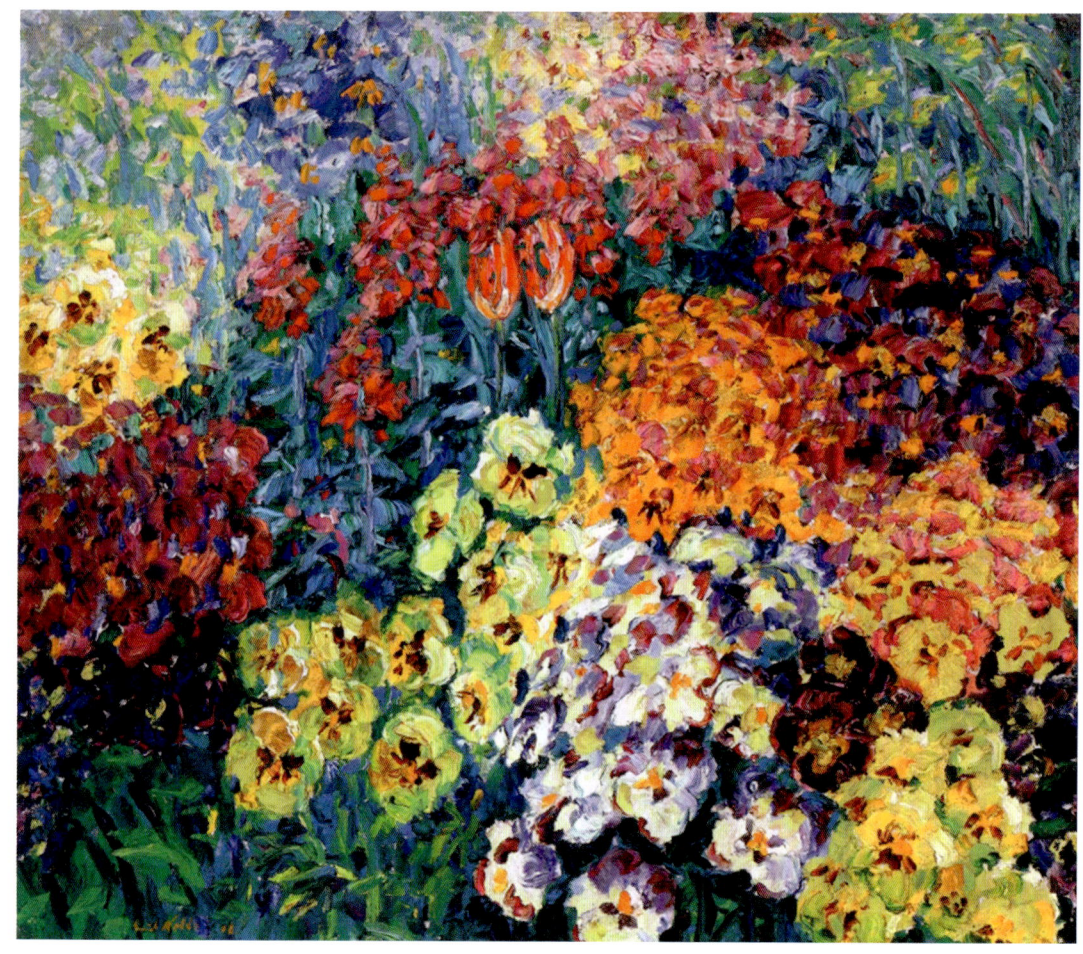

Emil Nolde

Flower Garden: Pansies, 1908
Oil on canvas, 73.5 × 89.5 cm / 29 × 35¼ in
Private collection

Flowers held an irresistible attraction for German painter and printmaker Emil Nolde (1867–1956). Even at a time of financial hardship when his wife, Ada, was enduring poor health, Nolde turned to flowers, painting this sensuous sea of cheerful pansies. As one of the twentieth century's greatest colourists, the German Expressionist found pansies, with their rich variety of colours, an ideal subject. Each flower is rendered with thick daubs of oil paint that reflect the influence of Vincent van Gogh (see p.47) and the French Post-Impressionist painters. The entire surface of the canvas is filled with a composition that is devoted almost solely to the vibrant exploration of colour, with little focus on depth or perspective. Although Nolde is often associated with landscapes and violent religious imagery, he painted flowers throughout his career, whether in the gardens of his friends or in his own garden at Seebüll in Neukirchen, Germany, which he planted himself and where he also built a Modernist house and studio.

Today, visitors to the garden can see irises, delphiniums, oriental poppies, geraniums and lupins. Nolde produced many flower paintings there, ranging from watercolours of single stems and fields of colourful blooms to still-life oil paintings of precisely arranged bouquets. Whichever medium he chose, each of his flower paintings is marked by the same intense colour and fluidity of paint for which all of his works are celebrated.

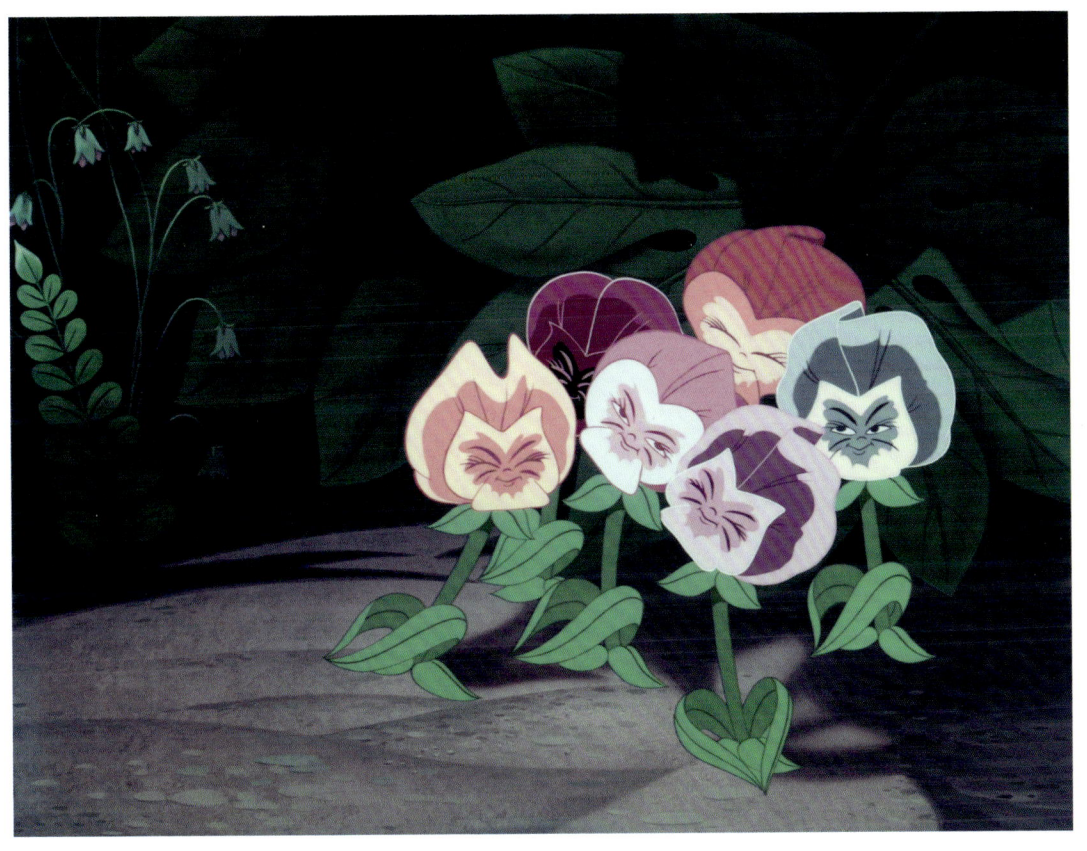

Walt Disney Productions

Pansies, from *Alice in Wonderland*, 1951
Animated film, dimensions variable

The fantastical anthropomorphic creatures of Lewis Carroll's *Alice* books proved irresistible to Walt Disney, whose animated feature film *Alice in Wonderland* (1951) brought them to life in vivid Technicolor. In this scene, a miniaturized Alice stumbles upon a garden of talking flowers, who serenade her with a jaunty song about themselves. A red rose conducts a choir of pansies as they sing 'All in the Golden Afternoon' accompanied by kissing tulips, dizzy daffodils and lazy daisies. A white rose performs a graceful solo, while a lily of the valley becomes a string of bells and thistles are pounded like kettledrums. Other flowers joining in with the merriment include tiger lilies, larkspurs and chrysanthemums. But, despite their cordial welcome, the flowers soon realize that Alice is not one of them. Concluding that she must be a weed, they chase her from the garden. The flower scene is inspired by the second chapter of Carroll's *Through the Looking-Glass* (1871), and while the flowers' song shares its title with the first line of the prefatory poem in *Alice's Adventures in Wonderland* (1865), the words and music are original to the film. The animators, including John Lounsbery (1911–76), drew inspiration from concept art by Mary Blair (1911–78), one of Walt Disney's favourite artists. Lounsbery was a prominent member of Disney's core animation team, and worked on nearly all of the studio's most famous feature-length films.

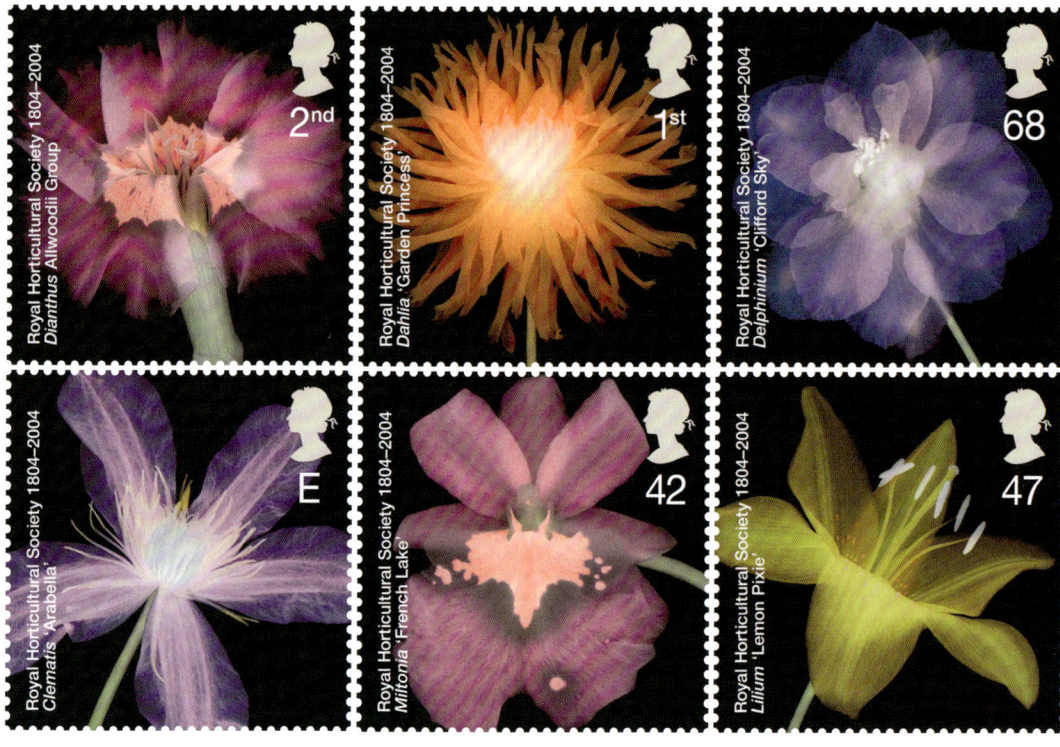

Barbara and Zafer Baran, Rose Design

Royal Horticultural Society 1804–2004
stamps, 2004
Gravure, gum PVA, each 3.5 × 3.5 cm / 1¼ × 1¼ in

Set against a black background are diaphanous yet vibrantly luminous depictions of *Dianthus* (Allwoodii group), *Dahlia* 'Garden Princess', *Delphinium* 'Clifford Sky', *Lilium* 'Lemon Pixie', *Miltonia* 'French Lake' and *Clematis* 'Arabella'. This elegant set of British postal stamps was commissioned by the Royal Horticultural Society in 2004 as a celebration of the organization's bicentenary. Each ethereal image was produced

by artists Barbara and Zafer Baran (born 1956, 1955) using a technique that reinvents the early photographic experimentations of pioneers Anna Atkins (see p.34) and William Henry Fox Talbot. During the first half of the nineteenth century, Fox Talbot placed leaves, stems and flowers in direct contact with photographic plates. The flatness of plants perfectly aligned with that of the photographic medium, thus enabling a subtle and spellbinding complicity between the two. Each photogram captured the precise imprint of vegetal form. The Barans' series is a technologically updated interpretation of the Victorian

photogram: instead of early photographic paper, the artists lay flowers on the screen of a scanner. As in a photogram, the outlines of each flower are painstakingly recorded, but the intensity of the scanning light penetrates the petals to also record their textural and structural characteristics. The results are ghostly and timeless portraits of flowers suspended between the accuracy of photographic reproduction and the soft nuances of illustration.

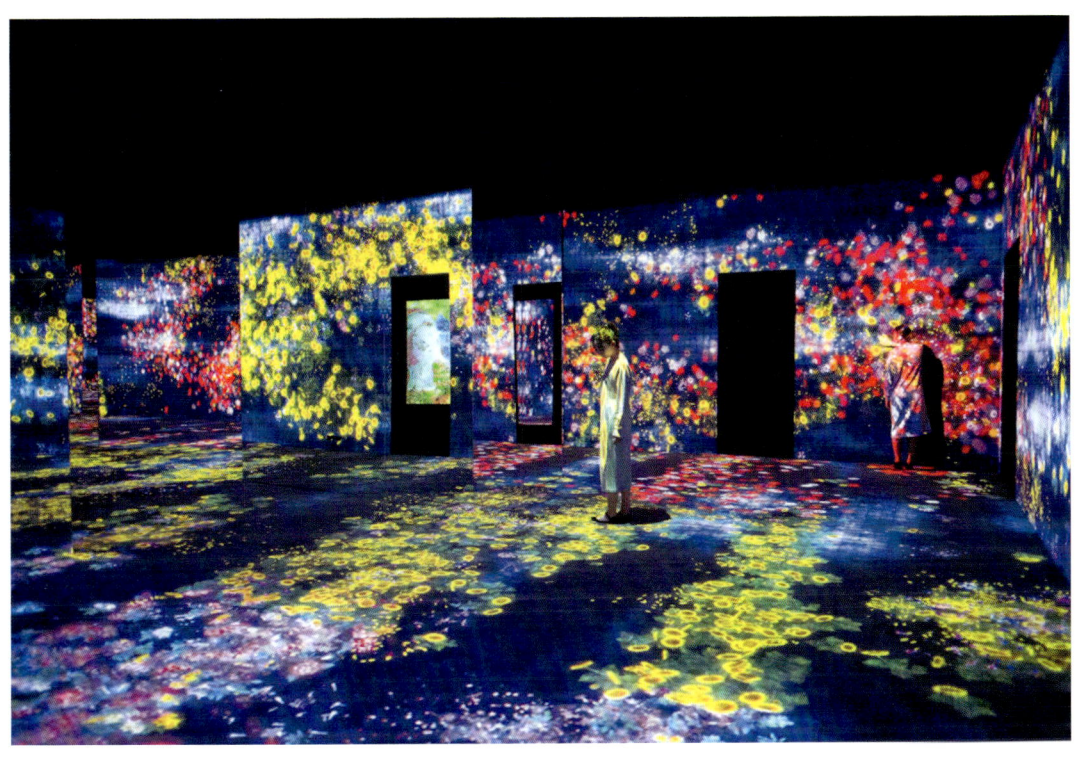

teamLab

Forest of Flowers and People: Lost, Immersed and Reborn, 2017
Interactive digital installation, dimensions variable

A profusion of digital flowers, budding and blossoming in response to visitors' movements, light up the walls and floor in this immersive installation by art collective teamLab. The flowers, of various shapes and colours, are rendered in real time by powerful computer programs and projected across the sprawling exhibition space. A network of sensors enables them to react to human presence: stand still and the flowers bud and blossom, but touch or step on them and they quickly wither and die, dissolving into nothing. The mesmerizing visuals mutate and evolve so that no part of the installation is ever replicated and each visitor's experience is unique. There is no prescribed route; instead, people are encouraged to move freely around the installation, exploring its many elements and witnessing the seasons gradually change. The creators at teamLab consist of artists, computer programmers, engineers, animators, mathematicians and architects. Since 2001, the cutting-edge collaborative practice has explored the intersection of art, science, technology, design and nature. The collective's interactive projects emphasize the notion that humans are not simply observers of nature but are an essential part of it. Visitors become collaborators, agents of change whose actions shape the artwork and the experience of fellow participants.

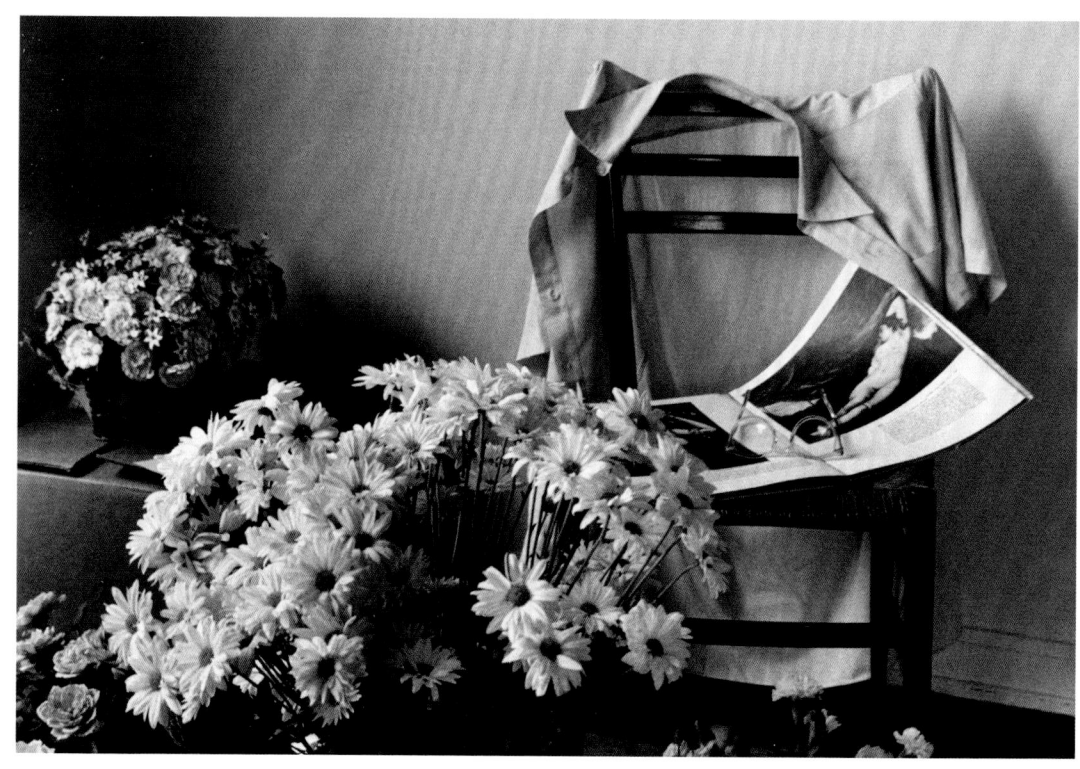

André Kertész

Flowers for Elizabeth, New York, from the portfolio
André Kertész / Still Life, 1976
Gelatin silver print, 16.5 × 24.4 cm / 6½ × 9¾ in
Museum of Fine Arts, Houston

This black-and-white photograph by Hungarian-born artist André Kertész (1894–1985) feels as if it is tinged with colour, daisies bounteously filling the bottom half of the composition. As the work's title indicates, the flowers are a gift for Elizabeth, the artist's wife of over four decades. With a shirt resting on a chair and a book opened to a page that depicts nude figures, this photograph acts

as a portrait of lovers – the lives of two people devoted to one another. Flowers, like these Shasta daisies (*Leucanthemum × superbum*), are so often gifted between people as a symbol of care, representing beauty, fertility and the new life of spring. Elizabeth died of cancer in 1977, a year after this photograph was taken, lending the image additional significance given the tradition that flowers often play in funeral rites. The couple had married in 1933 and emigrated from Paris to New York in 1936, fleeing the threat of German persecution and the looming war in Europe. Initially working for magazines as a photojournalist, Kertész began

to achieve international success in the 1940s and 1950s, and is generally understood as having four significant periods to his oeuvre: the Hungarian, French, American and International periods. He once said, 'I write with light', an approach evident in the chiaroscuro of this image, from the dark shadow in the top left-hand corner to the bright petals of the flowers themselves in the foreground.

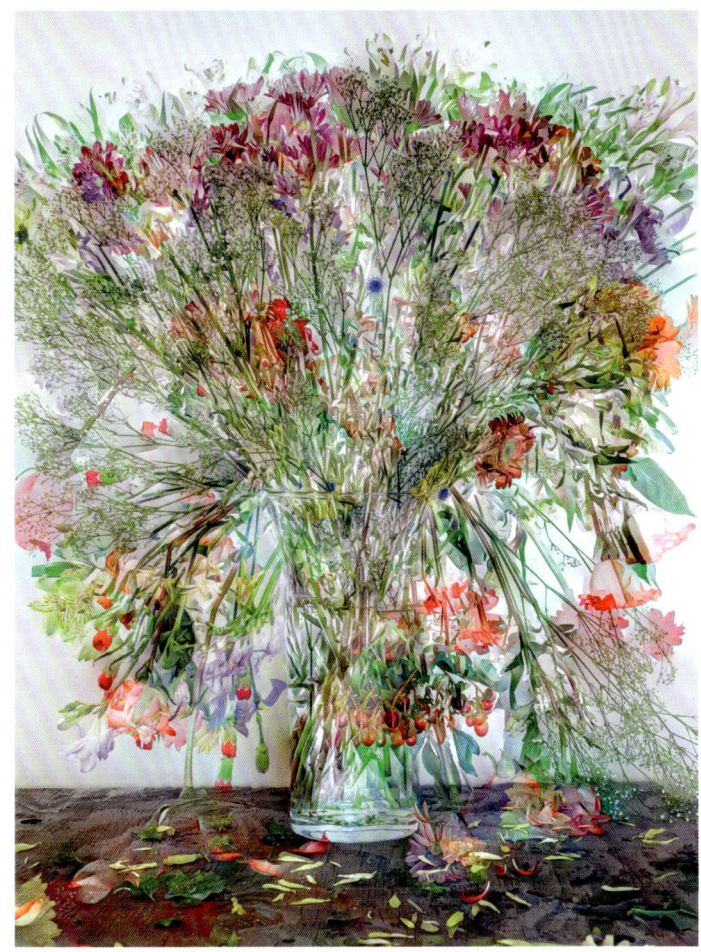

Abelardo Morell

Flowers for Lisa #1, 2014
Archival inkjet print, 1 × 0.8 m / 3 ft 4 in × 2 ft 6 in

Delicate sprays of gypsophila overlap with heads of gerbera, alstroemeria, carnations, roses and freesia in the chaotic array of *Flowers for Lisa*. The resulting arrangement creates a jungle of overlapping hues. Cuban-born photographer Abelardo Morell (born 1948) uses digital tools to sharpen colour to a spectrum brighter than life, ringing with hues of scarlet, orange, fuchsia, teal, yellow and purple. Created as a lasting love letter to his wife, Lisa – a birthday gift to outlast

the limited life of cut flowers – this image turns Morell's inventive photographic approach to the traditional floral still life. As with preceding projects in which Morell re-examined established techniques such as camera obscura, *cliché verre* (glass plate) or photograms, in *Flowers for Lisa* he explores the creation of a composite image from multiple digital frames. The original idea would grow to become an experimental series of seventy-six works executed over the course of three years. *Flowers for Lisa #1* is animated by many different bouquets captured individually in succession – with the same vase, the same table, the same

backdrop and simple daylight – then composed as a single image. Although Morell is fascinated by the mechanics of photography as much as composition, in this project he largely allows nature to take the lead.

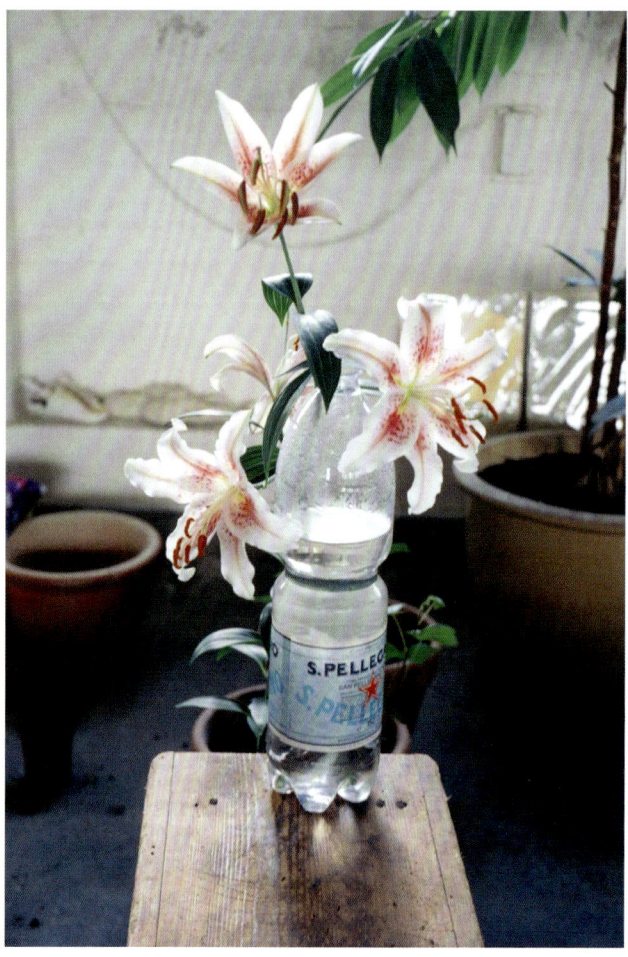

Wolfgang Tillmans

Podium, 1999
Photograph, dimensions variable
Private collection

A stem of an Asiatic lily flower has been placed apparently incidentally in a San Pellegrino bottle that doubles as a vase, sitting on a wooden bench surrounded by plant pots in a relaxed domestic space. With its petals marked by delicate pink spots and the anther of the stamen hanging heavy with orange pollen, the lily – a well-known herbaceous flowering plant with large flowers that is native to temperate environments in the northern hemisphere – takes centre stage. This photograph represents perfectly one of the core motives of German photographer Wolfgang Tillmans (born 1968) to 'take pictures, in order to see the world'. Tillmans came to prominence for his imagery capturing the spirit of his generation in the 1990s. He often works collaboratively with his subjects – including asking his friends to sit in nature on the branches of trees, wearing nothing but open overcoats. Tillmans later embraced a diverse range of subjects such as landscape, abstraction and still life, of which *Podium* is an example. While Tillmans has at times focused on issues of gender and sexual identity, at the heart of his work is the desire to observe and capture his surroundings faithfully and with absolute clarity.

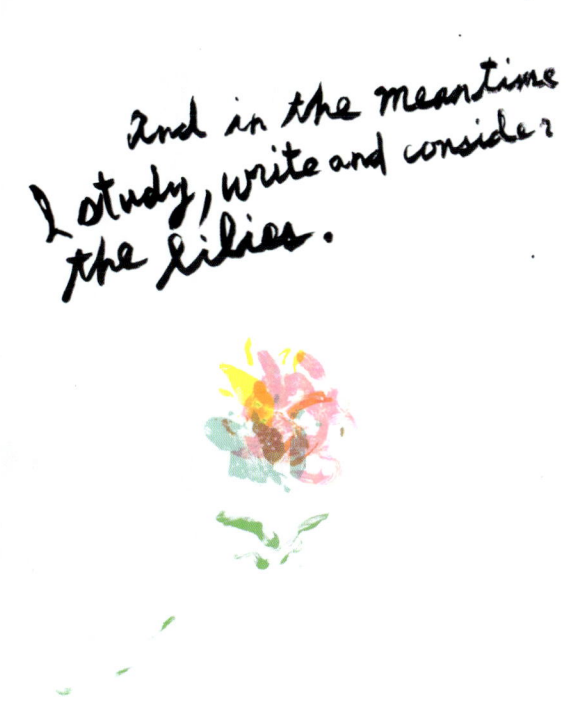

Raymond Pettibon

No Title (And in the...), 2018
Lithograph print on paper, 74.3 × 50.8 cm /
29¼ × 20 in

Over the course of his career, American artist Raymond Pettibon (born 1957) has developed a unique visual vocabulary. Images and language are invariably presented together and intertwine to generate an ephemeral, fragmented reality that does not seem to belong to any specific temporal dimension. Pettibon's early work, reproduced on the album covers and leaflets of bands such as Black Flag and Minutemen,

played a fundamental role in defining the aesthetics of American punk and hard-core music. His influences are rich and varied, however, and can be traced to artists such as Honoré Daumier and Ed Ruscha, as well as to literature and American cartoons. Most at home with crude and pulp imagery, Pettibon has occasionally engaged with more introspective, delicate subjects. This is the case of *No Title (And in the...)*, in which the flowers are sketched through a combination of colours – a minimal approach that reflects the artist's proclivity for discarding extraneous information as he grew better acquainted with his medium

of choice. The lily is effectively recognizable only when associated with the text on top: rendered in an intense bold black to counterbalance the over-lightness of the rest of the composition, it reads 'and in the meantime I study, write and consider the lilies'. The observation functions both as a reference to all the painters that have addressed the blossom in the history of art and as further evidence of the transitional nature of Pettibon's universe.

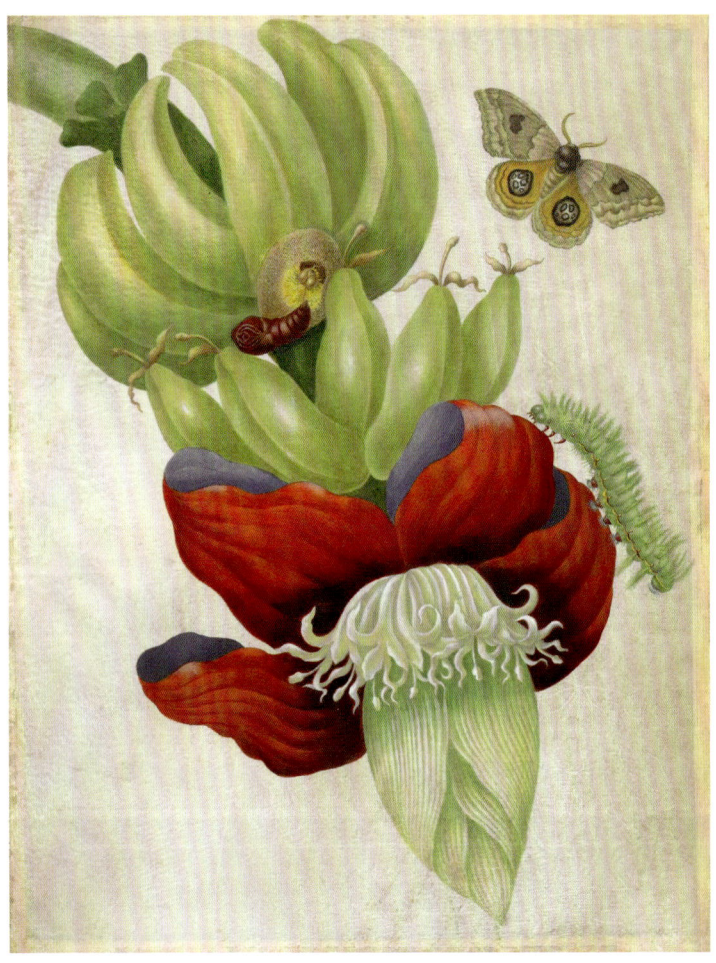

Maria Sibylla Merian

*Banana Plant with Red and Purple Flower,
and Fruit*, from *Merian's Drawings of Surinam
Insects &c, c.1701–05*
Watercolour and body colour with pen and grey
ink on vellum, 38.3 × 29.7 cm / 15 × 11¾ in
British Museum, London

A caterpillar crawls on a banana flower, a chrysalis clings to the fruit and an adult moth flashes an eye to foil a predator. These vital stages of insect metamorphosis fascinated the German artist Maria Sibylla Merian (1647–1717). Born into a family of printers and artists, including her stepfather Jacob Marrel (see p.101), Merian illustrated and published her observations of insect transformation. In Amsterdam she was captivated by collections of tropical butterflies and moths that presented wondrous patterns and colours. Later, she sailed with the younger of her two daughters to the Dutch colony of Surinam. There she collected, reared and painted insects no longer pinned and dislocated from their natural habitat. On her return to the Netherlands two years later, and with the assistance of both daughters, she completed the paintings that were engraved for her famous *Metamorphosis Insectorum Surinamensium* (1705). From each copperplate engraved for the publication, Merian also created a one-off work printed on vellum and finished in watercolour and gouache. While Merian may not have been correct in documenting which plant was associated with which insect, she was the first to conceive and portray this symbiotic relationship. Merian also noted that the banana in America 'serves in the place of apples ... and is good both raw and boil'd'. And in fact, today, banana flowers – the female flowers that develop into the fruit – are also commonly used in southeast Asian cuisine.

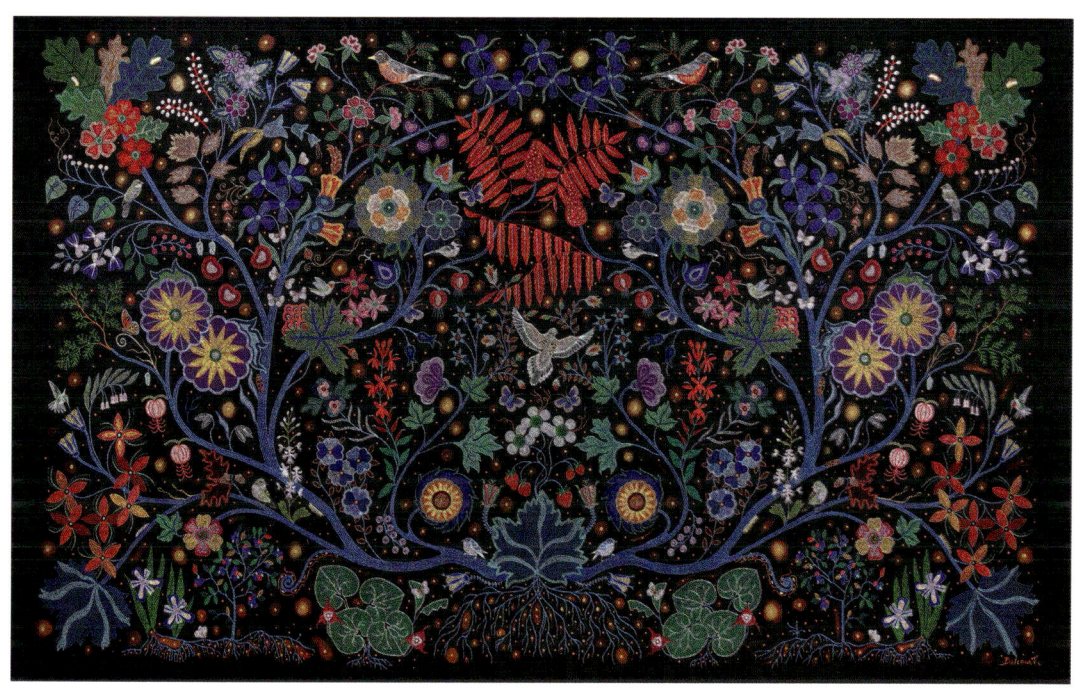

Christi Belcourt

The Wisdom of the Universe, 2014
Acrylic on canvas, 1.7 × 2.8 m / 5 ft 7 in × 9 ft 3 in
Art Gallery of Ontario, Toronto

Inspired by traditional Métis beadwork (see p. 83), this painting is a swirling, symmetrical celebration of biodiversity. A dazzlingly complex pattern of multiple hues and shapes creates striking aesthetic appeal, yet the message of the image is much deeper: it is a plea for us to respect wildlife and natural ecosystems instead of destroying them. More than 200 species of plants and animals are threatened, endangered or extinct in the Canadian province of Ontario alone. Among the intricately painted flowers that spring out from a central tree, Canadian artist Christi Belcourt (born 1966) has included dwarf lake iris (*Iris lacustris*), prairie fringed orchid (*Platanthera praeclara*) and blue-eyed Mary (*Collinsia verna*). Nestled among the blooming flora are the Acadian flycatcher, cerulean warbler and karner blue butterfly. At the centre, in flight, is a passenger pigeon, a once common species in North America infamously hunted to extinction by 1914, which has become a potent symbol for conservation. In this time of concern about climate change and the destruction of natural habitats, Belcourt's work takes on ever-deepening relevance. A member of the indigenous Métis community of Manitou Sakhigan in Alberta, she is inspired by love and respect for the natural world and celebrates its beauty and diversity. Politically active, Belcourt dedicates her life and work to achieving social change and justice for indigenous peoples.

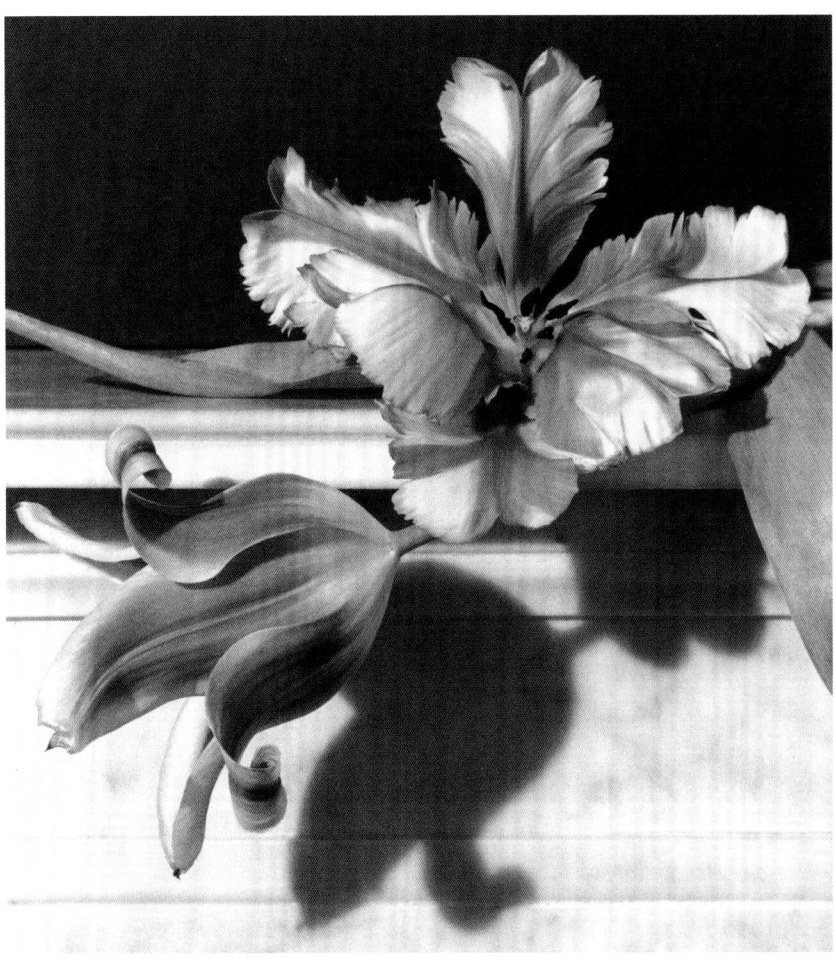

Horst P. Horst

Tulips, Oyster Bay, New York, 1989
Platinum palladium print, dimensions variable
Private collection

Caught in the kind of otherworldly stillness that only photography can bestow upon the living, the smooth petals of tulips appear as if carefully carved in marble by a neoclassical sculptor such as Antonio Canova. The ideals that underpinned the work of German-American photographer Horst P. Horst (1906–99) – one of as most iconic fashion photographers of the twentieth century – were at least in part derived from keen observation of the natural world. Horst's distinctive style capitalized on dramatic lighting and linear perfection, emphasizing elegance and simplicity in whatever he photographed. In 1946, Horst published his research on the surfaces, shapes and textures of plants, rocks, shells and butterfly wings in a book titled *Patterns from Nature*. This photograph of tulips retains Horst's sensitivity for iconic imagery while endowing the flowers with an unconventional sense of solidity and permanence. The marble balustrade upon which they rest summons the timelessness of classical Greek architecture, while the blackened background erases context, lifting the flowers from everyday life and rendering them immortal. In portraying the essential beauty of tulips, Horst challenged the norm of classical representation and chose to photograph two weathered flowers rather than fresh blooms. The curled edges of the downward-turned tulip and the burst-open petals of its counterpart are both distinctive signs that these flowers have lived.

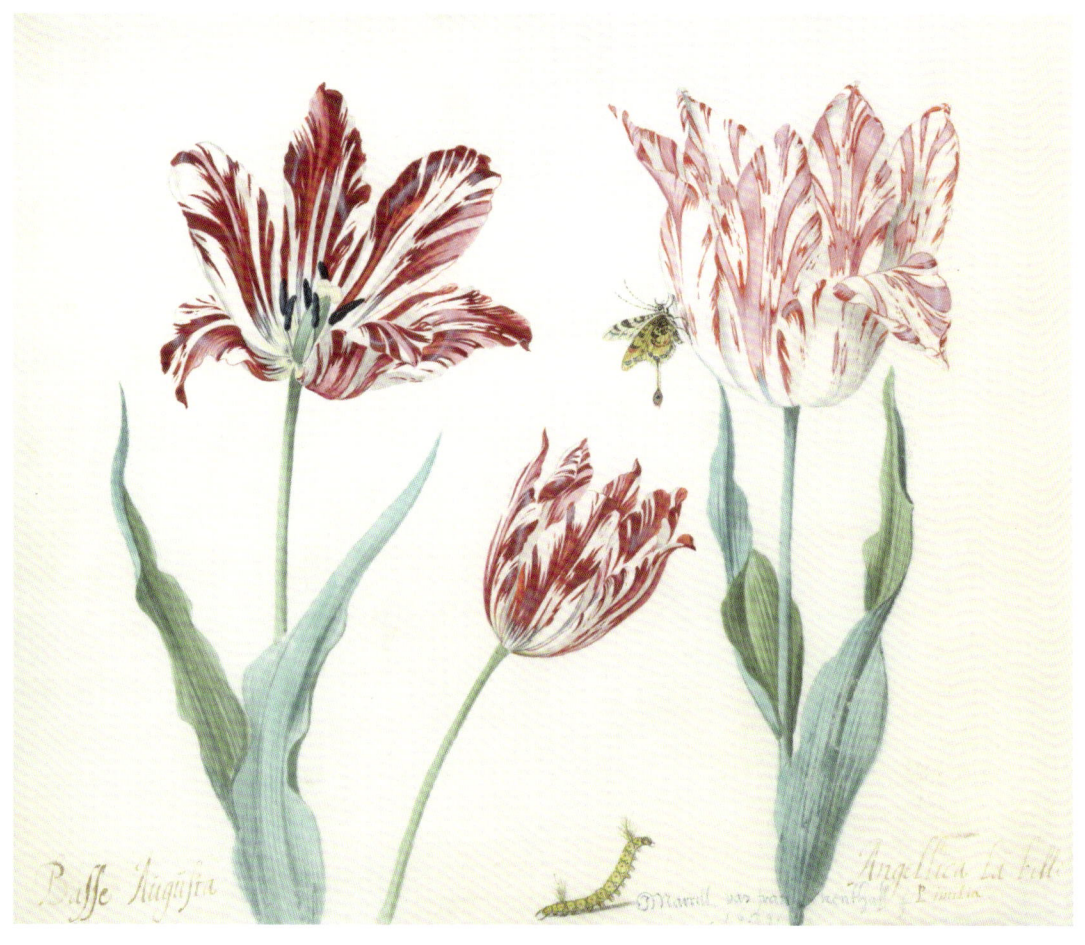

Jacob Marrel

Three Tulips with Caterpillar and Butterfly,
from *Album with Representations of Tulips*, 1639
Pencil and watercolour on parchment,
26.5 × 33.5 cm / 10½ × 13 in
Rijksmuseum, Amsterdam

Two tulip cultivars, a caterpillar and a butterfly
are beautifully depicted in this watercolour
on vellum – part of one of several watercolour
albums or *Tulpenboeken* made by German still-
life painter, print dealer and tulip trader, Jacob
Marrel (1613–81). On each sheet, Marrel's meticulously accurate blooms are supplemented by

images of insects, shells, berries and other flowers. Some sheets also include the weights and
prices of the tulip bulbs. The albums are remarkable documents of an extraordinary moment
in botanical and economic history, involving
a prized flower variety and its trade on the
stock market. Executed while Marrel was working in Utrecht during the late 1630s and early
1640s, his tulip books coincide with tulipomania, the period when the Dutch developed
a huge passion for the flowers, which had been
imported to Holland in the 1580s from Turkey,
where they had been cultivated by the Ottomans

since the beginning of the sixteenth century. The
craze for tulips, especially in variegated or mul-
ti-striped, forms resulted in wild speculation that
ended in 1637 with the ruinous crash of the bulb
commodity market. Marrel is a significant figure
in both the Utrecht and Frankfurt schools of still-
life painting, effectively linking the tradition
of flower painting exemplified by Ambrosius
Bosschaert the Elder (see p.177) with later masters, such as Jan Davidsz. de Heem (see p.125) and
Abraham Mignon. His stepdaughter was the
celebrated painter of flowers and insects, Maria
Sibylla Merian (see p.98).

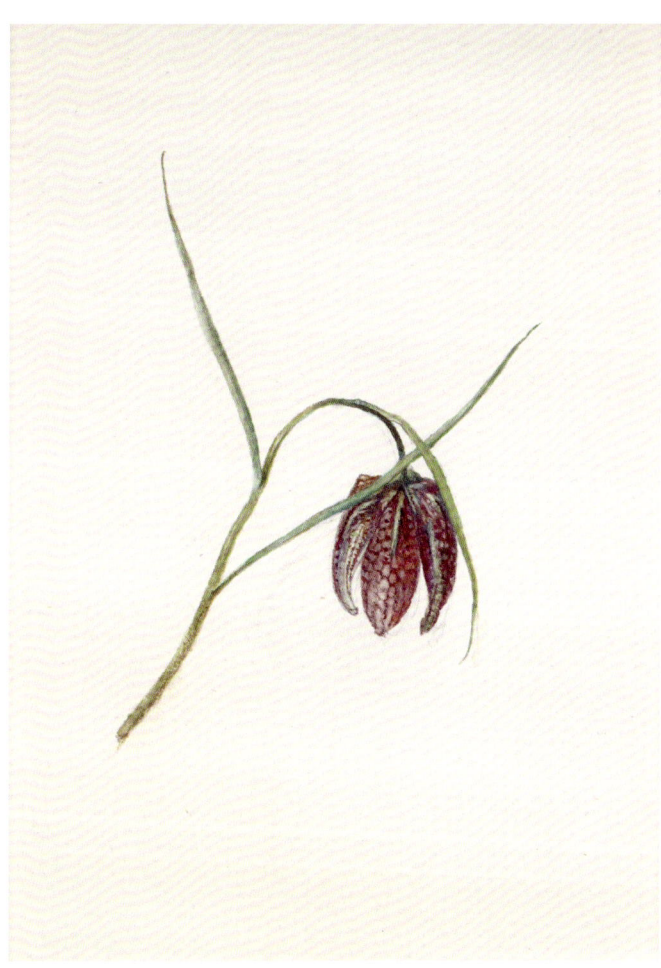

John Ruskin

Snake's-Head Fritillary, 1871
Watercolour and body colour over graphite,
34.4 × 25.9 cm / 13½ × 10¼ in
Ashmolean Museum, University of Oxford, UK

The snake's-head fritillary, a fleeting field lily found widely in spring, is shown as a lone stem with drooping petals minutely rendered in variegated purple hues. But, as the artist John Ruskin (1819–1900) noted, its isolation does not reflect where it grew. He also confessed that while 'the colour is fairly well observed', the outline in this study of the flower was 'utterly blundering and clumsy'. Ruskin donated the drawing as a visual reference for students at The Ruskin School of Drawing, which he established in Oxford in 1871, to sit alongside other examples carefully chosen to enable students to practice the art of drawing. Ruskin believed that seeing clearly – and especially seeing beauty – would imbue poetry, prophecy and religion in his students, thus achieving his vision for their greater pleasure of life. This graphite study with watercolour and body colour, outlined by a rough pencil frame, is not only a botanical observation of form and colour but also a portrayal of his feelings towards everyday – overlooked – blooms such as this. By isolating the study on the page, Ruskin elevates the humble subject matter and calls for us to look at it more closely. It both conveys his reverence for lilies – a plant family he considered to be the origin of handsome ornamental design – and also points to Ruskin's moral views and their intersection with truth and beauty.

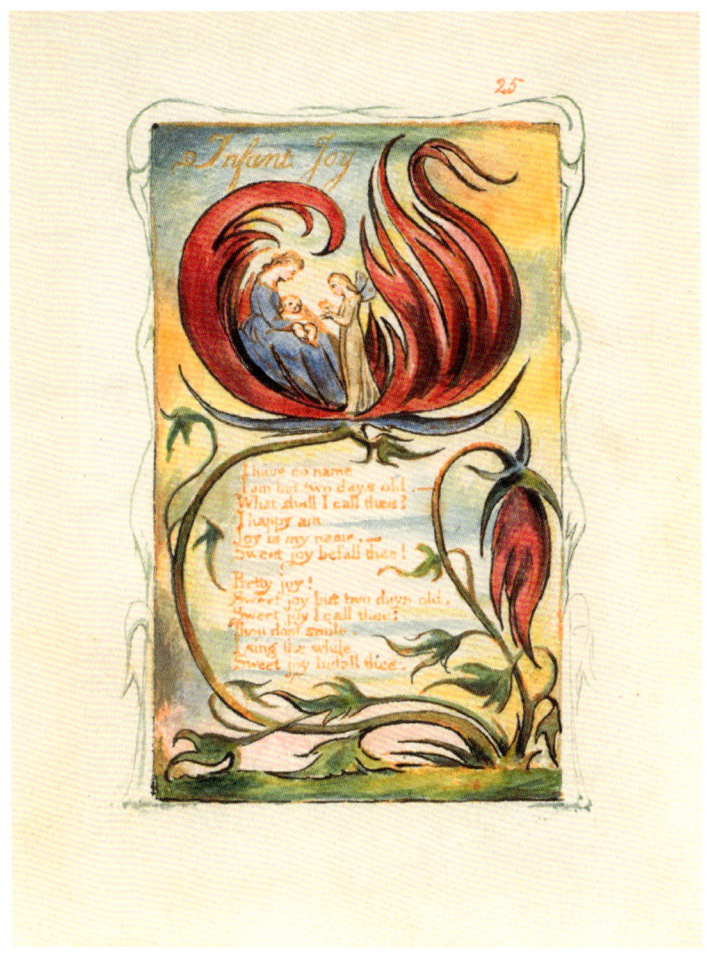

William Blake

Infant Joy, from *Songs of Innocence and of Experience*, c.1825
Relief etching printed in orange-brown ink and hand-coloured with watercolour and gold,
15.7 × 14.1 cm / 6¼ × 5½ in
Metropolitan Museum of Art, New York

A brightly coloured flower, perhaps inspired by a peony, swirls around this page from a book of poems by the famous English mystic artist and poet William Blake (1757–1827). The petals of the open flower encircle a mother cradling her newborn child, attended by an angel with outspread arms. Below are two verses of a poem that record an exchange between the baby – nameless and only two days old – and its mother, who expresses her joy at the birth and her hope for future happiness. Joy and warmth radiate from Blake's page, accentuated by the protective flame-like petals of the flowers and the golden background glow. The poem 'Infant Joy' was first published in 1789 in a volume entitled *Songs of Innocence* and later in an expanded collection called *Songs of Innocence and of Experience* (1794). The original publications were hand-printed, engraved and coloured by Blake himself. This involved a process known as relief etching (also called illuminated printing), in which the text was written on copper plates using an acid-resistant medium. The plates were then etched in acid to dissolve the copper and leave the design in relief. Critical of the established Church of England and of organized religion in general, Blake used his art and poetry to depict his mystical interpretation of Christianity, which for the time was highly unorthodox.

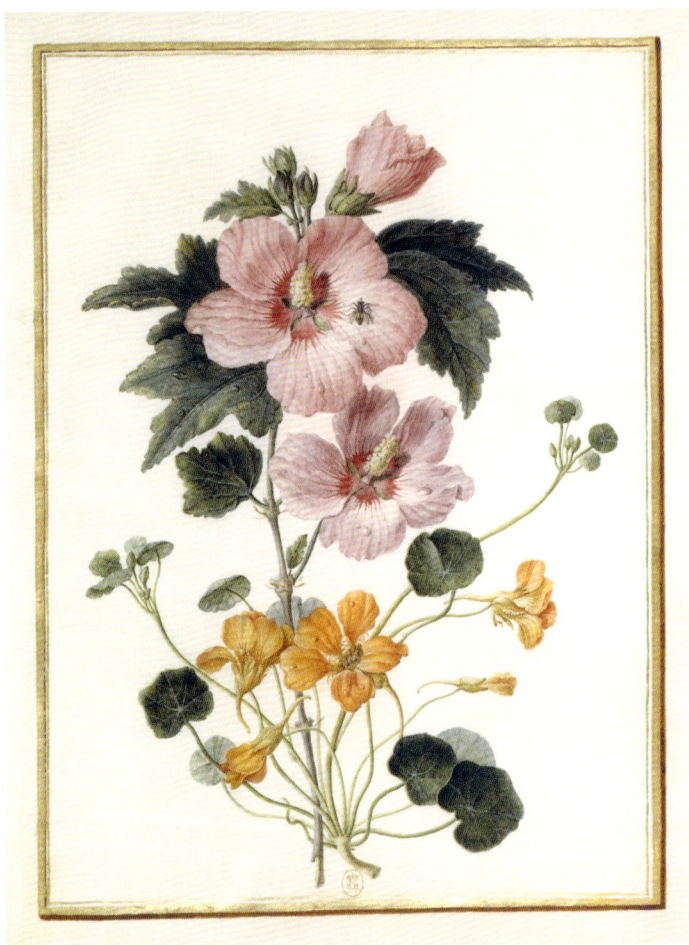

Madeleine Françoise Basseporte

Mallow and nasturtium, *c.*1750
Gouache on vellum, 30 × 38.7 cm / 11¾ × 15¼ in
Bibliothèque nationale de France, Paris

This study of two garden flowers combines a shoot of tree mallow (*Lavatera*) bearing broad pink flowers with the twisting flowering stems of a nasturtium (*Tropaeolum*). Characteristically, French painter Madeleine Françoise Basseporte (1701–80) has included water droplets and a fly resting on one of the petals to add to the vitality of the charming painting. Basseporte was an accomplished botanical artist who also gained

a reputation as a portrait artist for pastel paintings that depicted her subjects in almost photographic detail. In 1741 she was employed as Royal Painter for the King's Cabinet and Garden (the latter now the *Jardin des Plantes*) in Paris – the first female artist to be honoured with the position – which she held until her death in 1780. She is best known for her superb botanical illustrations, though she also painted animals, including birds and marine creatures. Her style combines artistic flair with strict botanical accuracy, which benefitted from Basseporte's contact with leading botanists of her time, including Carl Linnaeus (see p.208) and

George-Louis Leclerc, Comte de Buffon. She was commissioned by King Louis XV to teach his daughters how to paint flowers and is also said to have been consulted on interior decoration by Madame de Pompadour, the royal mistress. The renowned philosopher Jean-Jacques Rousseau is reported to have exclaimed, 'Nature gives plants their existence, but Mademoiselle Basseporte gives them their preservation.'

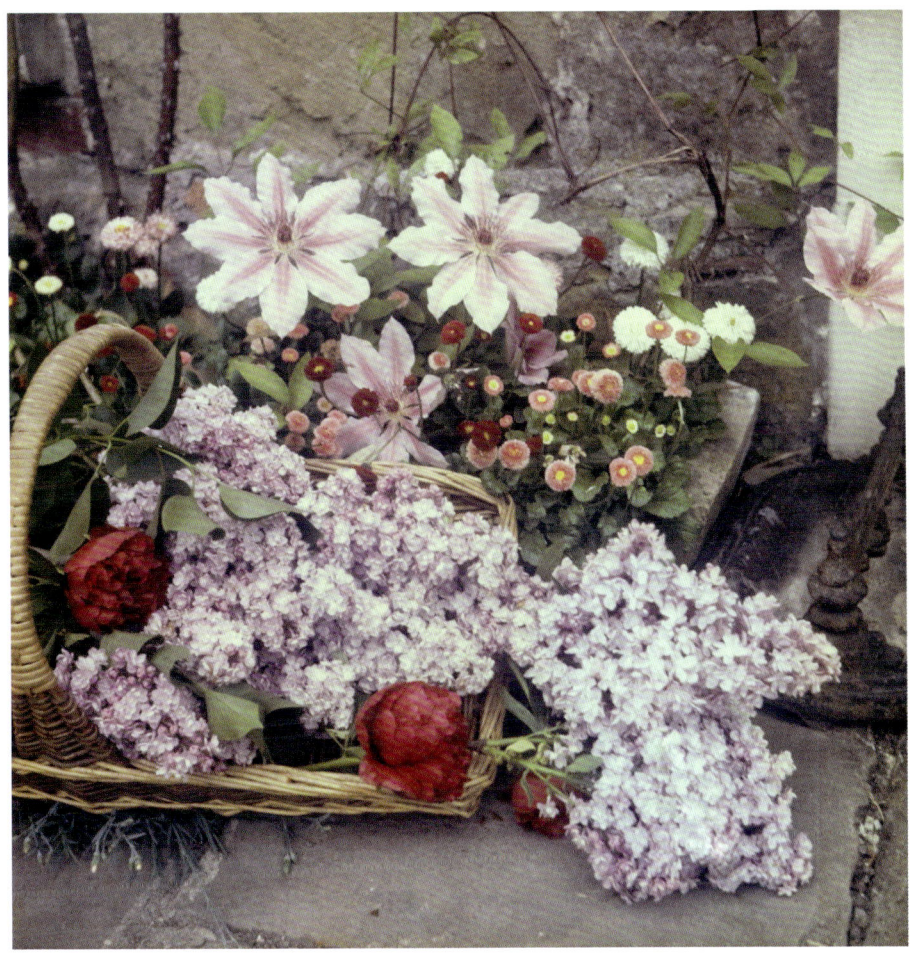

Cecil Beaton

A Basket of Flowers at Reddish House,
from *Vogue*, 1968
Photograph, dimensions variable

Two deep red peonies pierce the cloud-like soft-
ness of purple and white lilac blooms. Immediately
behind them, three large stargazer *Clematis* 'Nelly
Moser' are framed by a confetti-like scatter of pink
and red double-flowered daisies. The lilacs appear
to have just been picked, the basket that cradles
them only momentarily laid onto the ground by
an unseen hand. Everything seems effortlessly
composed, combining an elegant casualness
with a sense of privacy – although this might
not have been the case. The image was taken
by renowned British photographer and Academy
Award-winning stage designer Sir Cecil Beaton
(1904–80) in his beloved garden at Reddish House,
a country house surrounded by a five-acre garden
in Wiltshire's Chalke Valley. Beaton, whose work
regularly appeared in *Vanity Fair* and *Vogue*, often
picked flowers from the garden to use as adornments in his portraits of celebrities and royalty, but
this photograph is one of a handful in which
flowers take centre stage – and they likely represent more than one might at first assume. It is
no coincidence that the photograph should brim
with so many shades of pink, as it was one
of Beaton's signature colours. Given how much
Beaton loved his plants, it is inviting to read this
image as a subtle self-portrait of the artist himself.

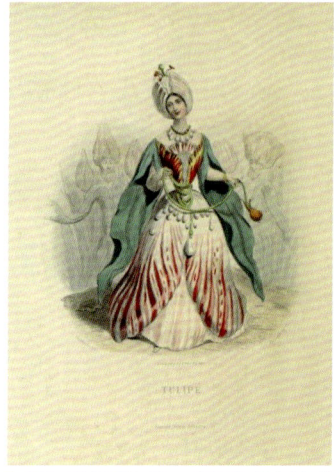

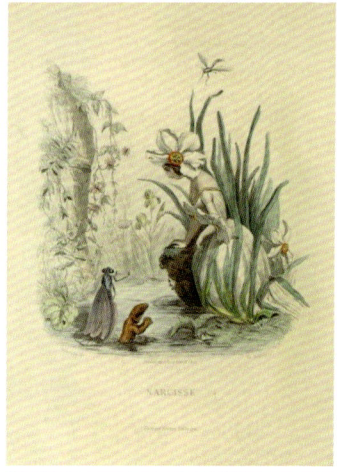

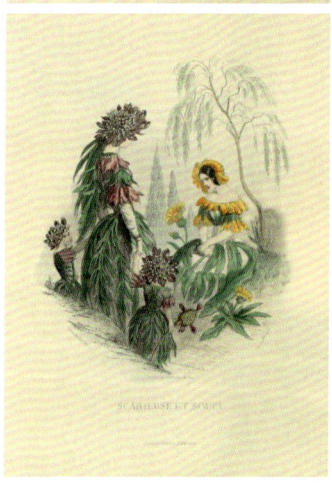

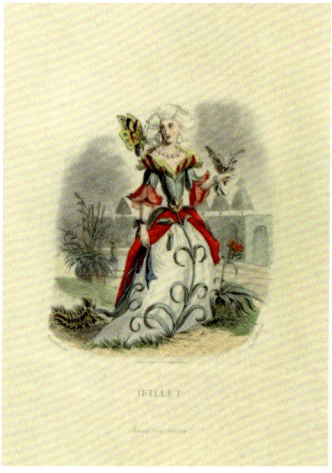

J.J. Grandville

Tulipe, Narcisse, Scabieuse et Souci and *Œillet*,
from *Les Fleurs Animeés*, 1847
Hand-coloured woodcut. 25.5 × 18 cm / 10 × 7 in
University of Ottawa, Canada

Blending the natural world with fantasy and
nineteenth-century fashion, the origin of these
charming 'flowers personified' was actually
a political caricaturist. French illustrator Jean
Ignace Isidore Gérard (1803–47), who worked
as J.J. Grandville, published his first work, *Les
Metamorphoses du Jour*, in 1828–29, and his cartoons appeared frequently in political periodicals
during the July Monarchy in France (1830–48).
Despite the disparate topics, Grandville employed
anthropomorphization across all of his work,
from depicting men as animals and birds to represent the social types in France to these more
delicate and romantic flower illustrations. Here,
Tulip is the vision of royalty with a dress of variegated petals and flowing sleeves made from the
plant's elongated leaves, accentuated with a necklace and sash of pearl-like bulbs. Narcissus kneels
on a riverbank, to converse with other denizens
of her natural habitat. Carnation, with sleeves
showcasing her pink hues and a bodice of striped
petals, appears in a courtyard visited by butterflies,
a setting appropriate for a desired garden flower.
Scabiosa, with her two young wildflowers, and
Dandelion sit together on a grassy hillside where
they might naturally grow together. Skilfully
mixing characteristics of both nature and humans,
Grandville is often cited as a precursor to the
Surrealists and as a possible inspiration for later
creatives, including John Tenniel, illustrator of
Alice's Adventures in Wonderland, and Walt
Disney (see p.91).

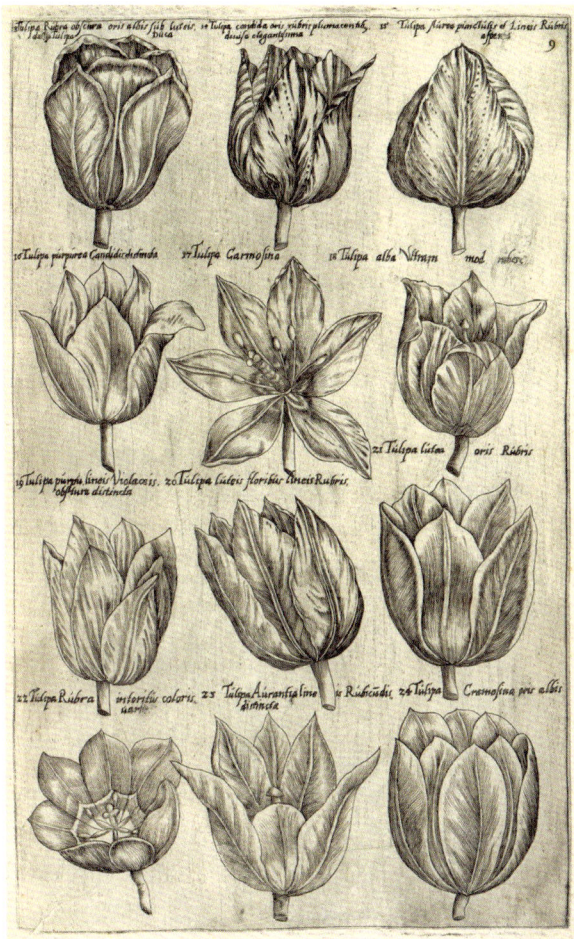

Emanuel Sweerts

Folio 9, from *Florilegium Amplissimum et Selectissimum*, 1612
Copper engraving, 39.8 × 26.2 cm / 15¼ × 10¼ in
Deutsche Fotothek, Dresden

The distinctive cup-like form of the tulip is unmistakable. This engraving by Dutch painter and nurseryman Emanuel Sweerts (1552–1612) showcases twelve varieties of the curvaceous flower, illustrating subtle variations across species. Some have pointed petals that arch outwards at the tips, while others are more rounded; several display variegated markings, such as stripes

or streaks, indicative of a virus that caused the flower's colour to split. The illustrations appear in Sweerts's florilegium of 1612, which concentrates on the ornamental qualities of flowering plants. As one of the first merchants to recognize the commercial value of tulips, Sweerts used his publication as a trade catalogue to advertise his wares. Its 110 plates feature more than 560 cultivated plants, including irises, hyacinths, anemones and tulips. By 1612, tulips had become an obsession among the rich, who desired brilliant and unusual colours as status symbols. The search for new varieties reached its zenith

in Amsterdam in the 1630s with a frenzy of speculation. At its height, tulipomania saw individual bulbs changing hands for prices that were equivalent to the cost of an Amsterdam townhouse. The mania was also highly lucrative for Dutch flower artists, who sold prints of rare tulips to those who could not afford the real thing. Eventually the bubble burst, and by the end of 1637 the market had collapsed. Sweerts's florilegium remained popular throughout the craze, and six editions were published between 1612 and 1647.

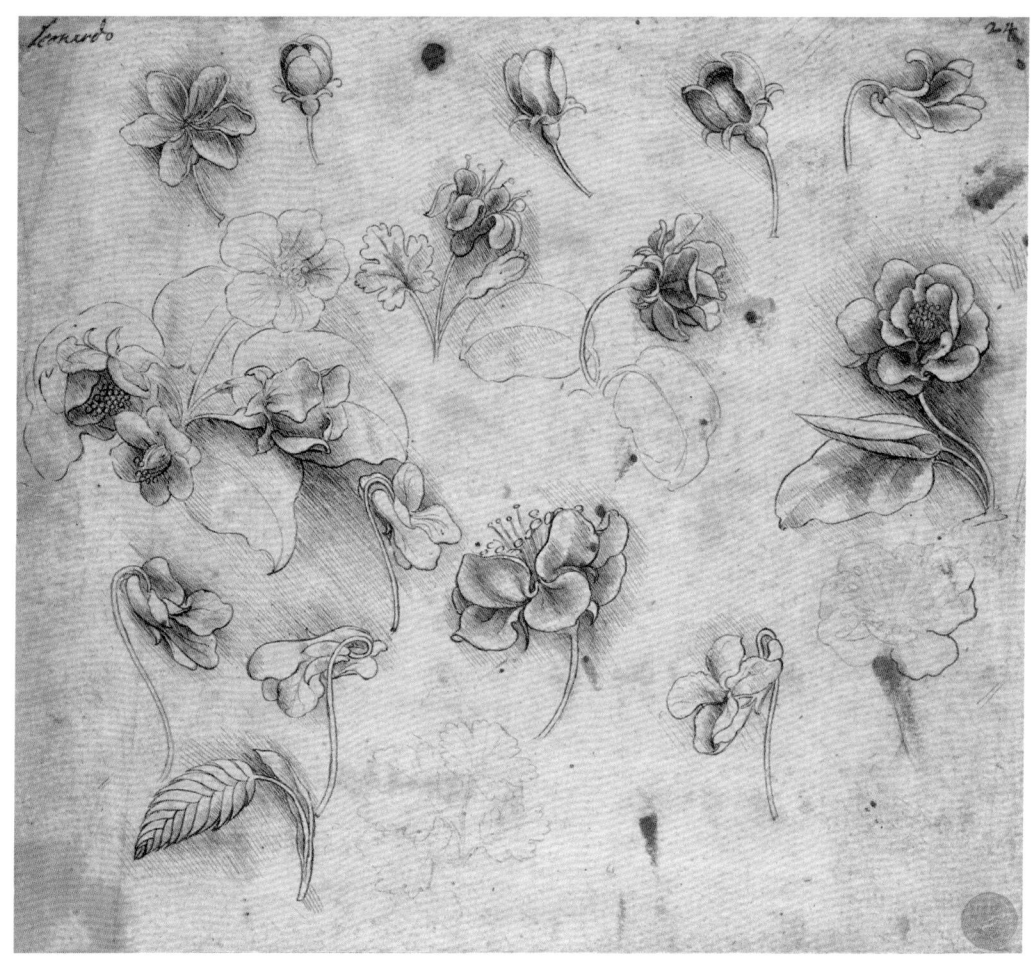

Leonardo da Vinci

Flower Study, 1486
Ink on paper, 18.2 × 20.1 cm / 7¼ × 8 in
Gallerie dell'Accademia, Venice

These delicate and highly detailed portraits of flowers not only mark a major departure from the stylized depictions of plants in medieval herbals, but such studies of flowers and plants also testify to broader cultural changes that informed human observation of nature during the Italian Renaissance. The Italian artist Leonardo da Vinci (1452–1519), celebrated as the archetypal 'Renaissance man', was among the pioneers of the accurate observation and precise depiction of animals and plants. In his quest for realism, he found an invaluable opportunity to both capture beauty and to gain insight into the functioning of life's most recondite mysteries. He carefully captured not only the shapes of leaves, petals and stems, but also the character of each individual species. To accomplish this, Leonardo drew flowers from different viewpoints, exposing the sculptural complexities of their forms while highlighting the structures beneath their graceful appearance. Although da Vinci mainly drew flowers and plants to perfect his skills in preparation for prestigious painting commissions, works like this laid the foundations of modern botanical studies. The plain background, linear precision and the arrangement of plants on the page to show as much detail as possible remain essential features of today's botanical illustrations.

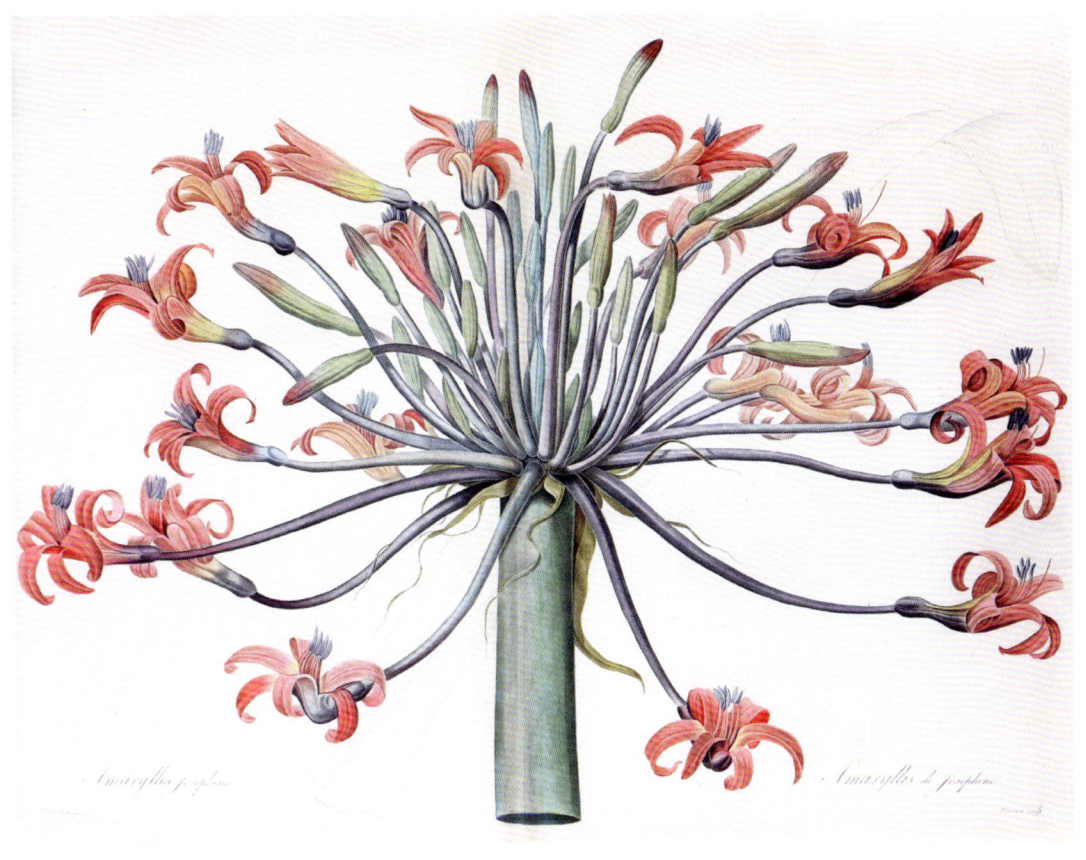

Pierre-Joseph Redouté

Amaryllis josephina from *Les Liliacées*, 1802–16
Stipple engraving printed in colours and finished
with watercolour, 55 × 72 cm / 21¼ × 28¼ in
Private collection

With a flowering head up to a metre (3 feet) wide
and averaging thirty to forty tubular red flowers,
this native South African amaryllis was a must-
have for French Empress Joséphine Bonaparte.
The specimen, brought to Holland from South
Africa, remained dormant for two decades; when
the amaryllis finally bloomed, Josephine pro-
cured it for herself and it continued to flower

under her care. In 1799, she purchased Château de
Malmaison on the outskirts of Paris and embarked
on an extravagant renovation of the gardens,
filling them with exotic plants and animals. Pierre-
Joseph Redouté (1759–1840), recognized for his
ability to paint flowers both naturalistically and
scientifically, was brought to her garden to illustrate *Jardin de la Malmaison* and shortly after was
named Joséphine's Painter of Flowers. As in life,
this amaryllis, named *Amaryllis josephina* in honour of the empress (now known as *Brunsvigia
josephinae*), can barely be contained on the paper;
it is one of 486 images in Redouté's lavishly

produced *Les Liliacées* – it appears on the single
folding plate included in the work. His original
watercolours were reproduced with stipple engraving *a la poupée* and, after printing, watercolours
were added to enhance areas of light and shadow.
Redouté's works produced for *Les Roses* and *Choix
des Plus Belle Fleurs* cemented his legacy as one
of the most important botanical artists of the nineteenth century and a major influence for contemporary botanical artists.

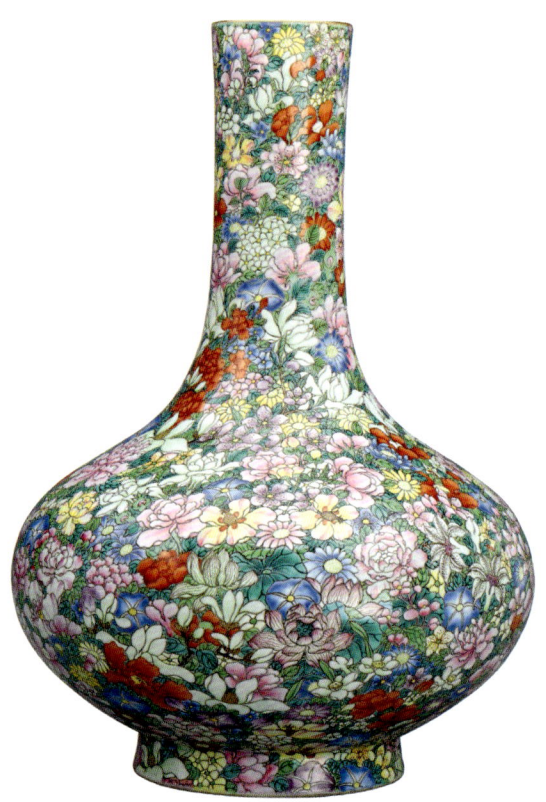

Anonymous

Vase with 'hundred flowers' decoration, 1736–95
Porcelain, 32.4 × 22.9 cm / 12¾ × 9 in
Asian Art Museum, San Francisco, California

Chinese artists and craftsmen, like their European
contemporaries, longed for the impossible dream
of experiencing the beauty of myriad flowers
blooming at the same time. This stunning porcelain vase makes that dream a reality through
a pyrotechnic burst of multiple species in a style
known as 'hundred flowers'. The many flowers
visible include morning glories, hibiscus, roses
of many colours, lotus flowers, wisteria, daisies,

chrysanthemums, magnolias, peonies and primroses. Despite the slightly exaggerated colours
and a sometimes approximated approach to form,
each flower retains enough characteristic traits
to make it possible to identify it accurately.
Although the design was not intended to categorize existing species, its sheer density provides
a snapshot of the popularity of certain varieties
of flowers in eighteenth-century China. This all-
over decorative scheme, the equivalent of *mille
fleur* in the West, is known in Chinese as *baihuadi*,
meaning 'hundred flowers ground'. It symbolized the enduring power of the Qing dynasty, one

of the longest-lasting of all Chinese dynasties,
which reigned from 1644 to 1911/12. Flowers in
bloom were taken as a sign of abundance and prosperity for the dynasty – and the hope was that
the reign of the Qing would last as long as flowers
continue to bloom.

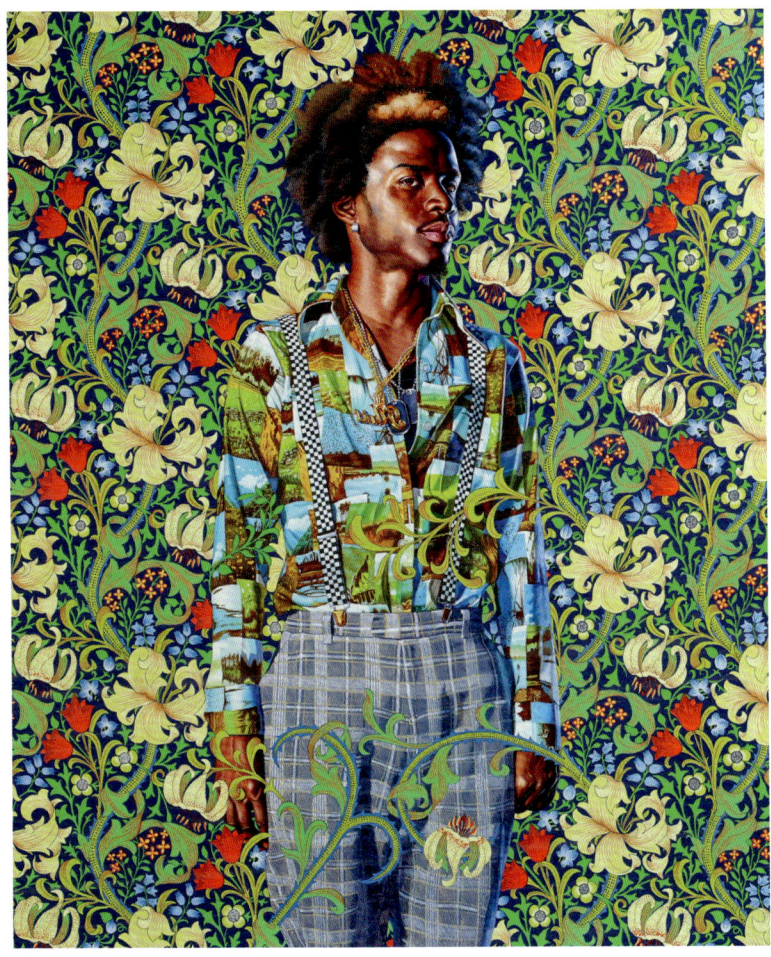

Kehinde Wiley

Portrait of James Hamilton, Earl of Arran, 2013
Oil on canvas, 1.8 × 1.5 m / 6 ft × 5 ft

Conceived at the Studio Museum in Harlem in the mid–2000s, *The World Stage* series by Nigerian-American artist Kehinde Wiley (born 1977) focused on urban black men striking poses typical of Chinese communist revolution propaganda posters. In the following years, the portraits would become more complex, investigating the troubled relationship countries such as Brazil, Israel, Nigeria, Senegal and Sri Lanka have with their colonial past. *Portrait of James Hamilton, Earl of Arran* was part of the seventh chapter of the series *The World Stage: Jamaica*. Borrowing from seventeenth- and eighteenth-century British portraiture, Wiley's painting juxtaposes the figure of a young Jamaican man with a floral pattern inspired by famed British textile designer William Morris (see p.160). The protagonist proudly stands at the centre of the composition, challenging the historical references of the setting he is repositioned in by putting his cultural heritage at the forefront. Morris's floral themes are rendered with uncanny tonal and structural precision – stylized lilies, tulips and other flowers intertwined with vining green foliage – and maintain the power of the message despite their harmonious nature. In February 2020, Wiley collaborated on an exhibition at the William Morris Gallery in London. Interacting with the black community in East London, Wiley remained true to the original spirit of his work, reconciling the two cornerstones of Morris's public persona: his iconic design and Victorian socialism.

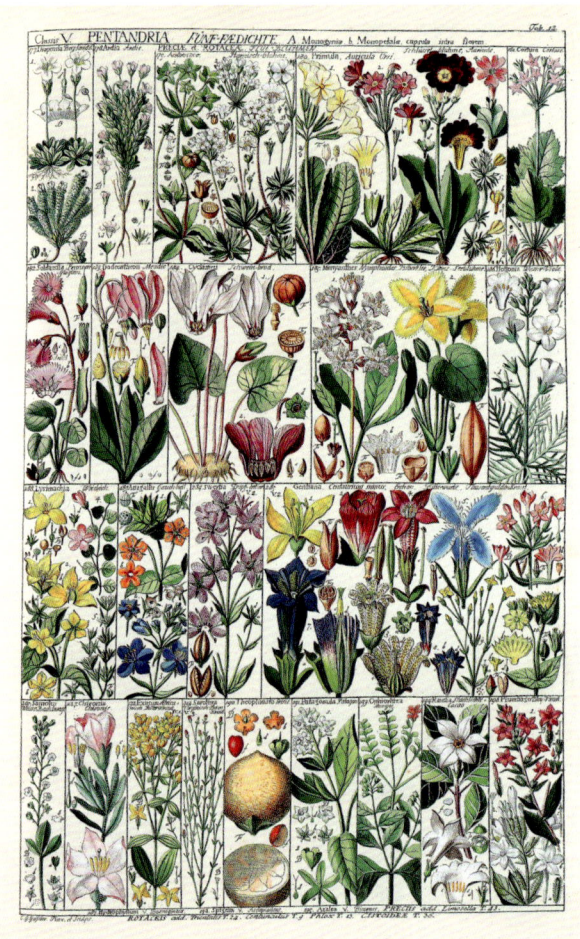

Johannes Gessner

Class V Pentandria, from *Tabulae Phytographicae Analysin Generum Plantarum*, 1795–1804
Hand-coloured engraving, 44 × 30 cm /
17¾ × 11¾ in
LuEsther T. Mertz Library, New York
Botanical Garden

Johannes Gessner (1709–90) created his fascinating *Tabulae Phytographicae* in an effort to illustrate the binomial classification system for plants, which had been developed comparatively recently by the influential botanist, zoologist and physician Carl Linnaeus (see p.208). Gessner conceived his book as a reference work that would set out the details of the different plant families in dense, tightly composed pictorial tables for ease of comparison. His illustrations follow Linnaeus in dividing flowering plants into classes based on the number of their stamens. This hand-coloured engraving illustrates the class of pentandrous plants – those with five stamens – including primulas, cyclamen and gentians as well the scarlet pimpernel, shooting star, water violet and plumbago, or leadwort. Gessner, a polymath Swiss botanist and physician, corresponded with Linnaeus from the early 1740s, exchanging ideas as well as plant specimens. Linnaeus held Gessner in high regard, praising him as 'a man I esteem above all other botanists'. Linnaeus did not live to see the work completed – nor did Gessner – but he was much impressed by the quality of the first two plates, drawn and engraved by Christian Gottlieb Geissler, copies of which Gessner sent him in 1763. The final work – two volumes with a total of sixty-four plates – was eventually completed in 1804, nearly a decade after Gessner began.

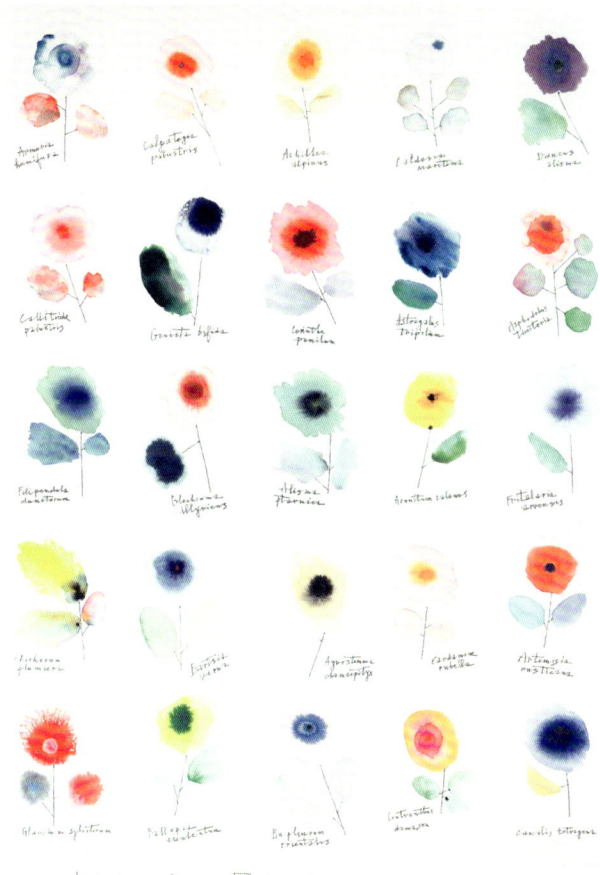

WILD FLOWERS

Alan Fletcher

Wild Flowers, 2002
Watercolour and ink on paper, 99.2 × 69.2 cm /
39 × 27¼ in
Fletcher Archive

Bringing together the serendipity of watercolour test sheets with the traditional art of botanical illustration, these interpretations of 'wild flowers' are perhaps even more whimsical than first meets the eye. The concentric watery circles forming colourful petals arranged in a regular grid are in fact experimental bleeds of colour that form the basis of this botanical conceit. Crisply illustrated with black ink details, their individual stems sit above titles that gave rise to a new fictional genus. By mismatching real Latin pairs of family and given flower names, British designer Alan Fletcher (1931–2006) created a wholly invented new catalogue of blooms. A reigning designer of the twentieth century and a founder of Pentagram, Fletcher shaped the look and feel of countless projects, ranging from books, posters and magazines to memorable corporate identities – each rendered with unusual inventiveness. Fletcher's work is imbued with a sense of wit, playfulness and a bold eye for colour, all of which are evident in this commission from the Very Interesting Paper Company. Released as a limited-edition colour lithograph poster and sent to the VIP Company's clients and friends, the work also informed a postcard book of all twenty flowers – including the imaginative, bright yellow bloom *Fallopia escultentum* and the fiery red-and-blue *Glancium sylvaticum*.

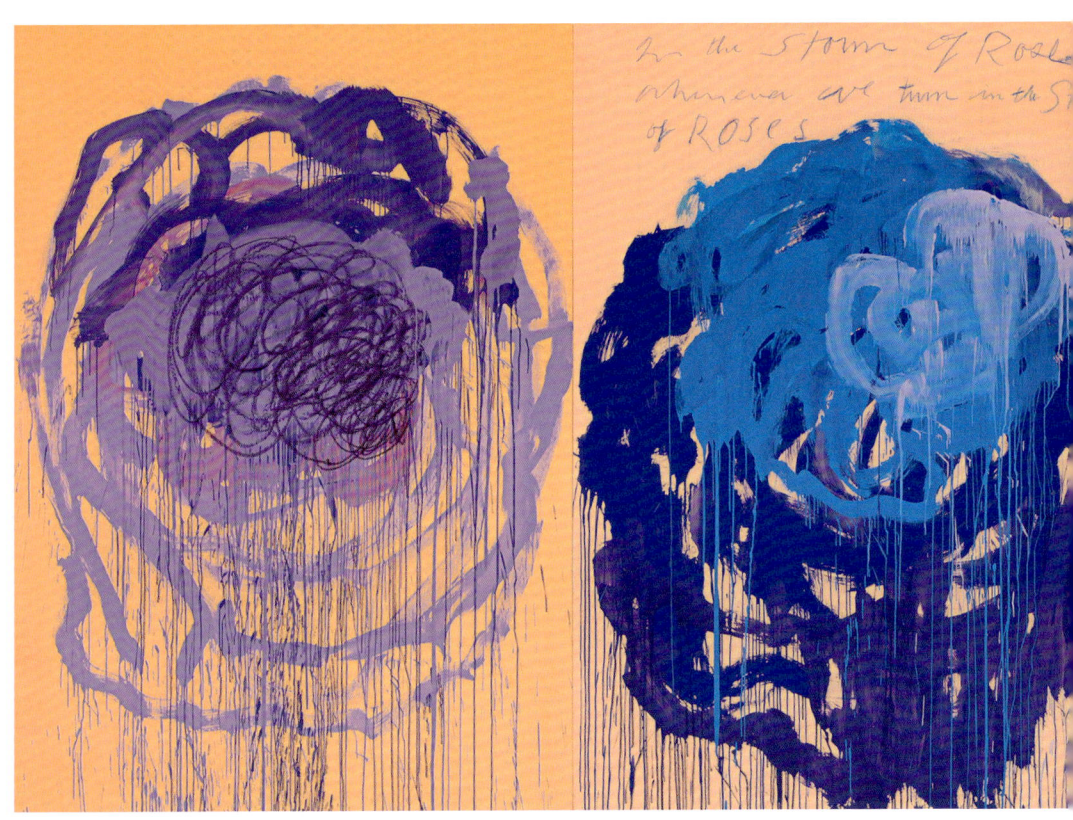

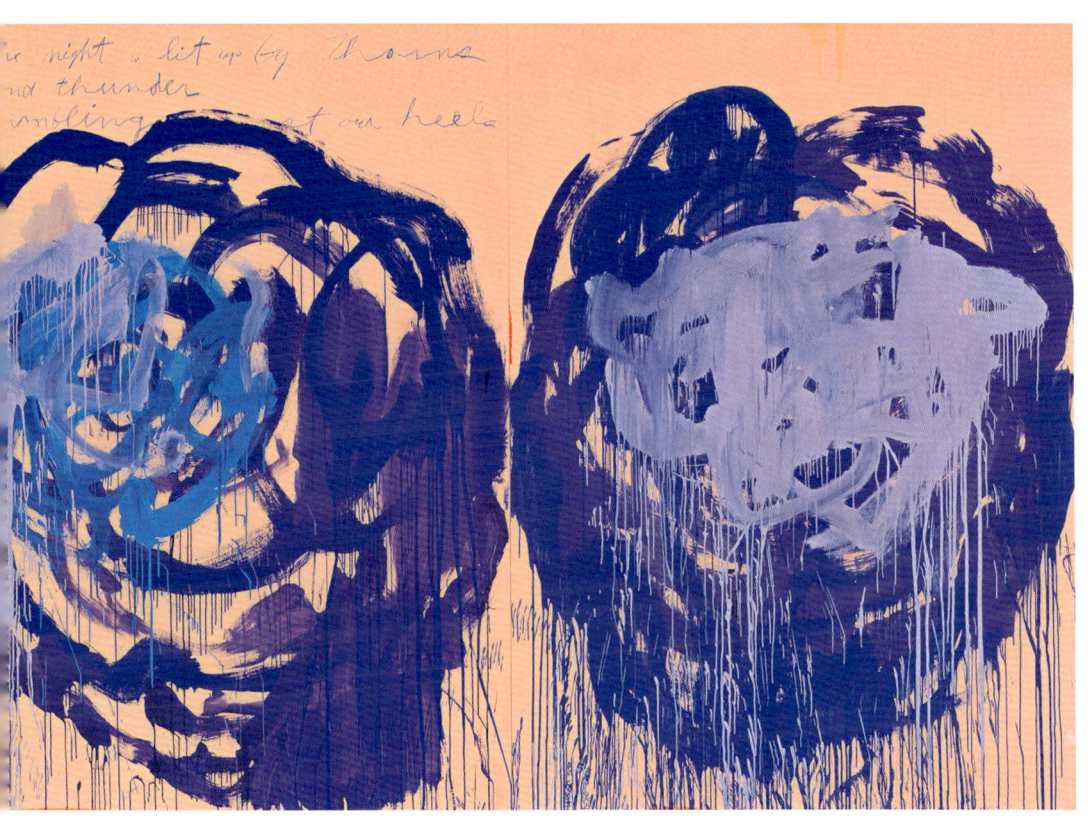

Cy Twombly

Untitled (Roses), 2008
Acrylic and crayon on wood, 2.5 × 7.4 m /
8 ft 3½ in × 24 ft 4 in
Bavarian State Museum Collections,
Museum Brandhorst

Four seemingly casually painted representations of rose heads float in repeated fashion across a canvas, each constructed out of a series of concentric circles in what could be one continuous paint stroke. The looseness of the painting, including drips of paint, builds up an idea of the flower heads rather than a strict representation

of how they appear in reality. The lines in the very centre of each head, where they are at their tightest, could almost be considered a scrawl. However, each brushstroke, shape and drip is intentionally executed by American artist Cy Twombly (1928–2011), who built his entire practice around an exploration of how gesture and the physical act of painting can create its own distinct artistic language. The mauve flower head Twombly paints is rare in real life, while blue roses – because of genetic limitations – do not exist in nature at all, so these flowers are largely made up or painted from his imagination. And although the title of the

'untitled' picture acknowledges the inspiration of roses, it seems as if Twombly may not be interested in the rose as such, but rather in using its form to explore a range of painterly gestures. Twombly explores the materiality of paint as he moves his brush across the canvas – describing the flowers and the act of painting them at the same time.

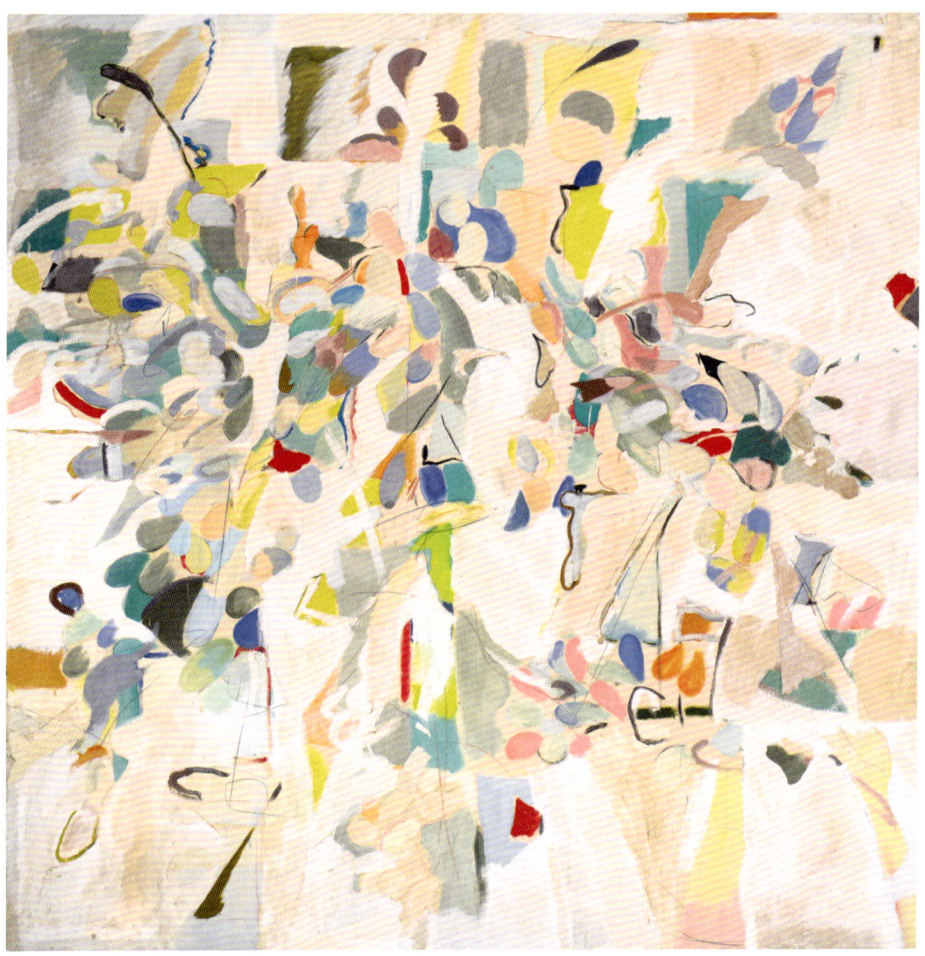

Derek Jarman

Flower Piece, 1965
Oil on canvas, 1.5 × 1.5 m / 5 × 5 ft
Private collection

Although better known today as a film director, stage designer, gay rights activist and creator of an iconic garden at Dungeness on England's south coast (see p.73), Derek Jarman (1942–94) originally trained as a painter at the the Slade School of Fine Art. Studying alongside noted artists Patrick Procktor and David Hockney (see p.211), Jarman eschewed the bold, comic book aesthetic of Pop art, preferring to work with

oils and often taking to landscapes as his subject. Like many of his paintings from the late 1950s and 1960s, *Flower Piece*, with its vibrant palette and dancing energy, almost seems like a harbinger of the garden he was to create and nurture in the shingle around his home at Prospect Cottage after being diagnosed with HIV/AIDS, the disease that was to kill him at the age of only fifty-two. Just as we can see a gardener's eye at work in this painting – one of around eighty pieces Jarman produced during the period – so we can see a painter's eye at work in his garden, with its unique mix of the cultivated and

the wild, and its sculptures made from found objects left behind by the sea. In *Flower Piece*, we see the fascination with space, movement and colour, reminiscent of the wildflowers, driftwood and pebbles of Dungeness, that was to shape his work in every medium for the rest of his life.

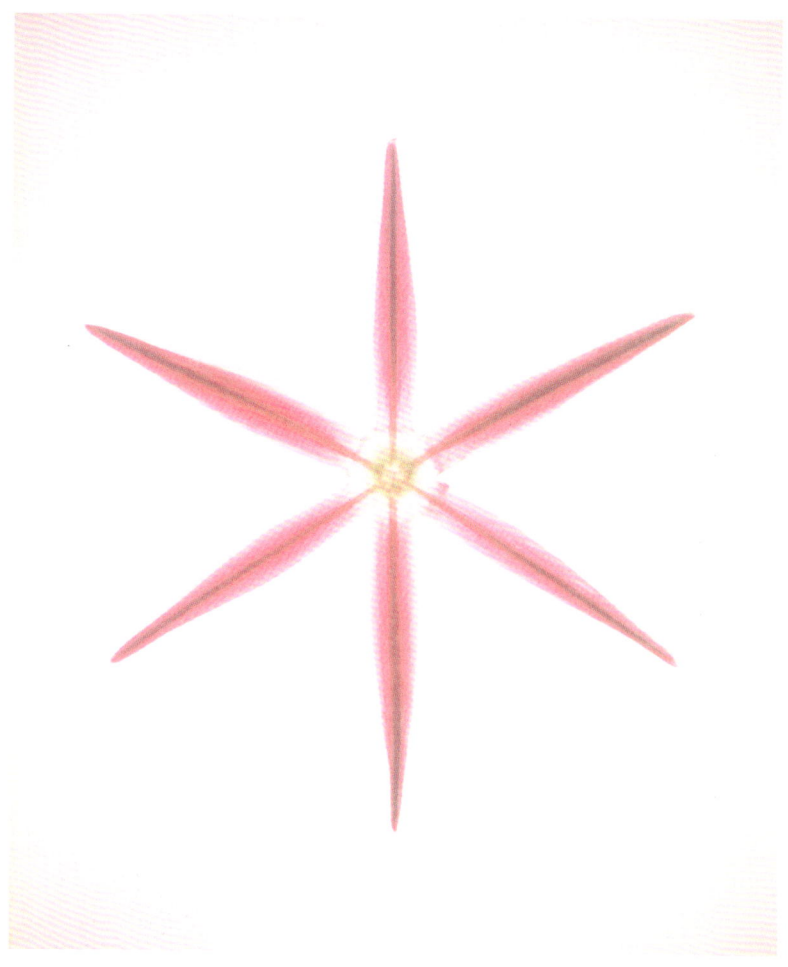

Garry Fabian Miller

Giant Allium, July 14th, 1997
Dye destruction print, 22.9 × 19.3 cm / 9 × 7½ in

This luminously beautiful image of one of the delicate star-like flowers that make up the globular flower head of *Allium giganteum* – the giant onion – was created by placing the flower itself in a photographic enlarger and using it as a transparency, passing light through it to be captured on sensitized paper. British photographer Garry Fabian Miller (born 1959) has been creating photographs without a camera since the early 1980s when, frustrated in his attempts to properly

capture the effects of sunlight shining through leaves and petals, he began to experiment with ways to reduce photography to the simplest methods and materials. He describes the essentials of his work as being 'the light, the gathered plant and a retaining paper containing the natural form as a light deposit, a radiant fossil'. There is an implicitly spiritual dimension to these images of plants, inspired by Fabian Miller's affinities with Quakerism, a faith that values simplicity and clarity and sees religion as integral to everyday life. The plants Fabian Miller uses generally come from his own garden, in a village on

Dartmoor in southwestern England, and he has long considered that tending the garden is part of the process of making the work, as it encourages a quiet contemplation that fosters a focus on detail. And light – the radiant essence behind Fabian Miller's photographs – is of course the sustaining element of life on Earth.

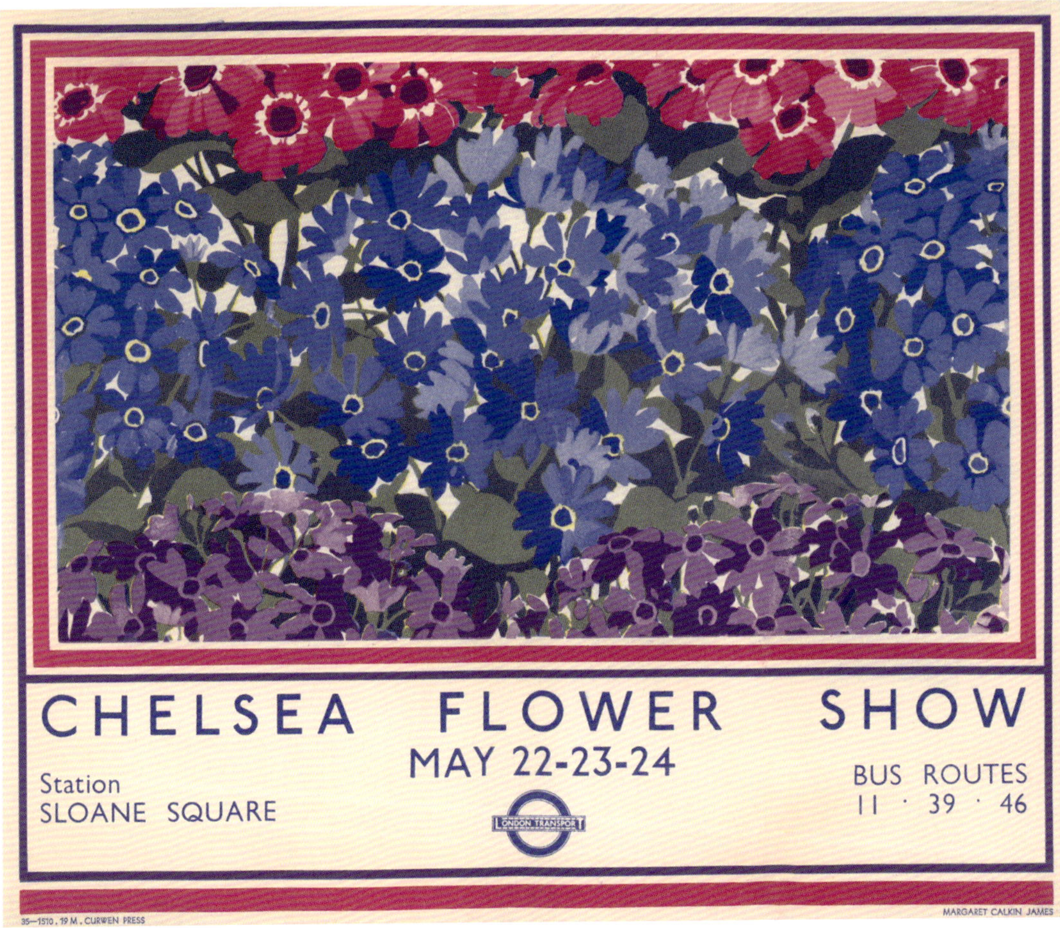

CHELSEA FLOWER SHOW
MAY 22-23-24
Station SLOANE SQUARE
BUS ROUTES 11 · 39 · 46
LONDON TRANSPORT

35—1510 . 19 M . CURWEN PRESS

MARGARET CALKIN JAMES

Margaret Calkin James

Chelsea Flower Show, 1935
Colour lithograph, 25.5 × 31.8 cm / 10 × 12½ in
London Transport Museum

This striking London Transport poster, with a profusion of bright pink, blue and purple cinerarias filling every corner of the frame like a tapestry, was a highly effective advertisement for the Chelsea Flower Show in 1935. Closely massed in bands of rich colour, the blooms mimic the style of dense display that was typical of the show at the time. Established in 1913 and held in the grounds of the Royal Hospital, Chelsea, the annual event served as a showcase where seed companies and nurseries would pre-sent their plants in floral displays and in landscaped gardens. New varieties and colours were crowded together to eye-popping effect, and British graphic designer Margaret Calkin James (1895–1985) used the same strategy in the design for her poster. Also an illustrator, painter and calligrapher, Calkin James made a number of watercolour studies of flowers in the 1930s and 1940s, adapting the motifs for posters and textile patterns. Her posters for London Underground and London Transport were created at the behest of its visionary chief executive, Frank Pick. Pick developed a strong visual brand in the 1920s and 1930s, and commissioned many gifted artists to design promotional posters. Some advertised specific routes or services while others pictured named destinations or special events – like the Chelsea Flower Show – but many were designed simply to encourage people to use buses and trains to discover the pleasures both within and outside of London.

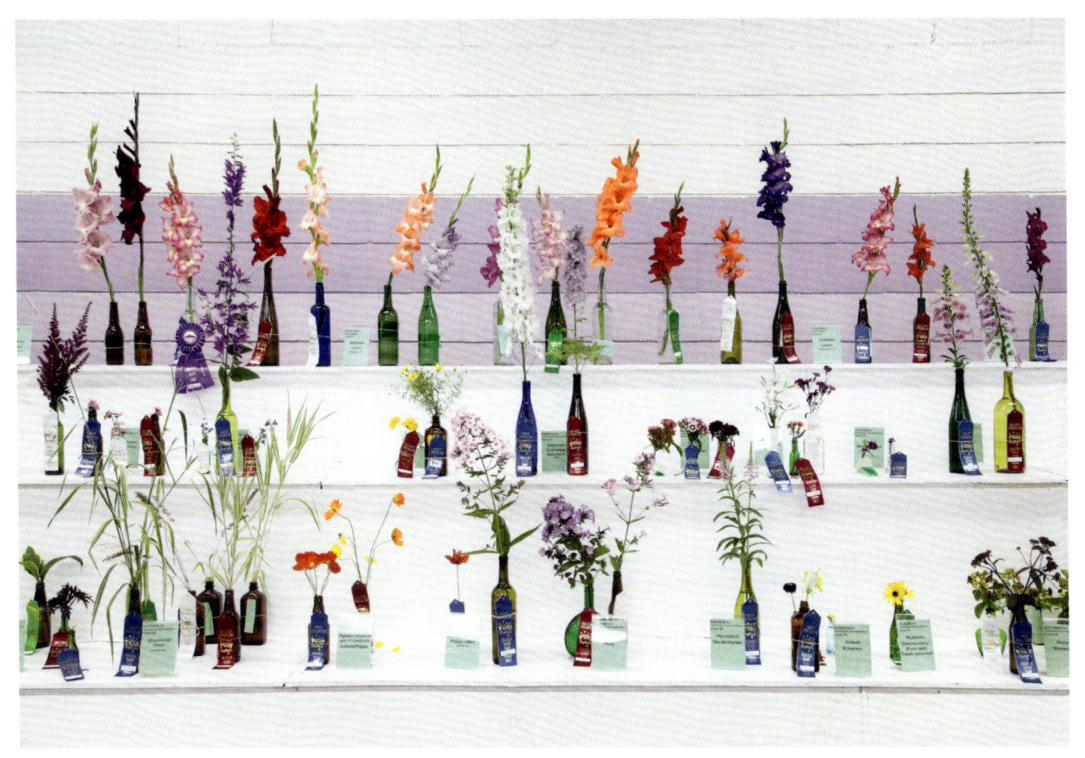

Sam Abell

Prize Winning Flowers, Alaska State Fair, 2013
Photograph, dimensions variable
Private collection

A selection of award-winning flowers from the Alaska State Fair are gathered together and exhibited as if they were on display in a shop window: gladioli dominate the top shelf, with delphiniums, dianthuses, poppies and other perennials below. Each specimen, whether a single stem or a very small bunch of flowers, attempts to meet the horticultural and aesthetic standards next to which these plants are judged in competitions. To avoid an ornate vase distracting from their beauty, the flowers have been placed in simple glass bottles, around which hang first-place and other ribbons; the large purple rosette indicates the overall division-winning flower, or 'best in show'. However, American photographer Sam Abell (born 1945) is not just interested in showing the best or most beautiful flowers. He photographs the plants from the front, rather than above, giving equal weight to the melange of random bottles, ribbons and labels in order to draw attention to the larger scene – the significance of such competitions as a whole – inviting us to think about flowers more broadly and the roles they play in our global cultures. Here, Abell seems to be asking us a question: what is it about the notion of the perfect specimen that we find so compelling? So compelling in fact, that we create, and take such pride in, elaborate annual rituals of competition to debate this very topic.

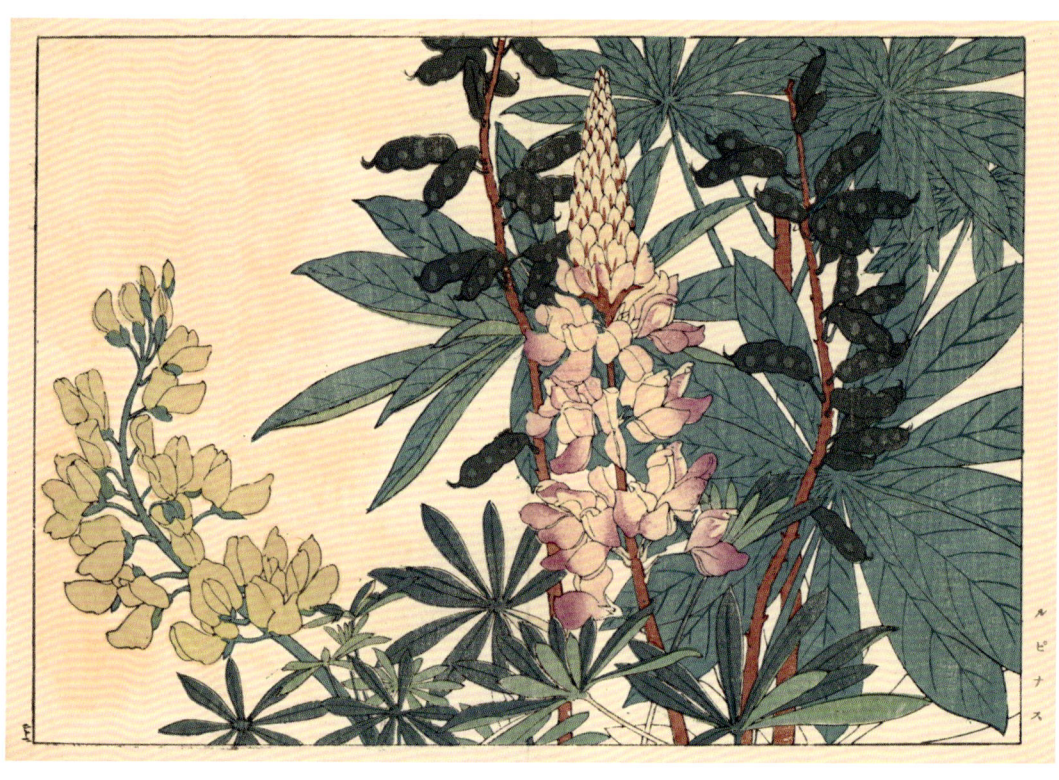

Tanigami Konan

Lupinus spp., from *Seiyō Soka Zofu* or *A Pictorial Book of Western Flowers*
Hand-coloured woodcut on rice paper,
27.8 × 37.5 cm / 11 × 14¾ in
Private collection

Following the height of *japonisme* that swept Europe in the late nineteenth century, Japanese artist Tanigami Konan (1879–1928) adapted traditional *kacho-e* (bird and flowers) art specifically to appeal to the Western eye, including illustrating flowers from outside Japan. Konan's *Seiyō Soka Zofu* was the first book produced

in Japan devoted to 'Western' flowers, and the artist used European techniques such as perspective and shading to supplement traditional Japanese simplicity of line in his compositions of lush foliage and flowers. Comprising five volumes – two for spring, two for summer and one for autumn and winter together – each book contains 125 plates and a centrefold. The subjects range from these lupins (*Lupinus luteus* and *L. polyphyllus*) to a striking combination of *Dendrobium* orchid with flamingo flower (*Anthurium* sp.), all accurately depicted, with minimal text at the outside edge of each plate.

Konan was born in Kansai and worked during the late Meiji era, when Japan was increasingly influenced by Western ideas. Traditional artists, including Konan, maintained *nihon-ga* – Japanese artistic conventions, techniques and materials – but in order to compete with new technologies, artists and printmakers adapted their approach to appeal to the Western market. Today, Konan's flower prints are usually referred to as *shin-hanga*, meaning 'new prints', coined in 1915 by prominent publisher Watanabe Shōzaburō for works that combined Japanese and Western techniques.

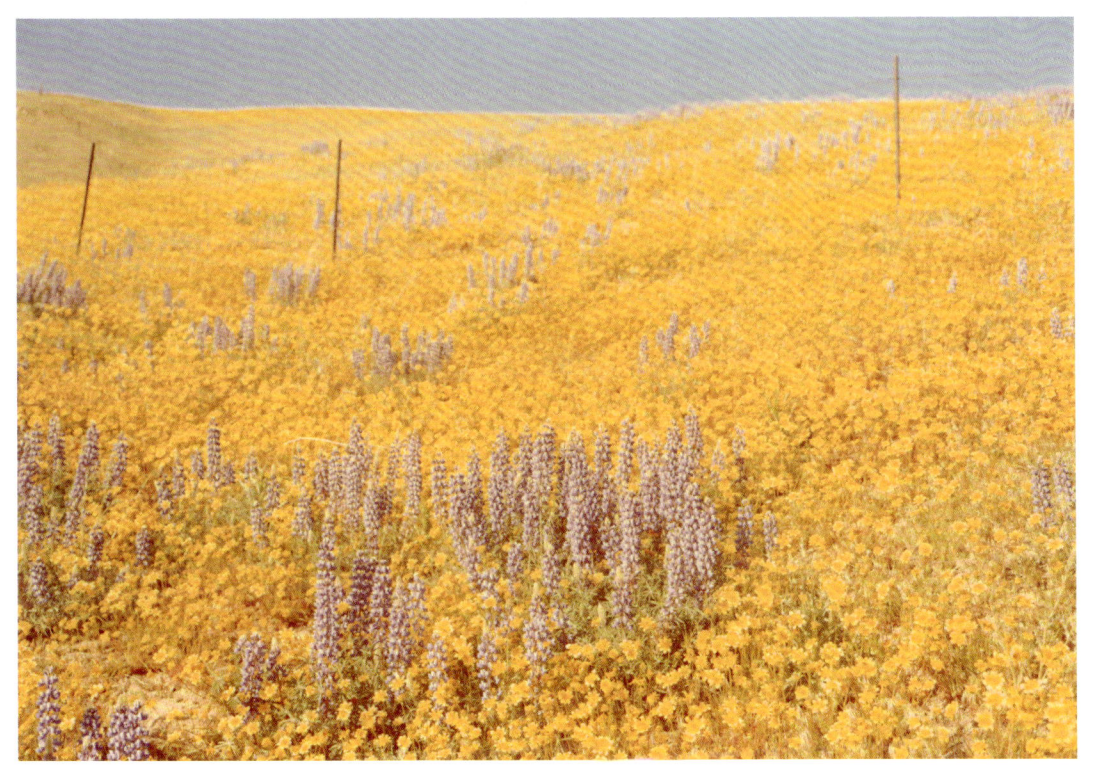

William Eggleston

Field of Daisies and Lupins, from
Morals of Vision, 1978
Chromogenic print, 17.2 × 25.4 cm / 6¾ × 10 in
J. Paul Getty Museum, Los Angeles

Clusters of purple lupins rise out of a carpet
of yellow daisies, blanketed by a grey sky, while
tilting fence posts act as grace notes. Lupins thrive
in the US state of Georgia, where winds disperse
seeds in the humid air; thus, this photograph offers
not only visual impact but also affects the sensory
imagination of smell, touch and sound. American
photographer William Eggleston (born 1939) was

a pioneer of colour photography from the mid-
1960s – when serious photography was always
black-and-white – and in the early 1970s discovered the complex dye-transfer printing process,
which resulted in an unprecedented richness
of colour saturation. In 1976 he was given a solo
exhibition at the Museum of Modern Art in New
York, a watershed moment in photographic
history: from that point on, colour photography
was accepted as art. Although Eggleston's style
has been called a 'snapshot aesthetic', it is a term
he rejects. Rather, his images – 'democratic',
in that no detail takes precedence over others

– compel the viewer to look beyond their banal,
mundane, everyday subjects. There is mystery
to his highly refined and often eccentric compositions, like movie stills pulled out of sequence;
the viewer's imagination provides the context from
which each subject was extracted. This image
is one of eight published in *Morals of Vision*, a portfolio of images taken around the small town
of Plains, Georgia, in 1978.

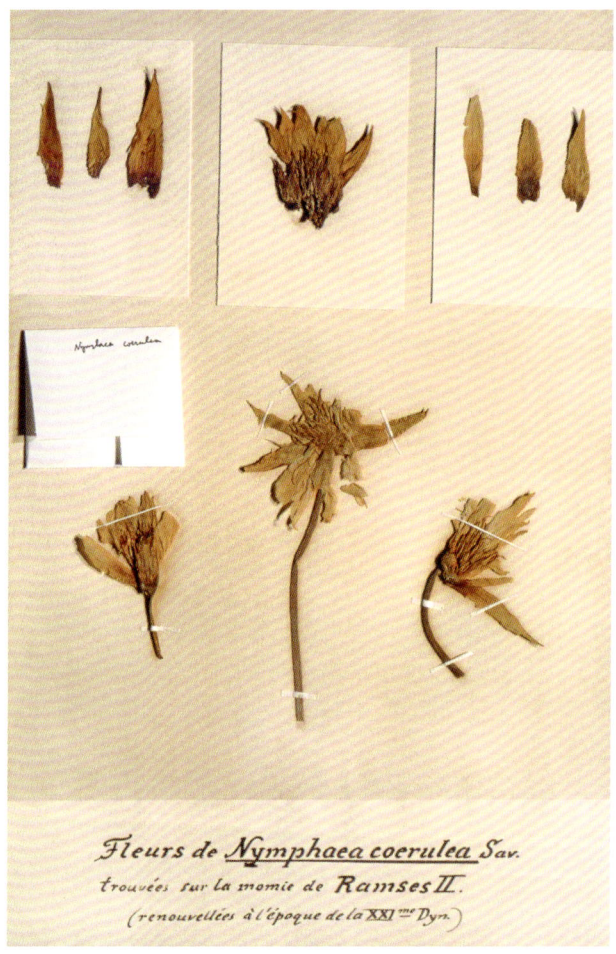

Fleurs de Nymphaea coerulea Sav.
trouvées sur la momie de Ramses II.
(renouvellées à l'époque de la XXI ᵐᵉ Dyn.)

Georg Schweinfurth

Flowers of Nymphaea caerulea Sav.
Found on the Mummy of Ramses II,
from *Garlands of Ramses II*, 1884
Herbarium sheet, dimensions variable
Musée National d'Histoire Naturelle, Paris

Funereal flowers have a very long history: these blue lotus, or blue water lily (*Nymphaea caerulea*), were buried with the Egyptian pharaoh Ramses the Great (reigned *c.*1279–1213 BC) more than 3,000 years ago. Ramses' mummified body was buried in the Valley of the Kings along with lavish grave gifts, which inevitably attracted looters. In the early eleventh century BC the body was rewrapped and transferred to a new tomb at Deir el-Bahari, on the left bank of the Nile opposite Karnak, along with the garlands of flowers buried with the king, which had been ignored by the tomb robbers. This final resting place was discovered by French archaeologists in the 1880s, who entrusted the preservation of the dried flowers to German botanist Georg Schweinfurth (1836–1925). Blue lotus, an aquatic plant native to the Nile, contains psychoactive alkaloids that were known to the ancient Egyptians. The flower often appears in Egyptian scenes of dancing and celebration, and in images depicting the passage of the dead to the afterlife. In Egyptian mythology, the supreme sun god Ra created the world by emerging from a blue lotus flower floating in primordial waters, and the flower itself is personified in the god Nefertem, depicted as a beautiful youth with blue water lilies around his head.

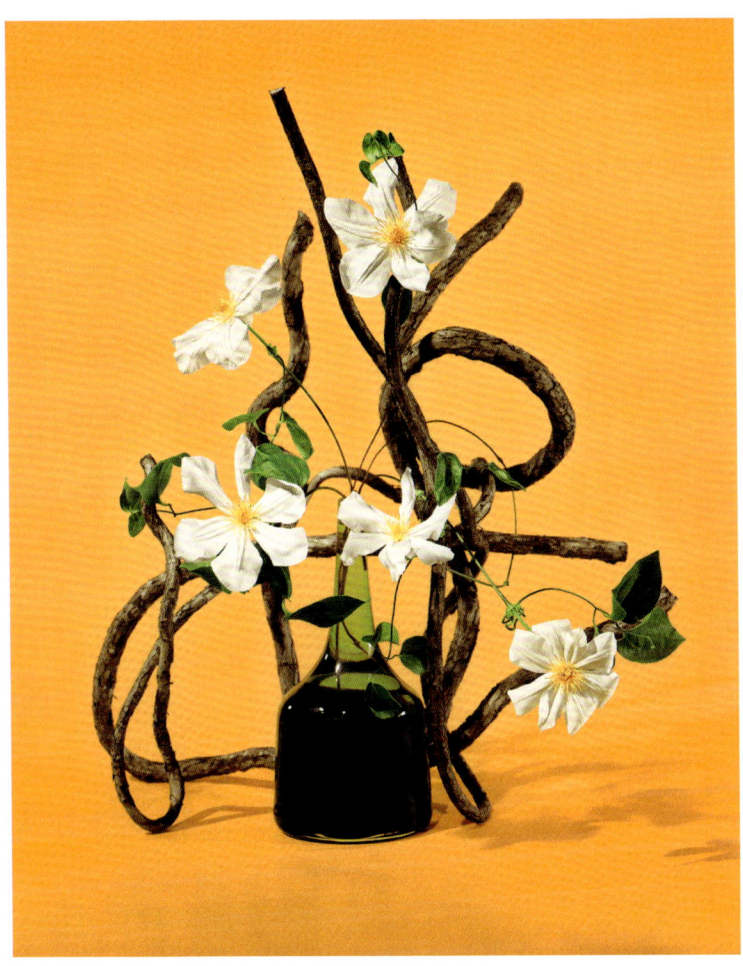

Sofu Teshigahara

Untitled, 1967
Floral arrangement with leather flower (*Clematis*),
tara vine (*Actinidia arguta*) and glass vase

This exquisite composition is the work of Sofu Teshigahara (1900–79), the founder of the Japanese Sogetsu School of *ikebana* flower arranging. This renowned art of displaying flowers arrived in Japan with Buddhism in the sixth century AD and inspired popular votive floral arrangements for temple altars during the seventh century AD. From these roots, ikebana evolved into a disciplined artform in which humanity and nature engage in a poetic dialogue of resistance and compliance. With compositions that are highly symbolic, ikebana master Toshiro Kawase described the art as being based on the notion that 'the whole universe is contained within a single flower'. Each flower is used to portray fundamental explorations of balance – between simplicity and beauty, light and shadow, life and death. Often crafted to reflect a specific season, ikebana relies on minimalism to induce a contemplative state capable of relaxing the mind, body and soul. Traditionally, the white clematis flowers seen in this composition by Teshigahara, arranged alongside the native Asian tara vine, were a symbol of ingenuity and cleverness according to *Hanakotoba*, the Japanese language of flowers. Teshigahara's school radically broke with tradition by believing that ikebana could be practiced 'anytime, anywhere, by anyone' and with any materials – using both flowers and untraditional elements. His experimental approach vastly enhanced the individualistic expressions of this ancient botanical art form.

123

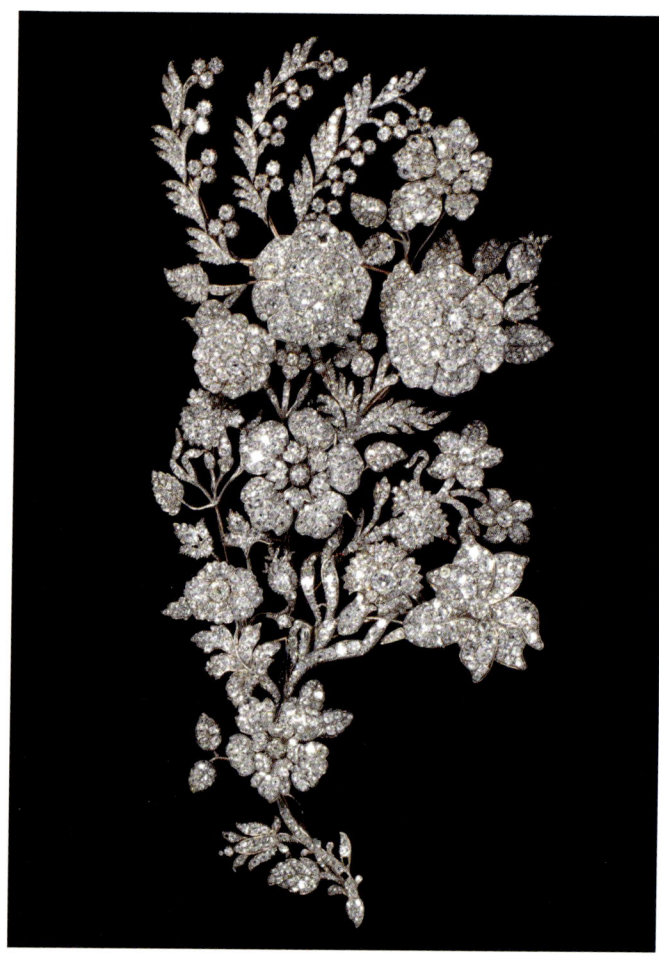

Anonymous

Bodice ornament, *c.*1850
Diamonds set in silver, backed with gold,
27.7 × 15 × 4.2 cm / 11 × 6 × 1¾ in
Victoria and Albert Museum, London

Georgian plant hunters and their feverish
obsession for collecting and showcasing exotic
species of the natural world set off the later,
more widespread Victorian fascination with
botanical allusions. The popular study of plants
infiltrated art, fashion and interior decoration,
while jewellers also saw the opportunity to work
their materials in foliate designs, of which this

ornamental setting is an example. This bodice
ornament translates precious stones and metals
into a lasting corsage, borrowing from the familiar
qualities of a fresh buttonhole. A sparkling array
of roses, carnations and other flowers created from
diamonds set in silver and backed with gold, the
large floral spray – measuring nearly 28 centimetres (11 inches) long – would have been an enviable
accessory that combined popular taste with the
height of fashion. Thought to be of English origin,
the bodice piece nevertheless adopts the technique of an *en tremblant* (trembling) setting, most
often associated with work from Parisian ateliers.

This delicate mechanism involved mounting
stones on fine, coiled springs of wire or gold. Set
in this way, the diamonds appear to quiver
as their wearer moves, amplifying the transfix-
ing effect of light bouncing off cut facets and
giving works a sparkling dynamism that is otherwise unusual for decorative jewelled settings.

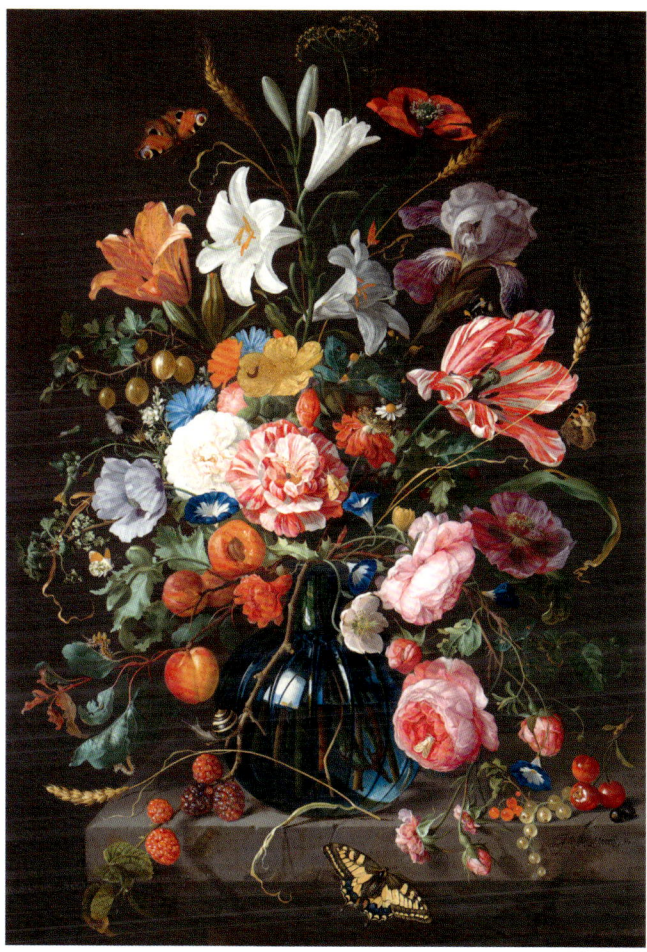

Jan Davidsz. de Heem

Vase of Flowers, c.1670
Oil on canvas, 74.2 × 52.6 cm / 29¼ × 20¾ in
Mauritshuis, The Hague, Netherlands

Emerging from a clear blue glass vase, roses, Madonna lilies, a tulip, an iris and other cultivars are combined with wildflowers – poppies, morning glories and even wild chicory – and a variety of small fruits. As with the majority of his flower pieces, this baroque floral still life was painted rather late in the career of Jan Davidsz. de Heem (1606–83/84) and he demonstrates all of his acquired skills in composition and handling of light and texture, as well as his ability to render details with meticulous precision. In a combination of subjects that was unusual in seventeenth-century flower paintings, de Heem inserted less expected species next to the typical flowers, such as the blossom of the pomegranate, holly and a daisy. And, as often in his floral still lifes, he has interwoven several ears of wheat that curve through the composition, inconspicuously adding to its liveliness. The viewer can go hunting for ants, bugs, caterpillars and butterflies, each of which looks as if it might start to move at any moment, just as a snail seems to be peering out from a branch of mulberries. The artist clearly emphasizes a sense of transience: the flowers are in various stages of bloom, with some roses still budding while others have finished flowering, and the tulip is already overblown. Many of the leaves show traces of gnawing, and the apricots have also suffered from foraging creatures. A painting like this can be read on several levels, from admonition to temporality to sheer amazement at the pictorial quality.

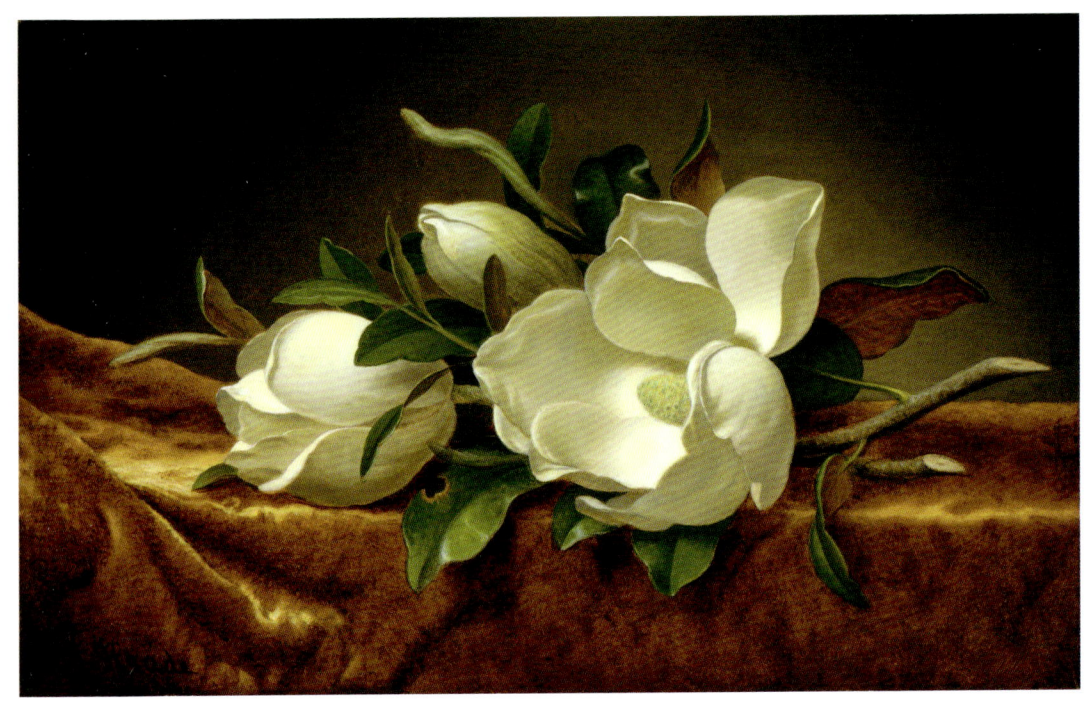

Martin Johnson Heade

Magnolias on Gold Velvet Cloth, c.1888–90
Oil on canvas, 37.6 × 61 cm / 14¾ × 24 in
Museum of Fine Arts, Houston, Texas

Evoking a sense of rarity and richness, the ivory petals of magnolias, cut just at the moment they have started to bloom, rest on a swathe of sumptuous gold velvet. Although he made his reputation as a landscape painter, American artist Martin Johnson Heade (1819–1904) began painting dramatically large flowers with glossy curving petals after he was inspired by the flora of the rainforests of Brazil and Central America, where he travelled frequently from 1863. Heade depicted mainly cattleya orchids, set alongside hummingbirds for greater appeal, against atmospheric backgrounds of lush trees and rain-drenched skies. In 1883 Heade ended his planthunting travels and retired to Florida, where he continued to compile his trademark rainforest paintings while also producing flower still lifes, again concentrating intensely on one type of flower in each composition. Magnolias were one of his common subjects, either laid on a cloth-covered surface or arranged in ornate vases. Native to southeastern North America, *Magnolia grandiflora* was considered a rare and rich species when it arrived in European gardens during the eighteenth century, followed later by species indigenous to China and Japan. Magnolias were comparatively late to global cultivation, but were among the earliest flowering plants, before bees existed, so they evolved with tough petals and modified reproductive structures that allow them to be pollinated by beetles.

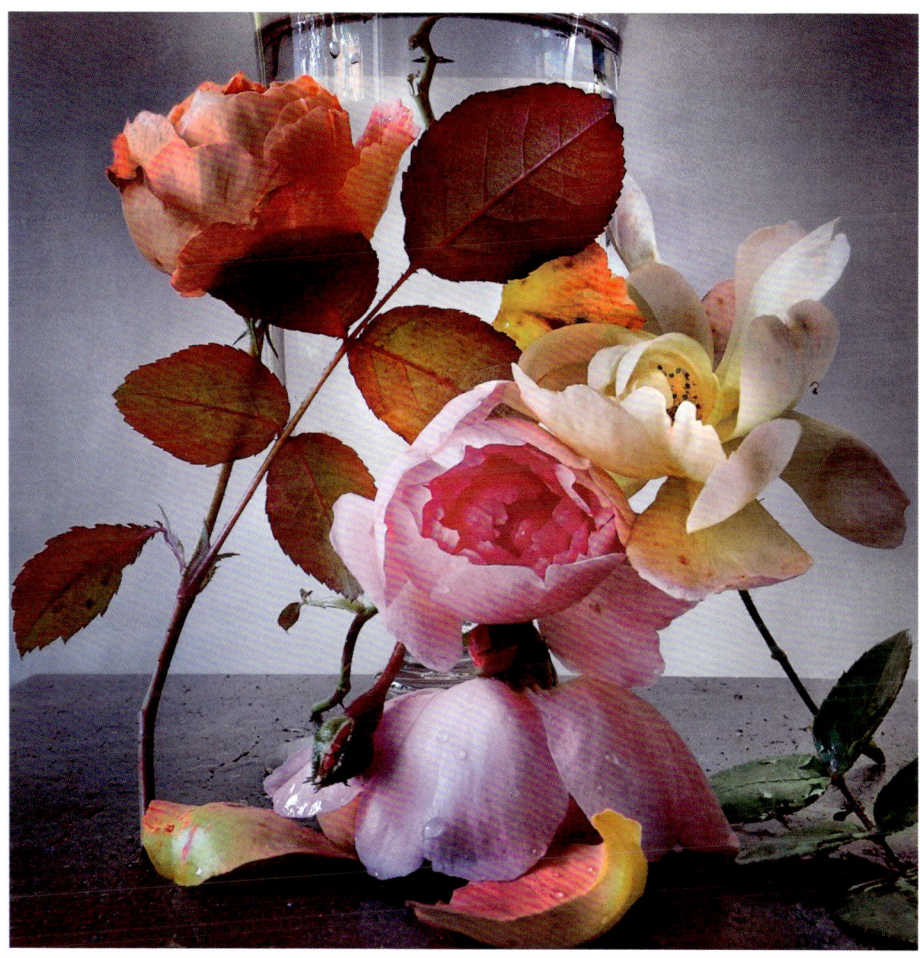

Nick Knight

From *Roses from My Garden* series, 2009
Hand-coated pigment print, dimensions variable

Focusing on the exquisite, ephemeral beauty of a collection of pink, lemon and apricot roses – including imperfections such as a tarnished leaf or fallen petals – this image is one of a series of photographs exhibited by British photographer Nick Knight (born 1958) in summer 2019. The still-life photographs, taken on an iPhone and then processed and published via Instagram, were part of a long-term project in which the fashion photographer cut roses from his

courtyard garden in Richmond, southwest London, and photographed them on a kitchen table using only natural daylight. Knight is a prolific image-maker and a vocal advocate of new technology. He produced his first book *Skinheads* while he was still a student in 1982 and went on to work for *iD*, *Vogue*, Alexander McQueen and John Galliano, and to create music videos for artists including Lady Gaga and Kanye West. In 2000, he founded the innovative digital fashion and film platform SHOWstudio. The images in his *Roses* series – which owe a debt to still-life paintings of the sixteenth and

seventeenth centuries and in some ways have evolved out of Knight's *Flora* series of the 1990s – are entirely rooted in their time. In order to print his original iPhone photographs at scale, Knight used new AI technology to sharpen the images, but the process also gives the pictures a texture and, in many cases, a painterly, ethereal quality that amplifies the tragic beauty of a cut flower.

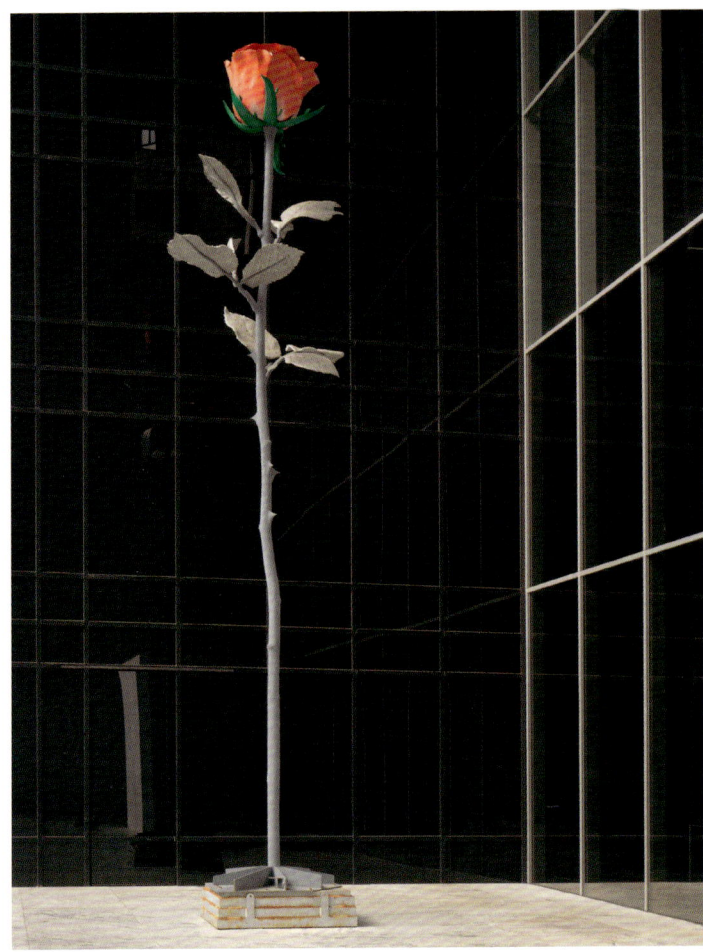

Isa Genzken

Rose II, 2007
Stainless steel, aluminium and lacquer,
10.9 × 2.9 × 1.1 m / 35 ft 9 in × 9 ft 6 in × 3 ft 7 in
Museum of Modern Art, New York

A single long-stemmed rose, with leaves, thorns and red lacquered petals sculpted from metal, soars upwards in front of a modern glass building façade. The creation of German artist Isa Genzken (born 1948), the towering sculpture has had varied iterations. It was first conceived in 1993 in Baden-Baden, a spa town in southern Germany renowned for an exceptionally broad and multicoloured rose garden and its annual international competition to find the best new variety of roses. When Genzken was commissioned to make a work by local collector Frieder Burda, she could not resist entering the contest on her own terms with an 8-metre (26-foot)-tall metallic rose. Although not site-specific, different versions of the piece have since appeared in different parts of the world, each time with a new significance. *Rose II* (2007) was created for the New Museum in New York City and is now permanently on display at the Museum of Modern Art's sculpture garden. Genzken also created *Rose III* (2016) in New York, this time as a gesture of affection for a city that always held a special place in her life. The sculpture found a permanent home in Zuccotti Park in lower Manhattan, ultimately elevating a flower normally thought of as an intimate gift to a city-wide collective tribute.

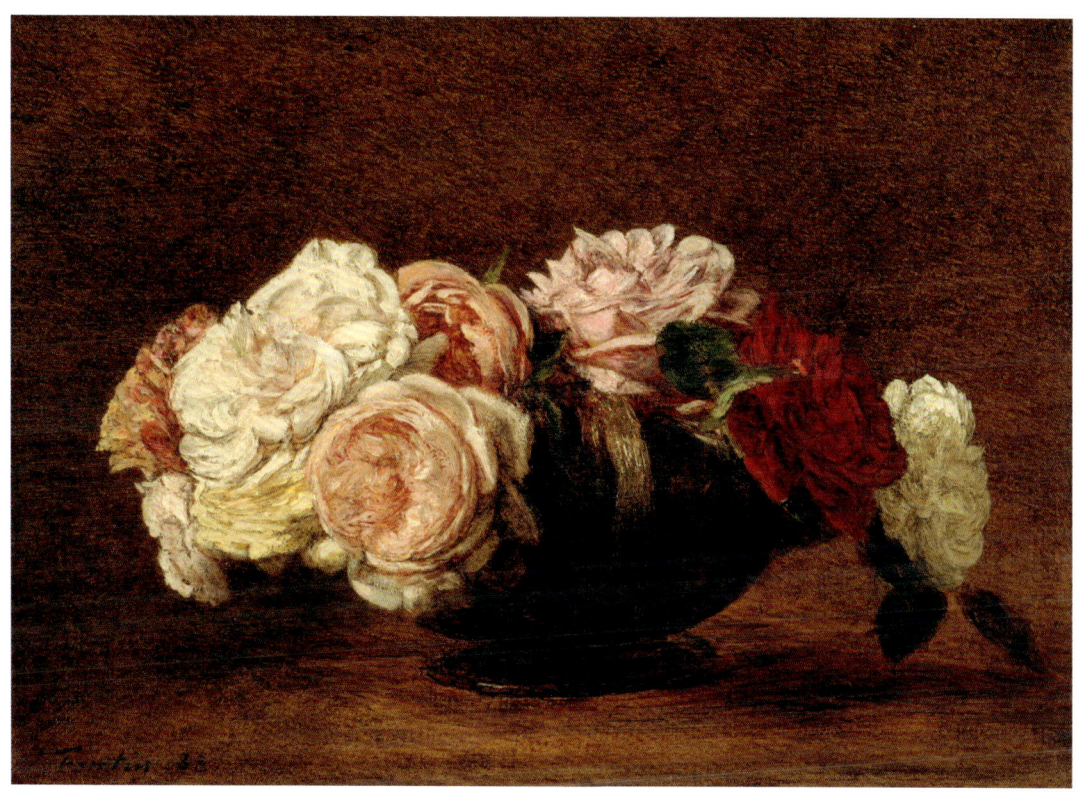

Henri Fantin-Latour

Roses in a Bowl, 1883
Oil on canvas, 29.8 × 41.6 cm / 11¾ × 16¼ in
Metropolitan Museum of Art, New York

The composition of this small painting of cut roses in a bowl, glowing with simplicity and freshness, might seem uncomplicated at first, but the fine details reveal a careful orchestration: a deeply crimson rose on the right steals the scene, surrounded by white, cream and light pink contenders. While roses in art have long been associated with love, this unembellished and intimate canvas by French artist Henri Fantin-Latour (1836–1904)

seems to deliberately bypass obvious symbolic meaning. The lighting and composition owe much to the style of Fantin-Latour's teacher and leader of the realist movement, Gustave Courbet, who rejected the opulence of classical still-life paintings and instead chose to represent the dignity of working-class life by depicting humble everyday objects. Fantin-Latour allows us to gaze unencumbered at the temporary serenity that rests on the petals of the roses, retaining an aura of honest realism through which he summons the genuine beauty of simple things. Despite being friends with Impressionist painters, Fantin-Latour chose not

to join the movement and focused on indoor flower painting instead. Unlike the Impressionist still lifes of Pierre-Auguste Renoir (see p.244) and Claude Monet (see p.169), his small paintings of flowers would prove particularly successful in England, where they were admired by, among others, James McNeill Whistler and John Everett Millais.

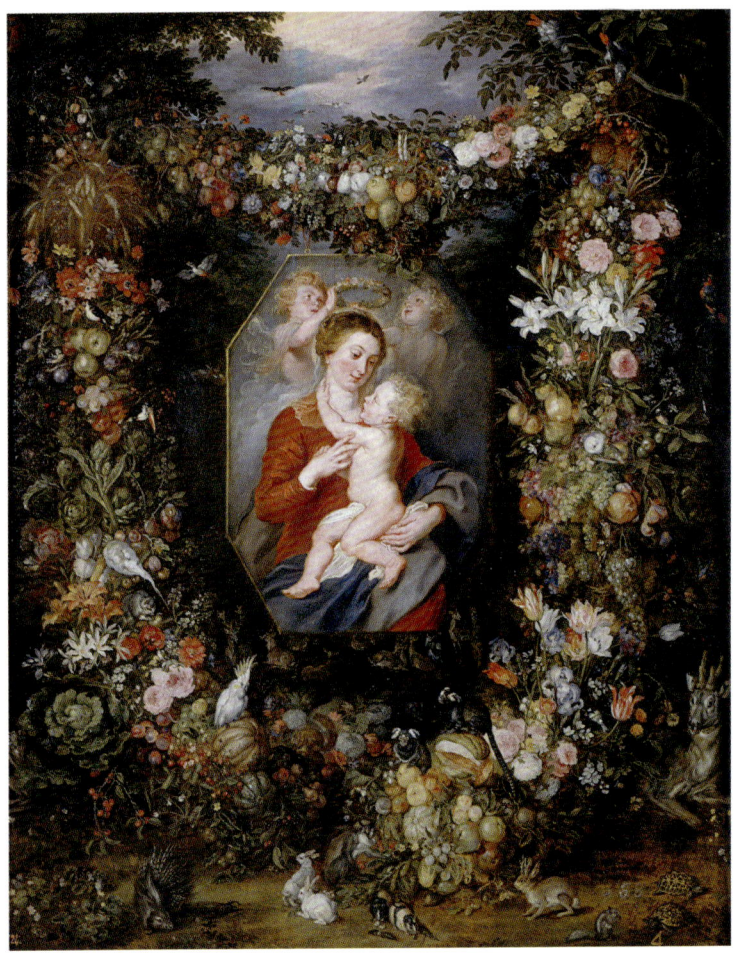

Peter Paul Rubens and Jan Brueghel the Elder

The Virgin and Child in a Flower Garland, 1617–20
Oil on panel, 79.7 × 63.7 cm / 31¼ × 25 in
Museo Nacional del Prado, Madrid

A bounteous garland of flowers and fruits forms a predominantly circular composition overflowing with pink roses, snowdrops and chrysanthemums, as well as grapes, plums and strawberries. White Madonna lilies, a symbol of purity following the Renaissance, bloom at the upper right. Animals rustle in the foliage, with rabbits, guinea pigs and even tortoises feasting on the bounty. Below the central image, a herd of deer rests peacefully on the grass, finding shelter behind the greenery. Within the central image, the Virgin Mary holds the baby Jesus, signified by the crown that is placed upon her head by flying cherubim. The painting is a collaboration of two masters – Jan Brueghel the Elder (1568–1625) (see p.268) and Peter Paul Rubens (1577–1640) – as a reaction against contemporary Protestant ideas that lavish images and decadent embellishment were improper in religious art or buildings of worship. Brueghel executed the garland, and is known for having produced numerous such panels of flowers surrounding holy figures, while Rubens painted the central panel. He used colour as a means of emphasizing movement and sensuality, here making Jesus's embrace of his mother's neck appear effortless. As close friends who often collaborated, Rubens and Brueghel were the most popular and prolific Flemish painters of the Baroque period and, as such, were dominant in the first three decades of the seventeenth century.

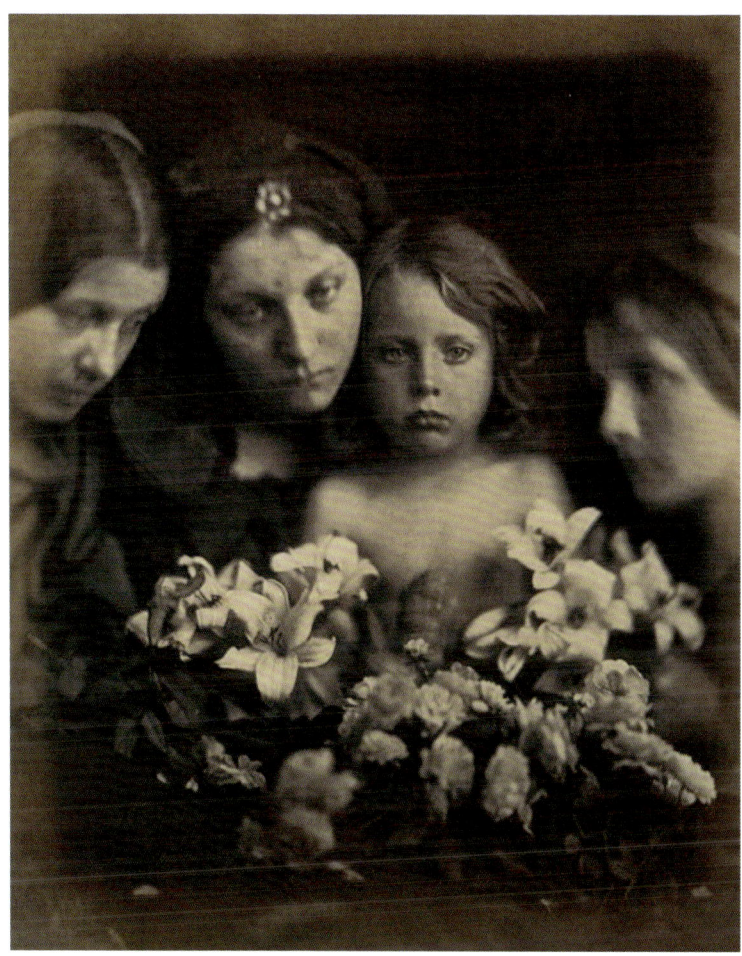

Julia Margaret Cameron

The Return After Three Days, 1865
Albumen print, 30.1 cm × 24.2 cm / 12 × 9½ in
National Science & Media Museum, Bradford, UK

This photograph – almost a floral still life of lilies and white roses – is unique in the oeuvre of British photographer Julia Margaret Cameron (1815-79), who is best known for her soft-focus portraits and tableaux. Cameron, who only took up photography at the age of forty-eight, was a devout Christian, and the work's title refers to the biblical story of the twelve-year-old Jesus's three days of disputation with religious teachers in the temple in Jerusalem, unbeknown to his searching parents. Cameron's tableaux were often not literal, but depended on the availability of friends, servants and children as models. This image conflates the story of Jesus in the temple with two further episodes from the life of Christ: the three women (Mary Kellaway, Mary Hillier and Mary Ryan) represent the three Marys who were present at his entombment and, later, were witnesses of his resurrection. The flowers, filling half the frame, suggest Christ's Passion. In Victorian floriography, the lily symbolized purity (the Easter lily is the symbol of the Virgin Mary), while white roses signified innocence, unity and love. The image has a very shallow field, with a relatively sharp focus on the foremost lilies and roses, in contrast to the soft focus of the surrounding elements. Of the figures, the face of the small boy (Freddy Gould) representing Jesus is central; his out-of-focus clasped hands are the result of inevitable movement over a long exposure time.

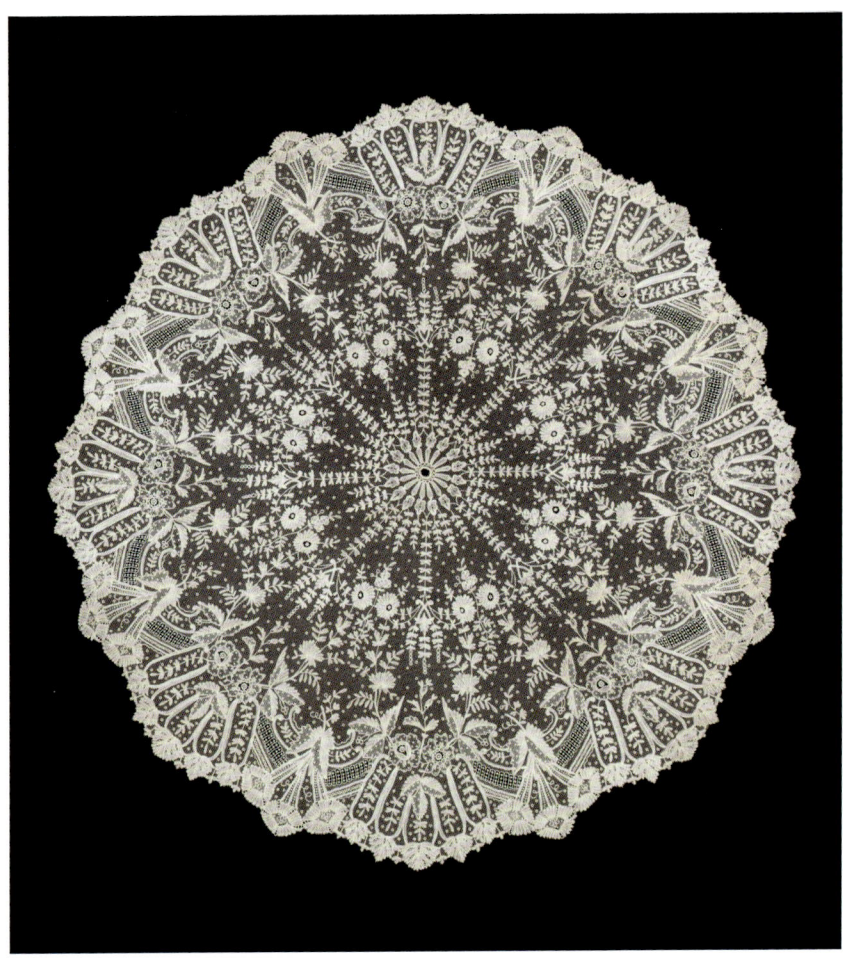

Anonymous

Parasol cover, 1880–89
Linen and silk, approx. diam. 65 cm / 25½ in
Metropolitan Museum of Art, New York

Like a delicate pressed flower, this gossamer-thin piece of lace woven by a master craftsperson in Belgium dazzles us with its symmetrical delicacy and refined detail. Although laid out flat here, this piece of material was originally laid over a sun parasol and therefore would have been viewed from the sides and in the round, rather than in two dimensions. Close up, the effect of the patterns of radiating flower heads, stems and leaves is stunning. In the middle of the parasol, the stems of a ring of chrysanthemum flowers arc back into the centre, dotted with leaves to create an almost stained-glass effect of rhythmic texture. The creator employs the full scope of the lace to dramatic effect, using different opacities to create depth and shape in the chrysanthemums; in the centre, the pistil is fully white but is held in place by six fine strands that create a negative space and make it pop out. The petals are thicker at the edges, giving them a three-dimensional form. It is fascinating to imagine an object like this in use, held by an elegant high-society lady, perhaps promenading by the seaside, the sun beating down as the lace creates an alluring mixture of dappled shade thrown across her figure.

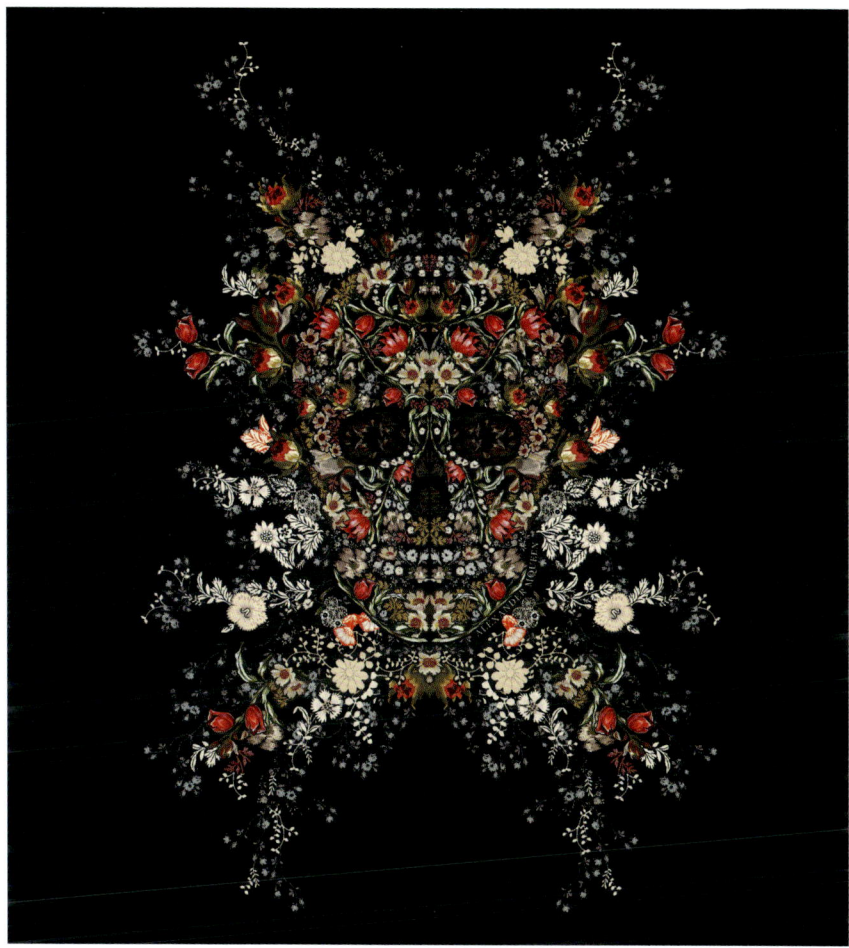

Alexander McQueen

Floral Skull, 2013
Textile print on cotton, dimensions variable

Life and death, darkness and light and the recesses of the mind were all themes that were channelled into the work of the London-based fashion designer Alexander McQueen (1969–2010). This stylized floral print is typical of his work, and the skull was a recurrent motif of McQueen's collections – used in prints, as jewellery or in accessories, and often appearing in portraits of the designer himself. Yet McQueen's predilection for the sinister and unsettling was always balanced by beauty; in this mirrored design, delicate spring blossoms including tulips, forget-me-nots, dianthus, astrantia and lily of the valley are repeated to form a graphic pattern around the skull – a modern *momento mori* printed onto an everyday garment. In a connection with the symbolism employed in seventeenth-century floral still lifes, McQueen was fascinated with the idea of flowers' fragility and fleeting beauty – in glorious bloom one day, wilting and dying the next. McQueen launched his own label in 1992. Four years later, at just twenty-seven years old, he was hired to head Parisian couture house Givenchy, and remained there until 2001. After his suicide in 2010, McQueen's work was the subject of *Savage Beauty*, a record-breaking fashion exhibition of 2011 at the Metropolitan Museum in New York. A 2019 exhibition in London, *Roses*, focused on garments inspired by the quintessential English bloom; summarizing one of the groundbreaking designer's inspirations, the byline read, 'the symbolism of flowers is rooted in the power of nature'.

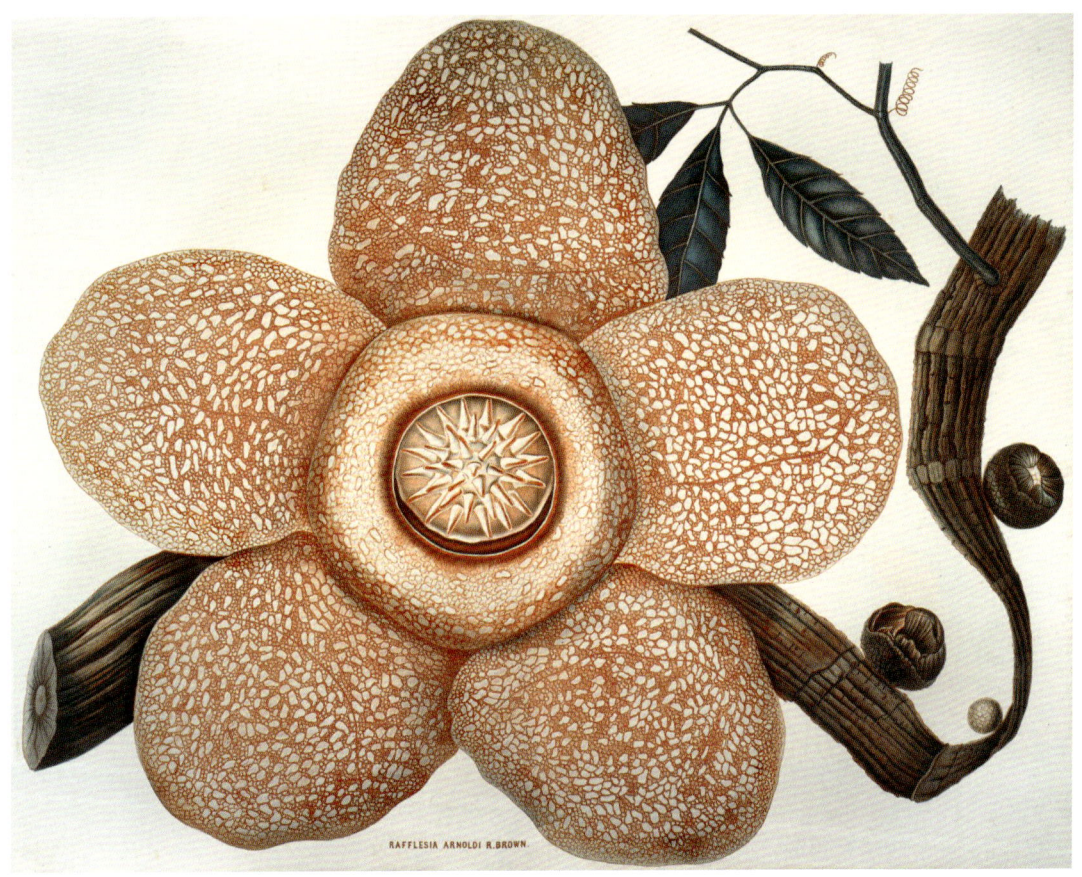

RAFFLESIA ARNOLDI R.BROWN.

Friedrich Anton Wilhelm Miquel

Rafflesia Arnoldi, from *Selection of Rare or Recently Discovered Plants Grown and Drawn in the Botanic Garden of Buitenzorg*, 1864
Lithograph, 54.5 × 74 cm / 21½ × 29 in
Missouri Botanical Garden, Peter H. Raven Library, St. Louis

This detailed depiction shows *Rafflesia arnoldi*, now commonly called the corpse lily, which is celebrated for producing the largest known individual flower in the world, up to 100 centimetres (39 inches) in diameter. A parasite, the plant has no roots or leaves and grows within the tissues of its host vine until the enormous flower bursts open, emitting a smell akin to that of rotting flesh which attracts the carrion flies that effect pollination and gives it its popular name. The plate's accompanying text quotes a Dr Arnold, who discovered the plant: 'To tell the truth, had I been alone, and had there been no witnesses, I should, I think, have been fearful of mentioning the dimensions of this flower, so much does it exceed every flower I have ever seen or heard of....' Dutch botanist Friedrich Anton Wilhelm Miquel (1811–71), under whose name this plate was published, was a professor at the University of Utrecht best known for his studies of the flora of the Dutch East Indies. This is the first plate in the 1864 book *Selection of Rare or Recently Discovered Plants Grown and Drawn in the Botanic Garden of Buitenzorg*. Buitenzorg was the Dutch name for what is now the city of Bogor in West Java, Indonesia, and which was the summer residence of the governor-general of the Dutch East Indies. Bogor Botanic Gardens, the first botanical garden in Indonesia, is now a renowned centre of research and conservation.

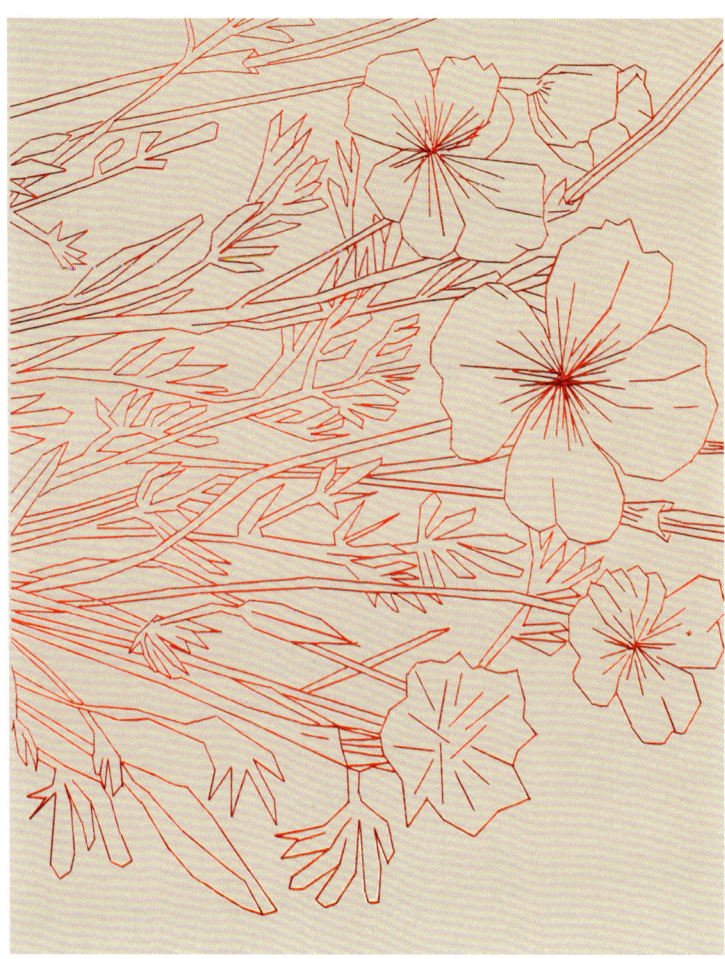

Franko B

View from the Ground from a Corpse, 2015
Cotton on unprimed canvas, 1.8 × 1.4 m /
5 ft 11 in × 4 ft 7 in
Private collection

The tangle of flowers stitched in blood-red cotton on a plain canvas are poppies, which is key to the disorienting perspective in which the stems protrude from the left edge of the work. As the title of this piece by Italian artist Franko B (born 1960) suggests, the perspective is that of a soldier who has fallen in battle amid a field of wild poppies – the flowers adopted to commemorate the victims of World War I (1914–18) on Remembrance Day, first enacted in commonwealth nations in 1919, inspired by the poppies that grew in abundance on the Western Front. The work was inspired by a song by the Italian *chansonnier* Fabrizio De André that became a popular anti-militarist anthem in the late 1960s, *La Guerra di Piero*, a protest against the sacrifice of human lives in war. The stitches on the canvas echo those of a sutured wound, while the red and white colours both represent the Red Cross (Franko B was raised in an orphanage run by the humanitarian organization) and recall the artist's early performative work, when he would shed blood on white-painted canvases. In the late 1970s, Franko B left Milan for London, where he expressed his objection to the military conscription that was still mandatory in Italy by making a collage that featured, among other things, a group of poppies – the theme he would return to almost thirty years later with *View from the Ground from a Corpse*.

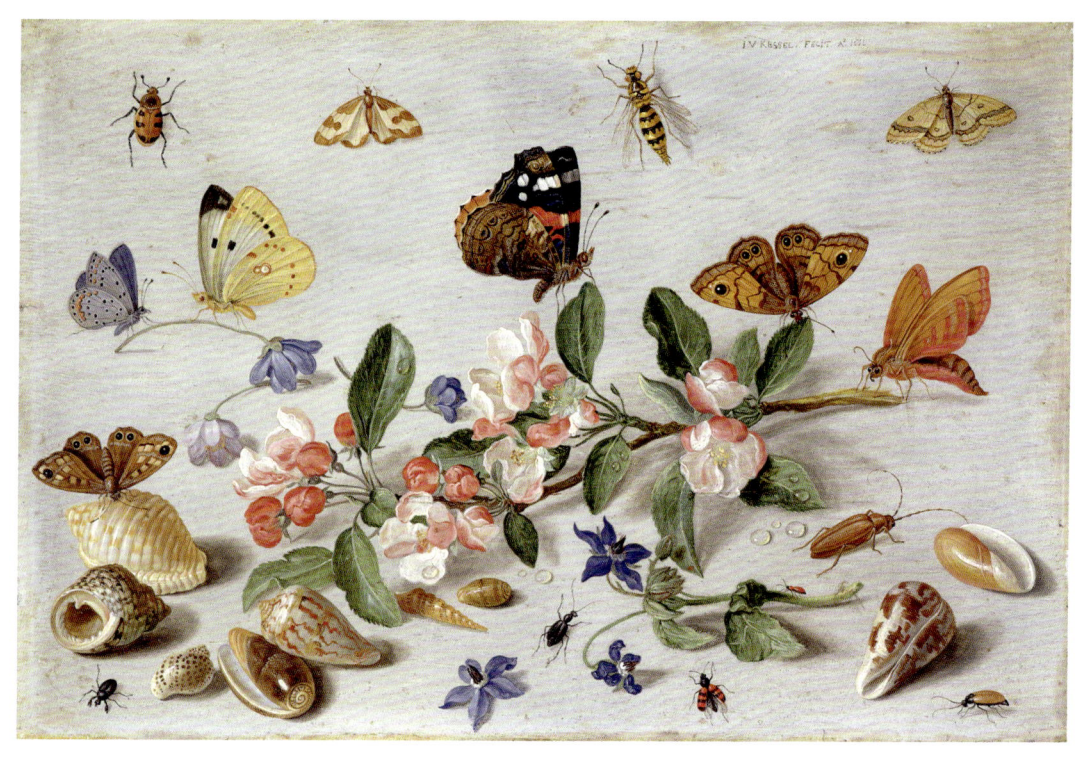

Jan van Kessel the Elder

Butterflies and Other Insects, 1661
Oil on copper, 19.3 × 29 cm / 7½ × 11¼ in
Fitzwilliam Museum, Cambridge, UK

Above a delicate sprig of apple blossom, scattered wildflowers, shells and butterflies, four insects along the top of this image look as though they have been plucked from life and pinned against a sheet of paper as entomological specimens. Perhaps it should not come as a surprise to learn that Flemish artist Jan van Kessel the Elder (1626–79) may have painted this miniature study as part of a series to adorn the facade of a *Kunstkast*,

or cabinet of art, in which a wealthy aristocrat of Antwerp might have housed his collection of exotic natural curiosities. Van Kessel, the grandson of Jan Brueghel the Elder (see p. 268), was a flower and still-life painter best known for miniature jewel-like studies of acutely observed and rendered flowers, insects and shells. Van Kessel was a master of the guild in Antwerp, and became renowned for his paintings in oil on copper – he produced upwards of 300 such panels in the 1650s and 1660s. The smooth hard metal allowed him to achieve remarkable depths of detail: droplets of water fall from the freshly picked apple blossom

and even the tear is visible at the end of the sprig, where it has been ripped from the tree; a minuscule red beetle tightrope-walks its way up a borage stalk, while two butterflies twitch their antennae towards each other as they balance on the delicate arched stem of a hepatica flower.

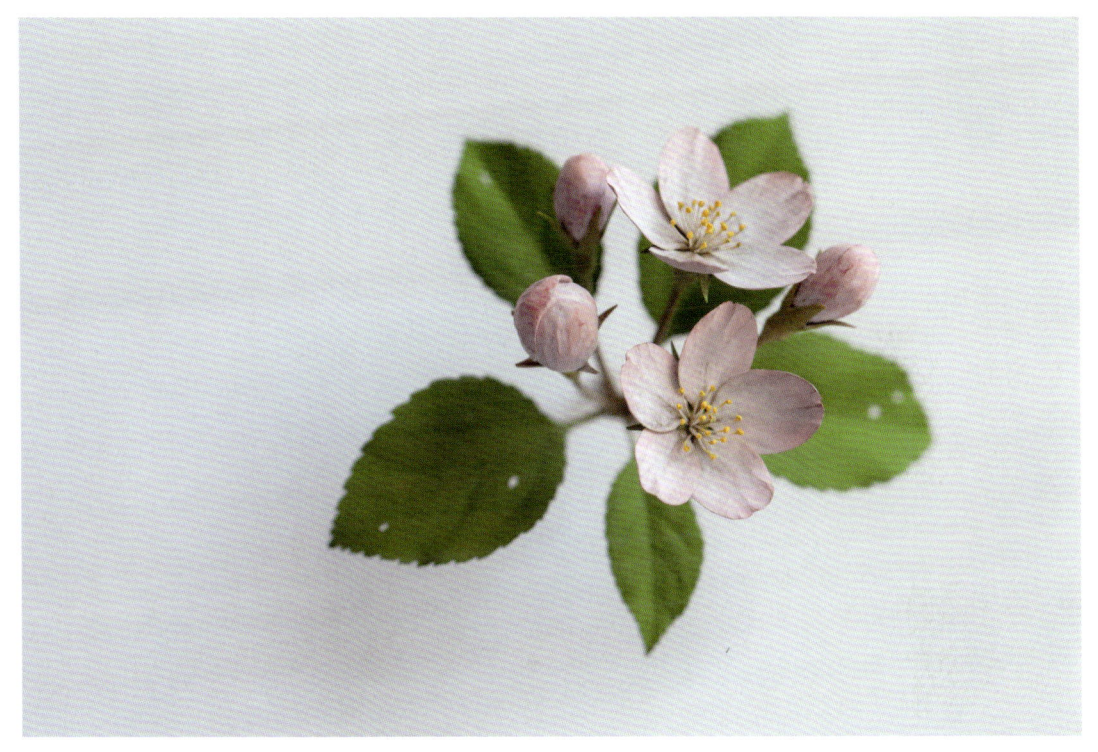

Yoshihiro Suda

Apple, 2015
Painted wood, dimensions variable
Private collection

Two flowers of a blossoming apple shoot open to reveal clusters of stamens with their bright yellow anthers, surrounded by three unopened buds, above a circle of five green leaves. So lifelike is the structure and so delicately painted that it is difficult to believe that it is carved from wood. The detail is remarkable, with each petal subtly shaded and shaped to mimic the living flower, and the leaves even bearing naturalistic imperfections.

This is the work of Yoshihiro Suda (born 1969), a Japanese master craftsman able to produce a work of art clearly based on close observation and study of the original flower. Unlike a painting, a carved flower resembles its natural subject more closely, and it simultaneously invites the viewer to pay close attention from different angles. Born in Yamanashi prefecture, Suda graduated from Tama Art University in Tokyo where he still lives and works. Suda fashions his works of art from magnolia wood, which he finds soft and easy to carve. It was after he moved to the city that he began to be interested in flowers, visiting florist

shops as well as noticing weeds struggling to survive along the sides of the streets. Part of his motivation is to foster attention and contemplation, especially as new devices and technology increasingly encourage a fast pace of life.

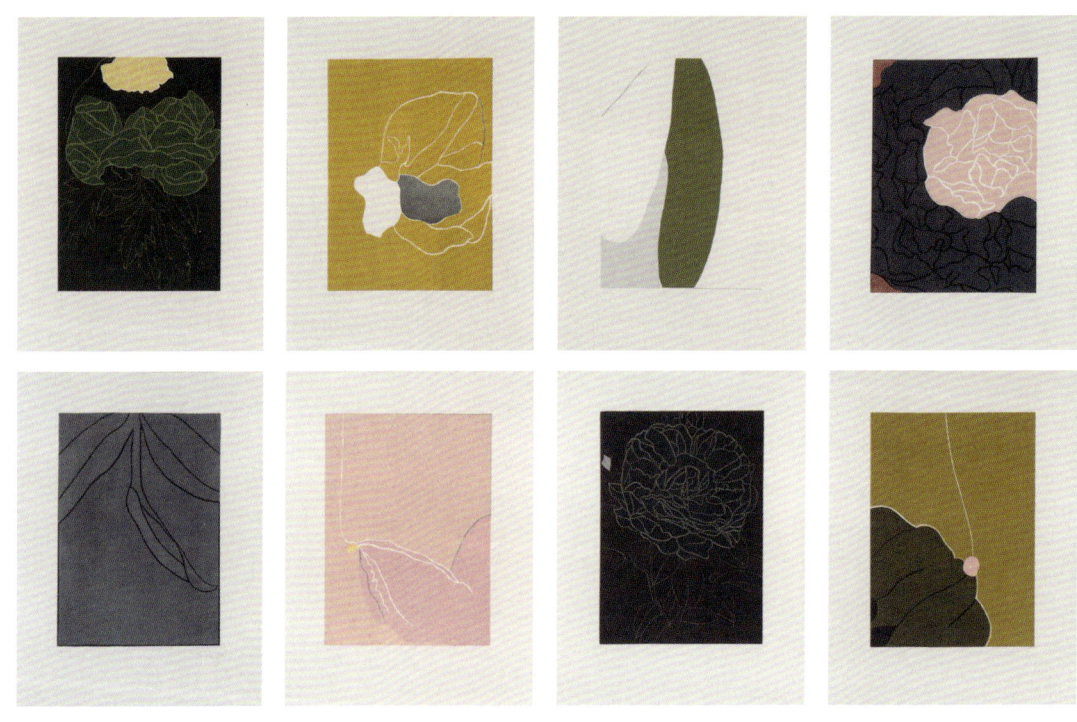

Gary Hume

Here's Flowers, 2006
Colour linocut prints, each 55.5 × 40 cm /
21¾ × 15¾ in
Private collection

Close-up details of flowers – forms that might have begun with petals, leaves, stems or seed pods – are simplified almost beyond recognition. Some take on an anthropomorphic quality, while others teeter into pure abstraction. Flowers have long been a central motif for British painter Gary Hume (born 1962) and are evidence of a deep connection to the natural world that informs his overall approach to image-making. Hume graduated from London's Goldsmith's College in 1988 and is considered one of the YBAs – a group of young British artists who came to redefine contemporary British art in the 1980s and 1990s. Unlike his colleagues, who were often known for their unorthodox techniques and bombastic personalities, Hume has exercised a quieter, more contemplative approach. His work is often characterized by large canvases of elegantly distilled forms painted in high-gloss industrial paints. In *Here's Flowers*, the medium is not paint but linocut, a printing technique in which an artist cuts lines into blocks of linoleum that are then printed on paper. This group of eight images were the first linocuts Hume made, and the artist adeptly used the medium to achieve his trademark combination of sensual lines and flat colours. The work's title is a quote from Shakespeare's *The Winter's Tale* and implies a gesture of giving – as if this is a bouquet we are being offered in gratitude or celebration.

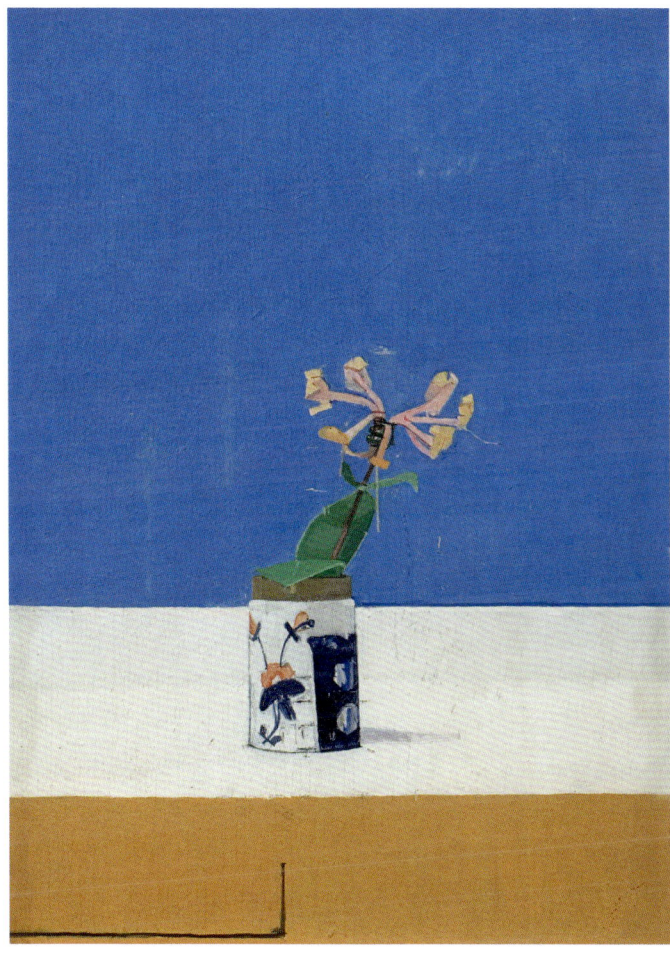

Euan Uglow

Still Life with Honeysuckle, 1968
Oil on panel, 37.4 × 26.9 cm / 14¾ × 10¾ in
Private collection

Against an electric blue wall in the artist's studio stands a single honeysuckle stem in a jar. Flowering from June to September, the honeysuckle calls to mind the height of summer, as reflected in the painting's vibrant colour palette. While the title implies a simple study from life, the composition is in fact a complex pictorial game in which British artist Euan Uglow (1932–2000) explores the challenges of representing the three-dimensional world in paint. Uglow provides few clues regarding depth, creating an indiscernible sense of space in the painting. The flower's pink and yellow petals seem to exist on the same plane as the blue wall behind, and like a printed pattern, their form is echoed by the motif on the container below. A single shadow on the white tabletop helps to make sense of the scene, as does the top of the jar, which disturbs the horizontal band of blue where the wall and table meet. This painting is a prime example of Uglow's fascination with modernist flatness, as well as his concern for creating a harmonious balance of colours.

Working directly from life, he adopted a slow and meticulous approach that involved taking many detailed measurements. Although best known for his carefully composed nudes, Uglow always maintained that such subject matter was merely a means to investigate the nature of painting itself.

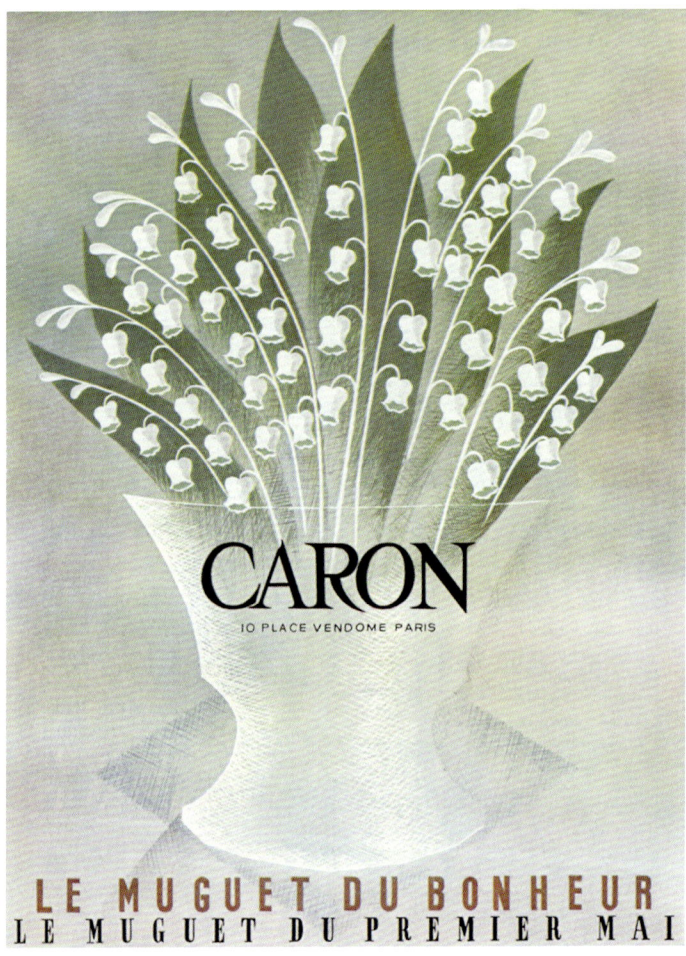

Caron

Le Muguet du Bonheur, 1958
Colour lithograph, 23.2 × 17.8 cm / 9 × 7 in
Private collection

A sprig of delicate lily of the valley flowers is gracefully arranged in a large glass vase, where the white, bell-shaped heads are contrasted by a fan of tapering green leaves. The vase is emblazoned with the logo of the legendary French perfume house Caron, whose scent Le Muguet du Bonheur is the subject of this stylish 1958 magazine advertisement. The feminine fragrance was created by Caron's celebrated perfumer Michel Morsetti

to celebrate the French custom of presenting bouquets of lily of the valley on May Day as tokens of good luck, friendship and appreciation. According to legend, the tradition of *Fête du Muguet* (Lily of the Valley Day) began in the mid-1500s when King Charles IX of France began distributing the spring flowers to the ladies of his court every first of May. With notes of lily of the valley, lilac, jasmine, magnolia, pear, heliotrope and musk, Morsetti's classic scent evokes the freshness and vitality of spring, though it can comfortably be worn all year round (one advertisement shows bottles of the perfume decorating a Christmas tree).

Caron has continued to produce Le Muguet du Bonheur for nearly three-quarters of a century and the fragrance remains popular today. The result of a successful partnership between perfumer Ernest Daltroff and artistic adviser Félicie Wampouille, Caron was founded in 1904 and is thought to be the second oldest perfume house in Paris.

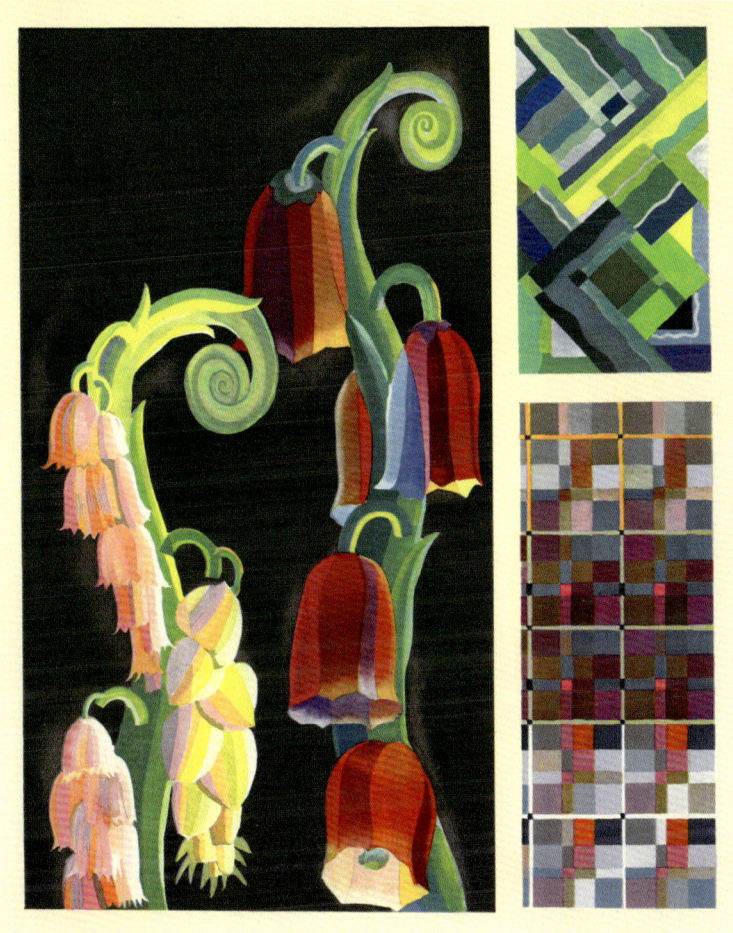

Édouard Bénédictus

Plate 3, from *Nouvelles Variations*, 1928–29
Stencil on wove paper, 46.8 × 26.5 cm /
14½ × 11⅜ in

These richly coloured, stylized flower forms, possibly loosely based on bellflowers (*Campanula*), coloured with bold stripes of red, pink, yellow, green and blue, take inspiration not only from nature but also from the avant-garde movement sweeping through European art and design in the early twentieth century. Created by French painter Édouard Bénédictus (1878–1930), the illustration belongs to his popular 1928 portfolio

Nouvelles Variations, which contained seventy-five colourful motifs across twenty loose sheets, intended to provide inspiration for professional designers of wallpapers, woven and printed textiles and upholstery. Floral and foliate motifs predominate, reflecting Bénédictus's association with Art Nouveau, a movement that drew much inspiration from nature, especially the sinuous curves and asymmetrical forms of plants and flowers. While Bénédictus's designs find inspiration in real flowers, his stems, leaves and petals are not botanically accurate and many are embellished or abstracted; several feature wholly abstract

patterns, reflecting the artist's interest in the visual languages of Cubism and Constructivism. Each plate in the portfolio was coloured by Jean Saudé, a French printmaker and master of *pochoir*, a highly refined stencilling technique renowned for achieving intense colours. Saudé's vivid and often synthetic colour choices are occasionally augmented with gold or silver highlights.

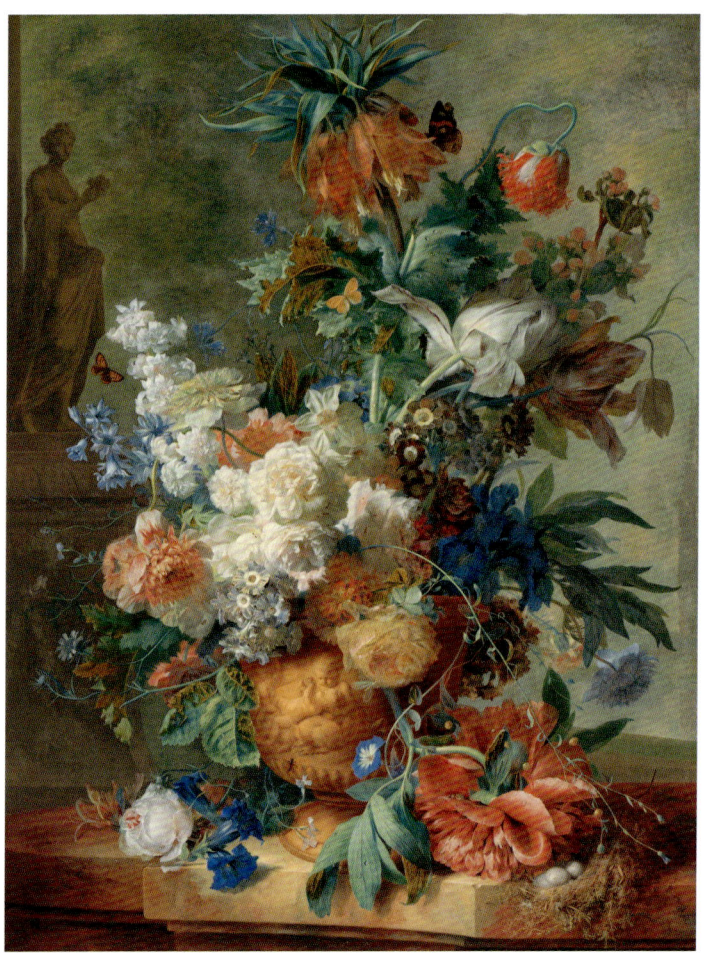

Jan van Huysum

Still Life with Flowers, 1723
Oil on panel, 81 × 61 cm / 32 × 24 in
Rijksmuseum, Amsterdam

The exuberant flower composition by Dutch painter Jan Van Huysum (1682–1749) is as impossible as it is beautiful. In the eighteenth century, cut flowers were a prerogative of the wealthy. Gathering these many varieties at once would have been not merely economically prohibitive, but unattainable at any cost, given that the flowers bloom at different times of the year. Van Huysum drew rare flowers from horticultural centres around Europe and adapted other rare species from botanical illustrations to put together a collage of flowers seamlessly united in their best possible form. Often Van Huysum's hyperrealist representation of leaves and petals is offset by bright backgrounds illuminating the scene. Unlike his predecessors, whose compositions were set indoors and shrouded in darkness, Van Huysum places his vase on the balustrade of a balcony, watched over from a distance by a statue of Flora, the classical goddess of flowering plants. Closer inspection reveals that the still beauty of the flower arrangement is counterpointed by a host of tiny insects. In classical Greek art, the delicate wings of butterflies symbolized the human soul, while the ants crawling across the plush, pink rose petals might refer to the importance of labour in life or to death itself, as the creatures are often seen carrying dead insects to their nests. These entomological accents complement the painting's overall concern with the passing of time and the transience of beauty, which the cut flowers embody so well.

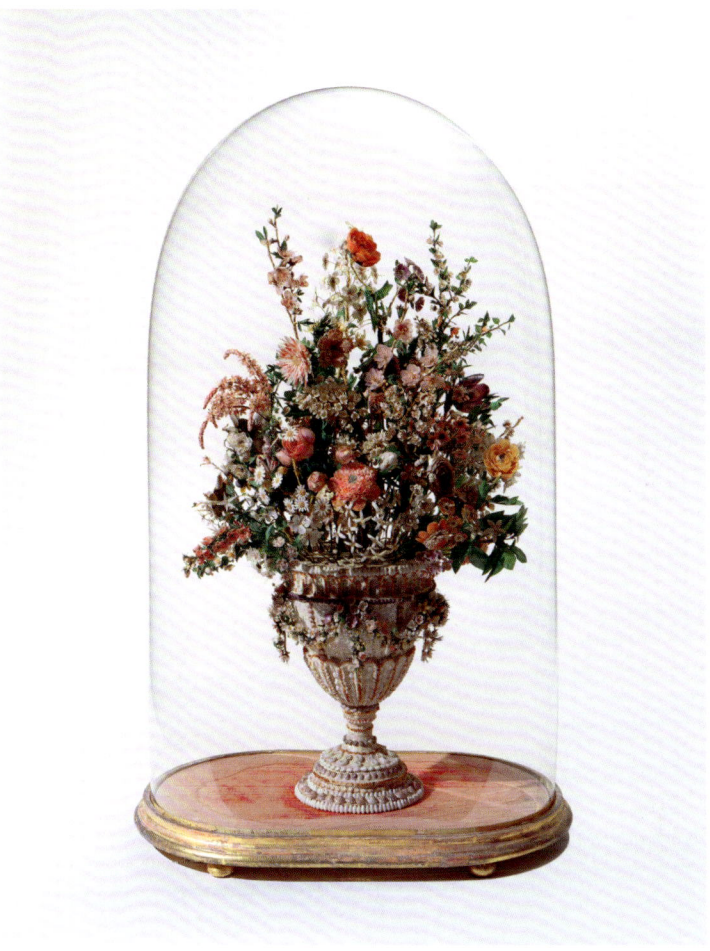

Mrs Beal Bonnell and Miss Harvey Bonnell

Shellwork vase of flowers, 1779–81
Shellwork with glass dome, 89 × 54 × 36 cm /
35 × 21¼ × 14¼ in
Victoria and Albert Museum, London

This gorgeous composition of mostly wildflowers can never wilt. Its colours and textures are as breathtaking as its vivid splendour, despite being more than 200 years old. Safe under a glass dome since the end of the eighteenth century, these flowers have been preserved neither by a magic spell nor by some kind of 'botanical taxidermy'. Close inspection reveals that, what

at first look like velvet petals, pistils and stamens, are actually created from countless miniature shells sourced from all over the world. Despite their utterly convincing naturalness, these flowers were individually crafted by securing shells with wires and supported by metal stems, with leaves made of paper to heighten and offset the naturalism of the flowers. The work of Mrs Beal Bonnell and her niece, Miss Harvey Bonnell, this vase is one of a pair. Its companion is said to have been presented to Queen Adelaide at the Bonnell home, Pelling Place, in Berkshire, England, but has since been lost. The flower

arrangement comprises more than 300 blooms, including lilacs, anemones, daisies and roses, along with many differently shaped varieties of foliage housed in an all-over shell-encrusted design enfolding the whole vase. This composition is one of the most impressive examples of naturalism in what is called 'shellwork', a form of craft that took European high-society circles by storm during the seventeenth and eighteenth centuries.

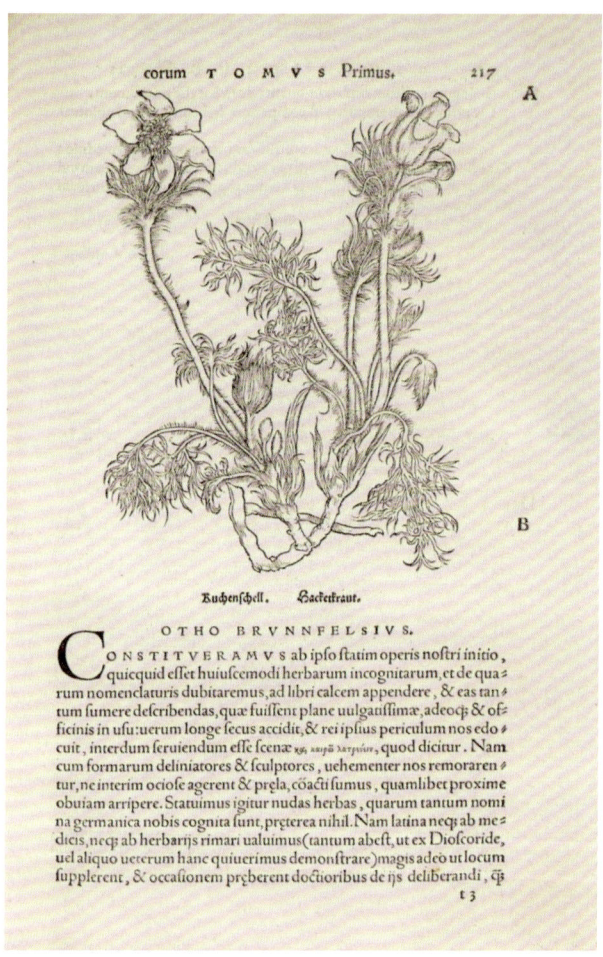

Buchenschell.   Backetkraut.

OTHO BRVNNFELSIVS.

CONSTITVERAMVS ab ipso statim operis nostri initio, quicquid esset huiuscemodi herbarum incognitarum, et de quarum nomenclaturis dubitaremus, ad libri calcem appendere, & eas tantum sumere describendas, quæ fuissent plane uulgatissimæ, adeocȷ & officinis in usu: uerum longe secus accidit, & rei ipsius periculum nos edo✣cuit, interdum seruiendum esse scenæ ϗϛ, καιρῶ λατρύσιν, quod dicitur. Nam cum formarum deliniatores & sculptores, uehementer nos remorarentur, ne interim ociose agerent & prela, cȏacti sumus, quamlibet proxime obuiam arripere. Statuimus igitur nudas herbas, quarum tantum nomina germanica nobis cognita sunt, præterea nihil. Nam latina neqȷ ab medicis, neqȷ ab herbarȷjs rimari ualuimus (tantum abest, ut ex Dioscoride, uel aliquo ueterum hanc quiuerimus demonstrare) magis adeo ut locum supplerent, & occasionem præberent doctioribus de ijs deliberandi, ȼȷ

t 3

Otto Brunfels and Hans Weiditz

Pasqueflower, from *Herbarum vivae eicones*, 1532
Woodcut, 31.2 × 21.4 cm / 12¼ × 8½ in
University of Padua Library, Italy

The pasqueflower (*Pulsatilla vulgaris*) is native to the Alps, but as a common alpine flower without curative properties, it had not featured in traditional pharmacological works before the *Herbarum vivae eicones* – literally 'living plant images' – a revolutionary work created by Otto Brunfels (*c.*1488–1534), one of the three 'fathers' of German botany, and German printmaker Hans Weiditz (before 1500–*c.*1536). Published

in three parts between 1530 and 1536, the work's primary goal was simply to document and illustrate plants observed directly from nature. Thanks to the great talent of Weiditz, a student of Albrecht Dürer (see p.295), the book marked the first time true portraits of plants were printed. Brunfels was a theologian and philosopher who studied plants in his spare time, as reflected in his accessible text, which gives simple descriptions of the plants and includes the common German names. Brunfels and Weiditz notably included a number of wildflowers, as here, that were excluded from medical

treatises of the sixteenth century as they did not have any medicinal uses. By depicting flowers in their entirety and showing development through different seasons, Weiditz made it possible to identify individual species, departing from the long tradition of representing plants in a schematic manner. With its masterly woodcuts, its concise and orderly exposition, and its readable roman type, the *Herbarum* set a new standard for the presentation of botanical books from that point on.

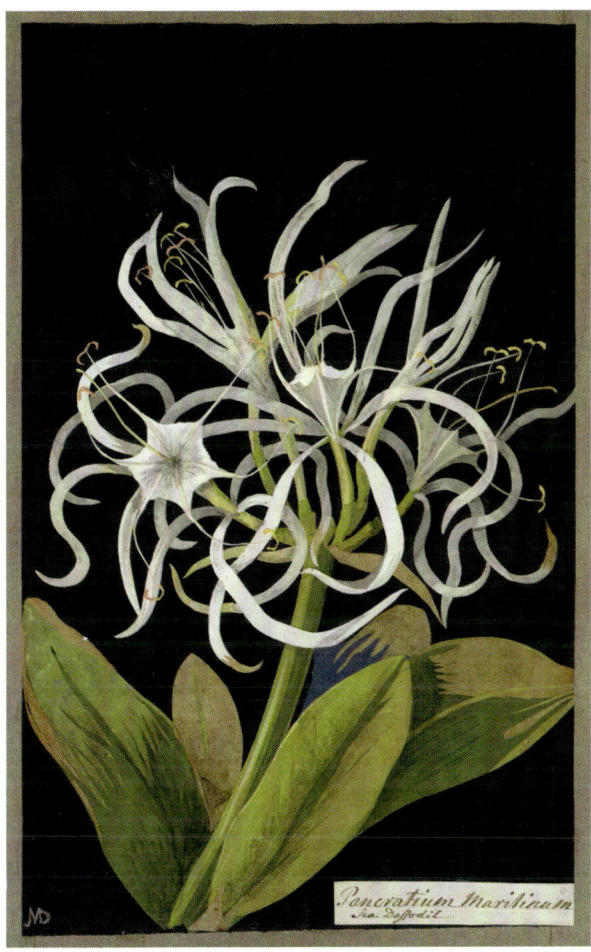

Mary Delany

Pancratium maritimum (Hexandria monogynia),
Sea Daffodil, 1778
Coloured paper, body colour and watercolour on
black ink background, 35 × 22.2 cm / 13¾ × 8¾ in
British Museum, London

The grace and detail of the slender stamen and
shaded white petals of this flower showcase an
intricate blend of art and science. British artist
Mary Delany (1700–88) called her unique method
'paper mosaics', produced by cutting out tiny
pieces of hand-coloured tissue paper in the shape
of petals, stamens and leaves, and then assembling

them against a dramatic black background. A lifelong artist, Delany came to this technique in her
seventies – she went on to produce nearly a thousand paper mosaics before her eyesight faded at the
age of eighty-three. Her skill won many frienships,
including that of Queen Charlotte, and unusual
and rare plants were brought to her for their
portraits. As a keen plantswoman, she had joined
the Duchess of Portsmouth's 'Hive' of scientific
patronage at Bulstrode, meeting luminaries
such as Joseph Banks and Georg Ehret (see p.20),
and learned to dissect flowers and examine
them through a microscope. Delany's scientific

interests are evident in her recording both the
Latin and common name for each flower, but also
the Linnaean classification (see p.208) and the
source of each plant. Delaney created her collages
of plants from all over the world. Although identified as the Mediterranean sea daffodil (*Pancratium
maritimum*), the flower seen here is in fact a close
relative from Jamaica, the spider lily (*Hymenocallis
fragrans*) – an understandable error, as the genus
and species were not named until 1812.

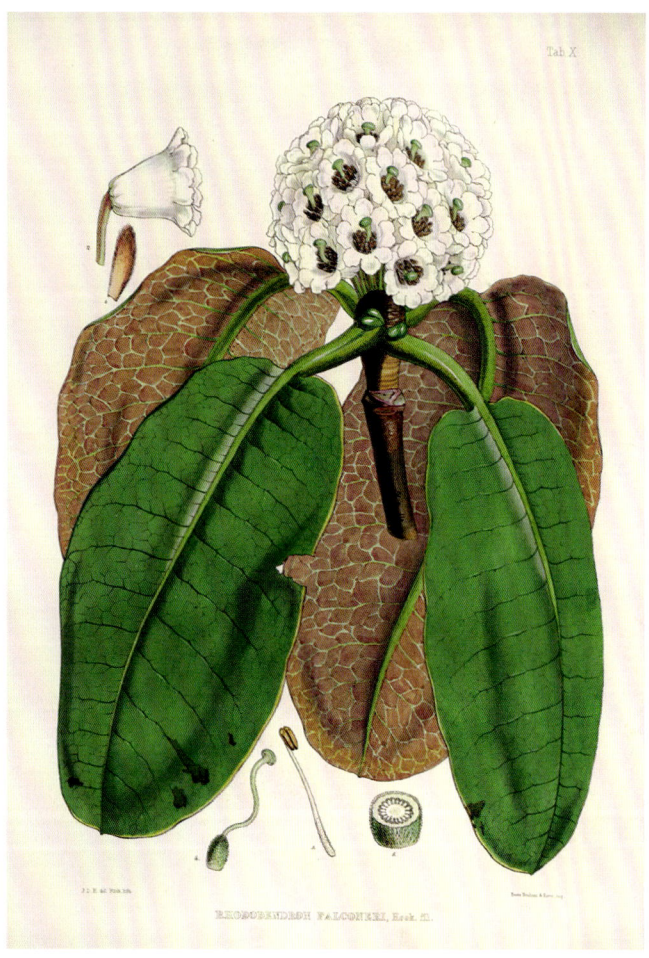

Tab. X

RHODODENDRON FALCONERI, Hook. fil.

Joseph Dalton Hooker and Walter Hood Fitch

Rhododendron falconeri, from *The Rhododendrons of Sikkim-Himalaya*, 1849
Hand-coloured lithograph, 50.1 × 36.8 cm / 19¾ × 14½ in
Missouri Botanical Garden, St. Louis

This depiction of a rhododendron, complete with details of petals and stamen, was among a series that helped inspire a craze for the plants, especially for the gardens of stately homes, and that ultimately stimulated an entirely new approach to horticulture – the wild garden. *Rhododendron falconeri* was first recorded after

Sir William Jackson Hooker, director of Kew Gardens in London, sent his son on a plant-collecting expedition to the Himalayas in 1847. Hooker was not disappointed. Joseph Dalton Hooker (1817–1911) endured monsoon rains, leeches, floods, snow blindness, frostbite and altitude sickness. He managed, however, to collect around 7,000 species of plants – including more than twenty-five new species of rhododendron unknown to European botanists and horticulturalists – and sent back seeds and plants to London in tin boxes. These shipments were accompanied by more than 700 drawings,

sketches and watercolours. Hooker's drawings and the notes that accompanied them were of such quality that they became the basis of the three volumes of *Rhododendrons of Sikkim-Himalaya*, edited by his father, with thirty lithographs by the outstanding botanical illustrator Walter Hood Fitch (see p.222). The work, which was published while Joseph Hooker was still in India, describes *Rhododendron falconeri* as 'if not the most showy ... certainly one of the most striking and distinct of the genus', with foliage similar to that of *Magnolia grandiflora*.

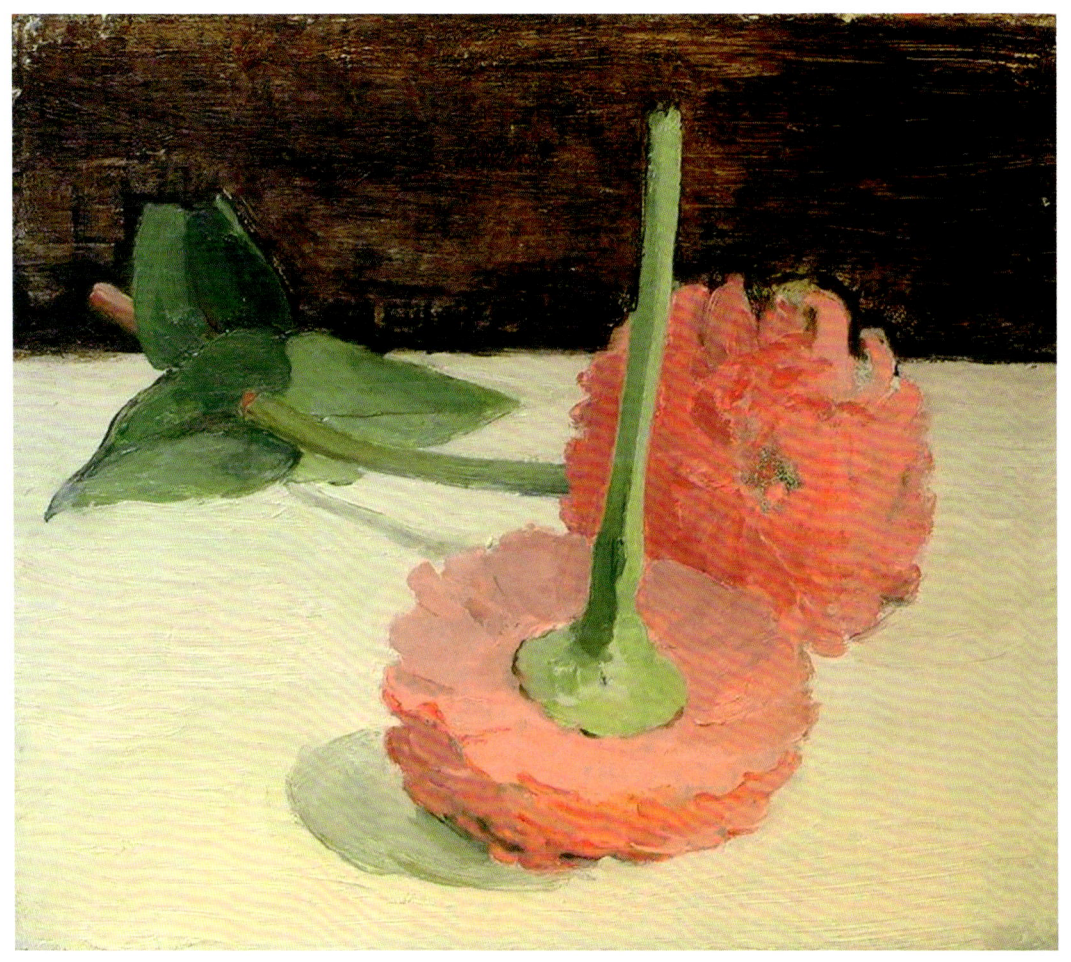

Albert York

Two Zinnias, c.1965
Oil on canvas mounted on wood, 23 × 27 cm /
9½ × 10½ in
Private collection

Two pink zinnias rest on a cream surface,
their contrasting green stems cut short, one stick-
ing straight up as the flower rests on its head like
a spinning top. When looking at the work
of American painter Albert York (1928–2009), one
feels the urge to whisper. His tiny paintings,
most no more than 30.5 centimetres (12 inches)
long, of landscapes, cows, figures and flowers,

are an intimate window into a quieter way
of looking at the beauty of the everyday world.
York shared this modest view through his
skilled painterly strokes on tiny wood boards
often produced in the early morning. His floral
studies seem to be his most vibrant and yet are
spare in their details, much like the style
of nineteenth-century Italian painter Giorgio
Morandi. York was also inspired by Édouard
Manet and Paul Cézanne, but his biggest influence was American painter Albert Pinkham
Ryder. After studying at Toronto's Ontario
College of Art and serving in the Korean War,

York moved to New York in 1952. He studied
briefly at the Art Students League, before finding
a job as a gilder with artist and framer Robert
Kulicke. A supportive friend and promoter of his
work, Kulicke introduced York to the Davis &
Langdale gallery in 1963, which represented him
until his death. York, not one for city life, left
Manhattan for the east end of Long Island with
his wife and stepchildren, sending paintings
to his gallery wrapped in brown paper, some still
wet on arrival.

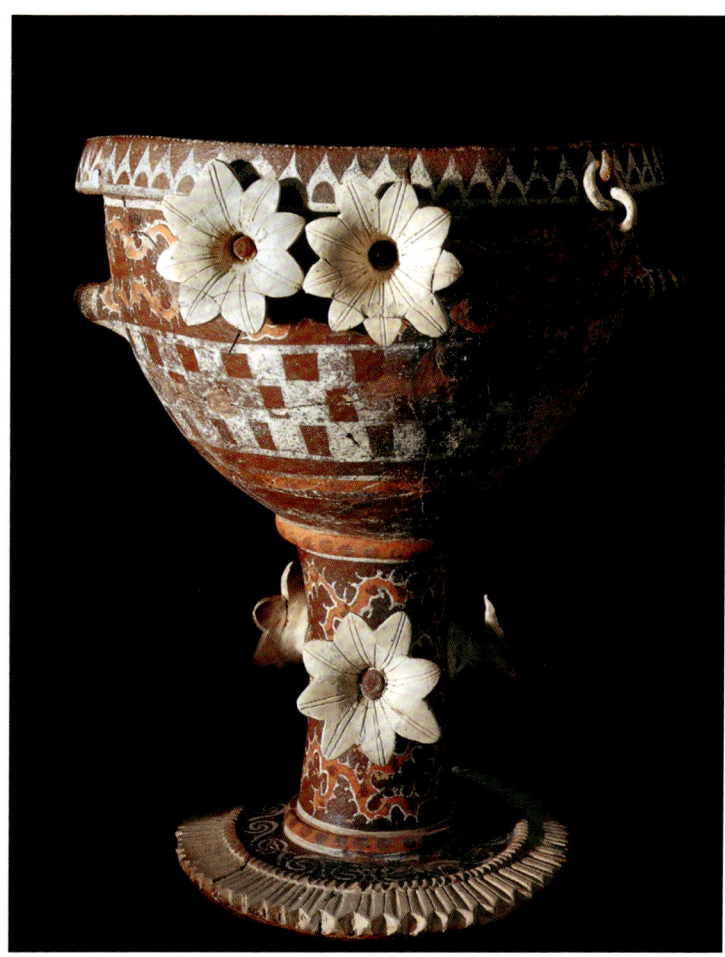

Anonymous

Kamares ware krater with moulded flowers,
*c.*1700 BC
Clay, H. 45.5 cm / 18 in
Heraklion Archaeological Museum, Crete

This highly adorned Minoan *krater*, sometimes referred to as a fruit stand, was excavated from the so-called Old Palace at Phaistos, an archaeological site in southern Crete. Kamares ware was an elite pottery, found only in or near Bronze Age palaces, and its style was highly sophisticated: abstract floral motifs, geometric patterns and marine motifs in complex schemes of

interlocking torsional curves that draw the eye around the body of the vase. Designs were typically executed in white, red and blue on a dark ground. This unique vessel was wheel-thrown in sections, and the flowers appear to have been created in a mould before being applied to the bowl and stem, leading to suggestions that the vase may imitate a type of metal vessel; this is also indicated by the clay links of a chain at the rim. The applied white flowers probably represent lilies (*Lilium candidum*), which appear in various colours in Minoan wall paintings at Knossos later in the second millennium BC. The flower was

especially popular among the inhabitants of Akrotiri on Thera (modern Santorini), where it occurs in wall paintings dating to 1700–1600 BC. The lily may have had some sort of religious significance for the Minoans, but even if this is not the case, the archaeological evidence makes it clear that Bronze Age Greeks had a deep appreciation for the natural world.

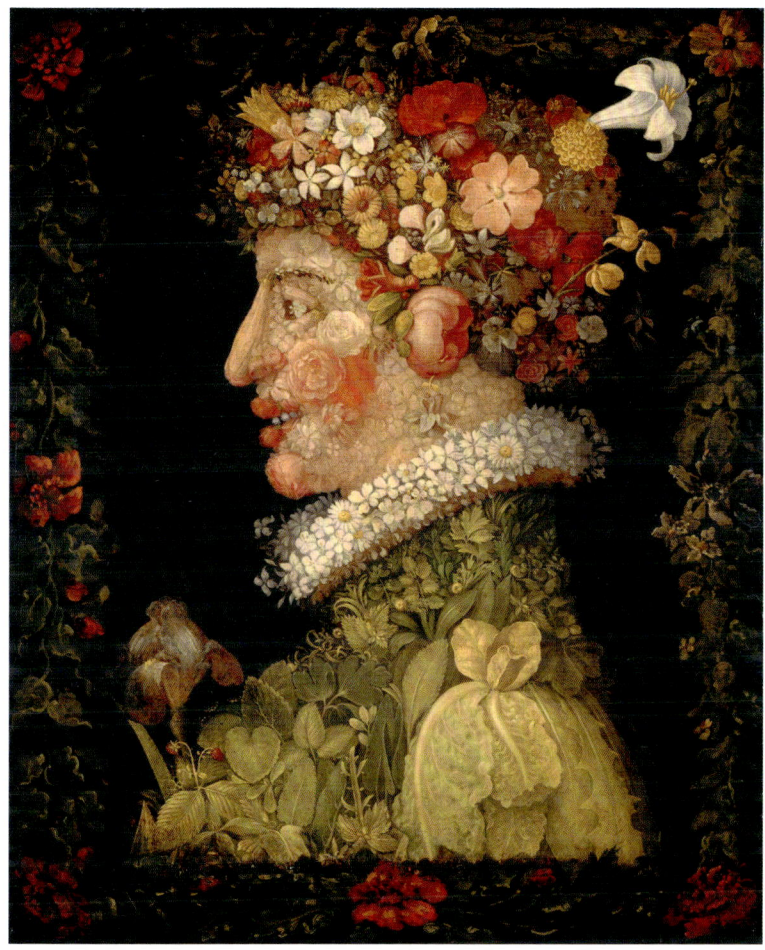

Giuseppe Arcimboldo

Spring, 1573
Oil on canvas, 76 × 63 cm / 30 × 24¾ in
Musée du Louvre, Paris

A surreal portrait emerges from hundreds of minus-cule, intricately detailed, flowers, buds, leaves and other vegetation: cheeks composed of roses, lips of rosebuds and teeth from lily of the valley; a coat of leaves spread out like a meadow; dian-thus, jasmine and wallflowers in a white garlanded collar; a jaunty white lily atop his head, an iris on his chest and a peony for his ear with a pome-granate flower above. One of four paintings representing the seasons, *Spring* was commis-sioned by Holy Roman Emperor Maximilian II from the Milanese artist Giuseppe Arcimboldo (*c*.1527–93). Arcimboldo is renowned for these composite portraits of the Hapsburg elite, some of which were recognizable depictions of the emperors themselves. Among the seasons, *Spring* is the only portrait composed of flowers; *Summer* and *Autumn* are made up of fruit and *Winter* is a grotesque face emerging from dead twigs and fungi. The composite series proved so popular, along with another entitled *The Elements*, that Arcimboldo produced many duplicates to be given as imperial gifts. Philosophy and science lurked beneath the fun: the paintings echo the Platonic concept of a substance that unifies all beings, while the flowers are depicted with such bota-nical accuracy that each is precisely identifiable. Arcimboldo drew on scientific explorations like those of his predecessor Leonardo da Vinci (see p.108) and the Hapsburgs' interest in collect-ing natural curiosities to incorporate exotic and rare plants, fruits and vegetables into the works.

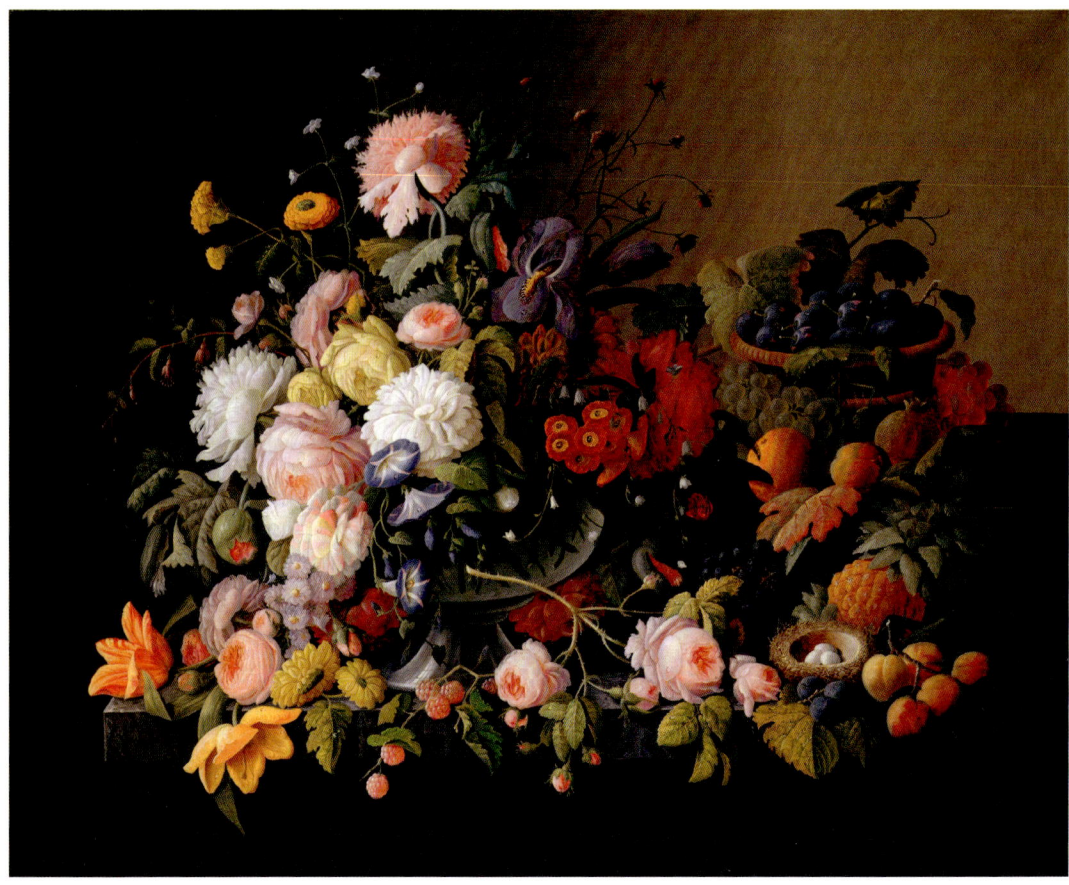

Severin Roesen

Still Life: Flowers and Fruit, *c.*1850–55
Oil on canvas, 1 × 1.3 m / 3 ft 4 in × 4 ft 2 in
Metropolitan Museum of Art, New York

A bounteous array of flowers and fruits, and a bird's nest with three white eggs nestled in its midst, is a reminder of the abundant fecundity of nature in this nineteenth-century American painting, echoing a European tradition of still life stretching back centuries. Spilling out of a glass vase are copious roses ranging in colour from pink to yellow and red, with other flowers including irises, peonies, chrysanthemums and tiny white snowdrops. Nearby, a terracotta pot of plums is surrounded by red and green grapes, peaches, a pomegranate, raspberries and even a pineapple, all delicately painted with fine brushstrokes. The scene is typical of the German-born American artist Severin Roesen (1816–after 1872), who made well over 300 still-life paintings during his lifetime, never veering from the genre. Roesen's style was influenced not just by seventeenth-century Dutch still-life paintings, crisply rendering light as it highlights nuances in colour and form, but also by his training as a porcelain painter in Cologne, which is reflected in his precision on the canvas. While relatively little is known about his life, Roesen began painting flowers in Germany before emigrating in 1848 to New York, where he began exhibiting his paintings at the American Art-Union. Roesen was notable for his meticulous attention to detail, as seen here in minute water droplets falling from petals, tiny thorns gracing the stems of roses and a gentle sheen illuminating the red flesh of raspberries.

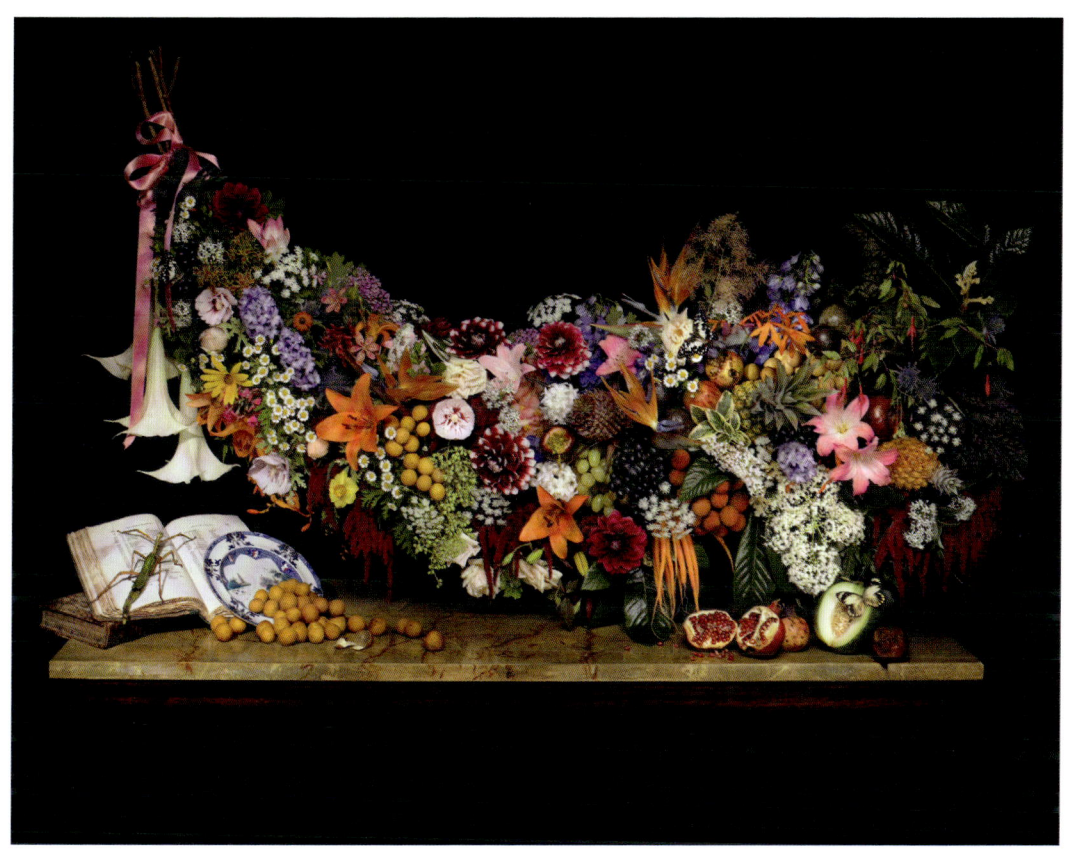

Robyn Stacey

Mr Macleay's Fruit and Flora, 2008
C-type print, 1.2 × 1.7 m / 3 ft 11 in × 5 ft 7 in

This monumental photographic print by Australian artist Robyn Stacey (born 1952) re-creates the staggering variety of flora and fruits that once made the garden of Elizabeth Bay House in Sydney world renowned. The garden featured Australian native plants alongside a remarkable collection of exotics from China, India, South America and the Cape of Good Hope. The house and garden were built by Colonial Secretary Alexander Macleay in 1835, but financial troubles eventually forced him to sell the property. Much of the garden has disappeared over time, swallowed by neglect and sprawling urban development, but despite the irreparable loss, memories of it survive in paintings and drawings – along with the names of all the plants that Macleay dutifully recorded in his notes. To create *Mr Macleay's Fruit and Flora*, Stacey researched each species in the Elizabeth Bay House archive. Once all the specimens had been sourced, the flowers were all cut on the same morning and she assembled them in the style of an extravagant Dutch Golden Age still life – a five-hour process. As a result, *Mr Macleay's Fruit and Flora* is a kind of ghostly homage to a garden that once was. Its exuberant opulence fully captures Macleay's burning passion for botany, as well as the nostalgia that underlies the loss of a truly magnificent collection of plants.

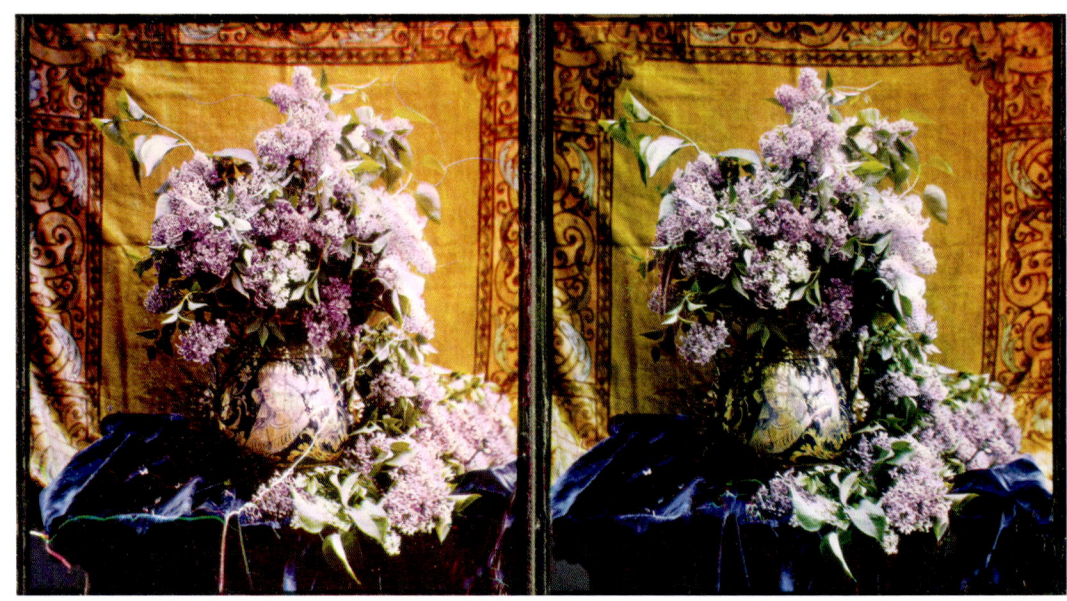

Lumière Brothers

Lilacs, *c*.1898
All-Chroma autochrome, 7 × 6.7 cm / 2¾ × 2½ in
J. Paul Getty Museum, Los Angeles

Although it seems conventional in appearance, this stereoscopic take on the history of Baroque still-life painting from the end of the nineteenth century represents a true technological innovation in the representation of flowers. This generous composition of lilacs in a vase comes from a period of experimentation with colour photography when floral subjects were often used to standardize the performance of new printing techniques, such as the autochrome process invented by French brothers Auguste (1862–1954) and Louis Lumière (1864–1948). Slight differences in tonal range between the two images, accompanied by a barely perceptible viewpoint discrepancy, substantially expanded the flat and limited range of hues that characterized early colour photography and produced the most vivid photographic representations then seen. While the Lumière brothers are most famous for inventing cinema in 1895, their experimentations with photographic processes are perhaps equally as notable. Contemporary audiences had developed a voracious appetite for ever-more realistic photographic images, in this instance the three-dimensional effect created by the doubling of the image when viewed through a special visor called the stereoscope. The phenomenon went global when Queen Victoria and Prince Albert saw cards similar to this one at London's 1851 Great Exhibition and became fans of three-dimensional photography.

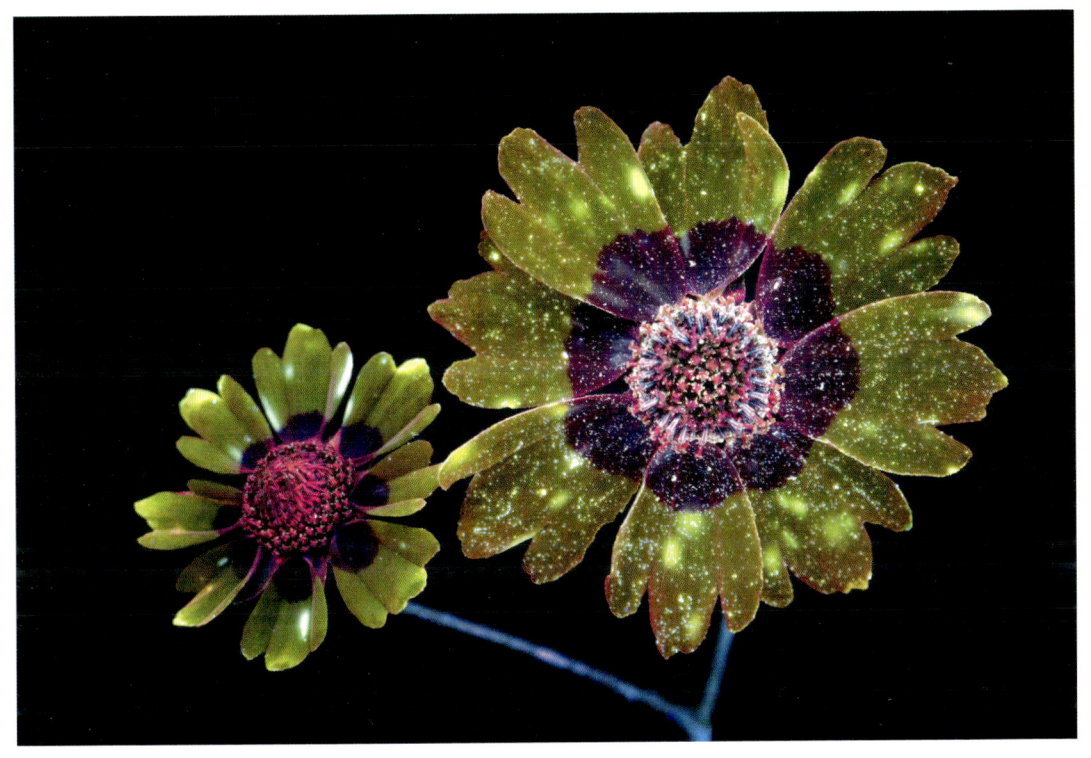

Craig P. Burrows

Plains coreopsis Pair 2, 2016
Digital photography (UVIVF), dimensions variable

Brimming with otherworldly saturated colours, petals, pistils and stems are transformed by American photographer Craig P. Burrows (born 1989) into luminescent botanical structures. Burrows is a specialist in the use of ultraviolet-induced visible fluorescence (UVIVF), a process that excludes the visible spectrum perceived by human eyes to elicit the natural glow that emanates from plants. The result emphasizes the outlines of the petals as well as the pollen that appears to dot the flowers like a scatter of glowing embers. Here, Burrows has photographed plains coreopsis (*Coreopsis tinctoria*), also commonly called golden tickseed or calliopsis, a wildflower common across much of North America. This type of photography is extremely complex to produce and can only be made in the still conditions of the studio, since it requires long exposure times. To avoid any blurring that might occur over the twenty seconds through which the camera shutter remains open, Burrows secures the flowers to a metal pole and holds his breath to avoid creating any air movement. While this image may not represent how bees or butterflies actually see flowers, it remains a reminder of the limited perceptual range of the human eye and invites us to look more closely. Because of its ability to reveal otherwise concealed colouration and other markings in plants, UVIVF has more recently been used by scientists to reveal hidden markings important to the classification of species.

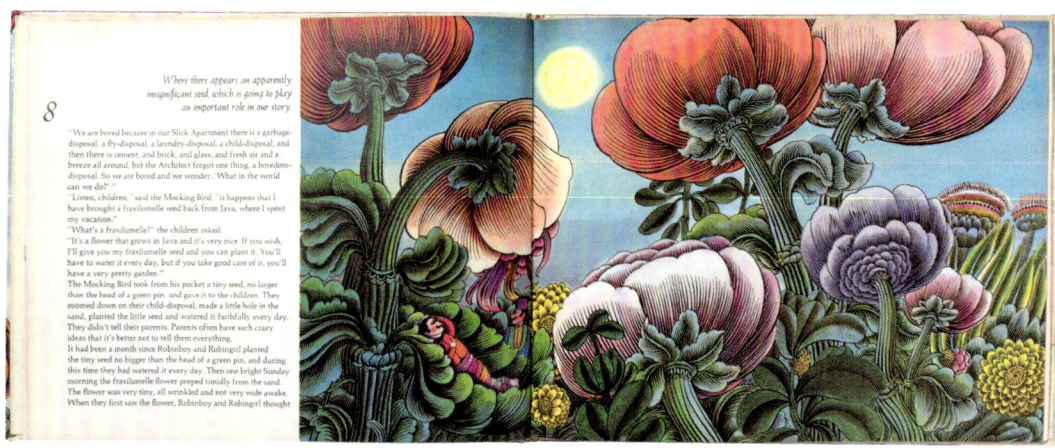

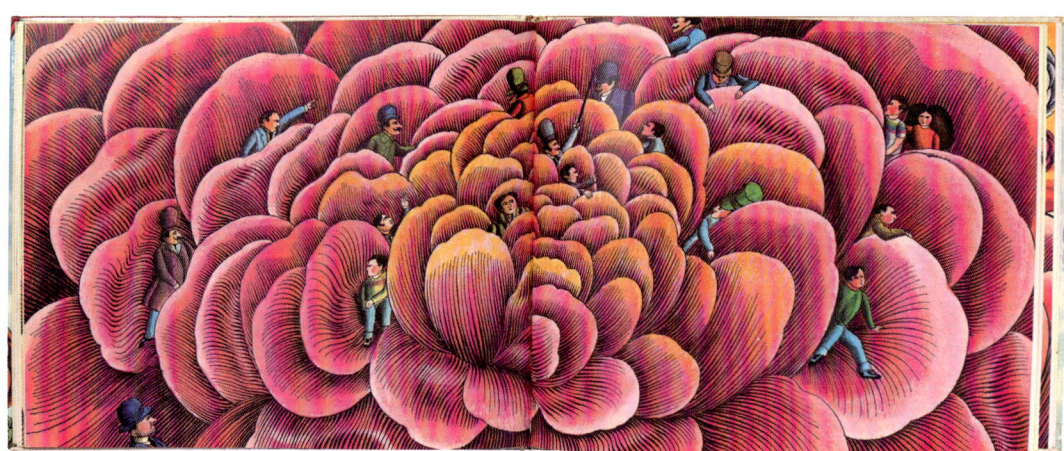

Alain Le Foll and Claude Roy

The Very Obliging Flowers, 1968
Colour lithograph, 21.6 × 27.3 cm / 8½ × 10¼ in
Private collection

A man lies hidden in the leaf of a gigantic plant, which envelopes him like a blanket, while behind him stems tower like fluted columns in a psychedelic landscape of gargantuan flowers. With no reference to the ground and a viewpoint that looks up at the underside of the flowers, the viewer, like the characters, feels a sense of being miniaturized and almost consumed by this jungle-like world. This beguiling scene is from

the children's book *The Very Obliging Flowers*, illustrated by French artist Alain Le Foll (1935–81) with text by the poet and journalist Claude Roy (1915–97). Originally published in French as *C'est le Bouquet* in 1964 by renowned publisher Robert Delpire, it was later published in English in 1968 by Grove Press. The book tells the story of Claudelun and Claudelune who, bored with the dreary, grey cityscape – based on the large complexes built in France in the 1960s – decide to plant a strange 'Fraxilumèle' seed brought by a bird from the island of Java. To their surprise the plant sprouts, and then – like their imaginations

– its flowers magically keep growing until they form a giant playground high above the urban surroundings. The children and their friends play hide-and-seek among the colossal blooms, while the adults get lost within the enormous pink petals, at first seeking to end the children's fun, but ultimately coming to accept the colourful new denizens of their city.

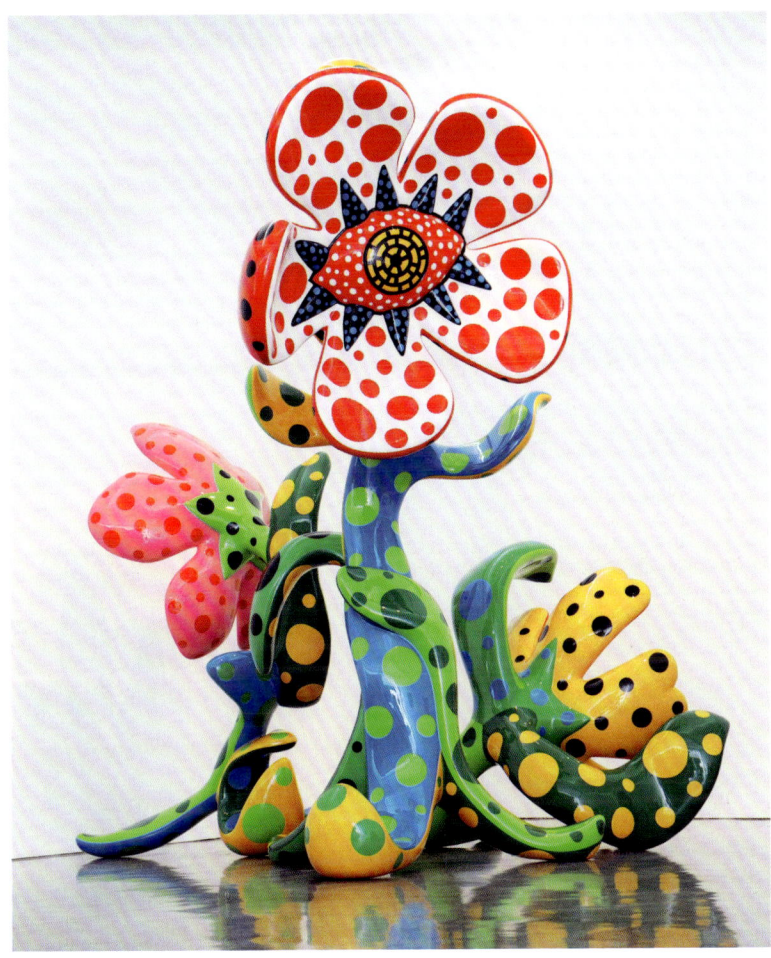

Yayoi Kusama

Flowers That Bloom at Midnight, 2009
Fibreglass-reinforced plastic, metal and
urethane paint, 3 × 1.8 × 2.1 m /
9 ft 10 in × 5 ft 11 in × 6 ft 11 in (left), 4.9 × 2 × 2 m /
15 ft 11 in × 6 ft 7 in × 6 ft 8 in (centre), 2.2 × 2.1 × 1.3 m /
7 ft 1 in × 6 ft 11 in × 4 ft 3 in (right)
Private collection

Towering over the viewer at monumental scale,
the brightly coloured flower sculptures by
Japanese artist Yayoi Kusama (born 1929) are larger
than life, vibrantly blooming into the world.
Marked with Kusama's signature polka dots, the
multicoloured patterns range from red on white
to yellow on green to red on pink, as the psychedelic petals pulse and shine with energy. Some
seem to have leaves for arms that expand to wave
at us, or stems as bodies that bend and curve.
The artist's obsession with dots stems from a hal-
lucination that she experienced as a child in
which the surrounding space was consumed with
repeating patterns. In the late 1960s, Kusama
enacted 'happenings', or performances, by placing
dot stickers or painting dots on people's bodies
or the environment. Kusama described this as
an act of 'self-obliteration', linking everyone and
everything – and even eliminating the ego –
via the contingency of the dots. As such, hers are
flowers of the imagination, with petals, leaves
and stamen sculpted to anthropomorphic effect.
A subject that Kusama has used continually
throughout her seventy-year career, flowers
appeared in some of her earliest works – even
as a young girl she sketched detailed portraits
of peonies – perhaps inspired by the flowers growing in her family's plant nursery and seed farm
at her childhood home in Matsumoto (see p.257).

155

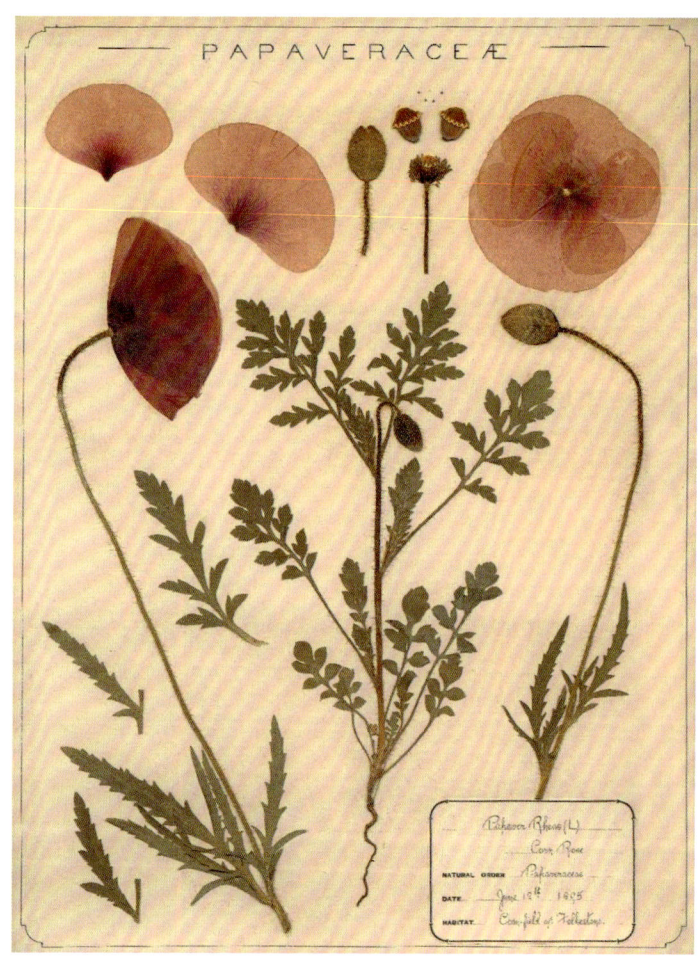

Páhaver Rhoeas (L)
Corr. Rose
NATURAL ORDER Papaveraceæ
DATE Jane 12th 1895
HABITAT Cornfield nr Folkestone.

Frances Giles

Herbarium specimen of common poppy
(*Papaver rhoeas*), 1895
Preserved plant specimen, 35.5 × 26.5 cm /
14 × 10½ in
Herbarium Collection, Royal Botanic Gardens,
Kew, London

The once brilliant red petals of this common
field poppy (*Papaver rhoeas*) still retain traces
of colour, though faded, despite being preserved
125 years ago. Herbarium specimens like this
use dried plants mounted on paper to accentuate
the characteristics that are important for their
identification. Often included are multiple flowers
showing different vantage points (side and frontal); the exact number of petals, stamens, fruit
and seeds; the position of leaves along the stem;
and root structures. This specimen also includes
a tag with the genus and species, the name of the
collector and the date and specific site (cornfield,
Folkestone, Kent) where the plant was collected.
This record of the location where a plant is found
growing on a specific date is today noted using
exact satellite coordinates. With such a precise
record, botanists and ecologists can compare
a historical record with the existing site in order
to determine if a species still flourishes or has
been impacted by changing environmental conditions. It was common for those using plants
for their medicinal purposes to create their own
personal herbarium of plants to aid in their acqui-
sition, as the pharmacist Frances Giles has
done here. For centuries the common poppy has
been used for its analgesic and sedative properties. More than just recording important data,
however, this specimen is beautifully arranged
on the paper in a composition that can be compared to any classical botanical illustration.

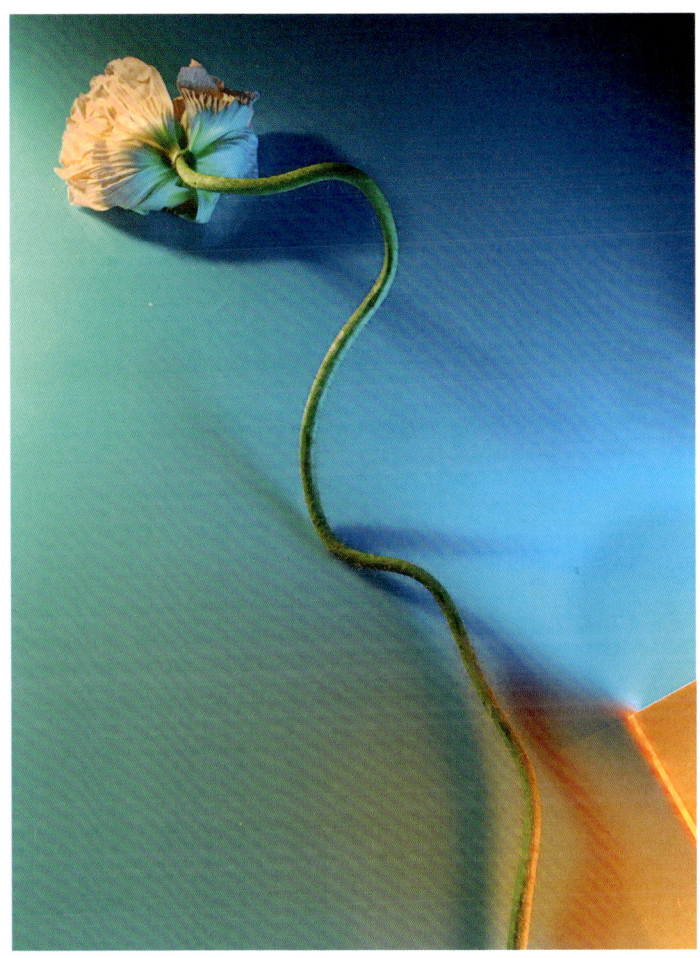

Doan Ly

Neon Poppy, 2018
Digital, dimensions variable

A white oriental poppy snakes across the neon surface of this photograph, its stalk bristling with tiny hairs as if sensing the curious emptiness around it. Vietnamese-American photographer Doan Ly specializes in the creation of contem porary floral still lifes that effortlessly combine the exuberant audaciousness of Baroque paint ings with the linearity and balance of early-twentieth-century botanical photography. Her palette regularly juxtaposes a limited range of warm and cold colours in a subdued but reso nant clash that heightens the sense of balance and gives an otherworldly feel to her images. The crêpe paper-like, bowl-shaped flowers of oriental poppies bloom in late spring, before the summer warmth induces the plant into a period of dor mancy that usually ends in September. The new shoots appear from the ground and stay green amid the winter snow. The beauty of oriental poppies was already appreciated in ancient Egypt and Mesopotamia, where the plant has been cultivated for ornamental purposes since 5000 BC. In 1702, botanist Joseph Pitton de Tournefort introduced the plant to France, where it became a sensation. The many differently coloured varie ties range from pure white to red, orange, pink and dark burgundy, the result of a complex hybridization process of three different species native to western Asia. Despite the physical simi larity to the famous opium poppy (*Papaver som niferum*), oriental poppies do not produce the alkaloids essential to the production of narcotics.

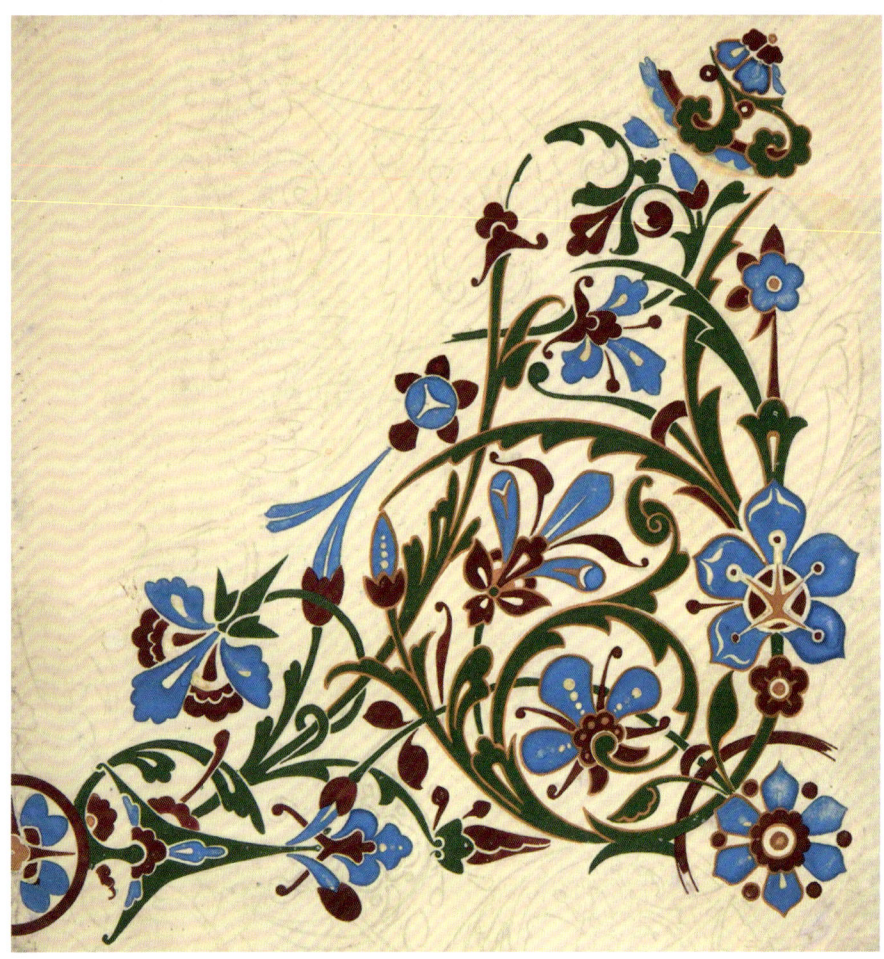

Christopher Dresser

Design for a floral pattern, 1883
Graphite, ink and gouache, 40.5 × 27.9 cm /
16 × 11 in
Metropolitan Museum of Art, New York

Stylized blue blossoms with swirling and sinuous leaves and stems reflect the emergence of the
Art Nouveau style in this floral pattern from the
late nineteenth century. Created by Scottish-born
designer Christopher Dresser (1834–1904), this
motif would have been used in fabrics, carpets
and wallpapers by any number of manufacturers
for which Dresser provided designs throughout

Europe and the United States. Considered
to be the first industrial designer, Dresser was
heavily associated with the design reform movement of the second half of the nineteenth
century, recognizing the opportunity created
by the Industrial Revolution and mechanization
to mass-produce affordable, well-designed products. Dresser's penchant for naturalistic themes
grew out of his education at the Government
School of Design in London, where he was introduced to botany. Possessed of a remarkable
facility for drawing plants in plan, elevation and
section, he was asked by the ornamentalist

Owen Jones to contribute a plate of botanical
forms to Jones's *The Grammar of Ornament*,
published in 1856. Dresser considered it to be the
duty of the artist to idealize rather than copy
nature, believing profoundly in the order, symmetry and geometric balance inherent in plants.
Dresser was equally influenced by the arts and
forms found in non-Western art. In 1882, he
published a groundbreaking book entitled *Japan:
Its Architecture, Art and Art Manufactures*, which
would continue the Victorian craze for *japonisme*
for the next two decades.

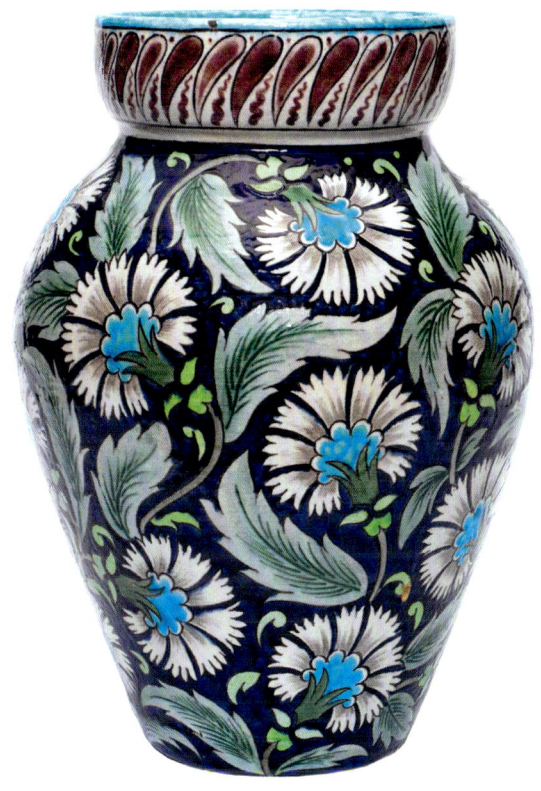

William De Morgan

Vase, c.1880
Ceramic with lustreware glaze, 39 × 25 cm /
15 × 10 in
Private collection

Crafted at the height of the Aesthetic movement
in the nineteenth century, this shallow-necked
oviform vase is a fine example of the ceramics
produced by English potter William De Morgan
(1839–1917) during his 'Chelsea Period,' when he
had a studio and kiln in Cheyne Row in Chelsea,
London. The kiln was safely tucked away in an
outhouse: De Morgan had been evicted from his

previous lodgings after the kiln he had built in the
chimney caused a fire that burnt the roof off the
house. The vase uses a palette De Morgan referred
to as his 'Persian colours', and the neck demonstrates his speciality: lustreware glaze. There
is also a discernible Iznik influence in the stylized
floral pattern of white carnations and scrolling
saz leaves – motifs featured repeatedly in Islamic
fritware (see p.72). De Morgan was passionate
about the art of the Middle East, an interest likely
aroused while working on the 'Arab Hall' of Lord
Leighton's home in Holland Park, when he was
charged with creating new tiles to match historic

Iznik, Persian and Damascan panels from the
sixteenth century. De Morgan produced a substantial quantity of similar homeware items, all
painted and glazed by hand in line with Arts and
Crafts ideology. De Morgan also manufactured
tiles to designs created by his lifelong friend
William Morris, who visited the studio on a weekly
basis to inspect the latest creations made for his
company Morris and Co. (see p.160).

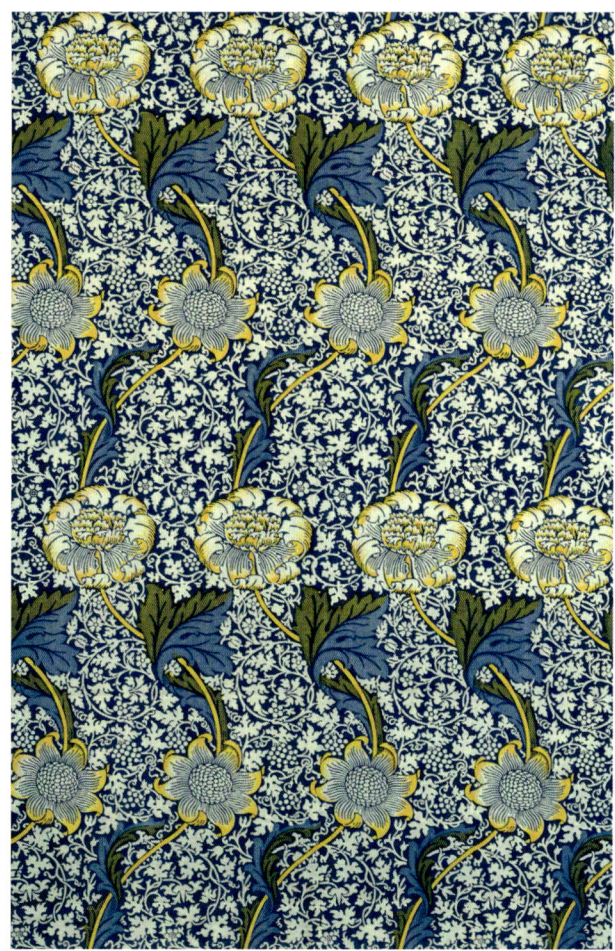

William Morris

Kennet, 1917–23
Cotton, indigo discharge and block-printed,
2.6 × 1 m / 8 ft 8 in × 3 ft 2 in
Metropolitan Museum of Art, New York

This iconic pattern of stylized, trailing flower heads and acanthus leaves on a background of smaller-scale vegetation has resonances in fifteenth- and sixteenth-century Italian textile designs, but is in fact barely a hundred years old. At a time when the Government Schools of Design were insisting that British design should reflect the ethos of industrial and economic progress, the Arts and Crafts movement, led by William Morris (1834–96), begged to differ. Morris, an avowed Socialist, condemned the social consequences of Victorian industrialization and rejected the cluttered, eclectic style of Victorian decoration, advocating instead for craftsmanship over mass-production, and drawing on pre-industrial English and medieval Celtic traditions for artistic inspiration. Most of his designs are based on natural forms – flowers, plants and trees – but as his work matured, Morris favoured the simple flowers of British gardens and fields over exotic foreign blooms.

He also believed that design should not attempt to precisely replicate nature, but, as here, should evoke natural forms in a stylized, ordered balance. Two-dimensional designs such as *Kennet* – which is still produced today in various colours – were well suited to reproduction on materials ranging from printed fabrics for upholstery and curtains, wallpaper, woven silk and carpets. Morris often drew floral inspiration from his own flower gardens at Red House in Kent and Kelmscott Manor in the Cotswolds.

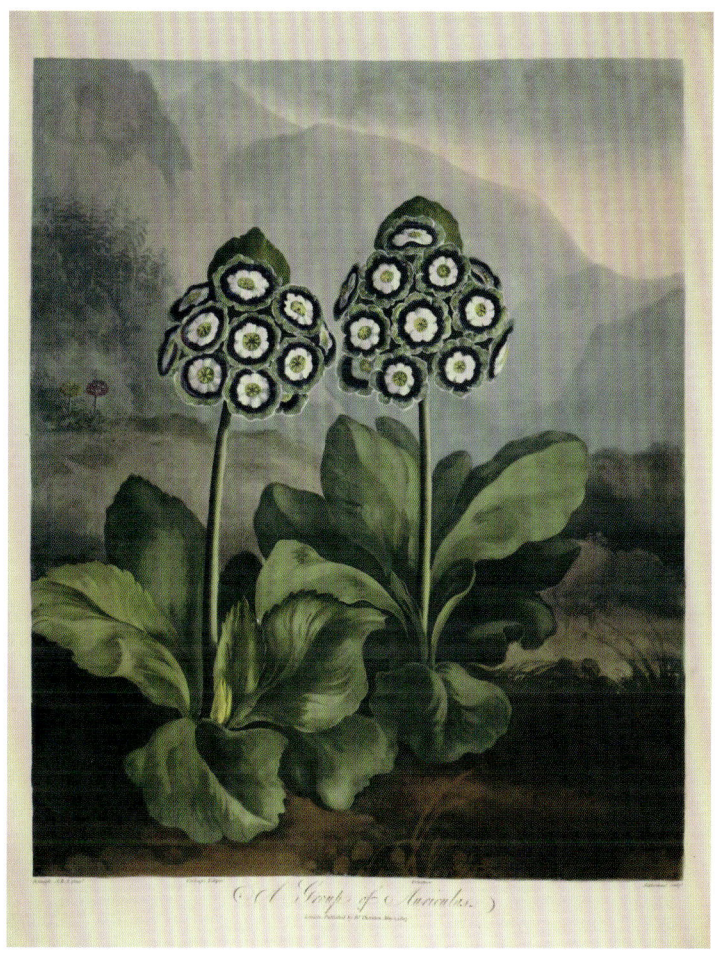

A Group of Auriculas, from New Illustration of the Sexual System of Carolus von Linnaeus ... and the Temple of Flora or Garden of Nature, 1807

Philip Reinagle and Robert John Thornton

A Group of Auriculas, from *New Illustration of the Sexual System of Carolus von Linnaeus ... and the Temple of Flora or Garden of Nature*, 1807
Colour aquatint finished by hand, 55.2 × 36.2 cm / 21¼ × 17¼ in
Missouri Botanical Garden, St. Louis

Set at the edge of a mountain forest, these auriculas are illustrated amid their native alpine habitat. First brought into cultivation by the eminent sixteenth-century Flemish botanist Carolus Clusius, auriculas are naturally soft yellow or mauve like other primulas, but breeders have developed rich

velvety shades ranging from red to green, which are especially valued when they contrast with the pale 'paste' in the centre of the flower and the dark rim. Here, *Primula auricula* 'Cockup's Eclipse' – named for the cultivator who first grew the variety – has been illustrated by English painter Philip Reinagle (1749–1833) for the *New Illustration of the Sexual System of Carolus von Linnaeus* published by English physician Robert John Thornton (1768–1837) between 1799 and 1810. The overambitious florilegium was published in three parts, the last being the well-known *Temple of Flora*, and used a number of artists and engravers to produce

large-format plates to illustrate the new binomial or sexual system of naming plants, based on the male and female parts of flowers, introduced by Linnaeus (see p.208). The rich landscape backgrounds were designed to match plants' natural habitats or dominant features in a 'picturesque' manner: tulips appeared with a Dutch windmill, the night-flowering cactus in moonlight with a church clock pointing to midnight, and blue water lilies in a lake beside a mosque. Despite the remarkable illustrations, the book failed to find enough buyers, and after more than a decade the project ultimately left Thornton bankrupt.

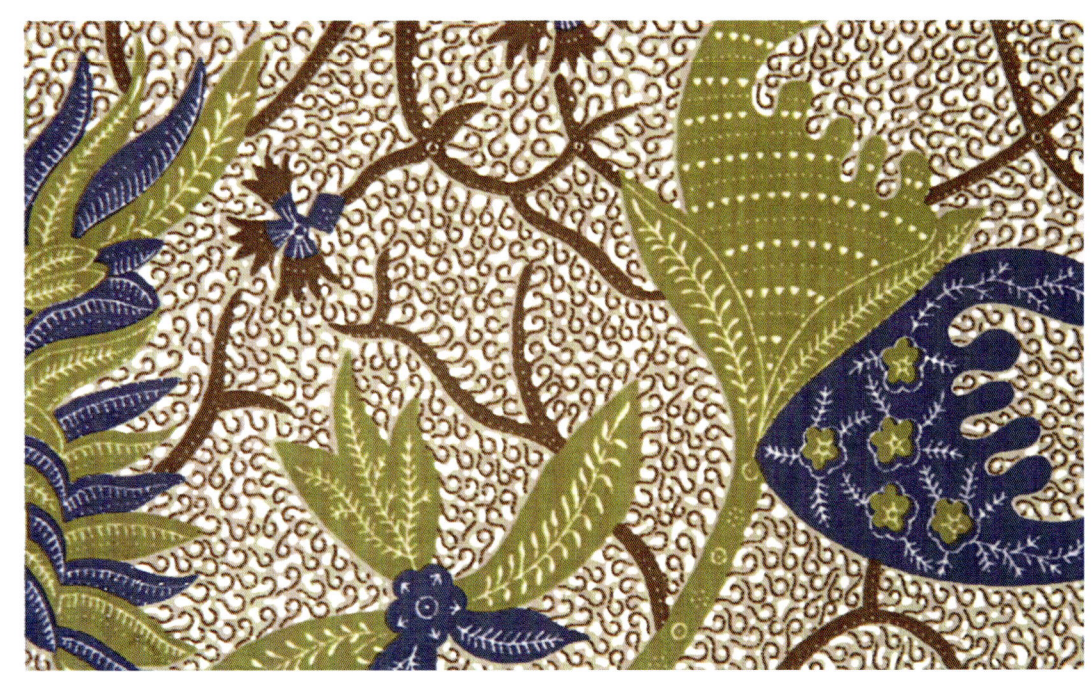

Anonymous

Textile sample, 1980
Printed cotton, 22.7 × 14 cm / 9 × 5½ in
Musée du Quai Branly, Paris

Geometric patterned branches are rendered in a rich brown hue while green leaves envelop blue blooms, unfurling like vibrant plumage – an intricate pattern set on a ground of pale fabric in a vestige of its origins. This swatch of colourful floral fabric, known as a Dutch wax print, is at once a useful piece of cloth and a potent crossbreed of geopolitical history. Dutch wax prints are widely recognized as an 'African' fabric, yet their complex origins span several continents. In the mid-nineteenth century, Indonesia – then the Dutch East Indies – was home to entrepreneurs such as Pieter Fentener van Vlissingen, who saw an opportunity to emulate traditional Indonesian batiks using mass-production. Unlike the original cloth, which employs handmade wax-resist dyeing, the Dutch machine-made methods of the late 1880s produced a new derivative. Less precisely executed, with crackled effects and over-bled dye, this version was unattractive to Javanese purists but instead found a market in West Africa, particularly in Ghana and the Coté d'Ivoire. Its myriad patterns, often employing floral and vegetal motifs and electric colours, created an identifiable calling card. By the early twentieth century Dutch wax-print cloth was a popular and widespread choice for cosmopolitan Africans, and it remains part of contemporary fashion. Laden with meaning, artists such as Yinka Shonibare have incorporated the fabrics into their works, creating a dialogue around their multilayered history (see p.61).

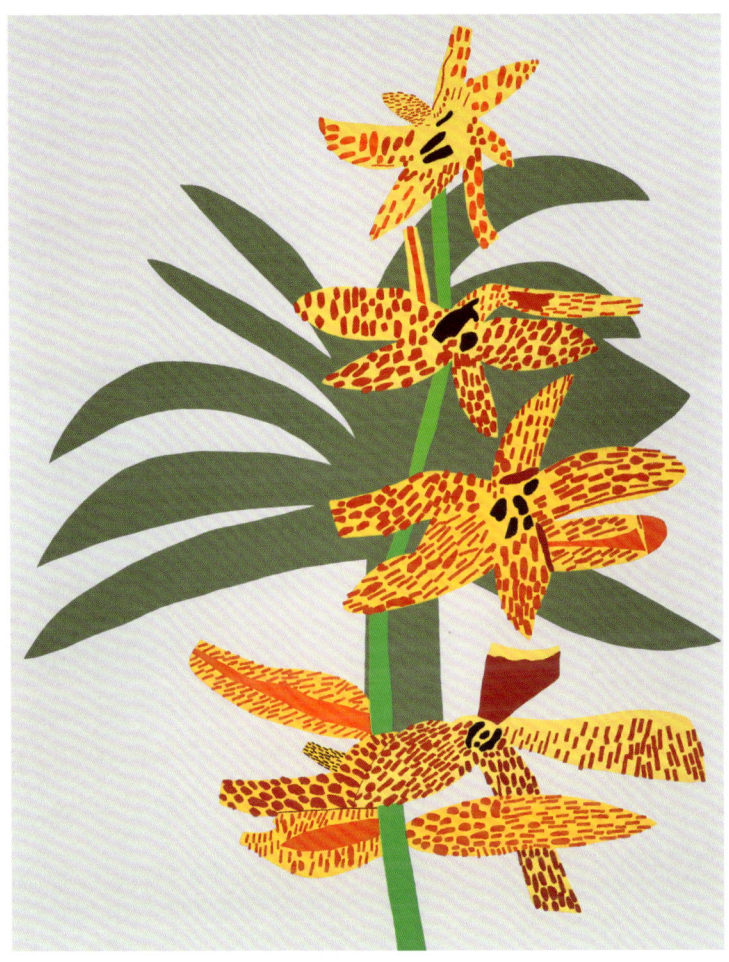

Jonas Wood

Clipping J1, 2015
Oil and acrylic on canvas, 2.2 × 1.8 m /
7 ft 4 in × 5 ft 9 in

An exotic tiger orchid stem is clipped and placed over a tropical leaf and petals and leaves overlap and protrude in a skewed and flattened perspective, all set against a grey background. This image by Los Angeles-based artist Jonas Wood (born 1977) is striking, but it is the scale, at more than 2 metres (7 feet) high, that hits the viewer. Clipping – reminiscent of 'cutting', a term instantly understood by any gardener used to snipping woody stems off existing plants to propagate a new seedling – refers to the forms Wood has taken from his previous work and then isolated in space. He 'clips' the flowers from their pots and enlarges them, leaving the flowers to be seen in detail in their flat two-dimensional perspective. By suspending these clippings in space, out of their original context, Wood explores geometry, shape, colour and repetition. Colours, cross-hatching, graphic lines and patterns push against each other in off-beat perspective and scale. But it is Wood's use of bold lines that defines him. His style – playful yet rigorous – is an answer to the challenge of capturing three-dimensional forms on a flat plane. By flattening, abstracting and exaggerating shapes and colour, he offers a colourful view of domestic settings. Wood works from photographs and sketches, cutting and pasting and making preliminary collages as the basis for his compositions. The final piece is usually a result of this fragmented and multilayered methodology.

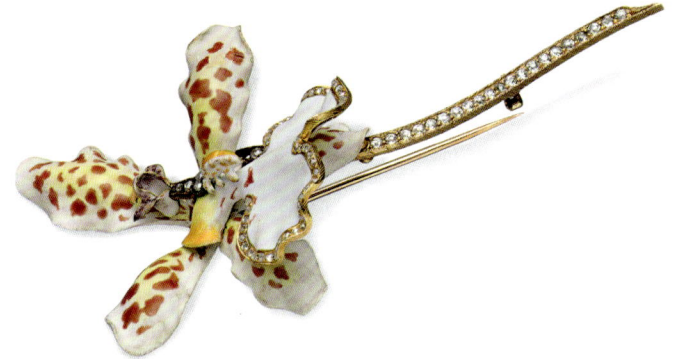

Paulding Farnham

Brooch, 1889–96
Gold, diamonds and enamel, 10.8 × 6.4 cm /
4¼ × 2½ in
Metropolitan Museum of Art, New York

This exquisite representation of the rare orchid *Oncidium jonesianum* by renowned jeweller Paulding Farnham (1859–1927) for Tiffany & Co. is composed of six enamelled petals framed by diamond accents, gold detailing and a gold setting. The firm's reputation as the leading jewellery house of the late-nineteenth century is largely due to two designers: its jewellery director, Edward C. Moore, and Farnham, who was made the firm's head designer in 1891. Together, the pair dared to combine unusual gemstones, historical references and, most notably, inspirations from nature to give Tiffany's work a leading edge. This brooch from the late 1800s exemplifies Farnham's trendsetting style. Exhibited at the 1889 Paris Exposition, it won Tiffany the gold medal for jewellery – the first time the honour was bestowed on an American firm. Farnham's skill with form, colour and technique meticulously translates the detail of the exotic specimen, turning a decorative work of art into a covetable object. Farnham's orchid pieces illustrate how the late-Victorian plant-hunting craze affected the decorative arts, creating a great demand for precious pieces based on natural forms. This particular orchid species was brought to England in 1878, after it was uncovered by a Brazilian–French plant collector in 1878 in northern Paraguay – one of the flower's native habitats, in addition to Bolivia, Brazil and northeast Argentina – and was named after a Reverend Morgan Jones, known as 'an enthusiastic lover of orchids'.

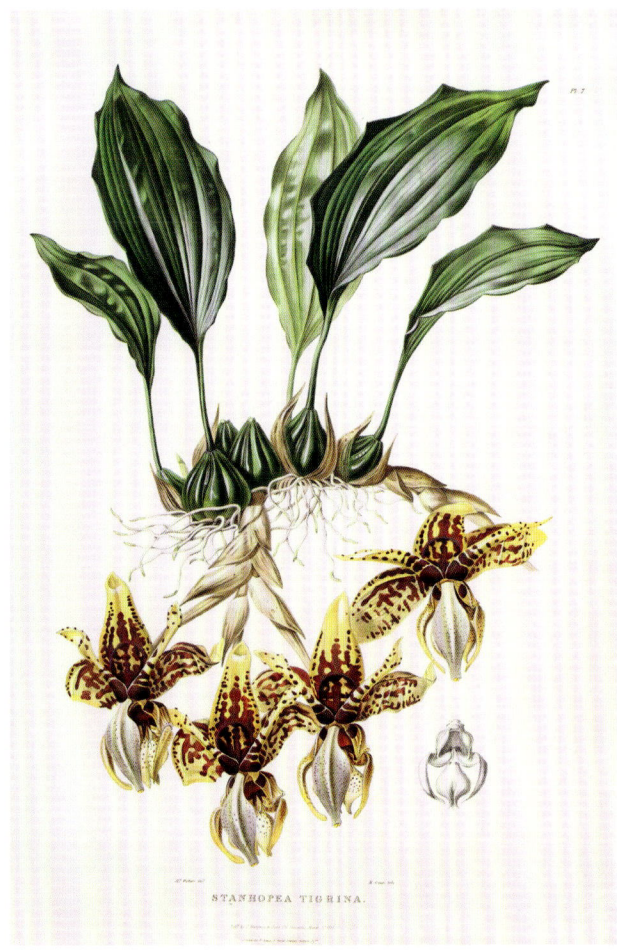

STANHOPEA TIGRINA.

Augusta Withers

Stanhopea tigrina, from *Orchidaceae of Mexico and Guatemala*, 1837
Hand-coloured lithograph, 73 × 51 cm /
28¾ × 20¾ in
Missouri Botanical Garden, Peter H. Raven Library, St. Louis

With the spotting of a wild tigrina, this spray of orchids (*Stanhopea tigrina*) makes for an intimidating composition. Created by British artist Augusta Withers (1792–1877), this plate is one of many portraying the sensational characteristics that fuelled the orchid mania of the Victorian era.

Nurserymen and wealthy landowners, such as James Bateman, satisfied their passion for collecting rare and unusual specimens by employing orchid hunters in the covert business of scouring the world for new species. Bateman's treatise *The Orchidaceae of Mexico and Guatemala* is a manifestation of this period in its number, rarity, scale and weight: forty images reproduced in just 125 copies, measuring 76 by 56 centimetres (30 by 22 inches) and weighing a remarkable 17 kilograms (38 pounds). It is thought to be the largest ever botanical book with lithographic plates. Of the forty species represented in the tome,

eleven were new discoveries and most had never before been published. Withers painted twenty-one of the orchids during the most prolific years of her career. She was appointed 'Flower Painter in Ordinary' to Queen Adelaide in 1830 and then to Queen Victoria in 1864, and her paintings were included in Royal Academy and Society of Female Artist exhibitions. Withers was also recognized for her dynamic botanical paintings published in *Transactions of the Horticultural Society of London* and horticultural serials such as *Pomological Magazine* (1828–30), *The Botanist* (1836–42) and *Illustrated Bouquet* (1857–63).

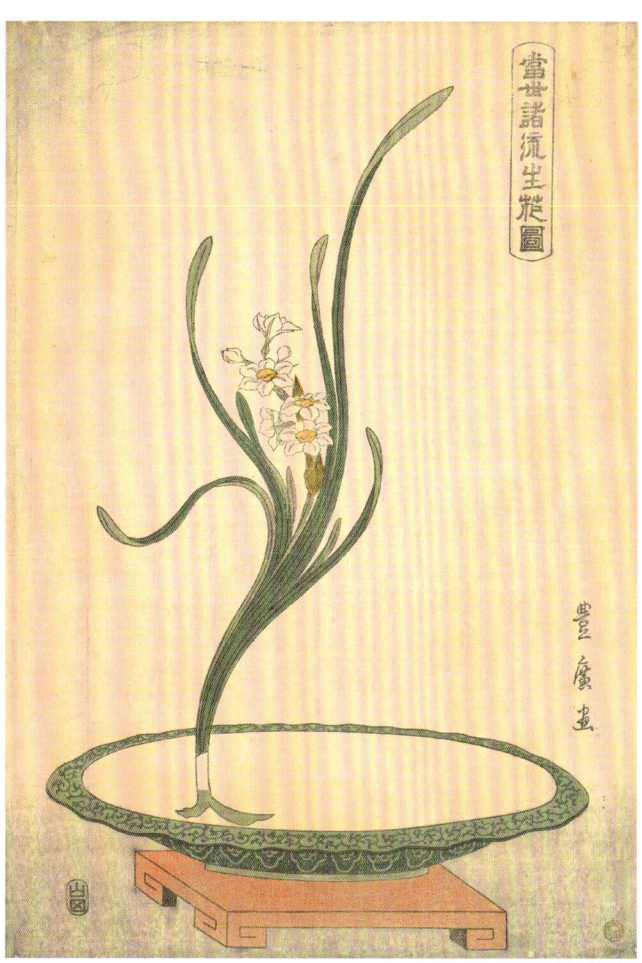

当世諸流生花圖

豊廣画

Utagawa Toyohiro

Flower Arrangement of Suisen (Narcissus) in a Flat Green Dish, Edo period (1615–1868)
Polychrome woodcut, 36.5 × 25.4 cm / 14¼ × 10 in
Metropolitan Museum of Art, New York

In Japanese culture this singular presentation of a white-petalled narcissus would be thought of as a complete flower arrangement, whereas in the West it would probably be considered too simple to be classified as such. In this woodcut by Japanese artist Utagawa Toyohiro (1773–1828), the waxy leaves probe skywards, creating curving arcs that frame the flower heads. Known as *ikebana* or *kadō*, this type of Japanese flower arranging has origins as far back as the seventh century. Ikebana can be translated as 'making plants alive', reflecting one of the aesthetic aims of the discipline – not simply to imitate nature but to enhance the essence of the plant so that it describes both itself and the broader natural world, the seasons and perhaps even the process of life and death itself. Here, we see the *Narcissus tazetta* – a wild narcissus species, which ranges across Europe to parts of Africa and Asia – as if it is wafting in the breeze, outdoors in nature. The lack of any shadows means that the plant is not grounded in any pictorial sense, but rather appears weightless in its dish. This work was made during the Edo period of modern-day Tokyo at a time when the city was expanding rapidly and was known for its large number of 'pleasure districts'. With a hedonistic attitude of *joie de vivre* and flourishing arts, the culture of the Edo period was referred to as *ukiyo* or the 'floating world'. Perhaps embodied in this narcissus is a world of heightened aesthetic perfection, where nature is both seductive and transformative.

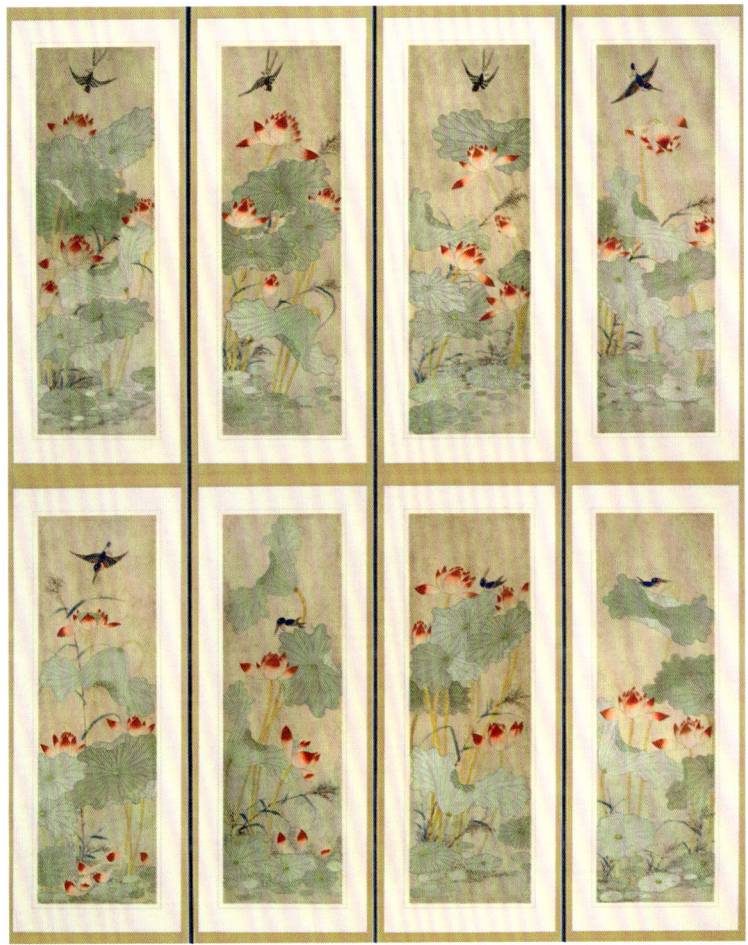

Anonymous

Lotus Flowers and Birds, late 19th century
Ink and colour on paper, 1.7 × 2.7 m /
5 ft 7 in × 8 ft 11 in
Minneapolis Institute of Art, Minnesota

The eight panels of this folding screen from late-nineteenth-century Korea each contain two main features – a flowering lotus plant (*Nelumbo nucifera*) and a single bird – to create a pleasing pattern of muted grey-green and beige, sprinkled with the red-tinged petals of the lotus blossoms. Although the individual components remain the same, no two panels are alike, and the vibrancy

and life in the paintings are created by the changing angles of leaves, stems and flowers, and the movements of the birds. On closer inspection, the variations between the panels appear almost as a story being told in sequence. At the base of each painting smaller leaves float at the surface of the water, above which strong aerial stems carry aloft the mature leaves, among buds bursting open to reveal pink and red lotus flowers in all their glory. The first three panels from the left show a swallow swooping towards the swampy scene below, while in the remaining panels a long-billed kingfisher dives down before finally

alighting on a lotus stem. Beyond the circular lotus leaves, a single stem of reed seems to sway in the breeze. In Buddhism, the lotus is highly symbolic, representing honesty and purity of body and mind, as well as faithfulness and humility. The bright lotus flowers contrast with the dark, muddy waters from which the plant grows, signifying transcendence over material attachment.

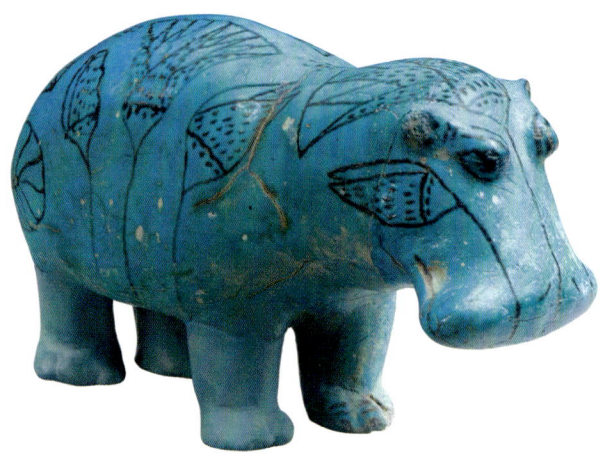

Anonymous

Hippopotamus ('William'), c.1961–1878 BC
Faience, 11.2 × 20 × 7.5 cm / 4½ × 8 × 3 in
Metropolitan Museum of Art, New York

Faience hippos from the Egyptian Middle Kingdom (c.2030–1650 BC) were often decorated with lotus flowers (*Nymphaea caerulea*) shown open and closed. Along with their leaves, the flowers were both indicative of the animal's natural habitat in the Nile and symbols of regeneration and rebirth: in a version of the Egyptian creation myth, the sun god Ra appears from a lotus that rises from the primordial waters.

As a grave gift, the lotus – either actual flowers or represented on a hippo – offered a link to Ra, with whom the dead hoped to be regenerated each morning. To the ancient Egyptians, the hippopotamus possessed a highly contradictory nature, symbolizing life, regeneration and rebirth as well as death, chaos and fear. Dangerous and destructive, hippos were associated in Egyptian mythology with the evil god Seth, who was defeated by Horus, the sky god who represented kingship. The pharaoh's successful hunt of a hippopotamus – frequently represented in relief carvings and paintings – symbolized the victory of order over chaos.

Hippos lived in the Nile, among the native lotus flowers, and like the river were associated with life and abundance. In 1931 the owner of a photograph of this hippopotamus wrote an article about it for the British humour magazine *Punch*, calling it 'William'; the piece was republished in *The Metropolitan Museum of Art Bulletin*, and William is now The Met's unofficial mascot.

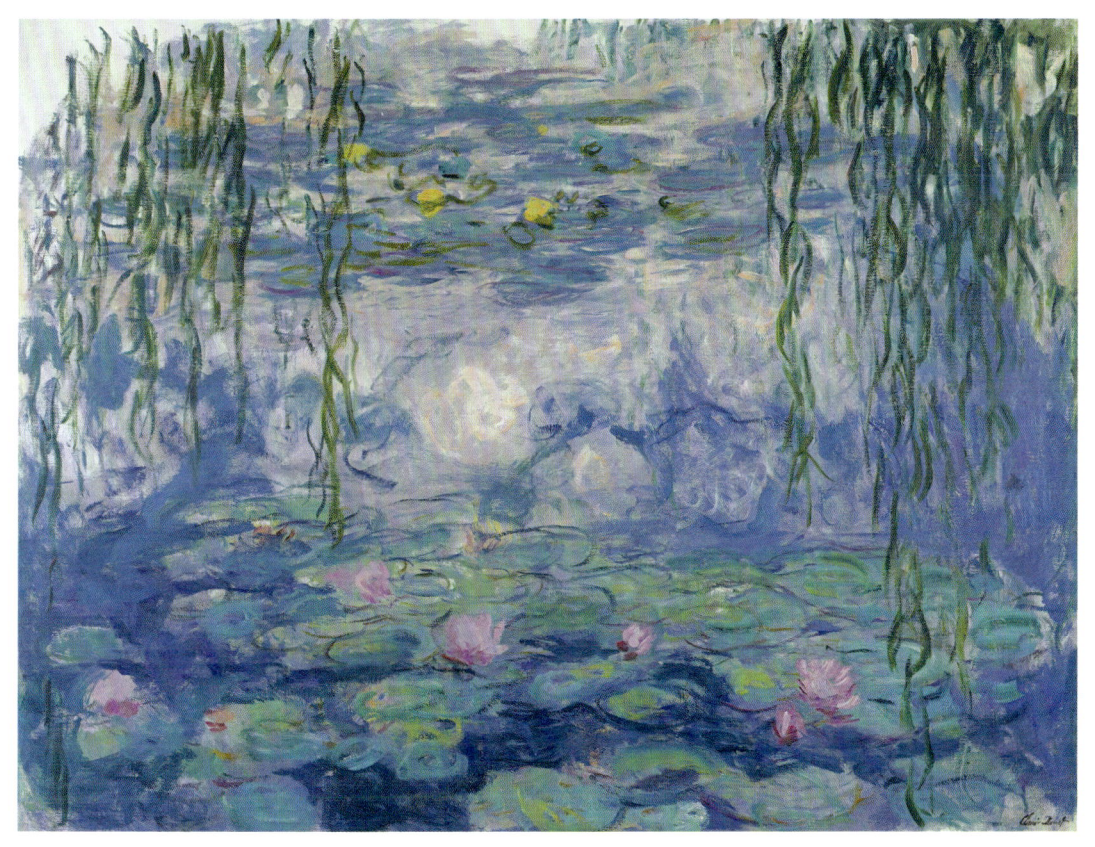

Claude Monet

Nymphéas, 1916–19
Oil on canvas, 1.5 × 2 m / 4 ft 11 in × 6 ft 6 in
Musée Marmottan Monet, Paris

Dangling fronds of weeping willow frame the
pink flowers and floating leaves of lilies of the
genus *Nymphaea*, beyond which the water reflects
the clouds above in a composition in which
water and sky meld together with an almost dreamlike quality. This oil sketch depicts possibly the
most famous water lily garden in the world:
that created in the small village of Giverny, some
80 kilometres (50 miles) northwest of Paris, by

French painter Claude Monet (1840–1926), who
bought a house there in 1890. Born in Paris, the
son of a grocer, Monet became the leading member
of the Impressionist group of landscape painters
which included Edgar Degas, Camille Pissarro,
Pierre-Auguste Renoir (see p.244) and Alfred Sisley
(his painting *Impression, Sunrise*, exhibited in
1874, gave the Impressionist movement its name).
Of Monet's thousands of works, the most iconic
are perhaps of his water lily garden. Around the
edge of the pond, Monet planted four European
weeping willows (*Salix × pendulina*), whose graceful silver-green branches appear in many of his

works, particularly those painted during World
War I (1914–18), when the guns of the Western Front
could be heard from Giverny. Painting *en plein
air* with a palette of blues, greens and white – and
a touch of pink and yellow for the lily petals –
Monet renders the natural scene before him with
quick brushstrokes, capturing the luminous and
changing daylight in a work that is the epitome
of Impressionism.

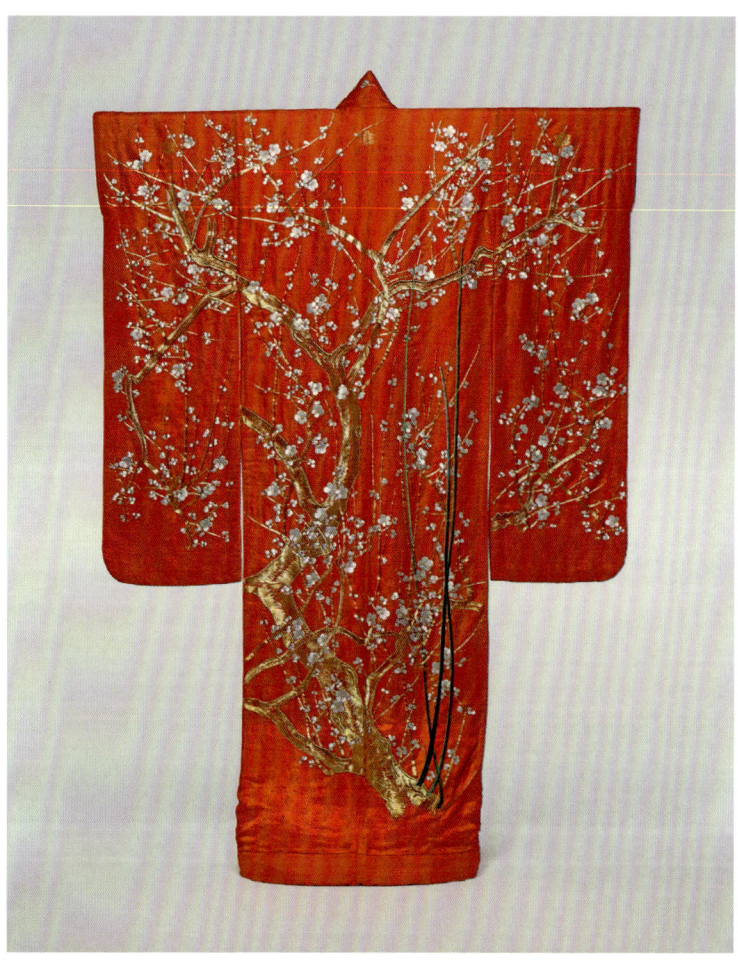

Anonymous

Furisode, 1801–68
Satin damask weave embroidered with silk and
gold-leaf-over-lacquered-paper-strip-wrapped
silk, 1.8 × 1.3 m / 6 ft × 4 ft 3 in
Art Institute of Chicago

A prismatic spray of white plum tree blossoms
decorates this Japanese kimono, tumbling down
the long sleeves from the branches lying across the
shoulders, while the trunk runs up the back as
if following the spine. This elaborate garment
is a *furisode*, or 'swinging-sleeve' kimono, that
would traditionally only be worn by an unmarried
woman on special occasions to denote her availability for marriage. The cloth is made out of sumptuous materials, including *rinzu* (a lustrous silk)
and gold, while the needlework is executed in such
a way as to create the illusion that the tree trunk
is three-dimensional and knotty, suggesting its
age. In Japan these varying symbols would have
been read to indicate different qualities: the old
tree indicated the nobleness of the wearer's family,
while the vibrant red colour was suited to be
worn by young women as it signifies glamour and
allure. The plum tree itself is associated with
winter, and as it is the first to blossom in the
spring, it represents renewal, longevity and perseverance. At the base of the tree three long
water sprouts – new growth created when a tree
is pruned – are sewn in black thread. If the tree
represents the old family, its heritage and, of course,
its wealth, then perhaps the water sprouts symbolize the vigour of the wearer's youth and her
potential as a partner in marriage.

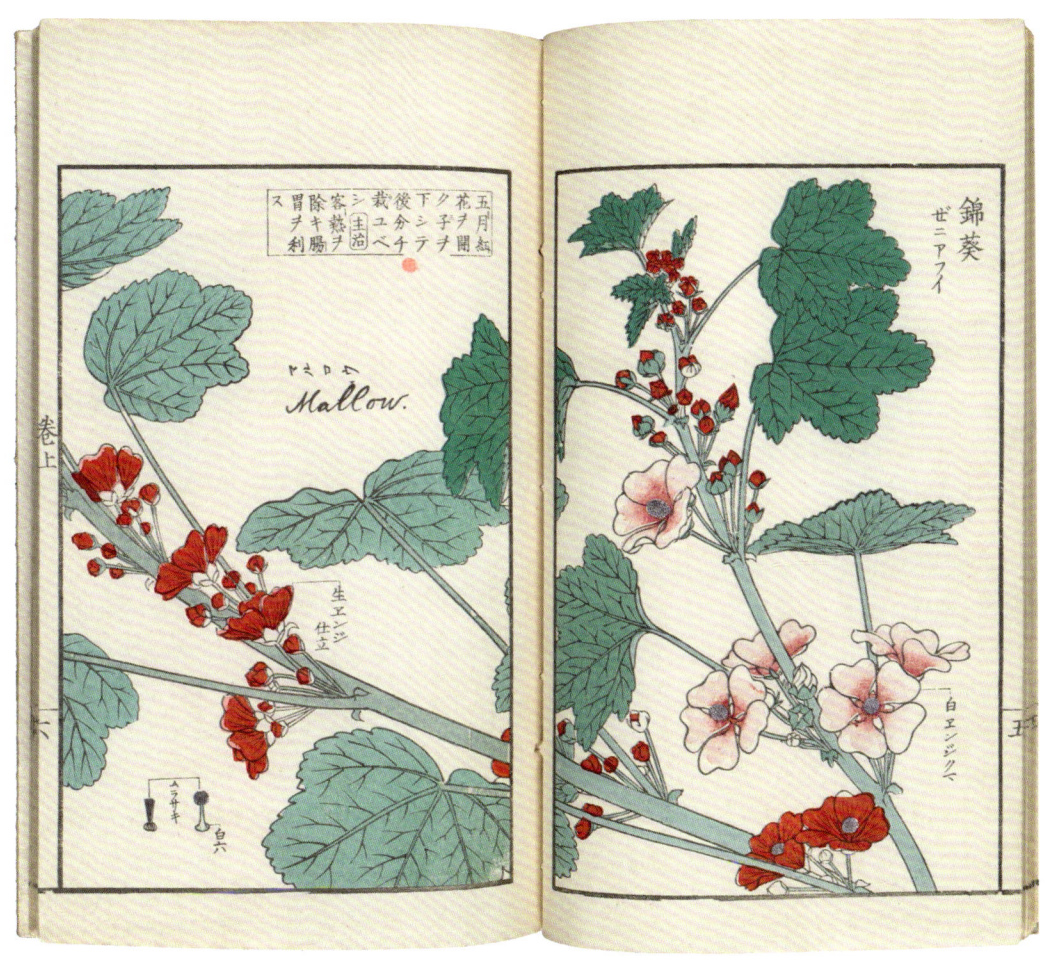

Kawahara Keiga

Mallow, from *Sōmoku kajitsu shashin zufu*, *c*.1836
Hand-coloured woodcut, 30 × 16 cm / 11¾ × 6¼ in
Library of Congress, Washington, DC

For more than a hundred years from the mid-seventeenth century, the Dutch East India Company's trading post at Dejima, an artificial island in Nagasaki harbour, was the only contact point between Japan and the outside world. One of the few Japanese people permitted to enter Dejima, Edo-period artist Kawahara Keiga (1786–1860) provided the island's residents and the wider world with a window on a hidden empire through his paintings of landscapes and everyday scenes, animals and, most famously, plants and flowers. Between 1823 and 1829, Keiga worked with Dejima's German physician – and avid natural historian – Philipp Franz von Siebold on a series of more than a thousand pictures of Japan's flora and fauna. In 1825, the European artist Carl Hubert de Villeneuve came to Dejima at von Siebold's request to instruct Keiga in Western painting techniques. Keiga combined these with traditional methods to create a distinctive style that recalls the Western natural history books of the era while remaining unmistakably Japanese. With its delicate precision and elegant colour palette, this image of common mallow (*Malva sylvestris*) displays Keiga's undoubted skill. The bold outlines of the mallow's leaves and flowers are reminiscent of a *ukiyo-e* (pictures of the 'floating world') woodcut print, while the dynamic diagonal composition shows how Keiga applied his own artistic sensibility to subvert the conventions of traditional European botanical art.

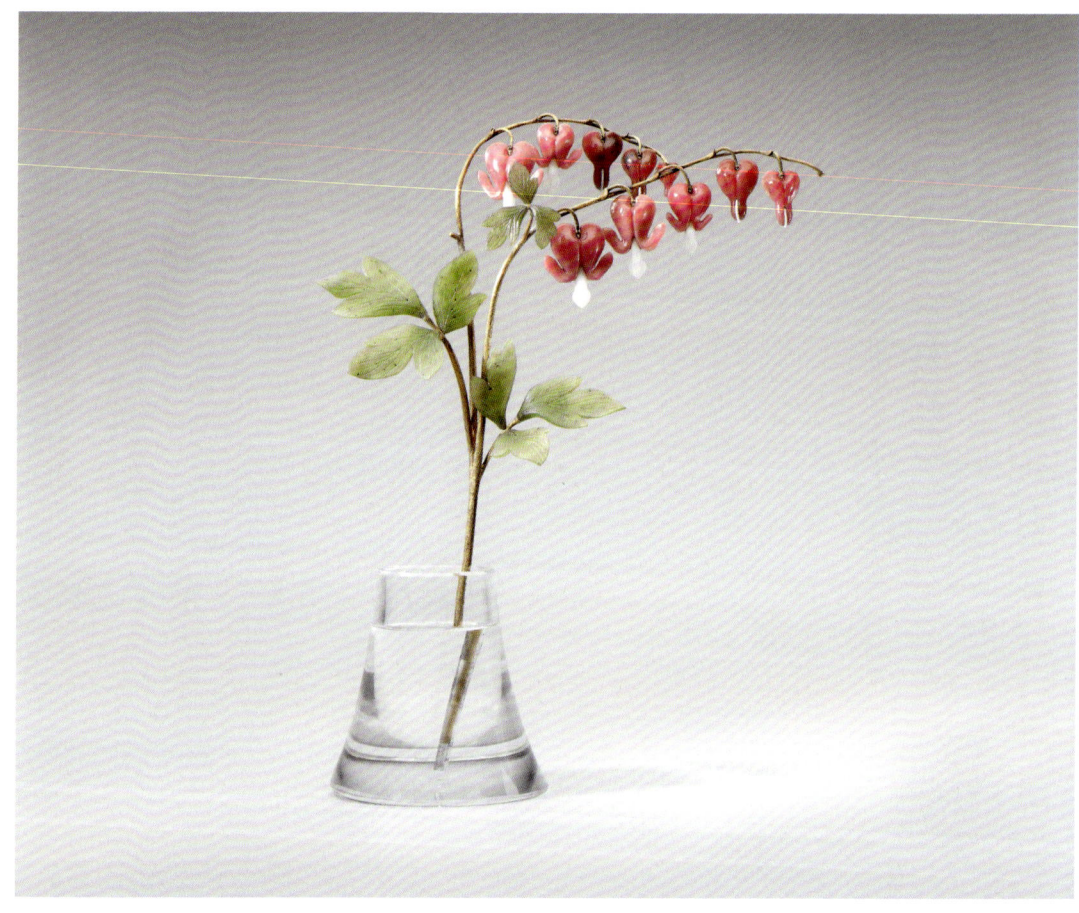

Fabergé

Bleeding Heart, c.1900
Rock crystal, gold, nephrite, rhodonite and
quartzite, 19 × 15.3 × 6.2 cm / 7½ × 6 × 2½ in
Royal Collection Trust, UK

This beautifully accurate botanical study
of a bleeding heart (*Lamprocapnos spectabilis*)
made in gold and hard stone is one of about
eighty designed by the celebrated Russian jeweller
Peter Carl Fabergé (1846–1920). An outstanding
example, the bleeding heart blooms are hinged
to the stem *en tremblant* so they can gently
swing in a breeze or when touched. Queen Mary
loved this one-of-a-kind, single-stem bleeding
heart so much she bought it in 1934. The purchase
might have been motivated as much by the
symbolism of the flower as by the delicacy of the
object itself. Beneath their innocent beauty,
the blooms of bleeding heart tell a tragic story
of unrequited love. According to Japanese legend,
the petals of bleeding heart faithfully resemble
gifts that a prince gave in vain to a beautiful girl
he loved. She barely glanced at the two pink bun-
nies (the outer petals), the exquisite earrings
or the pair of slippers (the inner petals). Too hurt
to live, the prince stabbed himself in the heart
with a dagger (the pistil). Only then did the
girl suddenly become aware of the prince's devotion and cry, 'I have done wrong. My own
heart is broken, too. I shall bleed for my prince
for ever more!'

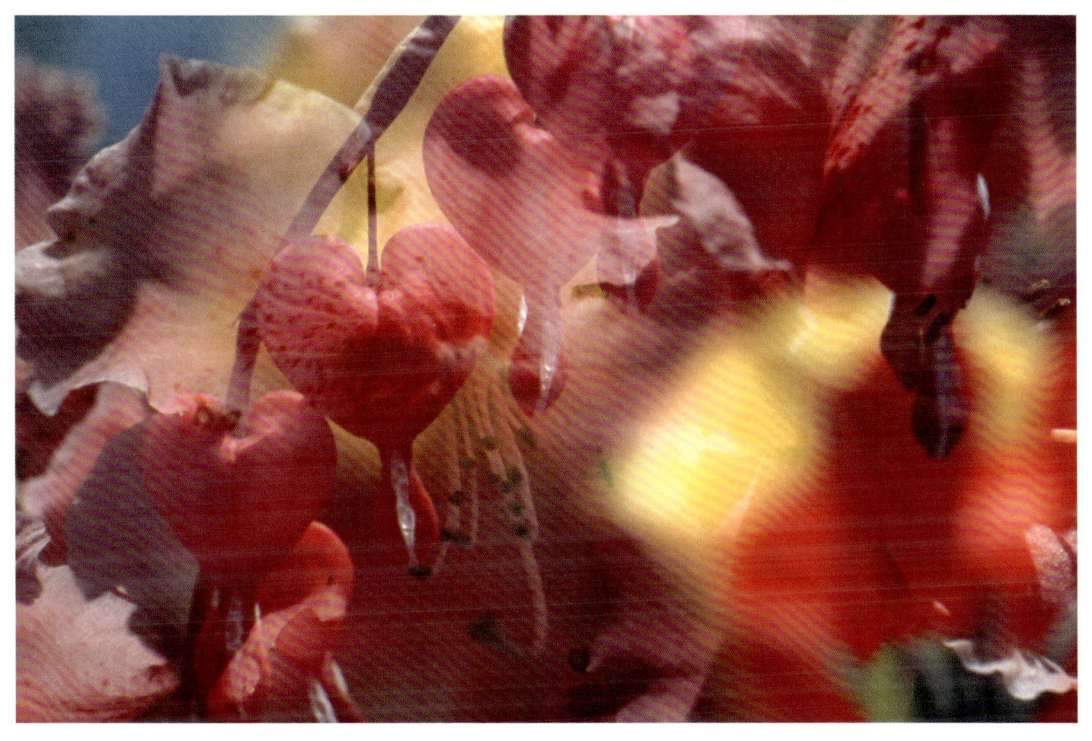

Peter Fischli and David Weiss

Untitled, 1997–98
Inkjet print

Imbued with deliberate romanticism, decadence and a dreamlike atmosphere, this striking image of bleeding hearts overlaid with pink azalea blooms is in fact intended to be just another pretty photograph of flowers, like millions of others. With a partnership that began in 1979, contemporary Swiss artists Peter Fischli (born 1952) and David Weiss (1946–2012) developed a reputation as anti-conformist, sometimes anti-establishment, *enfants terribles* of the art world. With characteristic wit and humour, Fischli/Weiss took pleasure in creating conceptual art that poked fun at the ever-serious art world through sculpture, video art, photography and installations. Flying in the face of 'high art' trends and conventions, in 1997 they adopted the characteristics of typical amateur photography to produce shamelessly beautiful images of what they perceived as a banal and clichéd subject: flowers. As with all their projects, Fischli/Weiss worked collaboratively on the series, using a double-exposure technique. One would photograph a garden or park, using up the entire roll of film, before the other photographed more flowers on the same film, creating a series of superimposed images. Although they discussed which subjects would overlap, there was always an element of unknown, leaving the end image up to the variances of their medium. Among the other 110 photographs in the series, Fischli/Weiss depicted a wide variety of garden flowers – some in bud, others wilting – as well as mushrooms and other fungi.

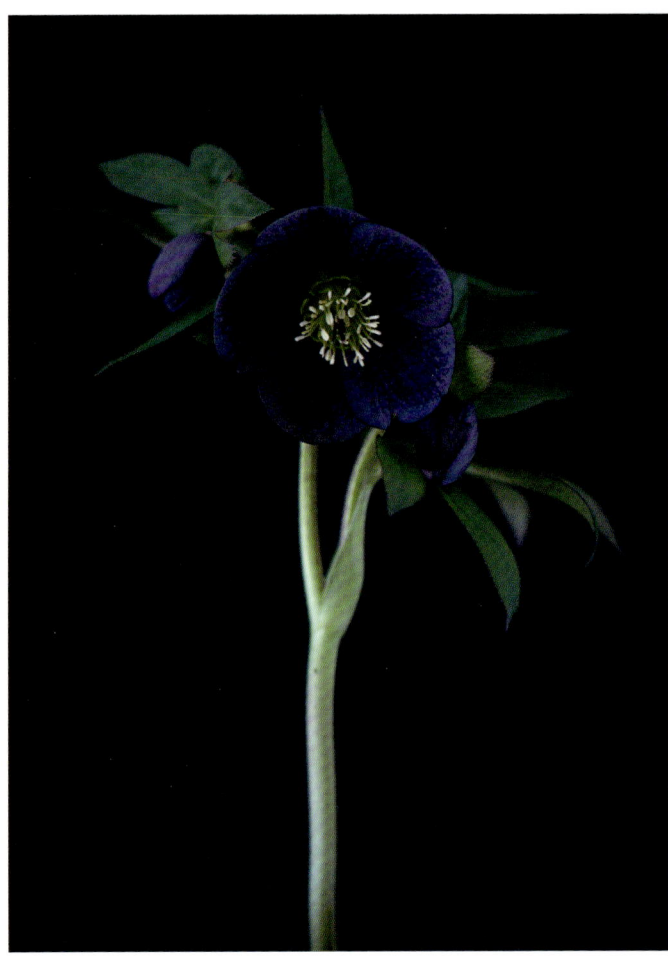

Britt Willoughby Dyer

Hellebore, 2020
Fine art print, 40.6 × 30.5 cm / 16 × 12 in
Private collection

A dark and broody hellebore flower summons all the mysterious essence of this unusual, late-winter-blooming plant. Closely related to the sunnier yellow buttercup, hellebore was documented by Hippocrates, Pliny and Dioscorides (see p.24) as a remedy for melancholy, an efficacious purgative and even a cure for insanity. The root of its genus name *Helleborus* points explicitly to the plant's poisonous attributes:

elein, in Greek, means to injure or destroy and *bora* means 'food'. Hellebore's extreme toxicity is caused by protoanemonin, a toxin released when the plant is wounded or crushed. This effective defence mechanism is a stark admonition to leave the species alone. Skin irritation and blistering are some of the less severe effects, but ingestion can often be fatal since it can cause cardiac arrest. The dark beauty of some varieties and lethal qualities of this flowering perennial make it one of the classic witchcraft herbs of medieval lore, the subject of legend and superstition. According to one, avoiding death when

digging up a hellebore depends upon drawing a circle around the plant and turning east to say a prayer. Another claims that powdered hellebore scattered into the air can make something or someone invisible. The hellebore seen here was grown by Farmyard Nurseries in Wales and captured by British photographer Britt Willoughby Dyer (born 1972). A skilled garden and lifestyle photographer with a global portfolio, Britt's personal passion is botanical fine art photography, documenting gems grown at home.

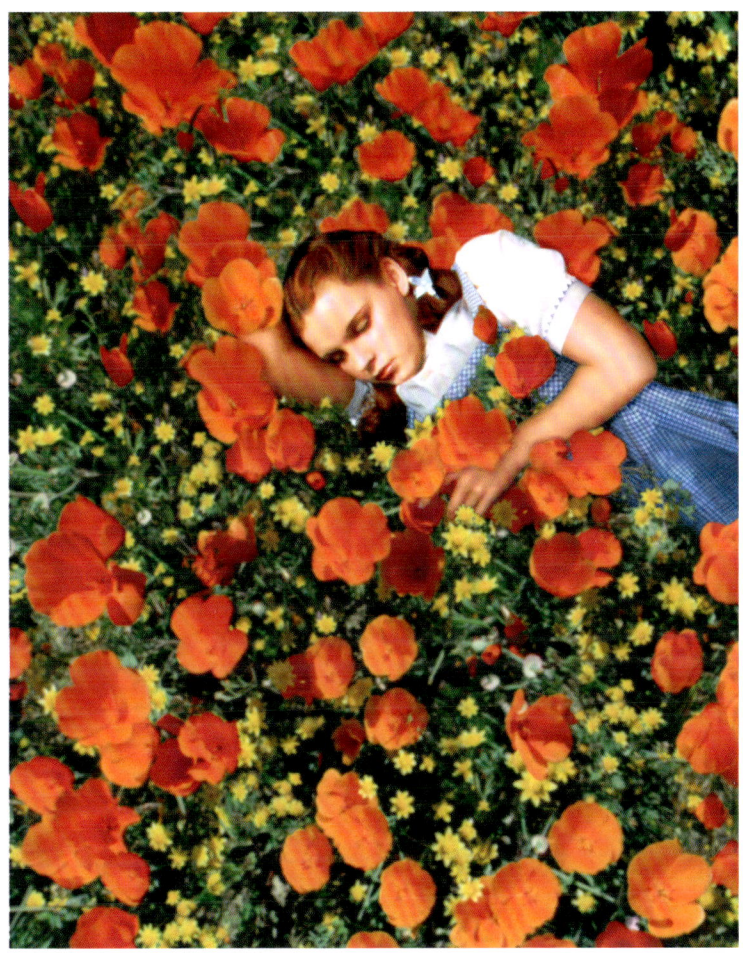

Metro-Goldwyn-Mayer

The Wizard of Oz, 1939
Film promotional image, dimensions variable

Many people will be instantly familiar with this promotional image of Dorothy – Judy Garland – falling into a deep and dangerous sleep in the middle of a field of super-sized, blood-red poppies. Scenes from the fantasy musical *The Wizard of Oz* have been etched into the memories of successive generations since the American film's release in 1939. In the story, the Wicked Witch of the West has conjured the field of flowers in a bid to stop Dorothy, her dog Toto, the Lion,

the Tin Man and Scarecrow from entering the Emerald City. As soon as they run into the field, all but the Tin Man and Scarecrow are rendered helpless, falling into a deep, potentially fatal, sleep. L. Frank Baum, author of the 1900 children's book and subsequent hit Broadway show that the film was based on, was inspired by the opium poppy (*Papaver somniferum*) and its ability to induce sleep – only in this case the Wicked Witch of the West does not intend for her victims ever to wake from their poppy-induced slumber, believing that she will be then be able to retrieve her sister's ruby slippers. As in the rest of the

film, which was directed by Victor Fleming with set designs by Edwin B. Willis, the poppy field – using the native California poppy (*Eschscholzia californica*) found in and around Hollywood – is hyperreal and dreamlike, typical of the dazzling sets that were filmed in Technicolour.

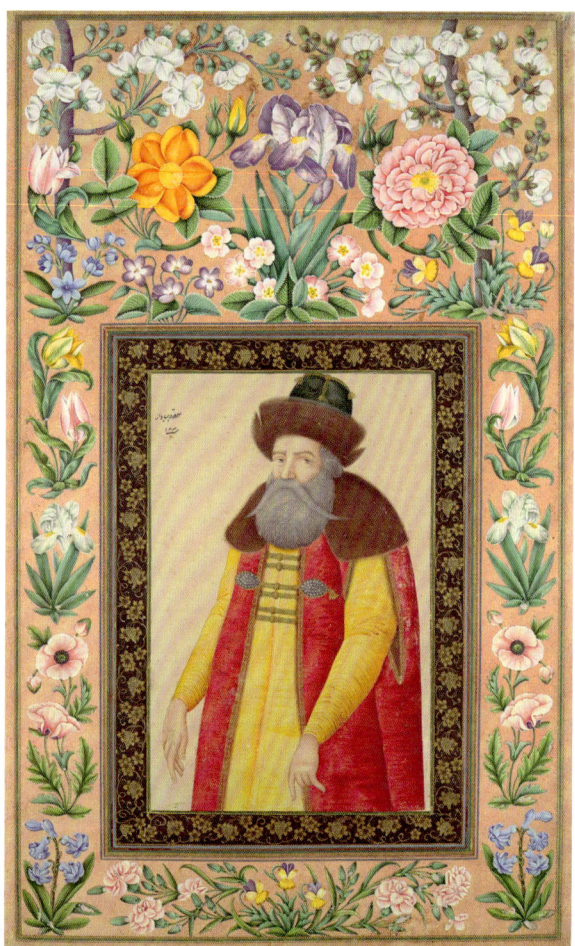

'Ali Quli Jabbadar

Portrait of the Russian Ambassador, Prince Andrey Priklonskiy, from *The Davis Album*, 1673–74
Ink, opaque watercolour and gold on paper,
33.3 × 21 cm / 13 × 8¼ in
Metropolitan Museum of Art, New York

A bountiful wreath of flowers frames a rich and powerful man. At the top are white apple blossoms; below, a cluster of jewel-like irises. Elsewhere and running down the sides of the image in a semi-symmetrical fashion are tulips, poppies and pansies, all in full bloom. The effect is one of regal splendour befitting

the portrait's main subject – the Russian ambassador Prince Andrey Priklonskiy, sent by Tsar Aleksey Mikhailovich to the Persian court of Shah Sulaiman. Priklonskiy is depicted by the leading Persian court artist 'Ali Quili Jabbadar (active 1642–late 17th century) in a golden tunic and velvet vest, his shoulders draped with a fur stole. Jabbadar was one of the first artists of what is now Iran to incorporate European styles into traditional Safavid painting. Prince Andrey would have been at court to represent the business interests of his homeland, including the silk and fur trades. Russian furs were traded all across

the Eurasian continent and were considered extremely valuable, representing an enormous income for the tsars. Jabbadar's portrait would have had an ambassadorial role in this game of wealth and power, and the flowers would have added to the effect. Beyond simply reminding the viewer of the importance and standing of the subject, as well as the abundance of the mother country, the flowers surrounding him – coming from so many different territories and climates – would have spoken to Russia's extensive trading networks and the vast and diverse lands over which it ruled.

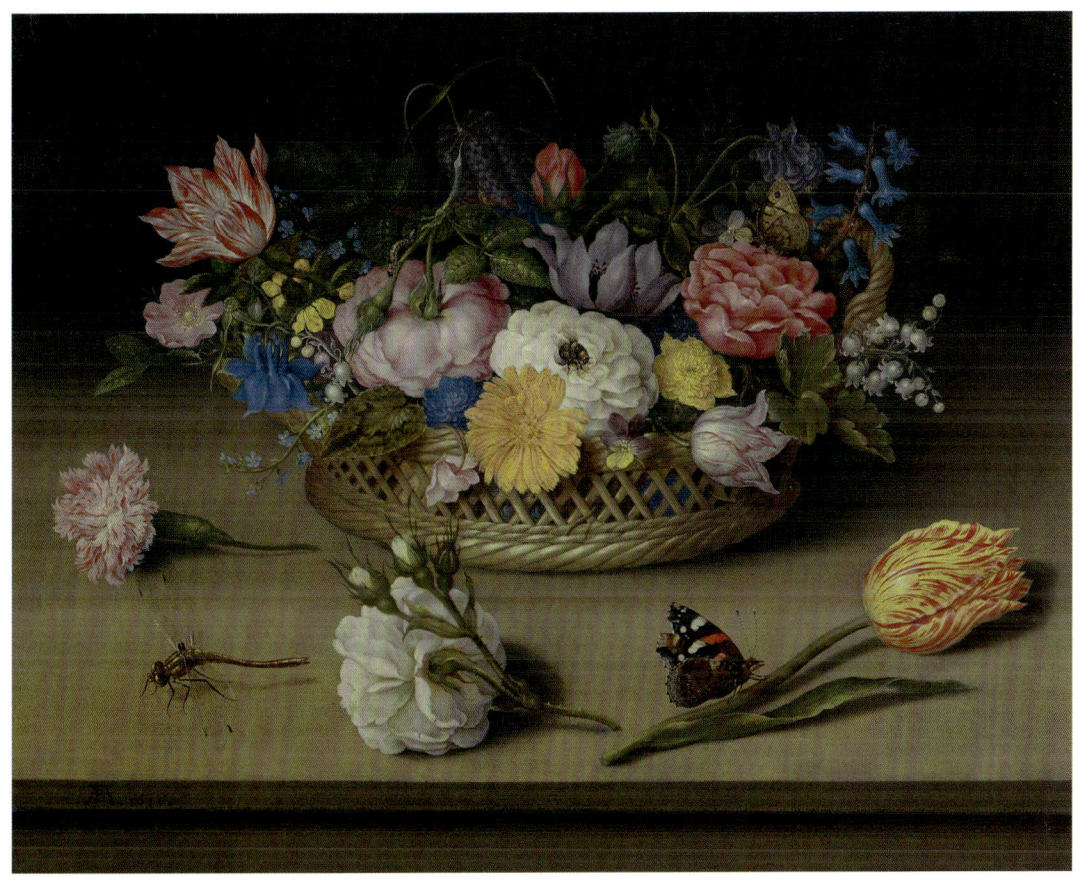

Ambrosius Bosschaert the Elder

Flower Still Life, 1614
Oil on copper, 30.5 × 38.9 cm / 12 × 15¼ in
J. Paul Getty Museum, Los Angeles

A basket rests on a table, full of flowers seemingly freshly picked from the garden – some even have butterflies, bees and other insects still clinging to the blossoms. In reality, it is an impossible arrangement: some of these flowers blossom in spring and others only in summer. Dutch painter Ambrosius Bosschaert the Elder (1573–1621) has created a beautiful illusion – a feast for the eye of the few privileged enthusiasts that

could afford such masterpieces. Bosschaert was one of the major pioneers of flower painting during the early Dutch Golden Age when his work tied in with the growing interest in botany in the Netherlands. Several of his individual flower depictions appear virtually identical across several paintings. Bosschaert made studies of each variety of individual flower before combining them in compositions in oils, often on copper – a stable and smooth support that allowed for fine rendering of the subtle details of plants and insects. *Flower Still Life*, which he painted in 1614, includes more than fifteen varieties, such

as several types of rose and tulip, fritillary, forget-me-not, cyclamen, columbine, poppy anemone, African marigold and lily of the valley. Bosschaert set an example for the many Netherlandish painters of flowers that would become active in the seventeenth century, but only few attained his level of quality – or the renown to charge 1,000 guilders for a single flower painting.

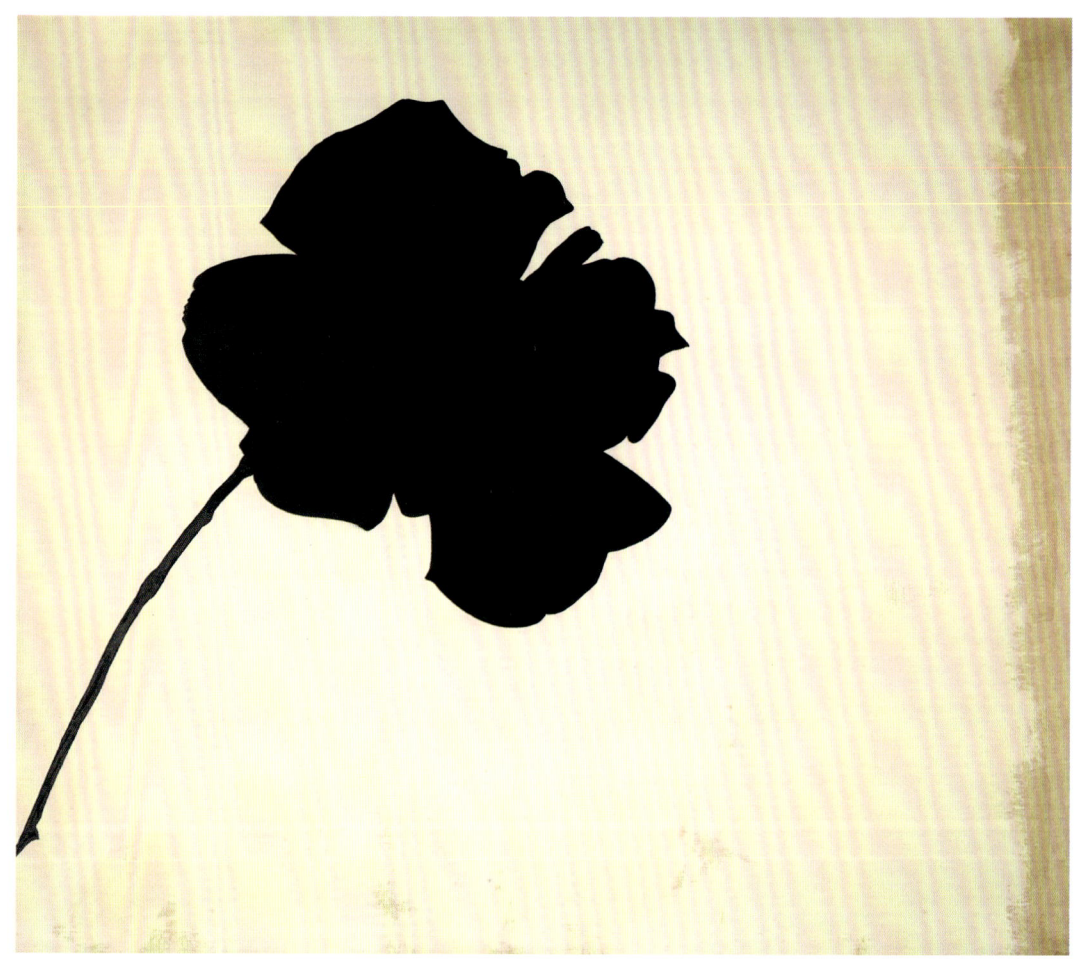

Jannis Kounellis

Untitled (Black Rose), 1966
Enamel on canvas, 2.2 × 2.6 m / 7 ft 4 in × 8 ft 6 in
Museo del Novecento, Milan

Immediately identifiable, a blossoming rose atop a long stem with a single thorn sits starkly in ink-black enamel on a partially primed white canvas. The Greek-Italian Jannis Kounellis (1936–2017) was a key exponent of Arte Povera, a movement that appeared in Italy in the late 1960s that advocated the use of discarded materials or natural elements such as soil or twigs to make art. A painter by vocation, Kounellis

created *Untitled (Black Rose)* as a transitional piece in his exploration of how to overcome the limits dictated by the artist's canvas. The following year, 1967, he again used the black rose as a subject, this time cutting the flower's silhouette out of black fabric and pinning it to a white, stretched canvas. By deliberately avoiding any pretence of realism, Kounellis questions the way flowers are traditionally depicted and gives the blossom a dynamism that could not be achieved by a simple flat depiction. Kounellis went on to explore flowers further, painting the rose on the shutter of his gallery in Rome and even putting

together a version of *Untitled (Black Rose)* where actual birds chirp around the rose. Perhaps his most memorable floral subject is an untitled piece from 1967: a flower-like form resembling a daisy, this time cut out of iron, with a live flame jetting out of the pistil. This 'fire daisy' signalled the artist's definitive departure from two-dimensional art, leaving *Untitled (Black Rose)* as the final testimony of his early period.

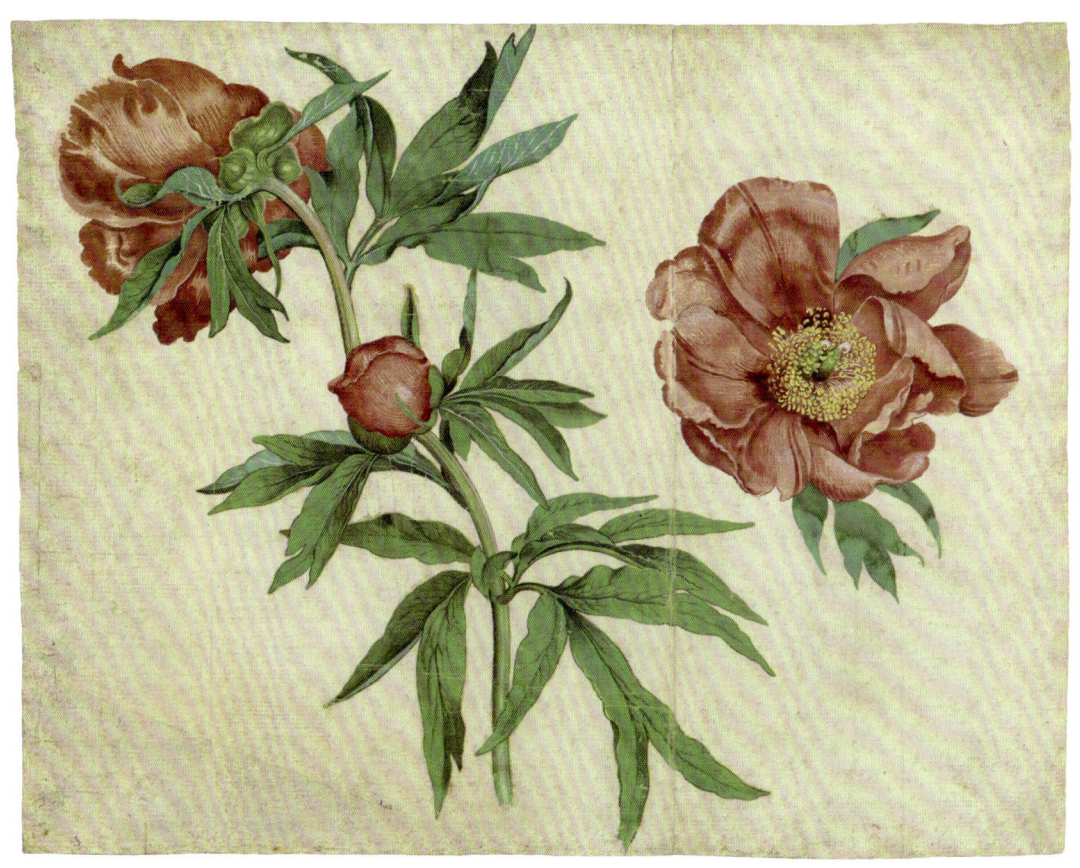

Martin Schongauer

*Studies of Peonies, c.*1472–73
Gouache and watercolour, 25.7 × 33 cm / 10 × 13 in
J. Paul Getty Museum, Los Angeles

Before the famed printmaker Albrecht Dürer rose to prominence, the Alsatian artist Martin Schongauer (*c.*1450–1491) was the leading painter and engraver of the German Renaissance, which occurred during the fifteenth and early sixteenth centuries. Schongauer's works typically depicted religious scenes, but this watercolour study of a peony is a true botanical record painted directly from nature, accurately capturing every

detail down to the bulging green sepals behind the petals. The study was used to inform one of Schongauer's only surviving paintings, *The Madonna of the Rose Garden* painted in 1473 for St Martin's Church in Colmar in northern France. In Schongauer's day, peonies, particularly *Paeonia officinalis*, were used medicinally as a treatment against pain and infection – correctly so, as botanists later confirmed that they possess antibacterial properties. Peonies were also associated with childbirth, a possible reason for their appearance in paintings of the Virgin and Child, to encourage women devoutly praying for

a safe delivery. Being similar to roses but without thorns, peonies also fit well into the poetic concept of the Virgin as a rose without a thorn. This exact study includes two angles plus a bud, but only the facing flower appeared in the final painting. When Dürer (see p.295) visited Colmar in 1492 hoping to meet Schongauer, he learned that the older artist had died the year before. Dürer acquired Schongauer's peony study and signed it – a confirmation that it inspired his own flower studies.

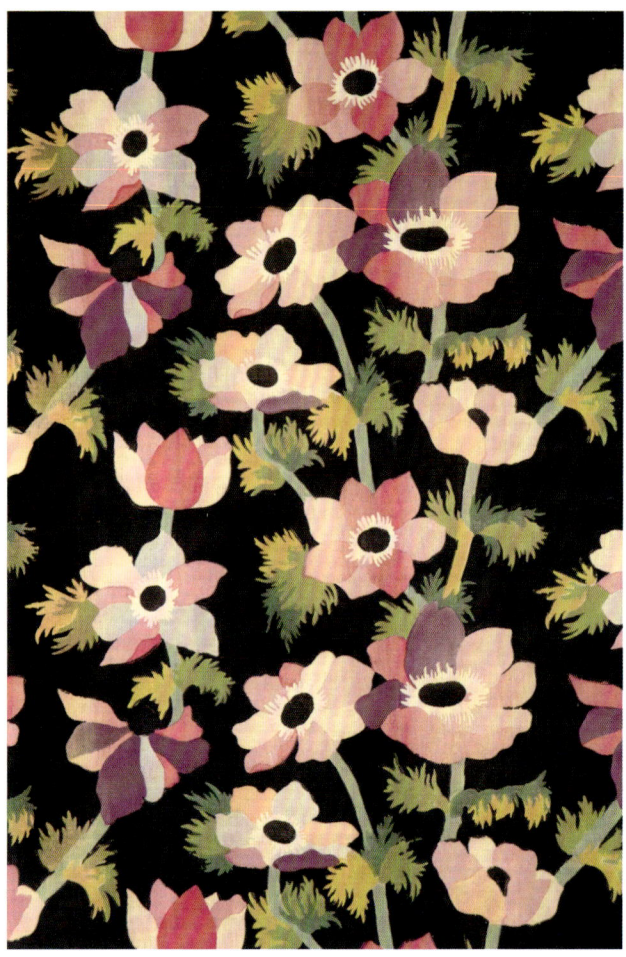

Paul Poiret for Atelier Martine

Les Anémones, 1912
Printed canvas, 1.1 × 0.6 m / 3 ft 5 in × 2 ft
Musée des Arts Décoratifs, Paris

Black anemone centres are flanked by petals in mauves, pinks and pale blues, with celadon and chartreuse-coloured stems linking the repeating motif. Set upon a black background, this eight-colour floral pattern was designed in the early twentieth century to be roller-printed on large bolts of canvas and cloth. Bold textile designs such as this, often produced in vivid colours, along with adventurous and boyish

silhouettes, were the signatures of master French couturier Paul Poiret (1879–1944), who effectively helped shape modern daywear. When he embarked on his career in the late 1890s, Parisian elites first considered his work too modern, but his unique approach built a popular following and, by 1910, he was in high demand. A year later Poiret established Atelier Martine, a design studio, school and shop that expanded his output to include home furnishings and textiles. Inspired by the practice of the Wiener Werkstätte (Viennese Workshops), the École Martine was embedded in the atelier, offering

a form of apprenticeship to artistically inclined girls from working-class backgrounds under the direction of Marguerite Gabriel-Claude Sérusier. Students were encouraged to capture naturalistic scenes inspired by outings to the zoo, museums, parks and gardens. The girls' compositions – unfiltered by schooled styles – formed the basis of prints like *Les Anémones*, which drew attention for their simplified yet vibrant aesthetic.

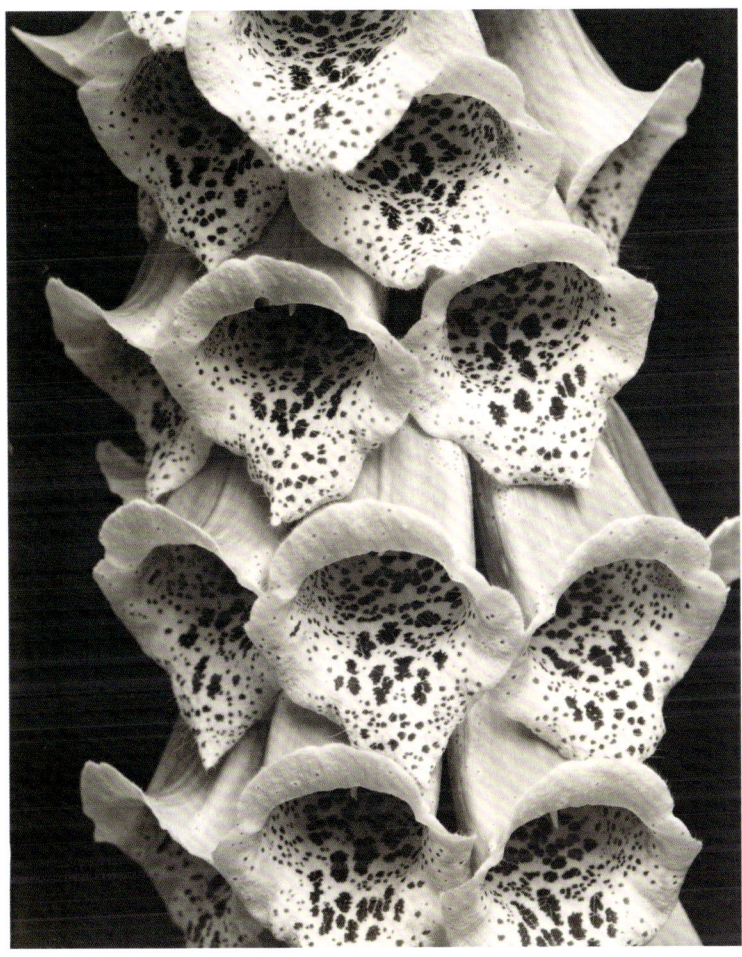

Edward Steichen

Foxgloves, France, 1925
Gelatin silver print, 25.2 × 20.2 cm / 10 × 8 in
Whitney Museum of American Art, New York

Seen in striking close-up, the cascading tubular blooms of the common foxglove lose their sense of scale, taking on an abstract and sculptural character. Strong contrast emphasizes the plant's formal qualities: the lighter tones of the distinctive flower heads jump out against the black background, while the plant's dark, speckled markings appear like spattered paint across the milky petals. The Luxembourg-born American photographer and artist Edward Steichen (1879–1973) argued that photographs such as *Foxgloves, France* were not merely documents of the visible world, but should be considered as objects of formal beauty, in the same way as paintings and sculpture. In this manner, Steichen played a significant role in photography becoming accepted as an art form in the early twentieth century. In the 1920s and 1930s, Steichen made his name as a commercial photographer for *Vogue* and *Vanity Fair*, and is often credited with inventing fashion photography. In 1947 he was appointed director of photography at New York's Museum of Modern Art (MoMA), where he organized the hugely influential *Family of Man* exhibition in 1955. Outside of photography, Steichen was a renowned horticulturist, known for breeding delphiniums on his farm in Redding, Connecticut. The flowers Steichen photographed were nearly all grown by him in his gardens in Redding or in Voulangis in France. In June 1936, MoMA exhibited a selection of delphinium varieties raised by Steichen in its first – and only – dedicated flower show.

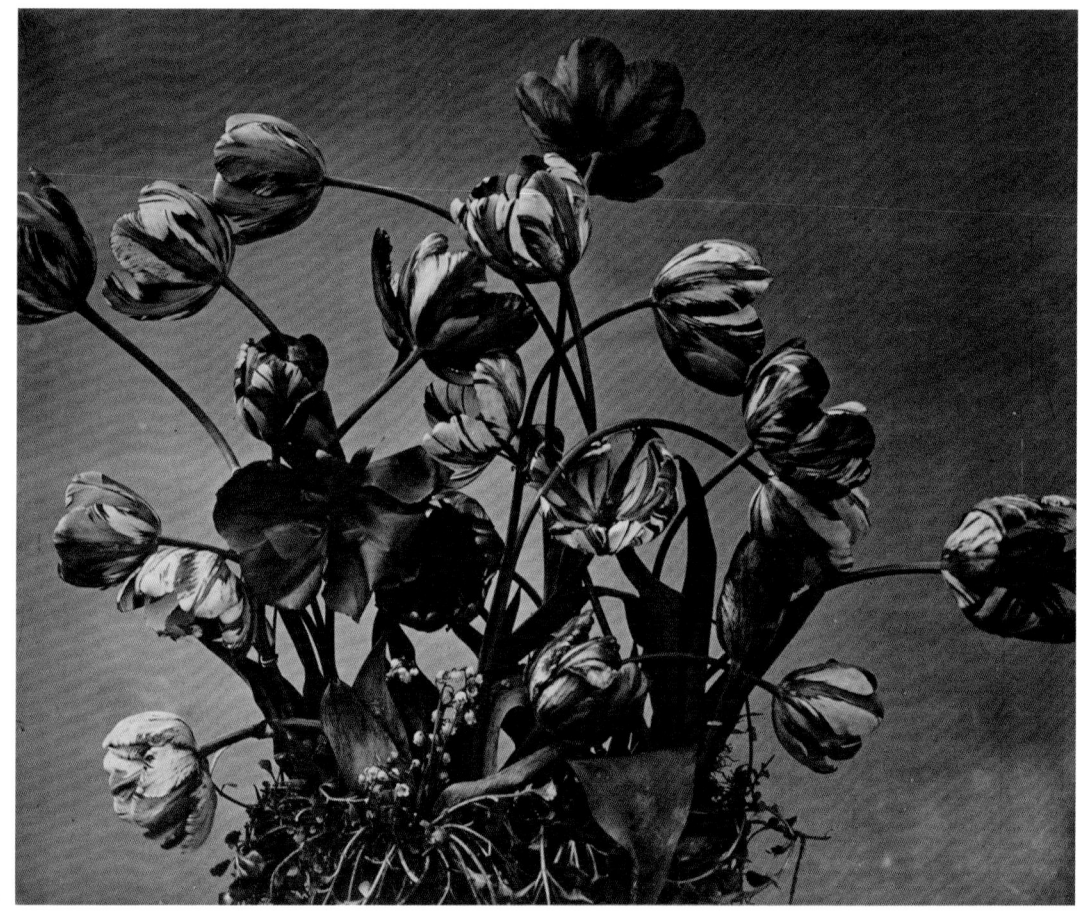

Adolphe Braun

Tulip Arrangement, c.1855
Albumen print photograph, 35 × 43 cm /
13¾ × 17 in
Collection of Fostin Cotchen

A lone stem of lily of the valley is almost lost at the front of this wild arrangement of variegated tulips in full bloom, which spill out of the frame of this photograph by French photographer Adolphe Braun (1812–77). *Tulip Arrangement* is one of thousands of images Braun produced in the late 1850s and 1860s, after abandoning his previous career as a creator of textiles and wallpapers

in 1853 to start to work with photography at the age of forty-one. Drawn to the relatively new wet collodion technique, Braun experimented with combining elements of traditional botanical illustration with the precision and vividness allowed by the new medium. The following year he produced a collection of floral still lifes, *Fleurs photographiées*, which he intended to be used as models for art students and designers, and also to be printed on fabric or wallpaper. Braun presented his book at the Exposition Universelle in Paris in 1855, where its technical skill and artistic quality earned a gold medal. Just as noteworthy,

the artist Pierre Bonnard praised Braun as 'le Nadar de la fleur', likening Braun to his contemporary Nadar, the great French photographer of celebrities and artists. In the early 1860s, Braun shifted his focus to photographing landscapes, which became in turn a major visual source for painters such as Gustave Courbet, Claude Monet (see p.169) and Rosa Bonheur.

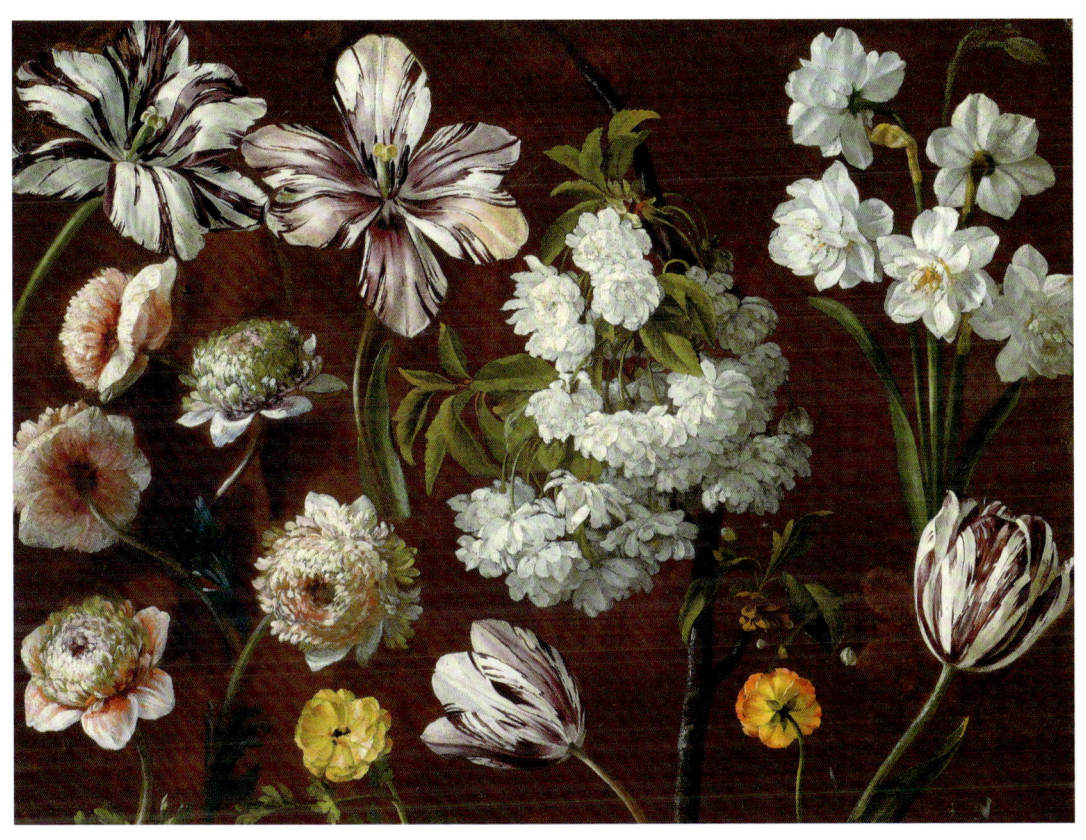

Pancrace Bessa

Purple Tulips, White Flowering Prunus, Narcissus and Pink Chrysanthemum, c.1830
Oil on paper, 44 × 57.5 cm / 17¼ × 22½ in
Private collection

In a carefully choreographed dance, purple varie-gated tulips and pink double-flowered anemones (identified incorrectly in the work's title as chrysanthemums) mingle with creamy narcissi and a sprig of white flowering prunus. On paper, canvas or vellum, French artist Pancrace Bessa (1772–1846) was one of the most talented flower painters of the late eighteenth and early nineteenth centuries. Bessa studied in the atelier of Gerard van Spaendonck (see p.201) in the last years of the ancien régime with fellow student Pierre-Joseph Redouté (see p.109), whose reputation has often overshadowed Bessa's own. During this time, Bessa learned how to study, interpret and repro-duce the tiniest details of a flower, plant or fruit under the guidance of the leading French bota-nists at that time in the Jardin du Roi, soon to become the Muséum National d'Histoire Naturelle and Jardin des Plantes in 1793. In 1823, Bessa was hired as *peintre des fleurs* for the famous *Vélins du Roi* – the Royal Vellums – one of a number of artists who contributed to the compendium of more than 7,000 paintings. Bessa is best known for the numerous vivid plates he painted and stipple engraved for successful books, including the *Herbier général de l'amateur* (1816–27). At his death in Ecouen in 1846, he left sketches in his atelier, such as this depiction of spring flowers in oil on dark paper; others represented summer flowers, such as matthiola, pink dianthus, ranun-culus and marigold; and others depicted wildflow-ers, including pink and blue morning glory, red poppy and larkspur.

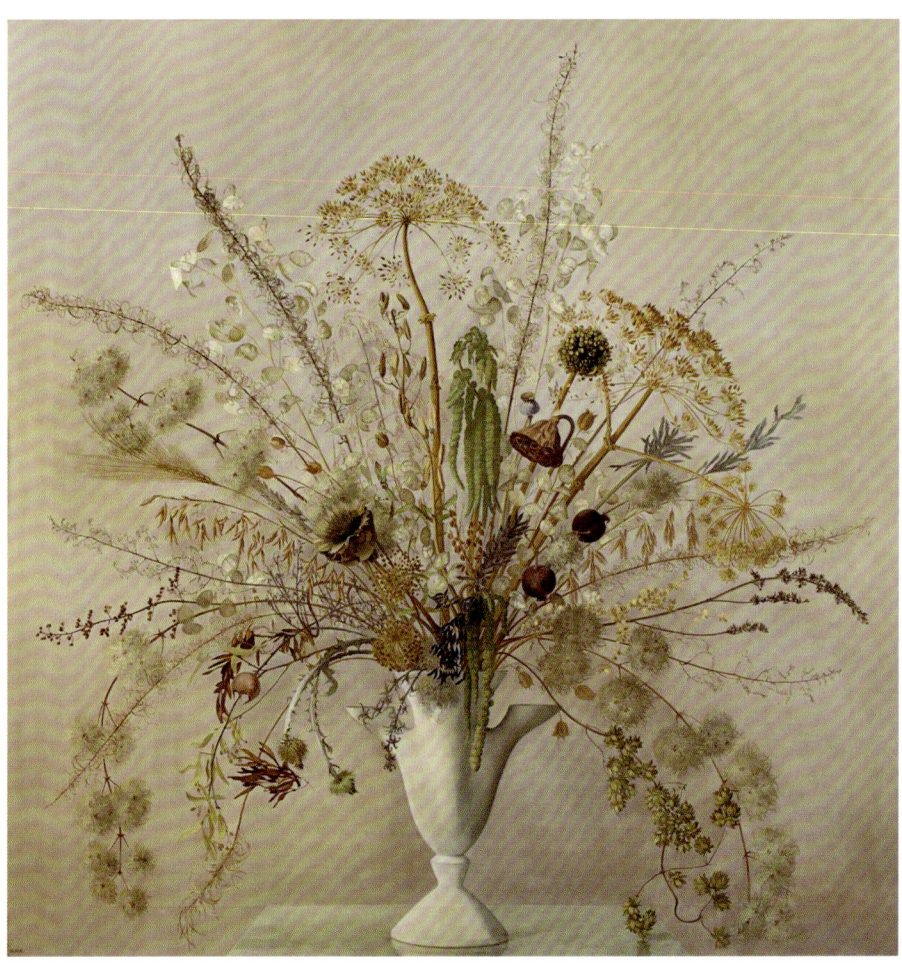

Hannah Gluckstein

Nature Morte, 1937
Oil on canvas, 1.8 × 1.8 m / 5 ft 10 in × 5 ft 10 in
Private collection

British painter Hannah Gluckstein (1895–1978) – known from the age of twenty-three as the genderless 'Gluck', by her own account – was a British painter who created controversial yet powerfully beautiful works of floral arrangements, landscapes and portraits. Born into a wealthy family, Gluck rebelled against the societal norms of her class and chose to travel in a more tolerant set, emerging in the twentieth century as a vocal lesbian artist, dressing in an androgynist style of men's clothes and cropped hair. Gluck's four-year relationship with society's floral darling, Constance Spry (see p.270), inspired a number of her own floral paintings. The almost transparent and virtually monochromatic *Nature Morte* shows her masterful handling of oil paint, her medium of choice. It is clearly a direct echo of Spry's iconic approach that all nature is fair game for the vase, thoughtfully depicting late-season seed heads cut from the fields and hedgerows, arranged in a loose, elegant form that comes together in a bone white ceramic vessel, likely a close resemblance to Spry's chosen vase. After the end of the affair with Spry, Gluck moved away from flowers as a subject and her style shifted, with a looser brushstroke and poignant portraiture taking over. As was Gluck's strong-minded way, even the actual medium of paint was not off-limits for her judgement: in the 1950s, she battled passionately with paint producers to demand better-quality oil paints, eventually securing a new standard with the British Standards Institute.

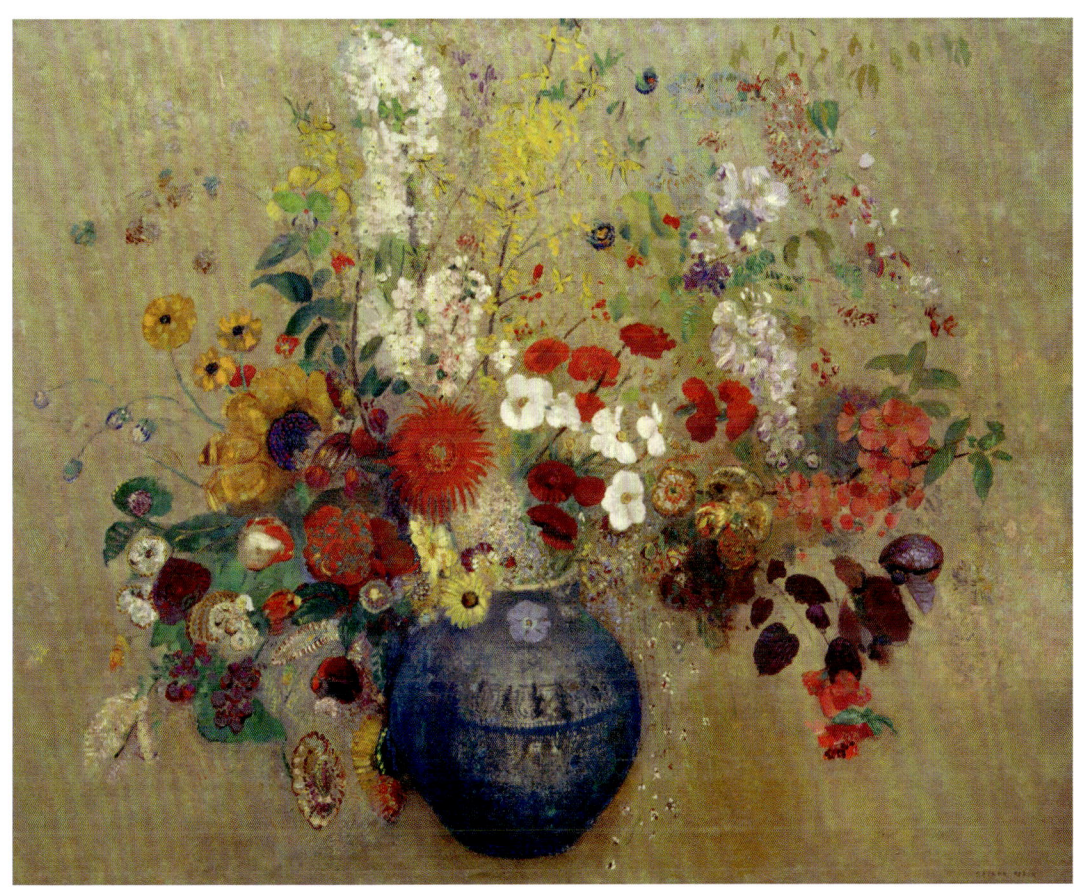

Odilon Redon

Bouquet de Fleurs, 1909
Oil on canvas, 0.8 × 1 m / 2 ft 8 in × 3 ft 3 in
Private collection

Most often recognized as a Symbolist, French artist Odilon Redon (1840–1916) is largely known for his supernatural compositions executed in charcoals and darkly inked lithographs of the late nineteenth-century. They contrast with his late period of flower paintings, where he set aside his sombre tools and took up a radiant palette of pastels and oils. Such floral works ushered in a dramatic aesthetic shift, but they also register

Redon's changing psychological mood. Beginning in his sixtieth year, he chose the subject matter and hues as an energizing means of joyful expression. *Bouquet de Fleurs*, which was completed in 1909, epitomizes his late body of work. Clustered in a blue vase – a vessel that reappears in other floral works of this period – is a loosely arranged collection of spring blooms that includes gerberas, daisies, poppies, forsythia and wisteria, as well as beech branches, likely from Redon's garden in Bordeaux. The untidy arrangement is depicted centrally on the canvas: the object of the artist's full attention. Painted in an unfussy style, the

exuberant bouquet has lively expression: daubs of oil build up the colour and texture of petals, as in foreground blooms like the tumbling wisteria. In contrast, a softer, almost scumbled paint treatment delicately articulates distant and fragile sprays of flora.

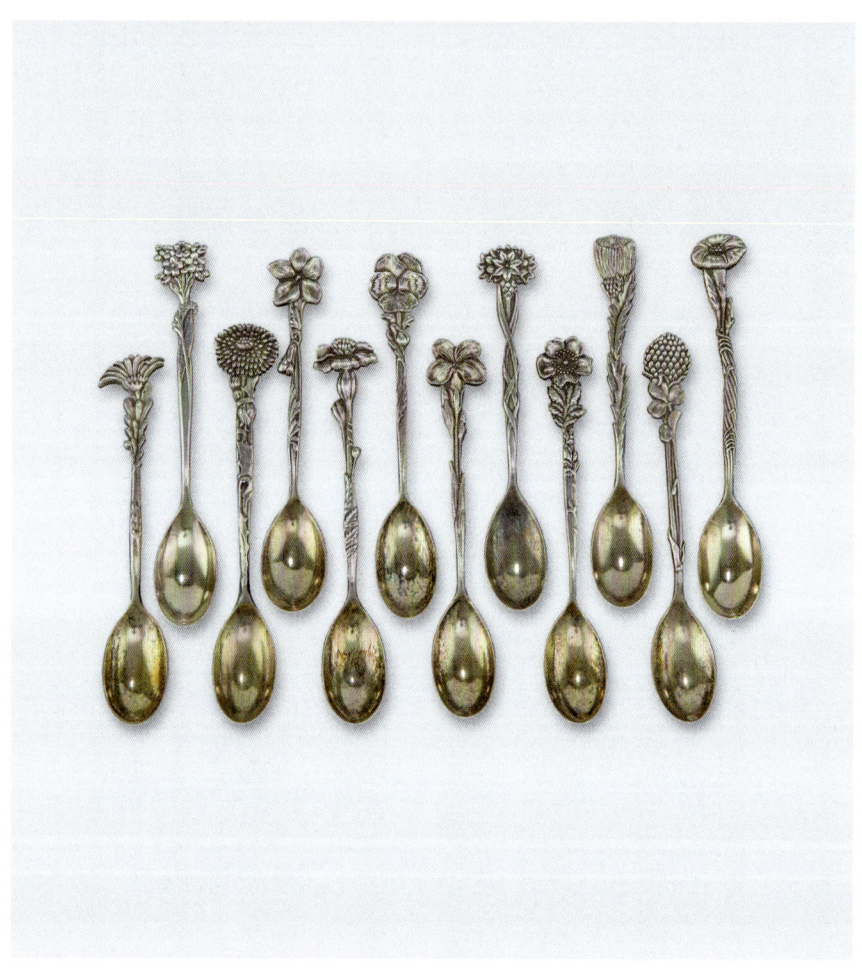

Tiffany & Co.

Floral demitasse spoons, *c.*1885
Silver and silver gilt, each H. 10.8 cm / 4¼ in
Private collection

These twelve delicate sterling silver spoons are
individually decorated with different flower
species, with the petals at the end of the handle
and the leaves and stem running along the
handle to the bowl section. This set of demitasse
spoons – intended to be used with small espresso
coffee cups – was created in the late nineteenth
century by the world-renowned American luxury
jeweller Tiffany & Co. in the Art Nouveau style,
which was typified by its sinuous forms inspired
by the natural world. The spoons would have been
a display of exceptional class, taste and refinement, whose elaborate decoration made them
also a status symbol that telegraphed the owner's
know-ledge of and adherence to a set of strict
rules about eating and drinking among the social
elite. It is also possible that each spoon was
intended to convey a particular meaning in the
widely popular Victorian 'language of flowers'.
Each of the flowers depicted has its own specific
meaning: daisy (innocence), forget-me-not
(memories of true love), dandelion (foresight),
violet (loyalty), marigold (despair or jealousy),
pansy (deep thought), gentian (ingratitude),
cornflower (delicacy), wild rose (beauty), thistle
(intrusion), clover (prudence) and morning
glory (affection).

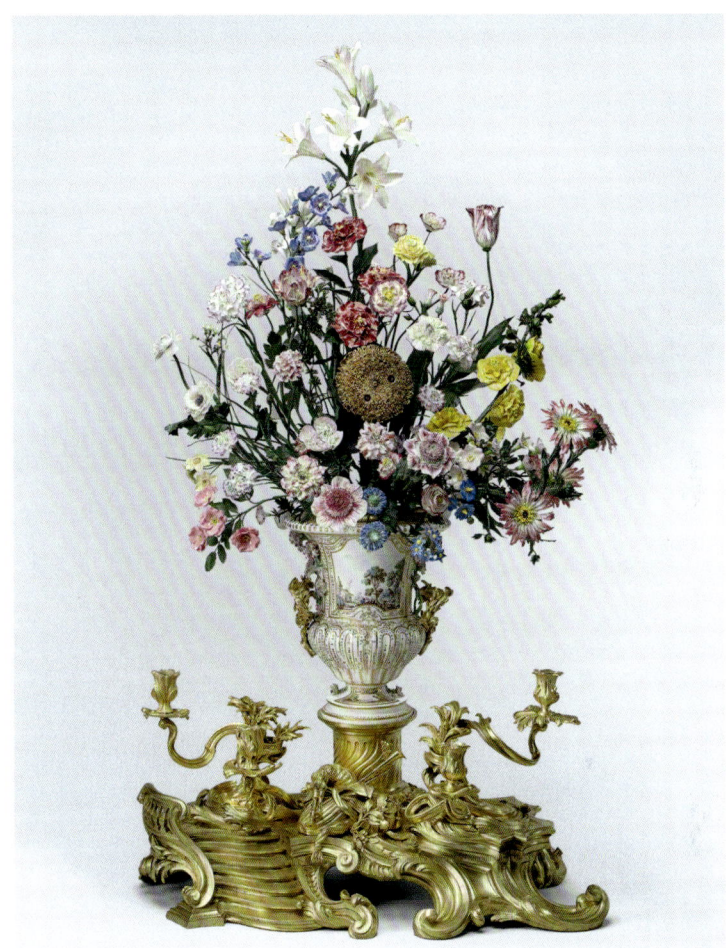

Vincennes Porcelain Factory

The Sunflower Clock, c.1752
Gilt bronze, copper alloy, soft-paste porcelain,
wire, lacquer and painted ceramics,
1.1 × 0.7 × 0.5 m / 3 ft 6 in × 2 ft 2 in × 1 ft 9 in
Royal Collection Trust, UK

A white, decorated porcelain vase rests on an elaborate bronze plinth with two coiled candleholders. The relative modesty of the vase is overwhelmed by its contents: a sumptuous bouquet of flowers that spread upwards in a combination of blooms including carnations and roses, topped by a stem of white lilies. Like the vase, the lifelike leaves and flowers are also crafted of porcelain, sprouting from stems of green lacquered brass wire. It might not be immediately apparent that this object is actually a clock, as the clock face itself takes the form of the centre of a sunflower almost overwhelmed by floral profusion. The clock is a symbol of Louis XIV, France's famous 'Sun King', and dates from the early 1750s, almost forty years after his death. The porcelain flowers are removable, and it is likely that in spring and summer the vase would have been filled with real flowers, the porcelain equivalents standing in during the winter months. The candelabra and the drum supporting the vase were later enhancements, dating from the early nineteenth century. The vase and most of the flowers were produced at the Vincennes porcelain manufactory near Paris, which was founded in 1740 to rival the Meissen factory belonging to the King of Saxony, and later moved to Sèvres. The manufactory developed a soft-paste porcelain that was whiter and purer than rival formulas, allowing the creation of delicate objects such as these remarkable flowers.

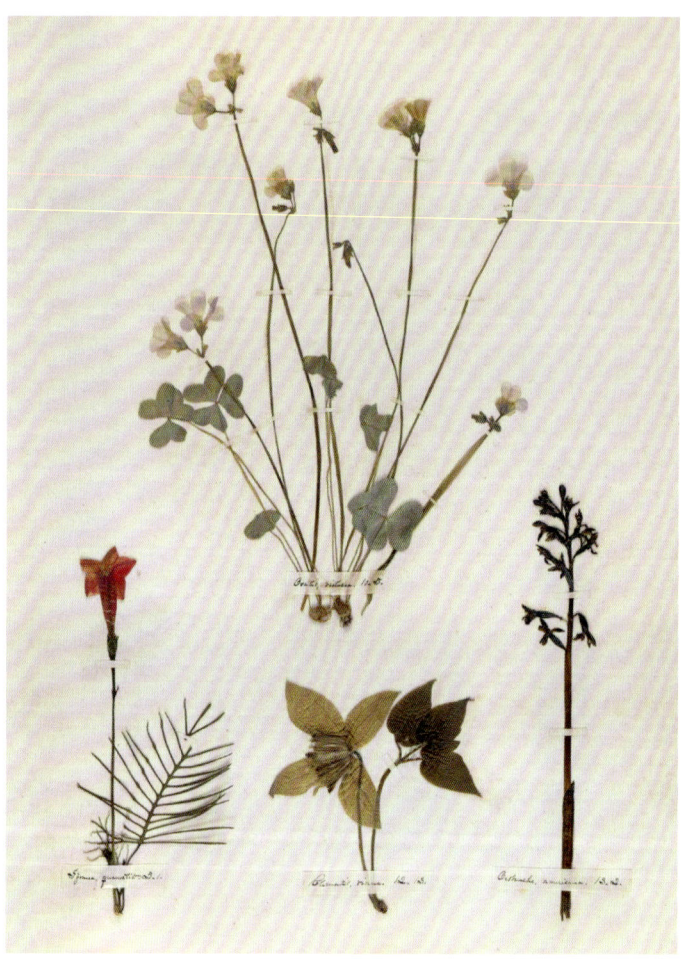

Emily Dickinson

Herbarium, *c.*1839–1846
Pressed flowers on paper, 37 × 28 cm / 14½ × 11 in
Houghton Library, Harvard University,
Cambridge, Massachusetts

In her poem 'With Flowers', American poet Emily
Dickinson (1830–86) writes: 'South winds jostle
them, / Bumblebees come, / Hover, hesitate, /
Drink, and are gone. / Butterflies pause / On their
passage Cashmere; / I, softly plucking, / Present
them here!' Dickinson's writing is intimately
attuned to the changing moods and lessons of
nature, with mentions of flowers in around a third
of her poems and half of her letters. Raised in
a New England home surrounded by gardens and
trees, and with a lifetime of customary long walks
in the woods, Dickinson created in her leather-
bound green *Herbarium* an early display of her sensitivity to art and natural science. Undertaken by
the teenaged author, this 'amateur' botanical study
of carefully assembled specimens was collected
from the local Amherst district of Massachusetts.
It presents 424 flowers ranging from native genera
to exotic plants, with each carefully annotated
with its Latin or common name (albeit sometimes
misspelled) on paper labels punctuating individual
stems: this page sets out *Oxalis violacea*, *Clematis
viorna*, *Ipomoea quamoclit* and *Cononopholis
americana*. It might be argued that this early book
of order flies in the face of Dickinson's later unorthodox approach to writing, but the *Herbarium*
remains significant for its nascent catalogue of the
exquisite observations on nature that would reappear in her poetry as an adult.

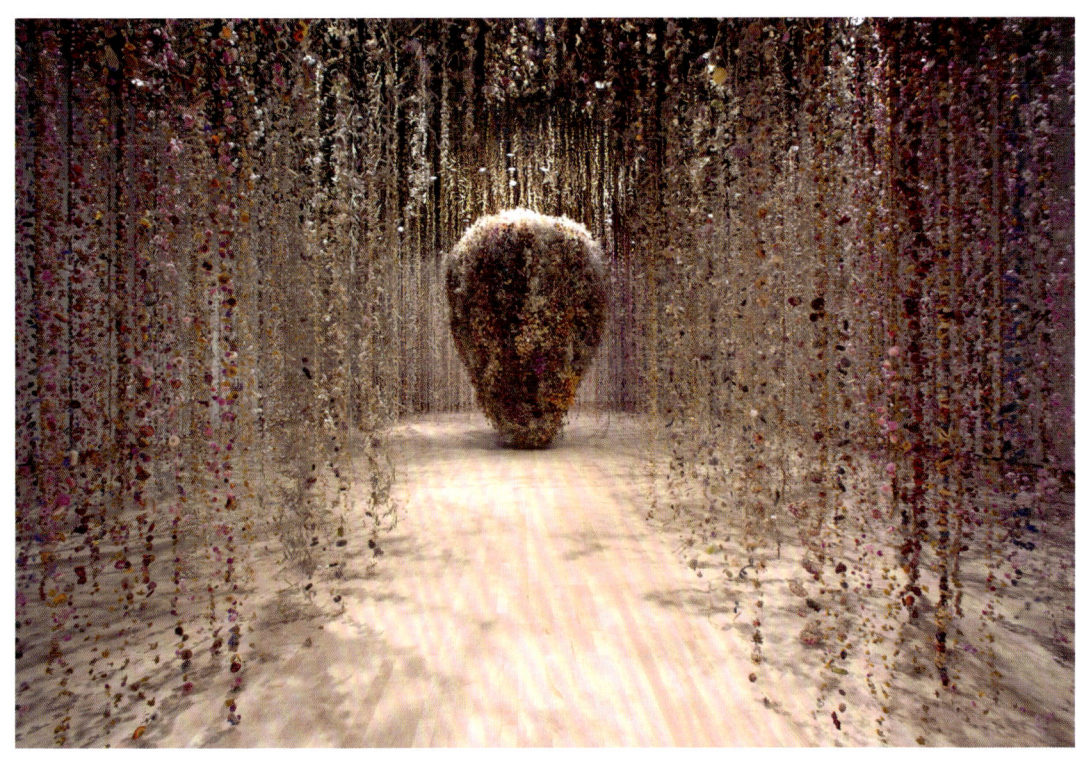

Rebecca Louise Law

The Womb, 2019
Mixed flowers and copper wire,
dimensions variable

This immersive sculpture by British installation artist Rebecca Louise Law (born 1980) explores the relationship between humanity and nature while illustrating the contrast between life and death. Nearly a million flowers and leaves gracefully decay over a period of five months as they envelop visitors in a womb-like experience, with the life-creating organ itself sculpted at the centre of the space, surrounded by protective veils of flowers individually strung on thin copper wire. Visitors are invited to return over the duration of the exhibition and experience the change of atmosphere as the natural materials evolve into different states of being. The installation is formed from dried, recycled plant remains preserved from Law's previous creations, supplemented with locally sourced fresh flowers, leaves and seed heads. Helichrysum, the everlasting straw flower, and crispy statice play dominant roles and bridge the gap between fresh and dried elements. There is an interplay between the delicacy of the raw product and the tensile strength of the malleable wires, which form about half of the final artwork and allow the sculptural elements to take shape. Flowers are utilized as brushstrokes in this ethereal painting in the air, enveloping the participant within a living and dying natural cocoon; they can also be seen as individual cells in the human body, forever repeating and dividing as they protect and nurture the growing life within.

Jules-Edmond-Charles Lachaise and Eugène-Pierre Gourdet

Wallpaper design (detail), 1830–97
Gouache on wove paper glued to cardboard,
47.4 × 31.3 cm / 18⅝ × 12⅜ in
Metropolitan Museum of Art, New York

The fleur-de-lis – depicted here in an elaborate wallpaper design of a type fashionable in France in the latter half of the nineteenth century – has been a symbol of the French royal family since the eleventh century. Although *fleur de lis* translates literally as 'lily flower', some argue that the three-petalled shape more closely resembles the white or yellow iris, *Iris florentina* or

I. pseudacorus. Used in ornamentation and heraldry since medieval times, the motif is based in one legend on the lily given by an angel to Clovis, the fifth-century king of the Franks, on his conversion to Christianity. The flower itself is said to have sprung from the tears shed by Eve as she left the Garden of Eden, and its three petals are variously seen as representing the holy Trinity; faith, wisdom and chivalry; perfection, light and life; or the three social estates of the medieval world – the Church, commoners and the nobility. The popularity of the motif has lasted for centuries, but it enjoyed a particular flowering during

the Gothic Revival of the late nineteenth century, with artists, designers and architects alike drawn to its rich symbolism, historical significance and representation of the highest ideals of the Middle Ages: the true flower of chivalry. This wallpaper was designed by Jules-Edmond-Charles Lachaise (died 1897) and Eugène-Pierre Gourdet (1820–1889), prolific interior design partners for the upper echelons of late-nineteenth-century European society, for whom botanical motifs were a recurring theme.

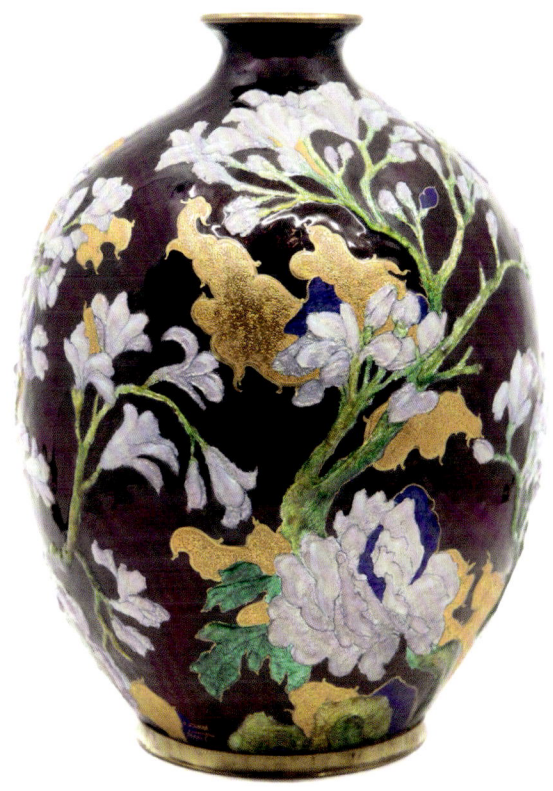

Camille Fauré

Plum ground copper vase, c.1925
Enamelled copper, 30.4 × 22.8 cm / 12 × 9 in
Private collection

Anchored by its glossy, deep plum-coloured
ground, this vase is embellished with a raised
surface scrolled with freesias, peonies and
abstract motifs in gold, malachite green, royal
blue and mauve. These elements – jewelled
colours depicting floral and abstract patterns,
with layers of enamelled colour thickly painted
on a copper surface to create *bas relief* – epito-
mize the distinctive style of French enamellist

Camille Fauré (1874–1956). Born in Perigueux,
Fauré moved to Limoges, Europe's centre of vitre-
ous enamelling since the early Middle Ages, where
he established his own workshop. The mark of
'Limoges' on Fauré's work indicates the city where
the piece was created rather than a particular
factory; although many porcelain and other facto-
ries have long been established in Limoges, the
term does not refer to a single manufacturer. From
modest beginnings as a painter of enamel street
signs, Fauré developed a technique to work enamel
in three dimensions on small art objects. This led
to the apotheosis of his work: geometric patterned

vases such as those exhibited at the 1925 Paris
Exposition des Arts Décoratifs – the exposition from which the term 'Art Deco' was coined.
Garnering acclaim for their unusual, abstracted
patterns, figurative style and bold finishes,
Fauré's work revived the previously unfashionable
art form of enamelling. His three-dimensional
representations in the Art Deco style are his most
identifiable motifs, along with vases that vividly
feature blooms such as irises, anemones and tulips.

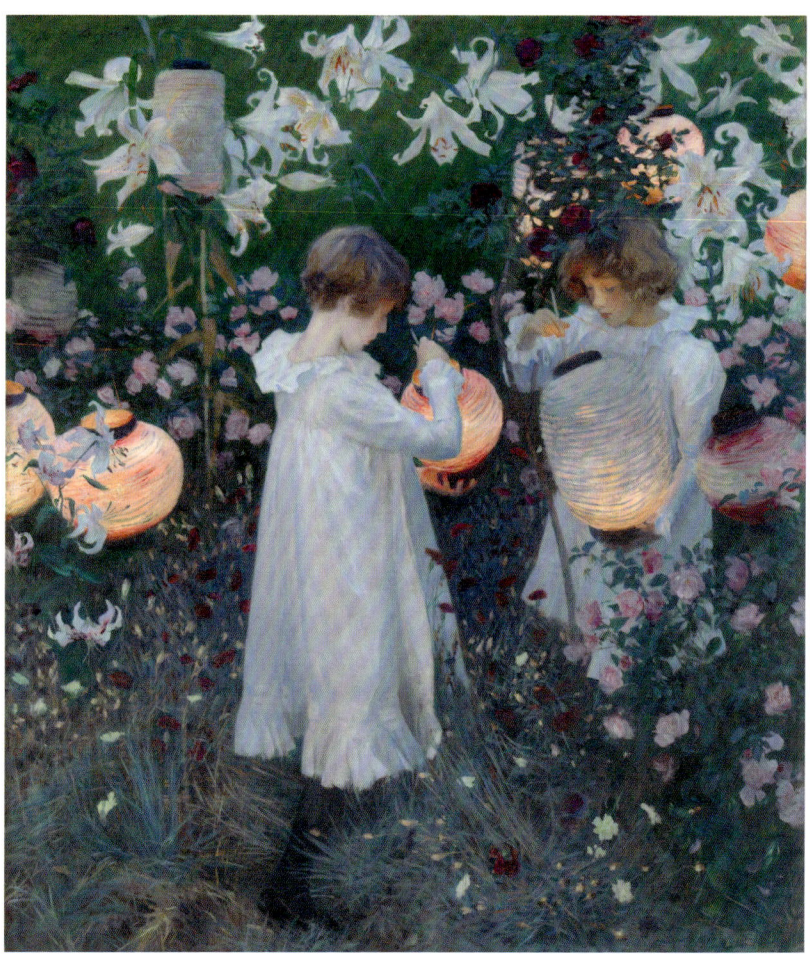

John Singer Sargent

Carnation, Lily, Lily, Rose, 1885–6
Oil on canvas, 1.7 × 1.5 m / 5 ft 8 in × 5 ft
Tate, London

Painted *en plein air* in a brief window of perfect glowing light lasting only a few minutes each evening, this oil painting is now arguably the most-loved work of American painter John Singer Sargent (1856–1925). Inspiration for the painting came from a twilight boating trip along the Thames, when Chinese lanterns hung from trees along riverbanks. The title – *Carnation, Lily, Lily, Rose* – on the other hand, is from the chorus of

a song popular in the 1880s named 'Wreath', which Sargent and his friends sang around the piano in the evenings at Broadway in Worcestershire, where the picture was painted in 1885 and 1886. Over the late summer months that Sargent worked in the dusk of the Cotswold garden, the different varieties of flowers would in turn wither and die, and gradually had to be replaced with artificial ones to keep the composition intact. The two young girls, pictures of innocence in their white cotton dresses, stand in drifts of carnations, their black-stockinged legs disappearing in the glaucous foliage. Around them are shrub roses, pale pink

and fully open, and towering white lilies heavy with pollen. The idyllic scene and the suggested aroma of the heady mingling scents is highly evocative of an English country garden. The lily, known as the golden-rayed lily (*Lilium auratum*), had only been introduced from Japan within the past twenty years, and was a complete sensation among its European audience.

INJUSTICE.

HOP.—*Humulus.*

" Lo, on auxiliary poles, the hops
    Ascending spiral, ranged in meet array."

Philips.

Injustice suffered this plant to be regarded
as a noxious weed, until we began to

" Brew in October, and hop it for long keeping."

———

INNOCENCE.

DAISY.—*Bellis perennis.*

" With silver crest and golden eye."

This " bonny gem" of Scotland's sweet poet,
is made the emblem of innocence, from its
forming one of the earliest floral amusements
of infancy.

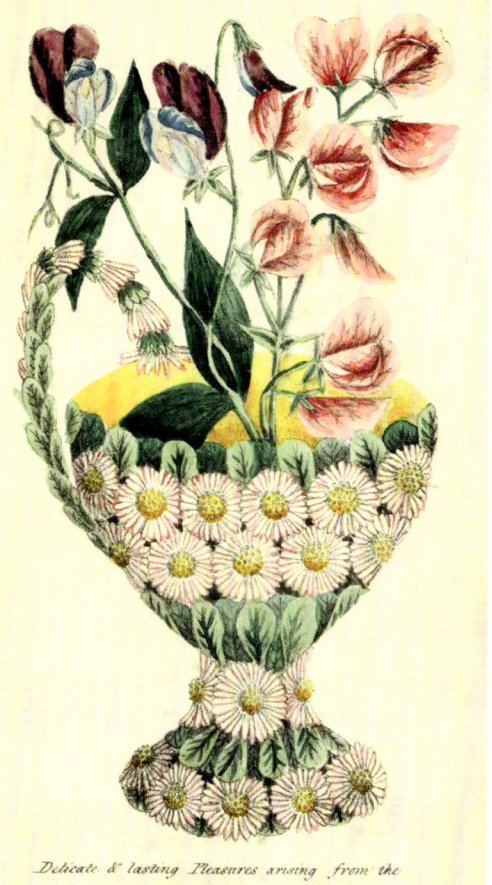

*Delicate & lasting Pleasures arising from the
Cup of Innocence*

Henry Phillips

Pages from *Floral Emblems*, 1825
Hand-coloured engraving, 22 × 14 cm / 8¾ × 5½ in
LuEsther T. Mertz Library, New York
Botanical Garden

———

In nineteenth-century England the Victorians were intrigued by the language of flowers – floriography – in which each species had a particular meaning. The foxglove symbolized youth, honeysuckle was associated with a bond of love, heliotrope represented 'intoxicated pleasure', larkspur with 'levity and fickleness' and so on. Here, sweet pea (*Lathyrus odoratus*) stands for 'delicate pleasure' and sits above a cup of daisies (*Bellis perennis*) the 'emblem of innocence'. The craze for floral symbolism was attributed to the Ottomans, and specifically to Lady Mary Wortley Montagu, wife of the British Ambassador in Turkey in the eighteenth century, who popularized the coded meanings of flowers back home in England. Floral symbolism had long existed in art, literature, garden design and dress across China, the Middle East and Europe, both informally in folklore and myth, and in everyday culture. Of the many illustrated dictionaries of flowers in the early nineteenth century, *Floral Emblems* was one of the most important. Published in London in 1825 with illustrations by an unknown artist, it was written by Henry Phillips (1775–1838), a botanist, landscape designer and teacher who dedicated his book to the poets and painters of Great Britain. The new language of flowers could be used as covert communication between friends or lovers, but it also reflected the growing interest in horticulture as plant hunters travelled the world looking for interesting species to bring home to grow in the nation's new glasshouses.

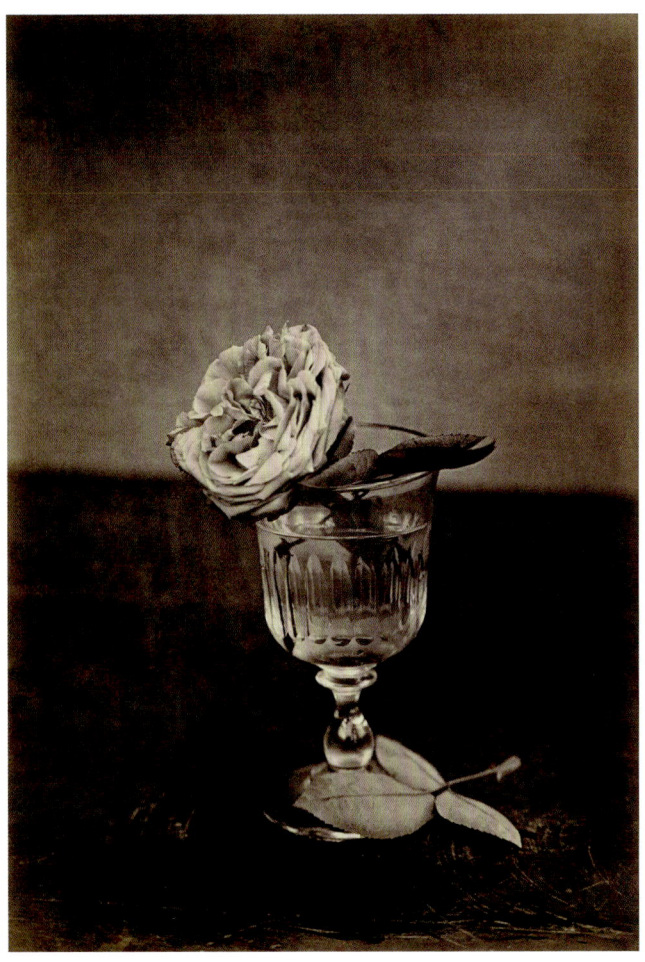

Charles Aubry

Rose in a Crystal Glass, 1864
Print on albumen paper, 34.3 × 23.8 cm /
13½ × 9½ in
Bibliothèque nationale de France, Paris

Placed in a French wine glass, a lone rose is the focus of a masterful composition of light and space, with its slightly asymmetrical composition and stark aesthetic. For Charles Aubry (1811–77), one of the pioneers of photography, this was more than a pretty picture of a cut flower brought indoors. Having spent more than thirty years as a designer of patterns for textiles and wallpaper manufacturers, Aubry embarked on a new venture in 1864, at the age of fifty-three. Spurred by the advances and experiments in the new medium of photography, he set out to create an archive of photographs and plaster casts that artists and designers could use as models to reproduce botanical subjects. In his first year, Aubry created around 150 negatives – including this one – and eventually found clients for his templates in drawing schools in France and abroad, and with companies such as the jewellers Tiffany & Co. and the textile manufactories Mulhouse and Gobelins. Aubry's images of flowers, fruits and leaves vividly captured the details and textures of the specimens, in some cases thanks to his technique of first dipping the plants in plaster to keep them looking fresh throughout the forty-five-minute exposure time required to make an image. His business proved short-lived, however, mainly due to the general lack of acceptance of photography as a medium at the time, and Aubry was forced to declare bankruptcy within a year. Despite his commercial failure, Aubry is today considered a master of early photographic still lifes.

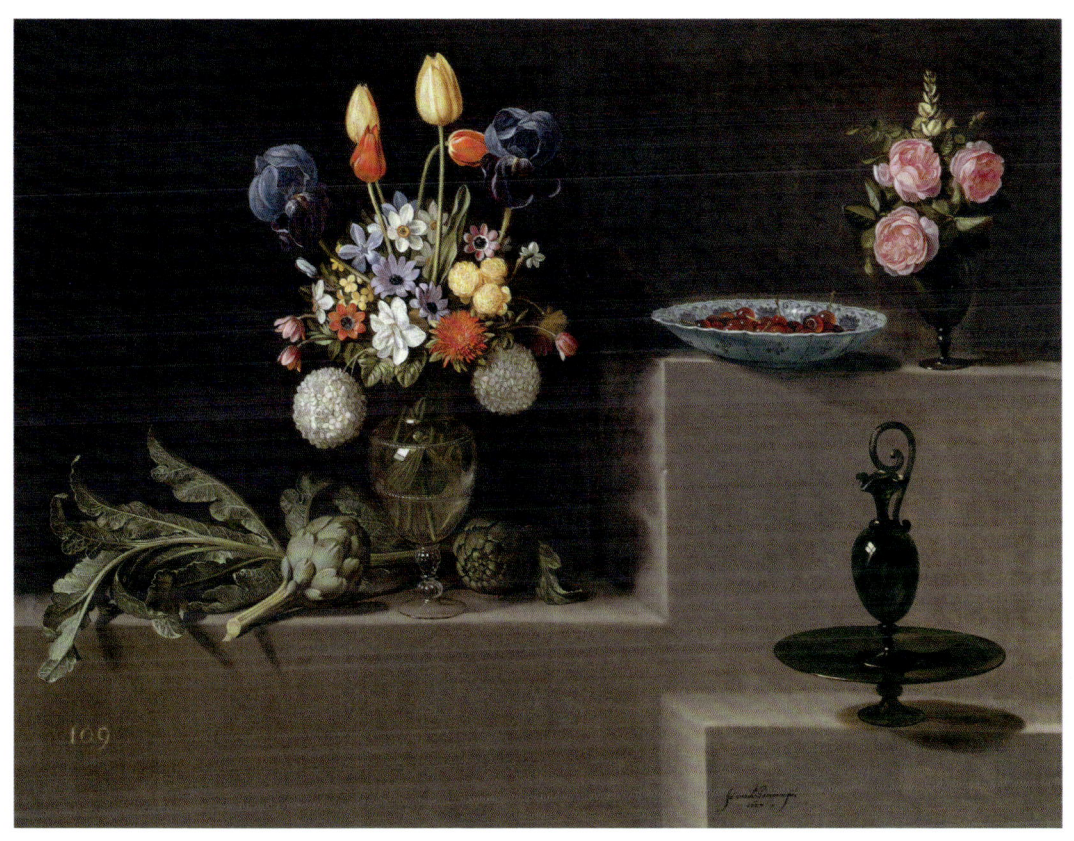

Juan van der Hamen y León

Still Life with Artichokes, Flowers and Glass Vessels, 1627
Oil on canvas, 0.8 × 1.1 m / 2 ft 8 in × 3 ft 7 in
Museo del Prado, Madrid

A large glass vase of tulips, irises, narcissi and the white orbs of *Viburnum opulus* 'Roseum', among other cut flowers is accompanied by a smaller vase containing sumptuous pink roses. Each bloom is rendered with exacting realism, as are the other objects, which include artichokes, a dish of red cherries and a piece of luxury glassware. The beauty of the flowers' delicate petals

contrasts with the coarse vegetables below, pitting the senses of sight and smell against that of taste. Contrasts are also drawn between the artificial and the natural, and between the ephemeral and the permanent. Spanish painter Juan van der Hamen y León (1596–1631) is regarded as one of the greatest still-life painters of the seventeenth century and was a master in the subgenre of flower painting. His style is clearly indebted to Flemish artists such as Jan Brueghel the Elder (see p.268), whose floral canvases were highly prized in Spain during the 1620s. Another key influence is Juan Sánchez

Cotán, whose still-life paintings similarly featured configurations of fruits and vegetables illuminated against dark backgrounds. Descended from a historic Flemish noble family, Van der Hamen served at the courts of Philip III and Philip IV; in addition to pioneering still-life painting in Madrid, he also painted allegories, landscapes and large-scale works for churches and convents.

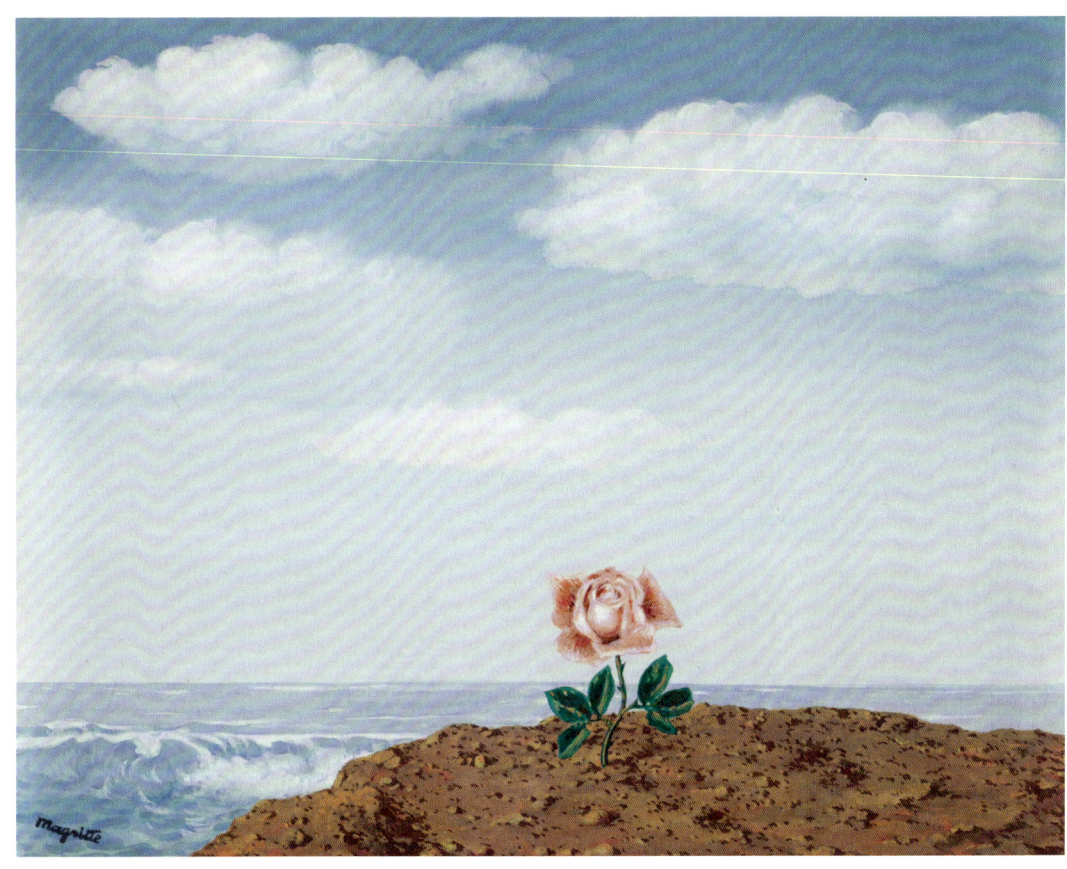

René Magritte

Utopia, 1945
Watercolour and gouache, 32.1 × 41.8 cm /
12¾ × 16½ in
Cleveland Museum of Art, Ohio

Few flowers carry as much cultural significance as the rose. Throughout human history, the rose has been used to symbolize a multitude of concepts and ideals, from war to peace and everything in between. Perhaps part of the rose's universal allure is the contradiction that lies at its heart: that despite the plump velveteen petals that create its dazzling beauty, its stem bears razor sharp spikes that any admirer knows can draw blood. The Belgian artist René Magritte (1898–1967) emphasizes this elemental contradiction by setting a blush-coloured rose on the edge of a barren cliff. Nothing else grows in this sandy and stony land, yet a single flower blossoms and thrives. As in the work of other Surrealists, basic logic and reason are dispensed with, leaving viewers to construct their own narratives. Behind the rose is a turbulent sea and a partially cloudy sky – and yet the rose casts no shadow. Magritte somewhat perversely titled this work *Utopia*; again, as with the subject matter, the title intentionally resists straightforward interpretation. Perhaps Utopia, or a type of perfection for the artist, might be the triumph of nature and life in impossible circumstances. Despite the salt of the sea, the glare of the sun and the barren soil, beauty can still thrive against all the odds.

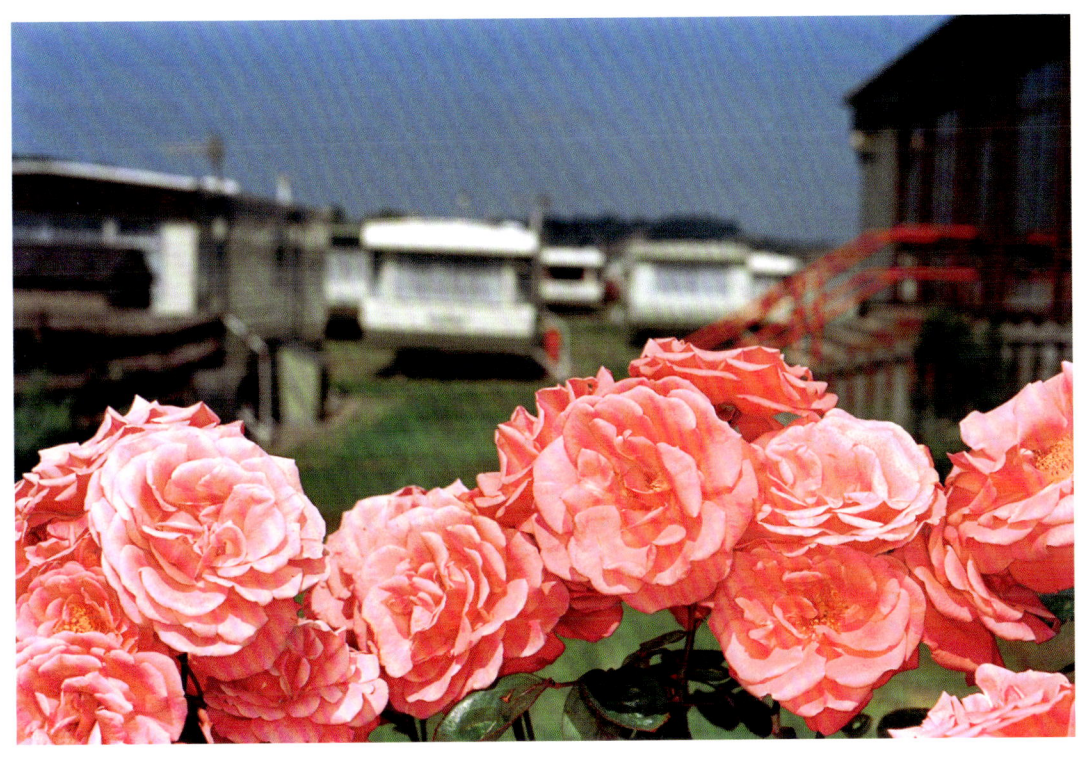

Martin Parr

Flowers on a Campsite, West Bay, England, 1999
Photograph, dimensions variable

Through his intimate, gently satirical images, British photographer Martin Parr (born 1952) takes the mundane and familiar – a motorway service station, a sandwich, a crowded beach on a hot summer's day – and presents them in such a way that we see them anew. While flowers may not be a typical Parr subject, this image – with its saturated, garish colour and caravan-park backdrop – nevertheless reflects many of the themes that run throughout his work: how and where we choose to spend our leisure time; the gulf between the world as it exists in our imaginations and how it actually is; and the subtle but immutable codes that define the English class system. In this close-up shot, the roses leap from the page, Parr's characteristic use of macro lens and daylight flash lending the already vivid pink blooms an almost surreal edge. In capturing this apparently unremarkable scene, he blurs the line between fiction and reality, and invests the everyday world around us with a kind of magic. Parr took to photography from a young age, going on to study at Manchester Polytechnic and undertaking his first solo exhibition, *Home Sweet Home*, in 1974. Since then, he has produced more than a hundred books of his photography and more than 350 exhibitions worldwide, earning dozens of awards for his achievements and important contributions to photography.

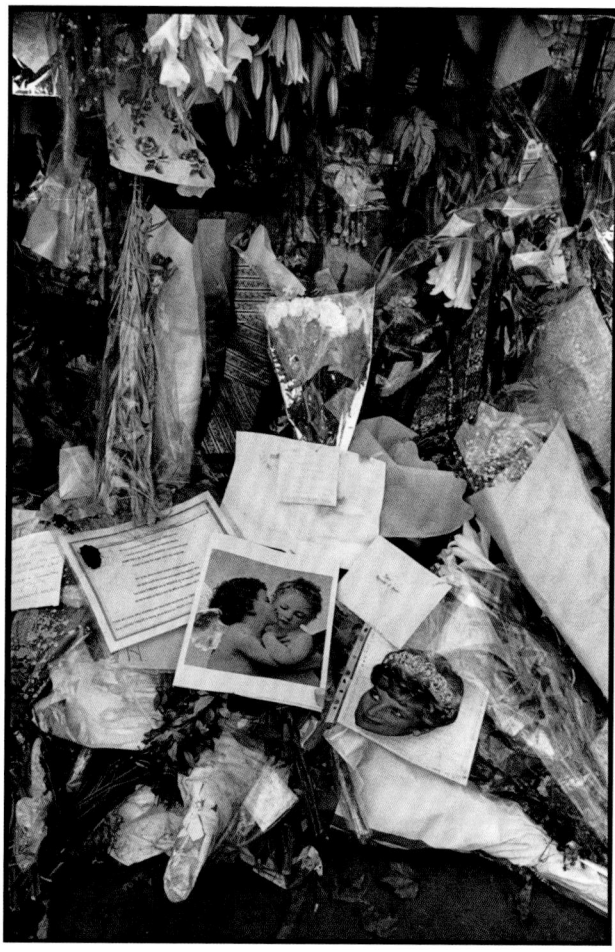

Henri Cartier-Bresson

*London. September 1997. After the Death
of Lady Diana Spencer*
Photograph, dimensions variable

On 31 August, 1997, Diana Princess of Wales and her lover, Dodi Fayed, died in a car crash in Paris. In the days following her death, a sea of flowers built up outside the gates of her former home, Kensington Palace in London, while bouquets also smothered the roads outside Buckingham Palace and St James's Palace amid an outpouring of public grief unprecedented in modern Britain. London's florists struggled to keep up with the demand as mourners flooded to the capital to honour a woman who had, until the previous year, been married to the heir to the British throne. It is estimated that nearly 13,500 tonnes (15,000 tons) of flowers were left in her honour, along with cards, pictures, toys and votive candles. Instead of trying to capture the occasion's magnitude, renowned French photographer Henri Cartier-Bresson (1908–2004) focused his lens on a small patch of cellophane-wrapped flowers. Amid the wilting plants and handwritten cards is a cut-out image of Diana's face, her eyes appearing to gaze at a reproduction of *L'Amour* *et Psyché, Enfants*, an 1890 oil painting by William Adolphe Bouguereau depicting the mythological figures of Cupid and Psyché. By highlighting this classical love story, Cartier-Bresson artfully underscores the tragic end of another, very public love affair.

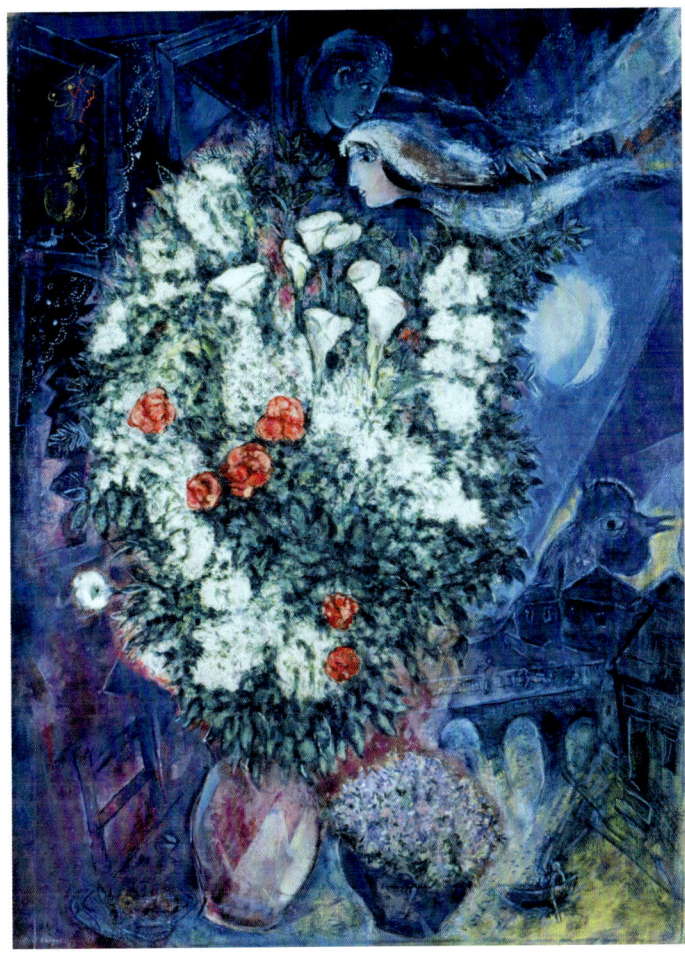

Marc Chagall

Bouquet with Flying Lovers, c.1934–47
Oil on canvas, 1.3 × 1 m / 4 ft 3 in × 3 ft 2 in
Tate, London

The tight bunch of mixed flowers that bursts from a tilted vase against an indistinct blue-toned background looks solid enough, but this painting by the French-Russian artist Marc Chagall (1887–1985) surely depicts a dream. Look more closely and several other images emerge: a rower crosses a river, a pedestrian and dog walk on an arched bridge, a cockerel raises its head from behind a row of houses against a moonlit sky, perhaps crowing to the golden yellow light of the rising morning sun. Memories of Chagall's past are echoed in the buildings, which represent the Russian town of Vitebsk (now in Belarus), where the artist was born. The viewer's eye, however, is drawn upwards from the bright whites of the bouquet to the two faces above – belonging, as the work's title indicates, to flying lovers – where the woman's bridal veil and dress stream out into the night, while the man, shrouded in shadows, reaches around to embrace her. Chagall started this painting in the 1930s, while he was living in Paris, but completed it slowly over several years, ultimately repainting this final version in 1947. His wife Bella died a short time before the painting was completed, and Chagall said that it expressed his feelings of sadness, loss and nostalgia.

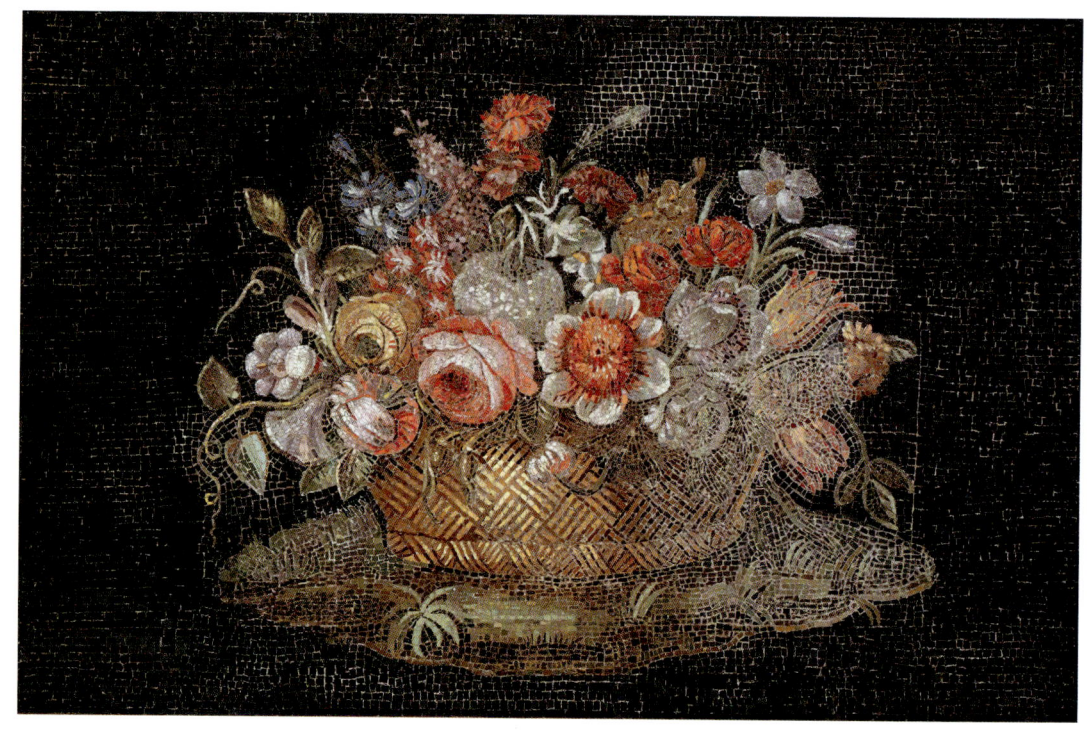

Anonymous

Basket of Flowers (detail), 2nd century AD
Mosaic
Museo Pio-Clementino, Vatican City

This exquisite image forms the central *emblema* of a mosaic floor, surrounded by black and white rectangular borders and a curving rope motif. The artful mixture of fragrant flowers – roses (*Rosa gallica* and *R. canina*, the dog rose), morning glory (*Convolvulus*), stock (*Matthiola incana*), lupin (*Lupinus polyphyllus*), mallow (*Malva sylvestris*), anemone (*Anemone coronaria*), possibly opium poppy (*Papaver somniferum*) and other varieties – includes plants native to southern Italy and well known from wall paintings in Rome, Pompeii and other Vesuvian sites. The blossoms were clearly chosen for their scent as well as their beauty, and the image might once have decorated the floor of a woman's *cubiculum*, a dressing room or bedroom. This mosaic is the earliest representation in Roman art of a floral arrangement in a container. The ancient Roman love of gardens and flowers is well exhibited in art, especially wall paintings, and in literature. Certain flowers and plants were associated with particular deities – the oak with Jupiter, the olive with Minerva, the grapevine with Bacchus – and the selection of flowers in this arrangement suggests that it was intended to remind the viewer of Venus, goddess of love, to whom the rose and anemone were sacred. When Adonis, beloved of Venus, was killed while hunting, it is said that anemones sprang from the blood he shed; another version of the myth has his blood turning white anemones red.

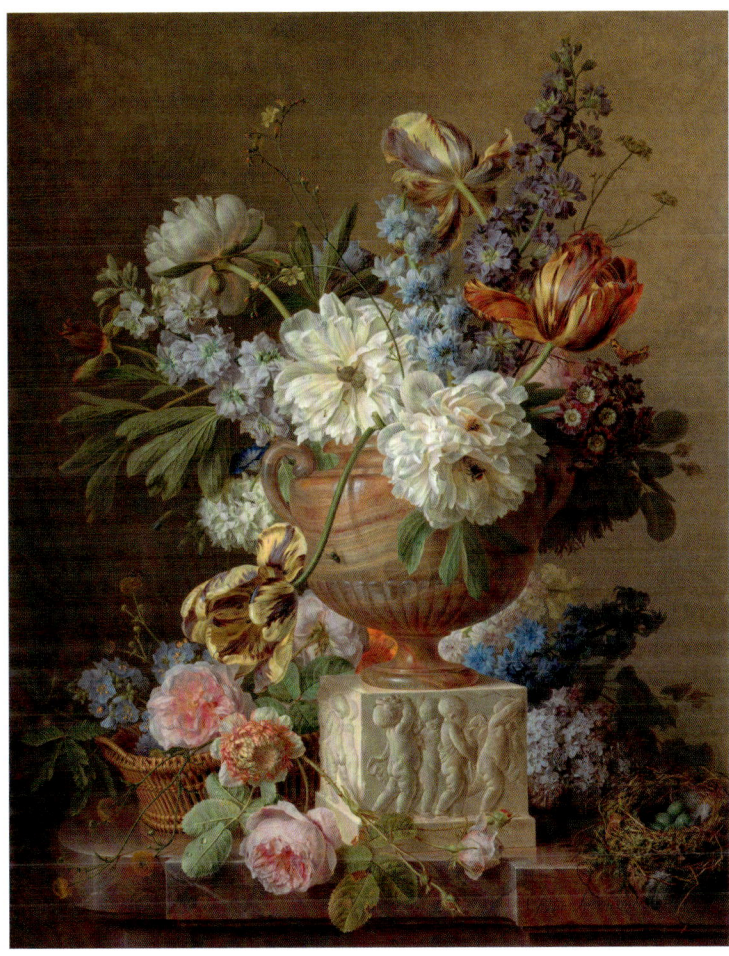

Gerard van Spaendonck

Flower Still Life with an Alabaster Vase, 1783
Oil on canvas, 80.5 × 64 cm / 31¼ × 25¼ in
Rijksmuseum, Amsterdam

The flower paintings of Gerard van Spaendonck (1746–1822), although painted in France, could perhaps be considered as the apotheosis of Dutch floral art. In this wonderful example, the alabaster vase and its white marble console with a relief of putti herald an appreciation of the classics. As with van Spaendonck's predecessors, roses, tulips and anemones play an important role in this still life, but they are overpowered by the white peonies and a rich variety of larkspur. Also included are auricula and lilac, rare flowers in earlier still lifes. The green eggs in the bird's nest – those of a blackbird – are a symbol of fertility, and the painting received particular acclaim for its lifelike rendering of the insects scattered among the bouquet. Born and trained in the Netherlands, van Spaendonck had a highly successful career in Paris, where he had moved in his early twenties. A few years later, in 1774, he was appointed flower painter to King Louis XVI. His main task was to produce botanical studies, but he also created still lifes of flowers and fruit, and had many pupils. His floral still lifes integrate the elegance of Willem van Aelst, the liveliness and fondness of little creatures of Jan Davidsz. de Heem (see p.125) and the brightness of Jan van Huysum (see p.142). In 1781, van Spaendonck was admitted to the prestigious Académie Royale. Although he had been painter to the king, his success and official positions continued after the French Revolution of 1789.

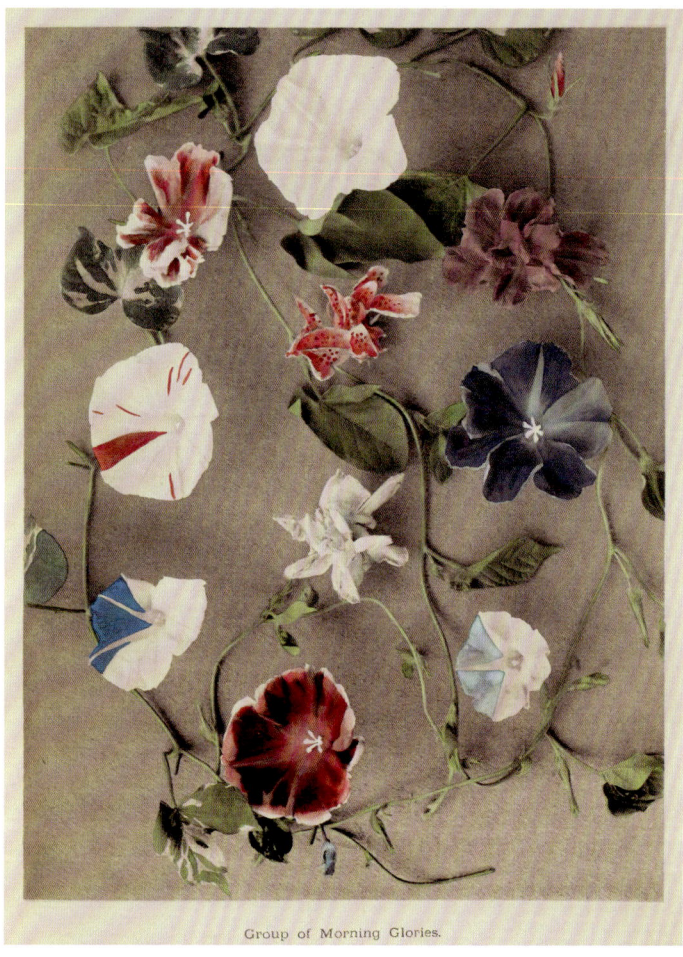

Group of Morning Glories.

Kazumasa Ogawa

Group of Morning Glories, 1896
Hand-coloured collotype, 28.1 × 21.3 cm /
11 × 8½ in
J. Paul Getty Museum, Los Angeles

This simple group of different morning glories physically intertwined as if they are all growing from the same plant, belies the importance of the image and the career from which it was produced. Kazumasa Ogawa (1860–1929) spent most of his life working with photographic images at a time in Japan when they were not widely seen as significant. He opened Tokyo's first photography studio and established Japan's first press using collotype (a dichromate-based photographic process used for mass production). *Group of Morning Glories* is a hand-coloured example of one such image where the simple yet dramatic reds, greens and blues are employed to give the flowers realistic three-dimensional form. This image would have been intended for sale as part of a range of books Ogawa produced for Western markets, featuring ritual customs, costumed geisha and, of course, flowers. Ogawa was not interested in photography as a medium to simply map reality; rather he wanted to expand photography's potential and explore how it might be experienced and disseminated in the world. Flowers were one of Ogawa's principal subjects, perhaps not simply because he found them beautiful but also because of their universal appeal to a mass market. Morning glories are renowned for their delicate petals that bloom at dawn – as captured here at the height of their beauty to delight an expectant audience.

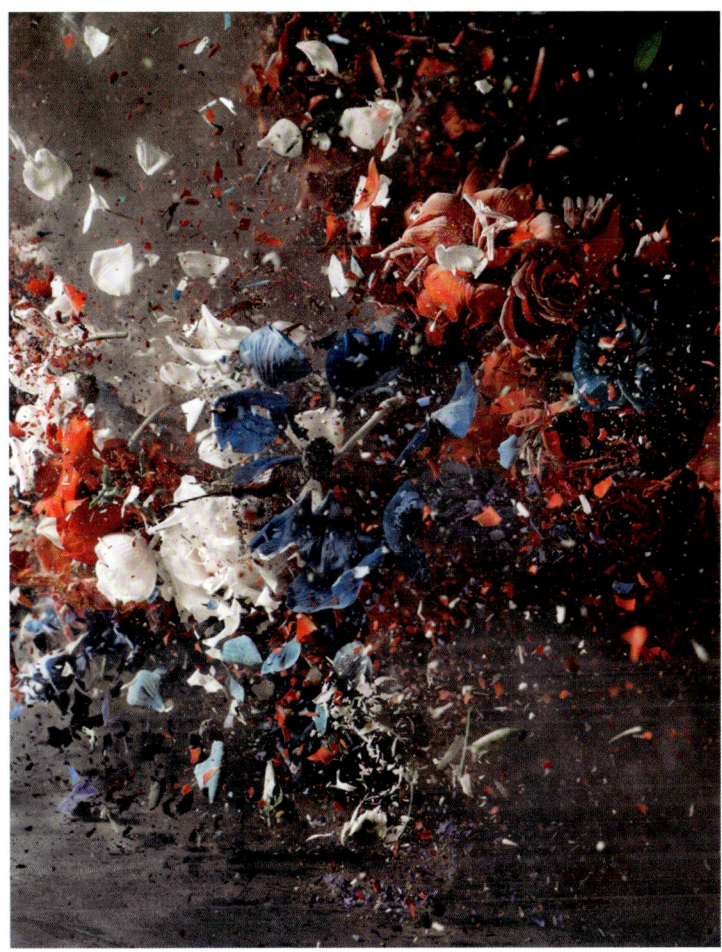

Ori Gersht

Blow Up 19, 2007
Lightjet print, 2.3 × 1.8 m / 7 ft 7 in × 5 ft 11 in

A moment of imagined brutality is captured and frozen in time by the Israeli photographer Ori Gersht (born 1967). As the detritus of shattered fragments is blown across the image, we can pick out the outlines of petals and, hidden to one side, the heads of roses – a suggestion of the form of what was there before. This is an image of a highly staged event: Gersht freeze-dried a bouquet of flowers in liquid nitrogen before using an explosive charge to blow them up,

capturing the moment with a high-definition digital camera using a shutter speed of 1/7500 of a second. Despite its aesthetic beauty, *Blow Up 19* perhaps points to darker artistic interests. Flowers have been common yet complex symbols during wartime. In contemporary times, the poppy has, since World War I, been a potent symbol of remembrance of the slaughter of the Western Front. In *Blow Up*, Gersht turns flowers into a metaphor for the physical act of war-like destruction itself: the petals no longer appear soft and supple, but rather they are splintered into shards like shrapnel. We are left as witnesses

to a terrible scene: the annihilation of something very human – a symbol of growth, renewal, love, even peace – leaving behind something quite macabre and deathly in its place.

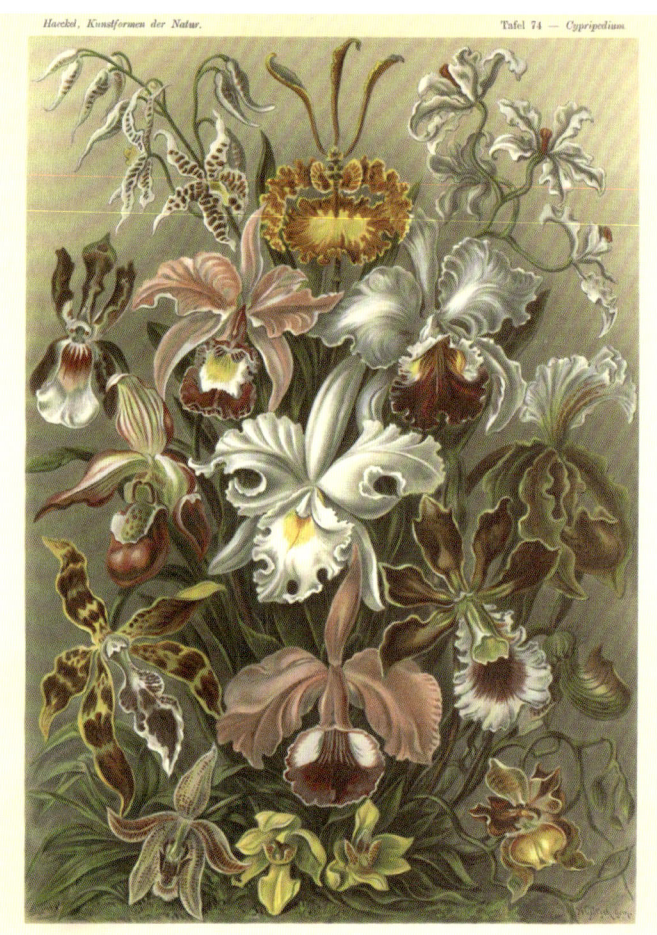

Orchideae. — Venußblumen.

Ernst Haeckel

Plate 74 – Cypripedium from *Art Forms in Nature*, 1904
Colour lithograph, 35 × 26 cm / 13¾ × 10¼ in
Private collection

German naturalist and artist Ernst Haeckel (1834–1919) gathered these sixteen different species of exotic orchids not simply to dazzle the eye but to highlight the recurring, distinctive traits that characterize the blooms of a related botanical family. A supporter of Charles Darwin's theory of evolution, Haeckel's revolutionary approach to the depiction of plants and animals used

clarity and beauty to emphasize the relationships between species and their evolutionary adaptations, luring readers with impactful images designed for the non-specialist nature lover. Scientific botanical illustrations would present a single representative of each species set against a white background, but Haeckel's slightly romanticized atmospheric effect emphasizes the flowers' exotic charm. He substantially changed the way we look at nature by underlining the importance of studying organisms within their environment – a study he was the first person to name ecology. Collecting orchids had become a pursuit of wealthy

Europeans around a century earlier, when the flowers became an exclusive status symbol. The trend began accidentally when the naturalist William John Swainson used dormant orchid plants as packing material for a shipment of other species he had collected in Brazil. A few months after their arrival in Britain, the unassuming orchids unfurled their glorious blooms, triggering a frenzy known as 'orchidelirium' – an obsession that would, in some cases, deplete entire family fortunes.

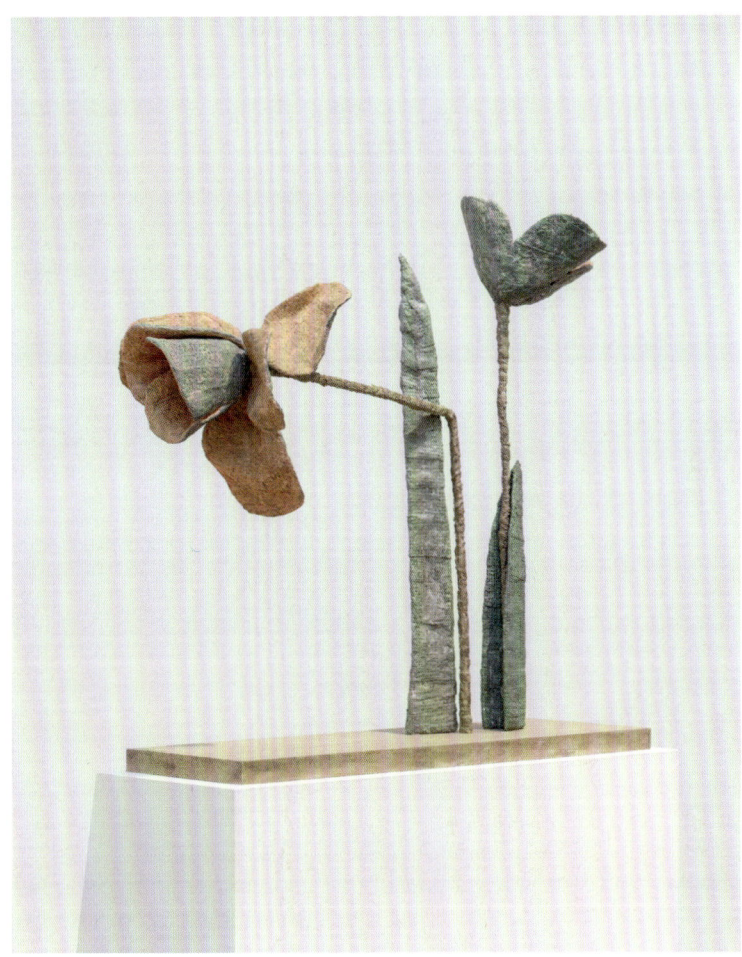

Georgie Hopton

Wounded Tulip (iii), 2012
Wire, plaster and acrylic paint, 48 × 49 × 15 cm /
19 × 19¼ × 6 in
Private collection

In contrast to the ample familiar depictions of joyous tulips, bursting with life and vivid colours, here British artist Georgie Hopton (born 1967) presents *Wounded Tulip*. The gentle bend of the flower subtly communicates its vulnerability. The ephemeral tulip, beautiful yet fading, reminds us of nature's transience and has a significance far beyond its humble character.

As is common in Hopton's work, the anthropomorphic flower speaks to a deep human emotion: tensions between life and death, attraction and repulsion, strength and submission are all central themes in her work. Hopton's broad working practice embraces a multitude of materials, from paintings and works on paper to photography, collage, sculpture, textiles and rugs. One element that unites her rich, multidisciplinary approach is a profound interest in the natural world. An avid gardener, Hopton takes much of her inspiration from the vegetable patch and flowerbeds she cultivates. Her harvest becomes both the subject

of her art as well as the implement she uses in making it. Reflecting her interest in the hand-made, Hopton's work incorporates common domestic materials such as clippings of yarn, found papers and, in this case, wire and plaster. In doing so, she elevates materials often associated with craft to the realm of fine art. Her holistic approach, always grounded in nature, is a constant balancing act between the humble and the profound.

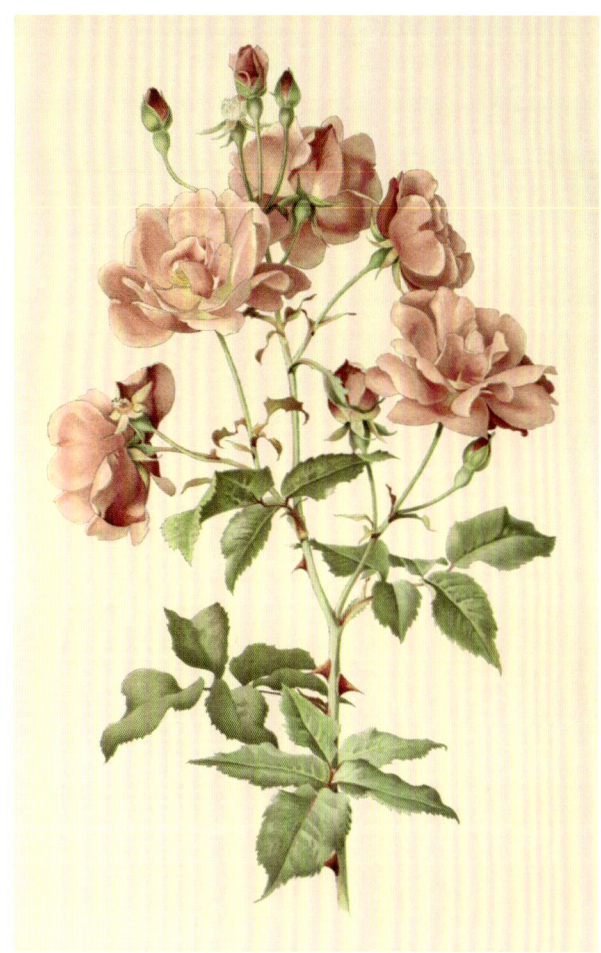

Alfred Parsons and Ellen Willmott

Rosa chinensis, from *The Genus Rosa*, 1910–14
Chromolithograph, 37.5 × 27.5 cm / 17¾ × 10¾ in
Harvard University Botany Libraries,
Cambridge, Massachusetts

This portrait of the Chinese rose (*Rosa chinensis*)
vividly captures the delicate shades of its pink
buds and blooms, borne on multi-flowering stems.
Roses have been cultivated for centuries in China,
where they were used for floral decoration and
in gardens as well as in traditional medicine.
Many modern garden-rose varieties have been bred
from the Chinese rose, a species particularly

valued for its continuous blooming over many
summer months and for the tea-like scent of its
flowers. In the wild, the flower is native to southwest China, and was first introduced to Europe
in the late eighteenth century. This watercolour
illustration is one of 132 colour plates created
by English artist Alfred Parsons (1847–1920) for
The Genus Rosa by Ellen Willmott (1857–1934),
published by John Murray in London between 1910
and 1914. Considered among the finest of all
depictions of roses, the original paintings are held
by the Lindley Library of the Royal Horticultural
Society (RHS) in London. Willmott was a wealthy

landscape designer and an enthusiastic horticulturist, whose work transformed the family home
of Warley Place in Essex into one of the most
famous gardens in England. The house was demol-
ished in 1939, after which the gardens reverted
to a wild state, now forming a nature reserve of the
Essex Wildlife Trust. For her services to horticulture, Willmott was awarded the RHS Victoria
Medal of Honour in 1897.

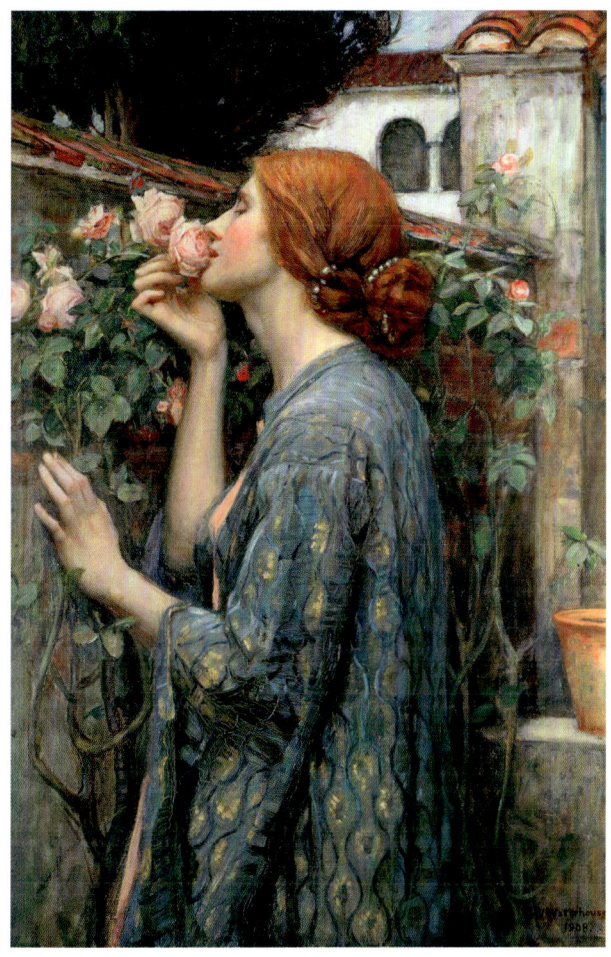

John William Waterhouse

The Soul of the Rose, 1908
Oil on canvas, 91.4 × 61 cm / 36 × 24 in
Private collection

This painting might almost be a classic portrait of synaesthesia, promoting through the eyes of the viewer the heady scent of the rose and the almost physical feel of the soft petals against the woman's lips and the rough wall beneath her hand. The inspiration is said to be a long and controversial narrative poem by Alfred, Lord Tennyson, called 'Maud' (1855), itself rich with sensation; the line 'And the soul of the rose went into my blood' comes from a scene in which the obsessive poet awaits Maud in a garden, having been denied entry to the house by her brother. The painting is not a direct representation of the poem, however – rather, English painter John William Waterhouse (1849–1917) takes the line, and the floral symbol of love, as a starting point for his own vision, creating a romantic scene of implied longing for lost love in a painting that activates the senses of touch, smell and sight. The setting is an imaginary walled court-yard, possibly meant to be in Tuscany, which evokes early Italian paintings such as works by Fra Angelico. Waterhouse himself was born in Rome and returned there as a young man, so such surroundings would have been familiar to him. The contrast of the enclosed cloister occupied by a lonely figure and the exuberant abundance of the climbing rose add a sense of ambiguity and mystery to the scene, suggestive of the scent of the rose in the sun.

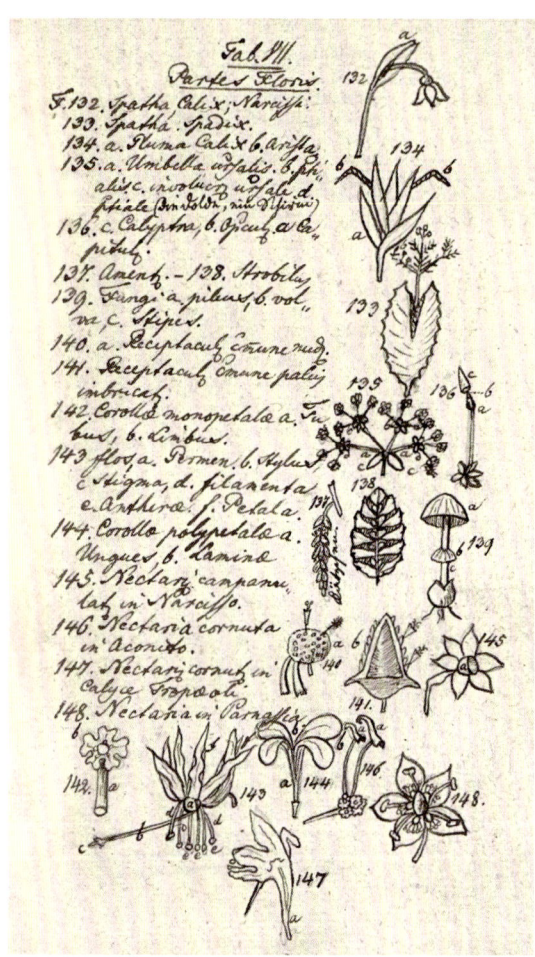

Carl Linnaeus

Botanical notebook, 1750–51
Ink on paper, 20 × 12 cm / 8 × 4¾ in
Slovenská Národná Knižnica, Martin, Slovakia

What might at first appear to be amateur field sketches have far more significance: they depict the beginnings of one of the founding principles of botany. Although these line drawings by Carl Linnaeus (1707–78) are of no great artistic merit, they demonstrate his attention to detail and desire to record the smallest elements of the flowers he encountered, especially the reproductive organs that he considered essential to enabling plant identification. It is important, too, that he transferred his observations to paper in the field, and meticulously annotated his sketches. Each drawing is numbered and has a brief accompanying description; here, the drawings include several plants such as narcissus, aconite and parnassia and also includes fungi. Linnaeus paid particular attention to the reproductive parts, with the female elements (stigma, style and ovary) and male elements (filaments and anthers) carefully noted. Linnaeus, also known as Carolus Linnaeus or Carl von Linné, was born in southern Sweden. He studied medicine at the universities of Lund and, later, Uppsala, before eventually moving to the Universiteit Leiden in the Netherlands. His great contribution to biology was to establish what is referred to as the binomial, or Linnaean, system for naming and classifying organisms, which is still used today. Each plant or animal is given a two-word name (a binomial), consisting of the genus and species names; a system that was famously published in detail in 1753, in the tenth edition of Linnaeus's major work *Species Plantarum*.

Pierre Jean François Turpin

Tableau XVI and *XX*, from *Leçons de flore*, 1819–20
Hand-coloured engraving, each 20 × 13.5 cm /
7¾ × 5¼ in
Bibliothèque nationale de France, Paris

These two plates from the early nineteenth century – one depicting flowers arranged in an inflorescence, a group or cluster of flowers atop a stem, with scabiosa, daisy and other plants; the other showing hermaphroditic flowers, which have both stamen (male) and pistil (female) reproductive parts – is remarkable for being painted by a French botanical artist who, unlike his renowned contemporaries, was almost entirely self-taught. Pierre Jean François Turpin (1775–1840), the son of a poor artisan, had only a rudimentary education before he enlisted in the French revolutionary army in 1789, at just fourteen years old. He was sent to the French colony of Saint Domingue in Haiti, where he met the botanist Pierre Antoine Poiteau, a former gardener at the Jardin des Plantes in Paris. The serendipitous meeting would lead to Turpin becoming one of the most distinguished plant illustrators of the Napoleonic Era. Protected by General Charles Leclerc and American consul Edward Stevens, a great plant enthusiast, Turpin

and Poiteau assembled a herbarium of more than a thousand individual plant specimens. Back in France, Turpin and botanist Jean Louis Marie Poiret collaborated on important publications, such as Alexander von Humboldt and Aimé Bonpland's *Plantes équinoxiales recueillies au Mexique* (1808) and their own *Leçons de flore*, from which these plates come. Published in 1819 to 1820, it aimed to teach the reader about plant and flower physiologies, depicted with brightly coloured engravings.

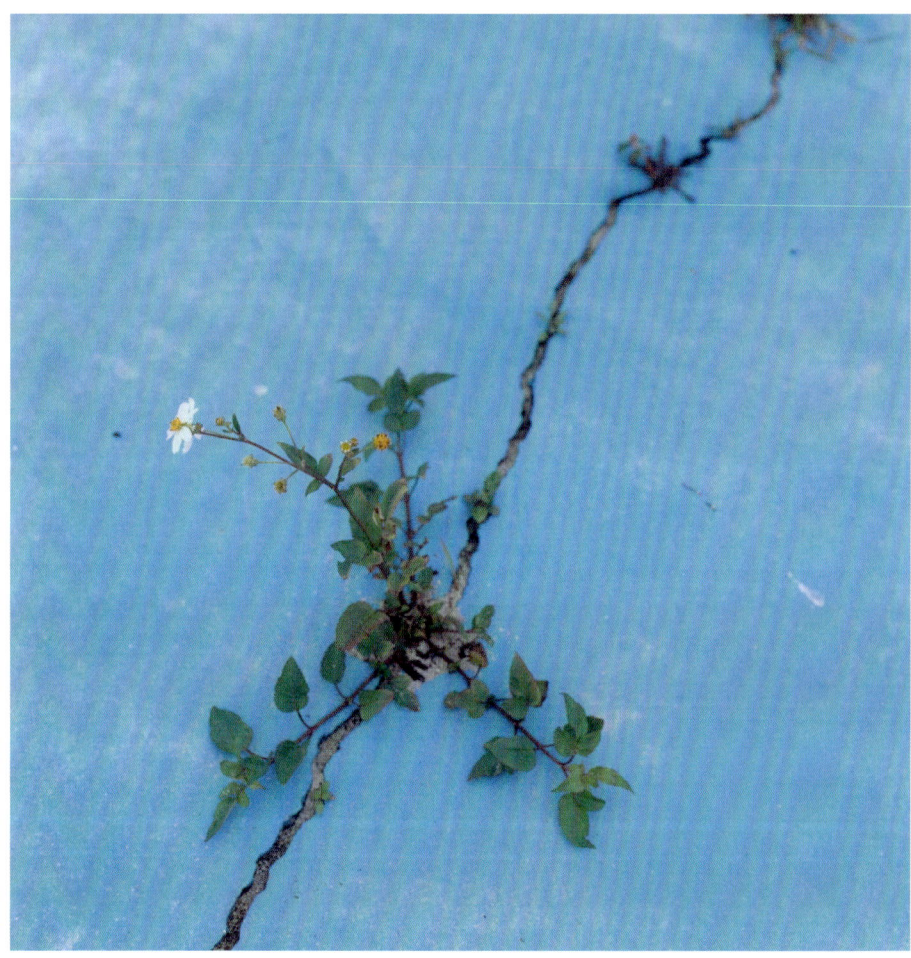

Rinko Kawauchi

Untitled, from *the eyes, the ears*, 2005
C-print, 29.8 × 25.4 / 12 × 10 in

A slender weed emerges determinedly from a cracked pavement. Japanese photographer Rinko Kawauchi (born 1972) heightens the plant's elegance by isolating its linear form against the uniform blue of the painted concrete. The single white flower, together with the yellow centres that have lost their petals and the sprawling green leaves, offset the otherwise monochromatic image, creating a point of interest while retaining the balance and simplicity that make the photograph so appealing. Central to Kawauchi's approach is the ethos of Japan's traditional religion, Shinto – in which every living thing has a spirit – a quality that is reflected in poetic images where mundane subjects are imbued with a dreamlike quality. Here, the flower's determination to reach the light is emblematic of the kind of resilience of which plants are capable: the herbaceous flowering blackjack weed (*Bidens pilosa*) has made its home in the unlikely place of a concrete crevice. Native to the tropical and subtropical regions of Central America and parts of South America, the flower was introduced into Japan during the Edo period (1600–1867). The species possesses an effective means of seed dispersal by humans, animals, wind and water, causing it to be spread widely and aggressively invade crops such as sugar cane. Despite its pernicious nature, the plant has been used in cultures worldwide for its anti-inflammatory medicinal properties to treat an extensive range of ailments.

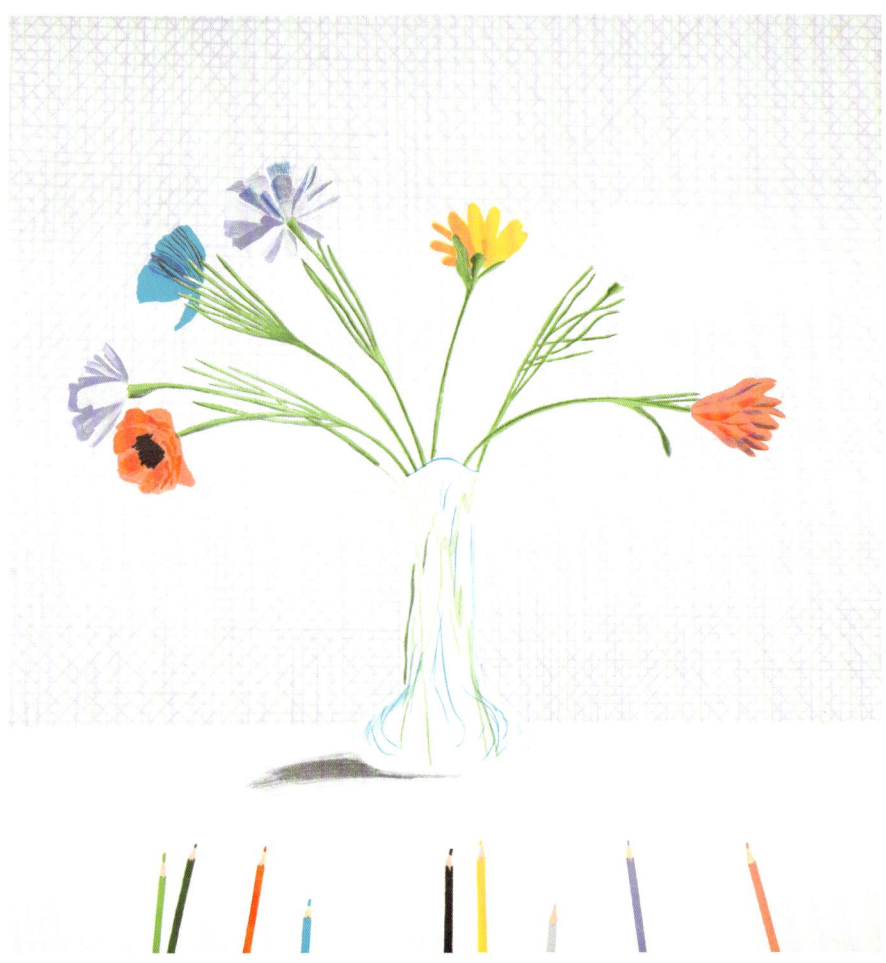

David Hockney

Coloured Flowers Made of Paper and Ink, 1971
Lithograph in colour, 99 × 95.2 cm / 39 × 37½ in

British artist David Hockney (born 1937) has never been able to resist a vase of flowers: from his earliest paintings to his most recent endeavours with digital technology, these still-life subjects have fascinated him for decades. Many of his most iconic portraits of friends and family include a flower still life, which he arguably gives as much prominence and care to as he does the sitters themselves. Created in London in 1971, *Coloured Flowers Made of Paper and Ink* was

made shortly after a trip to Japan, where Hockney became fascinated with traditional Japanese means of depiction, including the flattening of the picture plane and the simplicity of presentation. In this lithograph, Hockney makes the still life the central focus, firmly placing the tall vase and stylized array of flowers in the middle of the otherwise sparse composition. In an unusual inclusion, along with the flowers themselves, Hockney has also depicted the artist's tools – coloured pencils scattered along the bottom of the picture. This visual joke is a typical example of Hockney's witty sensibilities: here is my drawing and here is what

I've made it with. Adding to the playful humour is the fact that this work is not a drawing at all, but a lithograph – made not with coloured pencils but with lithographic wax and printer's ink.

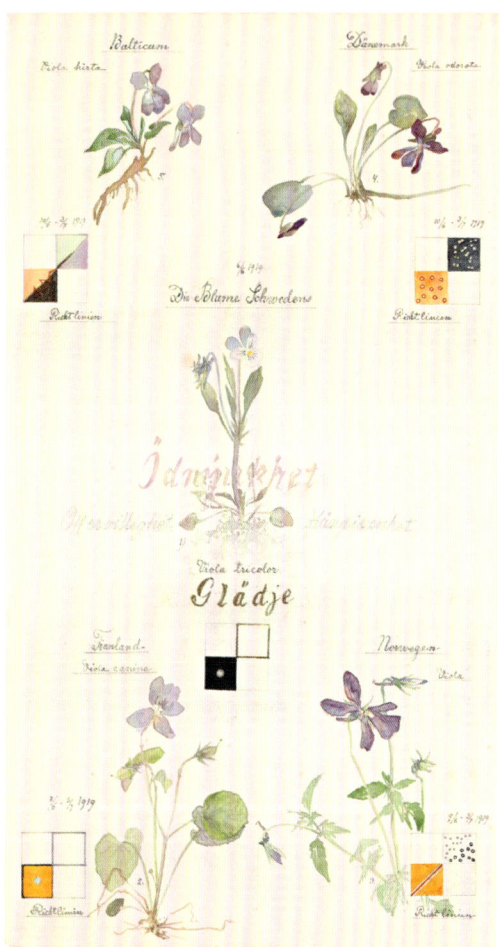

Hilma af Klint

Violet Blossoms with Guidelines, 1919
Watercolour, ink, graphite and metallic paint
on paper, 50 × 27 cm / 19¾ × 10½ in
Hilma af Klint Foundation, Stockholm

A central wild pansy (*Viola tricolor*) is painted in
delicate watercolour under the title 'The Flower
of Sweden' with descriptions of 'joy' and 'humility' layered beneath. In the four corners are *V. hirta*
from the Baltic, *V. odorata* from Denmark, another
Norwegian species and *V. canina* from Finland.
Each flower, executed with botanical accuracy,
is accompanied by a curious grid of four squares.

These are the 'guidelines', which for Swedish artist Hilma af Klint (1862–1944) represent the vital,
spiritual forces governing the growth and life of
the plants depicted: the true essence of these delicate flowers, and indeed of all life. Af Klint graduated from the Stockholm Royal Academy of Fine
Arts and developed an interest in spiritualism and
the occult, influenced both by Helena Blavatsky,
the founder of the Theosophical Society, and
by the anthroposophy of Rudolf Steiner. Upon her
death in 1944 at the age of eighty-one, she left
more than 1,200 works of art, including a trove
of some 150 annotated sketchbooks, all of which

she specified should be kept secret for at least
twenty years. In the late 1960s this collection
revealed a wide range of works, including large,
mystical abstract paintings that seemed to merge
geometric shapes with forms found in nature.
Af Klint believed that many of these were painted
directly through her by an unseen force guiding
her hand. She was a true pioneer of abstract art,
arguably equal in status to the more famous
Wassily Kandinsky.

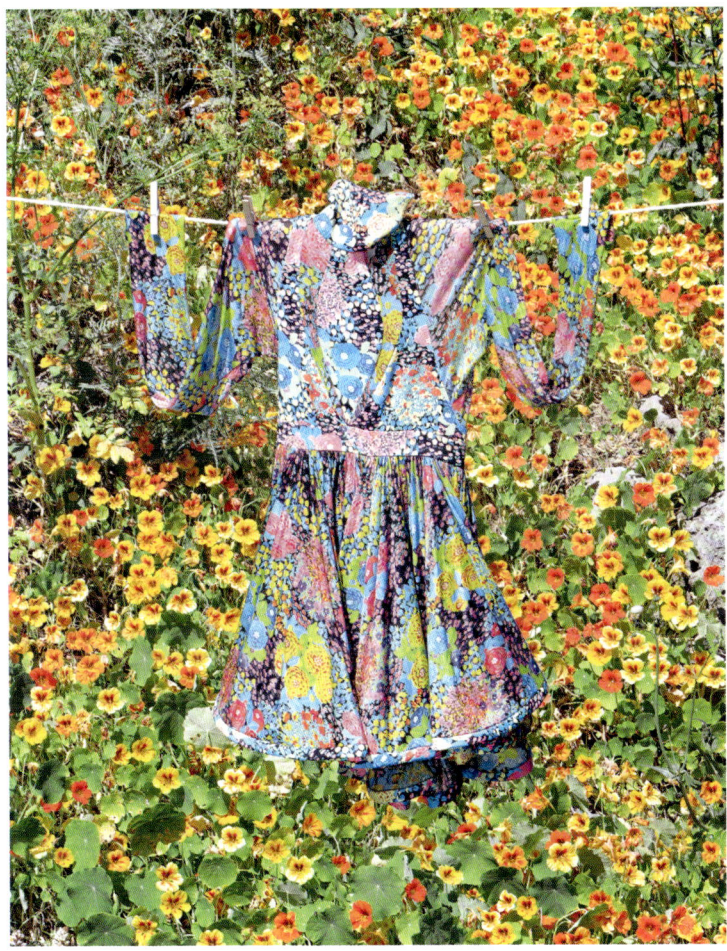

Alfred Seiland

Dress on Clothesline, Esporles, Mallorca, Spain, 2004
Digital print, dimensions variable

A high-necked, long-sleeved minidress in a vivid 'techno' floral in turquoise, fuchsia, orange and purple, designed by Nicolas Ghesquière for Balenciaga, hangs from pegs on a washing line. Behind, in stark contrast, is a sea of orange and tomato red nasturtiums (*Tropaeolum majus*) with their washed-out green foliage. This photograph by Austrian photographer Alfred Seiland (born 1952) was shot as part of a commission

Hanging Gardens: When the Bloom Is on the Line for *The New York Times* in the summer of 2004, in which the season's floral fashion from designer labels was hung on lines against backdrops of foliage, shrubs or trees. This image reflects the push to photograph contemporary fashion in more abstract or artistic ways around the turn of the century. Seiland is well known for distinctive landscapes that often feature deserted urban scenes or cultural sites, while his use of an analogue large-format camera and post-production that includes methodical corrections imbues his images with a slightly surreal perfectionism.

Here, the bed of sprawling nasturtiums appears almost flattened into a tapestry or wallpaper. Native to Peru, the trailing annual summer flowers are known for their lightly sweet fragrance and peppery tasting leaves; inspired by their flavour, the common name is derived from the Latin for 'nose twister'. The mostly red, yellow and orange blooms were introduced into Europe in the sixteenth century; in the Victorian language of flowers, they came to symbolize patriotism.

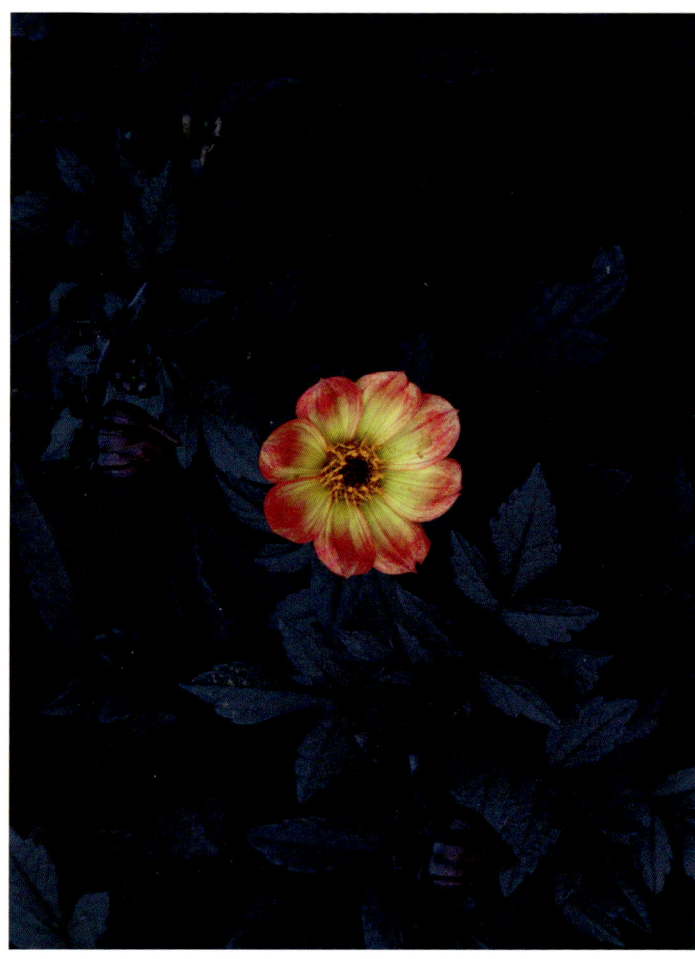

Rowan Spray

Untitled, from *Fieldwork 1*, *c.*2017
Photograph, dimensions variable

The dahlia was discovered in the mountainous regions of Mexico by Spanish botanists during the sixteenth century, but it was only 200 years later that the first tubers reached Europe. Today, more than thirty species of dahlia have been identified in the wild, while more than 20,000 cultivar varieties are available. But before becoming a garden favourite across the world for its beauty, the dahlia was grown as a vegetable, its crunchy tubers popular for stews and casseroles. It was only in the early 1800s that, thanks to Belgian botanists, the first large double-flower varieties stirred a breeding frenzy, reinventing the dahlia as a prized ornamental. By the 1840s, the plant's reputation was cemented as one of the most desirable exotics. A sign of this plant's long-lasting success, new dahlia hybrids are still produced today. The one captured here by British photographer Rowan Spray (born 1982) is *Dahlia* Star Wars (Dark Angel Series) – named after the blockbuster film saga by director George Lucas – a dwarf variety that grows to a maximum height of around 30 centimetres (11¾ inches). Appearing almost as if from a fairy tale, the orange-red flowers with yellow centres contrast starkly with the burgundy, almost black, foliage. Typical of Spray's work, the image reflects the inspiration she finds in the beauty and magic of nature, influenced by her childhood in the Forest of Dean in Gloucestershire, England. In addition to her field and studio work, Spray is a frequent photographer for the globally renowned McQueens Flowers School and studio.

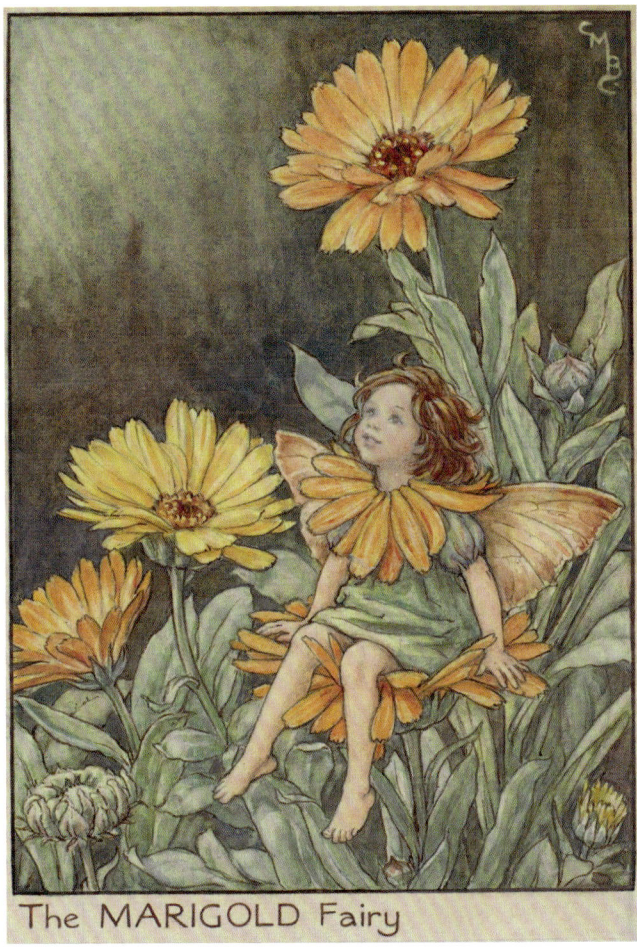

The MARIGOLD Fairy

Cicely Mary Barker

The Marigold Fairy, from *The Fairies of the Garden*, 1934
Ink and watercolour, 11 × 7.5 cm / 4½ × 3 in
Penguin Random House

A fairy girl with a necklace of vibrant orange petals and flaming ginger hair to match sits among a cluster of English marigolds (*Calendula officinalis*) – the garden flowers that are her namesake and with which she has been charged to look after. The creation of British author and illustrator Cicely Mary Barker (1895–1973), the Flower Fairies have been adored by children and adults since first published in 1923. Combining the charming innocence of childhood with the beauty of flowers, Barker's now classic series contains 170 original illustrations depicting fairies for each season and many types of garden flowers. Accompanying the illustrations are verses describing the distinct personality of each fairy derived from the respective flower. Here, the golden marigold is the flower of the sun, turning to watch the path of the sun as it moves across the sky. Barker was meticulous in her botanical accuracy, painting from local garden flowers as well as from specimens at London's Kew Gardens. She applied the same attention to her depiction of the fairies, which were largely based on the young pupils at her sister's nursery school, wearing costumes Barker constructed herself. During her lifetime, Barker wrote and illustrated more than thirty books, with additional works published posthumously.

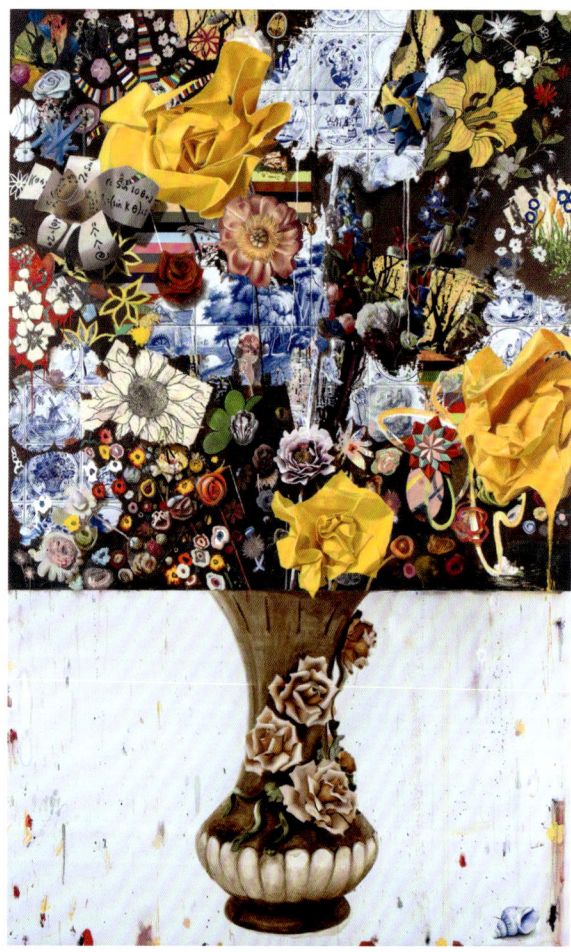

Keith Tyson

Still Life with Rose Vase and Seashell, 2015–17
Mixed media on aluminium, 3.2 × 2 m /
10 ft 6 in × 6 ft 6 in
Private collection, Switzerland

The tradition of a jewel-like still-life painting is disrupted by British artist Keith Tyson (born 1969). Its abiding lineage gives way to the artist's astute observation and use of paint, paired with a remarkable knowledge of art history and a curiosity about the mysterious forces of our universe. With a nod to seventeenth-century precedent, particularly perhaps the paintings of Dutch master Ambrosius Bosschaert the Elder (see p.177), Tyson's composition brings together aesthetic references from across place and time. Sieved through his particular outlook, this physical manifestation of logic and data creates a narrative *nature morte* – a depiction of inanimate objects in which the sheer exuberance and detail seem to radiate energy – rather than the kind of *memento mori* that floral still lifes often encompass. Above a moulded rose vase and a single seashell, elements dribble and collide: Dutch Delftware in blues and whites, exquisitely crafted spears of larkspur and lily, loops of algorithmic data petals, scrunched paper roses. Capturing an astounding array of chance and combination, the painting reflects the theme of Tyson's 2018 *Big Data* exhibition. A beautiful scrimmage, his work exchanges the genre's class-ical allegory of birth, life and death for a fecund translation of the traditional still life.

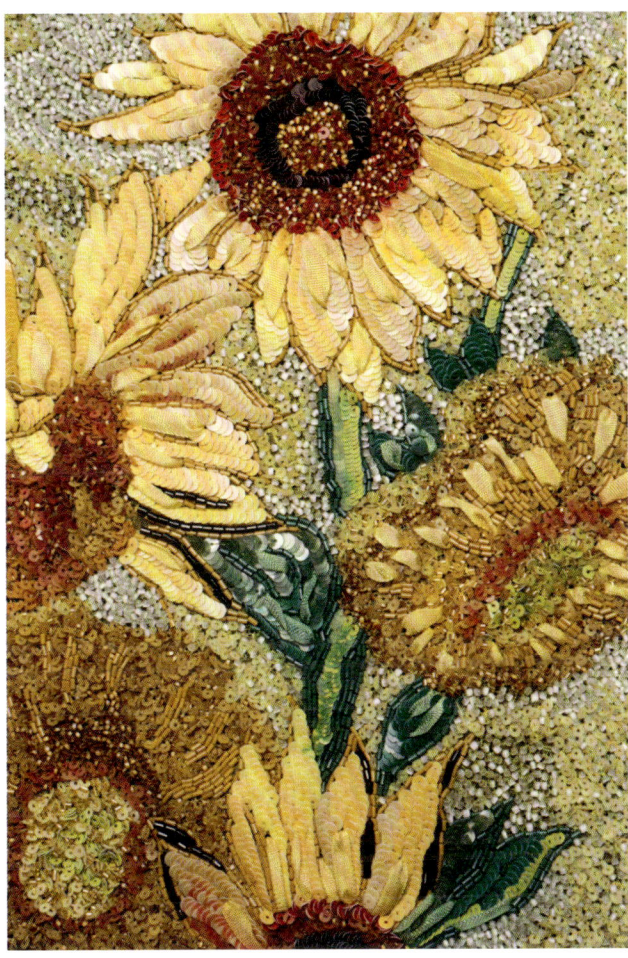

Lesage for Yves Saint Laurent

Sunflower embroidery sample (detail), 1988
Organza, sequins, glass beads and thread

In 1987 Vincent van Gogh's 1889 still life *Vase with Fifteen Sunflowers* was sold for £29 million at Christie's in London – at the time, the highest price ever paid for a painting at auction (see p.47). The following year, inspired by the painting, renowned French fashion designer Yves Saint Laurent (1936–2008) showed his 'Sunflowers' jacket on which this sample was based – a masterpiece depicting another masterpiece. By creating garments that echoed major works of art, Saint Laurent cemented the bond between art and fashion. From the middle of the 1980s, the couturier would write the word 'Musée' on the labels of garments destined for the archive; it appears alongside the name of the model 'Naome' (for Naomi Campbell) on the $100,000 Sunflowers jacket from his Spring/Summer 1988 haute couture collection. Created with French couture embroidery house Lesage, founded in 1924, the jacket was crafted from a yellow organza background lined with yellow satin silk and embroidered entirely by hand with hundreds of thousands of sequins, individually threaded

pearls and yards of ribbon. The embroidery alone took 600 hours and the jacket became one of the most expensive pieces Saint Laurent produced. Considered one of the most valuable haute couture garments ever made, the jacket was sold at auction in November 2019 to the National Gallery of Victoria in Melbourne, Australia, for €382,000 – the highest-ever auction price for a piece of clothing.

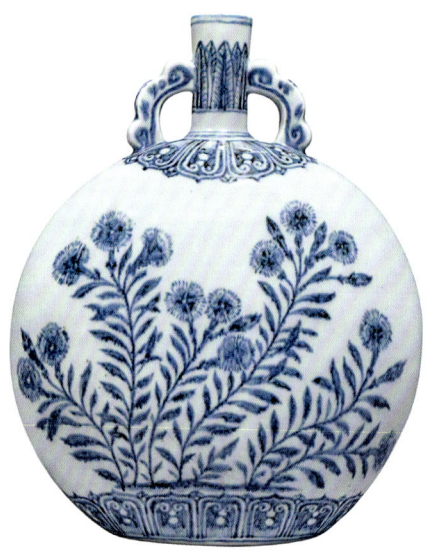

Anonymous

Yongle Moon Flask, 1403–24,
Porcelain, H. 28.8 cm / 11¼ in
Private collection

Painted with a bright blue derived from imported cobalt, these carnations and the unseen asters adorning this Chinese moon flask are a remarkably rare sight. In China, carnations symbolize marriage, while asters have traditionally been the symbol of faithfulness, yet their appearance is virtually unknown in Chinese blue-and-white porcelain. Where plants do appear, they generally form part of a stylized pattern, either in continuous scroll designs or as floating motifs. Unusually, the exquisitely painted flowers in this example are rendered naturalistically growing on a patch of uneven ground, as if in a garden setting. Painted on both sides of the fifteenth-century flask, they are presented between lotus-lappet bands that encircle the vessel's base and shoulder. Porcelain moon flasks such as this were produced in China from the fifteenth century. Quintessentially Chinese in style, the distinctive vessels have flattened, circular bodies and rounded scroll handles on their cylindrical necks. During the reign of Yongle, the third emperor of China's Ming dynasty, porcelain production was strictly controlled. Not only did the imperial court oversee the design and manufacture of porcelain wares, but also their distribution. At just under 30 centimetres (12 inches) tall, this fine example demonstrates the remarkably high standard achieved in the early Ming period.

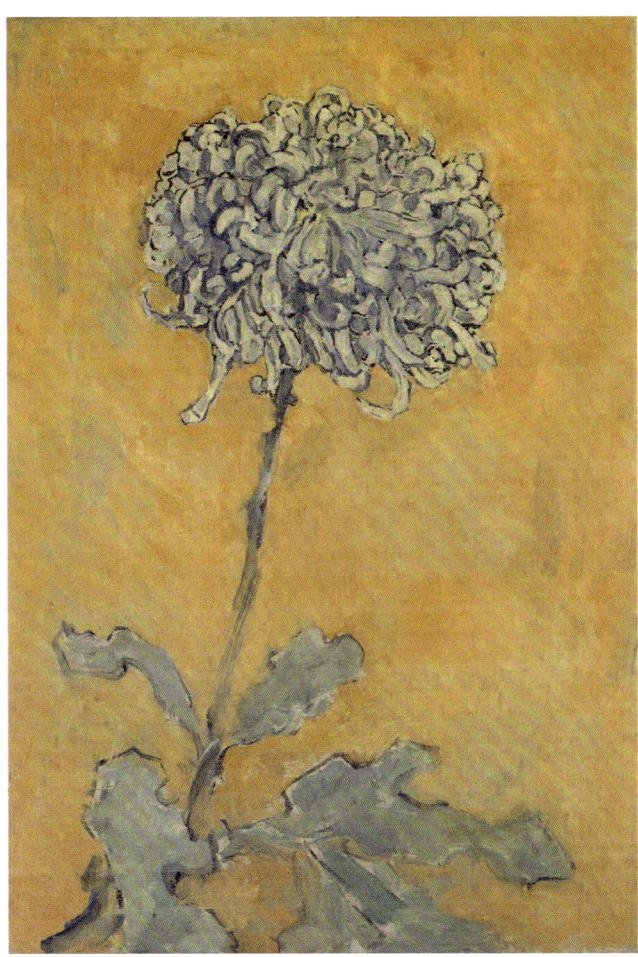

Piet Mondrian

Chrysanthemum, c.1911–44
Oil on canvas, 50.5 × 35.2 cm / 20 × 14 in
Private collection

A flurry of dark blue brushstrokes outline the complex structure of a tall chrysanthemum stem, while lighter washes of paint fill the flower's petals and serrated leaves, and a patchy field of golden yellow provides a simple backdrop. This loose, imprecise painting is the antithesis of the uncompromising hard-edged abstract canvases for which Piet Mondrian (1872–1944) is best known. But, in addition to his famous rectilinear black lines, white grounds and primary colours, the Dutch artist produced more than 200 flower paintings, many of which depict chrysanthemums, as well as lilies, roses and amaryllis. As here, Mondrian usually painted single blooms in an attempt to express the plant's essential 'plastic', non-representational qualities and what he described as their hidden deeper beauty. This notion reflects his interest in theosophy, a type of philosophical mysticism that claims to reveal hidden insights about the spiritual nature of reality. Nevertheless, many of Mondrian's flowers were actually painted simply as a way to generate income after he struggled to find a market for his abstract works. The placing of a single flower against a monochrome background recalls seventeenth- and eighteenth-century botanical drawings. Yet, despite the naturalistic approach to form, Mondrian's palette is deliberately unnatural, due to his conviction that the colours of nature could not be faithfully reproduced in painting.

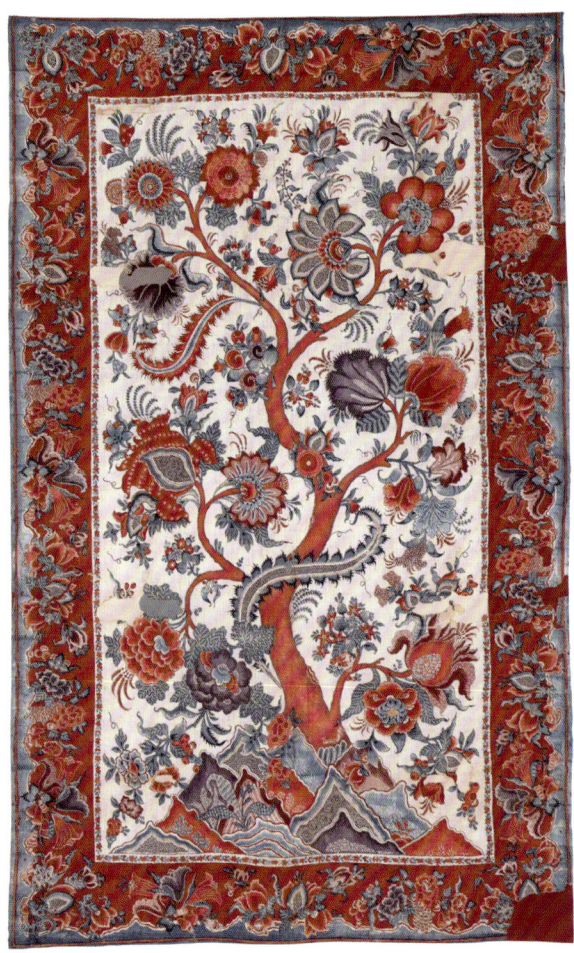

Anonymous

Palampore, early 18th century
Painted, resist and mordant-dyed cotton,
1.8 × 1.1 m / 6 ft × 3 ft 9 in
Metropolitan Museum of Art, New York

Bursting with floral vitality, this Indian palamp-ore, or bed cover, shows a serpentine tree erupting with exotic red, blue and indigo blooms. Its vivid colours jump out from a pale background, creating a dramatic counterpoint to the broad, meander-ing patterned border, which is also filled with floral motifs. The exuberant design is typical of the Indian textiles popular in Europe during the eighteenth and nineteenth centuries, particularly with the Dutch and English, who used them as bed and table coverings, wall hangings and cur-tains. This fine eighteenth-century example was, however, produced in India specifically for the Sri Lankan market, and was likely aimed either at European communities in South Asia or at native families who wanted to emulate Western taste. When it was made, India was the world's greatest exporter of textiles and its products were celebrated for their intricate designs and rich colours. The individual blooms in this palampore are coloured with different dyes: the vibrant red is derived from the roots of a herbaceous climb-ing plant known as *chay*, while the violet-blue indigo is obtained from the leguminous plant of the genus *Indigofera*. The complex mordant dyeing process ensured that colours did not fade, making these textiles among the most beautiful and most expensive of the period.

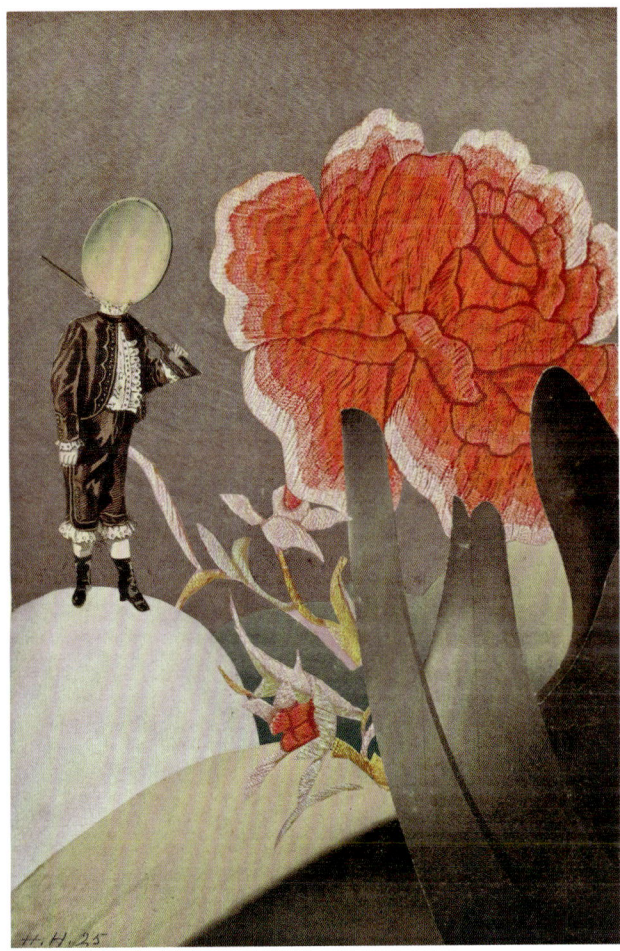

Hannah Höch

Watched, 1925
Cut-and-pasted printed paper on printed paper,
25.7 × 17.1 cm / 10 × 6¾ in
Museum of Modern Art, New York

Watched is an exemplary collage by German artist
Hannah Höch (1889–1978). A peony image
embroidered in graduated reds and pinks unfurls
glossily, filling the right side of the composition. It acts as an allegory for the feminine, with
its masculine adversary – a soldier – the colour-
less sentinel pasted left. With a rifle over his
shoulder, his blank egg-like head inclines towards

the blush flower in a scene of surveillance. *Watched*
conveys many of Höch's recurring motifs, notably
her astute use of collage, her inclusion of printed
matter from diverse sources and her voluble rejection of accepted social expectations. Höch's sharp
compositions began during the 1920s and can be
read in part as a reaction to the horrors and propaganda of world war. Part of the Dada movement
led by her partner Raoul Hausmann, Höch was the
only female artist in the collective. She and her
comrades took up satire and nonsense as weapons
to express their rejection of overt political coer-
cion and repressive social norms in the post-

war Weimar Republic. Gathering, cutting and
re-piecing printed matter – often everyday materials such as newspaper or posters – Höch developed a distinctive raw palette to articulate
these views. Her skill for surprising compositions
brings unlikely materials into stinging unison,
expressing her unerring eye and strident views.

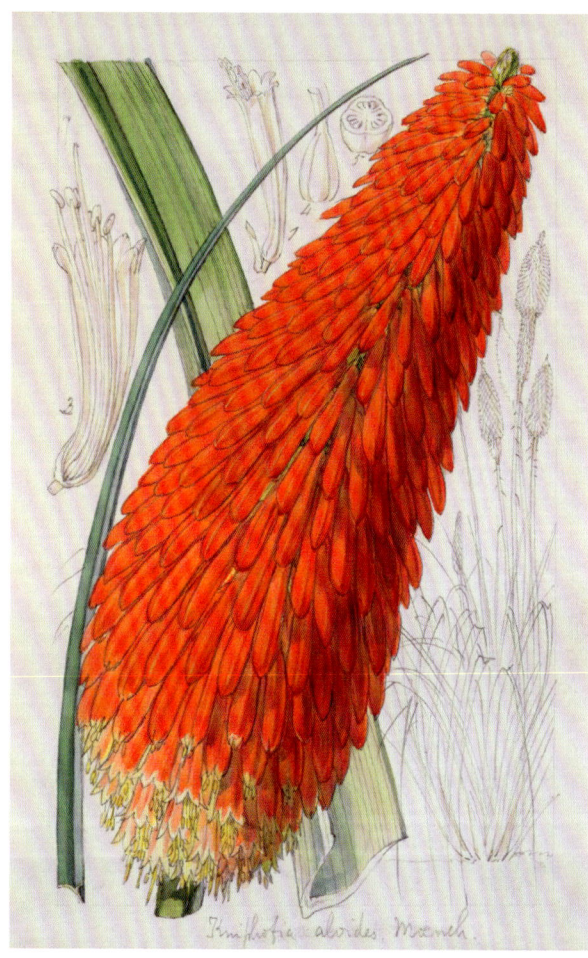

Walter Hood Fitch

Kniphofia uvaria, from *Curtis's Botanical Magazine*, Vol. 80, 1854
Watercolour and pencil on paper, 21 × 12.5 cm / 8¼ × 5 in
Royal Botanic Gardens, Kew, London

The tubular flower heads and thick stems of this fiery kniphofia flower – commonly known as red-hot poker or torch lily – dramatically fill the whole page in this illustration. The distinctive plant originated in South Africa and was introduced to English gardens around 1700. The flowers initially emerge red in colour and mature to orange and then yellow, giving the flower its iconic two-toned hue. The genus *Kniphofia* was named after German botanist Johann Kniphof, famous for creating a 'herbarium' by using nature printing; the species name, *uvaria*, denotes the resemblance of the flower head to a bunch of grapes. This detailed illustration is one of nearly 3,000 botanical plates produced by British artist Walter Hood Fitch (1817–92) for *Curtis's Botanical Magazine*, a British publication founded in 1787 by botanist William Curtis. For forty years, Fitch was the principal artist of the magazine, which presented its readers with illustrations of exotic and ornamental plants accompanied by texts describing their properties and characteristics. Thanks to his close relationship with William Jackson Hooker – the magazine's editor and director of the Royal Botanic Gardens at Kew – Fitch also illustrated many of Kew's publications. Considered the greatest botanical artist of his time, Fitch was remarkably prolific, publishing more than 12,000 illustrations in books and periodicals. His work was particularly valued by botanists for its precise detail, which was important in aiding plant identification.

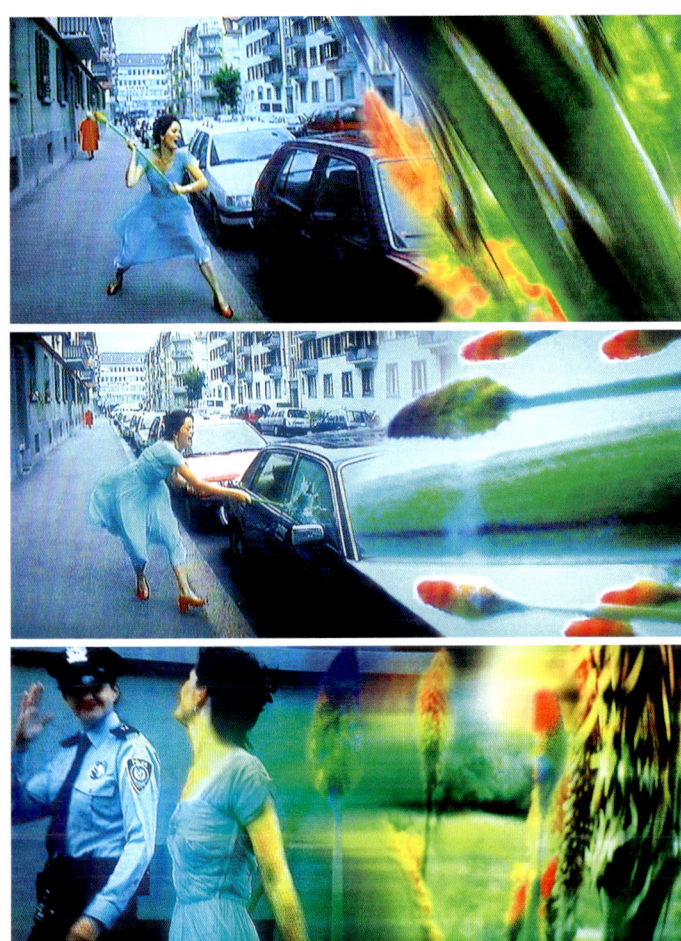

Pipilotti Rist

Ever Is Over All, 1997
Two-channel video installation with sound,
dimensions variable

In the early days of her career, Swiss artist Pipilotti Rist (born 1962) declared that her main objective was to 'create rooms where people can find themselves'. This position was reflected in her video installations gradually becoming more encompassing until reaching a turning point with *Ever is Over All*. Presented at the 47th Venice Biennale in 1997, the piece consists of two videos depicting two separate scenarios. In the first,

a woman sporting a blue dress and red shoes – a joint reference to *Alice in Wonderland* and the 1948 film *The Red Shoes* – can be seen joyfully wandering around an unidentified city, holding a red-hot poker (*Kniphofia*), a variety of flower native to South Africa that can reach up to 210 centimetres (6½ feet) tall. Occasionally she stops near a car and uses the flower as a club to smash its window – an activity that doesn't seem to be deterred by the presence of a policewoman, who surprisingly walks by and nods in approval. Rist's flower lends itself to multilayered interpretation. It could be read as an environmental fable, with nature taking

revenge on one of the world's primary causes of pollution, or as an empowering statement, with the feminine image of a woman holding a flower being subverted by her declared role as the ultimate avenger. This narrative fades into an overlapping projection of the second video, one with a misty atmosphere where flowers and blades of grass are closely inspected by a micro-camera, revealing all their visual appeal.

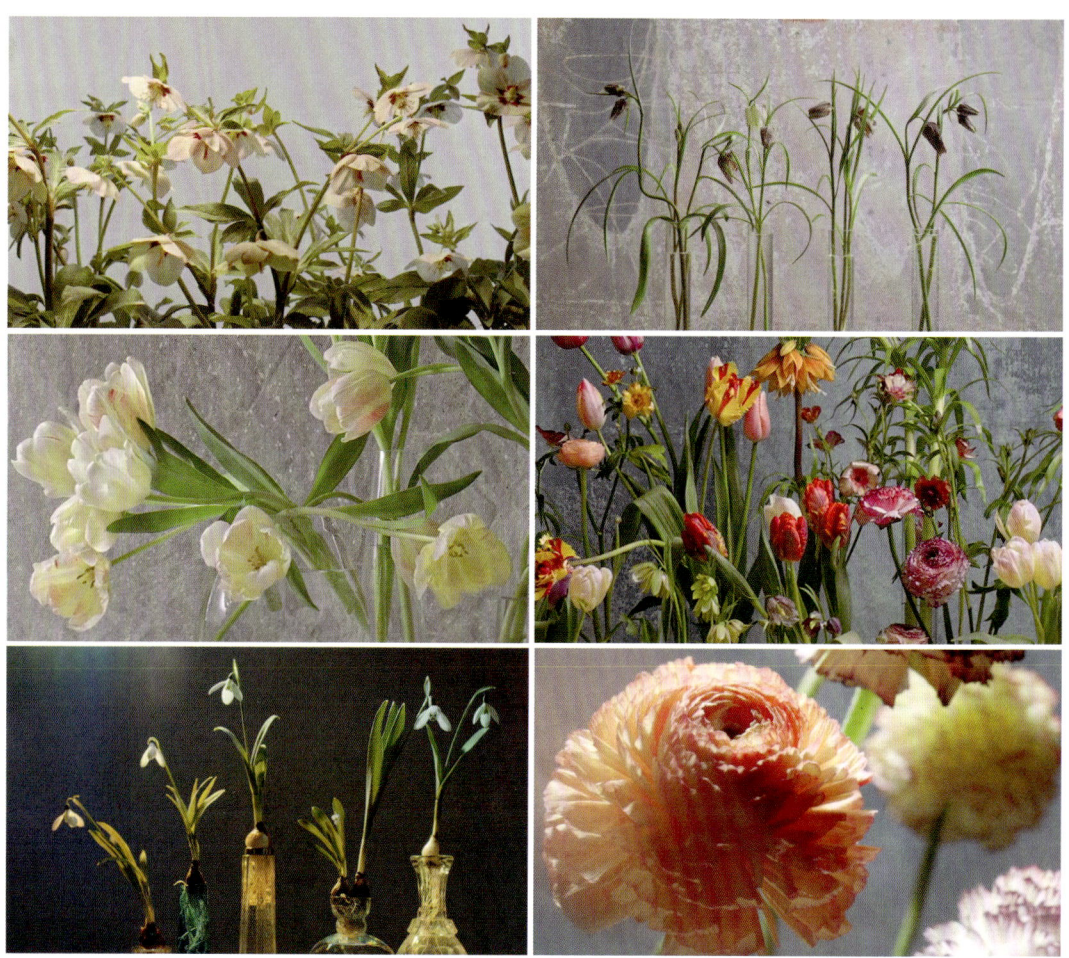

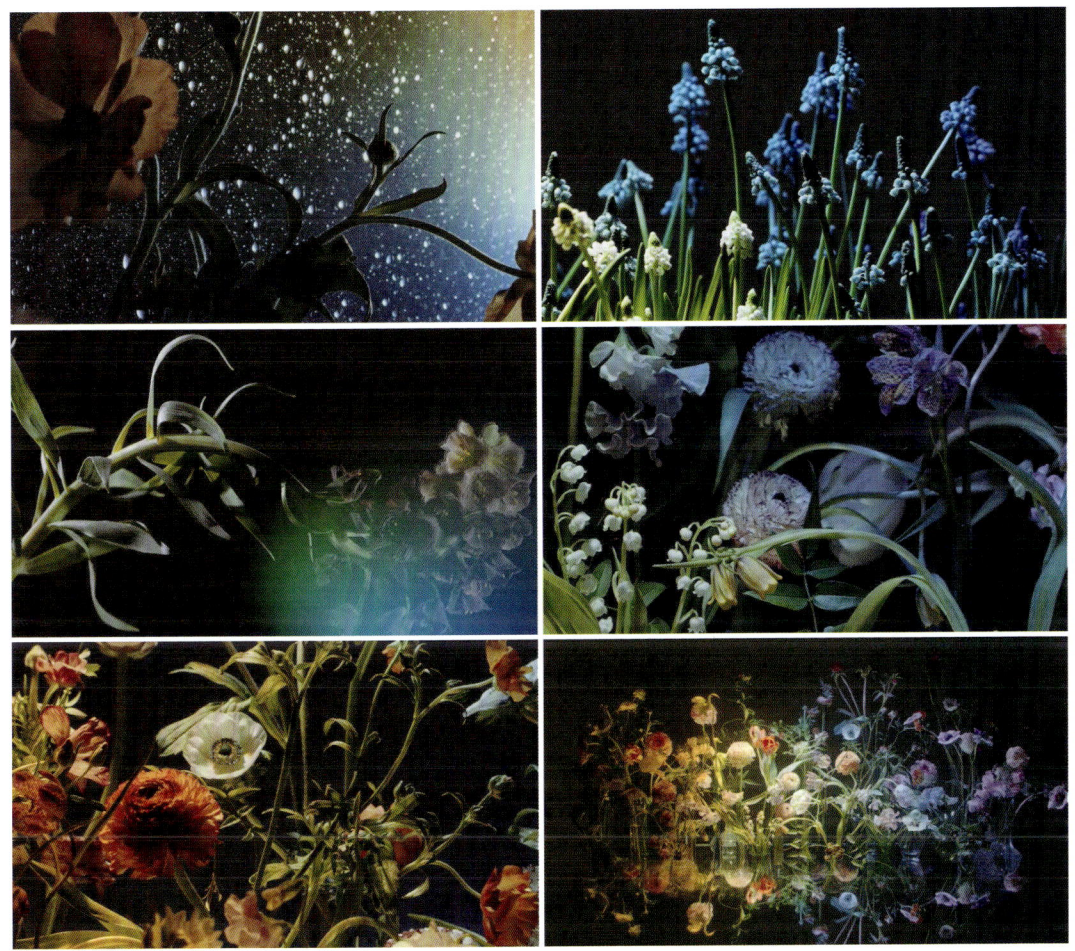

Flora Starkey

Spring Rites, 2018
Film

A tableau of delicate blue muscari and elegant white snowdrops emerges and blooms from an assortment of glass bulb vases; a row of snake's head fritillaries, with their unusual chequered pattern, dance in glass test tubes; a group of imperial fritillaries in rich orange, picotee pink ranunculus and tulips in carmine, white and blush pink twist and turn as they stretch for the light. These are just a few of the vignettes created by floral designer Flora Starkey (born 1974)

for her celebratory short film *Spring Rites*, which heralded the vernal equinox of 2018. Directed by James Stopforth and set to an ethereal contemporary score by sound designers Will Ward and Jack Wylie, the stop-motion film celebrates the miracle of flowers as they emerge from their winter dormancy and bloom into spectacular forms and colours, emphasized by moody or kaleidoscopic lighting that moves from light to dark throughout the nearly seven-minute duration. The flowers loosely chart the progression of spring, from early species such as snowdrops that emerge in the depths of winter through to

late spring blooms, including anenomes, lily of the valley and the unusual deep aubergine spires of *Fritillaria persica*. Starkey frequently cites her inspirations as Dutch and Flemish paintings of the sixteenth and seventeenth centuries, but continues to push contemporary boundaries, treating flowers not just as decoration but as a visual art form.

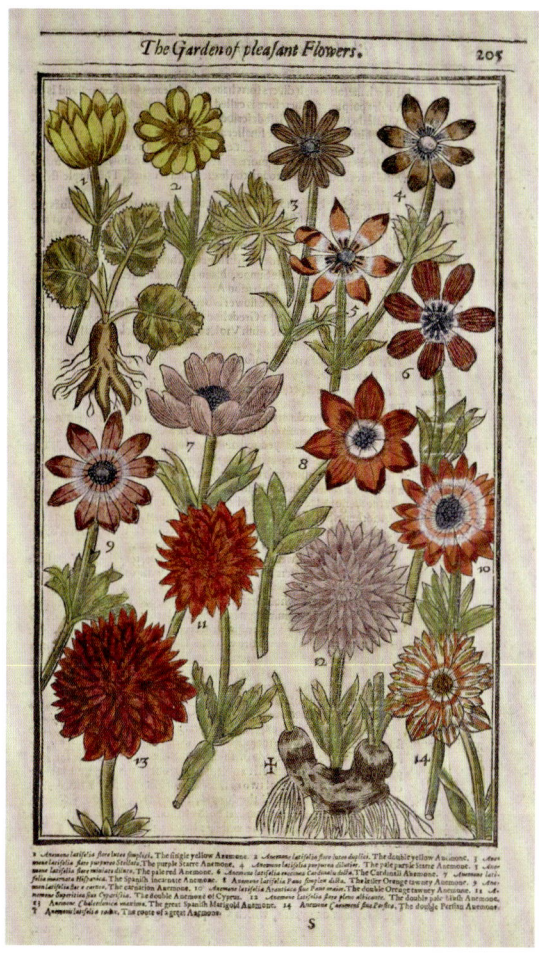

John Parkinson and Christopher Switzer

Anenome latifolia, from *Paradisi in Sole Paradisus Terrestris, or, A Garden of All Sorts of Pleasant Flowers*, 1629
Hand-coloured woodcut, 35.8 × 22.6 cm / 14 × 9 in
Getty Research Institute, Los Angeles

In the early seventeenth century, English herbalist and botanist John Parkinson (1567–1650) was pre-eminent in his fields and was granted appointments at court by both King James I as an apothecary and later to King Charles I as Royal Botanist. Parkinson was one of a group of bot-anists who eagerly collected, swapped and identified new plants arriving in Europe from Asia and the Americas. Parkinson also maintained his own walled garden in London, where he recorded 484 types of plants and his gardening experience in two monumental books. The first, published in 1629, was *A Garden of All Sorts of Pleasant Flowers* – the Latin title *Paradisi in Sole Paradisus Terrestris* was a pun on his own name: Park-in-Sun's Park on Earth. Divided into three sections on flowers, vegetables and fruits, the book illustrated almost 780 plants in its 108 full-page plates, mostly original woodcuts by German artist Christopher Switzer. Shown here are what Parkinson believed to be fourteen varieties of *Anemone latifolia*, meaning 'broad-leaved', but we now know that most are cultivars of *A. coronaria*, while others are not anemones at all – the top two yellow flowers are in fact the spring celadine *Ficaria verna*. Parkinson's second work, *Theatrum Botanicum*, was published in 1640 with descriptions of more than 4,000 medicinal plants, including previously unpublished native varieties. The most comprehensive herbal treatise in English at the time, it remained the definitive guide for apothecaries for a century after his death.

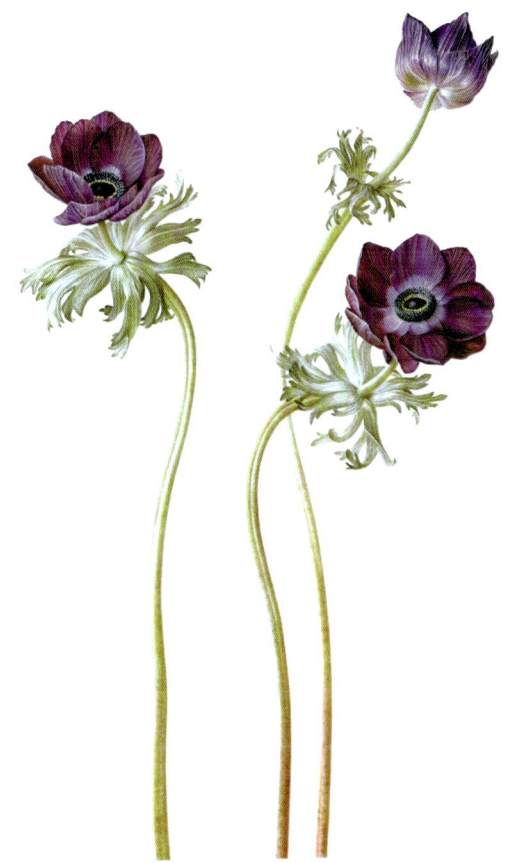

Lizzie Sanders

Blue anemones / Anemone coronaria cv., 2007
Watercolour on paper, 35.5 × 30.5 cm / 14 × 12 in
Private collection

Three velvety, cultivated anemones (*Anemone coronaria*) are dressed in their finest violet-blue ruffled collars. One faces the audience centre stage as another demurely turns away from the dance and its partner gently bows. Scottish artist Lizzie Sanders (1950–2020) used a white backdrop and theatrical lighting to accentuate the sinuous stances of her cast of characters. Combined with a dry-brush watercolour technique, the end result is a remarkably detailed rendering of flowers with a photographic, almost three-dimensional, quality. After a two-decade career in advertising and graphic design, Sanders began to focus on studies in botanical illustration and horticulture with leaders in both fields. Subsequently, she melded the influence of two Scottish artists – botanical painter Rory McEwen and figurative painter Alison Watt – into a fresh, individualistic perspective. Botanically accurate, her works fill the page with intriguing textures, forms and patterns of petals, stems, leaves and bark. As an instructor at the Royal Botanic Garden Edinburgh, Sanders was fortunate to have access to the plants that are the subjects of many of her paintings, including the world-famous collection of rhododendrons. Producing single, showy blooms, the *A. coronaria* depicted here – commonly called poppy anemones – are native to the Mediterranean. With petals that flutter in a breeze, the family name is derived from the Greek *anemos*, meaning 'wind', and *coronaria* indicates a possible traditional use in garlands.

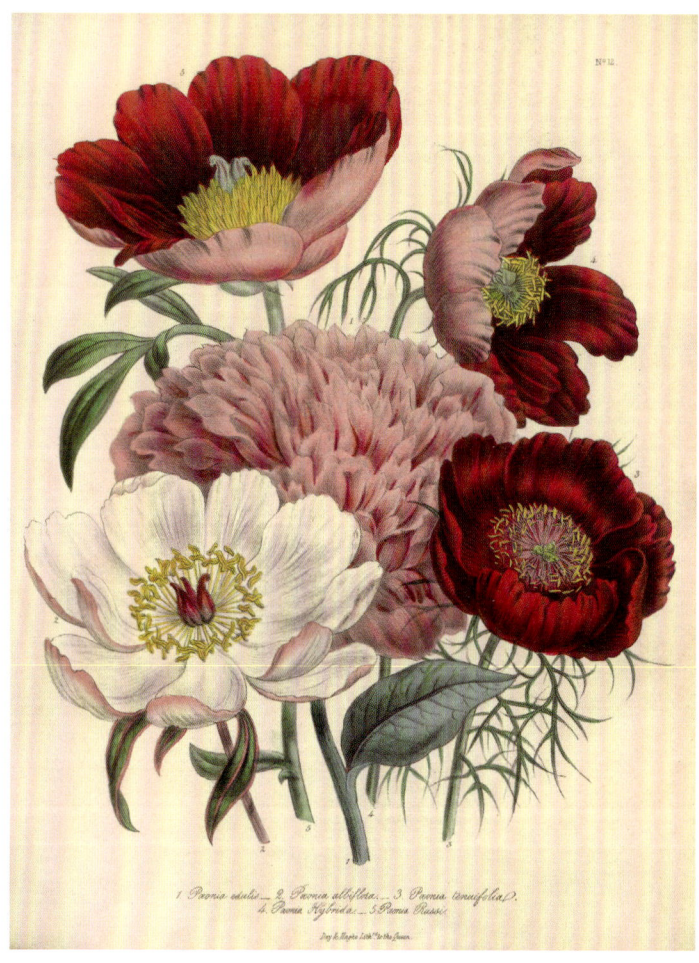

1 *Paeonia edulis* ... 2 *Paeonia albiflora* ... 3 *Paeonia tenuifolia* . 4 *Paeonia Hybrida* ... 5 *Paeonia Russii*

Jane Webb Loudon

Plate 12, from *The Ladies' Flower-Garden of Ornamental Perennials*, 1843–44
Hand-coloured lithograph, 27 × 22 cm / 10¾ × 8¾ in
Leiden University Library, Netherlands

This hand-coloured lithograph of red, pink and white peonies comes from *The Ladies' Flower-Garden of Ornamental Perennials* (1843–44), the first in a series of best-selling gardening books by the self-taught British horticulturalist and artist Jane Loudon (1807–58). Initially working alongside her husband John, a publisher, botanist and

garden designer, on technical books such as his *Encyclopaedia of Gardening* (1822), Loudon saw a gap in the market for an entry-level guide that would tap into the growing passion for gardening among the Victorian middle classes, particularly women. Her instincts proved correct. Books such as *Instructions in Gardening for Ladies* (1840) and *Botany for Ladies* (1842) sold tens of thousands of copies, thanks to their approachable, anecdotal style and Loudon's sumptuous illustrations. Loudon's great innovation was to show flowers grouped in bouquets, rather than as individual specimens, as if freshly gathered from a cutting

garden. Her success came to an abrupt end when John Loudon died in 1843, leaving Jane and her daughter, Agnes, virtually penniless. With the loss of her job as editor of *The Ladies' Companion at Home and Abroad* and sales of her books declining, Loudon was forced to ask for money from the Civil List and lived on a small pension until her own death in 1858. Today, Loudon is again lauded for her remarkable talent, resourcefulness and energy – and her determination to make gardening accessible to all.

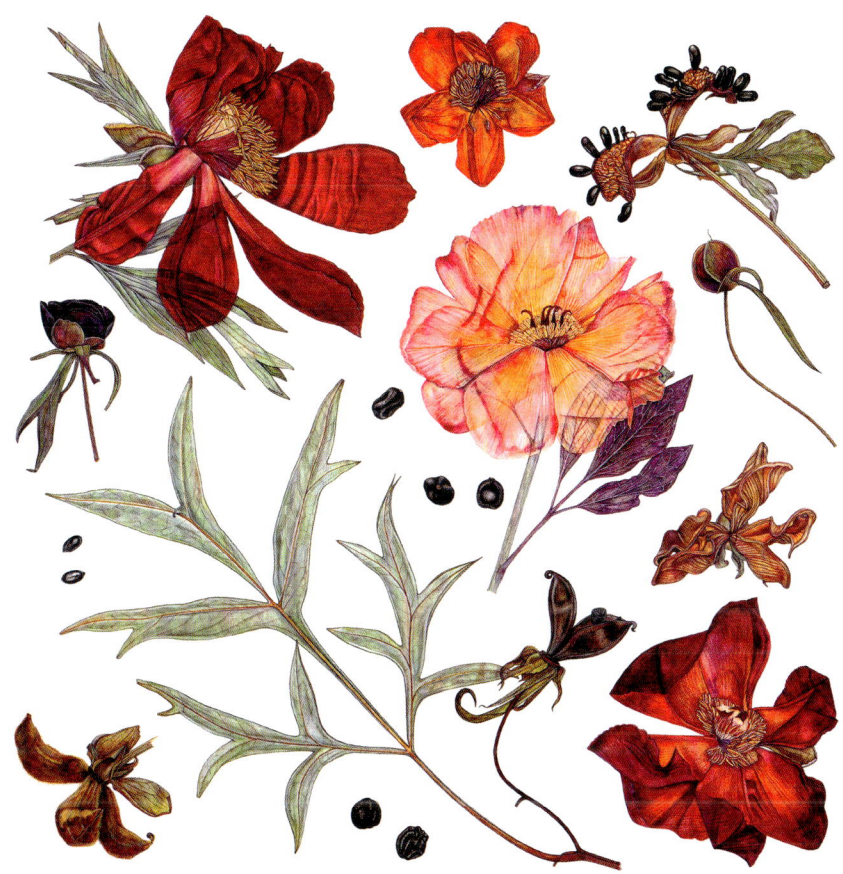

Rachel Pedder-Smith

Collection of Peony Specimens, 2011
Watercolour on paper, 29 × 29 cm / 11½ × 11½ in
Private collection

At first glance, the meticulously arranged peony specimens – flowers, buds, stems, leaves and seeds – appear to have been flattened and dried, perhaps presented as they appeared when found in the garden and set aside for future inspiration. Closer inspection, however, reveals a watercolour produced in stunning detail by British artist Rachel Pedder-Smith (born 1975). The negative spaces create a fluid movement around the edges of all of the bits and pieces of serration, translucency and minuteness, and tell a story of the cycle of vibrancy, fruiting, decline and dispersal of seed. Pedder-Smith's subject choices are often not those of typical beauty but those that represent intriguing forms, textures and ephemeral relationships as intricate tableaus from nature. In addition to flowers, specimens of bees, butterflies and other creatures often find their way into her paintings. As part of her doctoral thesis project in Communication, Art and Design from the Royal College of Art, London, Pedder-Smith painted more than 500 specimens from the herbarium of the Royal Botanic Gardens at Kew, over a period of nearly four years. This work culminated in a painting 5.5 metres (18 feet) long that represented the herbarium's history of collecting. Pedder-Smith continues to work as a natural history painter, instructor and participant in solo and group exhibitions, and she has received four gold medals from the Royal Horticultural Society, London.

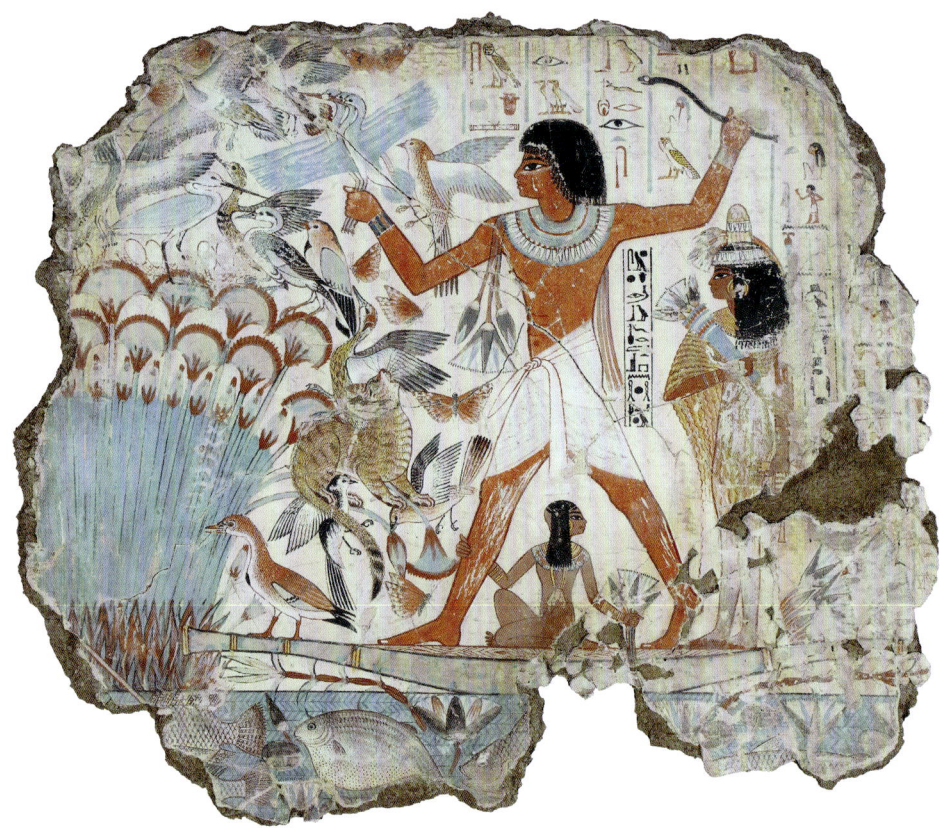

Anonymous

Fragment of wall painting from the tomb
of Nebamun, 1350 BC
Painted plaster, 1 × 1.2 m / 3 ft 3 in × 3 ft 9 in
British Museum, London

This watery scene of river lotus and papyrus
thickets originally decorated the mortuary chapel
of Nebamun, a scribe at the temple of Amun at
Thebes (modern Luxor). A middle-ranking official, Nebamun was wealthy enough to afford a
chapel above his grave on the West Bank of the
Nile, in which family and friends would leave
offerings and recite prayers; the paintings that

covered the walls were idealized visions of daily
life that he hoped would continue in death. Here,
Nebamun fishes and hunts fowls from a reed boat,
accompanied by his wife, daughter and hunting
cat. The cat has caught three birds startled from
a papyrus thicket, while fish swim among
broadleaved lotus plants. A bunch of lotus hangs
from Nebamun's arm, and another is held by
his wife. The flowers are shown in profile, white
petals edged by grey and green sepals, open flowers alternating with closed buds. A hieroglyph
in the form of a papyrus plant forms part of the
ancient Egyptian word *wadj*, meaning fresh and

thriving. Papyrus marshes were believed to be
areas of particular fertility, and amulets in the
form of the plant were worn for protection and
good health. At the same time, papyrus thickets
occupied a peripheral area at the edges of the
ordered world, symbolic of chaos. Thus they were
the settings for ritual hunts, in which a king or
noble metaphorically defeated the forces of entropy
that threatened the ordered Egyptian world.

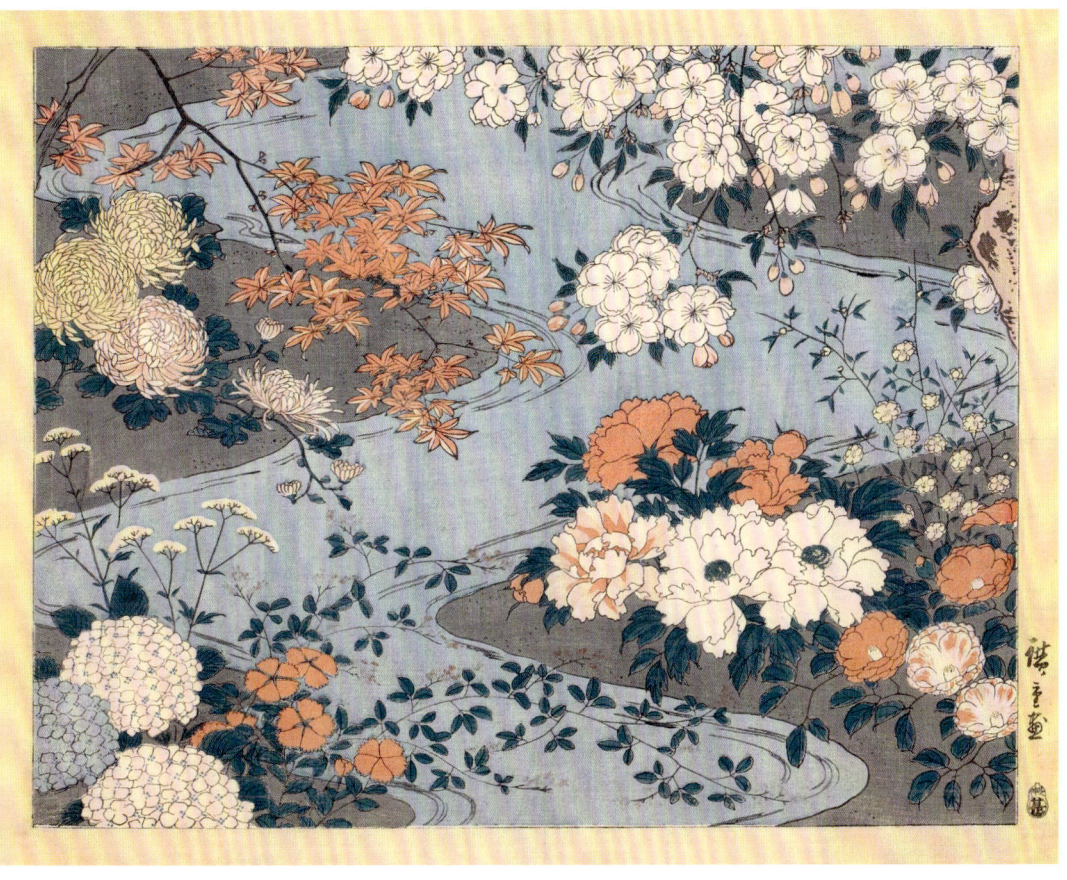

Utagawa Hiroshige

Flowers of the Four Seasons, c.1835
Nishiki-e (woodcut with colour blocks),
37.9 × 48.2 cm / 15 × 19 in
Honolulu Museum of Art, Hawaii

An elegant veil of flowers is draped lace-like over a Japanese rural scene, while a stream behind zigzags languidly across the page. Flowers grouped around each of the corners indicate the four seasons. Filling the top right are cherry blossoms in full bloom, a traditional sign of spring that flower across Japan as early as January in the south through to May in the north. At left, representing autumn and winter, are the leaves of a Japanese maple tree (*Acer palmatum*) hovering above chrysanthemum, yarrow (*Achillea*), hydrangea and dianthus. In the bottom left, peonies with a backdrop of delicate camellias herald summer. The groupings are arranged so that each flower is given strong prominence without disrupting the overall pictorial balance, imbuing the print with a remarkable sense of harmony and tranquillity. *Flowers of the Four Seasons* is one of more than 5,000 prints produced by the Japanese woodcut-print master Utagawa Hiroshige (1797–1858) in the *ukiyo-e* (pictures of the 'floating world') style. Hiroshige documented his many travels, most famously in the series *One Hundred Famous Views of Edo*, in which he created beautiful snapshots of contemporary life, imbuing each print with a particular *joie de vivre*. Here, we find the artist at his most meditative, completely in tune with nature. In the image the flowers float weightlessly, untroubled by the wind, their full beauty on display.

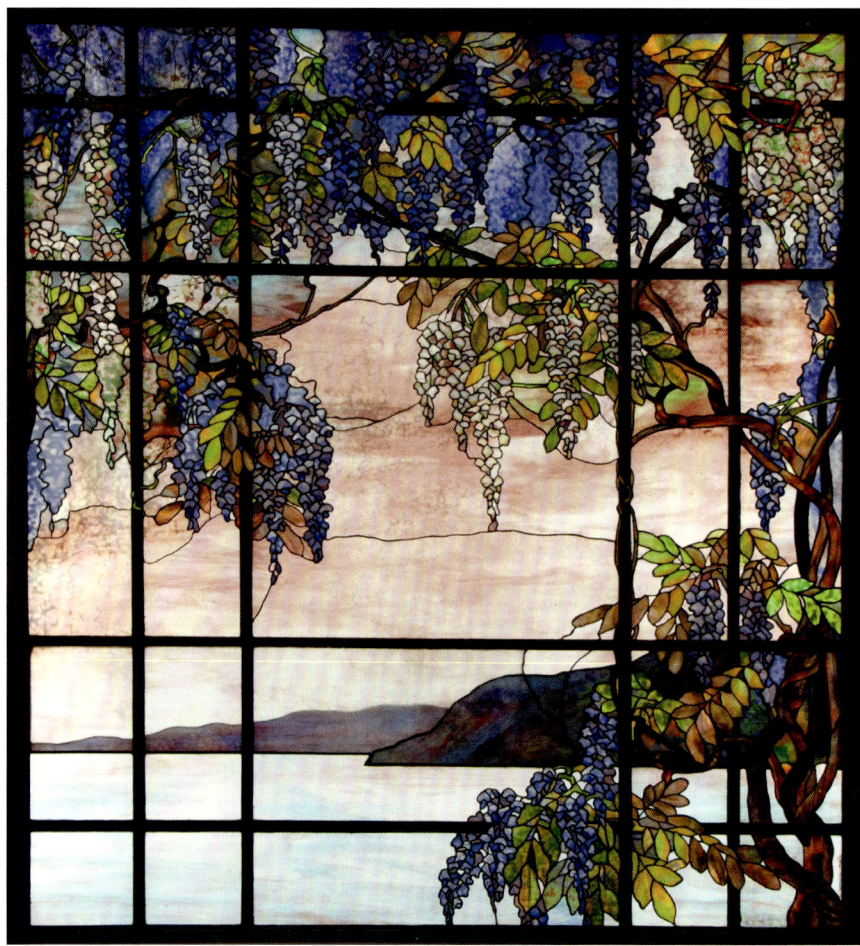

Louis Comfort Tiffany

View of Oyster Bay, 1905
Stained glass, 1.9 × 1.7 m / 6 ft 1 in / 5 ft 6 in
Metropolitan Museum of Art, New York

A view of Oyster Bay, New York, is beautifully framed by the arching, twined branches of a wisteria, the blue and purple flower clusters dangling among the subtly shaded green foliage. Beyond, distant headlands jut into the pale blue sea, forming a captivating vista. A remarkable coloured glass 'window', this piece was designed by American artist and designer Louis Comfort Tiffany (1848–1933) for the Manhattan home

of William C. Skinner, whose family house in Holyoke, Massachusetts, was named Wistariahurst. Tiffany's father, Charles Lewis Tiffany, founded the company that became synonymous with high-quality jewellery and silverware (see p.186), but instead of joining the business, Louis originally carved out his own career as a painter (he was appointed art director to Tiffany & Co. on his father's death in 1902). From the late 1870s, he became more concerned with decorative arts and interiors, especially involving the original use of glass. He developed a method of glass production that involved

blending colours in the molten state, thus achieving delicately shaded effects. This process, known as *favrile*, became a trademark, and features in much of his work. Here, the technique is used to render the wisteria flowers, evoking their fragrant summer blooms. Between 1902 and 1905, Tiffany worked on his country home of Laurelton Hall on Long Island overlooking Oyster Bay. Expressing Tiffany's aesthetic ideals, the home blended nature and exoticism, but was destroyed by fire in 1957.

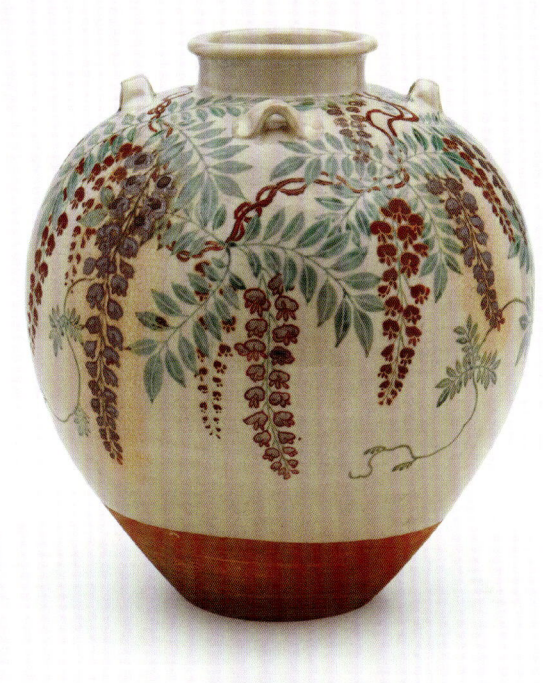

Nonomura Ninsei

Tea leaf jar, c.1646–66
Stoneware with overglaze enamels,
28.8 cm / 11⅜ in
MOA Museum of Art, Shizuoka, Japan

A designated national treasure of Japan, this decorated tea storage jar, or *chatsubo*, is perhaps the most famous work produced by Nonomura Ninsei (active c.1646–94). Born in Tamba, one of Japan's traditional pottery centres, Ninsei studied in Seto before moving to Kyoto some time around 1647. Here, he established the Omuro kiln and set about perfecting his elegant style. He worked closely with the renowned tea master Kanamori Sōwa, who described Ninsei's work – which included many pieces for the tea ceremony – as the epitome of *kirei-sabi*, or refined beauty. This jar, with its harmonious form and graceful decoration, is the perfect example of both Ninsei's aesthetic and his innovative methods. He was the first identifiable Kyoto potter to apply overglaze enamel designs such as this blooming Japanese wisteria (*Wisteria floribunda*) to stoneware vessels – previously enamel had only been used on porcelain – and also among the first to stamp his work with his name. Wisteria blossoms have been widely used in Japanese art and culture, including in family crests as well as in decoration for Imperial clothing – the colour purple was long associated with and at times restricted solely to being worn by the Imperial family and the highest-level officials. Here, the flowing composition, with the racemes seeming almost to dance in the breeze, fits perfectly with the jar's elegant shape, its uniformly thin walls a testament to the supreme technical skill of the man who came to be known as the father of *Kyo-yaki*, or Kyoto pottery.

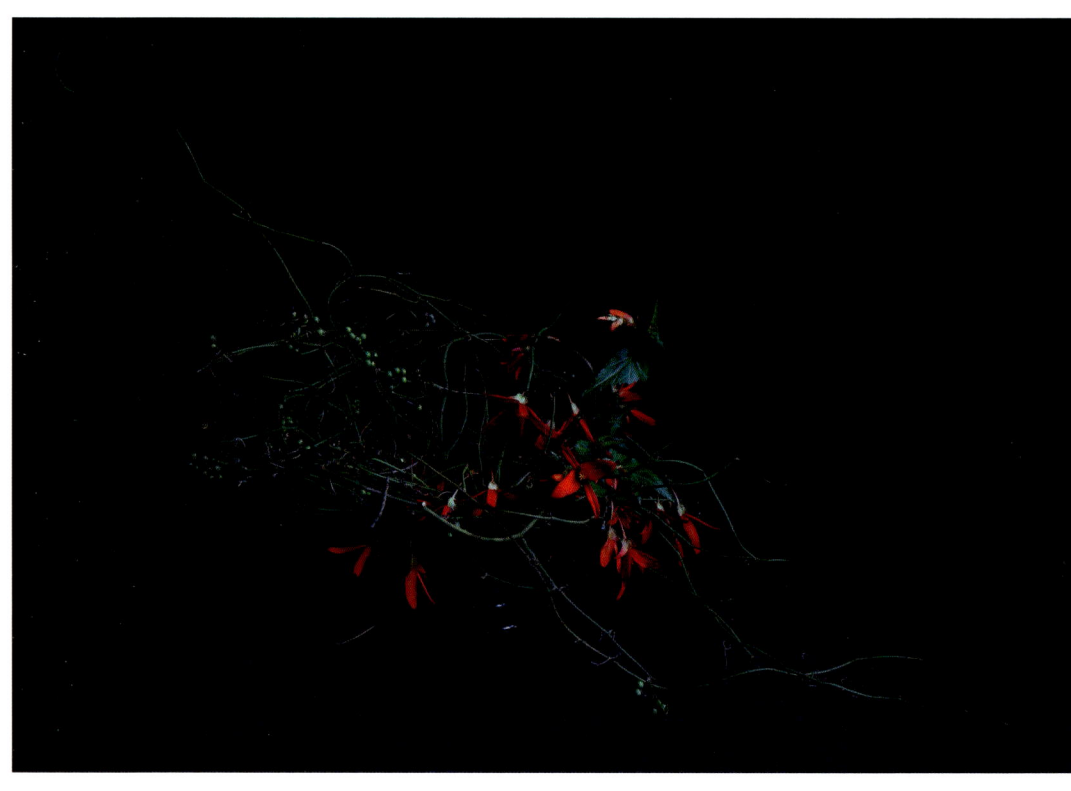

Emily Thompson

Study with Firecrackers, 2019
Floral arrangement

Hot, fleshy firecracker begonias (*Begonia boliviensis*) contrast with cool, thorny wild greenbriar (*Smilax rotundifolia*) in this intriguing floral composition. The work of American floral designer Emily Thompson (born 1973) might appear effortless, but she champions precision and intention in her choice of components, mirrored by the environmental integrity of their sourcing. For this study, the begonias were cut from local growing plants and the greenbriar was foraged from areas where it grows as a pernicious weed. Such unique and sometimes shocking combinations of the highly cultivated and the wickedly wild put Thompson's work on a completely different visual plane from most commercial floral designers. This 'fleuriste sauvage' turns to artists like the eighteenth-century English artist William Gilpin – proponent of 'the picturesque' – for inspiration. Like Gilpin, Thompson favours compositions that appear wholly designed by nature rather than man-made – and appreciates that a great deal of mental and physical exertion is required to achieve that seemingly effortless effect. Without a single focal point, her pieces invite the viewer to explore every angle of the arrangement. Here, the voluptuous begonias are bait to draw the observer in while the greenbriar is quite literally a snare to catch and keep them there. For Thompson, nature is always in charge, and her unique skill is to tame it *just* enough to bring it into the smart drawing rooms of Manhattan, enchanting and beguiling its audience.

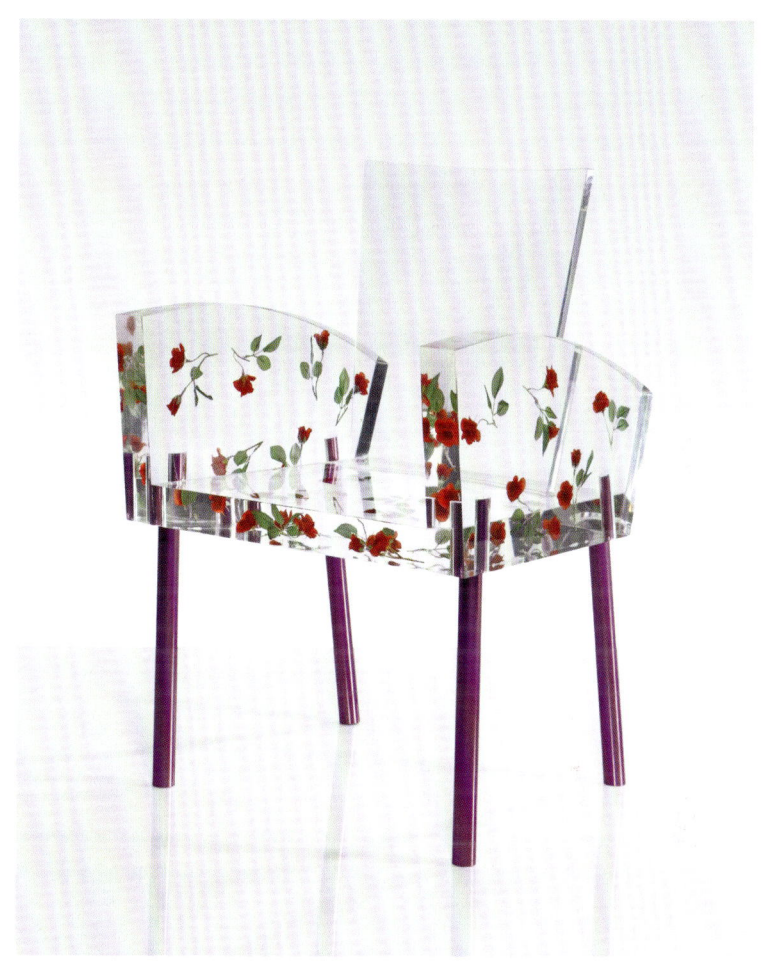

Shiro Kuramata

Miss Blanche, 1988
Acrylic, artificial roses and anodized aluminium,
92 × 63 × 61 cm / 36¼ × 24¾ × 24¾ in
Private collection

This remarkable artwork also happens to be a functional chair, with vibrant red artificial roses floating within thick panels of clear resin, their contrasting too-green stems and leaves dancing playfully among each other inside the seat and arms. The Japanese designer Shiro Kuramata (1923–91) fused whimsical ideas with a technical edge, such as his *Glass Chair* (1976), which was constructed solely from glazed panels, or *How High the Moon* (1987), made from a cloud-like mesh. *Miss Blanche* is perhaps his most recognizable piece. The chair encases run-of-the-mill artificial flowers in slabs of resin, creating a seat that appears clear as glass, accented by the red blooms and balanced on slim tubular legs of anodized aluminium. Named for Blanche DuBois, the central character in Tennessee Williams's 1947 play *A Streetcar Named Desire*, the reference is perhaps a riff on her illusory personality and veneer of propriety. Like Blanche, the chair is also a cunning sleight of hand: an apparently simple one-liner, the idea was deviously difficult to produce. Abandoning the original concept of using real roses, which the resin burned black, Kuramata made the limited-edition chairs individually in one-off moulds. Each required partially pouring a resin slab, inserting fake roses with tweezers before the liquid hardened and finally submerging them in an upper layer. Held in perpetual suspension, the effect is a chair graced with seemingly effortless floral animation.

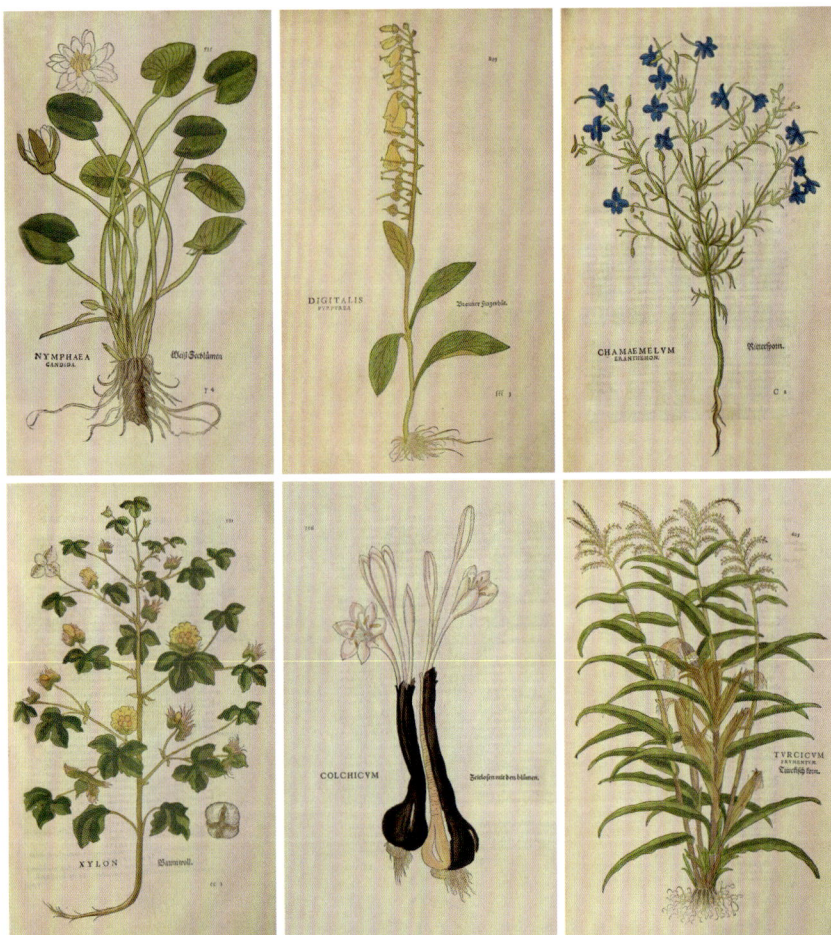

Leonhart Fuchs, Heinrich Füllmaurer, Albrecht Meyer and Veyt Rudolff Speckle

Six plates from *De historia stirpium*, 1542
Hand-coloured woodcut, each 39 × 27 cm /
15¼ × 10¾ in
Special Collections and Rare Books, University
of Missouri Libraries, Columbia

In the history of science, the years 1542 and 1543 mark a fundamental change of thought documented by three revolutionary books: *De revolutionibus orbium coelestium* by Nicolaus Copernicus, proving that Earth is not the centre of the universe; *De humani corporis fabrica* by Andreas Vesalius, the first evidence-based textbook on human anatomy; and *De historia stirpium* (The History of Plants) by German physician and botanist Leonhart Fuchs (1501–66). Fuchs's work consists of two disparate elements: the text, largely based on the writings of classical authors with a few new observations; and the botanical illustrations, which began a whole new era of plant documentation. True to nature and of remarkable quality, the illustrations are the result of the collaboration of Fuchs, a professor of medicine at Tübingen University, with the plant illustrators Heinrich Füllmaurer and Albrecht Meyer, while the woodcutter Veyt Rudolff Speckle prepared the printing forms. The book illustrates plants found in the wild and in gardens, but also includes a few copies based on pre-existing images, such as that of Levant cotton (*Gossypium herbaceum*) (bottom left). Of special interest are the plants recently introduced from the Americas, among them the first printed illustration of a maize plant (*Zea mays*) in flowering and fruiting stages (bottom right). Also depicted here are the dwarf white water lily (*Nymphaea candida*), foxglove (*Digitalispurpurea*), larkspur (*Consolida regalis*) and autumn crocus (*Colchcum autumnale*).

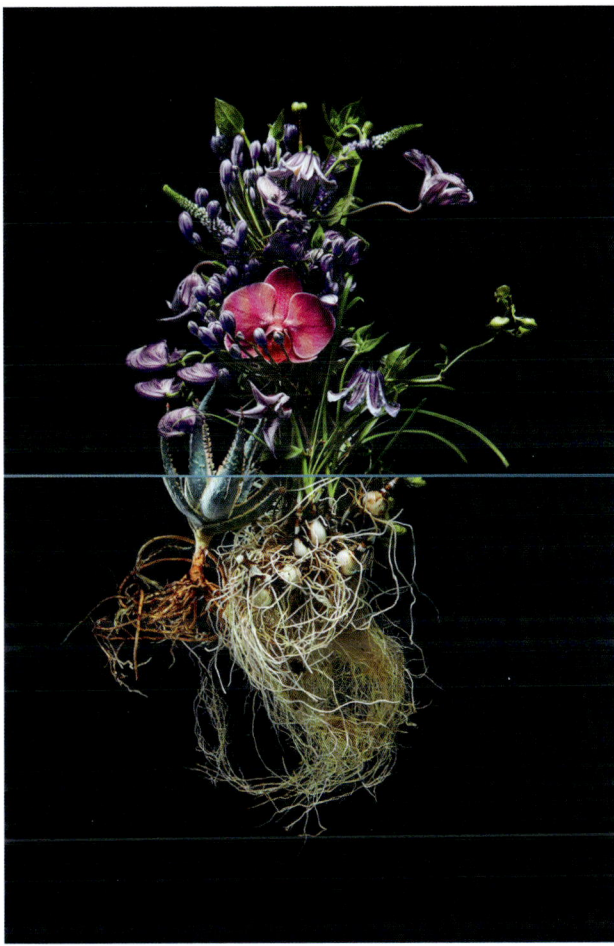

Azuma Makoto

Undersurface Flowers, 2018
Flowers and water, dimensions variable

Deep pink orchids sit alongside hyperreal aconitums, veronica and exotic foliage against a black background while their circling roots and bulbs sit beneath them. Created by Azuma Makoto (born 1976), the *Undersurface* series highlights one of the acclaimed Japanese artist and botanical sculptor's key concerns: showcasing a side of plants that we do not normally see. Through a series of still-life photographs, Makoto presents a stunning and meticulously arranged collection of flowers, but then also reveals the contrasting tangle of fibrous roots that keep the plants alive. His inventive concepts begin with experiments in his Tokyo haute-couture flower shop and laboratory, Jardins des Fleurs, which he co-founded with botanical photographer Shunsuke Shiinoki in 2002. Makoto has become widely known for remarkable botanical sculptures in which he takes the ephemeral nature of plant material to extremes, submerging arrangements into the depths of the ocean, setting them on fire, rocketing them into space or freezing flowers in ice. Highly original and thought-provoking, Makoto's mesmerizing work draws on *ikebana*, the classic Japanese art of flower arranging, and specifically the experimental practitioners of the 1970s.

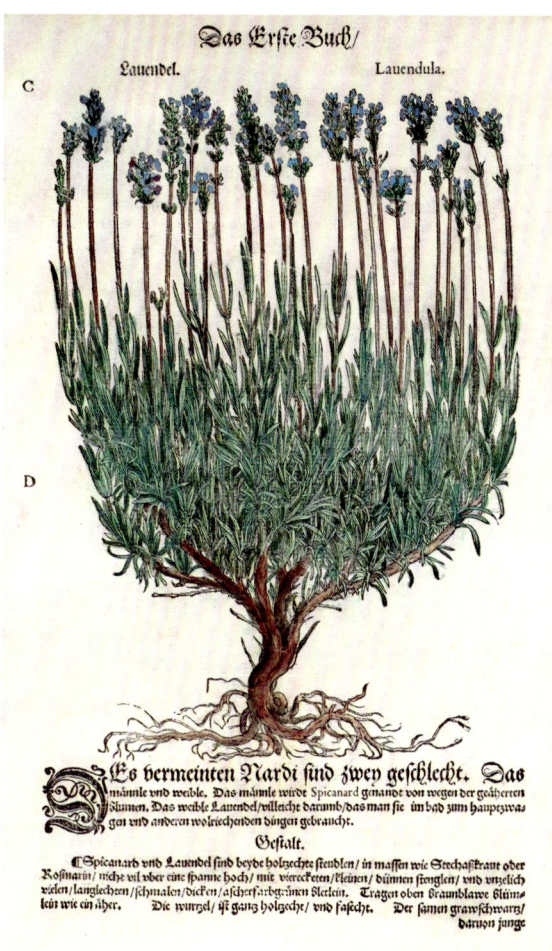

Pietro Andrea Mattioli

Lavender, from a German edition
of *New Kreüterbuch*, 1563
Hand-coloured woodcut, 37.2 × 23.5 cm /
14¾ × 9¼ in
Private collection

A lavender plant, perhaps one of the most instantly recognizable herbs in the world, is presented from flowers to roots in this sixteenth-century *Kreüterbuch* or 'book of herbs' by Italian botanist and physician Pietro Andrea Mattioli (1501–77). The *Kreüterbuch* was an enormous compendium of knowledge of the botanical world at that time. The lavender is shown growing vigorously as it reaches towards the sun, its flowers, leaves and roots healthy and strong. The illustrations, credited by some to Georgio Liberale and Wolfgang Meyerpeck, are deliberately accurate rather than stylized in any way, as one of the primary functions of the book would have been as an aid for identification of specific plants, in addition to noting, perhaps more importantly, their medicinal properties: failure and misidentification could leave a patient at best untreated, at worst dead. Much of Mattioli's material was built upon his knowledge of the *Materia Medica* of Dioscorides, the ancient Greek physician and botanist famed for his pharmacopoeia, which identified the compounds of drugs (see p.24). Lavender has long been used – as it still is – to treat stress, depression and pain. Although there is little scientific evidence behind these uses, the fact that it has been used in this way for hundreds, if not thousands, of years suggests that, if nothing else, the beautifully scented lavender flowers bring comfort to those being treated.

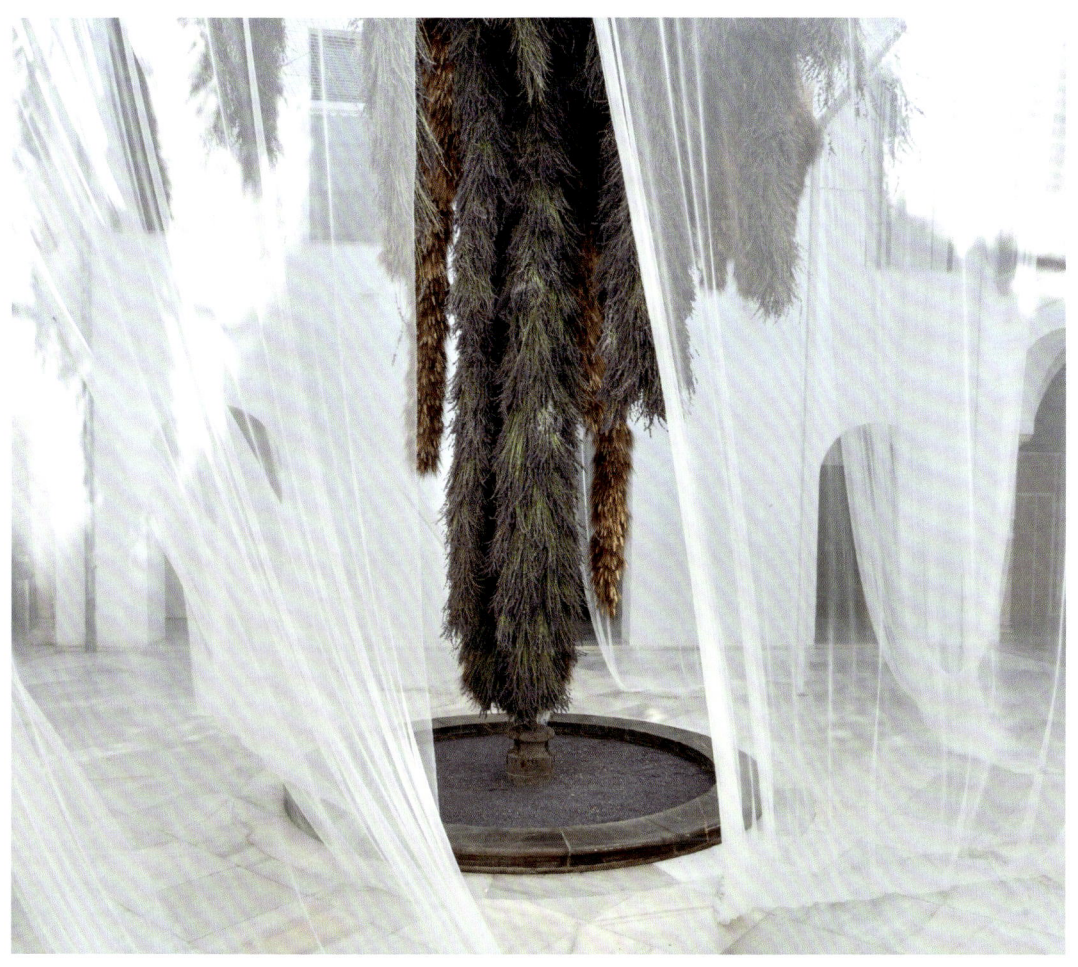

Mary Lennox

Fieldwork, 2019
Lavender, wheat, rope, iron, galvanized iron, plastic and tulle
FLORA International Flower Festival, Córdoba, Spain

Like a luxuriant chandelier, interleaved ropes of wheat and lavender in hues of gold and purple cascade in a bushy array. This aromatic immersive installation was suspended at the centre of the Palacio de Orive's Renaissance courtyard for the renowned Flora Festival in Córdoba, Spain, in 2019. *Fieldwork* by Australian-born floral designer Ruby Barber (born 1988) was inspired by a summer trip to La Mancha in central Spain, where she visited the famous fields of *Lavandula stoechas* in full bloom, which are flanked by rows and rows of wheat. Designed to evoke these agricultural landscapes, the installation transports viewers with the heady scent of lavender, which crunches underfoot, and the rustle of wheat in the breeze. The character and form of *Fieldwork* are indicative of Barber's innovative approach, which characteristically employs a hanging piece inspired by nature – biomimicry is integral to her design process. Her acclaimed studio, Mary Lennox – named for the central character in Frances Hodgson Burnett's novel *The Secret Garden* – migrated from Sydney to Berlin, where it is now based, and is distinctive for its inspired pairing of natural elements. Delighted to work with nature 'by the bucketful', Barber favours materials that are regularly foraged on adventurous field trips, including her calling card of hanging swathes of pampas grass (*Cortaderia selloana*). Each jaunt reveals unusual specimens that reflect specific locations and seasonal change.

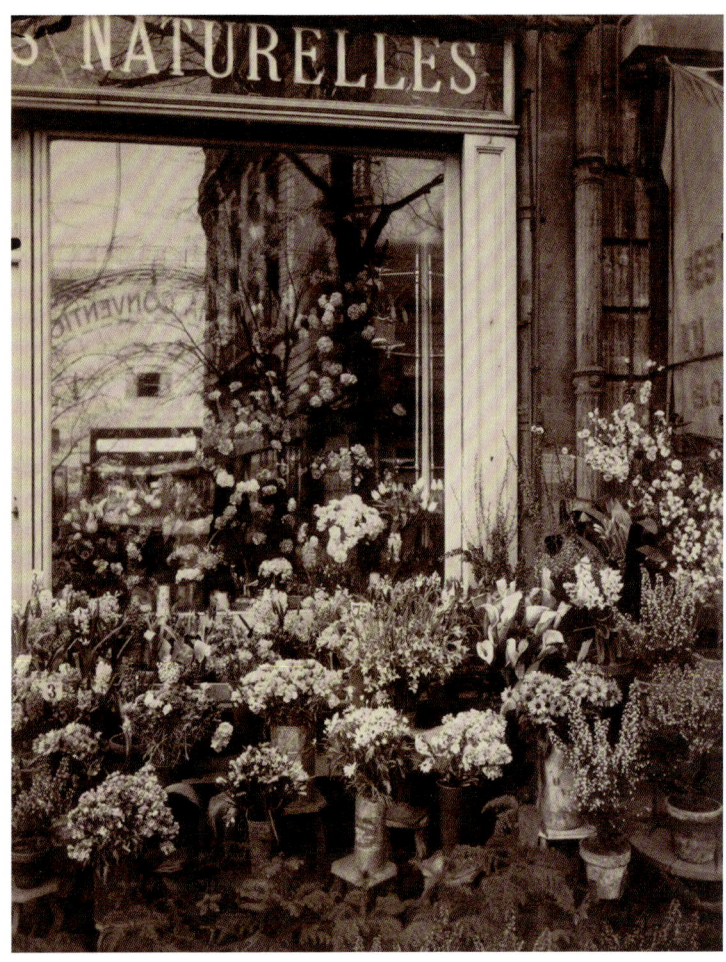

Eugène Atget

Boutique Fleurs, rue de Vaugirard, 1923–24
Matte albumen silver print, 22 × 18 cm / 8¾ × 7 in
Museum of Modern Art, New York

An array of cut flowers and potted plants floods the pavement outside a Parisian florist's shop, while more blooms can be seen through the large window that also reflects adjacent buildings and trees. By mingling exterior and interior views, this image by French documentary photographer Eugène Atget (1857–1927) creates a disorienting effect that is further compounded by the closely cropped composition, which isolates the shopfront from its surroundings. This kind of visual quirk greatly appealed to the Surrealists, who identified in Atget's photographs an uncanny, dreamlike quality. After initially training for the priesthood, Atget became a sailor and then an actor before finally settling on photography. In the late 1880s he began producing 'photographic documents' that included landscapes, animals, flowers, monuments and street scenes. Working both to commission and in response to public demand, Atget sold his photographs to architects, illustrators, painters, sculptors, sign painters, set designers and lovers of Paris. His own love for the old city fuelled his thirty-year quest to document its medieval streets, which were then being systematically bulldozed under Georges-Eugène Haussmann's modernization programme; buildings and shopfronts were swept away by the construction of boulevards, parks and public buildings. Atget's encyclopaedic inventory documents a city on the cusp of the modern era, although his work was not fully appreciated until after his death.

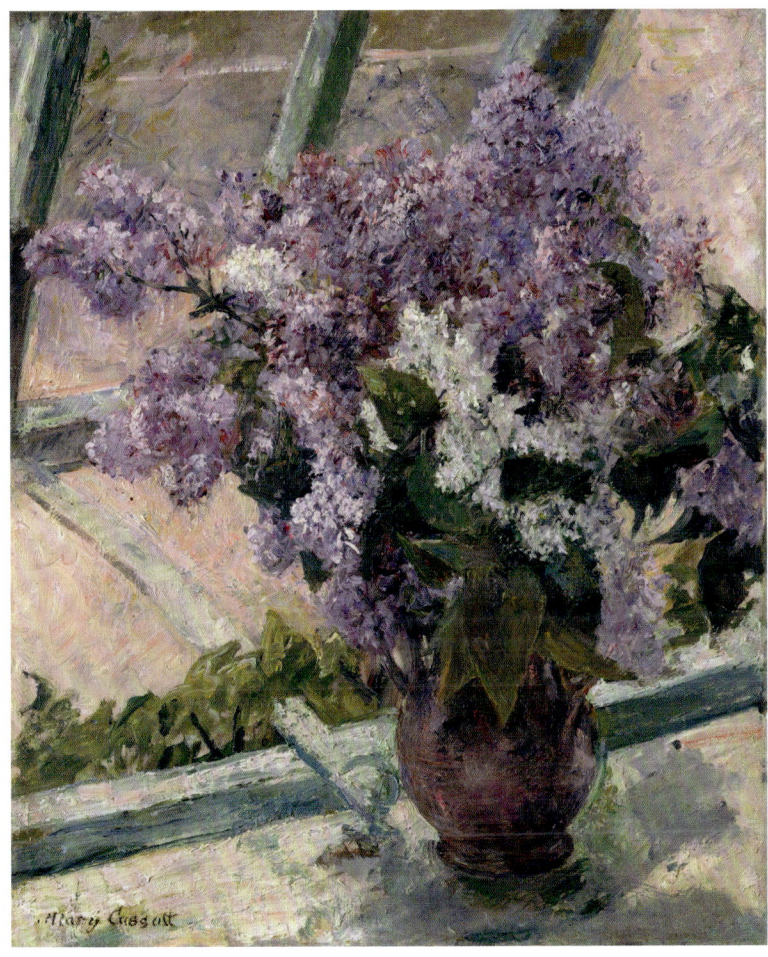

Mary Cassatt

Lilacs in a Window, c.1880–83
Oil on canvas, 61.5 × 51.1 cm / 24 × 20 in
Metropolitan Museum of Art, New York

Vibrant brushwork, swathes of emerald green and dashes of light purple immortalize the ephemeral beauty of lilac in this painting by American artist Mary Cassatt (1844–1926). Native to southeastern Europe and Asia, lilac blooms possess intense fragrance and striking colouration that was irresistible to nineteenth-century French gardeners, who propagated and hybridized many varieties, enhancing the plant's popularity around the world. At that time, still-life painting saw a resurgence among artists who did not take too seriously Claude Monet's invitation to only paint outdoors. Moreover, respectable women could not be seen alone on city streets, an imposition that greatly limited what female artists could paint. It is, therefore, no coincidence that gardens and balconies became some of Cassatt's recurring settings: safe outdoor compromises and quiet oases in which she could experiment with the nuances of natural lighting. Perhaps intentionally, Cassatt more than once included fences, railings and bars on windows, depicting the limitations that bound her practice instead of pretending the freedom she could not enjoy. While Impressionist artists rarely used symbolic meaning, favouring instead the plain portrayal of reality, it is difficult not to read Cassatt's vase as a subtle self-portrait – the poetic representation of a young life in bloom limited in her experience of the outside world by the confines men imposed upon her.

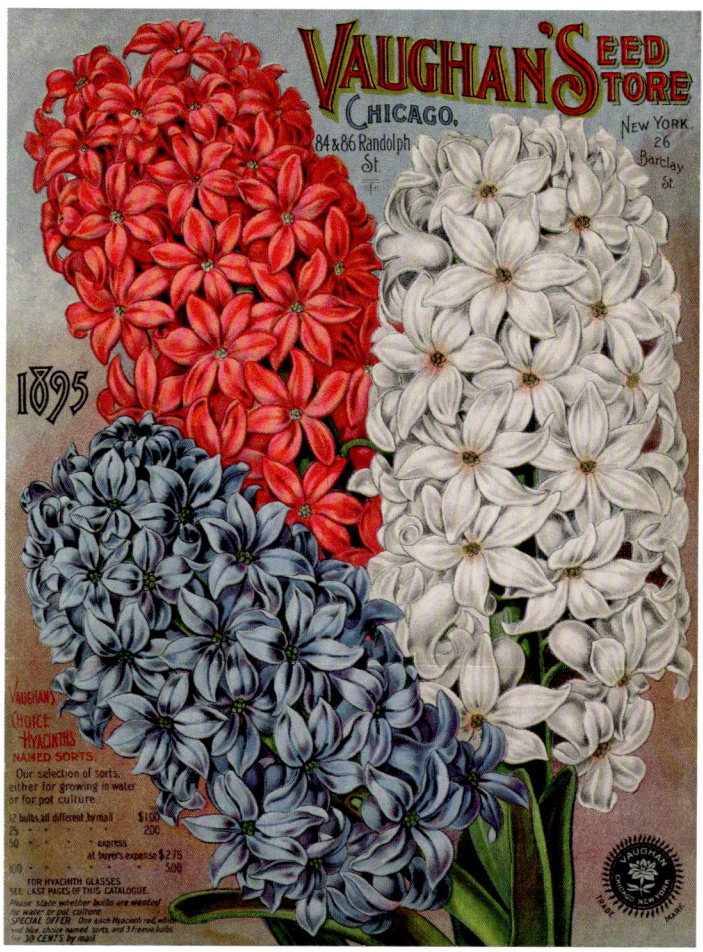

Vaughan's Seed Company

Gardening Illustrated, 1895
32 × 24.8 cm / 12½ × 9¾ in
Henry G. Gilbert Nursery and Seed Trade
Catalog Collection, Special Collections, National
Agricultural Library, Beltsville, Maryland

The brightly coloured covers of *Gardening Illustrated*, the Vaughan's Seed Store catalogue, were a warm reminder of spring's imminent arrival during the fiercely cold months of winter in the American Midwest. Gardening catalogues with beautiful illustrations bore the promise of a lush and green summer ahead, filled with botanical exuberance. In the Midwest, spring-flowering bulbs are one of the earliest signals of the end of winter, and this cover from 1895 is dedicated to a classic early bloomer of the region: hyacinths. The catalogue illustrations were produced by generalist artists rather than botanical specialists, with the result that the flowers appear slightly stylized or romanticized – the emphasis being on the overall appeal of the blooms, rather than a scientifically precise rendition. John Vaughan opened his Chicago seed store in 1876, and twenty years later his business was one of the largest wholesale seed and plant traders in the United States. In a pre-Internet world, printed catalogues were indispensable to commercial success. The first garden catalogue was published in 1612 by Dutch grower Emanuel Sweerts (see p.107) and featured over 560 hand-tinted plates of flowering plants and bulbs. As new technologies made it possible to expand the range of cultivated varieties, the popularity of catalogues grew exponentially in the late nineteenth century. Since the 1960s, however, new industrial printing and photographic processes have spelled the end for the charming illustrations so characteristic of the genre.

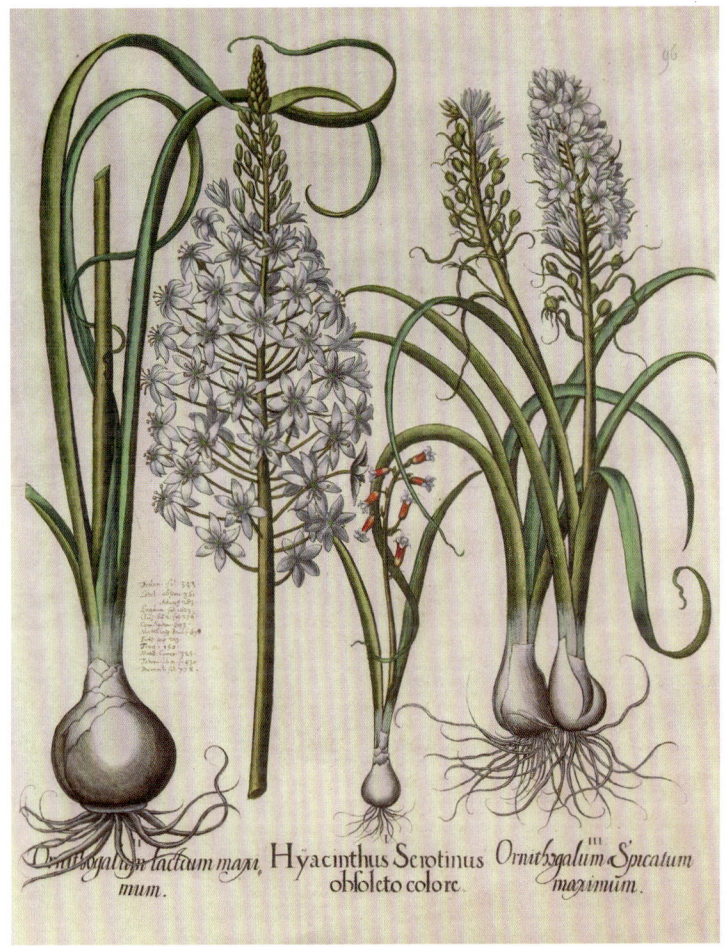

Basilius Besler

Plate 96, from *Hortus Eystettensis*, 1613
Hand-coloured engraving, 54 × 45 cm /
21¼ × 17¾ in
Teylers Museum, Haarlem, Netherlands

The *Hortus Eystettensis* is one of the most ambitious and beautiful botanical books ever published. The florilegium, literally a 'gathering of flowers', recorded more than a thousand flowering plants in the magnificent gardens of the Prince Bishop of Eichstätt, Bavaria, in 367 finely engraved plates. The work was compiled over a period of sixteen years under the supervision of Basilius Besler

(1561–1629), a Nuremberg apothecary, who also advised on the design and planting of the gardens. Boxes of flowers were sent regularly to a team of ten artists in Nuremberg so that all the plants could be drawn from fresh specimens, but then they were presented on the page with an emphasis on decoration rather than naturalism. The illustrations are ordered by their season of flowering; this page shows the central late hyacinth (now known as *Dipcadi serotinum*) with two varieties of Star of Bethlehem (the right now known as *Drimia maritima*) from the extensive 'Spring' sequence. The first copperplates made after the

original drawings were engraved in the Augsburg workshop of Wolfgang Kilian, but this work was later transferred to a team of engravers in Nuremberg. The *Hortus Eystettensis* was one of the first botanical books to be published with engraved illustrations, rather than woodcuts, and appeared in two editions, coloured and uncoloured. The coloured plates were painted with delicate precision, to ensure that the watercolours enhanced the fine details of the engraved lines rather than obscuring them.

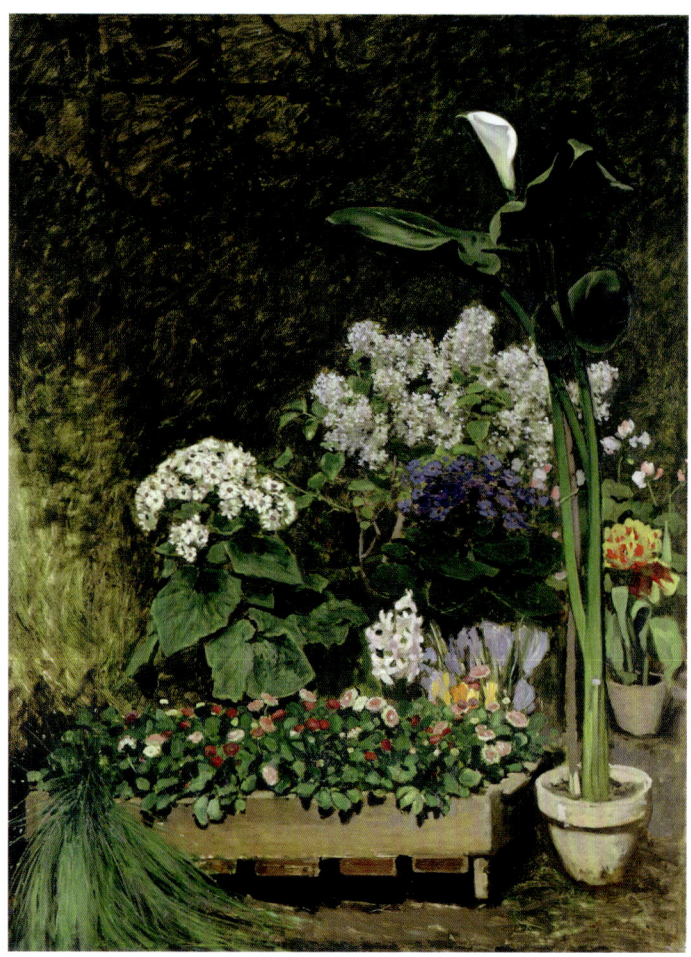

Pierre-Auguste Renoir

Flowers in a Greenhouse, 1864
Oil on canvas, 1.3 × 1 m / 4 ft 3 in × 3 ft 3 in
Hamburger Kunsthalle, Germany

Flowers in a Greenhouse is one of the finest and most original paintings of plants by French artist Pierre-Auguste Renoir (1841–1919). Predating his later fully Impressionist botanical compositions, it shows a more realist approach to the representation of leaves and petals. Indeed, such was Renoir's determination to paint the humble scene honestly that he even included the support-stake that holds up the slender and yet majestic canna

lily on the right-hand side of the painting. Elegantly composed and stylishly executed, the painting has a thoroughly modern feel thanks to the inclusion of the pots and containers in which the plants grow. In the still-life masterpieces of the Dutch Golden Age, flowers appeared cut and arranged in highly ornate vases. Their removal from the soil emphasized the ephemerality of their lives, thus alluding to the passing of time and the fading of youth and beauty. But Renoir's flowers nurture no existential ambition – they seem happy simply to thrive in the dappled lighting of a cool greenhouse. The true

originality of Renoir's painting lies in the spontaneous freshness of the growing plants. It may be a rather common and unassuming gathering, but flowers here do not represent the ending of life but a promise of abundance that will return again the following year.

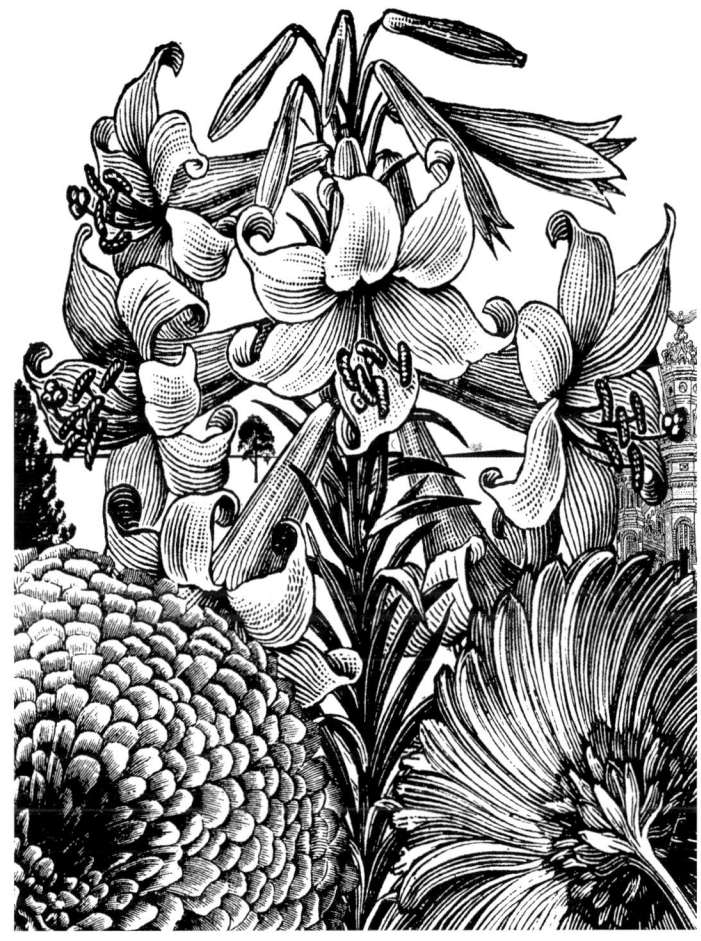

Paul Morrison

Untitled 10, from *Calathidium*, 2006
Screen print, 97.6 × 73.3 cm / 38½ × 28¾ in
Private collection

The distinctive forms of lilies, with their curling petals and spindly stamens, fill this black-and-white print, while large chrysanthemum and gerbera heads vie for attention in the foreground. Named after a botanical term for a particular type of flower head, *Calathidium* is a portfolio of ten screen prints by British artist Paul Morrison (born 1966). Other images in the series feature primroses, a passion flower and an anemone, with several dominating the page and blocking out much of the landscape behind. As with most of Morrison's prints, paintings and wall drawings, the image is devoid of colour as well as people, giving it an uncanny quality amplified by a skewed perspective in which some elements appear oversized and others seem strangely miniaturized. Human presence is implied here, however, by a building glimpsed at the far-right edge, suggesting that the flowers in fact belong to a tended garden. Like much of Morrison's work, the *Calathidium* series originated from compositions created using a computer. Elements drawn from a wide range of sources, including Disney cartoons, botanical illustrations and old master prints, are digitally collaged together before being translated into screen prints. Morrison's method results in unnatural-looking landscapes that recall children's colouring books or enchanted fairy-tale lands where different varieties of plants and flowers grow together in improbable combinations.

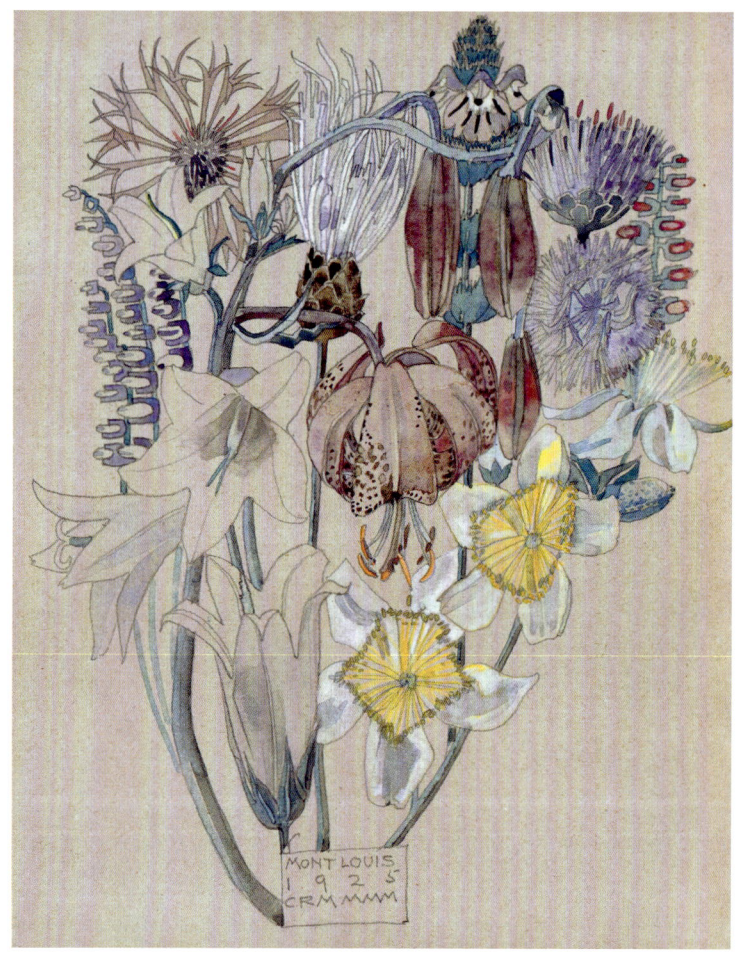

Charles Rennie Mackintosh

Mont Louis – Flower Study, 1925
Pencil and watercolour, 25.7 × 22.6 cm / 10 × 9 in
Private collection

Wildflowers from the pastures of the Pyrenean foothills are brought together in a mixed posy by the Scottish architect and artist Charles Rennie Mackintosh (1868–1928). The flowers include martagon lily (*Lilium martagon*) with its dark, mottled flowers and long dangling stamens; the open shiny flowers of a narcissus; and the large flowers of the Pyrenean bellflower (*Campanula speciosa*). Mackintosh's distinctive style combines detailed accuracy with an almost architectural feel for the structure of stems and petals. At the base of the image, he records the location and year, alongside his own initials and those of his wife, Margaret Macdonald Mackintosh. Having established what came to be known as the 'Glasgow Style' of art and design, Mackintosh spent much of his late career in England. He sketched and painted on the Suffolk coast at Walberswick, and in the south of France, where he and Margaret settled from 1923 to 1927. During that time he produced a series of paintings of the local flora of the eastern flank of the Pyrenees. From their base in Port-Vendres on the Mediterranean coast, he and Margaret would venture up into the hills to the ancient village of Mont-Louis, especially in summer, when the fields were full of wildflowers.

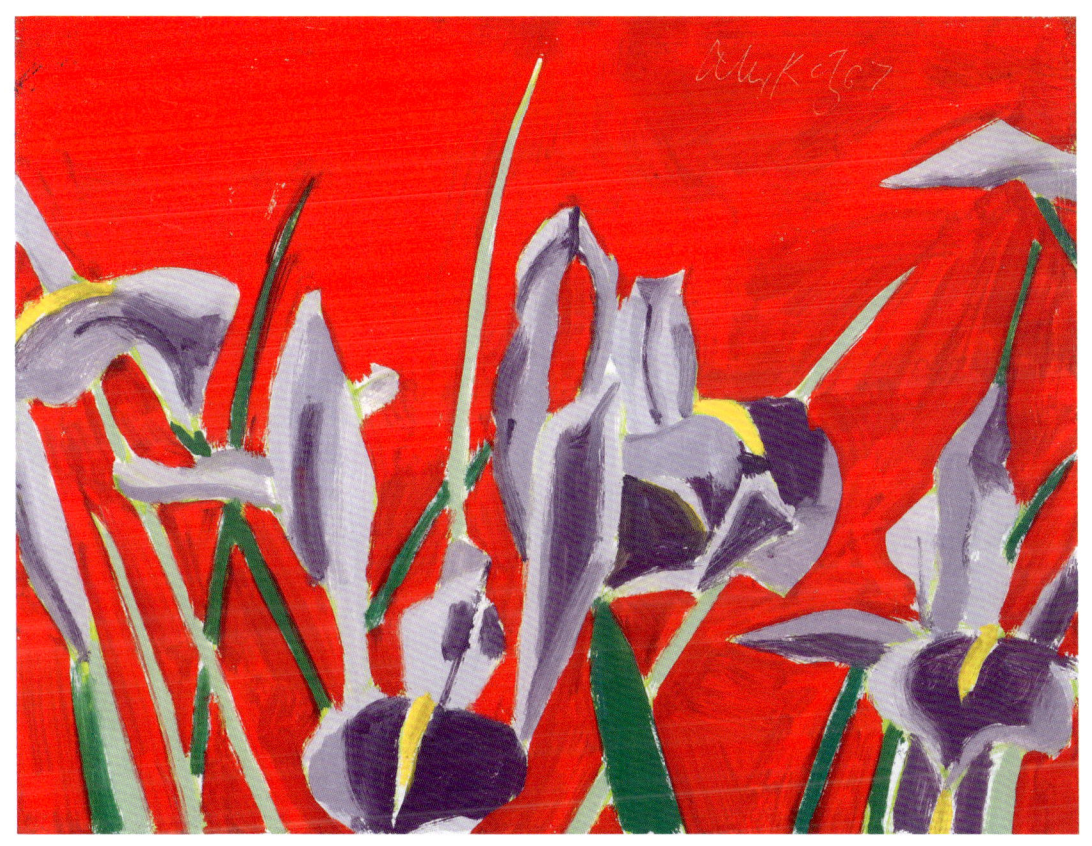

Alex Katz

Blue Flags, 1967
Oil on Masonite, 30.5 × 40.6 cm / 12 × 16 in
Private collection

Enriched by a lively red background, blue flag irises (*Iris versicolor*) display a vivid energy that transports them from the artist's memory right into the present tense. The petals appear as splashes of colour, and are entangled with each other in a way that makes it difficult to discern which petal belongs to which blossom. Reduced to their most basic traits and tightly arranged, the irises have a sense of intimacy that simultaneously communicates feelings of both tranquillity and agitation. *Blue Flags* is a prime example of the transition of American artist Alex Katz (born 1927) from portraiture to floral subjects. Although Katz is perhaps best known for his large-scale paintings, this work is in contrast a refined study on an unusually small canvas designed to capture the essence of the flowers. Katz's interest in flowers likely goes back to his days at the Skowhegan School of Painting and Sculpture in Maine, where he learned how to paint *en plein air* – indeed, blue flags are native to the wetlands of the American northeast and eastern Canada. In an interview a year after creating *Blue Flags*, Katz expanded on the idea, describing his paintings of flowers as a continuation of the group portraits he often painted. The flowers are overlapping volumes, and introduce a degree of movement and syncopation that reflects the rapid technique of the artist and his predilection for a physical approach not dissimilar to dance or free-form poetry.

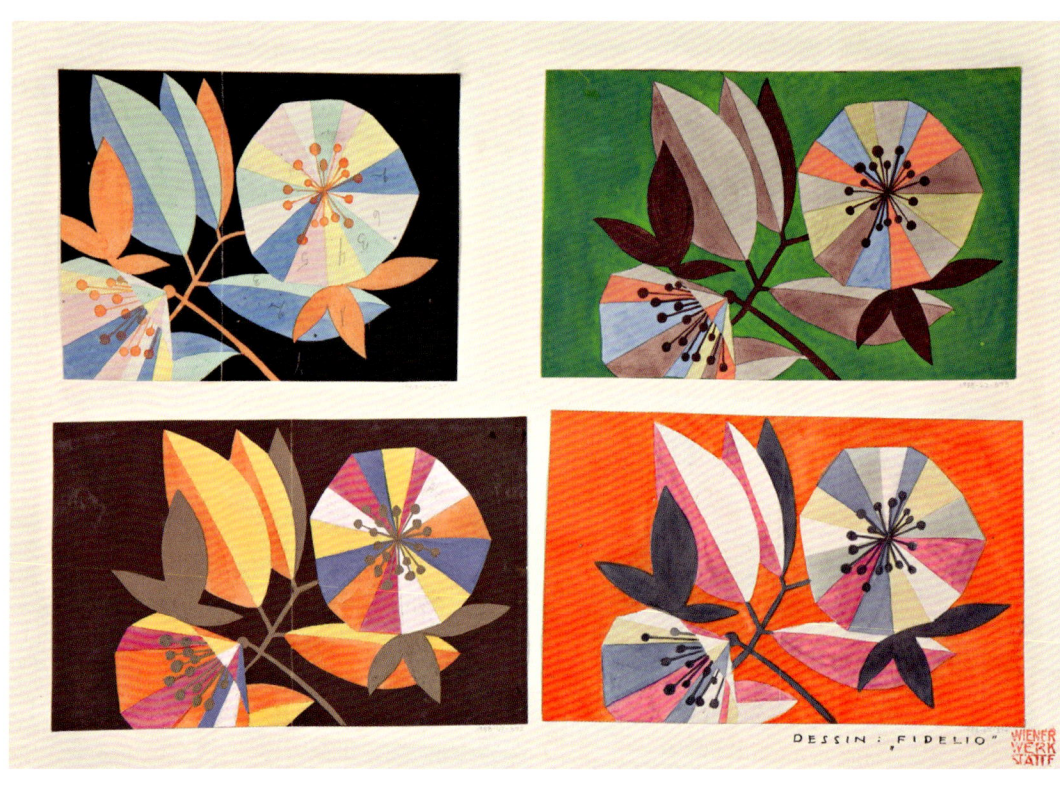

Maria Likarz-Strauss

Fidelio, 1924
Gouache on paper, 14.2 × 21.7 cm / 5½ × 8½ in
Cooper-Hewitt, Smithsonian Design Museum,
New York

The heads of two flowers and their leaves are transformed into a dance of dramatic and colourful geometric patterns in a page from the personal sketchbook of Austrian designer Maria Likarz-Strauss (1893–1971). Here, we see the same template repeated four times, with primary differences only in colour. The flowers are stylized to such an extent it is hard to identify any plant in particular. Likarz-Strauss is more interested in the patterns that the parts of the flowers create: the ring of petals becomes like a spinning windmill toy and the anthers and filaments appear like a game of Jacks. Likarz-Strauss was part of the famed Viennese design studio Wiener Werkstätte (Vienna Workshop), a cooperative of architects, artists and designers working in ceramics, fashion, furniture and the graphic arts who produced a range of influential products. *Fidelio* would ultimately become the design for a fabric, and these images record an important stage in Likarz-Strauss's design process as she experiments with different colour combinations. It is clear she had decided on the motif, but her relentless experimentation led her to visually ponder different tones for the background, as well as the petals, leaves and stems. The result is a cluster of flowers that spin and jump out excitedly into our vision.

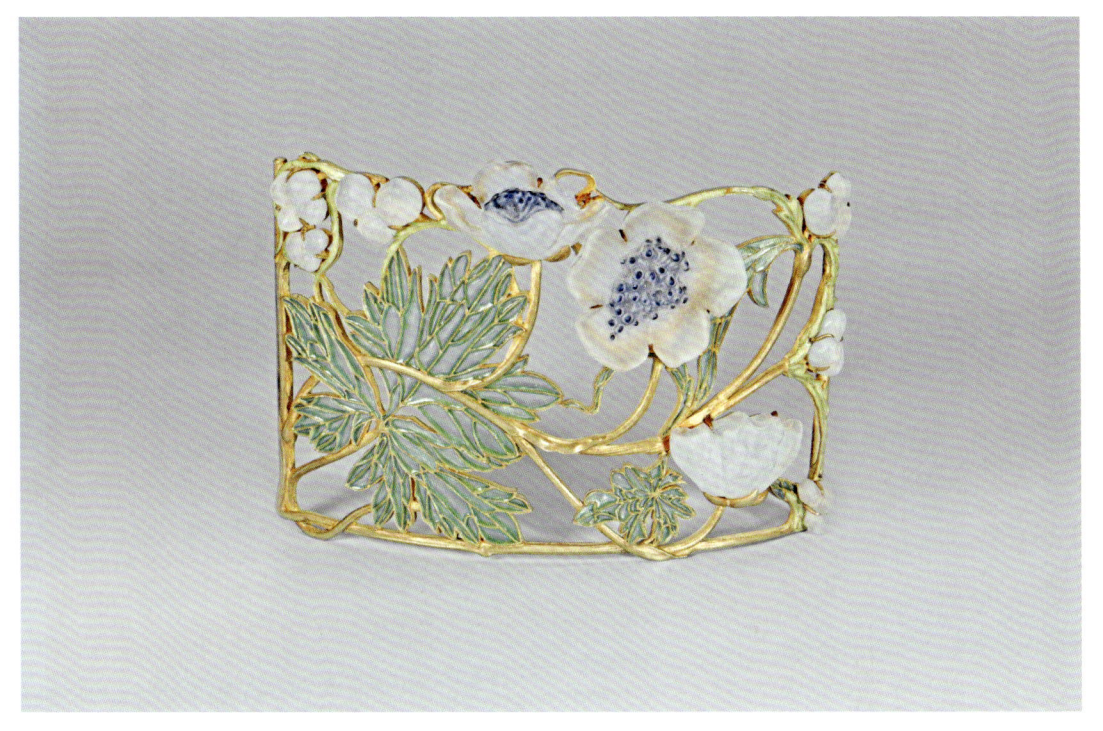

René Lalique

Neckpiece with Anemones, 1901
Gold, enamel and glass, H. 6 cm / 2¼ in
Staatliche Museen zu Berlin

With the vibrancy of living flowers, twisting golden stems frame white anemone blooms, the delicate shape of the leaves faithfully represented in a piece of wearable floral art. The *collier de chien* – 'dog collar' – was a 'choker' neckpiece fashionable during the Belle Epoque in France around the turn of the twentieth century, when it was often composed of a central curved plate mounted to a strip of fabric or with multiple strands of fine white pearls. This neckpiece, like so much of the work by French jeweller and glass designer René Lalique (1860–1945), is inspired by nature – particularly the countryside of his childhood in Champagne, where these anemones might have flourished. Lalique became a prominent trendsetter at the height of the Art Nouveau movement, having been apprenticed at the age of sixteen to Louis Aucoc, a leading Parisian jeweller, before studying at the École des Arts Décoratifs in Paris. By 1885 Lalique had his own workshop in the French capital, and in 1887 he opened a jewellery shop in the fashionable Opéra district. Winning the first prize at the Salon de la Société des Artistes Français in 1897 and achieving success at the 1900 Exposition Universelle firmly established him as a major figure in the world of high fashion and design. Upon meeting the perfumer François Coty in 1907, Lalique shifted his focus to creating glass perfume bottles and then expanded his glassworks operations in 1921 with a new factory in the north of France, exporting his remarkable pieces worldwide.

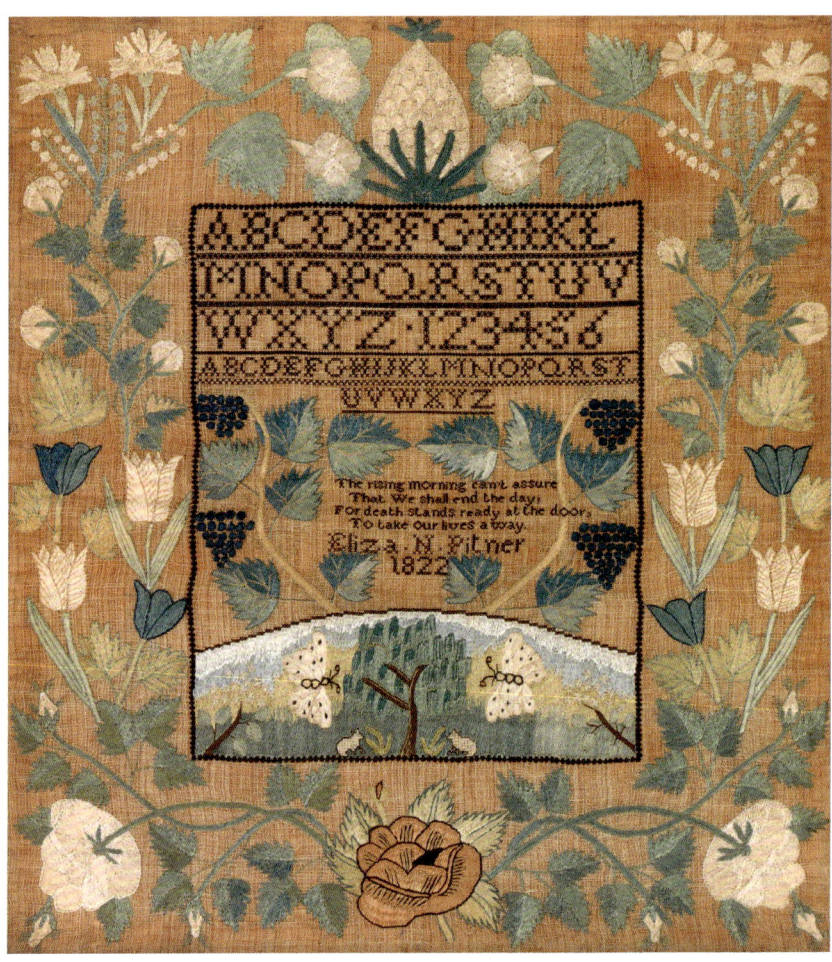

Eliza N. Pitner

Sampler, 1822
Linen embroidered with silk, 56.5 × 51.4 cm /
22¼ × 20¼ in
Metropolitan Museum of Art, New York

Tulips, roses, lily of the valley and other flowers combine with a border of winding leaves and stems around a central alphabet, an epithet and forest scene, all delicately stitched with silk thread not for any particular aesthetic purpose, but as an exercise in embroidery skills by Eliza N. Pitner (1802–after 1885) of Delaware. Samplers, which often had a seemingly eclectic collection of subjects, first appeared in North America in the Plymouth Colony in the mid-seventeenth century, and up until the late 1700s they remained the most common method by which girls and young women learned the basic needlework skills deemed necessary to run a household. A sampler also acted as a kind of sewing notebook. During a time when there were few printed patterns available for needleworkers, examples of new stitching patterns could be sewn for future reference. This is why different elements of the design have different appearances, such as the strong black outline of the central flower at the foot of the design, which is lacking from the other flowers. In the late eighteenth century, as more schools opened for young women, samplers became more elaborate displays of a woman's particular skill, showing pastoral or religious scenes, incorporating verses, and decorated with a wide variety of floral motifs, including both stylized blooms and those based on real flowers. A true testament to the painstaking work involved, samplers were often proudly 'signed' with the creator's name.

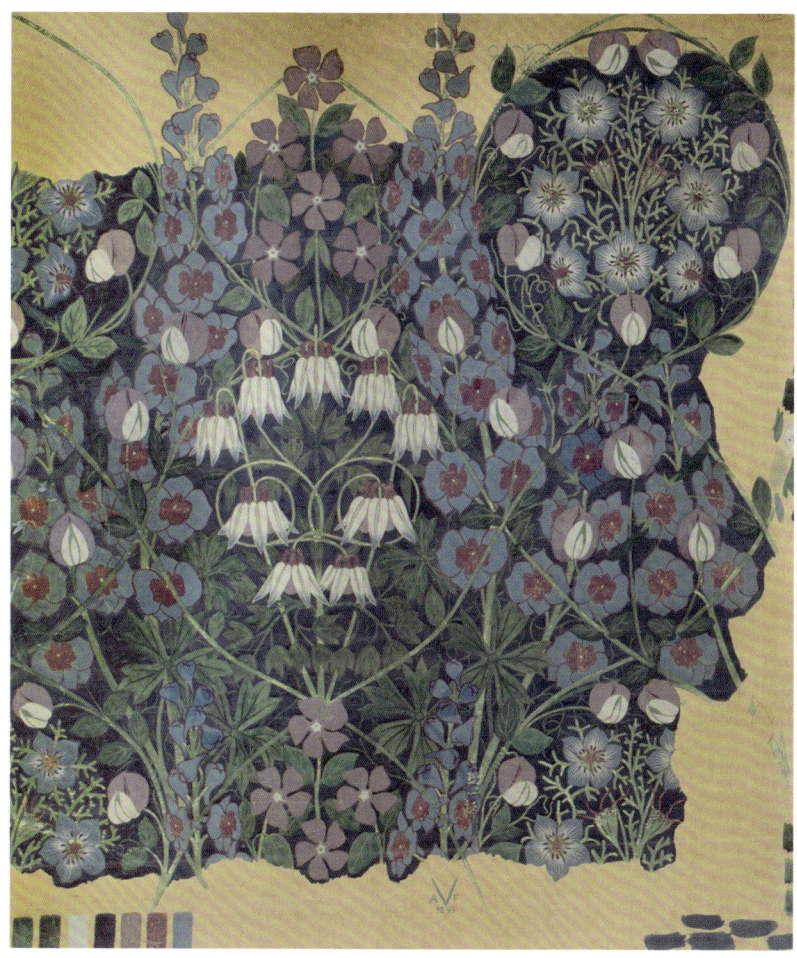

Allan Francis Vigers

Columbine, 1899
Body colour on paper, 77.5 × 61.6 cm /
30½ × 24¼ in
Victoria and Albert Museum, London

The white drooping blooms of columbine are flanked on either side by the tall spires of blue delphiniums in this richly detailed design by Allan Vigers (1858–1921). Typical of the British artist's distinctive approach to devising repeating patterns for wallpaper and textiles, it is naturalistic yet carefully formalized with a strong sense of symmetry. These typical English garden flowers are massed with other cottage-garden favourites which, although not botanically detailed, are rendered so accurately that they are readily identifiable as periwinkles, sweet peas and nigella (love-in-a-mist). There is no illusionistic modelling of the flowers and leaves, which are presented as flat forms, frontally or in profile; the highlighted stems, twining under and over, provide a supporting structure to this tight profusion, possibly a reflection of Vigers' training as an architect (he never practiced, choosing instead to work as a designer of wallpapers, textiles and furniture). The rich but muted colours demonstrate a sympathy with the principles of the late-nineteenth century Arts and Crafts movement, with its reverence for medieval decorative styles taken from tapestries and illuminated manuscripts. Vigers' patterns also show the influence of William Morris (see p.160), notably in his preference for dense all-over floral designs; most of his wallpapers, including this design issued in 1901, were produced by Jeffrey & Co., the London firm that also printed Morris's papers.

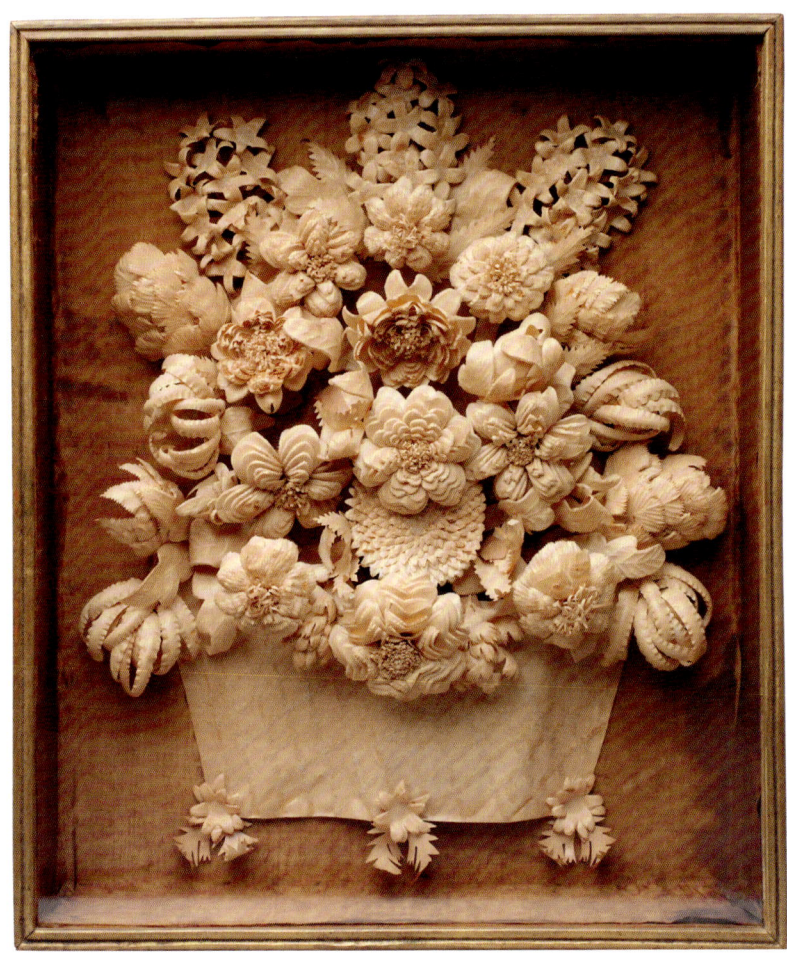

Myra Bates Willcutt

Quillwork shadowbox, *c.*1817
Paper, maple, pine and glass, 35.6 × 30.5 × 7.6 cm /
14 × 12 × 3 in
Metropolitan Museum of Art, New York

A row of three hyacinths stands at the top of an arrangement of flowers, while beneath it zinnia, dianthus and a central calendula are meticulously rendered from crimped and glued strips of paper. Quilling, or paper filigree, is the craft of working thin strips of paper into coils, twists and curls. Originally conceived in fifteenth-century France and Italy as a less expensive alternative to metal filigree or carved ivory, it was popularized by nuns and had its heyday in eighteenth-century England, when it was seen as a suitable pastime for gentlewomen. The craft features notably in Jane Austen's *Sense and Sensibility*, where Lucy Steele painstakingly decorates a basket with fili-gree. European settlers took the practice to North America, and this example, created by Myra Bates Willcutt (1798–1885) in Massachusetts around 1817, belongs to a distinctive American folk art tradition with its characteristically symmetri-cal, neatly organized layout of flowers and leaves. Similarities can also be drawn to still-life flower paintings from the Dutch Golden Age in terms of the composition and the choice of flowers, which would never be found blooming simulta-neously in nature. The work is staged against a veneer of maple wood and is set within a glazed pine shadowbox that both protects it and elevates it to the status of a framed art form.

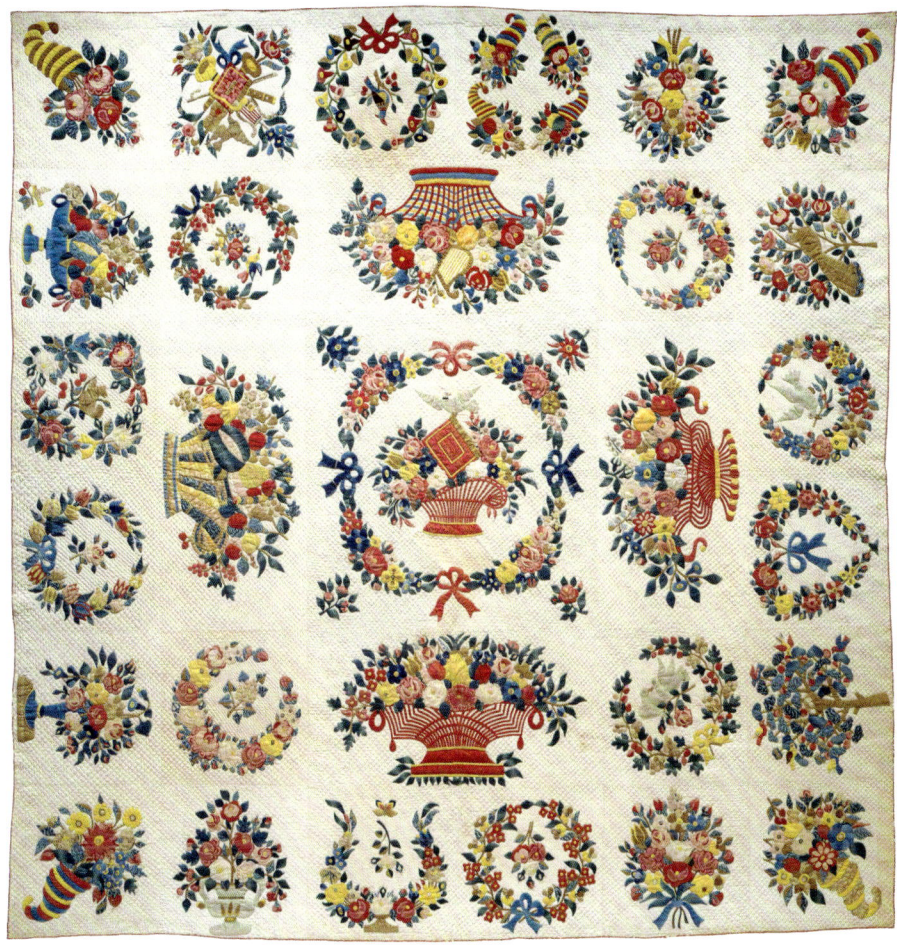

Mary Hergenroder Simon (attrib.)

Presentation quilt, c.1849
Cotton and silk velvet, 2.7 × 2.6 m /
8 ft 10 in × 8 ft 8 in
Metropolitan Museum of Art, New York

A multitude of colourful wreaths, laurels, bouquets, garlands and baskets of flowers adorn a quilt in a loosely symmetrical, block design that resembles that of an 'album quilt' – where each square is embroidered with a different motif and sewn by a different person. However, this is in fact a 'presentation' quilt sewn by a single maker in order to commemorate a specific event. The

quilt's design and construction are attributed to Mary Hergenroder Simon (1808–77), a Bavarian native who immigrated to Baltimore, Maryland, although the exact event it was intended to honour has been lost. On a nearly identical quilt by another maker, also created in 1849, an inscription describes the work as a wedding gift to a bride; on Simon's quilt, however, the inscription has been cut away and replaced with a patch of white fabric, perhaps indicative of a broken engagement. Among the flowers are the distinctive shapes of tulips, morning glories, daisies and roses, both in bud and in full bloom. Like other

high-end Baltimore quilts of the mid-nineteenth century, the flowers, baskets, bows and other elements have been given a three-dimensional effect by layering small pieces of fabric on top of one another, which distinguishes these later quilts from the flat quilts with single-layer appliqués popular earlier in Maryland. The floral, fruit and basket motifs would have commonly appeared in 1840s' Baltimore on other decorative wares, such as samplers, tea sets, vases and silverware.

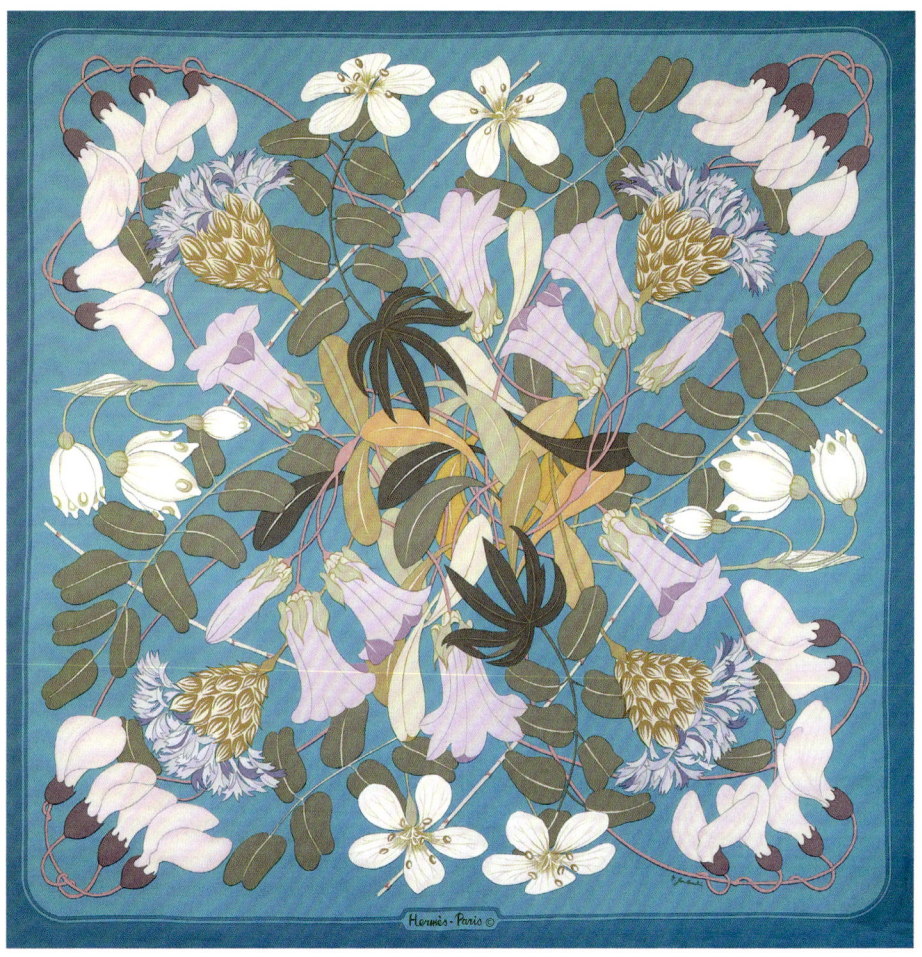

Niki Goulandris for Hermès

Hermès *Flora Graeca* silk scarf, 1983
Silk twill, 90 × 90 cm / 35½ × 35½ in
Hermès

In this scarf design for the Parisian luxury fashion house of Hermès, botanical artist Niki Goulandris (1925–2019) arranges flora from her native Greece, including *Centaurea* and summer snowflake (*Leucojum aestivum*), with exotic flowers such as the Mexican cup and saucer vine (*Cobea scandens*) and the Chinese *Wisteria sinensis*, in a formal symmetrical design. Although the flowers may have been based in part on the early nineteenth-century work *Flora Graeca* of John Sibthorp, illustrated by Ferdinard Bauer (see p.84), Goulandris was a well-known botanical artist in her own right, working for porcelain houses such as Haviland Limoges and Royal Copenhagen as well as Hermès. She was also a philanthropist and environmentalist who, along with her husband, Angelos, founded the Goulandris Natural History Museum in 1964, the first institution of its kind in Greece. In 1968 Goulandris published *Wildflowers of Greece*, which contained 114 watercolour plates of native flora. Since its establishment in 1937, Hermès has employed contemporary artists to create new 'carré' designs each year, often featuring natural history or tropes of the brand, such as equestrian paraphernalia. Now an iconic fashion accessory, the first Hermès silk scarf was based on a woodcut print by Robert Dumas; there have since been more than 1,200 designs, which are still made using silk-screen printing and hand-rolled and hand-stitched hems.

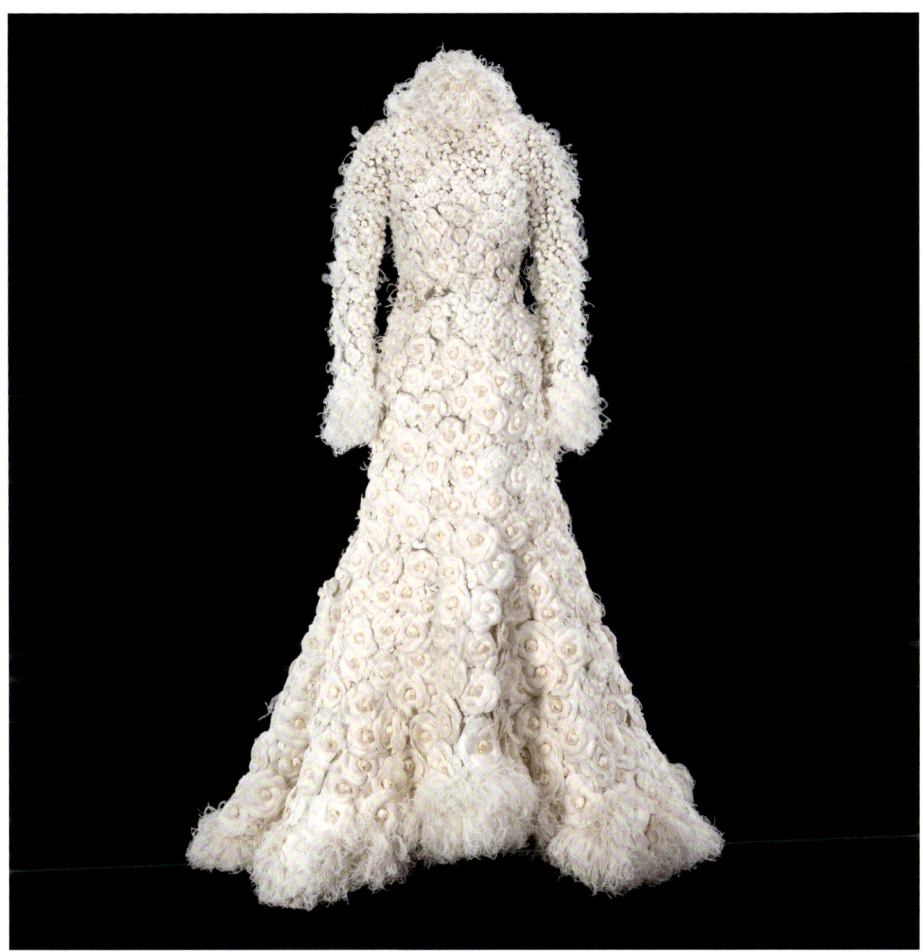

Chanel

Wedding ensemble, Haute Couture Autumn/
Winter 2005/2006
Silk tulle, organza, gelatin sequins
and ostrich feathers
Chanel Patrimoine Collection, Paris

The camellia, scentless and pure white and beloved by Gabrielle 'Coco' Chanel (1883–1971) has been a classic symbol of her fashion house since the early 1910s. Mademoiselle Chanel was enamoured with this genus of flower for its elegant simplicity as well as its association with Marguerite Gautier, the tragic heroine of Alexandre Dumas's novel

La Dame aux Camélias who wears the white bloom to show her purity. Here, a wedding ensemble, designed by Chanel's prolific creative director Karl Lagerfeld (1933–2019), is adorned with 2,500 silk versions of the house flower. Known in haute couture as *parurier floral* (artificial flowers), each exquisite bloom is painstakingly handmade by *atelier d'art* Maison Lemarié. Established in 1880, today the atelier produces more than 30,000 camellias for Chanel each year. The masses of camellias require hundreds of hours to create: petals are cut into a heart shape, crimped, then assembled individually, working atop a small

pillow. Intertwined with the overlapping blooms are delicate ostrich feathers and sequins, all hand-embroidered by Maison Lesage (see p.217). Featuring in the Metropolitan Museum of Art's 2016 spring exhibition *Manus x Machina*, this wedding ensemble is an elaborate example of meticulously hand-worked floral couture by a reigning fashion house.

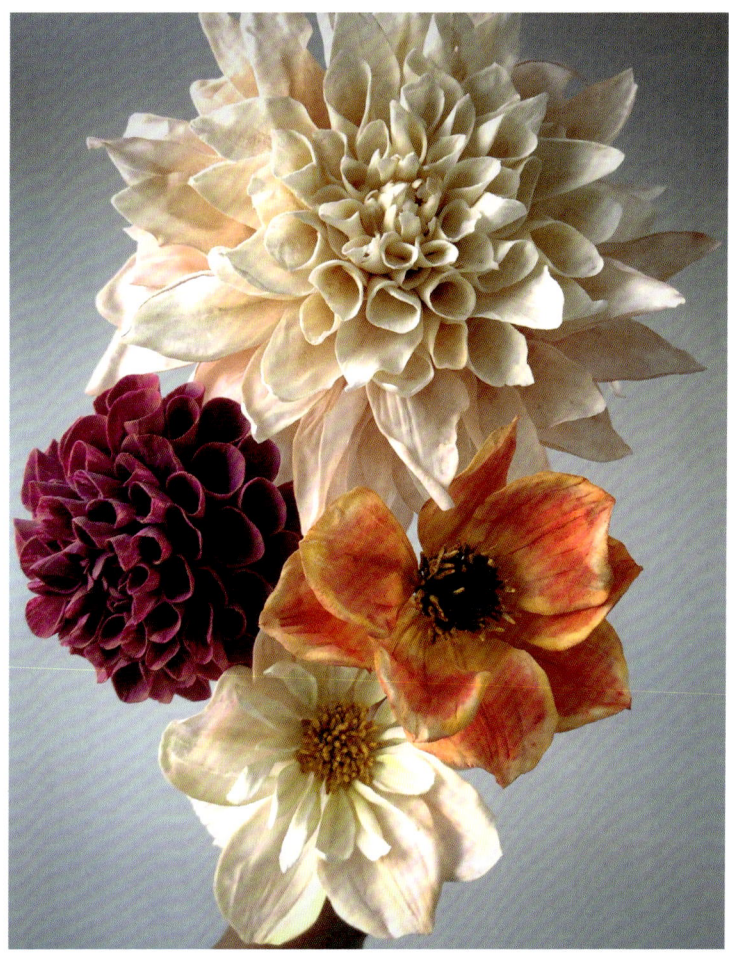

Natasja Sadi

Dahlias, 2019
Sugar with added colour, dimensions variable

A clutch of four dahlias burst into view: a pompon head of rich purple with deeply rolled petals stands at the left, while the cactus variety in soft, baby pink relaxes to open in naturalistic array above. Completing the composition are single dahlias in golden and peach tones marked by intricate central discs. A trademark of Dutch artisan Natasja Sadi (born 1975), each of these stunning flowers was painstakingly createdby hand to form remarkably realistic blooms, with petals rolled from sheets of fondant sugar paste icing, cut to shape, coaxed into sculpted array and then carefully painted to mimic a blossom's hues. Established in 2015, Cake Atelier Amsterdam is Sadi's labour of love. A dressmaker-turned-cake-baker, her latest career reflects a life fascinated by the beauty of flowers. Since swapping bridal haute couture for celebratory cake-making, Sadi has revealed an almost magical ability with sugar, butter and eggs, establishing her as a leading special-occasion baker. Inspired by historical Dutch Masters such as Rachel Ruysch (see p.86), Balthasar van der Ast (see p.267) and Jan Davidsz. de Heem (see p.125), flowers are her trademark and, as in nature, no flower is the same. Sadi's analysis of botanical detail ensures the scale and feature of each piece is exactingly correct; it is hardly surprising to learn that her edible arrangements are regularly mistaken for their living counterparts.

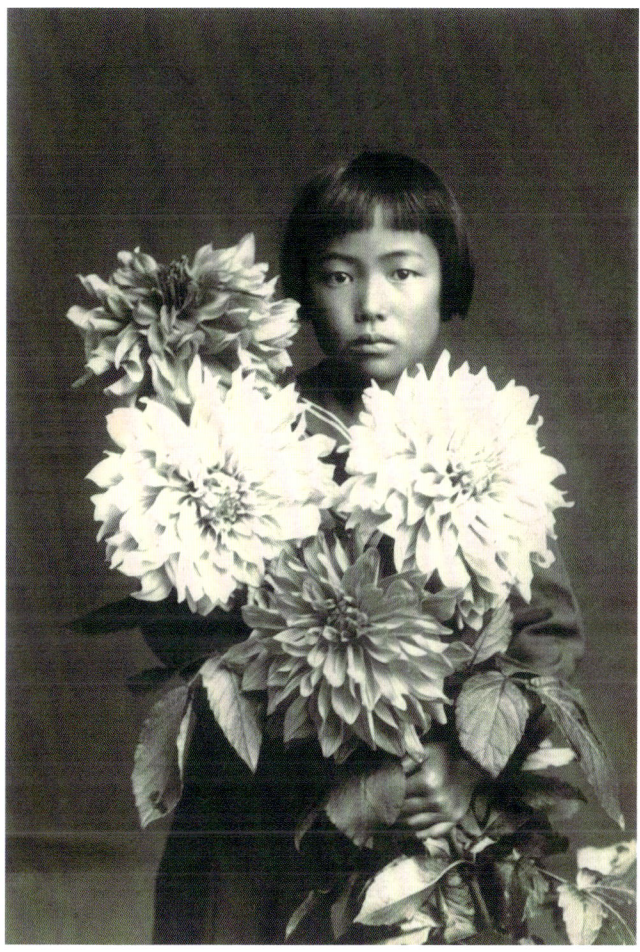

Anonymous

Yayoi Kusama at the Age of Ten in 1939
Photograph
Private collection

A girl holds four rare, giant dahlias, framing her face and shielding her from the world. A treasured flower in Japan, though originally from Mexico, dahlias signify 'good taste' according to *Hanakotoba*, the Japanese philosophy of the meaning of flowers. Although on the surface the composition underpins the fresh beauty of both flowers and girl, suggesting a sense of harmony and balance, the image captures more than it might initially seem. This portrait shows the artist Yayoi Kusama (born 1929) at just ten years old and bears the candid imprint of her psychological mindset, the essence of which has defined her artistic career. Kusama grew up in rural Japan, surrounded by the flowers her parents grew at their plant-nursery business. But despite the idyllic setting, Kusama's childhood was far from happy. Oppressed by her mother, the artist suffered hallucinations from an early age. As she recalls: 'I found myself trembling ... with fear, amid flowers incarnate, which had appeared all of a sudden. I was surrounded by several hundreds of violets ... with uncanny expressions ... chatting among themselves just like human beings.' It is no coincidence that floral motifs should often recur in Kusama's body of work (see p.155). Not only do flowers represent her past, but they also figure as emblems of transformation that suggest the possibility of changing an unpleasant situation into something beautiful. This photograph uncannily forebodes much of what has made Kusama's cre-ative journey so compelling.

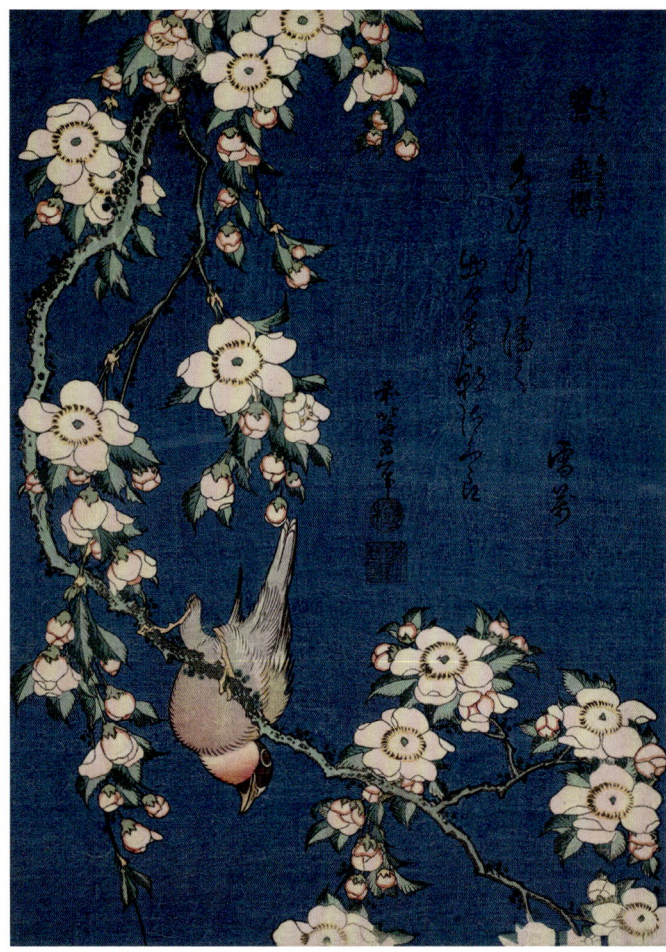

Katsushika Hokusai

Bullfinch and Weeping Cherry, from an untitled
series known as 'Small Flowers', *c*.1834
Woodcut, 25.5 × 18.7 cm / 10 × 7½ in
Museum of Fine Arts, Boston

A bullfinch dangles from the branch of a flowering cherry tree wet with morning dew. The bird
is beautifully framed by the tree's curled foliage,
adorned with flowers unfurling in the morning
light while others are still in bud. The sweeping
branch leaves a large space to the right in which
the artist has signed the piece and inscribed
a descriptive poem explaining that the work

captures a fleeting moment in nature. The haiku
is by a contemporary Edo-period poet from the
Setsumon school and reads: A single bird wets /
Its feathers and flits away / Morning cherry.
In Japan, the bullfinch is a bird of special significance as it plays a central role in new year
ceremonies at Tenjin shrines. At the start of the
new year, a bullfinch made of wood is formally
exchanged for a new model bird, which is then
blessed in order to guard against misfortune in
the coming year. Katsushika Hokusai (1760–1849)
is one of Japan's most famous artists, with a prolific and much-revered output. Hokusai started

painting at around six years old and continued
almost to the end of his life. It was in his seventies that he began to concentrate on birds and
flowers, striving by careful observation to under-
stand their essential nature.

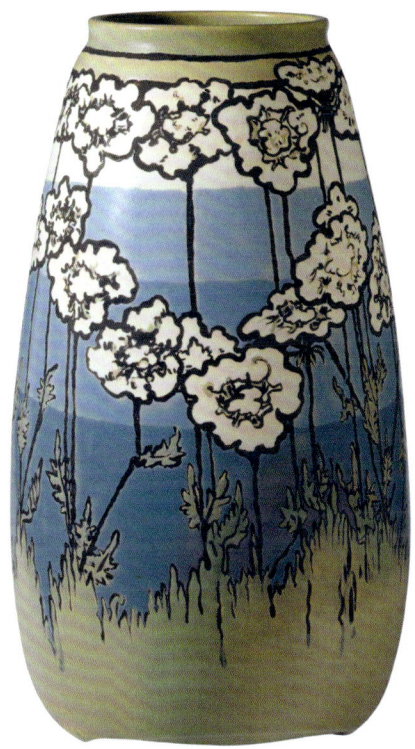

Sara Galner for Paul Revere Pottery

Vase, 1915
Earthenware, 40.6 × 22.9 cm / 16 × 9 in
Metropolitan Museum of Art, New York

In a bold interpretation of the white flowering plant Queen Anne's lace (*Daucus carota*), commonly known as wild carrot, American artist Sara Galner (1894–1982) uses a heavy black outline around the pristine blossoms. The flower – whose name is derived from a tale of Queen Anne pricking her finger while tatting lace, giving the centre of the flower its characteristic hue – is shown in various stages of bloom: some petals are barely peeking out of their buds, while others emerge in full. The flowers grow from the earth and rise into the sky like huge pluming clouds. The colour palette of the vase is gentle, defined by shifting shades of blue that go from dark to light as they lift into the sky, while the earth is the palest of greens. This vase is typical of Galner's refined technique and the designs, set on a solid matte ground, were a signature of the renowned Paul Revere Pottery in Boston. At the turn of the twentieth century, Galner was a poor Jewish immigrant from Austria-Hungary living in a tenement in Boston's North End.

On weekends, she attended story readings at the Saturday Evening Girls Club, a group founded by three women in the 1890s to educate immigrant girls in the arts as a way to better their lives. The club went on to found its own pottery in 1908, naming it after the local hero Paul Revere, and the girls who worked there, including Galner, became important contributors to the Arts and Crafts movement.

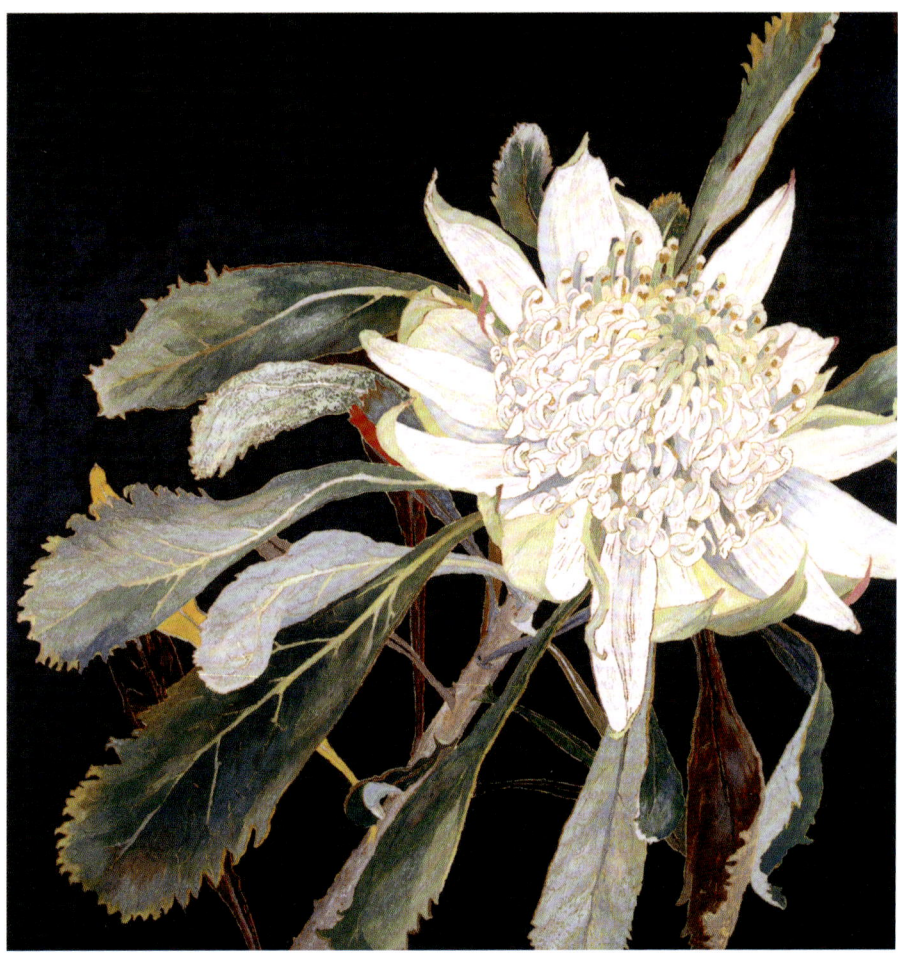

Cressida Campbell

White Waratah, 2000
Woodcut print, 57 × 51.5 cm / 22¼ × 20¼ in
Art Gallery of New South Wales, Sydney

A rare white waratah blooms across the page, its leaves extending past the confines of the edges – a hint by renowned Australian artist Cressida Campbell (born 1960) at the size of the plant. The waratah (*Telopea speciosissima*) is one of Australia's most iconic flowers, growing up to 3 metres (9 feet 10 inches) in height. It is typically red and grows naturally in New South Wales in eastern Australia, where it is the state emblem. Australia's Aboriginal people tell creation stories about the rare and sacred white waratah, including those that describe how blood was shed onto the white parent and thereafter the progeny grew red flowers. During the Arts and Crafts movement of the late nineteenth century, the waratah was a popular subject for Australian designers and artists as they sought to realize a national identity. Artist Margaret Preston (see p.85) reflected the flower's appeal in the twentieth century with her bold woodcut prints. Knowledge of the isolated locations of white waratah was limited to few people. Botanist and conservationist Thistle Stead was instrumental in bringing the plant into cultivation with cuttings taken from a single known surviving tree in 1972. In 1986 the *Telopea speciosissima* 'Wirrimbirra White' was registered as a cultivar. This print was inspired by a 'Wirrimbirra White' given to Campbell by the Australian arts impresario Leo Schofield in 2000. Campbell's usual practice is to carve a woodblock, meticulously hand paint it in a watercolour pigment and make one impression only.

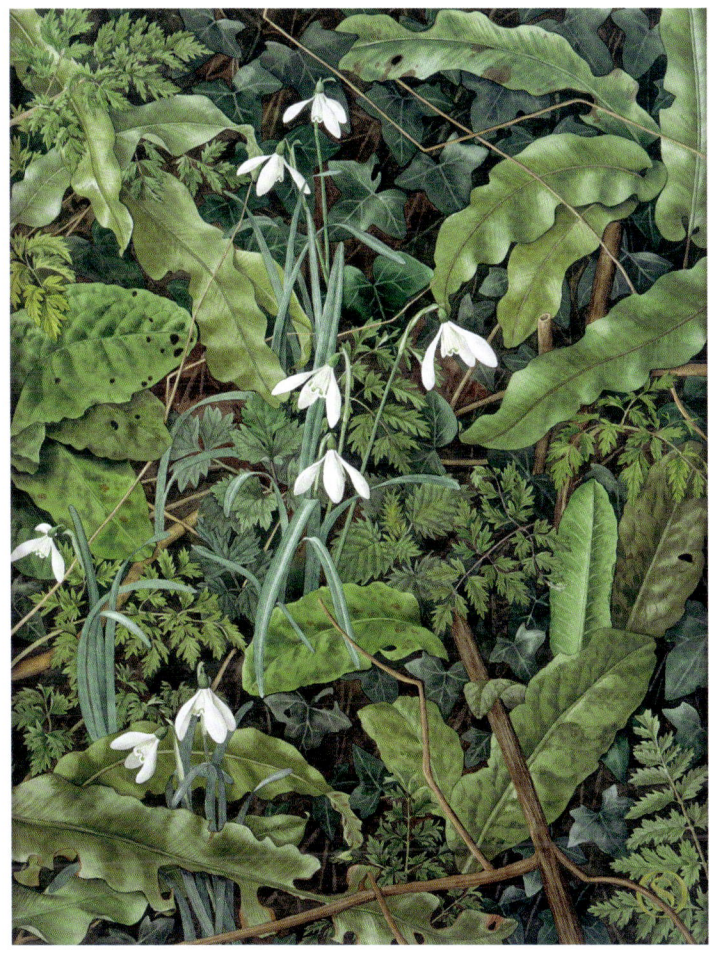

Susan Ogilvy

Snowdrops, Churchyard, 2000
Watercolour on paper, 45.7 × 35 cm / 18 × 13¾ in
The Shirley Sherwood Collection

Delicate, milky white snowdrops emerge from a layered green hedgerow of undulating fern and ivy leaves. Unlike the white background and frontal perspective used in traditional botanical art, British artist Susan Ogilvy (born 1948) fills the page with a downwards view depicting the flowers among their natural habitat. In *Snowdrops, Churchyard* Ogilvy captures an intimate and joyful moment, reminiscent of the view one might have upon unexpectedly discovering the flowers on a walk in early spring. Considered a symbol of hope, common snowdrops (*Galanthus nivalis*) are often one of the earliest varieties to flower after winter; they are hermaphroditic, meaning that they have male and female reproductive organs, and so can self-pollinate in addition to being pollinated by insects. Ogilvy originally trained as an art therapist and went on to focus primarily on botanical watercolours, later winning a gold medal from the Royal Horticultural Society. She was one of a select number of artists invited to document flowers and plants from the Prince of Wales and Duchess of Cornwall's estate gardens at Highgrove, and the flora at Prince Charles's two estates in Transylvania. *The Highgrove Florilegium* (2008) and the *Transylvania Florilegium* (2018) rival the spectacularly illustrated florilegia of the seventeenth to nineteenth centuries.

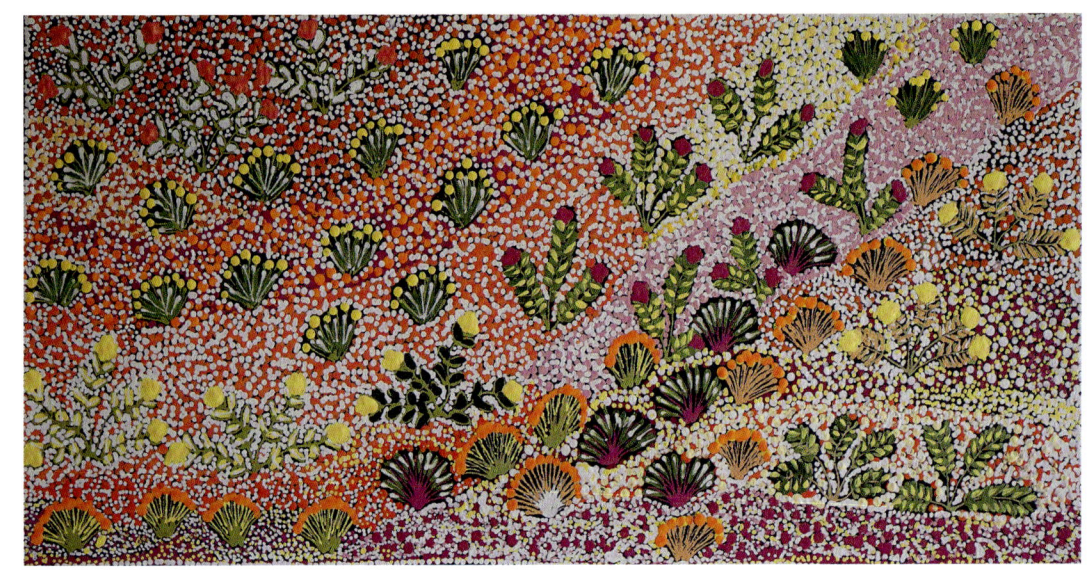

Julieanne Ngwarraye Morton

My Country and Bush Medicine Plants, 2019
Acrylic on canvas, 30 × 61 cm / 11 × 24 in
Private collection

Using the application of fine dots on linen
in a rich palette of colours, Aboriginal artist
Julieanne Ngwarraye Morton (born *c*.1975)
expresses her deep connection with landscape.
Morton paints the layered narrative of folk
stories, walks and veiled symbols of her roots.
A member of the Ampilatwaja community,
Morton is instantly identified by her work
as coming from the central and western desert

areas in Australia. Her images resonate with
an energy given by the endless hypnotic rows
of bush flowers, spinifex grass clumps, rocks,
and the oranges and reds of the desert. The composition omits the sky, presenting two viewpoints
simultaneously: a frontal view and an intriguing
aerial perspective. Neither appear to have a focal
point. Both reveal the natural contours of the land
as well as the abstract and metaphysical forms
that hint at the hidden stories of Aboriginal culture. This harks back to the tradition of reading
the land for tracks when hunting and requires
an intimate relationship with the landscape.

Despite the disruption of the twentieth century
that threatened to wrench the Aborigines
of Ampilatwaja away from a land and way of life
that was previously unchanged for thousands
of years, Morton's paintings not only say much
about indigenous Australian culture, but also
reveal a spirit of optimism, energy and inventiveness that gives hope for the future.

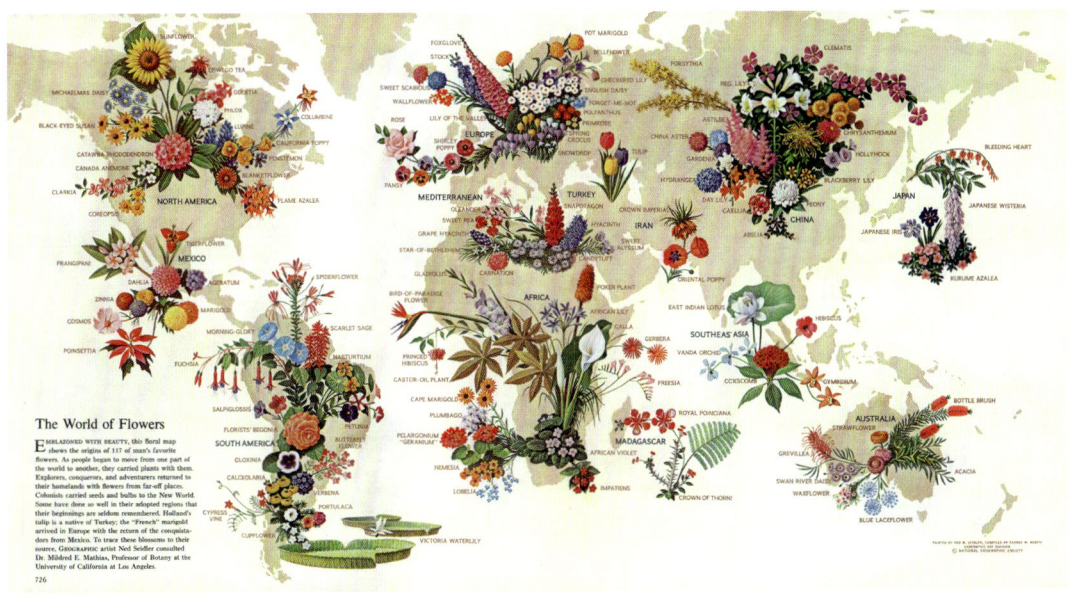

The World of Flowers

Emblazoned with beauty, this floral map shows the origins of 117 of man's favorite flowers. As people began to move from one part of the world to another, they carried plants with them. Explorers, conquerors, and adventurers returned to their homelands with flowers from far-off places. Colonists carried seeds and bulbs to the New World. Some have done so well in their adopted regions that their beginnings are seldom remembered. Holland's tulip is a native of Turkey; the "French" marigold arrived in Europe with the return of the conquistadors from Mexico. To trace these blossoms to their source, GEOGRAPHIC artist Ned Seidler consulted Dr. Mildred E. Mathias, Professor of Botany at the University of California at Los Angeles.

726

Ned Seidler

A Map of the Dispersion of Flowers Around the Earth, 1968
Lithograph, 25.4 × 39.4 cm / 10 × 13¾ in
National Geographic

The desire of plants to colonize the world is visible in the sophisticated design of their seeds, enabling them to migrate far and wide. Spiky seed pods hitch long rides on hides and feathers, while fluffy filaments or blade-like wings sweep them up into the air. Other plants have found an even more ingenious way to spread across the globe: seduce humans. Throughout the history of civilization, plants with beautiful blooms have persuaded people to take them on journeys to faraway lands. Their colours and scents have become indispensable reminders of beauty and love – essential parts of our identities, traditions and celebrations. So accustomed are we to flowers' ubiquitousness, we often forget where they originated. This blooming world map, created for *National Geographic* magazine by artist Ned Seidler (1922–2007) in consultation with Dr Mildred E. Mathias (1906–95), professor of botany at University of California, Los Angeles (UCLA), displays some of the most beloved flowering plants to remind us that, like humans, flowers have countries of origins – and that they, too, can adapt to life far away from their birthplace. British garden favourites, such as fuchsia, nasturtium and petunia, travelled from South America, for example, while common plants in American gardens, such as forsythia, chrysanthemum and hydrangeas, migrated from Asia. This borderless map is a beautiful invitation to discover the wondrous journeys, histories and realities that have made flowers and people travel the globe.

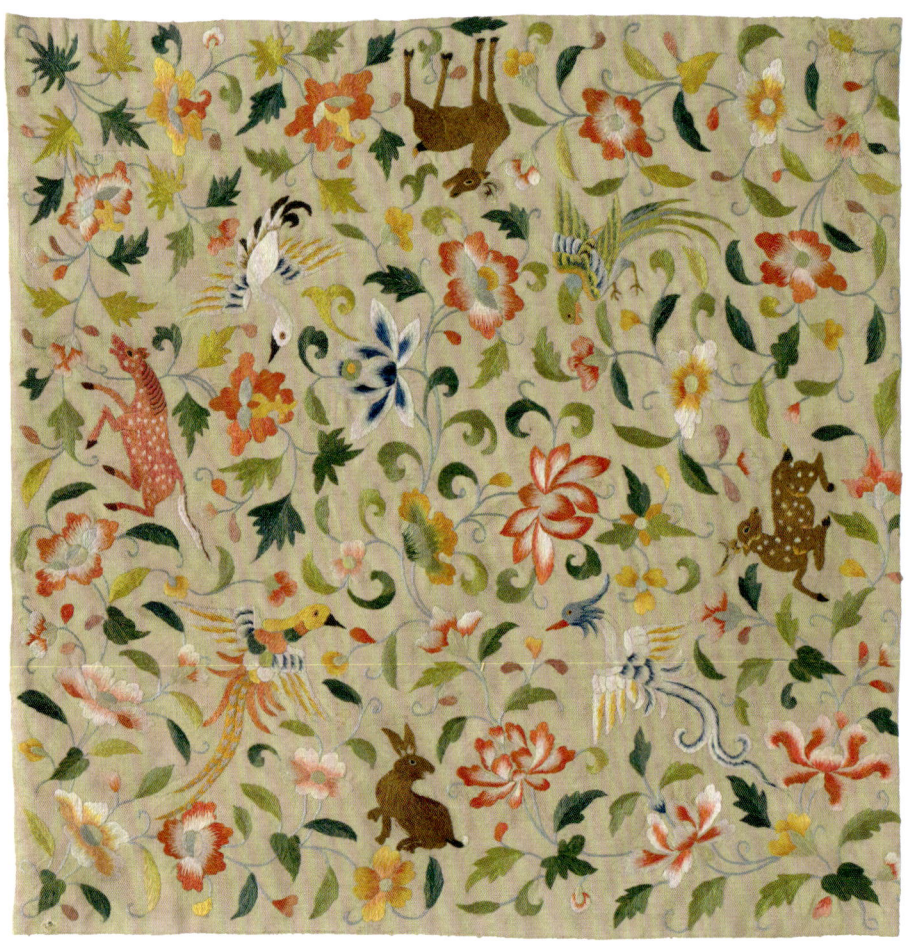

Anonymous

Embroidery square with animals, birds and flowers, late 12th–14th century
Silk thread on silk, 37.1 × 37.8 cm / 14¾ × 15 in
Metropolitan Museum of Art, New York

A swirling pattern of blue, pink, yellow and white blossom with vining leaves and stems intertwines with birds and animals in this remarkably detailed silk square, embroidered more than six centuries ago. Created in eastern Central Asia sometime between 1150 and 1400 AD, the textile and the detail of its design exemplify the long-standing character of recurrent motifs in the region's art. A dappled horse, a rabbit and two antlered deer or antelope are arranged at the four cardinal points of the composition, in a configuration that first appeared during the Han dynasty in China (206 BC–220 AD). Four birds of exotic plumage set at the midpoint between the animals – wings spread as if in flight – include a striking green and turquoise parrot, which had entered the Central Asian decorative vocabulary during the Tang dynasty (618–907 AD), a second period of strong Chinese influence. Central to the vibrant botanical motif are lotus blossoms and leaves, as well as trefoil leaves. Lotus designs had begun to appear in work produced in Central Asia and North China, but they only became widespread during the Yuan dynasty (1271–1368). Little is known about the exact origins of this textile, but it may reflect the varying artistic and cultural influences following the dissolution of the Tang, when Buddhist imagery was sponsored by the kingdoms in northwest Asia, Islamic rule dominated in West-central Asia and the Mongols began to invade from the north.

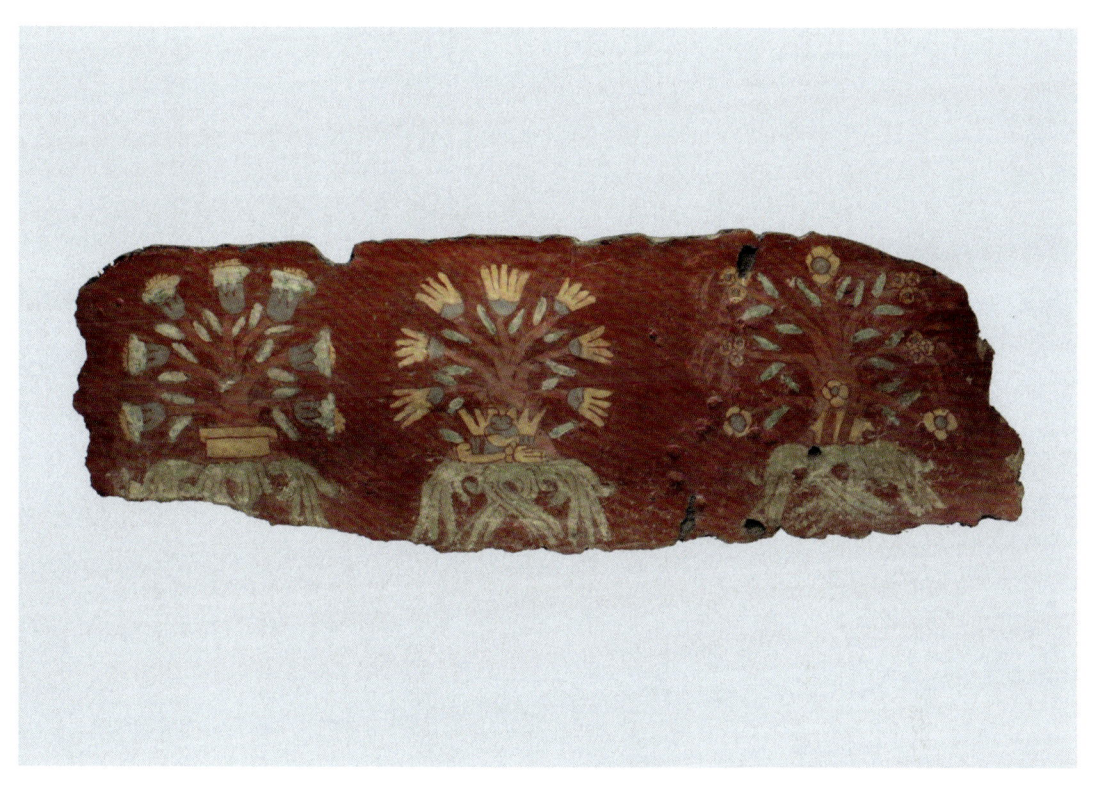

Anonymous

Teotihuacana wall painting, c.100 BC–900 AD
Pigment on plaster
Museo Nacional de Antropología, Mexico City

Three otherworldly plants adorn this ancient fragment of wall from Mexico. The artist has flattened out the flowers as if they have been pressed and then arranged as graphic patterns at the ends of their stems, but has virtually disregarded the leaves, which are depicted as small and insignificant. In contrast, the roots are elaborate, swirling and rippling almost as if they were in water. This fragment was discovered in Teotihuacan,

the most important and largest Mesoamerican city in Mexico, where it flourished nearly a thousand years before the arrival of the Aztecs. Located 50 kilometres (30 miles) northeast of modern-day Mexico City, Teotihuacan had a population of more than 125,000, and a central ceremonial avenue lined by pyramids. More than just depictions of the natural world meant to decorate a building, these three figures are toponyms: glyphs, or pictorial characters, which represent both important earthly and mythological locations. The writing system of Teotihuacan has not yet been fully deciphered, but the

meanings of certain elements have been extrapolated from the culture's known belief system. A core belief in the Teotihuacan cosmology was that the souls of warriors who had fallen in battle would transform into butterflies, and live on in a supernatural place known as 'Flower Mountain' – a realm often represented by depictions of three mountains with flowers blooming from their sides.

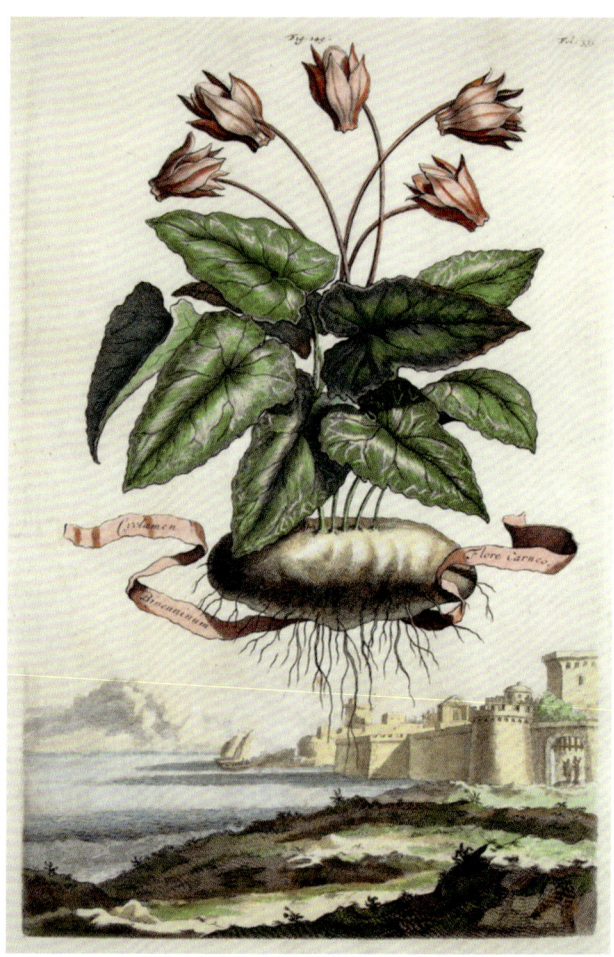

Abraham Munting

Cyclamen Bipenninum Flore Carneo,
from *Accurate Description of Terrestrial Plants*, 1696
Hand-coloured copperplate engraving,
39.1 × 25.6 cm / 12½ × 10 in
Private collection

In this remarkable example of botanical illustration, a cyclamen (*Cyclamen hederifolium*) floats in the sky as if it has just been grabbed by its stems, pulled out of the soil, roots and all, and held up to be examined. Dutch botanist and botanical artist Abraham Munting (1626–83) reveals the plant's heavy corm from which its roots protrude and its stems grow, around which wafts a pink ribbon bearing the full title of the work, *Cyclamen Bipenninum Flore Carneo* ('the cyclamen with flesh-coloured, two streaked flowers'). Set in a strange Dutch landscape featuring a fortified town, portcullis and a ship setting sail, the cyclamen levitates like some imagined medieval UFO. The heads of the flowers, although they are recognizable, are stylized so that they are ridged and look almost like the heads of dragons due to the upswept petals. Upon closer inspection, the red stems of the flowers do not actually grow from the corm as the green stems for the leaves do. While we might postulate that the cyclamen is set in this landscape to demonstrate where it might grow, the lax accuracy of the illustration perhaps points to something else. This illustration is just one from Munting's most famous work, *Naauwkeurige Beschryving Der Aardgewassen*, literally translated as 'Accurate Description of Terrestrial Plants'. Rather than the stated aim of accuracy, it could be seen as a form of popularization of scientific methodology aimed at a general readership rather than scholarly study – as perhaps evidenced by the success of Munting's book.

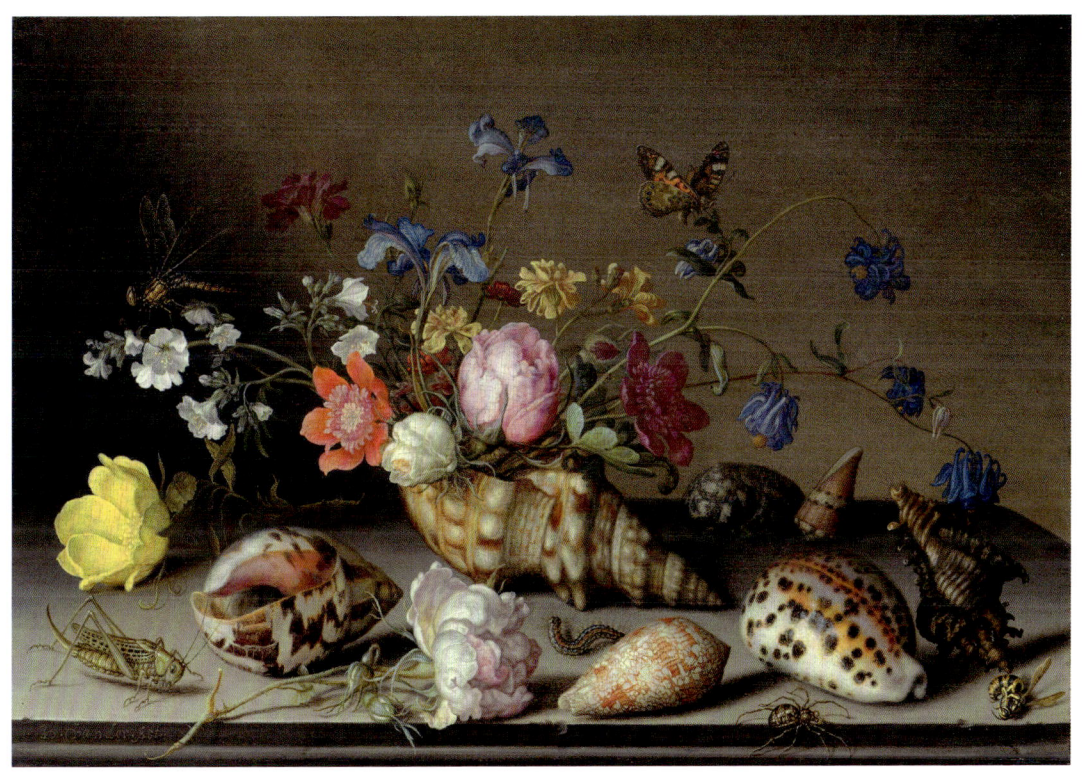

Balthasar van der Ast

Flowers in a Snail Shell, Insects and Conches, c.1640
Oil on panel, 23.8 × 34.5 cm / 9¼ × 13½ in
Private collection

A variety of delicate flowers – budding roses, anemones, columbine, Siberian iris – are arranged in a rather curious container: a large Triton shell (*Charonia lampas*). Strewn on the table are various other types of seashells and two more varieties of roses. Flowers and seashells were favourite subjects of the Dutch Golden Age painter Balthasar van der Ast (1593/94–1657). The flowers chosen here are mostly summer flowers, while a similar still life, probably its companion, depicts close species that bloom in spring. Exotic shells were costly rarities at the time, brought to the Netherlands from distant shores by merchant ships of the Dutch East and West India Companies; they match the sense of exclusivity borne out by van der Ast's delicate and exotic flowers. The painter also delighted in including a variety of creatures in his still lifes: here, a dragonfly, a grasshopper, a spider, a dead wasp, a caterpillar and a butterfly. The combination of the last two, because of their metamorphosis, could be intended to remind the viewer of the cycle of life and thus of his or her own transience. Van der Ast painted this still life in Delft, where he had moved from Utrecht in 1632, probably around 1640. The soft lighting and atmospheric impression seem to anticipate the works painted after the mid-1650s in the same town by Johannes Vermeer, who doubtlessly knew several of van der Ast's still lifes.

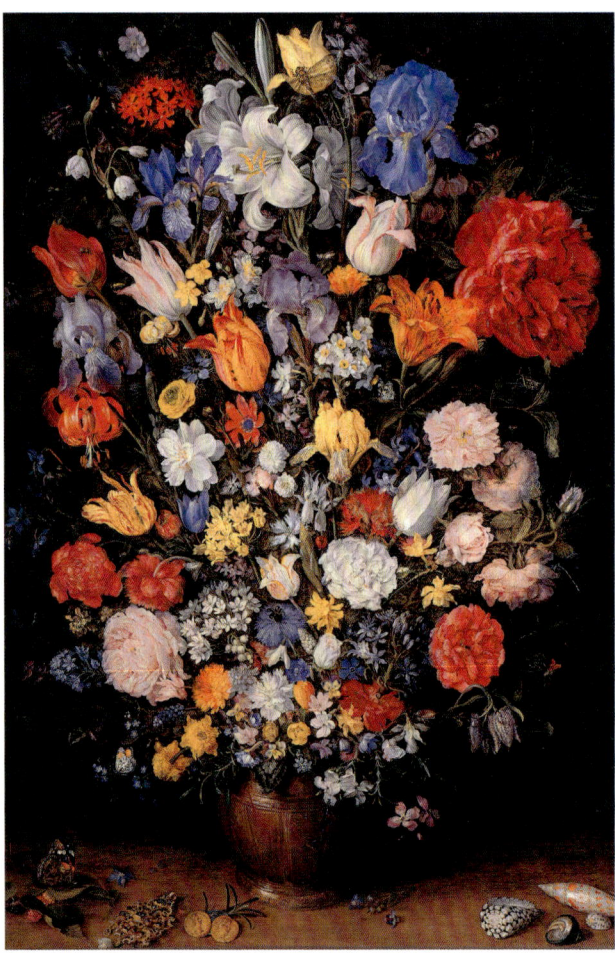

Jan Brueghel the Elder

Vase of Flowers with Jewel, Coins and Shells, 1606
Oil on copper, 65 × 45 cm / 25½ × 17¾ in
Veneranda Biblioteca Ambrosiana, Milan

In a veritable painted catalogue of floral species, Flemish painter Jan Brueghel the Elder (1568–1625) went out of his way to include more than a hundred flowers in a single image, all rendered in immaculate detail. Various tulips, lilies, irises and roses sit next to snowdrops, peonies, cyclamen and a number of rare varieties. There is almost no overlap and, characteristic of this early type of flower painting, the bouquet gives

the impression of being a tapestry of flowers rather than a nat-urally rounded bunch. Brueghel painted the still life in 1606 for Cardinal Federico Borromeo in Milan, who had become the artist's patron when he visited the city in 1596. In correspondence with Borromeo, Brueghel excused himself for the delay in delivering the painting, explaining that he had to wait for the spring to portray some fresh blooms. He painted them 'from life', he wrote. This does not mean that Brueghel ever had a bouquet like this in front of him; in fact, he composed it from individual floral studies of real-life specimens in the botanic

gardens of Archduke Albert and Archduchess Isabella in Brussels. Brueghel painted a jewel in the lower part of the image, by which he sought to indicate that the value of his work was equal to that of the jewel. The cardinal himself remarked on this, and consequently wrote, 'This is the price we paid to the artist.'

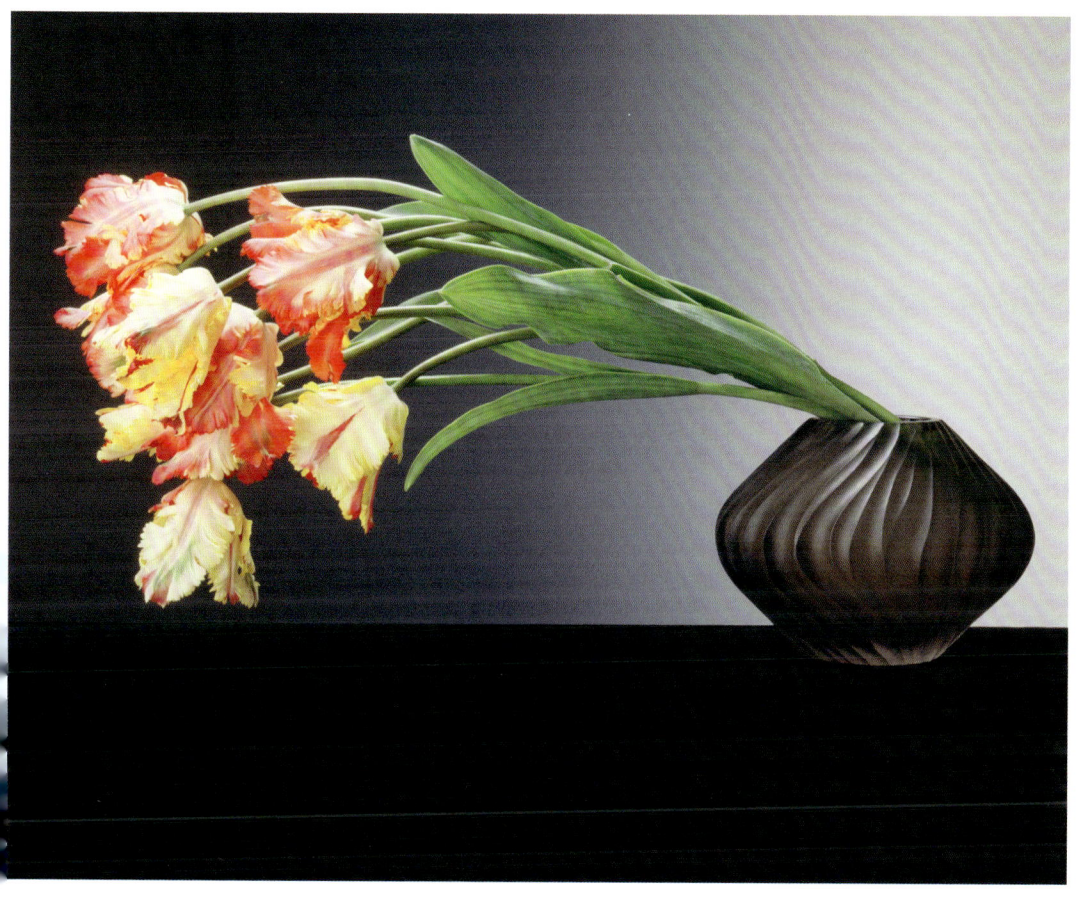

Robert Mapplethorpe

Parrot Tulips, 1988
Dye transfer print, 61 × 76.2 cm / 24 × 30 in

In an effort to better familiarize himself with the technical opportunities offered by the camera, American photographer Robert Mapplethorpe (1946–89) first experimented with flowers in the early 1970s, capturing them in Polaroids. A decade later, when he was already a popular if controversial name, Mapplethorpe's continued exploration of floral subjects helped to perfect his knowledge of light and exposure within his trademark black-and-white images. Each morning he sent his friend and studio assistant, Dimitri Levas, out to flower markets to pick up the varieties with the most interesting architectural forms and shapes. Mapplethorpe would then explore different backgrounds, luminosities, angles and families of flowers, roaming from irises to orchids, daisies and tulips – including these stunning parrot tulips. While the sombre mood and the fragility of some of Mapplethorpe's later floral arrangements have been noted as proof of the artist's coming to terms with his own mortality, the formalism and geometrical precision of others resonate soundly with his earlier work. The erotic element that characterized his portraits can easily be detected in his still-life photographs as the tulips especially testify. Mapplethorpe himself seemed satisfied with having found a subject that could convey his vision to a broader audience. 'Sell the public flowers,' he once declared, 'things that they can hang on their walls without being uptight.'

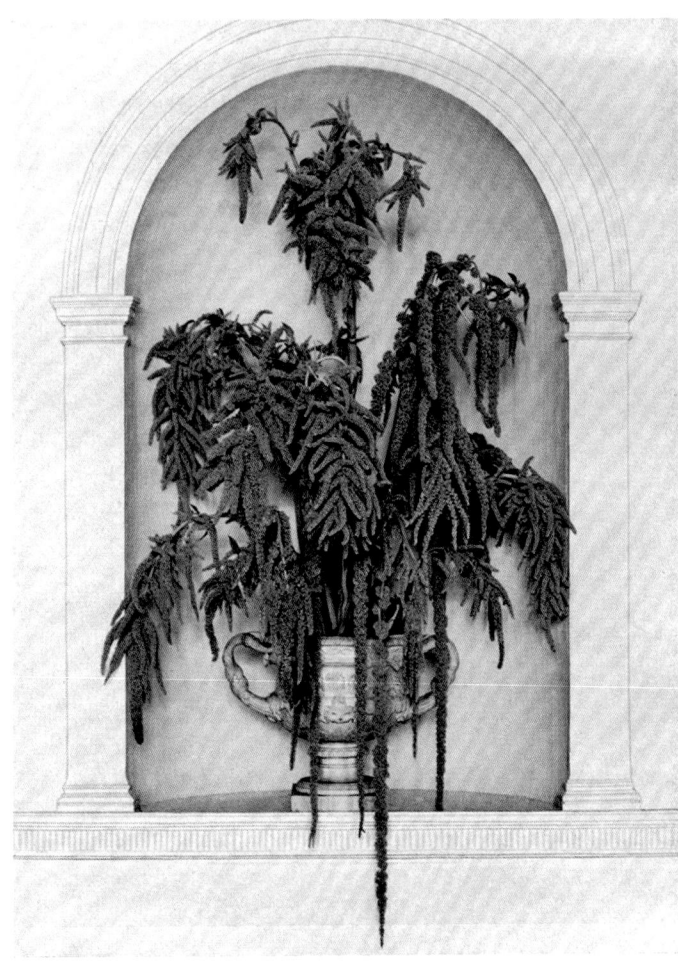

Constance Spry

Love-lies-bleeding (*Amaranthus caudatus*) arranged
in a stone urn, from *Flower Decoration*, 1934
Floral arrangement

A fountain of love-lies-bleeding (*Amaranthus caudatus*) erupts from a marble urn and tumbles from a stone niche. This 1930s design by pioneering English floral decorator Constance Spry (1886–1960) has lost neither its novelty nor its ability to intensify our appreciation of the quirks of this unique petal-less flower: Spry noted that the long, delicate trails are more easily appreciated cut than growing, with the 'rough

and coarse' leaves removed. When Spry opened her first shop in London in 1929, she pointedly called it 'Flower Decoration' to distinguish it from the standard florists' shops of the time. While she recognized many of the traditional techniques of floristry, Spry approached flowers with the care and innate instinct of an artist choosing paints. A gardener with a botanist's eye, she observed each flower's natural characteristics and arranged it precisely to enhance those attributes, mixing colours or flower types and drawing in the viewer to appreciate its particular beauty. She often selected unconventional flowers and vegetation

– such as her infamous use of kale – paired with more traditional blooms, and had a varied choice of containers for her works, from ornate urns to Fulham pottery she designed herself. Starting with a seemingly eclectic array of materials, Spry's works both showcased and tamed the wildness of nature – at times in simple, sparse forms, and at others in opulent, baroque displays. Her aesthetic was revolutionary, and Spry's influence has carried through to the new guard of floral designers today.

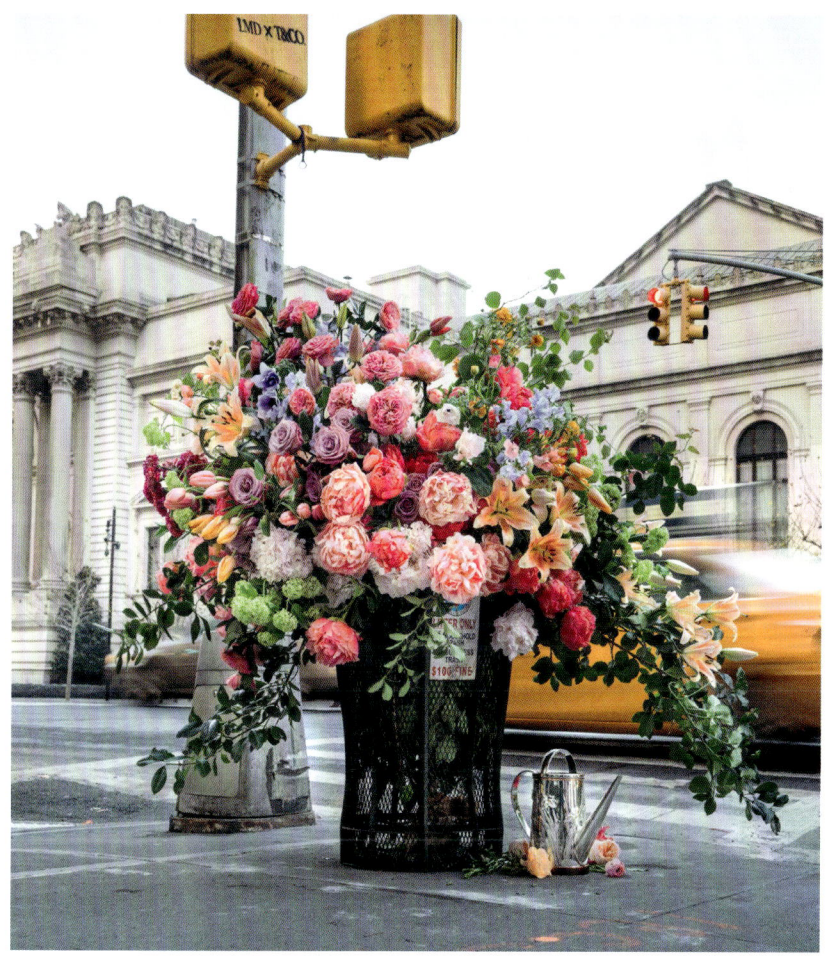

Lewis Miller Design

Flower Flash, 2018
Floral installation, New York

An enormous arrangement of exuberant summer stems spills out from a New York City trash can: luscious pink peonies, lilac and pink roses, orange and peach lilies, pink tulips, blue sweet peas and delicate orbs of *Viburnum opulus*. Behind them a yellow taxicab whizzes along the street and the creamy facade of the Metropolitan Museum of Art provides an elegant backdrop. This is a Flower Flash, the brainchild of Lewis Miller (born 1974), whose guerrilla installations

of over-the-top blooms pop up in the most unprepossessing spaces: a disused post office, bus shelters, traffic signs, roadworks and subways all over New York. Miller founded his eponymous studio in 2002, working on private events for fashion and luxury brands such as Bulgari, Valentino and Tiffany, and in 2016 he began creating his impromptu public displays as a way to use up leftover flowers and foliage from events that would otherwise go to waste. The first was at the John Lennon Memorial in Central Park, which Miller circled with 2,000 dahlias and carnations. Each display is put together by a small

team in around fifteen minutes in the early hours of the morning to bring some joy to the city's commuters as they rush to work. Occasionally, an individual takes a few stems for themselves – but it's all part of the fun.

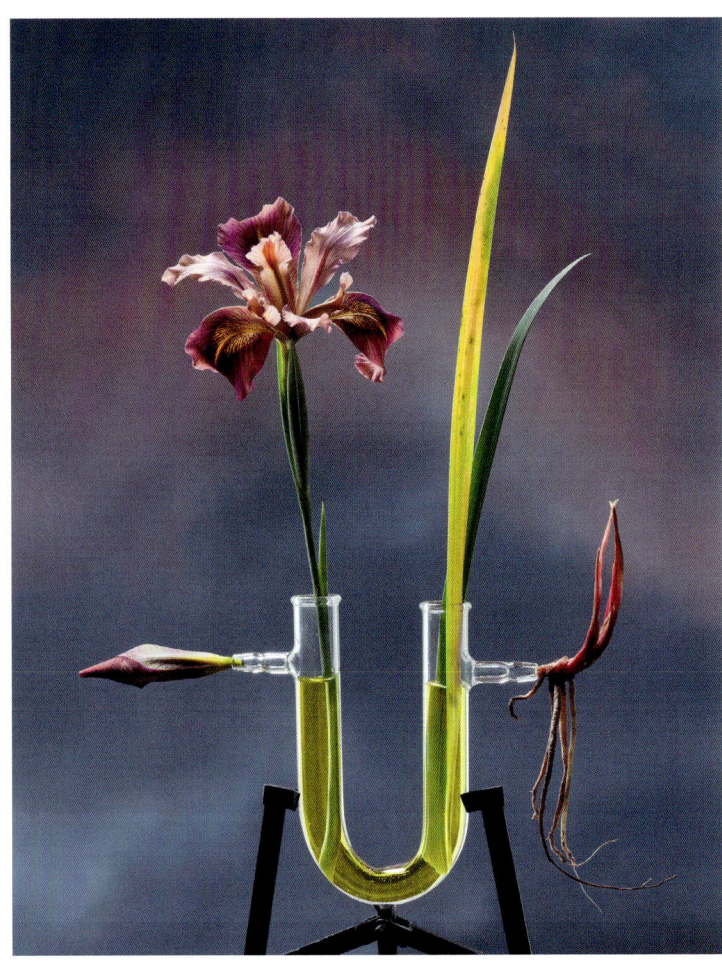

Jo Whaley

Iris ser. Californicae, 2012
Archival pigment photograph, 66 × 50.8 cm /
26 × 20 in

A Pacific Coast iris (*Iris ser. Californicae*) with
richly coloured pink and gold petals sprouts
from a U-shaped test tube filled with luminous
yellow liquid. Is it the product of a dubious scientific experiment: a flower modified to resist
disease, drought and pests? Or are we witnessing
a laboratory disaster about to unleash unintended
consequences into the world? This photograph
is part of the *Botanical Studies* series by American
photographer Jo Whaley (born 1953), which
explores the intersection of nature and technology and expresses anxieties about biotechnology
and genetic modification. As an avid gardener
– she grew many of the *Botanical Studies* subjects in her California garden – Whaley is deeply
concerned with nature. Humans have been
manipulating the natural world for their own
ends for centuries, but modern developments
in genetics have raised serious moral and ethical
questions. While some proclaim great benefits,
others warn of irreversible damage to the planet's
ecosystems. Whaley began her career as a scenic
painter for theatre and, like stage productions,
her photographs are a fusion of the imaginary
and the real. Each image is elaborately constructed in her studio, often over the course
of several days. Eschewing digital manipulation,
she employs meticulous lighting, props, painted
backdrops and coloured gels to achieve her
distinctive aesthetic, which references a blend
of still-life painting, advertising photography
and botanical illustration.

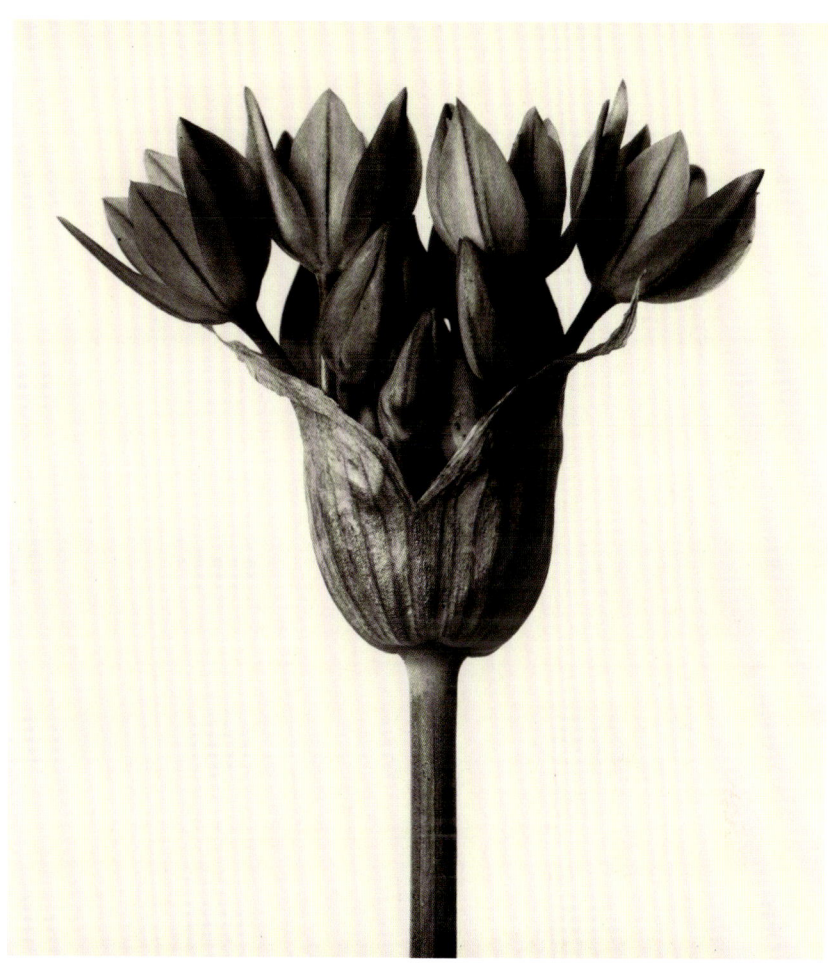

Karl Blossfeldt

Allium ostrowskianum, Knoblauchpflanze, 1928
Gelatin silver print, 25.9 × 20.4 cm / 10¼ × 8 in
J. Paul Getty Museum, Los Angeles

Clearly outlined against a plain background, this depiction of *Allium oreophilum*, the pink lily leek, embodies the solemnity of a carving from a gothic cathedral. It is typical of the work of German photographer Karl Blossfeldt (1865–1932), whose close-up images of plants are among the most original representations of the vegetal world. Blossfeldt's simplicity of style revealed the architectural essence

of leaves, stems and flowers, and his *Urformen der Kunst (Art Forms in Nature)*, a series of photographic plates published in 1928, became instantly iconic by casting the botanical world as the source of natural blueprints of architecture and design. Blossfeldt saw plants as true artistic expressions in their own right, 'artistic educators' in which the specific forms and shapes of plants no longer bore any symbolic meaning. They are an invitation to look anew through the photographic lens – an opportunity to rediscover plants by embracing their silent stillness and to appreciate them for that alone.

From the late nineteenth century, photography changed the way people look at plants and split scientific opinion. While some heralded the arrival of a new medium capable of capturing minute details with objective precision, others condemned photography's inability to neatly focus all parts of a plant and portray colour appropriately. Blossfeldt's work demonstrated that, used in a particular way, photography could provide an alternative and important view of plants that elegantly straddles the domains of art and science.

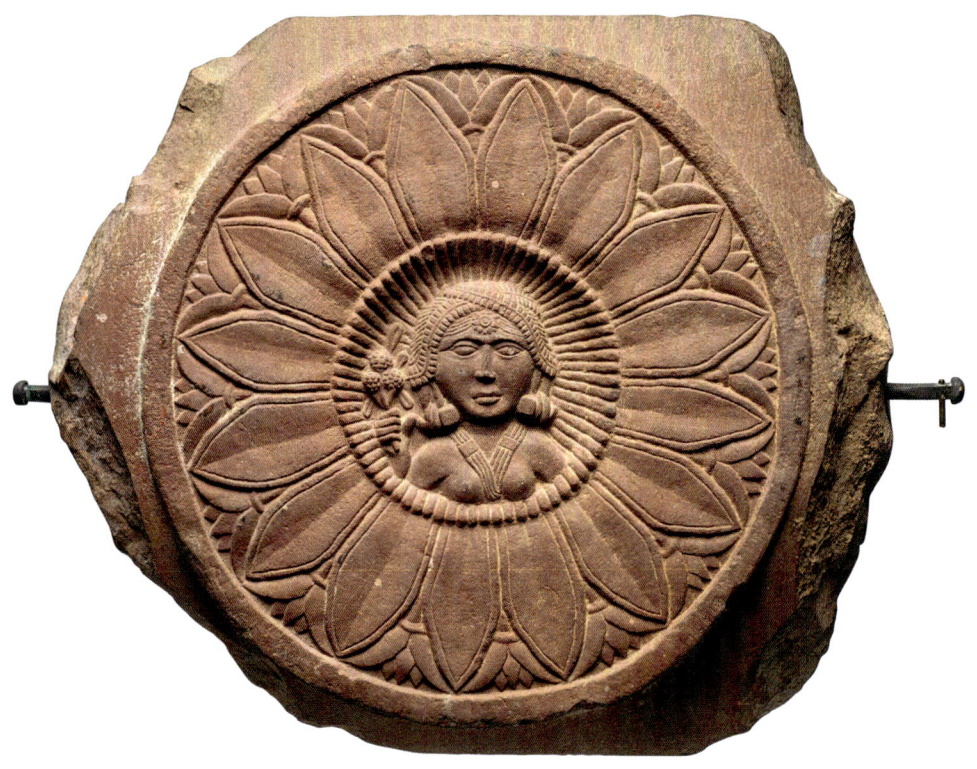

Anonymous

Crossbar with a female figure from a railing,
c.150 BC
Sandstone, 55.9 × 66 cm / 22 × 26 in
Cleveland Museum of Art, Ohio

A female figure sits at the centre of an Indian
lotus-flower medallion carved from plum-
coloured standstone. Embodying the life-giving
forces of nature, she likely represents a *yakshi*,
a type of nature spirit found in Buddhist teachings. Neither gods nor demons, the divine spirits
are strongly associated with sacred groves –
small plots of woodland that have religious

connotations for the local community – which
they help to protect. In her hand, the figure holds
a posy of three *kadamba* flowers (*Neolamarckia
cadamba*), from a tropical tree native to India
and southeast Asia and recognizable for its dense
orange globe-like flower heads. Adorning her
forehead, where one might find the Buddhist
'third eye' – the eye of consciousness – another
lotus-shaped ring echoes the larger design
encircling the image. The reverse of the medallion employs the same lotus motif, this time
with a male worshipper at its centre. In Buddhist
symbolism, the coupling of male and female

represents birth and prosperity. This fragment
is one of many grouped together on the large
stone 'railing' or gateway that demarcated the
entrance to the sacred space surrounding the
Buddhist *stupa* at Bharhut in Madhya Pradesh,
India, which was built in around 150 BC. Lotus
motifs were used widely on stupas for their
association with purifying waters, life and abundance in Buddhism.

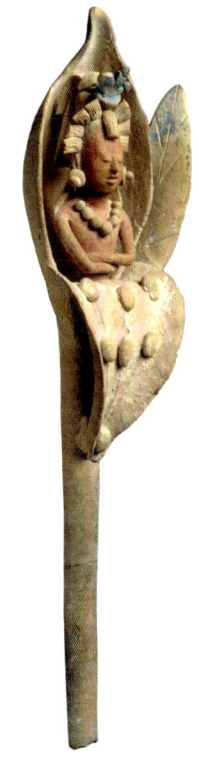

Anonymous

Figure emerging from a water lily, 600–900 AD
Ceramic, pigment, 21 × 5.4 × 4.3 cm /
8¼ × 2 × 1¾ in
Brooklyn Museum, New York

The sleeping figure of a man is unveiled – his private moment broken – by the peeling back of single petal of a water lily. One is surprised by this discovery, not least because the man is in full ceremonial regalia: an impressive head-dress coloured blue with natural pigment, large earrings and a bold beaded necklace. This is one of many hundreds of models and sculptures, many of them ceramic, that have been uncovered on Jaina Island, off Mexico's Campeche coast on the Yucatán Peninsula. Thought to be derived from the Maya phrase *Hail na*, Jaina's name translates literally to 'watery house'. The island played an important role as an elite burial ground during the pre-Columbian Maya civilization: more than 20,000 tombs have been discovered at the site. In Maya culture the water lily was associated with the underworld, or *Xibalba*, where the gods of death, such as Hun-Came ('One-Death'), were found. The temptation is to read this object as a funerary item – especially as the lily could be considered coffin-like – but the prominent seeds, indicated by the six clay ovals below the figure, may instead symbolize this man's new life after death.

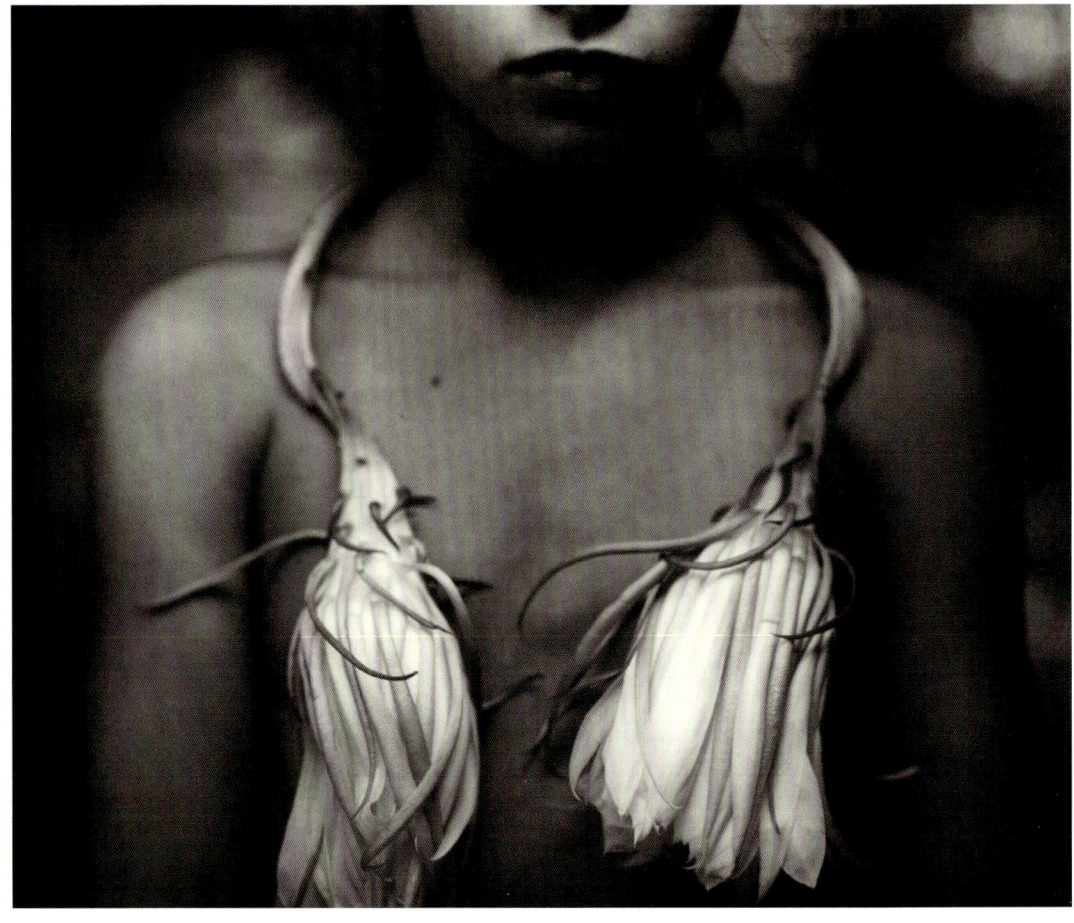

Sally Mann

Night-blooming Cereus, 1988
Gelatin silver print, 50.8 × 61 cm / 20 × 24 in

Still a child, a girl with chiselled shoulders and dark lips recedes into the background as the framing of the photograph leads the eye to the swan-like flowers covering her chest. In this image taken in 1988 by American photographer Sally Mann (born 1951), we see her seven-year-old daughter, Jessie, wearing a wreath of night-blooming cereus (*Selenicereus grandiflorus*). An example of Mann's coming-of-age depictions, the photograph deliberately uses the cereus

flower as a metaphor for the ephemeral nature of childhood. The night-blooming cereus, also known as queen of the night, has trumpet-shaped flowers with creamy white, waxy petals. Large and fragrant, the flower can measure up to 30 centimetres (11¾ inches) in diameter and only blooms after sunset for one night each year, wilting by sunrise. Mann first came to international prominence in 1992 with *Immediate Family*, a series of complex and controversial images of her children photographed with the unnerving intimacy and honesty of a mother. Captured at home in rural Virginia, the children are

surrounded by nature, sometimes posing in ways reminiscent of photographs by Julia Margaret Cameron (see p.131). But as much as Mann's documentary approach captures an intimate narrative, it also has a magical dimension. When developing and printing her images, she brings out a luminous tonal range of silvers that gives them a dreamlike quality. Is this a childhood as it really existed? Or is it the childhood only as preserved in memories?

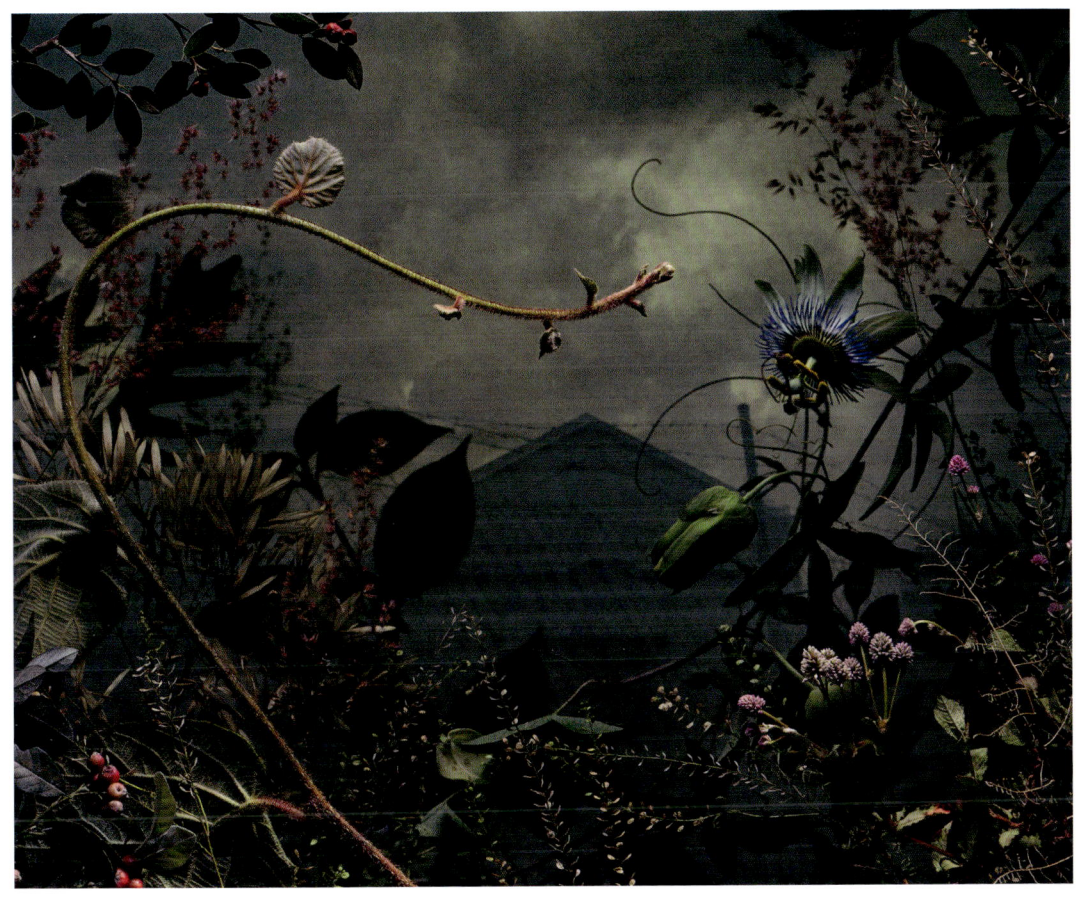

Daniel Shipp

Restricted Storage Area, from the series
Botanical Inquiry, 2019
Pigment ink-jet print, 68.5 × 86 cm / 27 × 33¾ in
Private collection

A passion flower among a tableau of other botanical subjects projects an uncanny presence: petals and leaves seem to quiver in the breeze and tendrils snake and whirl. At first glance, the dramatically darkened skies and the subtly lit details of each flower, leaf and stem might look very much like a seventeenth-century painting, but this is a modern creation by Australian photographer Daniel Shipp (born 1972). Despite being photographed through a digital camera, Shipp's images of flowers are not the result of extensive Photoshop collaging. Each specimen is collected and brought back to the studio, where he builds a complex diorama. It is in his studio that Shipp exerts maximum control over the lighting, atmosphere and composition of each scene to produce dramatized effects as we see here. The image is produced using techniques that made the Viewmaster 3D slides and Disney animation technology so successful during the 1950s. This might, at least in part, explain the vintage atmosphere that pervades his work. But Shipp is after more than breathtakingly beautiful and impossible images. His dioramas suggest possible narratives in deserted and forgotten urban sites. It is the juxtaposition between the mysterious and somewhat menacing architectures in the background – with the strands of barbed wire – and the vibrancy of the foliage, stems and flowers in the foreground that suspends this image in a somewhat tense and eerie mood.

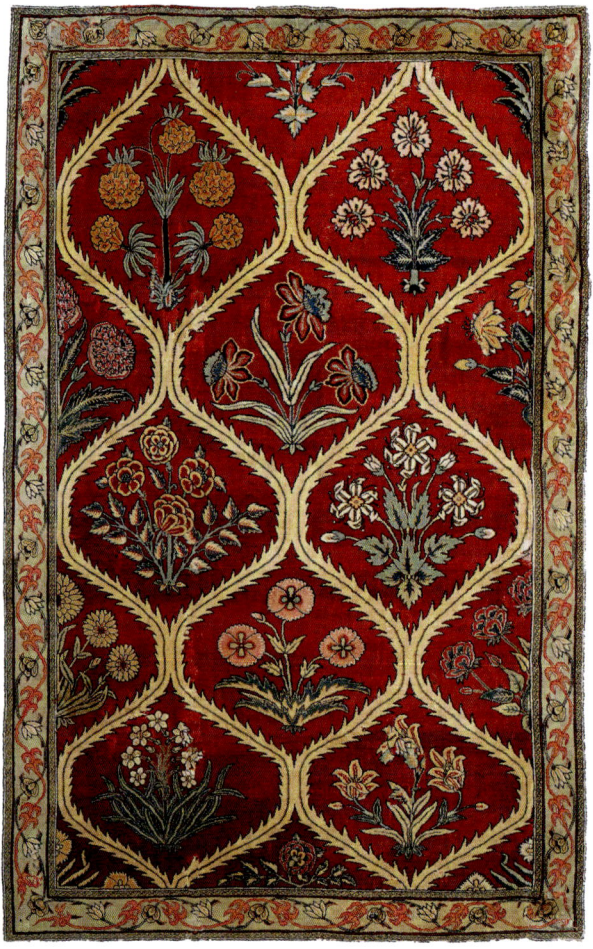

Anonymous

Carpet, *c*.1650
Knotted-pile pashmina on silk, 1.4 × 0.9 m /
4 ft 7 in × 1 ft 11 in
Victoria and Albert Museum, London

Gently waving serrated stems form a trellis
enclosing eight compartments, each containing
a different flower, all beautifully set against
a red background. The use of pashmina (goat hair)
woven into warps and wefts of silk results in a
dense pile capable of displaying patterns and
objects in considerable detail. The central floral
design – roses, tulips, carnations, poppies,

narcissus and other flowers – is surrounded
by a narrow border of intertwining leaves and
white flowers on a pale background. The craftsman who created this superb carpet is unknown,
but it is likely to have been woven in Kashmir
or Lahore. Its probable date places it within the
rule of the Mughal Emperor Shah Jahān (ruled
1628–58), who is best known for building the
famous Taj Mahal at Agra as a tomb for his wife.
Shah Jahān continued to encourage the creation
of many works of art, a tradition started by earlier
Mughal emperors, notably his father, Akbar
(ruled 1556–1605). Akbar established workshops

that specialized in producing splendid paintings
and objects in gold, as well as carpets that were
richly decorated with depictions of flowers, trees
and animals. Shah Jahān's palace in Agra also
included a 'carpet house' that organized carpets
to be woven to order, either locally or traded,
notably from the royal factory in Lahore.

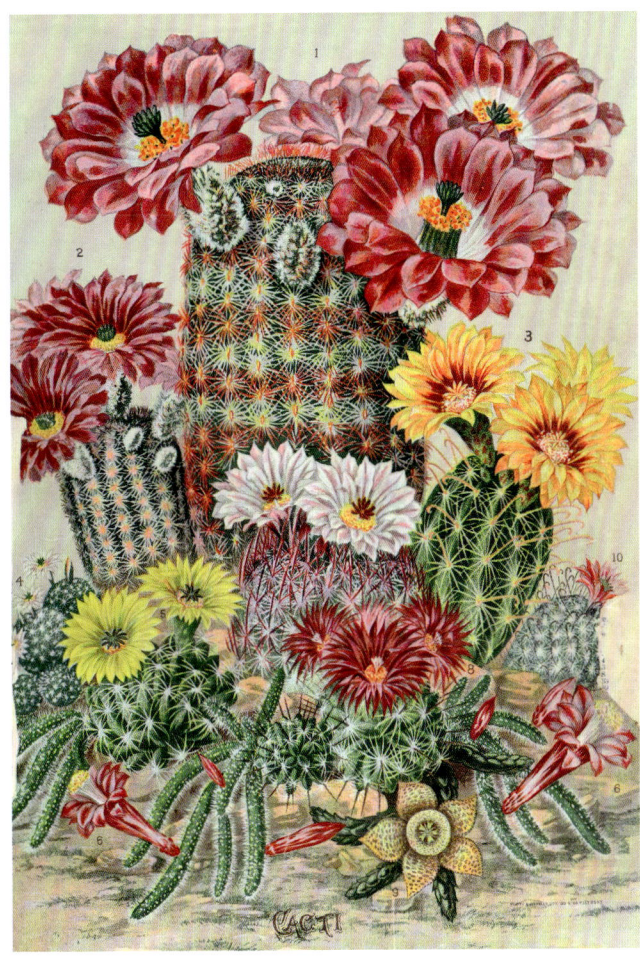

John Lewis Childs

Cacti, from *New, Rare and Beautiful Flowers*, 1891
Colour lithograph, 25 × 17.3 cm / 10 × 6¾ in
LuEsther T. Mertz Library, New York
Botanical Garden

Illustrated in vivid colour, this print from the late 1800s showcases a profusion of native Mexican cacti, including: *Echinocereus candicans* (1), *E. pectinatus* (2), *Echinocactus setispinus* (3), *E. simpsoni* (8), *Mammillaria pusilla*, also known as *M. prolifera* (4), *M. decipiens* (5), *M. childsi* (7), *M. grahamii* (10), *Cereus flagelliformis* (6) and *Stapelia variegata* (9). Seed catalogues like this are the unsung textbooks of garden history – time capsules that chronicle the patterns and trends of an entire industry. For many gardeners in the nineteenth and twentieth centuries, there was no feeling quite like that of opening the mail to a new seed catalogue and the promise of new beginnings, with images that sparked the imagination, inspiring vegetable beds and fields of daffodils. The illustrations and delightful descriptions of the flowers and vegetables changed year to year. The John Lewis Childs catalogue – *New, Rare and Beautiful Flowers* – was renowned as one of the most beautifully illustrated seed catalogues. John Lewis Childs (1856–1921) himself was a committed plantsman from childhood who started his seed company in 1875. His first catalogue had just eight pages and only six hundred copies were printed, but the lavishly illustrated publications quickly found success and soon he was sending seeds and plants around the world. He eventually bought up parcels of land just outside Queens, New York, and named it Floral Park.

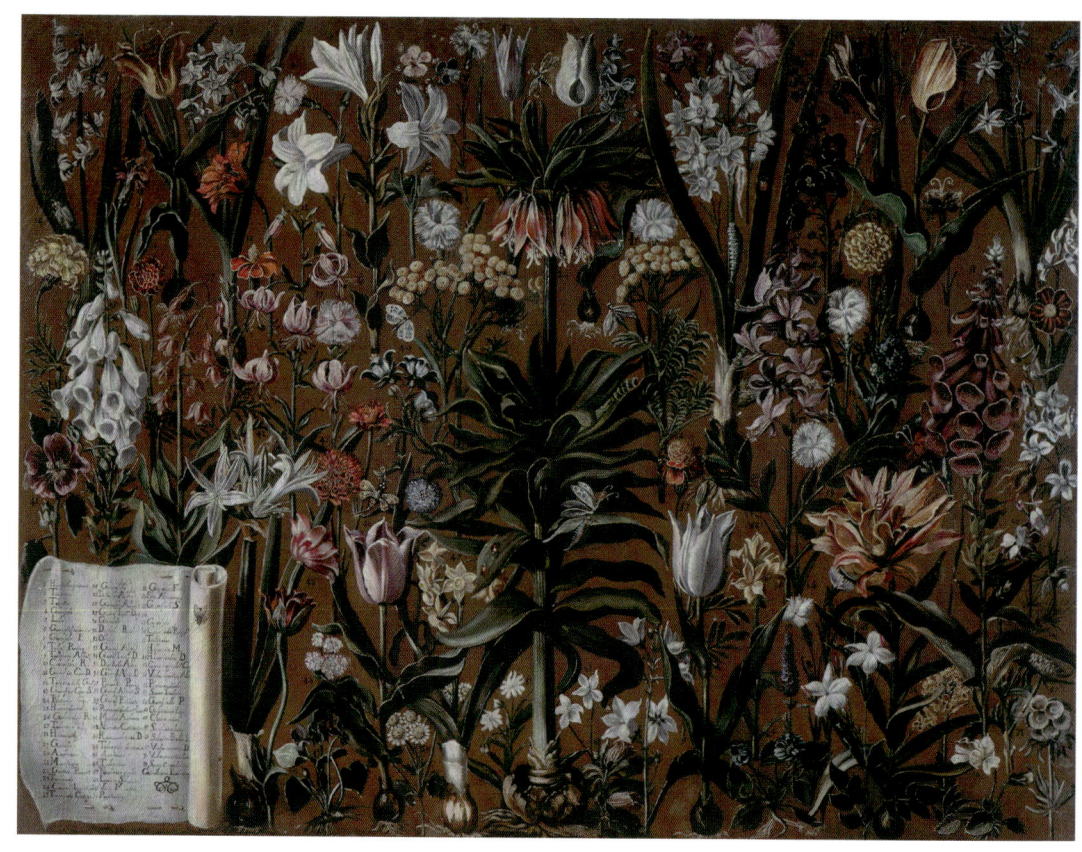

Girolamo Pini

Étude de Fleurs, 1614
Oil on canvas, 0.9 × 1.2 m / 3 ft × 3 ft 11 in
Oak Springs Garden Foundation,
Upperville, Virginia

Believed to have come from the Tuscan city of Pistoia, little is known about the seventeenth-century botanical artist, Girolamo Pini (active 1610–20). During the period in which Pini was working, Florence was an important centre for scientific illustration, drawing notable artists specializing in the subject, such as Jacopo Ligozzi, who produced many botanical paintings for the Medici family. Where Ligozzi typically produced works that concentrated on a single plant, Pini, influenced perhaps by examples of contemporary florilegia, characteristically filled his canvases from edge to edge with intricate compositions involving multiple specimens. In this work, an autograph replica of the original painting held at the Musée des Arts Décoratifs in Paris, the central crown imperial (*Fritillaria imperialis*) is surrounded by seventy-one separate species of flower, including tulip, foxglove, narcissus, lily and carnation. Each plant is numbered, corresponding to a list of common names for the flowers on the scroll in the lower left corner of the canvas. An emphasis on bulbous species is a feature of Pini's work, as is the earthy hue of the dark brown background and the scattering of meticulously rendered insects – here, Pini has included butterflies, caterpillars, a variety of exotic winged creatures and beetles. While the plants appear to be floating free in some exquisite botanical ballet, with their exposed roots and bulbs, this dream-like quality is countered by the realism of Pini's mastery of colour, light and detail.

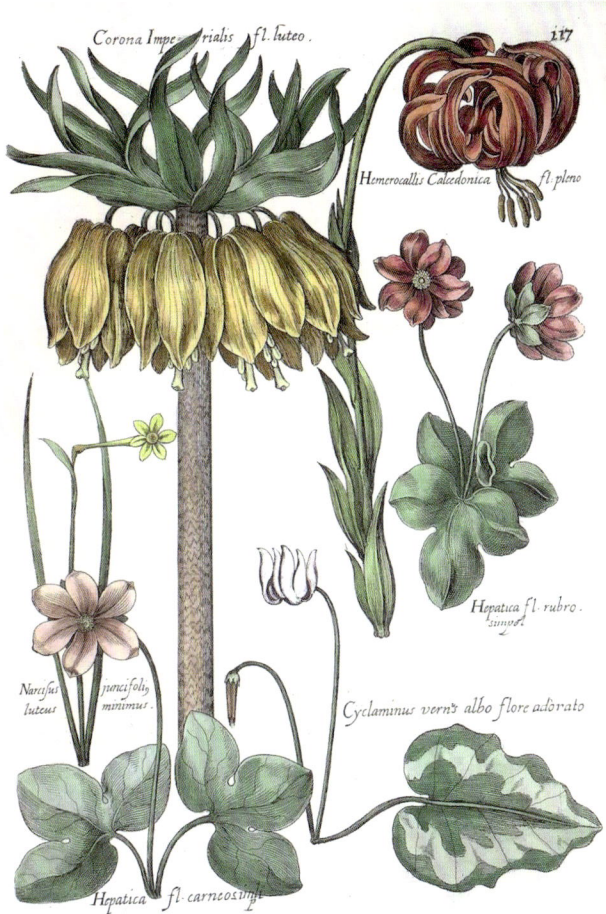

Corona Imperialis fl. luteo.

117

Hemerocallis Calcedonica   fl. pleno

Hepatica fl. rubro.
simpl.

Narcisfus juncifolij
luteus   minimus

Cyclaminus vern's albo flore adorato

Hepatica fl. carneosimpl

Johann Theodor de Bry

Fritillaria or Crown Imperial, Cyclamen, Daylily,
from *Florilegium Novum*, 1612
Hand-coloured copperplate engraving,
31.7 × 20.3 cm / 12½ × 8 in
Private collection

With all the grandeur of its name, the *Fritillaria
imperialis* 'Lutea'– also known as crown imperial,
imperial fritillary or Kaiser's crown – is the pre-
siding presence within this engraving of mainly
spring-flowering plants. Although the species
is usually red-flowered, here the golden fritillary is surrounded by *Cyclamen vernus* (now

C. repandum), two colour variants of *Hepatica*,
Narcissus juncifolius (or rush-leaved daffodil)
and *Hemerocallis calcedonica* (now known
as *Lilium martagon*). The illustration is part of the
Florilegium Novum, comprising more than fifty
botanical plates, published by the Strasbourg-
born engraver Johann Theodor de Bry (1561–1623)
in Frankfurt in around 1612. De Bry was from a
family of established engravers, and Johann took
over the family printing house after the death
of his father, Theodor, in 1598. He also collaborated with his brother Johann Israel on a variety
of works such as emblem books and a grotesque

alphabet. A second version of the *Florilegium
Novum* was produced in 1613 and contained more
than twenty additional engravings. Then, in 1641,
the work was expanded again by the Swiss
engraver Matthäus Merian, father of the botanical artist Maria Sybilla (see p.98), who had moved
to Frankfurt to work for de Bry. Merian married
de Bry's daughter and took over the publishing
house upon de Bry's death in 1623. Matthäus
Merian's additions to the florilegium included
plates depicting exotic flowers and plants growing
in gardens in and around Frankfurt.

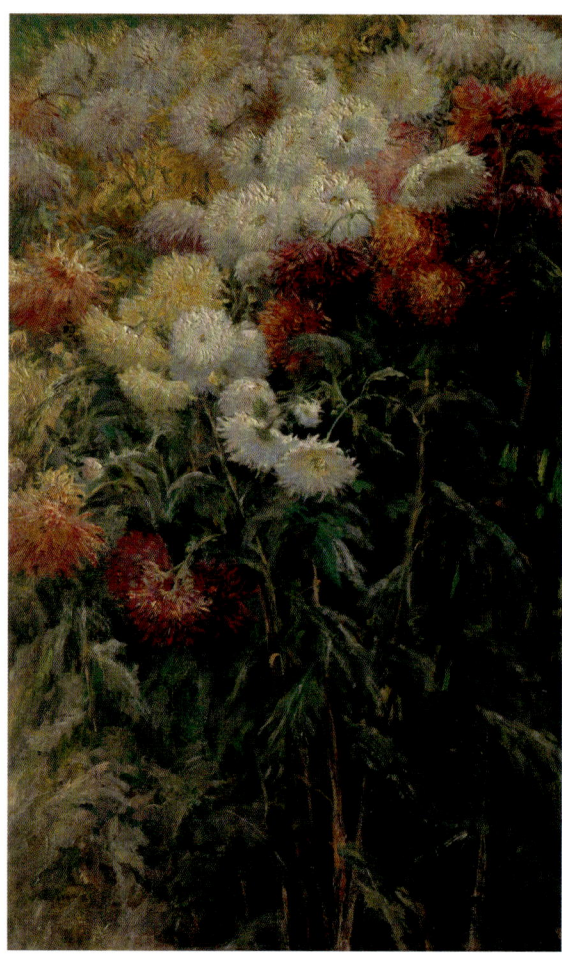

Gustave Caillebotte

Chrysanthemums in the Garden at Petit-Gennevilliers, 1893
Oil on canvas, 99.4 × 61.6 cm / 39 × 24¼ in
Metropolitan Museum of Art, New York

Framing a bed of chrysanthemums in close-up, French painter Gustave Caillebotte (1848–94) has lovingly captured the flowers' silky petals, autumnal colours and untidy leaves – all from the best possible viewpoint. Inspired by photography and Japanese prints, both novelties for Parisians at the time, Caillebotte experimented with perspective angles and dramatic shadows, resulting in an unusual portrait of a familiar and beloved flower. Chrysanthemums were popular in France during the late nineteenth century, with their bold colours and, under the influence of Orientalism, as tokens of the exotic East – they had long been cultivated in China and Japan, where large blooms and varied colours had been developed with names like jade basin and purple crab's claws. Cultivating his garden at Gennevilliers, a small community in the northwestern suburbs of Paris on the Seine, was one of Caillebotte's many lifelong enthusiasms, but it was not until later in life that he turned to flowers as a subject for his paintings. Among his Impressionist friends, he was closest to Pierre-August Renoir (see p.244) in style, while he also shared similarities with Claude Monet (see p.169), with whom he corresponded at Giverny about plants as well as paintings. Caillebotte, who had inherited wealth, helped to finance and organize many Impressionist exhibitions, buying a number of paintings to support his contemporaries long before there was an appreciative market for them.

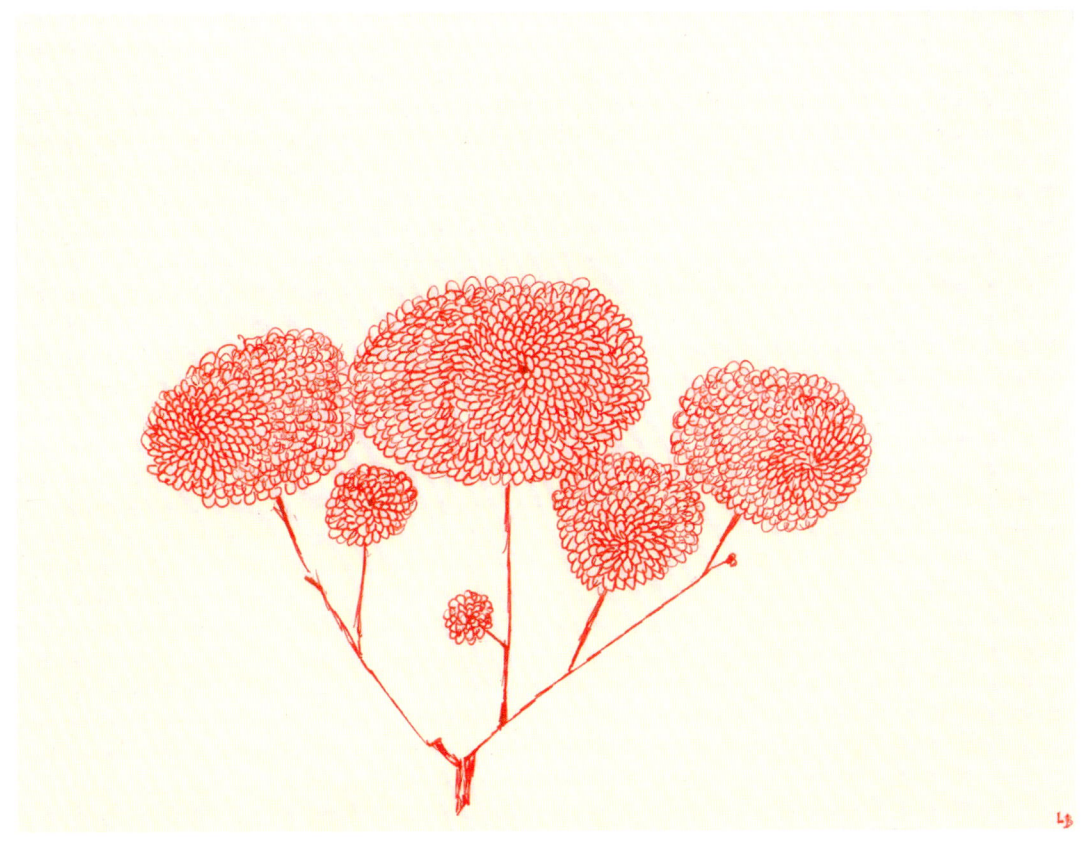

Louise Bourgeois

The Insomnia Drawings, 1994–95
Ink on cardboard, 22.9 × 30.5 cm / 9 × 12 in
Daros Collection, Zürich

Drawn with precise circles in red ink on a contrasting cream sheet, these imaginary, abstract flowers might suggest a dreamlike quality – and the reality is not far off. This work is one of 220 completed by French-American artist Louise Bourgeois (1911–2010) during bouts of insomnia from November 1994 to June 1995. It has been widely assumed that Bourgeois used flowers, like most subjects in her art, as a metaphor for the body, but while floral qualities such as growth, reproduction and fragility have a clear association with the human body, Bourgeois's interest in flowers and the different ways she depicted them over a seventy-year career indicate more complex relationships. Even when Bourgeois fully exploits their allegorical power, her flowers seldom display the sense of darkness and hopelessness present elsewhere in her work. It is perhaps a remnant of an idyllic childhood memory: while growing up in Choisy-le-Roi, Bourgeois and her two siblings were each allocated a small plot for gardening by their father. The children set to work with alacrity, planting roses and geraniums. As Bourgeois entered early adulthood, however, a series of unexpected events – the loss of her mother, her decision to drop out of university and a move to New York to follow her husband – forced her to experience death and displacement in quick order, and her art began to reflect her fears, inner conflicts and vulnerability. Uniquely in her output, however, her flowers seem to have escaped the cloud of the artist's bleakest moments.

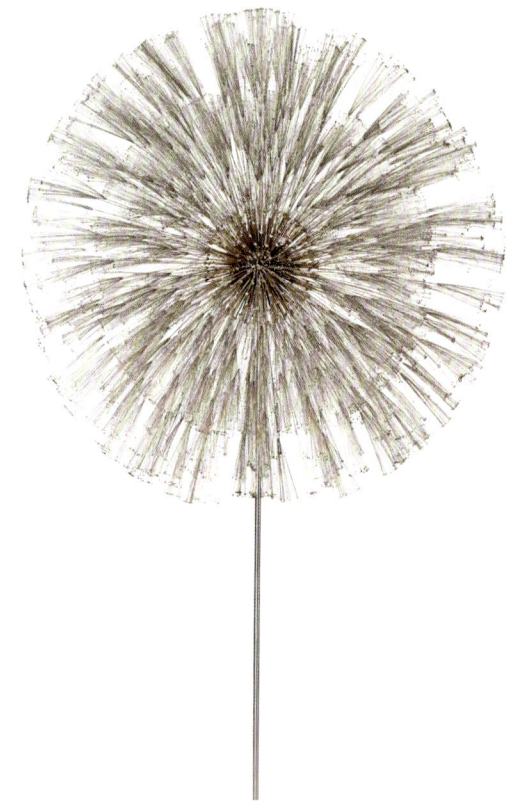

Harry Bertoia

Each of the hundreds of delicate rods clustered in regular arrangement around a central orb in this huge stainless steel sculpture – some 3.5 metres tall – was hand-welded by Italian émigré artist and designer Harry Bertoia (1915–78). The diaphanous sphere mimics the structure of a dandelion: an ellipse evenly clustered in florets or perhaps the plumed seeds or pappus. The sculpture reflects the influence of Bertoia's adopted home in the United States, and the mid-century modern period in which he practised. Bertoia trained at Cranbrook Academy of Art in Michigan, where he was exposed to European modernism and met a group of like-minded artists, designers and architects, including Charles and Ray Eames, Walter Gropius and Florence Knoll. Following a period as the head of Cranbrook's metals department, Bertoia left for Pennsylvania, where Knoll offered him a large workshop in which to experiment and to design modern furniture. In pieces like his distinctive Diamond and Bird chairs, Bertoia combined refined welding techniques with sculptural form and an originality that launched his career. In the late 1950s, he began making a series of dandelions that united his fascination with the natural world and his technical exactitude, transferring skills learned from design production to meticulously welded forms in copper, brass and steel. The radiant results and their arresting impact led to many high-profile commissions, including this example for the Hilton Hotel in Denver, Colorado.

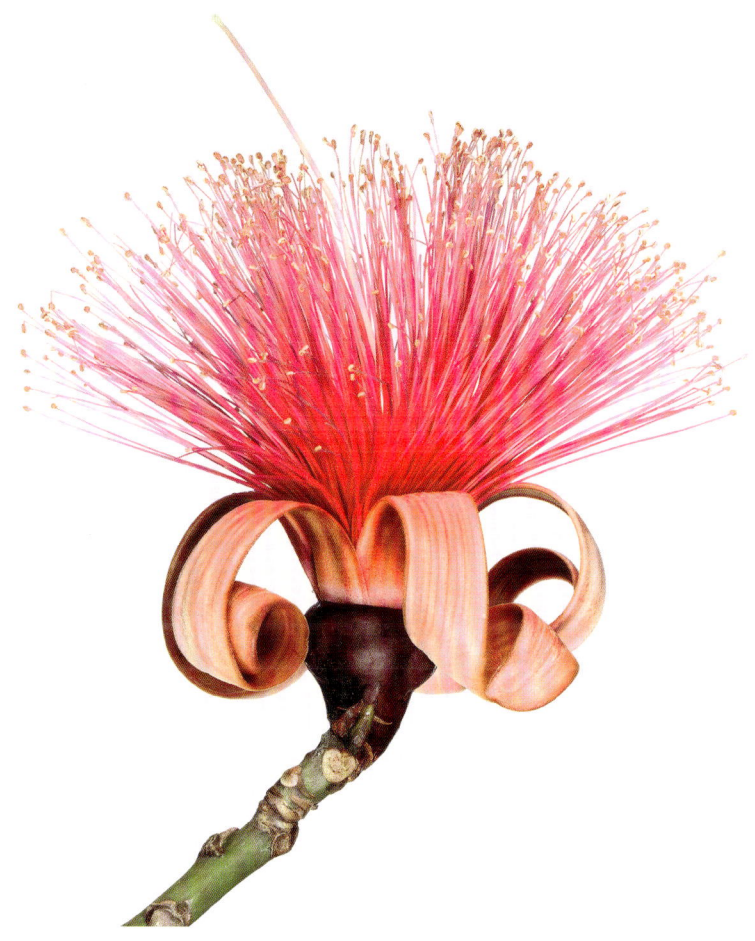

Andrew Zuckerman

Pseudobombax ellipticum, 2012
Archival pigment print, 1 × 1 m /
3 ft 4 in × 3 ft 4 in
Private collection

With pin-sharp focus set against a stark white background, the delicate structure of this remarkable, almost fantastical flower is fully showcased. Captured by American portrait photographer and filmmaker Andrew Zuckerman (born 1977), the flower of a shaving brush tree or amapola (*Pseudobombax ellipticum*) is given an almost lifelike, three-dimensional quality from the precision and clarity of the image. Fascinated by nature, Zuckerman uses his skill to reveal the botanical and zoological worlds in all their complexity and beauty. After publishing volumes on animals, birds and other subjects, in 2012, he completed a project of 150 flower portraits, including *Pseudobombax ellipticum*. The shaving brush tree is found in the wild from southern Mexico to El Salvador, Nicaragua and Honduras. A member of the mallow family, this tropical tree takes its common name from the similarity of its flower to an old-fashioned shaving brush. From a shiny chestnut base, the flower opens to reveal a dense array of filaments, each with a yellow pollen-bearing anther at its tip, from the centre of which protrudes a long style with a terminal stigma. Bees, hummingbirds and small mammals such as bats visit the flowers to sip nectar, but the tree can also pollinate via the wind.

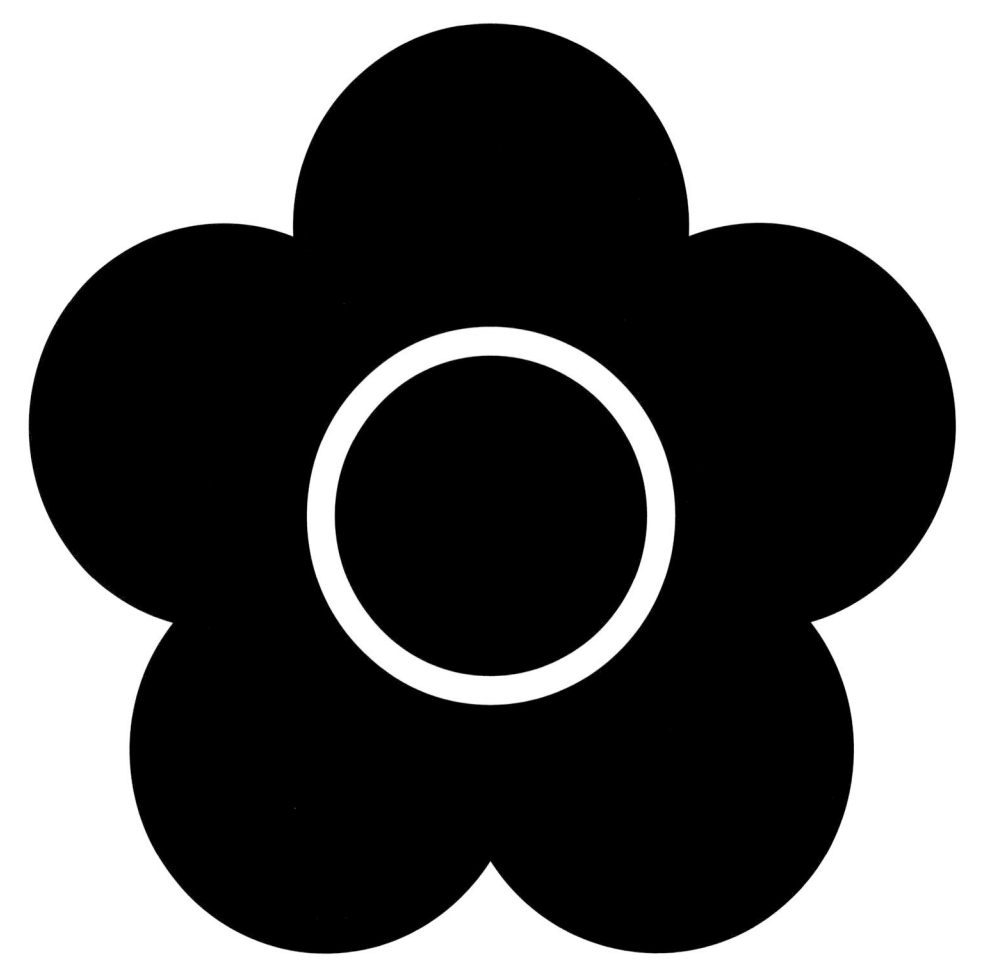

Mary Quant

Brand logo, 1966
Digital, dimensions variable

Mary Quant (1930–2023) epitomized the rebellious spirit of the 1960s and dressed a generation of young women in the playful yet practical look of the decade. Quant opened her first boutique in 1955 and went on to design and register her monochromatic and graphic daisy motif in 1966 – the same year she launched her cosmetics line and was also appointed Officer of the Order of the British Empire (OBE) for her contribution to the fashion industry. Her distinctive packaging set the benchmark for fashion branding, and Quant herself was a marketer's dream with her catchy name, bold personal style and striking Vidal Sassoon haircut, which only amplified her singular, instantly recognizable brand. The bold, Pop-art–influenced logo is symbolic of the fresh aesthetic that Quant ushered in – joyful, liberating and fuss-free, with easy tunics, miniskirts and colourful hosiery, as well as knitted cardigans and pieces inspired by men's tailoring. Quant's approach to fashion, which was inspired by music and youth culture, was entirely democratic. Operating at the height of the counter cultural flower power movement, fostered by American poet Alan Ginsberg and French photographer Marc Riboud's famous protest image (see p.326), Quant's daisy logo was emblematic of the era. Over the following decade she became a household name, and then a global one, as she broadened her business to cover lifestyle and homewares, beauty and bedding, and even a limited edition of the iconic 1960s' Mini Cooper automobile.

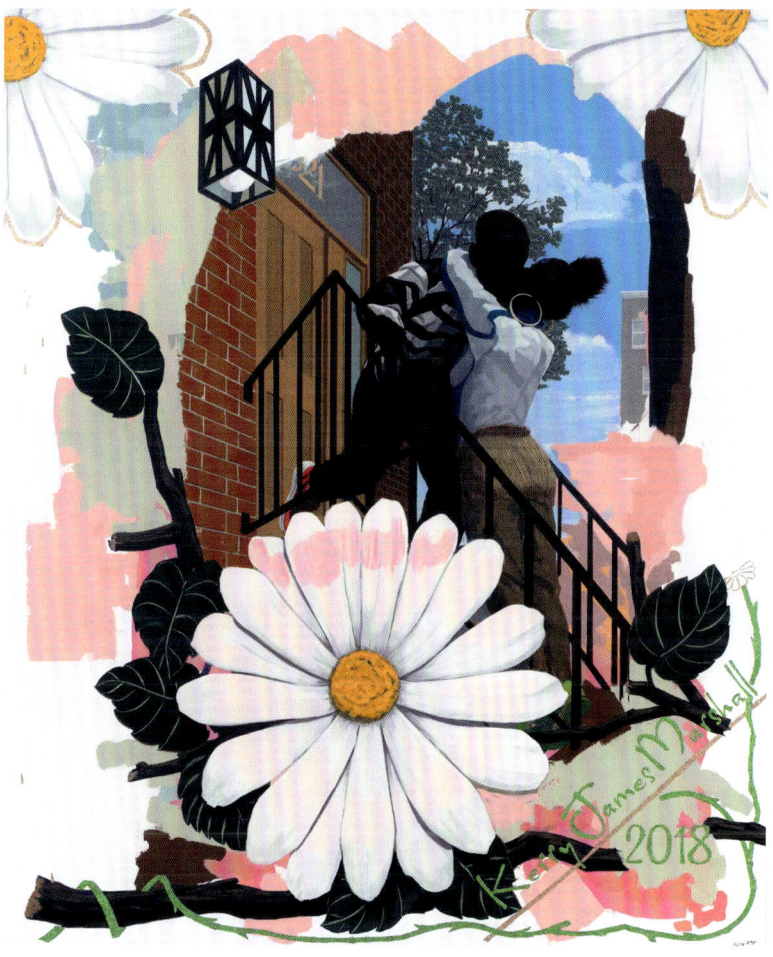

Kerry James Marshall

Vignette (The Kiss), 2018
Acrylic on PVC panel, 1.9 × 1.5 m / 6 × 5 ft
Private collection

Framed by three large daisies among a joyously coloured border, a young black couple kisses on the steps outside an urban house. The boy seems slightly taken by surprise as the girl embraces him, pulling his body towards hers. The romantic scene is one of numerous paintings in the *Vignette* series by American artist Kerry James Marshall (born 1955). The series, which began in 2003 and still continues, seeks to defy cultural expectations by

portraying black couples in love rather than in scenes of violence or tension. Inspired by Jean-Honoré Fragonard's late-eighteenth-century cycle of paintings *The Progress of Love*, the vignettes make explicit reference to the flamboyance of French Rococo painting, with its sensuality, floral motifs and strong sense of theatricality. Since the late 1970s Marshall has dedicated his career to challenging the marginalization of African Americans in art. Celebrating the history of black identity, his representational paintings exclusively feature people of colour – figures that have been historically excluded from the Western

artistic canon – creating a new vocabulary of such imagery within art history and visual culture more broadly. The composition is based on an actual event that Marshall glimpsed from his car window while driving through a Chicago neighbourhood. A moment of pure, unadorned, everyday love, surrounded by flowers laden with meanings of happiness and innocence.

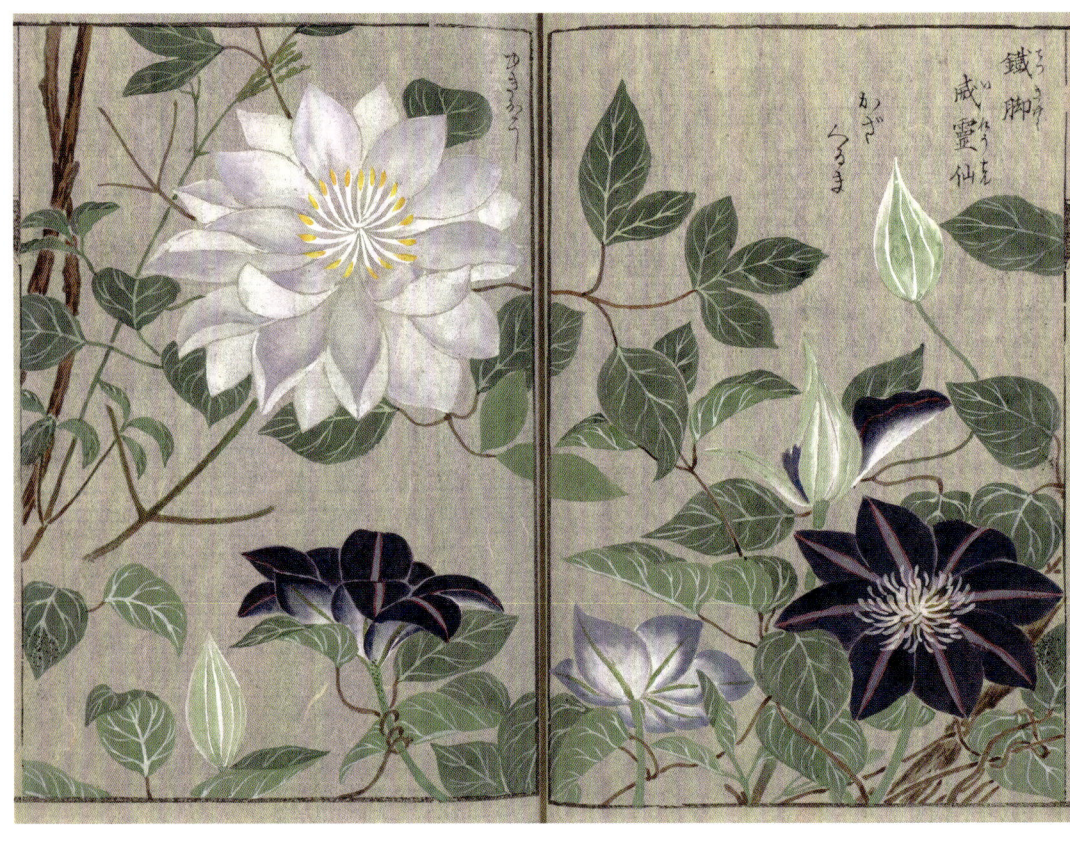

鐵脚
威靈仙

ひらうこう

かざ
くま

Kan'en

Clematis, from *Honzo Zufu or Illustrated Manual of Medicinal Plants*, 1828
Woodcut on paper, each 25.2 × 17.8 cm / 10 × 7 in
Royal Botanic Gardens, Kew, London

A brilliant white *Clematis florida* appears in full bloom above a trio of darker indigo-coloured clematis, surrounded by a tangle of vining leaves and buds. This exquisite image is a very early woodcut print from the *Honzo Zufu*, a chronicle of Japanese flora and medicinal plants compiled from 1786 to 1842 by Iwasaki Kan'en (1786–1842). Kan'en, also known as Iwasaki Tsunemasa, was

a Japanese botanist, zoologist, entomologist and samurai in the service of Tokugawa shogunate during the Edo period (1603–1867). He was a leader in plant propagation in Japan and was integral to the country's horticultural history. The *Honzo Zufu* is an important botanical work with detailed illustrations and descriptions, primarily of plants of Japanese origin; the clematis, which is native to China and was introduced later to Japan, is an exception. Originally distributed as hand-coloured manuscripts, it was not until 1920 that the work was printed as a whole in more than ninety volumes, with two full volumes of

indices. The technique of woodcut printing originated in China as early the eighth century, if not before, and a century later was adopted in Japan, where it became an important tool to document text. During the Edo period, however, the Japanese developed a way to create multiple blocks, allowing different colours to be applied and allowing the creation of illustrations as well as texts. Woodblock-printed images flourished, and the technique has come to define the Japanese aesthetic.

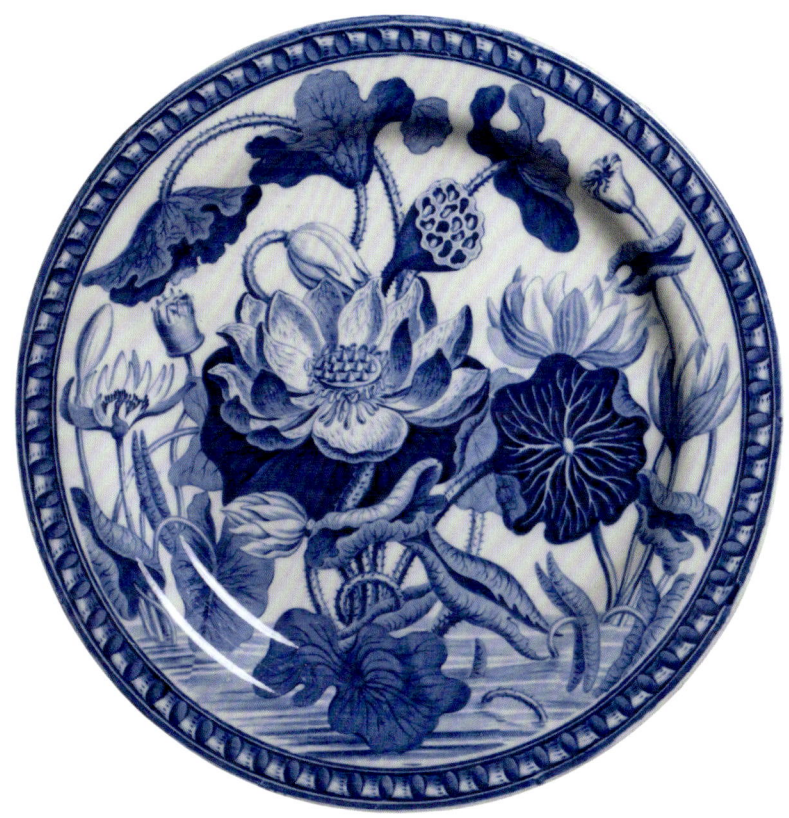

Josiah Wedgwood and Sons

Water Lily plate, from the *Darwin* service, *c.*1811
Lead-glazed earthenware transfer printed in blue
underglaze, Diam. 24.8 cm / 9¾ in
Victoria and Albert Museum, London

Three different water lilies, at the time newly
arrived in Europe from Asia and Africa, adorn this
handsome Wedgwood plate from the early 1800s.
To the left is the dainty *Nymphaea stellata* from
Southeast Asia; to the right is the blue-flowered
Nymphaea lotus, used in ancient Egypt to make
garlands for mummies; while the centre is dominated by *Nelumbo nucifera*, the sacred lotus of

Buddhism, native to India and China, its characteristic edible seed case instantly recognizable.
Designed by John Wedgwood (1776–1844), the
flowers were based on three different botanical
illustrations created between 1803 and 1806. John,
the son of Josiah, the founder of the Wedgwood
potteries, was an enthusiastic horticulturist who
helped to found the Horticultural Society of
London (now the Royal Horticultural Society)
in 1804. He introduced many floral patterns into
the Wedgwood repertoire, including this design
created for his brother-in-law Dr Robert Darwin
– although the first Darwin dinner service was

brown, the blue version proved more popular.
Later, in the mid-nineteenth century, the
so-called 'Darwin' plate surged in popularity
as Charles Darwin's theories of evolution
gained fame. These three water lilies can be
seen as evidence of evolutionary variation,
which, even in the time of Charles's grandfather
Erasmus Darwin, was prompting scientific
minds to investigate evolution.

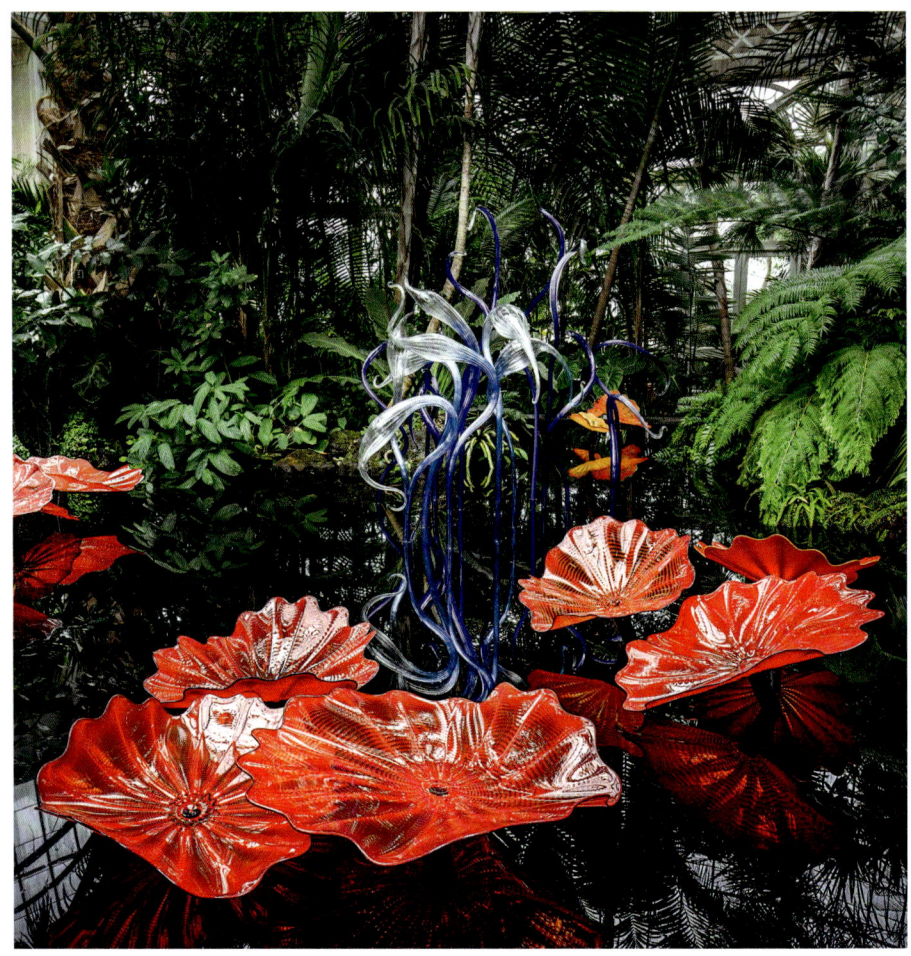

Dale Chihuly

Persian Pond and Fiori, 2017
Blown glass
New York Botanical Garden

Evoking the mystery and magic of 'the East' –
a place of luxury and refinement, science and art,
poetry and song – these asymmetrical, swirling,
floral forms give the impression of water lilies floating alongside pond irises. The installation, by
American glass sculptor Dale Chihuly (born 1941),
combines his *Persians* series with the swaying
verticals of his *Fiori* series at the entrance to the
Haupt Conservatory of the New York Botanical

Gardens. *Persian Pond and Fiori* is a reflection of
Chihuly's lifelong appreciation of glasshouses
and his interest in weaving together living plants
and glass forms in a dramatically organic setting.
Here, the ephemeral and the everlasting share
their worlds. Early in his career, Chihuly rejected
the constraints of glasswork as a craft object that
was either functional or insulated in a vitrine,
in favour of increasingly florid sculptural installations in which huge glass elements hang from
ceilings, climb the walls and occupy outdoor
spaces on an equal basis with nature. He takes
as much inspiration from Andy Warhol (see p.23)

in his collective Factory years and from Jackson
Pollock's passion for process and artistic imagination as he does from the traditions of Murano
glassblowing and the work of the Venetian
Renaissance artist Vittore Carpaccio. The human
passion for non-utilitarian, utterly superfluous
beauty has been described as one of the four main
drivers of cultural evolution: its presence is unmistakable in Chihuly's work.

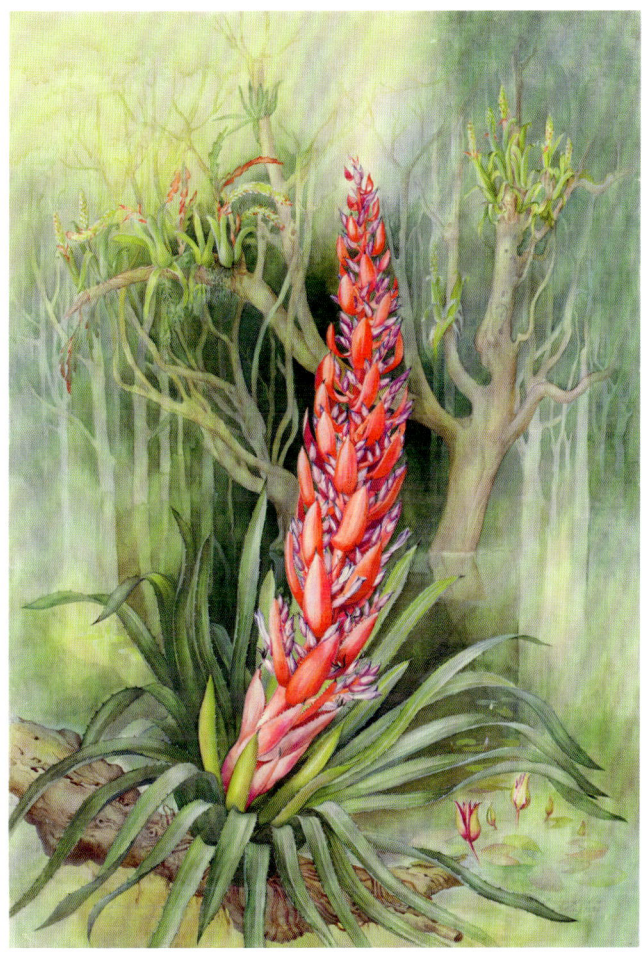

Margaret Mee

Streptocalyx poeppigii, 1985
Pencil and gouache on paper, 71.8 × 50.5 cm /
28¼ × 20 in
Margaret Mee Collection, Royal Botanic Gardens,
Kew, London

This flame-like, flowering bromeliad, now
known as *Aechmea vallerandii*, is both epiphytic
and terrestrial, either growing on another plant
for support while absorbing moisture and nutrients
from the air – as here – or flourishing alone in
rocky soil. British artist Margaret Mee (1909–88)
portrays her subject in a flooded rainforest to
show the interdependency of plants. Mee relocated to São Paulo, Brazil, in 1952 at the age of
forty-two, and became enamoured with the flower
forms of the region. In a span of more than thirty
years she embarked on fifteen expeditions along
the tributaries of the Amazon to paint and collect
a vast array of bromeliads and orchids, many for
cultivation at the Rio de Janeiro Botanical Garden.
She travelled by motorboat and dugout canoe,
slept in swaying hammocks and endured stifling
heat, torrential rains, capsized boats, lost provi-
sions, unreliable guides and the occasional illness.
With each journey, she witnessed the growing
devastation of vegetation and pollution of rivers,
and became increasingly determined to document
rare species before they disappeared. While in
England in 1988 for an exhibition of her paintings
at the Royal Botanic Gardens at Kew, however,
Mee died in a car accident. Created in her memory,
the Margaret Mee Fellowship Programme to study
at Kew has greatly benefitted Brazilian artists
and ecologists as they endeavour to continue her
mission of understanding and documenting the
biodiversity of Amazonia.

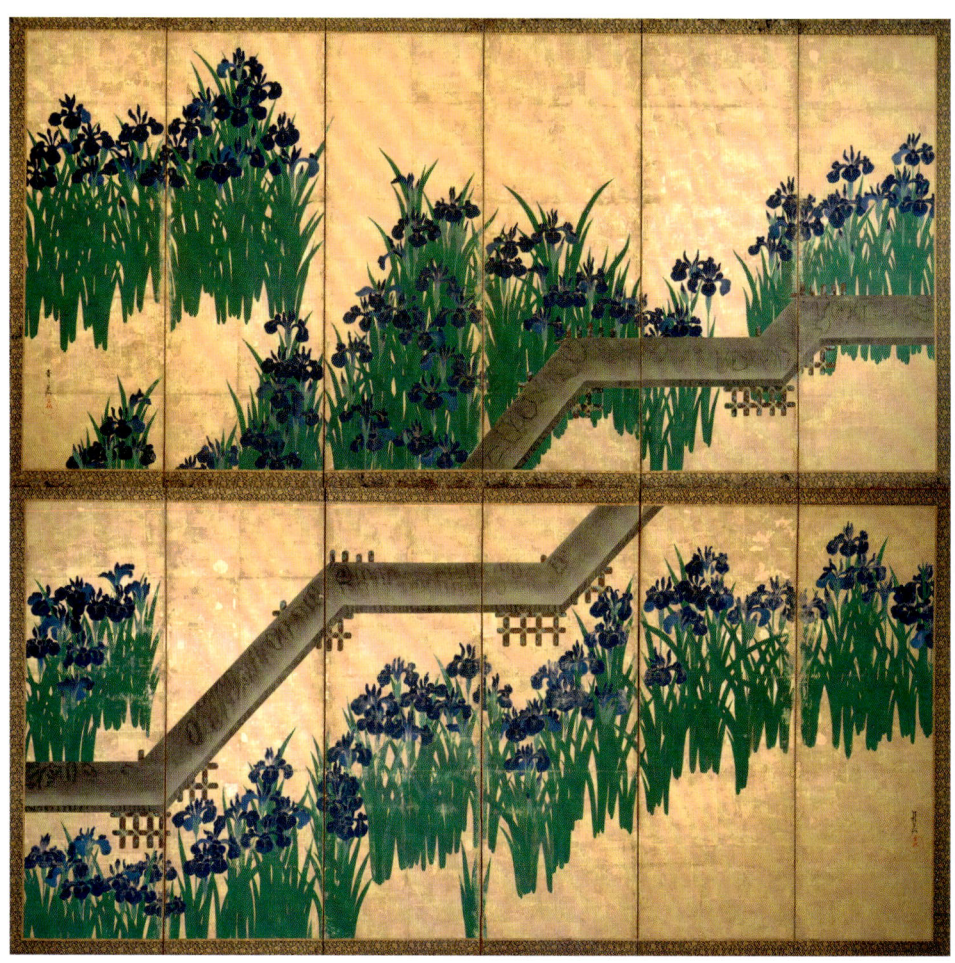

Ogata Kōrin

*Irises at Yatsuhashi (Eight Bridges), c.*1709
Pair of six-panel folding screens, ink and colour
on gold leaf on paper, each screen: 1.8 × 3.7 m /
5 ft 10 in × 12 ft 2 in
Metropolitan Museum of Art, New York

Designs based on irises were a recurring theme
in the lacquerwork of Japanese artist Ogata Kōrin
(1658–1716), but here they reach their apotheosis
on these folding screens: gorgeous in ultramarine
and verditer on a glowing background of gold
leaf, the three-dimensional composition adding
depth and dynamism to the whole. As one of the

pieces produced by Kōrin after he was awarded
the honorific *hokkyō*, the third-highest rank for
a Buddhist artist, *Irises at Yatsuhashi* is considered one of his masterpieces and an outstanding
example of Rinpa, the interdisciplinary design
aesthetic first established fifty years before in
Kyoto by the artists Tawaraya Sōtatsu and Hon'ami
Kōetsu. The image is based on an episode from
the tenth-century romance story *Ise monogatari*,
in which a poet in exile from Kyoto stops to rest
at Yatsuhashi where the river splits into eight chan-
nels, each with their own bridge. Here, he com-
poses a wistful elegy both to a lost love and

a lost city, the first letter of each line forming the
Japanese word for irises, *kakitsubata*. This is a
work steeped in Japanese folklore and artistic
tradition, yet it is also profoundly modern. In revi-
talizing Rinpa, Kōrin became part of the story
of successive waves of artistic revival in Japan. Its
influence reaches down through the centuries to
Vincent van Gogh's exuberant irises, the blocky
constructions of Paul Cézanne, the abstractions
of Henri Matisse and perhaps most of all the decorative finishes and abstracted natural forms that
characterize Art Nouveau.

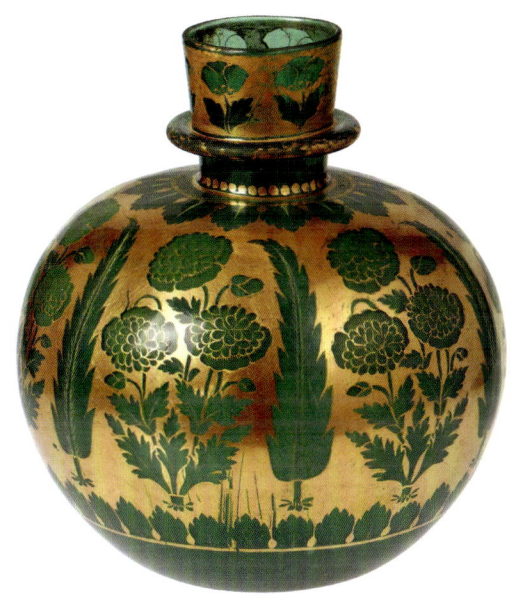

Anonymous

Huqqa (water pipe), early 18th century
Emerald-green glass decorated with gold
and yellow enamel, H. 19.4 cm / 7⅝ in
Inventory no. 10/2010,
The David Collection, Copenhagen

Made of transparent emerald-green glass, this
water pipe was made in India in the early eighteenth century, during the days of the Mughal
Empire. The *huqqa*, or hookah, was introduced
to Mughal India after being invented by Abu'l-
Fath Gilani, a Persian physician, as a means of
using water to partly purify tobacco smoke.

Painted with gold, the negative shapes depicted
include poppy flowers and cypress trees, which
appear to blow gently in the wind. Interspersed
in a regular pattern around the circumference
of the pipe, the poppies are abnormally enlarged
to match the height of the cypress trees. The
cypress is an evergreen coniferous tree that grows
in northern temperate regions, defined by its tall
pinnacle shape and rounded woody cones. Poppies,
of the family *Papaveraceae*, are herbaceous plants
that often grow with red petals. The habitual
use of opium was common at the time among
all classes of society, from emperors to manual

workers. Water pipes like this were used to smoke
opium mixed with tobacco and were often adorned
with images of the flowers. Opium, derived from
Papaver somniferum, is the latex that is taken from
the seed capsules of the flower; it is collected
through a labour-intensive process of scratching
the seeds, collecting the liquid and then drying it.

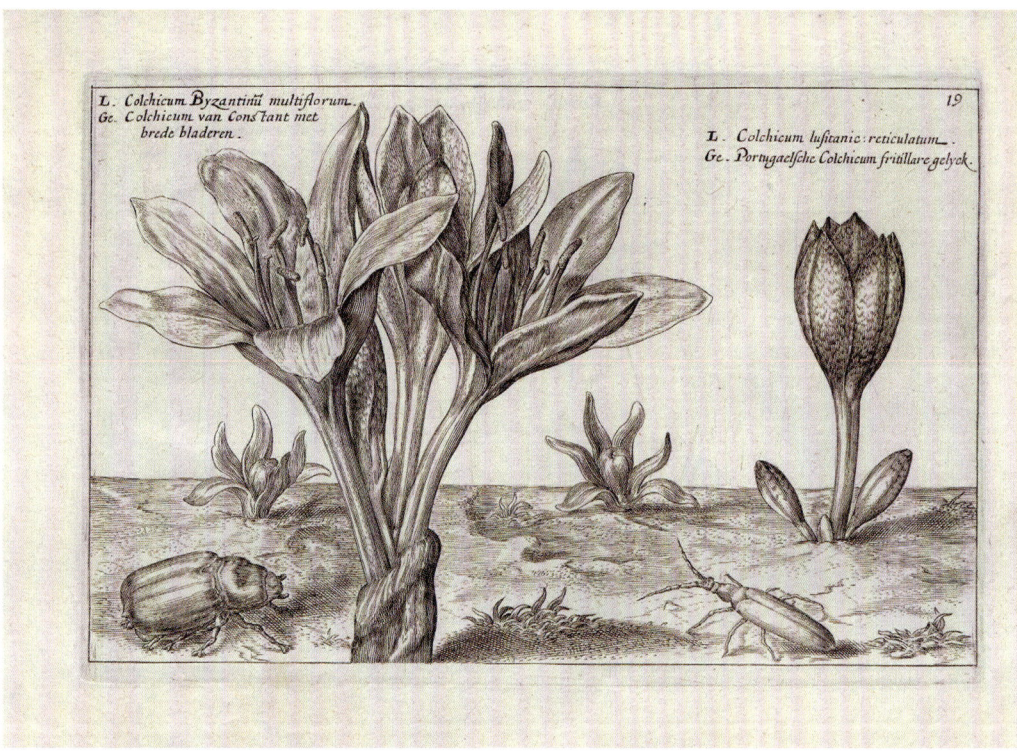

L. Colchicum Byzantinū multiflorum.
*Ge. Colchicum van Cons̄tant met
brede bladeren.*

19

L. Colchicum lusitanic̄: reticulatum.
Ge. Portugaelsche Colchicum fritillare gelyck.

Crispijn van de Passe II

Plate 19, from *Hortus Floridus*, 1614
Copperplate engraving, 17 × 26 cm / 6¾ × 10¼ in
Utrecht University Library

This engraving of two varieties of autumn flowering colchicum, a bulbous plant often mistaken for
the common crocus, was created as part of the
Hortus Floridus, one of the most popular botanical
books ever published, by Crispijn van de Passe II,
or the Younger (1593–1670), when he was just
seventeen years old. This plate depicts the large,
broadleaved saffron of Constantinople at the left,
each of its four flowers unfurled to reveal several
delicate stamens. To the right is the smaller
Portuguese saffron, with its upright petals and distinctive chequered patterning. The illustration is
one of 175 from the book drawn by van de Passe,
who belonged to a printmaking and publishing dynasty. Grouped by season, each engraving
shows a bulbous or tuberous plant growing in the
soil, attracting the interest of butterflies, bees and
other insects. The *Hortus Floridus* is of particular
significance in the history of botanical illustration
as its copper engravings provided more detail
than the common woodcut techniques of the day,
allowing van de Passe to depict his plants with
greater accuracy and artistic flourish. The book
capitalized on the contemporary appetite for
tulips and other bulbous plants among wealthy
Europeans. The Dutch edition, titled *De Blom-hof*,
even featured a list of leading tulip enthusiasts,
while later editions included an appendix dedicated
entirely to the flower, anticipating the tulipomania that would grip the Netherlands in the 1630s.

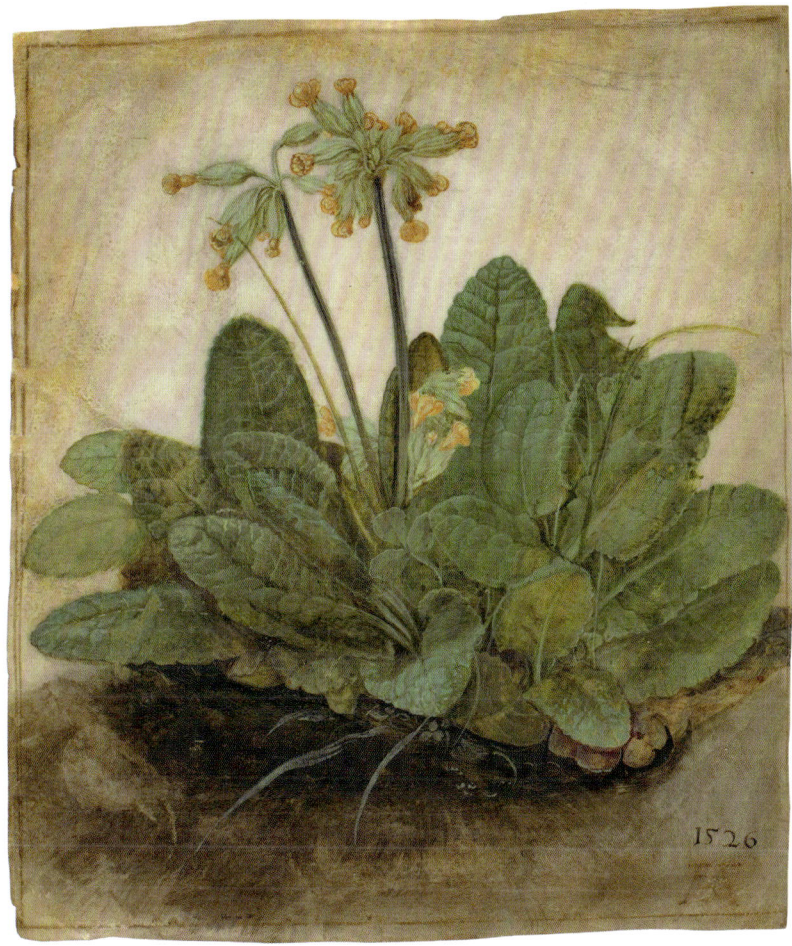

1526

Albrecht Dürer

Tuft of Cowslips, 1526
Gouache on vellum, 19.3 × 16.8 cm / 7¾ × 6¾ in
National Gallery of Art, Washington, DC

Sprouting from a patch of soil, a cluster of cow-slips (*Primula veris*) appears with stalks of golden flowers reaching above its lush green leaves. Once as common as buttercups, cowslips would have been a familiar sight for renowned German print-maker Albrecht Dürer (1471–1528), growing in spring among the pastures and meadows across Europe. *Tuft of Cowslips* is attributed to Dürer – likely working from a live plant in his studio

in Nuremberg – painted in the final years of his life, a period of relatively little output compared to the remarkable prolificacy of his earlier career. The son of a goldsmith, Dürer learned engraving from an early age, going on to apprentice with a local painter and woodcut illustrator in Nuremberg. He revolutionized the art of printmaking in the late fifteenth century, drawing significantly from works of the Italian Renaissance and contempo-raries such as Leonardo da Vinci (see p.108), who strove for the accurate depiction of both human and botanical subjects. Dürer influenced, and may have trained, Hans Weiditz (see p.144), who in

1530 produced the first lifelike plant illustra-tions for a printed herbal. Dürer breathed similar life into the flowers he created primarily for inclusion in religious paintings and altar-pieces. Cowslips often appeared growing beside the Virgin and Child because of their religious symbolism. In German the folk name for cow-slips, *Himmelsschlüssel* ('heaven's key'), linked them with entry into heaven.

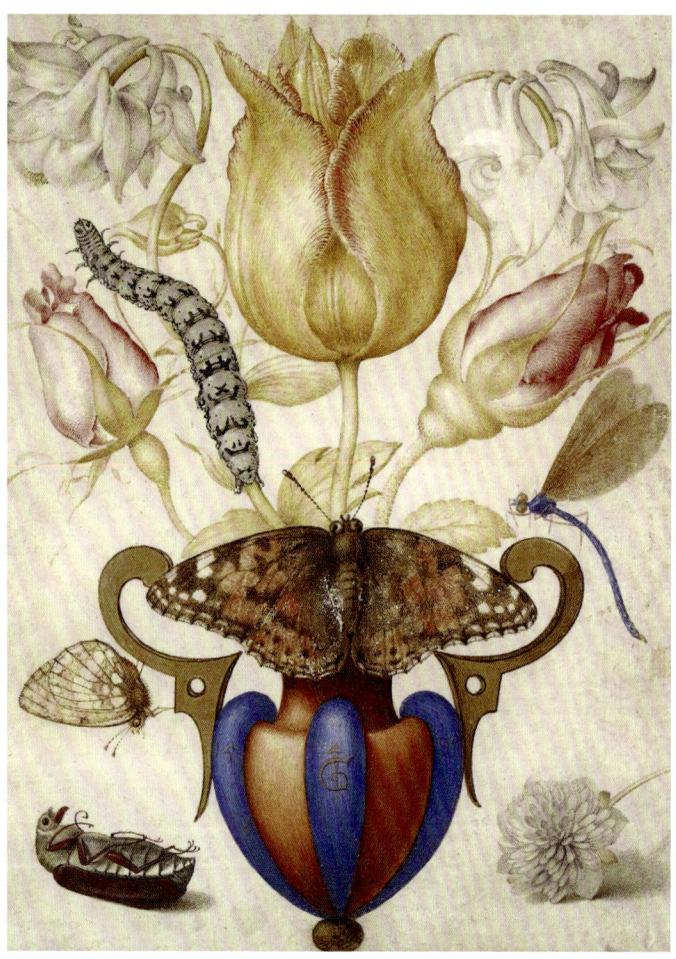

Joris Hoefnagel

Arrangement of Flowers in a Vase, with Insects, 1594
Body colour and watercolour with gold leaf
on vellum, 16.1 × 12 cm / 6¼ × 4¾ in
Ashmolean Museum, University of Oxford, UK

This exuberant depiction of a vase of flowers
and insects by Flemish artist Joris Hoefnagel
(1542–*c.*1600) effectively launched a new genre
in 1594: the floral still life. Hoefnagel was born
into a merchant family in Antwerp whose
wealth allowed him to travel to France, Spain
and England in his twenties, sketching the landscapes, flora and fauna as he went. He returned

to Antwerp, but left when the city was invaded by
the Spanish in 1576, going on to work in Augsburg,
Rome and Munich producing miniatures, illuminated manuscripts and emblems for various
courts. In 1591 Hoefnagel arrived in Frankfurt and
embarked on a successful career at the court
of Emperor Rudolf II, who had amassed a large
natural history collection, specimens from which
feature in Hoefnagel's illuminated manuscripts.
Here, the vase is from Rudolf's *Kunstkammer*,
or cabinet of curiosities, and holds flowers first
cultivated by Hoefnagel's friend Carolus Clusius,
a leading botanist and a fellow exile from the

Netherlands. The central golden tulip 'feathered'
with pinkish red was introduced from Turkey
around 1560, with an astonishing tendency to
form bicoloured patterns; yellow flowers streaked
with red were known as *bizarres*. The white aqui-
legias were a variant on the usual blue, and the
rosebuds may be double centifolias. The butterflies
and dragonfly hover as if the flowers were real,
while the caterpillar hints at a threat and the dead
beetle is a *momento mori*, which became characteristic in the still-life genre.

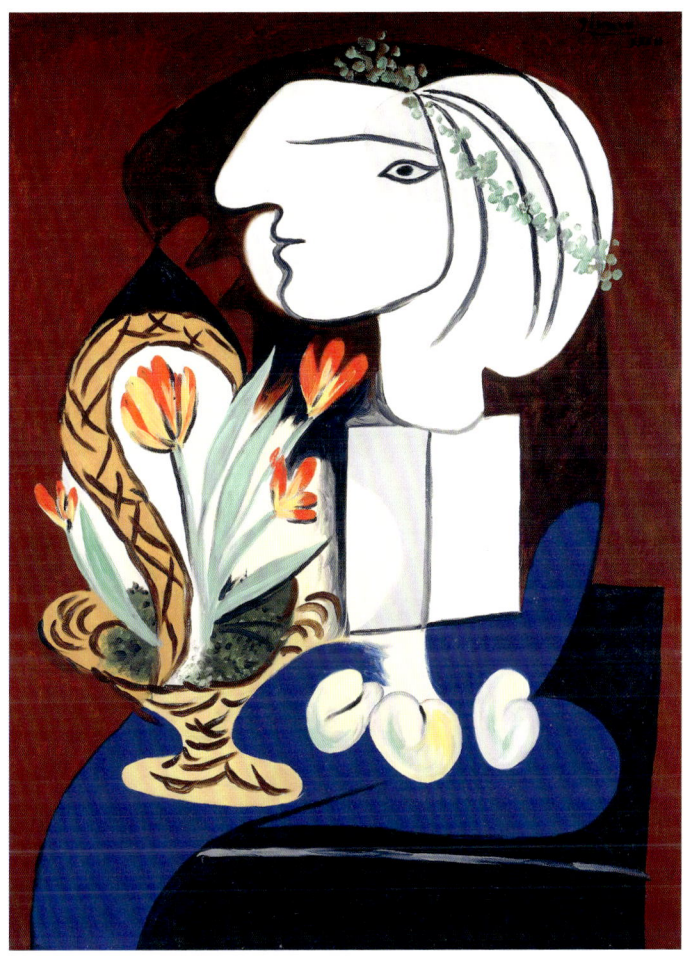

Pablo Picasso

Still Life with Tulips, 1932
Oil on canvas, 1.3 × 1 m / 4 ft 3 in × 3 ft 2 in
Private collection

A woman appears as a white marble bust on a plinth, crowned with a floral coronet. A wicker basket holds red and yellow tulips that blossom within a corona of white light, and the intense blue tablecloth and plum-like white bulbs take on obvious erotic allusions. In early 1932, the renowned Spanish artist Pablo Picasso (1881–1973) was preparing his first major retrospective, detemined to silence the critics who believed he was

yesterday's artist, no longer contemporary. In his personal life, his marriage to Olga Khokhlova was faltering, and he was in the midst of a passionate affair with the twenty-three-year-old Marie-Thérèse Walter. The painter's relationship with Walter was probably the most artistically fertile of his long life, and she was the inspiring muse of this remarkable period. Though he had known Walter since she was seventeen, when the affair began in 1927, Picasso had attempted to hide her presence in sculptures and paintings, concealing her from his wife. But something changed, and in the first months of 1932

he produced a rush of inventive portraits of his lover. In March, over the course of twelve days, he painted six large canvases – an astonishing series of masterpieces of which the first was *Nature morte aux tulipes* (*Still Life with Tulips*) where Walter appears as the marble bust. A number of Picasso's works of the time feature flowers and foliage that seem deliberately to constrain the nude body of a woman; here, however, Walter gazes beyond the tulips like the goddess Athena over the offerings of her worshippers.

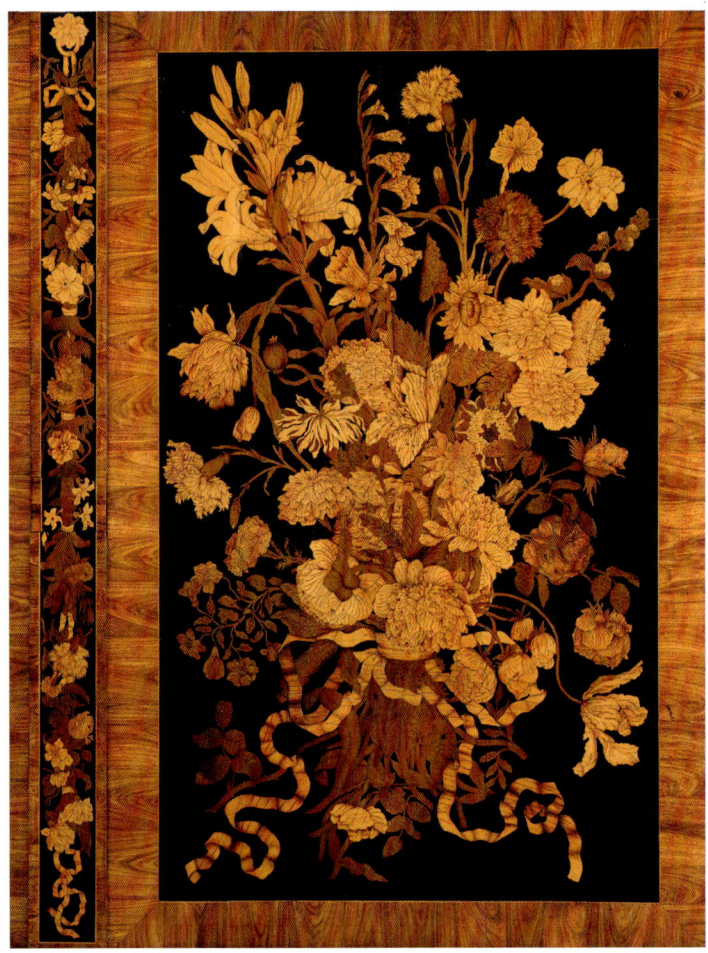

Jan van Mekeren (attrib.)

Detail of cabinet on stand, *c.*1700–1710
Oak veneered with rosewood, olivewood, ebony, holly, tulipwood, barberry and other partly green-stained marquetry woods, overall: 1.8 × 1.4 × 0.6 m / 5 ft 10 in × 4 ft 6 in × 1 ft 10 in Metropolitan Museum of Art, New York

Such is the transportative skill of the marquetry of Dutch cabinetmaker Jan van Mekeren (1658–1733) that it is as if we are looking not at a solid wooden object but rather the soft and delicate petals of a multitude of flowers gathered into a bouquet and tied gently with a ribbon. Every

bloom seems to be vying for centre stage: daffodils, carnations and tulips compete with peonies, lilies, roses and gladioli, among others. Each flower inlay – of which there are over 200 – was created separately and then combined into delicate arrangements that cover every possible surface of the household linen cupboard with flowers: the front, the sides, the horizontal bands, the stretcher and even all the way down the legs. Clearly at the height of his creative power, van Mekeren uses wood as if it were paint, creating a still-life tableau of remarkable realism. Different woods – kingwood, ebony, rosewood, olive, sycamore

and others – were selected for their ability to create light and shade, helping to provide depth, while staining and etching into the wood creates the illusion of reality. The overall shape of the cupboard is simple in its form so the marquetry has maximum impact, as van Mekeren elevates this functional piece of everyday furniture and instead seduces with the sheer powerful beauty of the flowers.

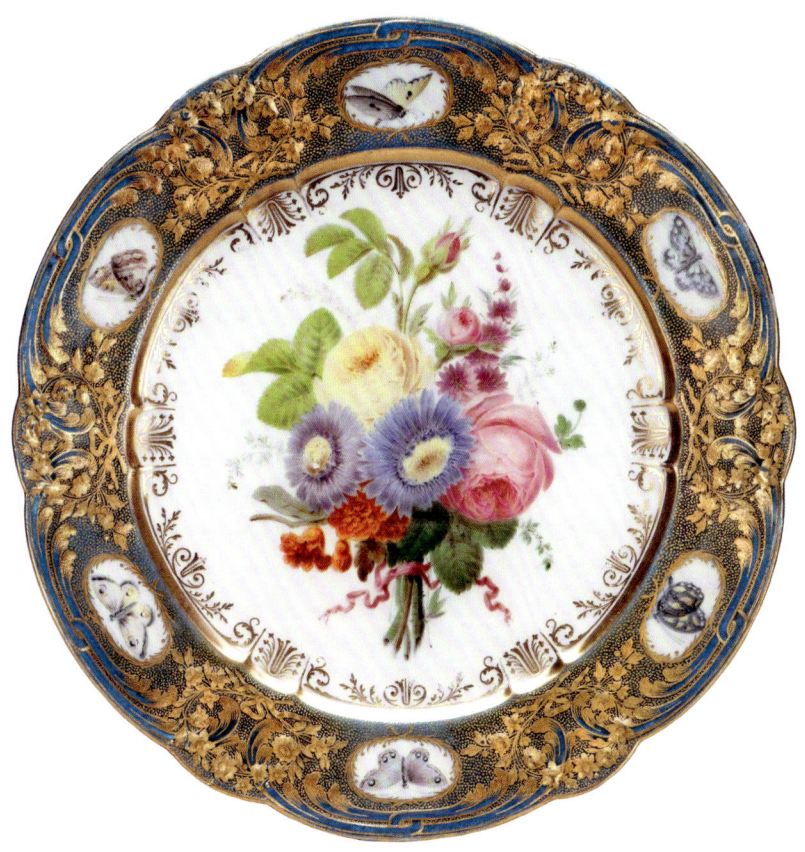

Sèvres Porcelain Factory

Plate with floral decoration, early 19th century
Soft-paste porcelain, light blue ground and gilded
decoration, Diam. 25.1 cm / 9⅞ in
Royal Collection Trust, UK

A central bouquet featuring pink and pale yellow
centifolia roses, blue China asters, pink mallow,
and a sprig of double-flowered pomegranate tied
with a pink ribbon is encircled by a vibrant blue
border with scalloped edges and intricate gilding
of flowers, bows and scrolls. This pretty porcelain
plate was made by the Sèvres Porcelain Factory
in the early nineteenth century and was part of a

set of eighteen acquired by George IV for
England's royal household around 1820. The edge
of turquoise ground, typical of the French porcelain house, is set with six ovals, each featuring
a single butterfly. Delicate and highly prized, porcelain had originally been shipped from East Asia
at great expense, but in the early eighteenth century German alchemist Johann Friedrich Böttger
discovered how to make hard-paste porcelain
and European houses such as Meissen emerged.
In France, soft-paste porcelain was made at a factory in Vincennes from 1738 but as its popularity
grew, fuelled by King Louis XV, a new factory

was built at Sèvres in 1756. It was known for its
deep *bleu céleste* background, intricate gilding and
delicate hand-painted designs, all of which made
it highly prized. The factory was also skilled
in keeping records of painters and gilders, many
of whom added their mark to the pieces they had
worked on. In turn, these craftsmen became
well-known for their specialisms; flower painters
such as Edmé-François Bouillat père, who created ribbon-tied bouquets, were well paid and
became lifelong employees of the manufacturer.

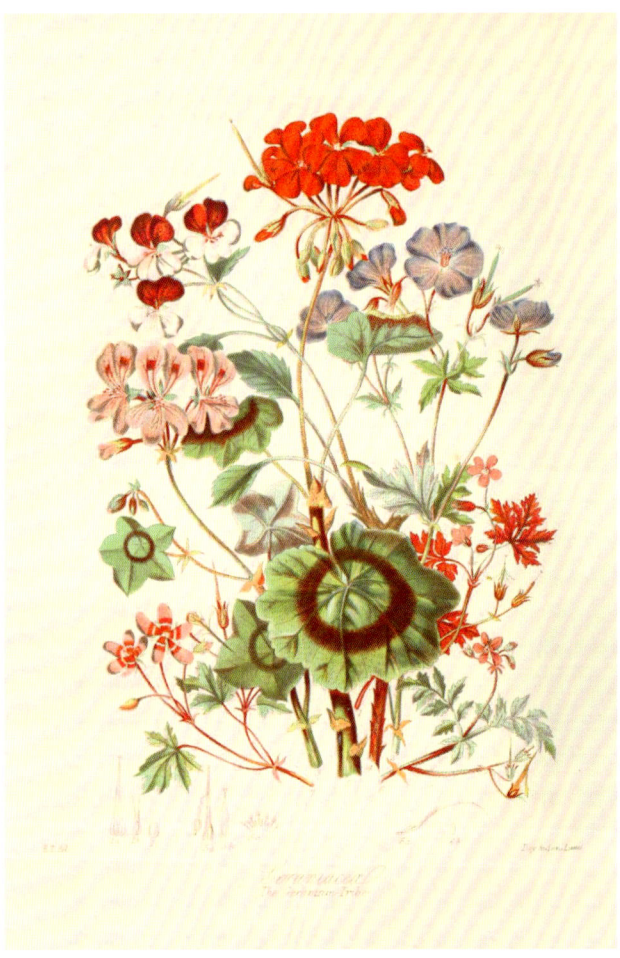

Elizabeth Twining

Geraniaceae; The Geranium Tribe, from
*Illustrations of the Natural Orders of Plants
With Groups and Descriptions*, 1868
Hand-coloured lithographs, 25 × 15 cm / 9¾ × 6 in
University of Illinois, Urbana-Champaign

Herb Robert (*Geranium robertianum*) with its striking red autumnal leaves and the pale blue wild
meadow geranium (*G. pratense*) are drawn alongside the diminuitive redstem stork's bill (*Erodium
cicutarium*) and *E. incarnatum (*now known
as *Pelargonium incarnatum*). The arrangement also
includes more tender species from the Cape of

Good Hope, such as the ivy geranium (*P. peltatum*)
and the three-coloured variety, *P. tricolor*. This
hand-coloured plate by English artist Elizabeth
Twining (1805–89) is one of 160 in her book
Illustrations of the Natural Order of Plants. First published in 1849 with the second volume in 1855,
Twining's work aimed to demystify plants: she
used simple and nontechnical language to describe
plants that she grouped by genus, outlining their
key characteristics and geographical origins.
Twining was born into the famous British tea-
merchant family and dedicated her life to writing
and drawing plants as well as philanthropic

causes, many of which were local to her home
in Twickenham in London. From an early age she
recorded flowers, re-creating flower paintings
in miniature for her doll's house. As the British
Empire expanded, the nineteenth century saw
an increasing interest in plant hunting as explorers
sourced interesting plants around the world
that could be grown in glasshouses and gardens
back in Europe. Concurrently, there was a renewed
interest in botanical art. Twining recorded plants
at the Royal Botanic Gardens at Kew in London
as well as at Lexden Park in Essex.

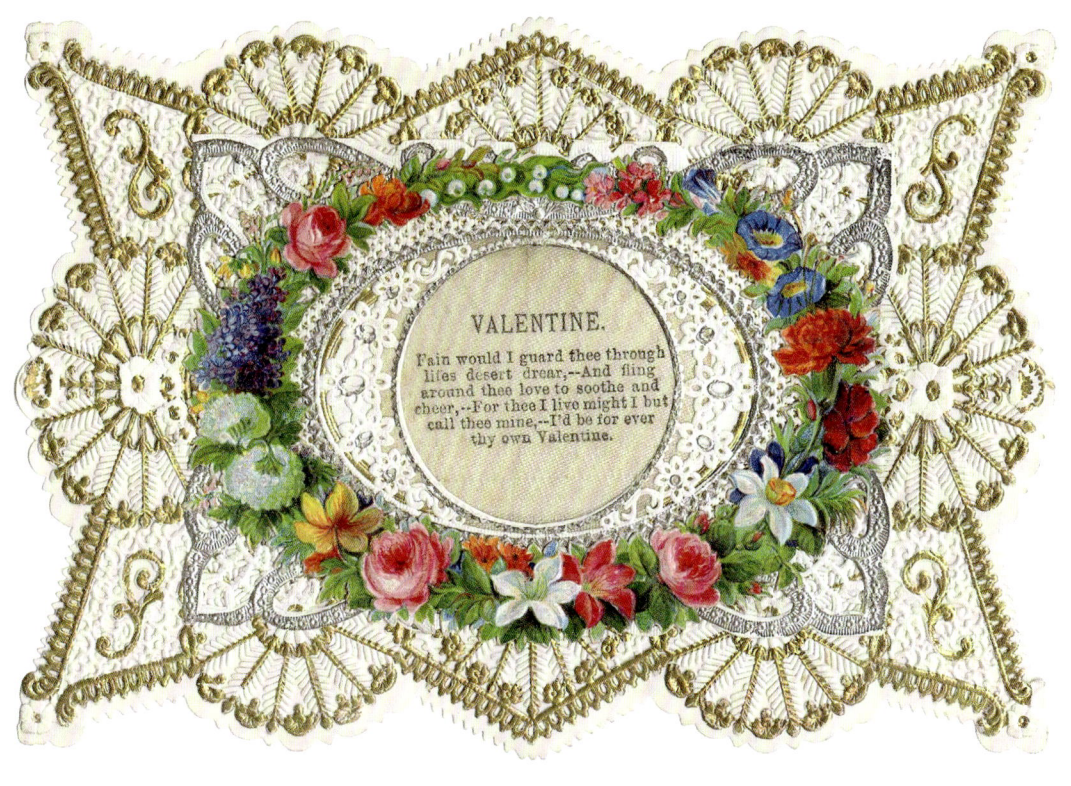

VALENTINE.

Fain would I guard thee through
lifes desert drear,--And fling
around thee love to soothe and
cheer,--For thee I live might I but
call thee mine,--I'd be for ever
thy own Valentine.

Anonymous

Valentine's Day Card, *c.*1800s
Cut paper and chromolithograph
Private collection

Delicately crafted roses, lilies, narcissi, lilacs, morning glories and other flowers woven into lush green foliage encircle a love poem – and not just any poem, but a valentine. The annual tradition has its origins in the ancient Roman Lupercalia festival, celebrated in mid-February. In the fifth century, the Catholic Pope effectively replaced the 'pagan' holiday, declaring the 14th of February as St Valentine's Day. Romantic notions were not associated with the holiday until the late fourteenth century with Chaucer's mention in *The Canterbury Tales* of birds choosing their mates on that day. In the 1820s, Londoners alone sent more than 200,000 valentines every February. The more decorative the card, the more expensive – and thus the more desirable the valentine. Recipients could expect a fanciful paper construction heavily detailed with costly effects such as embossing, colour printing and hand-dyed elements. These were flanked with further flourishes, such as romantic poetry, decorative lace and foiling, as well as coloured paper bouquets, cherubs and even real bird's feathers. The popularity of sending valentines increased through the century, and by the time the standardized penny post arrived in the 1840s, around 400,000 cards were sent each year. Although the cards were often sent anonymously, they also became an element of formal Victorian courtship. The custom was tied with the giving of flowers, as it remains to this day: more than 200 million red roses are produced for the holiday each year.

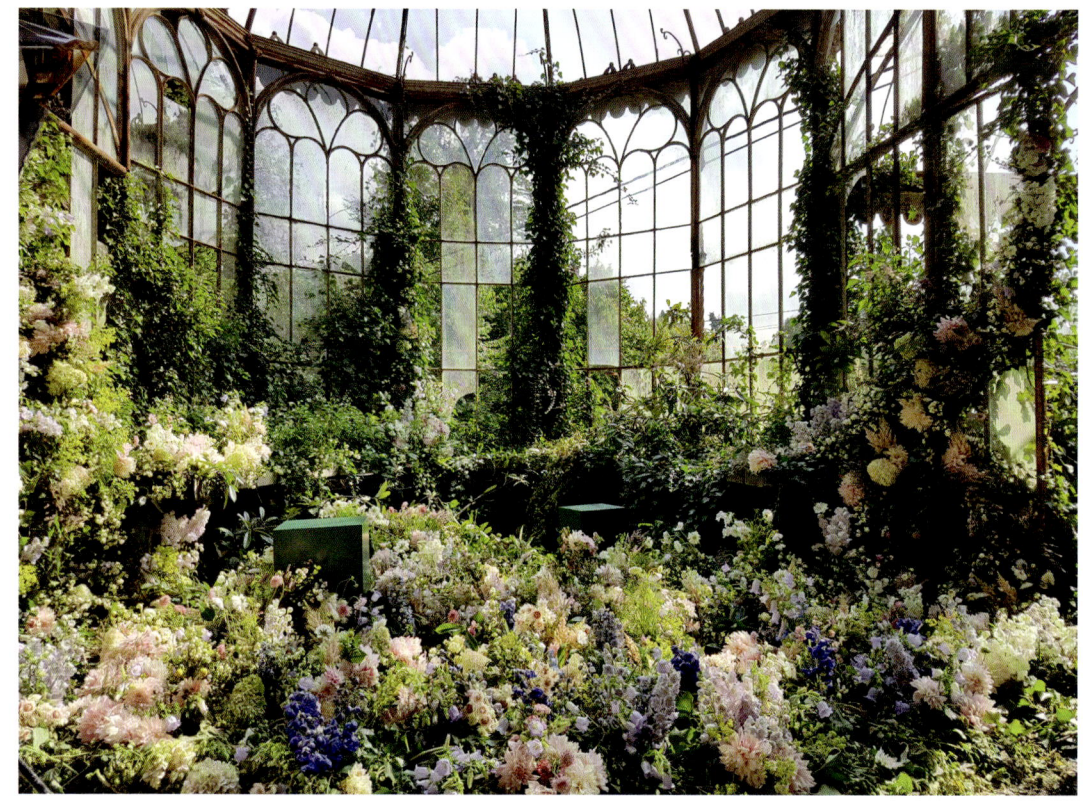

Thierry Boutemy

Lost Garden, 2006
Floral arrangement, 6 × 5 m / 20 × 16 ft

A rusted nineteenth-century glasshouse in Belgium provides a melancholy backdrop for a lush, exuberant floral installation of soft pink, blue and white flowers, including dahlias, scabiouses, panicle hydrangeas, bellflowers, cosmos, roses and trailing foliage that evoke a country garden in the middle of summer. This immersive, transportive work for a private event is typical of the evocative scenes created by Thierry Boutemy (born 1969), the French-born and Brussels-based florist who

works on fashion shows and events for luxury brands including Hermès and Dries Van Noten as well as parties and events for private clients: most famously, he created a remarkable floral wall for Kim Kardashian's marriage to Kanye West in 2014. Boutemy's ability to conjure up fantastical, dreamlike spaces has made him not only sought-after but hugely influential. He was catapulted onto the international stage when he designed eighteenth-century-style floral arrangements of luscious anemones, ranunculus, periwinkles and wild roses for Sofia Coppola's 2006 film *Marie Antoinette*. That spirit is tangible here

in the broken panes of glass and pillars covered in rambling evergreens. Boutemy is a potent storyteller with flowers and plants, but all of his work is anchored by a sense of naturalism – even if it's sometimes based in a hyperreality – and a reverence for nature that was nurtured from his childhood in Normandy.

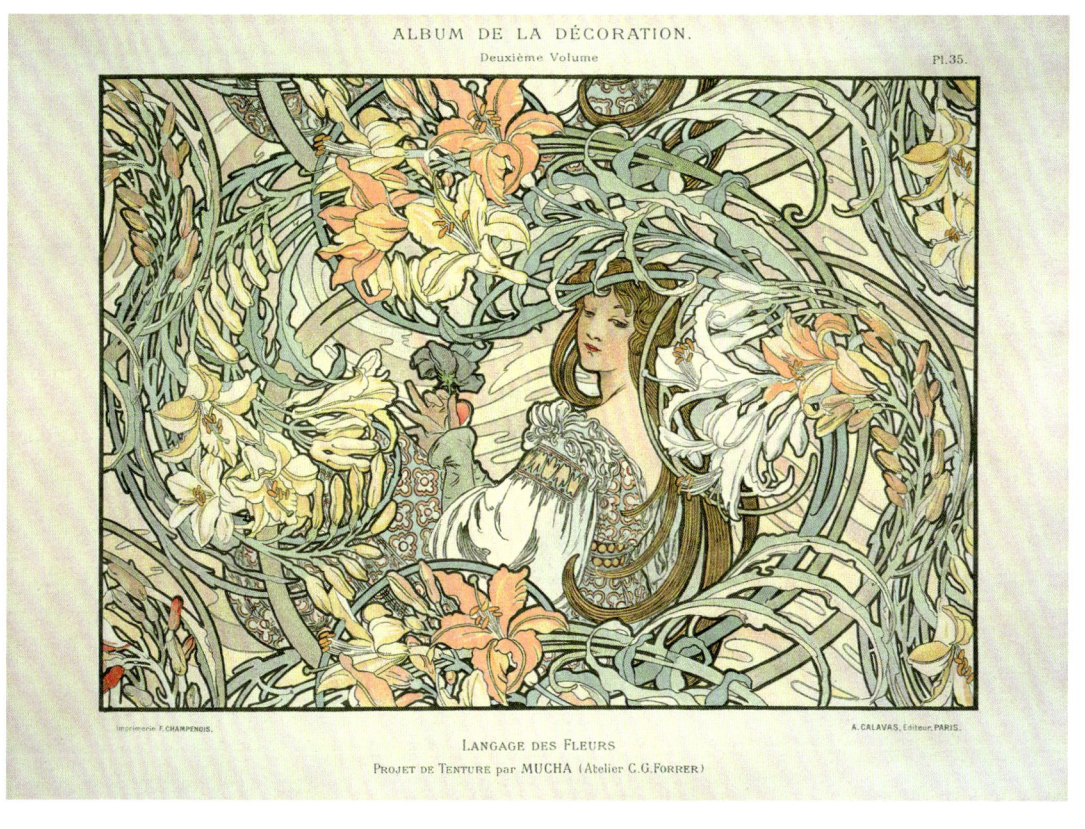

Alphonse Mucha

Langage des Fleurs, from
Album de la Décoration, 1900
Colour lithograph, 26.5 × 36.5 cm / 10½ × 14¼ in
Private collection

Flowing locks of auburn hair and swirling stems of pastel coloured lilies are typical of the designs that the Czech-born artist Alphonse Mucha (1860–1939) painted at the start of the twentieth century. His instantly recognizable style was synonymous with the Art Nouveau movement in France and beyond. This lithograph, part of a loose-leaf folio collection of prints by various artists, was printed by the Imprimerie Champenois in Paris. The album was intended to provide models for adaptation by designers of textiles, wallpaper, ceramics and jewellery. The printing firm and publisher signed an exclusive contract with Mucha in 1896, making him a household name by mass-producing his work in the form of theater programmes, books, menus and postcards. Mucha also credited the *Exposition Universelle* staged in Paris in 1900 with helping spread his style internationally by 'bringing aesthetic values into arts and crafts' and into the domestic sphere. He succeeded in his aim to make high-quality, affordable art available to ordinary people. The title of this print, translated as the 'Language of Flowers', stemmed from the Victorian obsession with floriography. The lily represents purity, reflected by the coy expression of the beautiful young woman at the centre of the stylized labyrinth of flowers. Her pose and billowing white dress stand in contrast to many of Mucha's earlier poster designs of bewitching and provocative beauties – although the notion of purity is perhaps belied by the arc of her bare neck and shoulder.

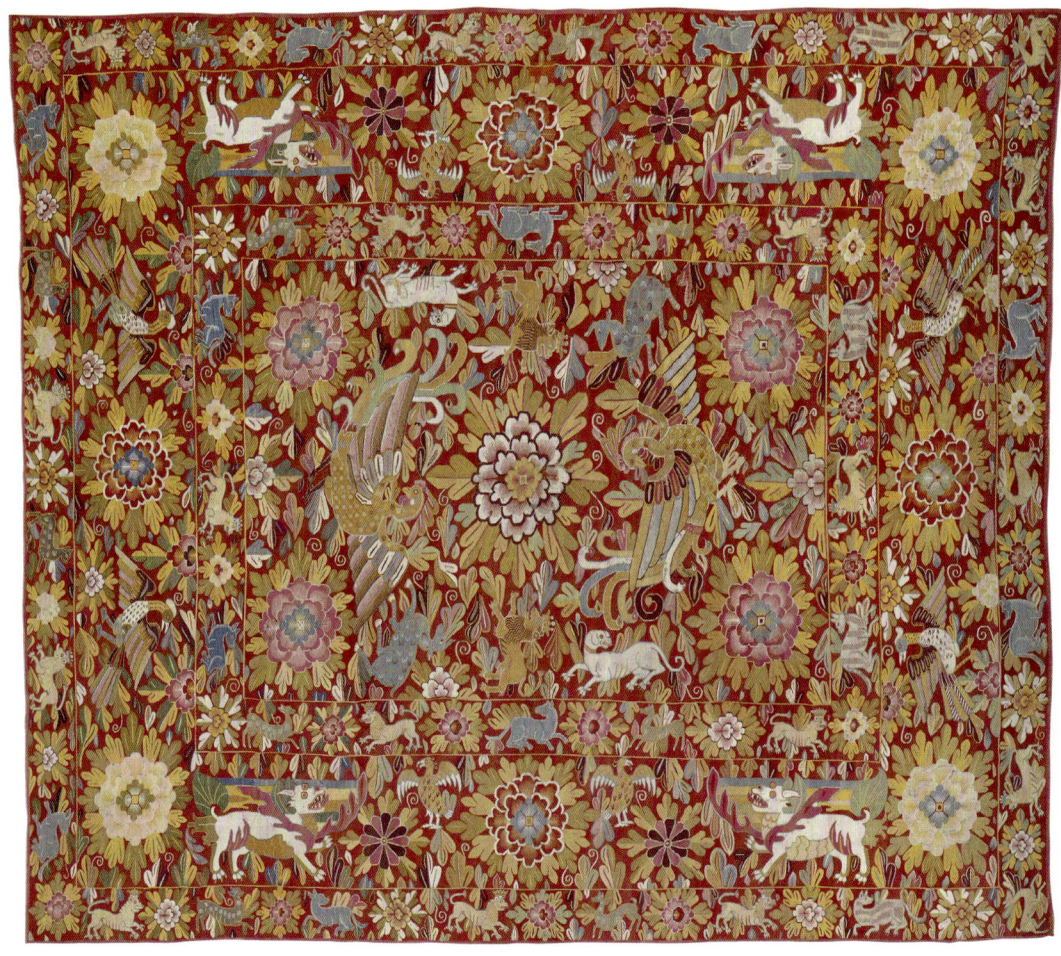

Anonymous

Cover, late 17th–early 18th century
Wool, silk, cotton, and linen interlocked
and dovetailed tapestry, 2.4 × 2.1 m /
7 ft 10 in × 6 ft 10 in
Museum of Fine Arts, Boston

Although the imagery in this spectacular tapestry
is based directly on figures from Ming and Qing
dynasty silk embroideries, it was created not in
China but Peru by weavers who incorporated local
flair into a wild, kaleidoscopic scene that is evidence of the globalization of Asian artistic influence in the Americas in the decades around

1700. Stylized flowers and animals run alternately
in bands: the flowers – based on peonies, which
are a traditional Chinese symbol of wealth and
honour – are shown in full bloom, radiant, with
an extra corona of leaves; the animals are based
on Chinese mythical beasts called *xiezhi*. In the
centre, two birds open their spectacular wings
as if in full flight, inspired by Chinese phoenixes.
The whole composition seems to rotate on a central axis, with each pictorial element weighted
so that it is perfectly balanced and no one element takes precedence. Red, the most auspicious
colour in China, fills the background; but here,

the colour is much deeper than its counterpart
would have been in Asia, thanks to the traditional
Peruvian technique of using cochineal beetles
collected from local cacti to create a striking crimson dye. Asian influence in American visual arts
began in the sixteenth century and reached its
height in the popular chinoiserie decorative style
of the mid-eighteenth century.

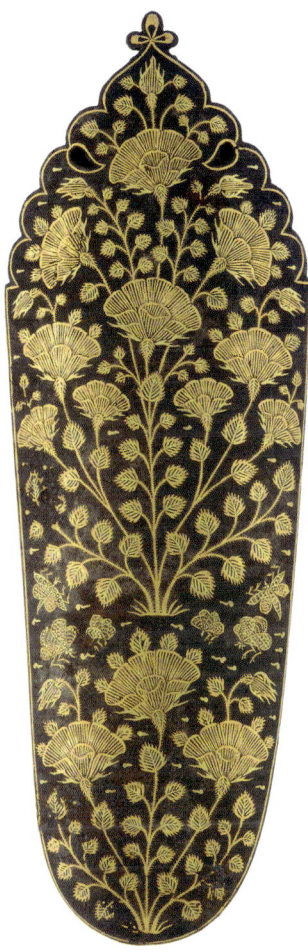

Anonymous

Chape of a scabbard, 17th century
Iron inlaid with gold, 11.2 × 3.8 × 1.6 cm /
4½ × 1½ × ½ in
National Museum of Asian Art, Washington, DC

The beauty of these shimmering golden flowers belies what this object was designed to cover and protect: this is an iron chape for the tip of a scabbard that carried a sword or knife. The tip of the blade sat in the rounded bottom of the scabbard, while the two holes at the other end would have helped attach it to the leather case. The flowers are poppies, rendered in such a way as to suggest they are swaying in a breeze, with the decorative impact heightened by the leaves and a few insects – all laid out in a radiant symmetrical pattern. This artefact was made during the Mughal Empire that controlled large swathes of India and Pakistan in the sixteenth and seventeenth centuries. The empire has been praised for both its religious tolerance and its refined culture, best represented in the building of the Taj Mahal. An object such as this reminds us of the refinement of the higher classes at the time, and is an example of the use of flowers to communicate a sense of cultural exclusivity. However, as with any empire, the Mughals came to power and often ruled through violence. This object represents that contradiction, at once threatening and beautiful, the pattern of flowers camouflaging the potential of repression and the threat of violence.

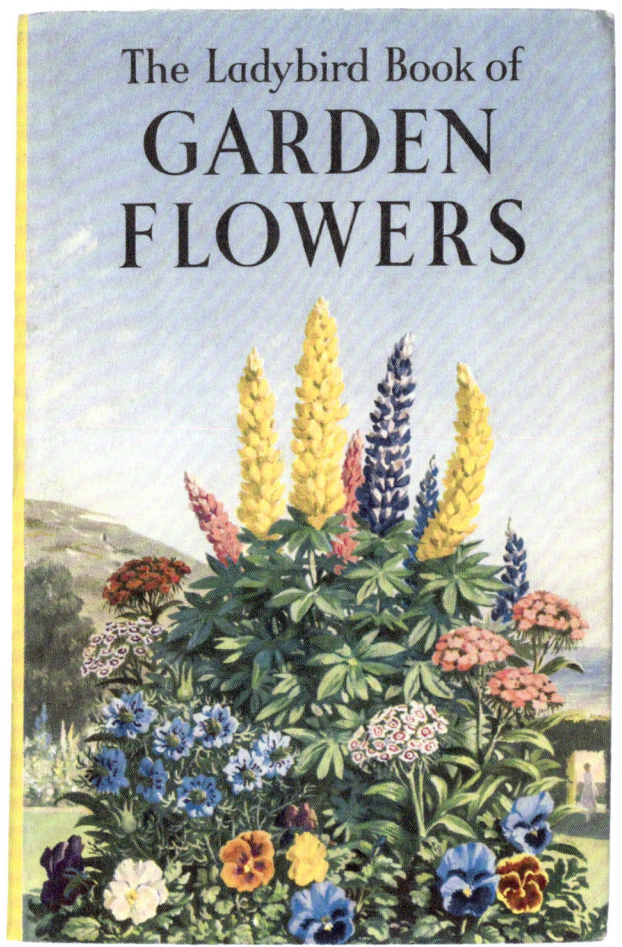

The Ladybird Book of

GARDEN
FLOWERS

John Leigh-Pemberton and Brian Vesey-Fitzgerald

The Ladybird Book of Garden Flowers, 1960
Colour lithograph, 18 × 12 cm / 7 × 4¾ in
Private collection

This profusion of lupins, sweet Williams, pansies and nigella, or love-in-a-mist, sums up the early summer peak of a garden near the English coast, with the sea glimpsed beyond the rising hills in the distance. The illustrations by British artist John Leigh-Pemberton (1911–97), based on original oil paintings, are familiar to generations of young Britons, for whom Ladybird books were an introduction to reading and a first guide

to many aspects of daily life. Wills & Hepworth first began publishing the Ladybird imprint in 1915, but it gained widespread popularity only after World War II. Informative and entertaining, its titles included both fiction and nonfiction covering all aspects of post-war life. *The Ladybird Book of Garden Flowers* comes from the *Nature* series launched in 1953 and is characterized by the accessible but authoritative writing of Brian Vesey-Fitzgerald (1900–81), a distinguished naturalist and prolific author. Inside, the format follows the course of the gardening year. Each right-hand page is filled with an image of a garden in bloom,

from the first snowdrops of the year to the helle-bores, or Christmas roses, via tulips, larkspur, sunflowers and red-hot pokers; the left-hand pages contain a key and a short description of each flower, including its family, flowering times and practical hints and tips on cultivation. Idyllic though the gardens may be, this was no mere picture book. Rather, it is intended to inspire young readers to pick up watering cans and garden tools and go about creating their own floral worlds.

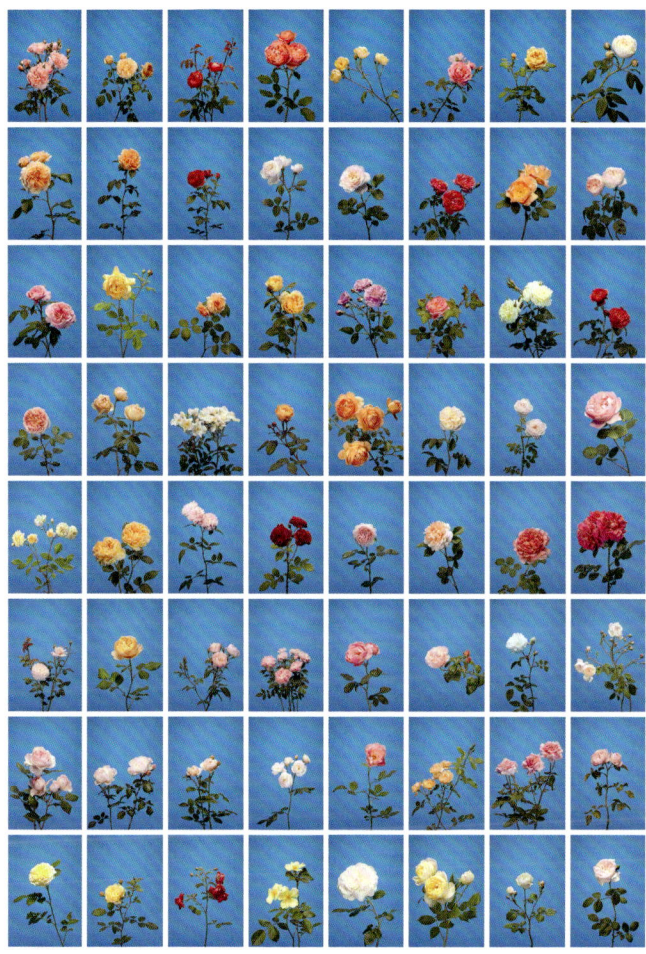

Luke Stephenson

The English Rose, 2019
Printed poster, 59.4 × 42 cm / 23½ × 16½ in

Showcasing the rich diversity of the English rose, the national flower of England, British photographer Luke Stephenson (born 1983) assembles sixty-four modern varieties in this vibrantly colourful grid. Traditionally associated with royalty, religion and beauty, the symbolic flower has for centuries dominated the nation's poetry, art and literature. However, the modern English rose was popularized in the 1960s by David Austin. The celebrated British breeder crossed antique varieties

(those introduced before 1867) with modern roses (hybrids and floribundas) to create plants that have the character of old garden roses but are able to flower for longer. Stephenson spent two summers at the headquarters of David Austin Roses, photographing the flowers in a small makeshift studio. He shows each stem in isolation against a rich blue backdrop with a retro quality reminiscent of 1970s flower books. The colour gives the flowers a rich luminosity, intensifying their lush pinks, deep crimsons, lemon yellows and milky whites. Each rose is named after a famous English person, such as the Roald Dahl, whose

peach-coloured bloom evokes the eponymous fruit from the celebrated author's children's tale *James and the Giant Peach*. Another, the Maid Marion, is named after the companion of legendary Robin Hood in English folklore and has clear mid-pink, saucer-shaped rosettes. Others are named for Emily Brontë, Dame Judi Dench, Anne Boleyn and Austin's own daughter, Claire.

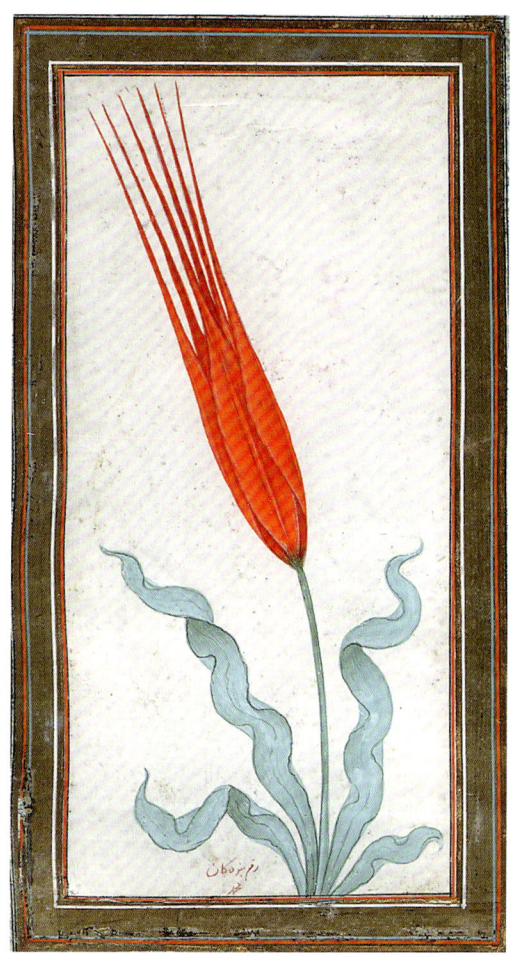

Mehmed Bendegân

Plate from *Sultan Ahmed III's Tulip Album*, *c.*1725
Watercolour and body colour, full page:
30.9 × 21.7 cm / 12 × 8½ in
Private collection

The Istanbul tulip, with its distinctive dager-shaped petals with needle-like points, is preserved in the precious albums created during the reign of Ottoman Sultan Ahmed III (1673–1736). Ahmed ushered in a period of prosperity and artistic achievement known as the Tulip Era after the craze for the flowers that swept the Ottoman elite. Much like the earlier tulipomania in the Netherlands, the demand for tulip bulbs among the wealthy, especially for unique varieties, increased exponentially, and bulbs were bought and sold for small fortunes. In the gardens of the Topkapı Palace in Istanbul, the flowers were staged on wooden pyramids, while at night the grand vizier's tulip gardens were lit with mirrored lanterns and candles carried on the backs of tortoises. Tulip councils ensured standards of perfection, and the best blooms were given fabulous names: the albums record 'scarlet swallow', 'one that confuses reason', 'pomegranate lance' and the yellow 'vizier's finger'. The first Istanbul tulip, 'Light of Paradise', was cultivated in the sixteenth century, and by the time Ahmed's reign ended in 1730, more than 2,000 individual varieties had been named. The craze began to disappear by the 1750s and the tulips were all but lost by 1800, surviving primarily on Iznik tiles (see p.72) and later-period ceramics and textiles. Today, the form of the Istanbul tulip can still be found in the species *Tulipa acuminata*. Ahmed's tulip festivals remain legendary, however, and are still celebrated each spring in Istanbul.

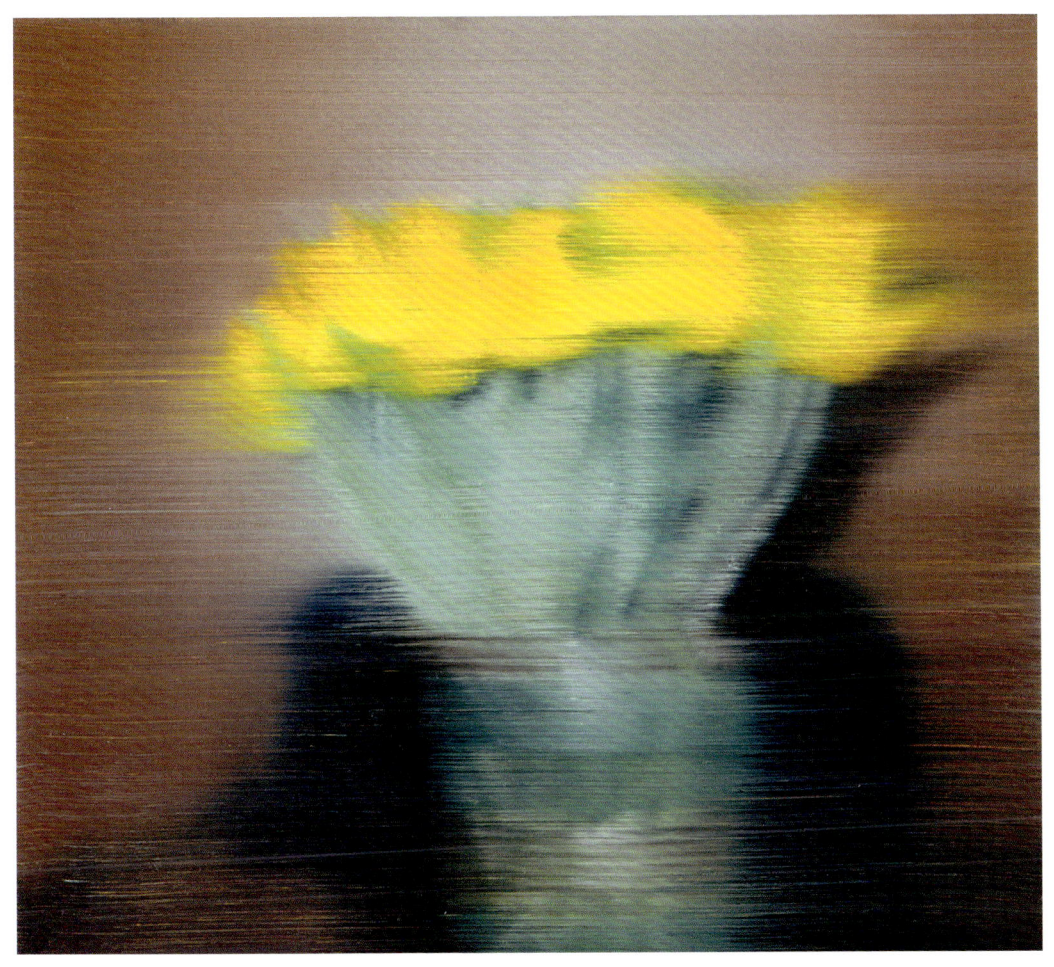

Gerhard Richter

Tulips, 1995
Oil on canvas, 36 × 41 cm / 14¼ × 16 in
Österreichische Galerie Belvedere, Vienna
(on loan from a private collection)

In the traditional language of flowers, tulips are a declaration of love, and yellow tulips signify a loving, sunny smile. This painting by German artist Gerhard Richter (born 1932) can be seen as a personal celebration of the artist's new wife, Sabine Moritz, and their newborn son. It was painted at the same time as a series of paintings Richter made of his wife and son that, with what

has been called their 'almost palpable tenderness', are among the most intimate of the artist's works. Richter is known for the variety of his painting styles and subject matter, often incorporating visual effects from photography, most famously a blurred, out-of-focus rendition. He has written that 'the photograph is the most perfect picture', and he describes blurring as simply a way of equalizing transitions and making the elements of a painting fit together, wiping away excess detail. A similar principle dates back to the fifteenth-century Italian Renaissance, and can be seen in the *sfumato* technique of Leonardo da Vinci

(see p.108). Richter begins by projecting a photograph onto the canvas and tracing its form; basing his palette on the original photograph, he replicates the image and applies his blur – sometimes gently with a soft brush, sometimes aggressively with a homemade squeegee. The bleary haze of *Tulips* suggests the flowers in motion and blurs the line between figuration and abstraction.

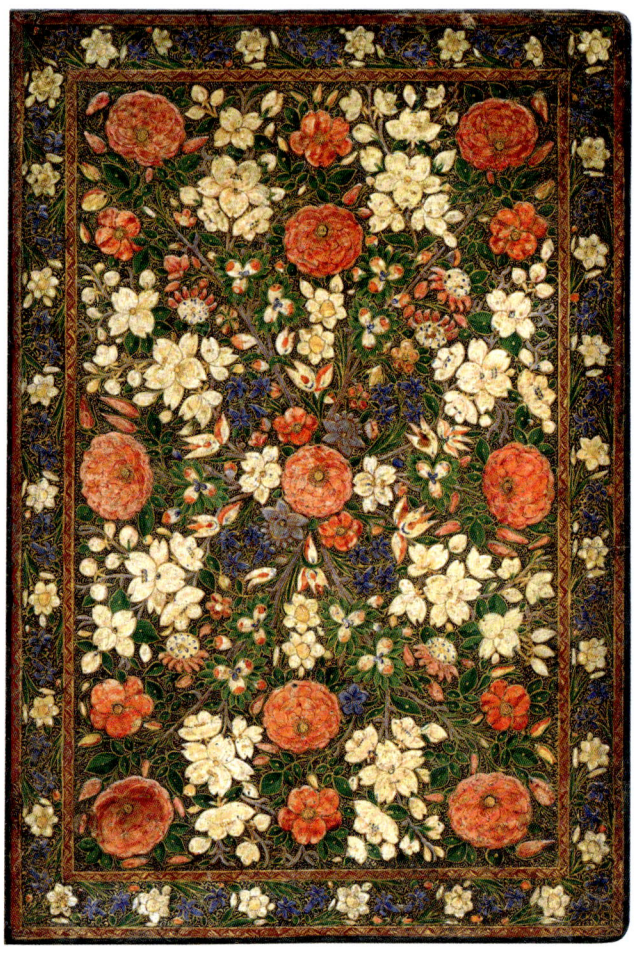

Anonymous

Kashmiri book cover, early 19th century
Lacquer painting on papier-mâché, 33.5 × 25 cm /
13¼ × 9¾ in
British Museum, London

An elaborate papier-mâché design of flowers and
stems radiates from the centre of this book cover
in the Kashmiri *hazara* (thousand flowers) style.
The dominant red Persian roses link the design
to the introduction of papier-mâché techniques
to Kashmir in the fourteenth century, when the
scholar, poet and mystic Shah-i-Hamadan is said
to have migrated from Iran to Kashmir with

hundreds of skilled artists and craftsmen, who
taught the local population many of the crafts still
in use today. Stems of bright blue hyacinths grow
from the heart of the pattern, surrounded by two
paler blue scilla flowers and small clusters of the
Lady Tulip (*Tulipa clusiana*) – a species native to
the western Himalayas with red and white pointed
petals. Sprays of cherry blossom extend to the
border of white blossom and hyacinths. The cover
would have been made in two stages by different
specialist artisans. The *sakhtasaz* formed the base
structure by moulding pulp paper and repeatedly
rubbing it smooth, while the *naqqashi* painted the

freehand design with brushes made of cat, goat
or donkey hair. Highlighted with fine gold-leaf
scrollwork, the black background was likely created from charred dung. Pigments were derived
from vegetables and minerals: blues and violets
from indigo leaf, red from cochineal or saffron and
brown from walnut skins. Once the painting was
completed, it was polished again with a jade stone
and then coated in layers of lacquer to create the
trademark shine and impressive durability.

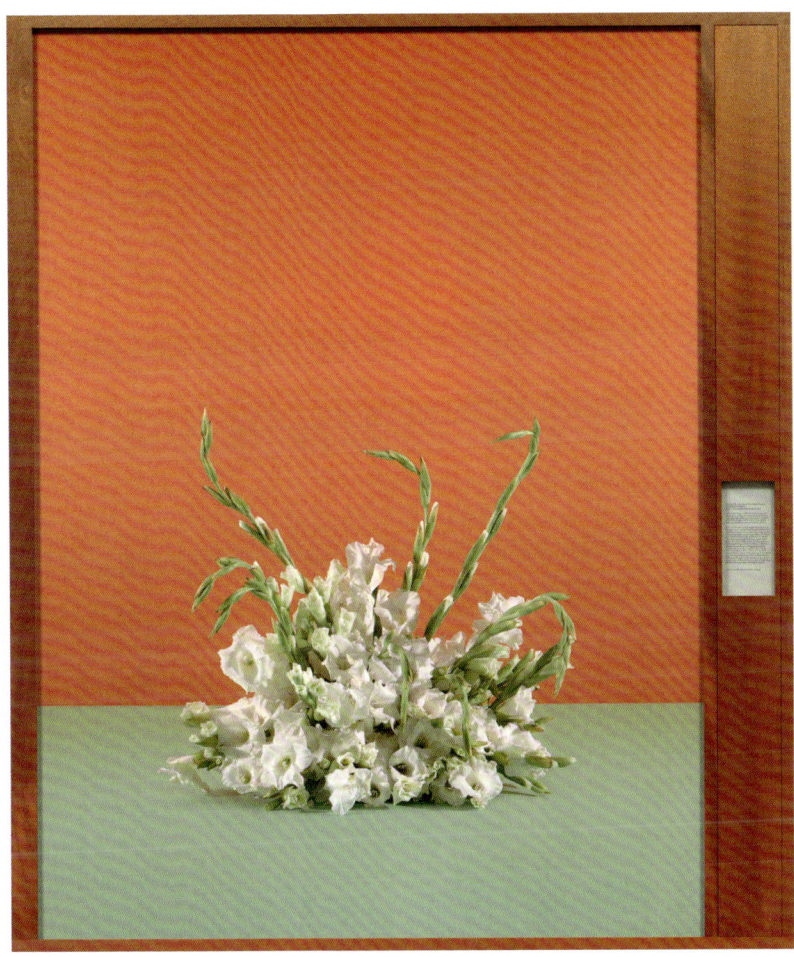

Taryn Simon

Agreement for cooperation on China's Beidou Navigation Satellite in Pakistan, Aiwan-e-Sadr, Islamabad, Pakistan, May 22, 2013, from *Paperwork and the Will of Capital*, 2015
Archival inkjet print and text on archival herbarium paper in mahogany frame, 2.2 × 1.9 × 0.1 m / 7 ft 1 in × 6 ft 1 in × 3 in
National Gallery of Canada, Ottawa

In her *Paperwork and the Will of Capital* series, American artist Taryn Simon (born 1975) sets sumptuous floral centrepieces against minimal colour fields. Re-created from archival

photographs of the signings of political treaties and decrees, the dramatic flower arrangements, along with their flag-like backgrounds, underscore the pageantry and performance of governmental power. This arrangement of *Gladiolus* hybrids is a re-creation of a centrepiece made to commemorate the signing of a political accord in 2013. China, concerned by the dominance of the United States' Global Positioning System (GPS) satellites, cemented a deal to enhance China's own satellite system, 'Beidou', with its ally Pakistan in the presidential palace Aiwan-e-Sadr in Islamabad. Embedded in the frame on the right side Simon

provides a piece of contextual information: 'Establishing Beidou ground stations in Pakistan could bolster Pakistan's national defense technology by enhancing the reliability and accuracy of various guided weapons systems.' The work points towards Simon's wider interests, including the examination of hidden histories, and the contours and mechanics of state-led power and its effects both globally and locally. Simon invites us to consider striking arrangements of flowers as agents carrying meaning, representing accord, alliance, perhaps even peace between nations – all the while building greater state-level powers.

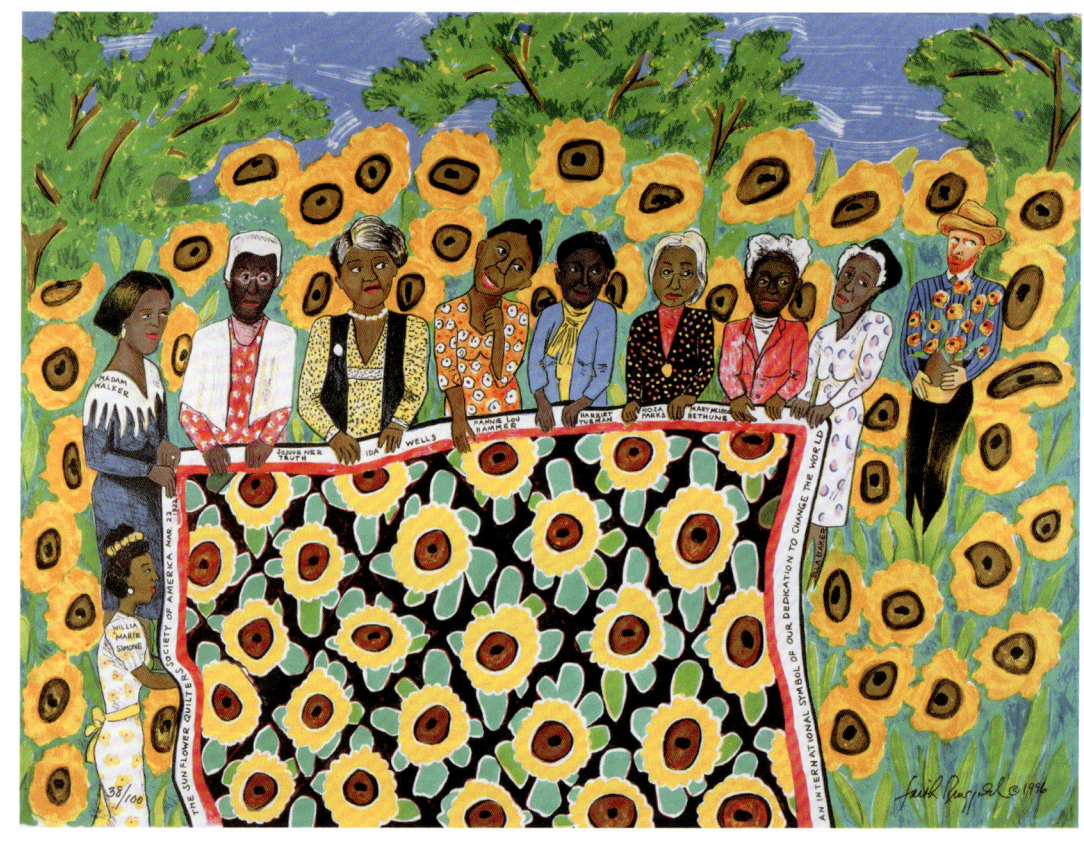

Faith Ringgold

The Sunflower Quilting Bee at Arles, 1996
Colour lithograph, 55.9 × 76.2 cm / 22 × 30 in
Philadelphia Museum of Art, Pennsylvania

It's March 1922 and the Sunflower Quilters Society of America has gathered amid a field of sunflowers in southern France to create a colourful new quilt. The fictional group, created by American artist Faith Ringgold (1930–2024), includes eight prominent women's and civil rights activists from African-American history: Madam C.J. Walker, Sojourner Truth, Ida Wells, Fannie Lou Hammer, Harriet Tubman, Rosa Parks, Mary McLeod Bethune and Ella Baker. A ninth figure on the lower left is the artist's alter ego, Willia Marie Simone. Ringgold's print shows the women holding up their vibrant quilt, which is adorned with sunflowers and represents their communal dedication to changing the world. Behind them is Vincent van Gogh; the vase of sunflowers in his hands refers to the many paintings he made of the subject (see p.47), but his presence is also a more general symbol of Western art history. Ringgold contrasted the notion of the heroic white male painter with the collective and traditionally female activity of quilting, whose roots lie in the slave culture of pre–Civil War era America. Ringgold is celebrated for paintings, quilts and murals that explore issues of race, gender and cultural identity. An activist since the 1960s, she had consistently challenged perceptions of African-American identity and gender inequality, both in the art world and in society at large.

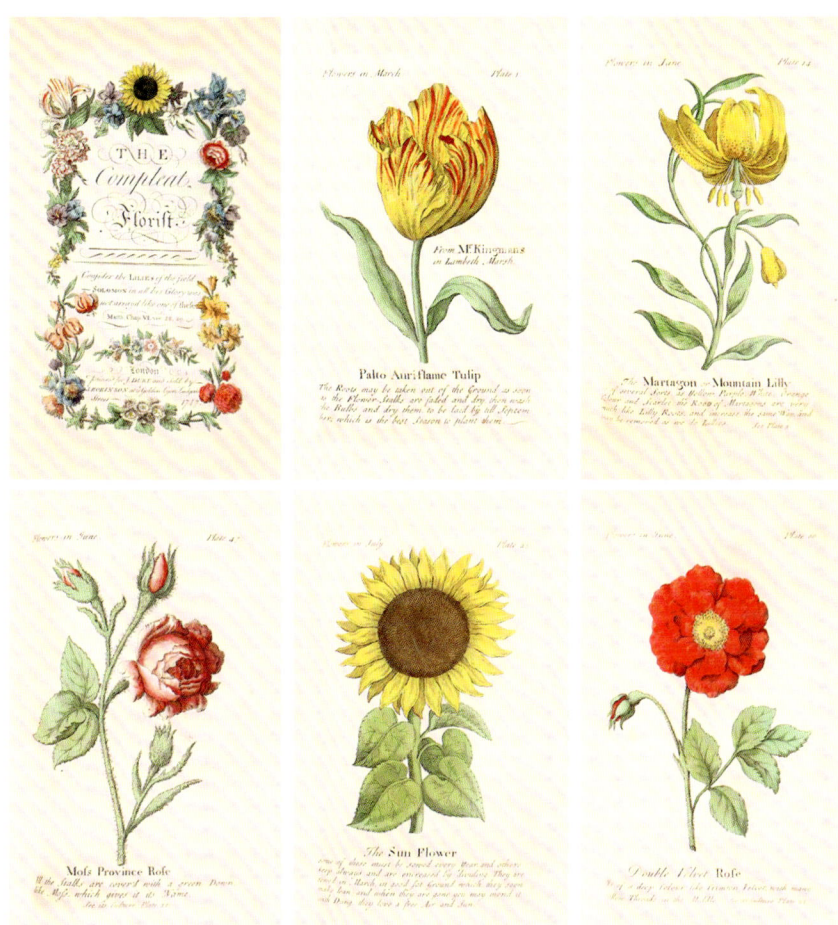

John Carwitham

Pages from *The Compleat Florist*, 1747
Hand-coloured engraving, 22.8 × 13.3 cm /
9 × 5¼ in
Private collection

The elaborate title page of *The Compleat Florist*
by John Carwitham (active *c*.1723–41) features
a floral border showcasing the flowers to be found
within the book's pages – anemones, tulips, lilies,
carnations, roses, irises, auriculas – while the
selection of plates depict the Palto Auriflame tulip,
the yellow flowered Pyrenean lily, moss Provence
rose, sunflower and double velvet rose. Each

of the one hundred plates in this exquisitely illustrated eighteenth-century herbal, engraved by
an unknown artist, includes detailed information
about the plant, its growing habit and flowering
season. The representation of each plant generally follows traditional botanical illustration:
a single plant against a white background in its
full-flowering glory, the leaves and blooms turned
towards the reader to showcase the essential
traits of the plant. But while the illustrations might
make *The Compleat Florist*, first published in two
parts in 1740, resemble any other eighteenth-
century herbal, it was in fact more of a plant

catalogue. Listing the species in fashion at the
time, it was designed to appeal to and be accessible
for professional and amateur growers alike: the
word 'florist' at the time referred to any cultivator
of flowers. Unlike more scientific herbals, the book
also included growing and caring instructions.
As such, Carwitham's work offers a rare glimpse
of the cultural tastes of plant growers around
Europe at a specific moment in history – one
when the study and cultivation of plants began
to increase dramatically in popularity.

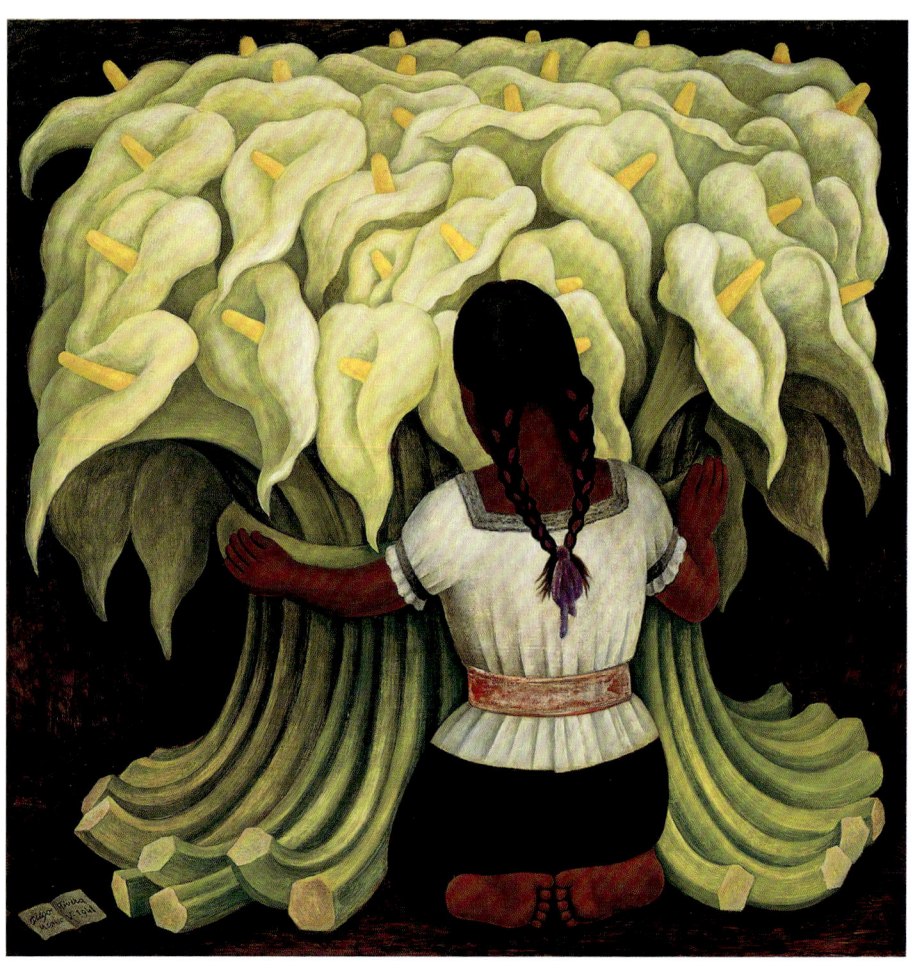

Diego Rivera

The Flower Vendor (Girl with Lilies), 1941
Oil on Masonite, 1.2 × 1.2 m / 4 × 4 ft
Norton Simon Museum, Pasadena, California

A young flower seller, shoeless and simply dressed, kneels before an enormous bundle of calla lilies in an almost devotional pose. The waxy, funnel-shaped flowers dwarf the girl's small frame; her dark, plaited hair and olive-brown skin contrast with the lilies' ivory petals and light yellow stamens. The artist Diego Rivera (1886–1957) intended the painting to honour the everyday life of workers in his native Mexico. The calla lil-

ies, often associated with funerals and death in Mexican culture, are both a tribute to the splendour of indigenous Mexican cultures as well as their suffering. These lilies (*Zantedeschia aethiopica*) were introduced to the Americas from South Africa in the seventeenth century. The image of the flower seller was a recurring motif in Rivera's works on canvas, as well as in the celebrated large-scale public murals he painted in Mexico and the United States. Rivera, who is regarded as one of the most influential Mexican artists of the twentieth century, was highly political, and his images of indigenous people

served to highlight the social inequality and poverty that many experienced following the Mexican Revolution (1910–20), which brought significant shifts in the country's economy, culture and society. Along with the work of his wife, the artist Frida Kahlo, Rivera's paintings and murals attempted to define a new national identity for Mexico by promoting the notion that its indigenous communities and traditional cultures should be recognized as the foundation of the Mexican society.

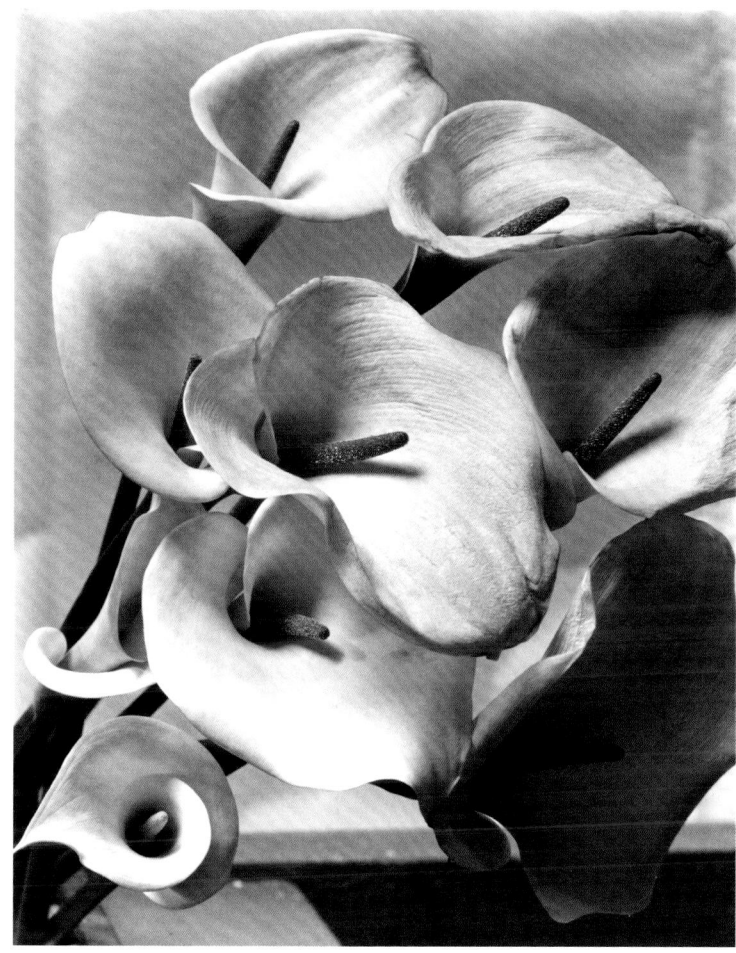

Imogen Cunningham

Callas, c.1925
Gelatin silver print, 24.1 × 19 cm / 9½ × 7½ in
Imogen Cunningham Trust

Both a scientist and a sensualist, Imogen Cunningham (1883–1976) was one of the most influential American photographers of the twentieth century. Her deep understanding of the chemical processes involved in photography led to significant technical breakthroughs, while her images – from nudes to landscapes to botanical studies – pulse with energy and life. Cunningham first began photographing plants in the botany department at the University of Seattle as a way of paying for her tuition, but it was not until moving to San Francisco in 1917 that her interest in the flora of California really took hold, producing bold, graphic forms. The series of studies she produced throughout the 1920s – of plants including magnolias, agaves and these elegant sculptural calla lilies – are among her best-known works, and brought her into the orbit of contemporaries such as Ansel Adams (see p.30) and Edward Weston. Together, they formed a loose association known as Group f.64, bound by a set of aesthetic principles that included a focus on natural forms and found objects, tight framing and a shunning of artifice in all forms, including the use of artificial light. Precise and filled with detail, this carefully composed monochromatic study is the perfect expression of the new modernist aesthetic that was emerging at this time, and of the unbridled pleasure Cunningham took in the natural forms of the world around her.

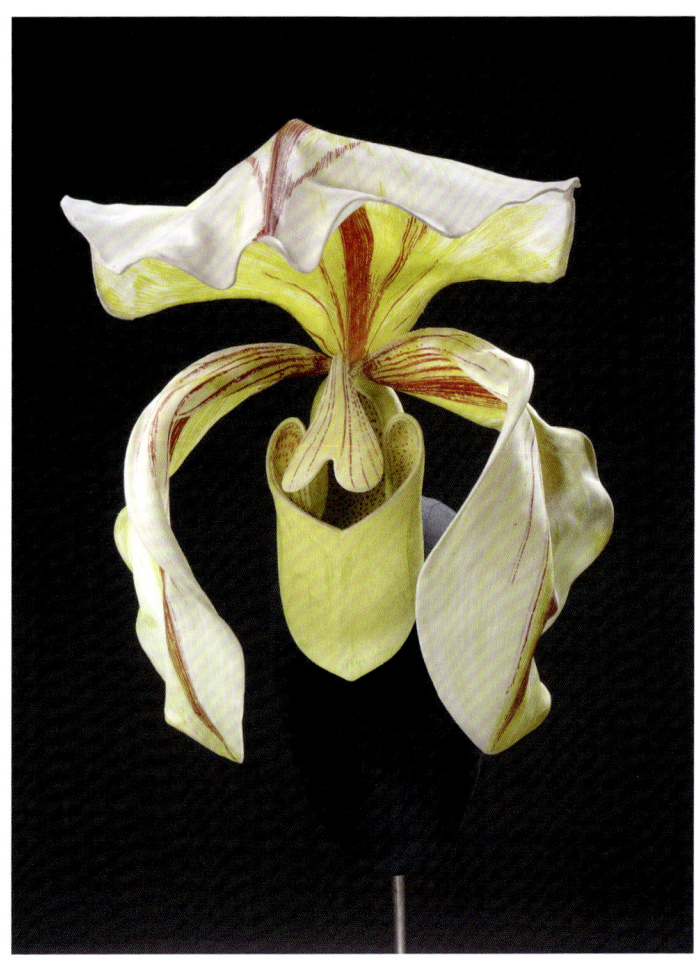

Philip Treacy

Orchid Hat, 2011
Hand-painted silk with wired edges,
25.5 cm / 10 in
Victoria and Albert Museum, London

After visiting Singapore, the Asian heartland of orchid floristry, in the late 1990s, avant-garde British milliner Philip Treacy (born 1967) was bewitched by the beauty of one of nature's most intriguing flowers. Known for creating fantastical haute couture hats since the late 1980s, Treacy used the exotic forms of the orchid as the inspiration for a number of hats. Here, he was inspired by the lady slipper (*Paphiopedilum*), crafting its petals from sculpted silk and hand-painting the streaks of chartreuse and red. The Latin name stems from the Greek myth of Aphrodite being born out of the sea and landing at Paphos (*Paphio-*), while its shape resembles that of a slipper (*pedilon*) suitable to a goddess. The actual purpose of the flower's form is to lure insects into a shoe-shaped pouch containing nectar, pollinating the flower by becoming temporarily trapped. Treacy noted that, 'The orchid's anatomy revolutionized my perception of beauty' – a remarkable statement considering his already successful career.

After graduating from the Royal College of Art in London, Treacy was introduced to the legendary fashion editor Isabella Blow, who had a distinct penchant for quirky hats. Blow introduced Treacy, then just twenty-three years old, to Karl Lagerfeld at Chanel (see p.255), launching a career that would see him design for Alexander McQueen (see p.133), Givenchy and Valentino, as well as supermodels, celebrities and the British royal family.

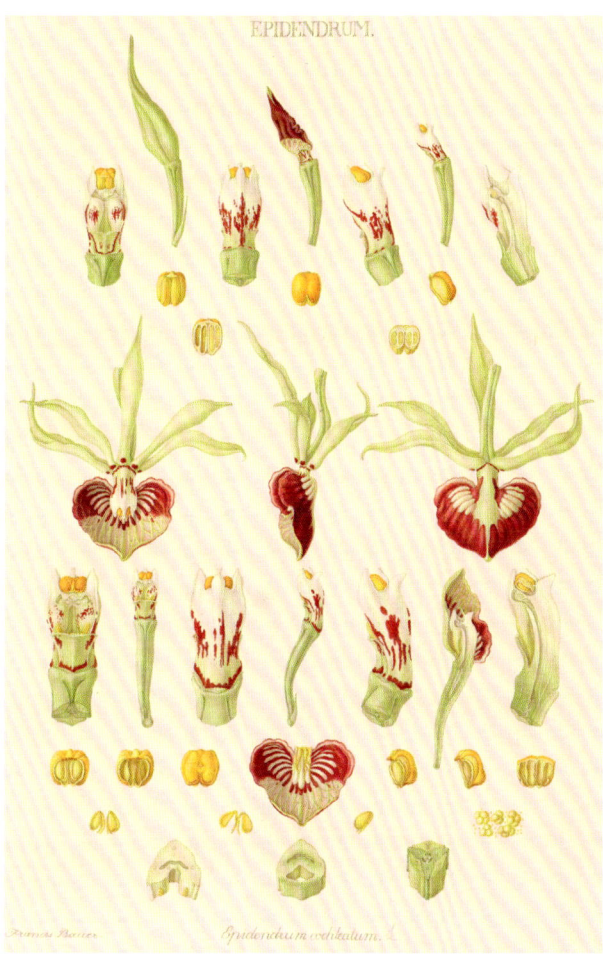

Franz Andreas Bauer

Epidendrum cochleatum, from *Delineation of Exotick Plants Cultivated in the Royal Garden at Kew*, 1796
Colour lithograph, 62 × 48 cm / 24½ × 19 in
Natural History Museum, London

Born into a family of artists, Austrian botanical illustrator Franz Bauer (1758–1840) began his education alongside his younger brother Ferdinand (see p.84) under the local Abbot of Feldsberg, learning to draw flowers in the monastery's medicinal garden. From there, the brothers moved to Vienna, working for the Baron Nikolaus von Jacquin on a florilegium of the Schönbrunn Imperial Gardens. While Ferdinand travelled the world documenting the flora of Greece and Australia, Franz went to London in 1788, where scientist Sir Joseph Banks persuaded him to become the first resident botanical artist at the Royal Botanic Gardens at Kew in 1790. Franz spent the rest of his life in the position, meticulously recording exotic plants as they arrived from Africa, Asia and the Americas. In an exacting process, Bauer recorded all the internal parts of the flower, following the new Linnaean system of classifying plants, which depended on identifying their sexual characteristics. The remarkable detail of such small elements was thanks to Bauer's pioneering use of a microscope. Here, Bauer's study of the cockleshell orchid (now known as *Prosthechea cochleata*) is an example of this method, dissecting an epiphytic orchid native to Central America, the West Indies, Colombia, Venezuela and southern Florida, where it grows on trees. The flower grows upside down compared to other orchids, but Bauer has mistakenly reversed this – not surprisingly, given that he only ever saw a cut specimen rather than a live plant.

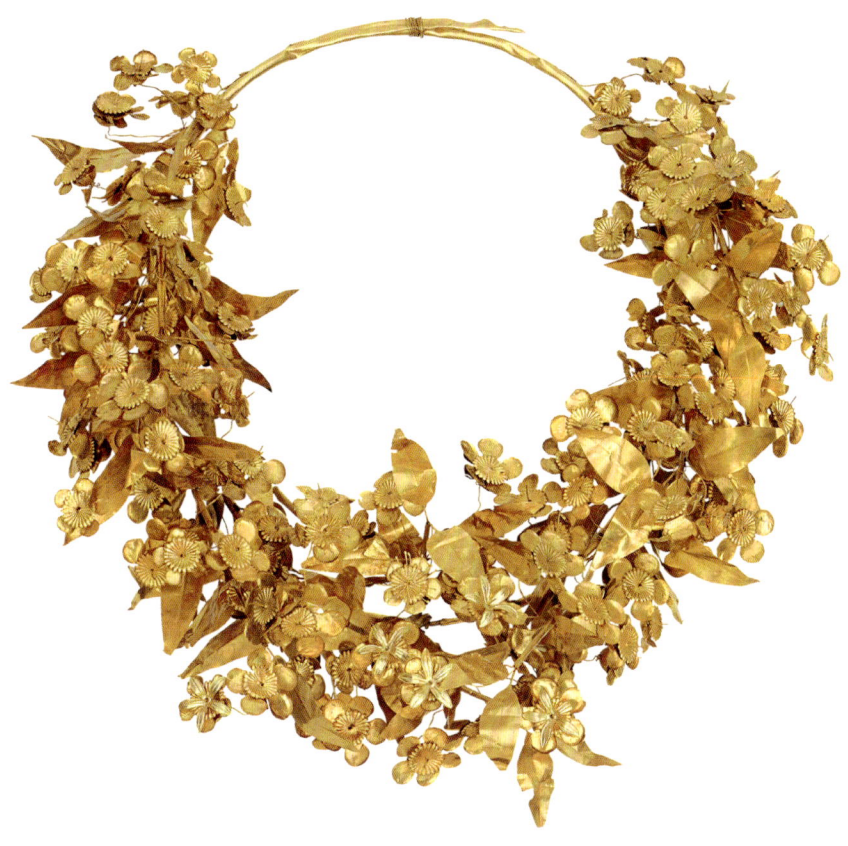

Anonymous

Golden Myrtle Crown of Queen Meda,
c.350–336 BC
Gold, Diam. 18.5 cm / 7¼ in
Museum of the Royal Tombs of Aigai,
Vergina, Greece

Made of hundreds of tiny, twisted twigs, 80 myrtle
leaves and 120 myrtle blossoms (*Myrtus commu-
nis*), each created from individually moulded
petals and stamens, this exquisite gold diadem
was found in the anteroom leading to Tomb II
at Vergina, in Greek Macedonia. It lay inside
a gold larnax (casket) containing the cremated

bones of a woman wrapped in a gold and purple
cloth, all within a marble coffin. There has been
much scholarly debate about the occupant of Tomb
II – whether he was Philip II, father of Alexander
the Great, or Philip III Arrhidaeus, Alexander's
half-brother, who assumed the throne after
Alexander's death in 323 BC. It is now assumed
by most archaeologists that the tomb belonged
to Philip II, and that the woman in the antecham-
ber was Meda, his Thracian queen and his fifth,
sixth or seventh wife. Meda was a member of the
Scythian Getae tribe, who were known to prac-
tise *suttee*, meaning the queen may have died

voluntarily on her husband's pyre. Philip was
assassinated in 336 BC, possibly on the orders
of Olympias, mother of Alexander. In ancient
Greece, crowns made of actual stems of oak,
laurel, ivy or other plants were traditionally
bestowed on winning athletes, victorious soldiers or royalty. Wreaths like this one, too
fragile to be worn, were created as grave gifts
to be buried with the dead as a symbol of their
triumphs in life. The representation of myrtle
in this crown alludes to the goddess of love,
Aphrodite, to whom the plant was sacred.

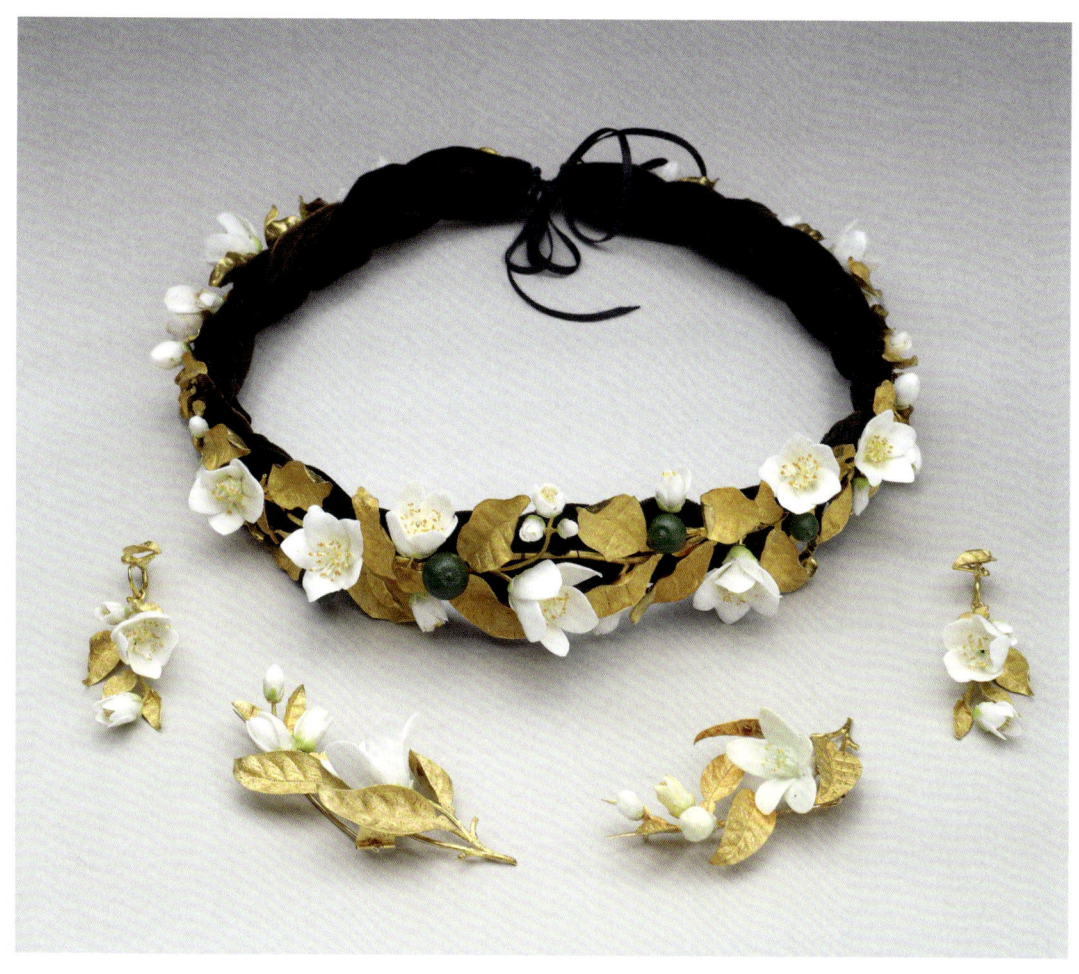

Anonymous

Queen Victoria's Orange Blossom Parure, 1839–46
Gold, porcelain, enamel, velvet and silk,
dimensions variable
Royal Collection Trust, UK

'My beloved one gave me such an unexpected present, a wreath ... made to match the brooch and earrings he gave me at Christmas. It is entirely his own design and beautifully carried out. The leaves are of frosted gold, the orange blossoms of white porcelain and four little green enamel oranges, meant to represent our four children.' So wrote Queen Victoria in her journal upon receiving this headdress from Prince Albert on their sixth wedding anniversary in 1846. The headdress completed the parure, or set of jewellery, that had begun with the gift of a brooch to mark the couple's engagement in 1839. Then came a second matching brooch and a pair of earrings in 1845, and finally the headdress of orange blossom, leaves and myrtle berries sewn onto a band of black plaited velvet, tied at the back with fine silk ribbons. The choice of flower was not incidental. In the Victorian lexicon of floriography, orange blossom (*Citrus sinensis*) represented purity and fertility. Queen Victoria wore freshly cut sprigs of the blossom entwined with myrtle at her wedding, when it decorated even the wedding cake. Victoria adored the parure and wore elements of it on every wedding anniversary until Albert's death in 1861. After the Queen's death in 1901, the pieces were placed on display in 'Albert's Room' at Windsor Castle. She had decreed that the jewellery never be worn by any of the couple's descendants, a wish that has been adhered to.

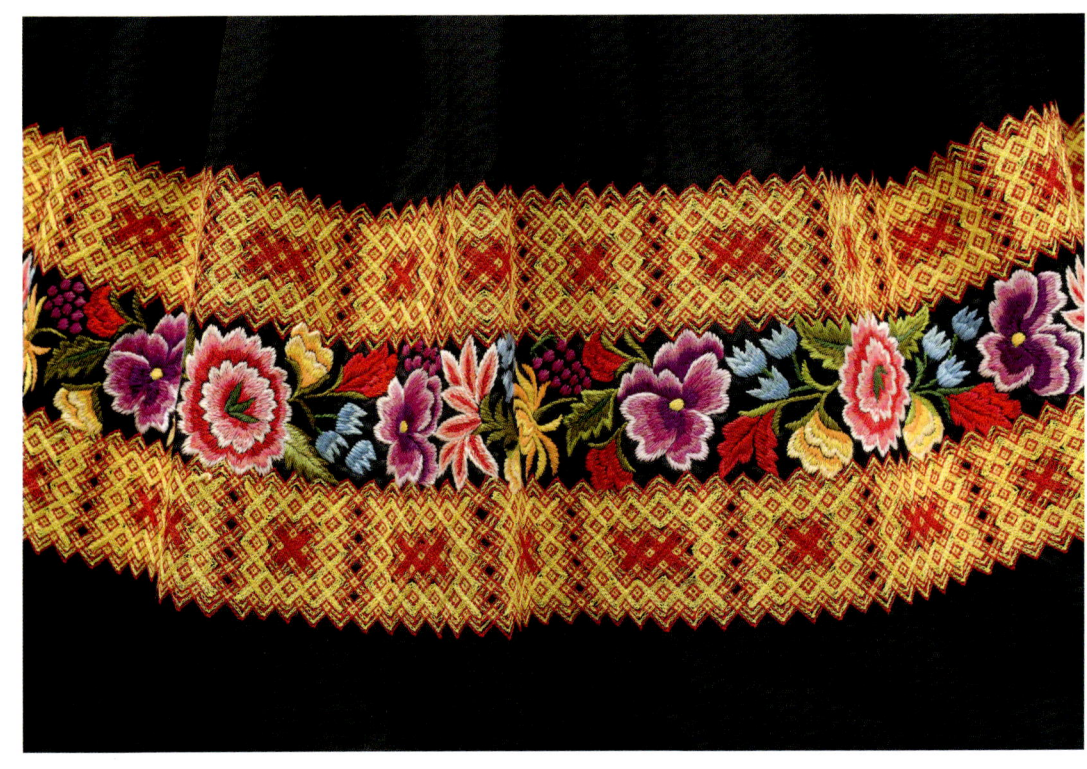

Anonymous

Tehuana skirt with chain stitch and floral
embroidery (detail), 20th century
Embroidered satin
Museo Frida Kahlo, Mexico City

Running in between yellow and red geometric
borders, vibrant embroidered flowers with petals
of pink, purple, blue and red, together with lush
purple grapes, are stitched against the black background of this satin skirt. The bright floral motifs
are typical of the now widely produced styles
of the traditional indigenous dress of Tehuanas –
Zapotec women from the Isthmus of Tehuantepec

in Oaxaca, Mexico. Part of the collection of the
celebrated artist Frida Kahlo, this detailed skirt,
or *enagua*, was embroidered by sewing machine
using a chain stitch: the introduction of the Singer
sewing machine at the start of the twentieth
century generated the 'fast fashion' of the region;
previously, the designs had been hand-sewn.
Kahlo was renowned not only for her paintings
but also for her range of bright indigenous clothing
and floral headware from Mexico and Guatemala.
The artist often combined clothing from different
regions, including woven *huipiles* (sleeveless
tunics), Puebla cotton blouses and beautifully dyed

rebozos (shawls), all intricately linked with
Mexican cultural identity. Such traditional garments used texture and pattern to decorate
clothing not only with flowers, but also with birds,
animals and geometric forms. Kahlo frequently
painted herself with flowers, not least in her portrait *Self-portrait as a Tehuana* (1943), where she
depicts herself in a Tehuana ceremonial *resplan-
dor*, a lace headdress, with a centrepiece of white
and purple flowers among green foliage from which
black vines emerge.

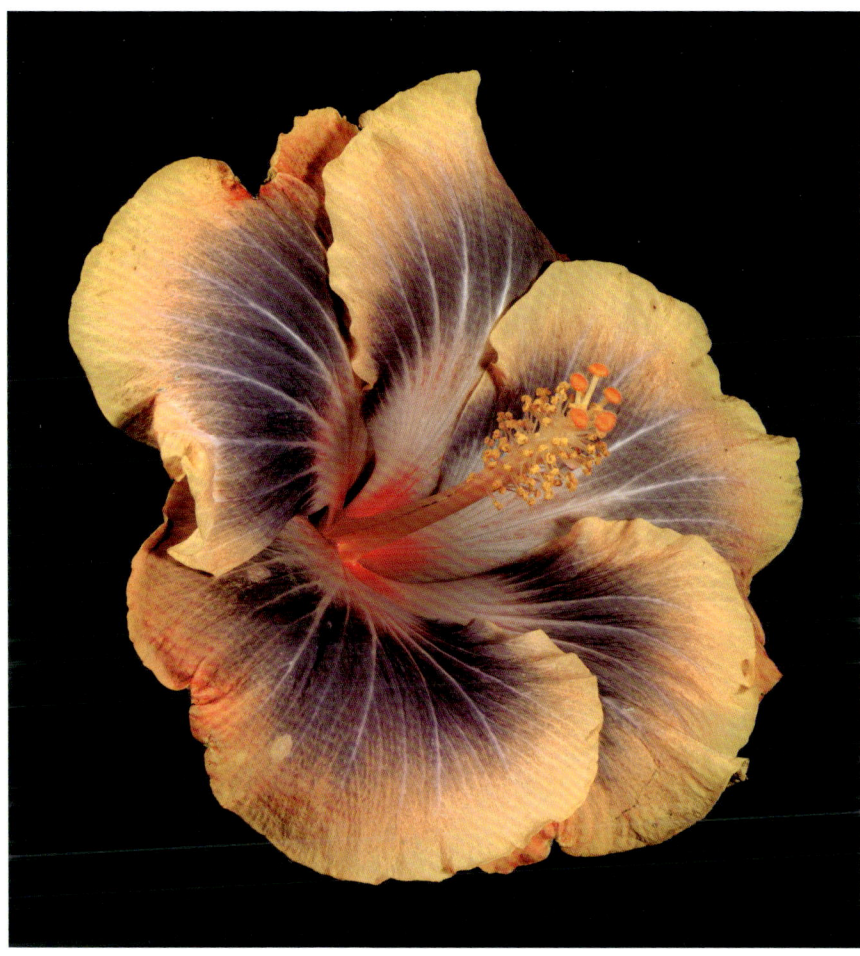

Jonathan M. Singer

Hibiscus 'Silver Memories', from *Botanica Magnifica: Portraits of the World's Most Extraordinary Flowers and Plants*, 2007
Digital photograph on Japon paper,
1.2 × 0.9 m / 3 ft 11 in × 3 ft

Emerging from a pitch black background, this gloriously colourful hibiscus flower bears the photographic hallmark of American photographer Johnathan M. Singer (1949–2019), one of the most original contemporary photographers of flowers and plants. Singer worked as a podiatrist until, in the 1970s, he met Ansel Adams at his gallery in Yosemite National Park and was inspired to change careers. Today, his collected photographs have been published in five volumes comprising *Botanica Magnifica*, with texts by W. John Kress, vice president for science at the Smithsonian National Museum of Natural History, and Marc Hachadourian, senior curator of the orchid collection at the New York Botanical Garden. The tome includes 250 photographs, each a scientifically identified plant species, grouped in themes of horticulture, plant form, orchids, gingers and rare species. The dark background is more reminiscent of baroque paintings than the clarity and brightness of traditional botan-ical illustration; it removes the flower from its natural context and elevates it to the status of a timeless icon. The photograph shows one of the many hybrid varieties of *Hibiscus rosa-sinensis*, an extremely popular tropical cultivar originally from China. Tropical hibiscuses have excited breeders and collectors around the world for hundreds of years. There is almost no limit to the stunning colour combinations that can be made to appear on its petals, but the intense beauty of each flower lasts only a day or two.

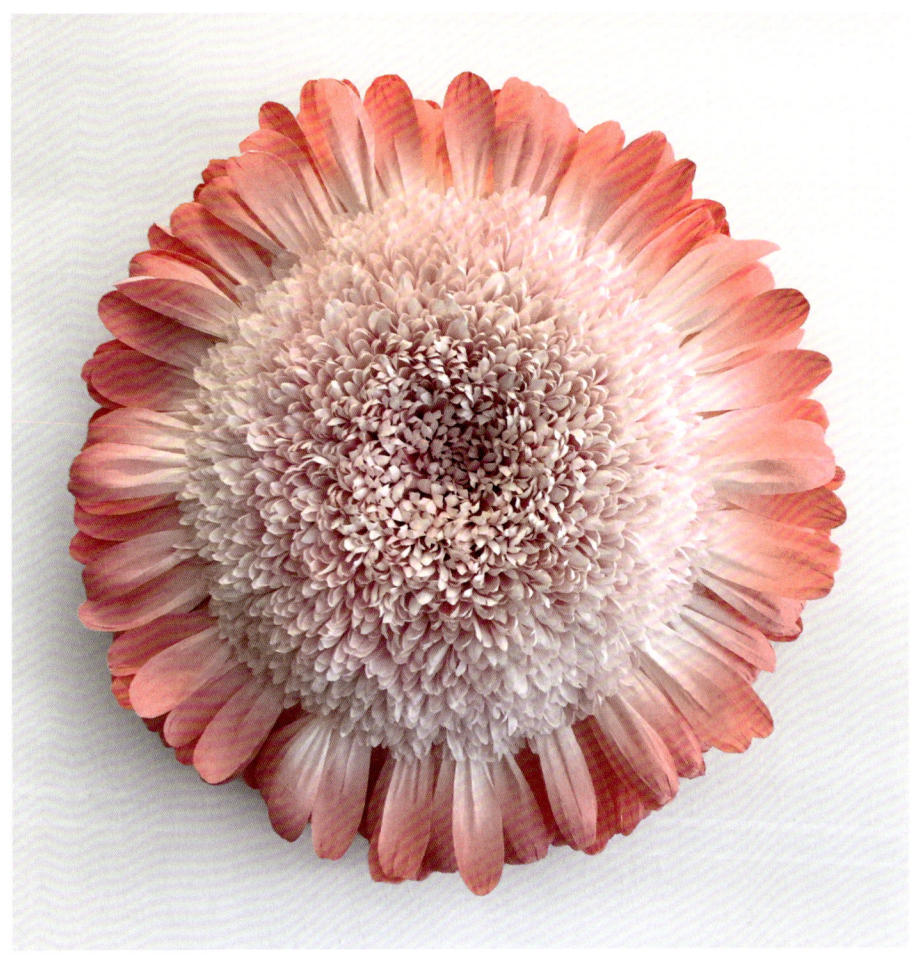

Tiffanie Turner

Cremon Mum, 2016
Paper mâché and Italian crepe paper,
1.3 m / 4 ft 4 in
Private collection

Every delicate petal of this enormous cremon chrysanthemum – over 1.3 metres (4 feet) in diameter – was individually crafted from paper by American artist Tiffanie Turner (born 1970). Dominating the gallery wall, the blushing pink sculpture celebrates the complex structure of these flowers, faithfully replicating their form, texture and colour. Turner began engineering paper flowers in 2012, initially creating life-sized pieces before supersizing her work. Made from thousands of hand-cut paper fragments, each of her lifelike flowers takes between 250 and 400 hours to complete. Turner cuts, stretches, curls and pleats each petal by hand from high-quality Italian crepe paper. The huge scale of her flower heads often reveals commonly over-looked details, enabling viewers to appreciate a flower's intricate forms afresh. In addition to closely observing the structure of flowers them-selves, Turner also studies the floral paintings of sixteenth- and seventeenth-century Dutch masters, such as Jan Davidsz. de Heem and Ambrosius Bosschaert the Elder (see pp.125, 177). Another influence on her work is Charles Rennie Mackintosh (see p.246), whose botanical draw-ings and paintings are stylized yet accurately show the structure of each plant. While Turner is drawn to the vibrancy of flowers in bloom, she is also fascinated by their ephemerality. Although her sculptures arrest decay, Turner uses her work to open up conversations around ageing, vanity and life's transience.

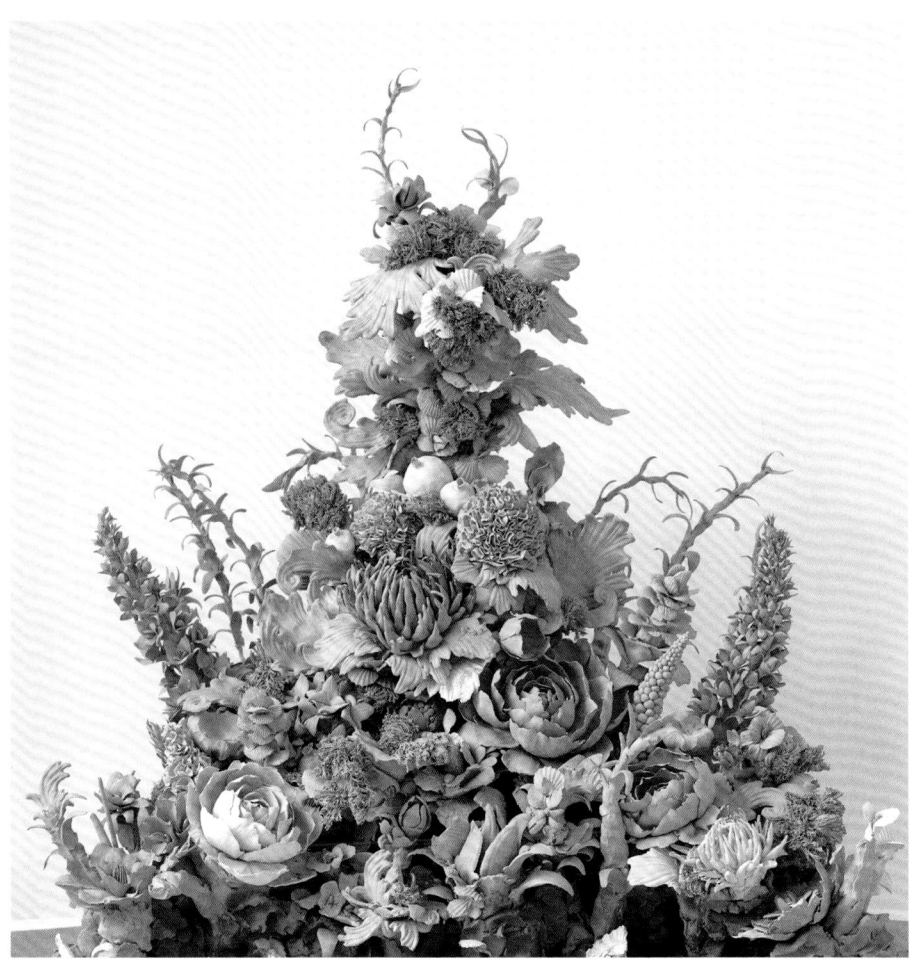

Phoebe Cummings

Triumph of the Immaterial, 2017
Clay and water, approx. 80 × 50 × 40 cm /
31½ × 19¾ × 15¾ in
Victoria and Albert Museum, London

Sculpted in a greyscale of raw clay, flowers including roses, Japanese chrysanthemums and grape hyacinths fold in upon themselves in this artwork, delicate petals and leaves curling at the ends amid lush foliage, fruit and lichen. The flowers emerge from a bedrock of clay carefully crafted by British artist Phoebe Cummings (born 1981), who leaves her works unfired and unglazed –

and therefore vulnerable: temporary sculptures and installations destined to disintegrate, following a life cycle defined by blooming and decaying in the same way as a real flower. The clay is then gathered and used again in new sculptures, as the seasonal pattern begins again. The different handcraft techniques Cummings uses are evident in the scallop-shell lines of some petals, baroque in their grandeur, or the fine-stringed filaments of others. The artist's method is both ephemeral and performative because her works are often made for and encountered in specific sites. Using inspiration from the history of art, natural forms

and verdant vegetation are commonplace in her work, recalling landscape paintings or decorative art motifs. In 2010 Cummings created an installation as artist-in-residence at the Victoria and Albert Museum in London, reproducing flowers and other plants from prints and paintings in the museum's collection.

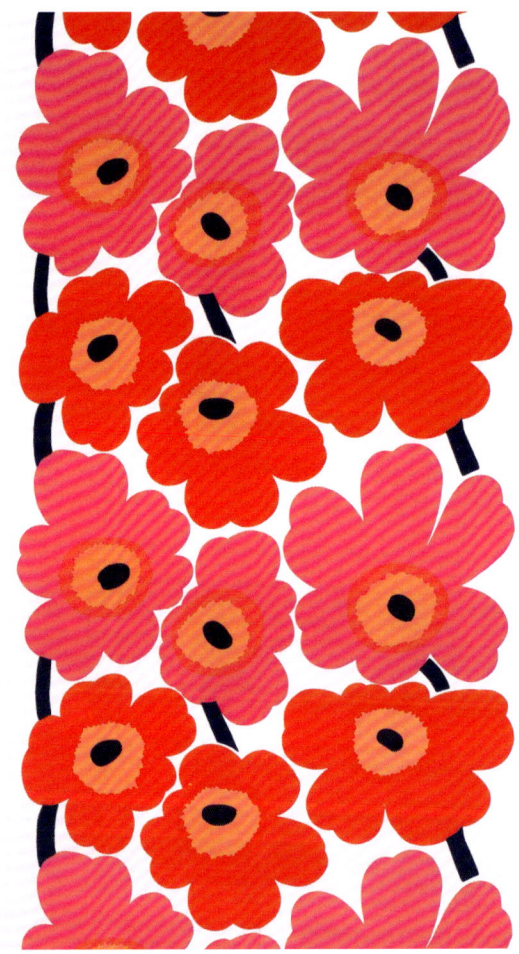

Maija Isola for Marimekko

Unikko, 1964
Screen-printed cotton, 3 × 1.4 m /
9 ft 11 in × 4 ft 6 in
Cooper Hewitt, Smithsonian Design Museum,
New York

This bold and joyful poppy print featuring red and pink flowers on a white background – one of the best-known designs of the Finnish lifestyle brand Marimekko – was designed by Maija Isola (1927–2001), who created more than five hundred prints for the house over thirty-eight years. Isola's designs were inspired not only by modern aesthetics, but also by traditional folk art and the natural world. Her first thematic series of around thirty designs, *Luonto* (nature), was based on pressed flowers and plants. The graphic floral motif is typical of the simplistic, colourful patterns used for the brand products. Marimekko was founded in 1951 by Armi Ratia, who had studied textile design in Helsinki before working for an advertising agency. Initially designing liberating, easy clothing and prints herself, Ratia later employed a team of designers so she could focus on expanding the company. The Finnish firm became known globally for uplifting fabrics that often used bold stripes, checks, spots and florals, reworked in a kaleidoscope of different colourways. In 1964 Ratia banned her designers from creating any further floral prints – Isola's response was to produce an entire collection of designs. Ratia was so taken with the unique patterns, she put eight of them into production, including *Unikko*. The poppy print has appeared on T-shirts, dresses and children's clothes as well as homewares including trays, cups, napkins and teapots, bedding and towels – and even on a hot-air balloon and a Finnair aircraft.

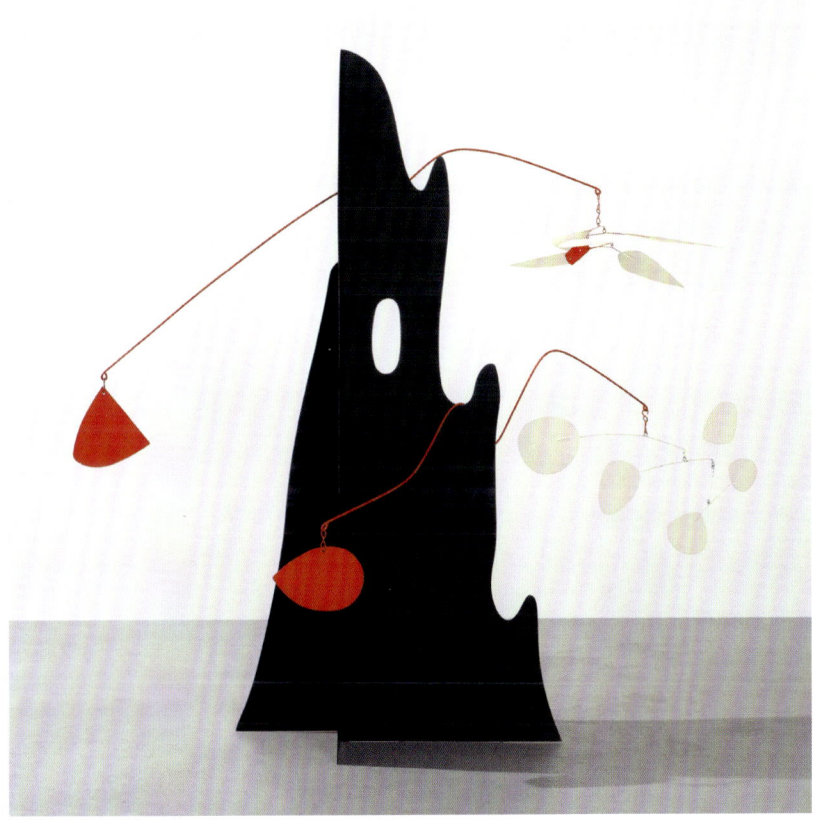

Alexander Calder

Crag with White Flower and White Discs, 1974
Painted sheet metal and wire, 1.9 × 2.2 × 1.2 m /
6 ft 4 in × 7 ft 2 in × 4 ft
Private collection

The solidity of a black, undulating form, reminiscent of a nineteenth-century Japanese landscape painting, is offset by delicate wire mobiles balancing white and red discs – an assemblage of biomorphic shapes in their simplest forms, one of which might recall a flower. Created by American artist Alexander Calder (1898–1976) for the exhibition *Crags and Critters* of 1975, the sculpture integrates Calder's concept of the 'mobile', so named by Marcel Duchamp in 1931, and the 'stabile', an ironic term for Calder's static works coined in 1932 by artist Jean Arp. It exemplifies Calder's use of disparity in form, colour, size and weight to create artwork of arresting and enchanting appeal. Generous of spirit, Calder was born in Pennsylvania to artist parents, earned a degree in mechanical engineering, and maintained a bond between physics and aesthetics throughout his career. He explored the interrelationships between space, time and kinetic energy, and revolutionized sculpture in the twentieth century. As in Calder's other sculptural work, abstract elements appear in their simplest forms in mobiles, many of them large, that capture the ethereal dynamics of nature in wire and metal, as with the subtly moving white mobile here and its dramatic flash of red. In such works, Calder brought a new appreciation of nature's forces to diverse audiences.

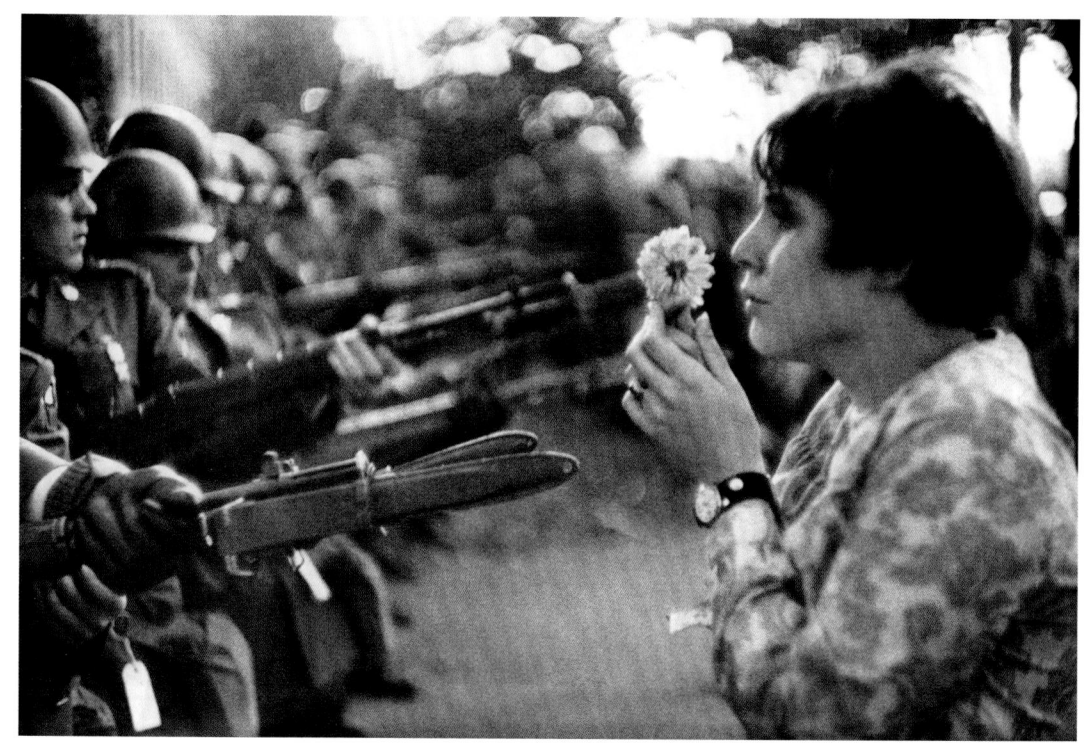

Marc Riboud

The delicate soft petals of a chrysanthemum flower stand in stark contrast to the pointed bayonets of the American National Guard outside the Pentagon in Washington, DC, in this image that came to represent the social tensions of the late 1960s in the United States. Taken by French photographer Marc Riboud (1923–2016) on 21 October, 1967, this image documents the day nearly 100,000 people marched on Washington to protest peacefully against the Vietnam War. The last frame in Riboud's roll of film caught this now iconic image, which depicts seventeen-year-old Jan Rose Kasmir confronting the soldiers deployed to control the protesters. She cups the flower in her hand in a gesture of both offering and protection from the cold metal thrust in her direction. Opposition to the Vietnam War began in 1964 and grew into a strong social movement that shaped polarizing debates within the United States in the late 1960s and early 1970s. As the police increasingly used violence against those taking part in peaceful protests, beat poet Allen Ginsberg published his manifesto *How to Make a March/ Spectacle* in 1965, suggesting that protesters hand out flowers to police, press and other spectators to quell any fears of violence. 'Flower power' was born, and two years later Riboud's photograph became the enduring visual symbol of the movement.

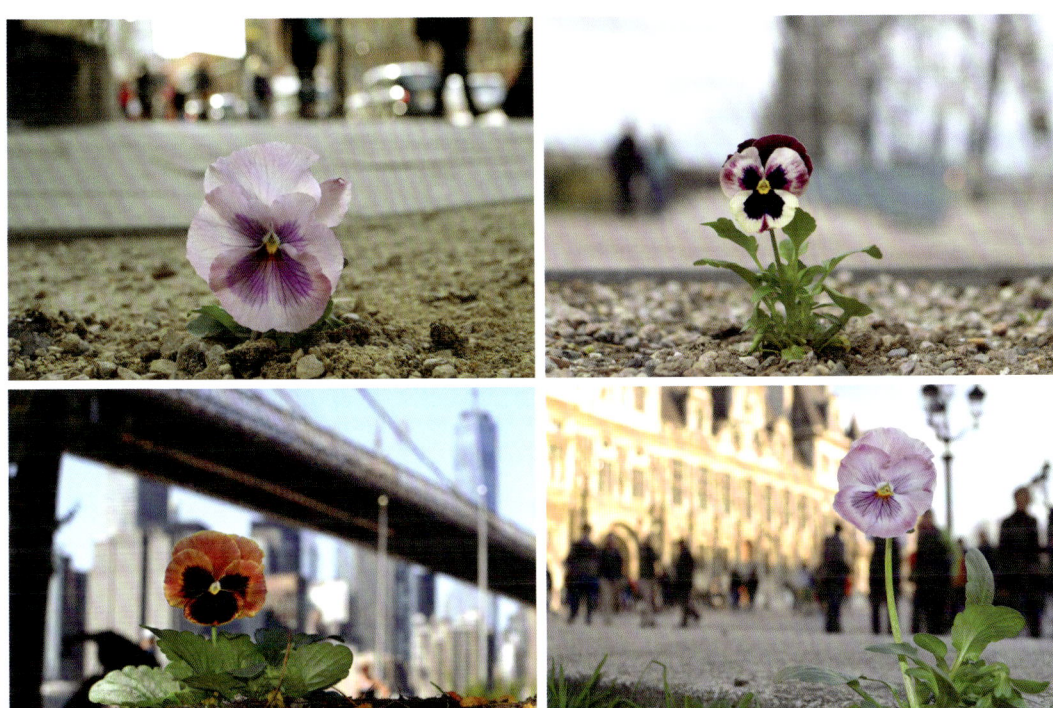

Paul Harfleet

Clockwise from top left: *'Batty!' Kings Cross,*
London, 2013; *'Nice Shoes, Faggot!' For Alain*
Brosseau, Alexandra Bridge, Ottawa, 2019; *'Les*
pédés au bûcher!' Hôtel de Ville, Paris, 2005;
'Misbegotten Pansies', Brooklyn Bridge, New York,
2019, from *The Pansy Project*, 2010–19
Colour photographs, dimensions variable

These lonely pansies blooming at the edges
of busy pavements are portraits of both fragility
and defiance. The flowers did not grow spontane-
ously, they were planted by British photographer
Paul Harfleet (born 1970) at a site of homophobic
abuse. The Pansy Project began in 2005 – marking
ten years, nearly to the day, of an incident where
Harfleet and his partner endured a series of verbal
homophobic attacks in Manchester, England.
To the photographer, situating a living plant where
the abuse occurred can change the energy of the
location – it replaces the negative memories associated with that place, adding a sense of positivity
and the possibility of personal growth. In the
English language, the word 'pansy' is often used
as a derogatory term for a gay man and has been
laden with negative connotations of being effem-
inate, weak or frail. In the mid-fifteenth century,
the flower designated a man who thinks 'too
much', perceived as a feminine attribute. The
analogy emerged from the word French *pensée* –
the past tense of 'to think' – which well suited the
pansy, with its bowing head suggesting a pensive
demeanour, but it wasn't until the late 1920s that
the word was used as a pejorative remark. Harfleet
has created an extensive collection of photographs for the Pansy Project, with around 300 sites
worldwide. The title of each photograph is a quote
from the abuse hurled at its victim, while the colours and flamboyant petals of each pansy signal
hope for a better world.

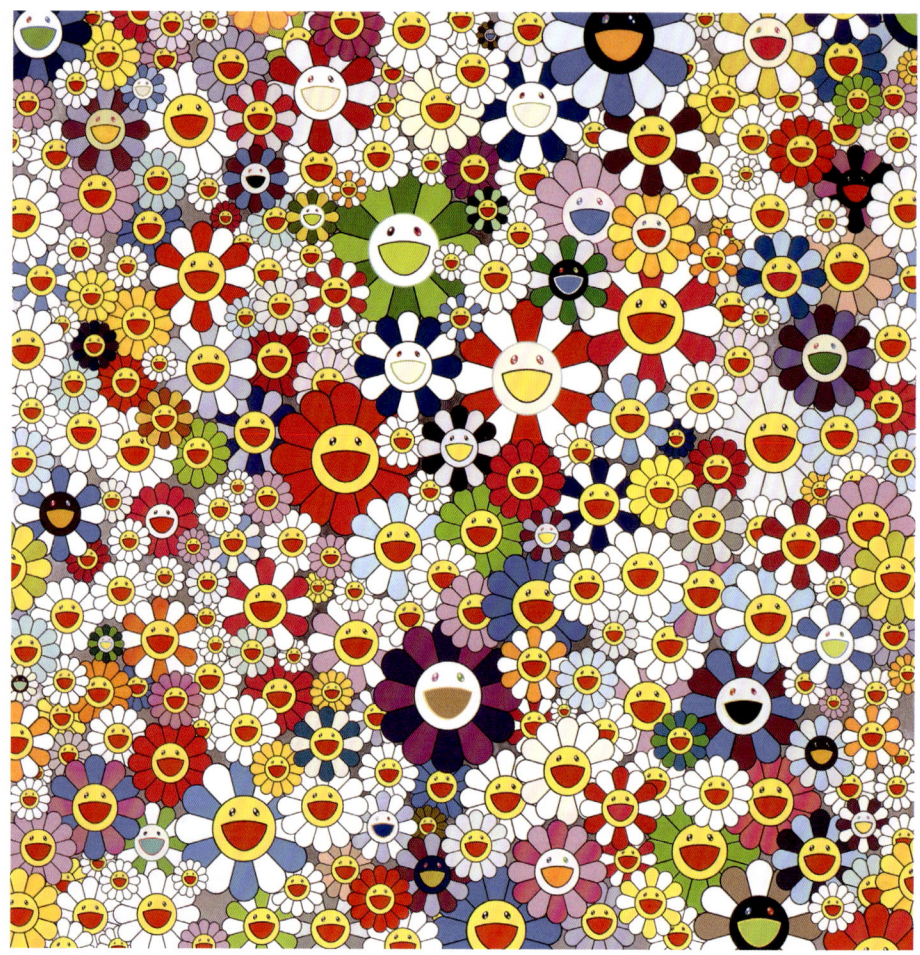

Takashi Murakami

If I Could Reach That Field of Flowers, I Would Die Happy, 2010
Offset lithograph, 60 × 60 cm / 23½ × 23½ in
Private collection

A manic crowd of cartoon flowers assaults the viewer, relentlessly happy, loud – perhaps even garish or brash. This is not a representation of an idyllic field of wild summer flowers, but rather a more Warholian translation of a flower that was perhaps once a daisy but is now transformed into a symbol for something else by the Japanese artist Takashi Murakami (born 1962).

Influenced in part by contemporary Japanese anime and manga, Murakami has given new life and meaning to the simple flower form – literally giving flowers a new face. Like looking at an explosion of emoticons found in text messages between best friends or lovers, Murakami's flowers stand in for a profusion of unrestrained love and joy. Joyous but also so obsessive and maniacal that they could actually be seen as quite frightening and disturbing. The work's title, *If I Could Reach That Field of Flowers, I Would Die Happy*, might give a final clue to Murakami's intent. This image is about achieving a perfectly

zen-like blissful state before an inevitable end: an ideal that eludes the artist as the flowers laugh at his idea of perfect happiness, reminding him that he is human and that such ideals only exist in truly synthetic spaces.

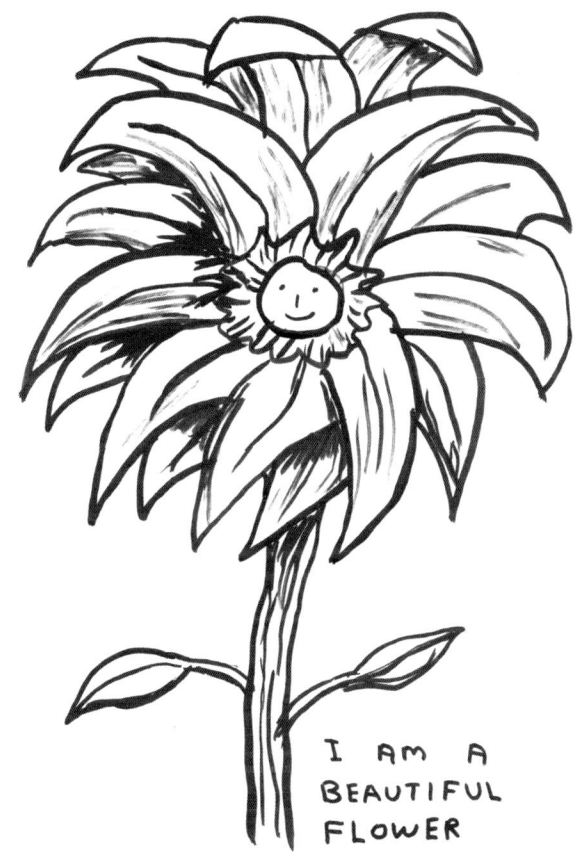

I AM A
BEAUTIFUL
FLOWER

David Shrigley

I am a beautiful flower, 2012
Ink on paper, 42 × 29.7 cm / 16½ × 11¾ in

This rudimentary cartoon of a flower with a smiling face is typical of the quirky style of British artist David Shrigley (1968). Accompanying the plant is a handwritten phrase taken from a quote by the prominent motivational author Louise Hay, which declares: 'I am a beautiful flower that is blossoming more and more each day. I delight in my world, and my world delights in me'. By juxtaposing Hay's words with a dishevelled, almost weed-like, flower – anything but beautiful to

traditional gardeners – Shrigley gently mocks the self-help mantra with his signature sardonic wit. Shrigley's crude drawings are characterized by deadpan humour and mordant commentary that often expresses his angst about modern life. His themes range from the absurd and surreal to weighty issues such as unemployment and child welfare, employing subjects from talking flowers, animals and birds to shopping trolleys, tea sets and stick figures. Despite being nominated for the Turner Prize in 2013, he still describes himself as an art world outsider. Quick and spontaneous, his technique falls somewhere between

handwriting and drawing, and while he never makes corrections, elements are sometimes scrubbed out to comic effect. Drawing remains at the heart of his practice, but Shrigley has also made animations, published books, produced large-scale public sculptures and designed album art for musicians including David Byrne, Franz Ferdinand and Bonnie Prince Billy.

Shane Connolly
Founder, Shane Connolly & Company Flowers, London and Royal Warrant Holder to HM The Queen and HM The King.
—

Humans are drawn to flowers – instinctively, impulsively and irresistibly – by their scent, their colour and their beauty. We have woven flowers into our myths and our religions; we have used them to cure mental and physical illnesses; and, above all, we have used flowers to comfort each other and to speak for us when we struggle to find the right words, or *any* words at all.

We have imbued flowers with countless meanings throughout our long history of interacting with them. Long before 'the language of flowers' – a lexicon of floral meanings – gave nineteenth-century lovers a means of communicating in an age of emotional repression, these symbolic characteristics were recognized. And for centuries, artists have used flowers, chosen with knowledge and care, to emphasize or define their subjects, as well as the intentions and messages behind their artworks.

On the following pages is a selection of flowers that appear in this book and a short history of their lives and their significance across cultures – a brief compilation to inspire a deeper exploration of the rich symbolism of flowers.

Amaryllis (*Hippeastrum*)
Amaryllis arrived in the West from Peru in the late nineteenth century. The Latin genus name *Hippeastrum* comes from the ancient Greek for 'Knight's Star' after its resemblance to the morning star used in medieval heraldry. The common name, amaryllis, was not a grand knight at all, but a mythological shepherdess. However, the flower was still associated with pride and noble beauty from the time of its arrival.

Anemone (*Anemone coronaria*)
According to Greek myth, anemones sprung from Aphrodite's tears at Adonis's death; in another, a jealous Chloris, the goddess of flowers, turned a beautiful nymph into an anemone to nip an affair with her husband, Zephyrus, in the bud. It is no surprise that the flowers have traditionally symbolized romantic abandonment and the transience of love.

Auricula (*Primula auricula*)
Auriculas are no doubt the grandest of the primula family. In the late eighteenth and early nineteenth centuries they were highly coveted and became a symbol of avarice and greed. With their extensive colour palette, auriculas also became a symbol of 'The Arts'.

Bluebonnet (*Lupinus texensis*)
The native bluebonnet is the state flower of Texas, and now has many cultivated forms thriving in Europe as well. Lupins are highly toxic to humans and so are associated with danger and dejection. But with their colourful flowers, they have also been used to illustrate vivid imagination.

Buttercup (*Ranunculus acris*)
The plain country cousin of the sophisticated florist shop ranunculus, the wild meadow buttercup is associated with simple, good things – epitomized in the childhood game of placing the yellow blossom under someone's chin to see if they like butter. It has also represented the riches of heaven in early Christian art, childishness and cheerfulness, and is used for homeopathic remedies to treat self-doubt.

Cactus (*Cactaceae*)
Cacti have uniquely adapted to living in arid regions. The family has many species, in all shapes and sizes, with the common traits of toughness and robustness. Cacti are associated with warmth and endurance based on their ability to survive their usual hot habitats. Thought to be a plant with caring qualities, Native Americans have used cactus pulp medicinally, and cactus flowers have become associated with a mother's unconditional love.

Camellia (*Camellia japonica*)
Native to Japan and the Far East, where they have been cherished for centuries, the *Camellia* family is large and includes the tea plant (*C. sinensis*). In the Shinto religion, gods visited earth and lived in camellia flowers. In Alexandre Dumas's novel *La Dame aux Camélias*, the central courtesan carries white camellias to signify her 'available' days of the month and red camellias for the other 'resting' days. Nineteenth-century trendsetter Empress Josephine grew camellias in her gardens at Malmaison, making them supremely stylish. Inevitably, they were then used in secret messages of love and passion: white camellias for 'perfect loveliness', red for 'a flame in my heart' and pink to say, 'I am longing for you'.

Carnation (*Dianthus caryophyllus*)
The carnation has been so extensively cultivated for the past 1,500 years that its precise origin is not known,

although they were a mainstay of floral crowns in ancient Rome, Greece and Turkey. The genus name *Dianthus* is possibly derived from the ancient Greek *dios* and *anthos*, meaning 'divine flower' or from its later link with the Roman goddess Diana. The carnation has had many contradictory associations, often specific to the flower colour. Red carnations are linked to love, but they are also a long-standing symbol of socialism and the Labour Party in the UK. Since Ottoman rule in Turkey, the same red carnation has represented Muhammad, while in Portugal it became a symbol of the 1974 'Carnation Revolution'. In China carnations are associated with weddings, but in Italy they are traditional funeral flowers. Purple carnations are linked to whimsy and capriciousness, while striped ones traditionally symbolize unrequited love.

Cherry Blossom (*Prunus*)

Cherry blossom, or *sakura*, is the unofficial national flower of Japan. Celebrated every spring since at least the tenth century, the short-lived blossoms became a symbol of the transience of life. During World War II, the cherry blossom was a motivational motif painted on suicide bombers' aircrafts and afterwards it became an emblem of remembrance. The Japanese diaspora carried cherry blossom trees around the world and they have been embraced by many disparate cultures as symbols of hope and spiritual beauty.

Chrysanthemum (*Chrysanthemum*)

The golden chrysanthemum is the official national flower of Japan and its Imperial House is known as 'The Chrysanthemum Throne'. In traditional Chinese art, this flower is one of 'The Four Noble Ones', along with plum blossom, orchid and bamboo. The yellow chrysanthemum symbolizes nobility, long life and revitalization, while white is associated with adversity and sorrow. In certain European countries, incurved blooms are seen as a symbol of death and only used at funerals. Despite that, the year-round and long-lasting cut blooms were a popular florist's flower throughout the nineteenth and twentieth centuries and were rechristened with more romantic meanings.

Columbine (*Aquilegia vulgaris*)

Resembling a circle of birds, the upturned flower of columbine, gets its name from the Latin *columba*, for 'dove' and its genus name from *aquila*, for 'eagle'. In the Middle Ages, the Christian Church adopted it as an emblem of the Holy Ghost, a symbol of grace and redemption. Paradoxically, it was also

used to signify cuckoldry – as its spurs look like the shameful cuckold's horn – and often appears in Pre-Raphaelite art to represent folly and caprice.

Daffodil (*Narcissus pseudonarcissus*)

Daffodils have been the national flower of Wales since 1911 when Prime Minister David Lloyd George wore one on St David's Day. Like all early spring flowers, and especially yellow ones, daffodils are associated with optimism, survival and hope. In Christianity, daffodils have long been part of the Easter celebrations and are also linked with the more ancient fertility festivals of Oestrus. But as a member of the narcissus family, they have also been used to symbolize unrequited love and wasted youth (see **Narcissus**). In the language of flowers, daffodils have also been used to suggest respect and gallantry.

Dahlia (*Dahlia*)

Dahlias are native to, and now the national flower of, Mexico, where the tubers were a staple of the Aztec diet. There was even a failed attempt by early Spanish settlers to substitute it for the potato back in Europe. They also used the hollow stems to hold water, creating associations with inner strength and survival, which were later reinforced by the flower's preference to grow without competition from other plants. Later hybridization in the Netherlands produced the decorative and popular garden plant known today and the dahlia became synonymous with Victorian elegance and good taste.

Daisy (*Bellis perennis*)

'Daisy' originates from the Old English 'Day's-Eye', as the flowers reflect the path of the sun. Historically, daisies were sacred to goddesses of love, beauty and fertility and, as the Virgin Mary replaced them, they became linked with purity. In the fifteenth century, daisies were known as 'love's flower', perhaps reflecting the myth that pulling off their petals, one by one, might tell if someone 'loves me' or 'loves me not'. Daisies also have a strong association with childhood and youthful activities such as daisy chains and daisy caterpillars. 'Pushing up the daisies', on the other hand, is a charming euphemism for death.

Foxglove (*Digitalis purpurea*)

Foxgloves are highly toxic but also contain the powerful compounds digoxin and digitalin, which can either kill or cure, creating associations with insincerity, deception and unreliability. With the threat of death also comes the perception of power and even respect. Foxgloves appear in many folk tales and myths of magic and witchcraft, linking them with secrecy, riddles, mysticism and faith. In medieval gardens, they were planted in honour of the Virgin Mary.

Honeysuckle (*Lonicera*)
Honeysuckle entwines and embraces everything in its path, and so has ancient links with love and passion. In Scottish folklore, it was planted on a home to ward off evil and keep its occupants sweet natured. Its clinging, honey-scented flowers are the symbol of a devoted marriage, as seen in stylized, ornate Victorian railings designed to indicate the domestic bliss within the home. Pre-Raphaelite artists sometimes used honeysuckle ironically to hint at the infidelity or sexual abandonment of their subjects.

Hyacinth (*Hyacinthus*)
According to Greek legend, Hyacinthus was a handsome young boy with whom Apollo, the sun god, and Zephyrus, god of the wind, were both in love. As Apollo and Hyacinthus played a game of quoit, a jealous Zephyrus blew the discus off course and killed the boy. Hyacinth flowers grew where his blood had spilled and endowed the flower with enduring symbolic links: to sport, to the constancy of love, to jealousy, and to sorrow and forgiveness. Poets also invoked the phrase 'hyacinthine hair', as the flower's petals resembled beautiful, curly locks.

Hydrangea (*Hydrangea*)
Requiring a lot of water to thrive, 'Hydrangea' fittingly comes from the Greek word for a water vessel. When hydrangeas were first brought to Europe, their demanding ways soon had them associated with coolness and arrogance. The flowers also seemed to magically change colour (actually caused by the acidity of the soil), which linked them to the traits of vanity and boastfulness. As they produce very few seeds, hydrangeas are sometimes used to symbolize frigidity and heartlessness. In Japan, however, they can be used to convey an apology, and in Korea, they represent 'the beat of my heart'.

Iris (*Iris*)
In ancient myth, Iris travelled to earth on rainbows to deliver the messages of the Greek gods and to collect mortal prayers in return. To this day, Greeks plant irises on graves to help the souls of the dead find their way to heaven. In this way, irises are associated with death and the afterlife, but they have also

symbolized good news or good luck, wisdom, hope and faith. For centuries the iris was the emblem of French royalty as the stylized fleur-de-lis, and it is now the national flower with associations of brightness, purity and freedom.

Lilac (*Syringa vulgaris*)
In one version of a Greek myth, the nymph Syringa turns herself into a lilac bush to avoid the amorous advances of the god Pan. It didn't work; the plant has hollow stems and Pan fashioned himself some pipes to play so Syringa could never escape. The Celts believed the intoxicating lilac scent could magically seduce a lover. In European culture, lilacs became associated with love and loving memories. The Victorians used purple lilac to represent first love, while white lilac symbolized memories of youth and youthful innocence.

Lily (*Lilium candidum*)
The white lily of Greece is said to have appeared when Hera, wife of the Greek god Zeus, sprinkled her own breast milk onto the earth. They later became a Christian emblem of Mary, the mother of God – their perfect whiteness and heavenly perfume symbols of her purity and innocence. Lilies were used at funerals to help the deceased's soul become pure again – and their strong scent had practical uses in the days before widespread embalming. In China, Korea and Japan, lilies have had both culinary and medicinal uses. And they are, in part, the national flower of France: the stylized fleur-de-lis may actually be an iris, but when it was chosen as a symbol of French royalty in the Middle Ages, the lily's strong links with the Virgin Mary would undoubtedly have held more appeal for devout Catholic monarchs.

Lily of the valley (*Convallaria majalis*)
Although used in traditional medicine to treat heart complaints, the fragile appearance of the sweet-scented lily of the valley is deceptive and, in fact, highly toxic. The association stuck, though, and the flower has been linked with restored health and happiness in all matters of the heart. Lily of the valley was sacred to the Germanic goddess of spring, Ostara, and considered the farmer's friend, as they herald better weather and the end of frosts. They were a traditional medieval springtime gift and in France they have been associated with May Day since 1561 when King Charles IX gave them to the ladies of his court – a tradition that continues to this day. The flowers are sometimes called 'Lady's Tears' or 'Mary's tears' as they were thought to have sprung from

the Virgin's tears as she followed Jesus to his crucifixion and so were often used as a symbol of humility and devotion in early religious art.

Myrtle (*Myrtus communis*)
For thousands of years, myrtle was used medicinally for pain relief, and we now know that it contains salicylic acid, which is related to aspirin. It was thought to have originated in the Garden of Eden, and in ancient Greece and Rome, myrtle was sacred to Aphrodite and Venus, goddesses of love, so it became associated with love, marriage and fidelity. Ancient Greeks also wore wreaths of myrtle in council meetings to symbolize their willingness to compromise. It has been a popular symbol of marriage and a contented, successful union since Queen Victoria established the custom of a sprig being carried in the wedding bouquets of all her family in perpetuity.

Narcissus (*Narcissus*)
In the well-known Greek myth, the nymph Echo falls desperately in love with the handsome youth Narcissus but he cruelly spurns her. As punishment, the gods decide that he should see his own beautiful reflection in a pool of water. Transfixed and unable to move away, he starves to death and in his place, narcissus flowers grow. Thereafter the flowers were synonymous with self-absorption and egotism, and in Renaissance art they were a symbol of fallen and wasted youth. But the name comes from the Greek word for 'narcotic', as their scent was thought to be powerful enough to induce trance-like states. In one version of the myth, Narcissus, paralyzed by the fragrance of the flowers, is forced to stare at his own reflection forever. The language of flowers accentuated these negative connotations, with the exception of delicate jonquils, which conveyed the message – in memory of Echo – 'Please return my affection.'

Orchid (*Orchis* family)
In ancient times, ground-up orchid roots were used as an aphrodisiac. In fact, their name comes from the ancient Greek word for testicles. So, naturally, they have been linked with the more carnal aspects of human behaviour and were used in art, literature and floriography to embody capricious lovers, voluptuous beauties and promiscuity.

Pansy (*Viola* × *wittrockiana*)
The name 'pansy' originated in the fifteenth century from the French *pensée*, the past tense of 'to think', and was confusingly used for all violas. But today's large-flowered pansies are the result of early nineteenth-century hybridization and are closely related to wild heartsease, a plant much used in folk medicine to cure all ills, and used today in homeopathic remedies to give a boost of energy. In the language of flowers, the pansy was symbolic of both platonic and romantic loving wishes.

Peony (*Paeonia*)
Peonies are named after Paeon, personal physician to the gods of ancient Greece. They were used to treat many ailments, from hepatitis to arthritis. Christianity later adopted them as a symbol of the Virgin Mary – the rose without thorns – and the flower became linked with modesty and devotion. In the eighteenth century, the tree peony (*Paeonia suffruticosa*) arrived in the West from China, where its flowers had traditionally been used in poetry to describe the blushes of a young girl.

Poppy (*Papaver*)
Poppies have been cultivated since around 5000 BC and they were believed to make soil more fertile (in fact, they simply grow best in soil disturbed by cultivation). The ancient Greeks used poppies as an emblem of Nyx, Hypnos and Thanatos, the gods of night, sleep and death. They have been widely used medicinally, and opium poppies (*Papaver somniferum*) are the source of several narcotics, including morphine and heroin. Poppies have been used for centuries to bring relief, sleep and even oblivion to those suffering emotionally or physically. They were respected for their seemingly magical power to annihilate as well as restore. Poppies grew in profusion on the lacerated battlefields of France in World War I, and afterwards became a lasting symbol of loss, but also of comfort, in reflection of their ancient meanings.

Rose (*Rosa*)
Throughout history, roses have been associated with love in all forms. The sacred flower of Venus and Aphrodite, roses were synonymous with passion and sensuality; Cleopatra was said to have had her pillows stuffed with fresh rose petals every night; and Roman orgies were awash with them, too. But they were also linked with Brahma, Buddha, Vishnu and Confucius, and finally, the Christian Church adopted them as a symbol of the Virgin Mary – the rosary her perpetual prayer. Roses were also used in medicine and to replenish physical and emotional well-being – a 'rosy glow' is still considered a sign of health and happiness. A rose is the national

flower of both the United States and England. In the nineteenth century, the language of flowers used roses to convey more loving meanings and messages than any other flower. And the Empress Josephine's contemporary rose gardens at Malmaison helped guarantee its place as the most fashionable and desirable flower of all time.

Snowdrop (*Galanthus nivalis*)

Snowdrops are native to Europe and have long been a favourite flower of late winter, marking the start of spring and establishing associations with new beginnings, hope and purity. In ancient Greece, they were even used as an antidote to poison. Queen Victoria carried a small posy of snowdrops when she married Prince Albert in 1840. And, in the original fairy tale of 'Snow White', her name is the German word for 'snowdrop'.

Sunflower (*Helianthus*)

From the Greek *helios* meaning 'sun' and *anthos* for 'flower', the sunflower is quite literally the flower of the sun. According to Greek myth, the nymph Clytie fell in love with the sun god, Apollo, and when he did not return her love, she was transformed into a sunflower so that she could gaze at him forever – interpreted as the reason the flower head follows the direction of the sun. The plant we call a sunflower today was introduced to Europe from North America in 1510, so the Greeks were in fact referring to the native *Helianthemum*. Nevertheless, the myth gave the sunflower associations with loyalty and fidelity, and 'your devout admirer' in the language of flowers. But Apollo's cool detachment also gave the flower connotations of hauteur and pride, as well as unrequited love.

Sweet pea (*Lathyrus odoratus*)

Annual sweet peas have been cultivated since the seventeenth century for their exquisitely scented flowers, in spite of the fact that the peas or seeds it produces are mildly toxic to humans. They were extensively hybridized in the nineteenth century and became even more floriferous, sometimes at the expense of scent. The quantity of flowers made them ideal gifts, and sweet peas became associated with gratitude, departures and sometimes death as well. Their fragile, short-lived flowers led them to symbolize 'delicate pleasures' in Victorian floriography.

Tulip (*Tulipa*)

Persian poets waxed lyrical about tulips centuries before they were known in the West. Highly prized and cultivated by the Ottomans, tulips were both tokens of romantic love and a sacred symbol of Allah – painted, carved and printed in every way throughout the empire. Tulips reached Vienna in 1554 and Holland in 1593. Never before or since has a flower caused such a sensation; they were bred and hybridized to produce an array of colours, shapes and prized 'broken' or striped patterns. Between 1634 and 1637 speculation on the prices of tulip bulbs reached fever pitch and tulipomania almost destroyed Holland's economy. The legacy was that tulips were used in western art to convey fame, riches, greed and power – and they also became the national flower of Holland. But the tulip's more ancient links with love and devotion were revived in the floral lexicons of the nineteenth century, with different colours given specific messages: red to declare love, yellow to symbolize hopeless love, and stripes to say 'you have beautiful eyes'.

Index

Publisher's Acknowledgements

A project of this size requires the commitment, advice and expertise of many people. We are particularly indebted to our consultant editor Anna Pavord for her vital contribution to the shaping of this book and her exhaustive knowledge.

Special thanks are due to our international advisory panel for their knowledge, passion and advice in the selection of the works for inclusion:

Lugene B. Bruno
Curator of Art and Senior Research Scholar, Hunt Institute for Botanical Documentation, Carnegie Mellon University, Pittsburgh

Dr James Compton
Botanical adviser to *Gardens Illustrated* magazine and former Post Doctoral Research Fellow, Department of Plant Sciences, University of Reading, UK

Shane Connolly
Founder, Shane Connolly & Company Flowers, London and Royal Warrant Holder to HM The Queen and HM The King

Anne-Pierre d'Albis-Ganem
President and Director, Parcours Saint-Germain, Paris

Celia Fisher
Art historian and author of *The Medieval Flower Book*, *The Golden Age of Flowers* and *Flowers of the Renaissance*

Susan M. Fraser
Vice President and Director, LuEsther T. Mertz Library, The New York Botanical Garden

Victoria Gaiger
Founding Editor and Creative Director, *Rakesprogress* magazine, London

Elizabeth Hammer
Senior Specialist, Classical and Modern Chinese Paintings, Christie's, New York

Daisy Helman
Founder, *Garden Collage Magazine*, New York

Catherine Hess
Chief Curator, European Art, Huntington Library, Art Museum, and Botanical Gardens, San Marino, California

Pascale Heurtel
Library Director, Conservatoire National des Arts et Métiers, Paris

Dr Lisa Hostetler
Curator in Charge, Department of Photography, George Eastman Museum, Rochester, New York

Lyndsey Ingram
Founder, Lyndsey Ingram Gallery, London

Professor Dr Hans Walter Lack
Botanic Garden and Botanical Museum Berlin, Freie Universität Berlin

Dr Fred G. Meijer
Independent art historian and expert of Dutch and Flemish seventeenth-century painting

Colleen Morris
Landscape heritage consultant, Sydney and former National Chair, Australian Garden History Society

Polly Nicholson
Founder, Bayntun Flowers, historic tulip and antiquarian book specialist, Wiltshire, UK

Lynn Parker
Curator, Illustration and Artefact Collections, Royal Botanic Gardens, Kew, London

Anna Pavord
Gardener and author of *The Tulip*, *The Naming of Names* and *The Curious Gardener*

Gill Saunders
Senior Curator of Prints, Word and Image, Victoria and Albert Museum, London

Lindsey Taylor
Garden designer, floral stylist and writer, Lindsey Taylor Design, New York

Anatole Tchikine
Curator of Rare Books, Garden and Landscape Studies, Dumbarton Oaks Research Library and Collection, Washington, DC

Betsy Wieseman
Chair of European Art from Classical Antiquity to 1800 and Paul J. and Edith Ingalls Vignos, Jr. Curator of European Paintings and Sculpture, 1500-1800, Cleveland Museum of Art, Ohio

We are grateful to Sarah Bell and Annalaura Palma for their picture research, and to Jamie Ambrose, Caitlin Arnell Argles, Sara Bader, Vanessa Bird, Tim Cooke, Dr James Compton, Diane Fortenberry, Simon Hunegs, Helen Miles, Ava Miller, Rebecca Morrill, João Mota, Celia Ongley and Michele Robecchi for their invaluable assistance.

Finally, we would like to thank all the artists, illustrators, photographers, collectors, libraries, institutions and museums who have given us permission to include their images.

Text Credits

The publisher is grateful to Anna Pavord for writing the introduction and Shane Connolly for the texts on the meanings of flowers.

Additional thanks go to the following writers for their texts:

Giovanni Aloi: 11, 27, 33, 35, 44, 46, 52, 63, 67, 92, 100, 105, 108, 110, 123, 120, 142, 143, 151, 152, 153, 157, 172, 173, 174, 194, 204, 210, 214, 241, 242, 244, 257, 263, 273, 277, 313, 321, 327; **Louise Bell:** 21, 36, 73, 116, 171, 190, 197, 228, 233, 292, 306, 315; **Lugene Bruno:** 20, 66, 79, 98, 109, 156, 165, 227, 229, 261, 291; **Shane Connolly:** 234, 270; **Clare Coulson:** 15, 55, 56, 60, 62, 127, 133, 175, 193, 213, 225, 237, 254, 271, 286, 299, 300, 302, 324; **Louisa Elderton:** 26, 32, 51, 89, 94, 96, 130, 150, 155, 259, 293, 320, 323, 326; **Celia Fisher:** 14, 18, 61, 84, 126, 145, 149, 161, 179, 226, 282, 289, 295, 296, 308, 316, 317; **Diane Fortenberry:** 29, 39, 47, 59, 121, 122, 131, 146, 148, 160, 168, 200, 207, 230, 290, 297, 309, 318; **Victoria Gaiger:** 41, 48, 50, 57, 82, 163, 217, 262, 276; **Daisy Helman:** 30, 279; **Pascale Heurtel:** 106, 144, 182, 183, 209; **Lyndsey Ingram:** 23, 65, 138, 205, 211; **Hans Walter Lack:** 43, 236; **Fred G. Meijer:** 86, 125, 177, 201, 267, 268; **Alison Morris:** 19, 24, 71, 83, 101, 158, 264, 280, 281; **Colleen Morris:** 120, 260, 325; **Polly Nicholson:** 72, 136, 159, 189, 192, 252, 303, 310, 319; **Michele Robecchi:** 58, 68, 69, 97, 111, 128, 135, 178, 223, 247, 269, 283; **Rebecca Roke:** 34, 42, 70, 85, 88, 95, 102, 113, 124, 162, 164, 180, 185, 188, 191, 216, 221, 235, 239, 255, 256, 284, 301; **Gill Saunders:** 25, 112, 117, 118, 243, 251; **James Smith:** 10, 16, 27, 28, 38, 40, 76, 78, 81, 115, 119, 132, 154, 166, 170, 176, 186, 196, 202, 203, 231, 238, 248, 250, 253, 265, 266, 274, 275, 298, 304, 305, 311, 328; **Lindsey Taylor:** 147, 184, 288; **David Trigg:** 12, 37, 45, 53, 64, 77, 90, 91, 93, 107, 139, 140, 141, 181, 195, 198, 218, 219, 220, 222, 240, 245, 272, 287, 294, 307, 312, 314, 322, 329; **Martin Walters:** 31, 49, 54, 75, 80, 87, 99, 103, 104, 134, 137, 167, 169, 187, 199, 206, 208, 212, 215, 232, 246, 249, 258, 278, 285.

Picture Credits

321: Courtesy Abbeville Press from *Botanica Magnifica: Portraits of the World's Most Extraordinary Flowers and Plants* by Jonathan M. Singer, W. John Kress, Marc Hachadourian, photographs by Jonathan M. Singer, 2009; 119: Sam Abell; 185: akg-images; 303: akg-images/Mucha Trust; 43: The Picture Art Collection/Alamy Stock Photo; 120: Florilegius/Alamy Stock Photo; 232: Peter Horree/Alamy Stock Photo; 81: The Albertina Museum, Vienna. The Batliner Collection/© 2025 ADAGP, Paris and DACS, London; 84: Allport Library and Museum of Fine Arts, Tasmanian Archive and Heritage Office; 141: Courtesy The Annex Galleries, Santa Rosa, California; 295: The Armand Hammer Collection; 290: © ARS, NY and DACS, London 2020; 99: Art Gallery of Ontario, Canada/Purchased with funds donated by Greg Latremoille, 2014. © Christi Belcourt; 170: Gift of Gaylord Donnelley in memory of Frances Gaylord Smith/The Art Institute of Chicago; 61: © 2025 Yinka Shonibare CBE. All Rights Reserved, DACS. Photo: Stephen White. Artimage 2019; 110: Asian Art Museum, The Avery Brundage Collection, B65P13. Photograph © Asian Art Museum of San Francisco; 215: © The Estate of Cicely Mary Barker, 1944, 1990; 76: Photo: Ian Bavington Jones; 49: © 2025 Estate of Vanessa Bell. All rights reserved, DACS; 18, 104, 209: Bibliothèque nationale de France; 112, 134, 146, 161, 165: Biodiversity Heritage Library/Missouri Botanical Garden, Peter H. Raven Library; 206: Biodiversity Heritage Library/Harvard University Botany Libraries; 226: Biodiversity Heritage Library/The Getty Research Institute (archive.org); 300: Biodiversity Heritage Library/University Library, University of Illinois Urbana Champaign; 159: Bonhams; 29, 37, 39, 66, 71, 75, 78, 102, 136, 169, 244, 274, 296, 317: Bridgeman Images; 126: Museum purchase funded by the Alice Pratt Brown Museum Fund, and gifts of Isabel B. Wilson and The Brown Foundation, Inc./Bridgeman Images; 167: Mary Griggs Burke Collection, Gift of the Mary and Jackson Burke Foundation/Bridgeman Images; 19: Photo © Christie's Images. Bridgeman Images © 2025 Succession H. Matisse/DACS; 183, 246, 267, 308: Photo © Christie's Images/Bridgeman Images; 284: Photo © Christie's Images/Bridgeman Images. © 2025 ARS, NY and DACS, London; 297: © Christie's Images/Bridgeman Images/© 2025 Succession Picasso/DACS, London; 304: Denman Waldo Ross Collection/Bridgeman Images; 17: © The Lucian Freud Archive/Bridgeman Images; 207: By courtesy of Julian Hartnoll/Bridgeman Images; 59: Gift of Mrs. Inez Grant Parker in memory of Earle W. Grant/Bridgeman Images. © 2025 Georgia O'Keeffe Museum/DACS; 94: © 2020 Estate of André Kertész/Higher Pictures/Gift of Susan and Peter Wilkes Tucker/Bridgeman Images; 58: Gift of Mr and Mrs Jonathan Marshall/Bridgeman Images; 178: Mondadori Portfolio/Electa/Luca Carrà/Bridgeman Images/© 2025 DACS; 90: © Nolde Stiftung Seebüll/Bridgeman Images; 70: Photo © Luisa Ricciarini/Bridgeman Images; 312: Gift of Anne d'Harnoncourt, 1996/Bridgeman Images/© 2025 Anyone Can Fly Foundation/ DACS; 20: The Stapleton Collection/Bridgeman Images; 268: © Veneranda Biblioteca Ambrosiana/Paolo Manusardi/Mondadori Portfolio/Bridgeman Images; 38: Werner Forman Archive/Bridgeman Images; 98, 145, 230, 310: © The Trustees of the British Museum; 132: Brooklyn Museum Costume Collection at The Metropolitan Museum of Art, Gift of the Brooklyn Museum, 2009; Brooklyn Museum Collection; 275: Brooklyn Museum, Dick S. Ramsay Fund, 70.31; 153: Craig P. Burrows; 140: Courtesy Caron, Paris; 255: © CHANEL/Photo Antoine Dumont; 196: Courtesy of The Cleveland Museum of Art. © 2025 ADAGP, Paris and DACS, London; 83: Courtesy of The Cleveland Museum of Art; 30: Collection Center for Creative Photography, University of Arizona © The Ansel Adams Publishing Rights Trust; 191: Photo Michael Fallon/Collective Hudson; 100: Horst P. Horst, Vogue © Conde Nast; 105: Cecil Beaton, Vogue © Conde Nast; 324: Maija Isola and Marimekko © 2019. Cooper-Hewitt, Smithsonian Design Museum/Art Resource, NY/Scala, Florence digitale (1); 48: © Sharon Core. Courtesy of the artist and Yancey Richardson, New York; 79: The Corning Museum of Glass, Corning, NY; 46: Courtesy of the artist; 53: Courtesy of the artist; 311: Courtesy of the artist; 51: © Gregory Crewdson. Courtesy Gagosian; 315: © Imogen Cunningham Trust, 2020; 151: Courtesy of the artist & Darren Knight Gallery, Sydney; 293: © The David Collection, Copenhagen/Pernille Klemp; 147: Courtesy of Davis & Langdale Company, Inc.; 323: Sylvain Deleu; 154: © Estate of Joséphine et Camille Le Foll/Photo: Ian Bavington Jones; 55: Dior; 91: © 1951 Disney; 174: © Britt Willoughby Dyer; 283: Photo: Christopher Burke © 2025 The Easton Foundation/VAGA at ARS, NY and DACS, London; 301: East News Press Agency; 95: Courtesy of Edwynn Houk Gallery; 121: © Eggleston Artistic Trust/The J. Paul Getty Museum, Los Angeles; 173: © Peter Fischli and David Weiss, Courtesy Matthew Marks Gallery; 113: By kind permission of Raffaella Fletcher; 32: Fondation Custodia, Collection Frits Lugt, Paris; 182: The Fostinum: The Collection of Fostin Cotchen https://www.fostinum.org; 135: © 2025 Franko B. All rights reserved, DACS; 35: Courtesy Frantic Gallery; 305: Freer Gallery of Art, Smithsonian Institution, Washington, D.C.: Purchase – funds provided by Rajinder K. Keith and Narinder K. Keith in honor of Mahinder Singh Keith, F1994.5; 276: © Sally Mann. Courtesy Gagosian; 16: George Eastman Museum, gift of the 3M Foundation, ex-collection Louis Walton Sipley; 203: © 2025 Ori Gersht. All rights reserved, DACS; 24: Science & Society Picture Library/Getty Images; 148: Leemage/Getty Images; 177: Digital image courtesy of the Getty's Open Content Program 83.PC.386; 273: Digital image courtesy of the Getty's Open Content Program; 217: Photo by Julio Donoso/Sygma via Getty Images; 80: Courtesy T.M. Glass; 327: Courtesy of Paul Harfleet, The Pansy Project; 188: MS Am 1118.11, Houghton Library © President and Fellows of Harvard College; 52: Courtesy Cig Harvey; 254: Drawing by Androniki Goulandris © Hermès Paris, 2020; 211: © David Hockney Photo Credit: Richard Schmidt; 68: © Jim Hodges, Courtesy the artist and Gladstone Gallery, New York and Brussels/© 2020. Christie's Images, London/Scala, Florence; 231: Honolulu Museum of Art, Gift of James A. Michener, 1991 (21657); 205: © 2025 Georgie Hopton. All Rights Reserved, DACS; 138: © 2025 Gary Hume. All Rights Reserved, DACS; 262: Caroline Hunter; 41: Image courtesy the Artist; 65: Lyndsey Ingram; 116: © Keith Collins Will Trust/courtesy Irish Museum of Modern Art; 202: The J. Paul Getty Trust; 152: 84.XP.463.11 The J. Paul Getty Museum, Los Angeles; 179: 92.GC.80